Applied Multivariate Analysis

Ira H. Bernstein

Applied Multivariate
Analysis

With Calvin P. Garbin
and Gary K. Teng

With 37 Illustrations

Springer-Verlag
New York Berlin Heidelberg
London Paris Tokyo

Ira H. Bernstein
Department of Psychology
University of Texas at Arlington
Arlington, Texas 76019
USA

Gary K. Teng
Technical Evaluation and Management
   Systems, Inc. (TEAMS®)
Dallas, Texas 75240
USA

Calvin P. Garbin
Department of Psychology
University of Nebraska at Lincoln
Lincoln, Nebraska 68588
USA

Library of Congress Cataloging-in-Publication Data
Bernstein, Ira H.
  Applied multivariate analysis.
  Bibliography: p.
  Includes index.
  1. Multivariate analysis.   I. Garbin, Calvin P.
II. Teng, Gary K.   III. Title.
QA278.B457   1987   519.5′35   87-15174

Typeset by Asco Trade Typesetting Ltd., Hong Kong.
Printed and bound by R.R. Donnelley & Sons, Harrisonburg, Virginia.
Printed in the United States of America.

9 8 7 6 5 4 3 2 1

ISBN 0-387-96542-4 Springer-Verlag New York Berlin Heidelberg
ISBN 3-540-96542-4 Springer-Verlag Berlin Heidelberg New York

To Linda, Cari, Dina
and
the memory of Jum C. Nunnally

Preface

Like most academic authors, my views are a joint product of my teaching and my research. Needless to say, my views reflect the biases that I have acquired. One way to articulate the rationale (and limitations) of my biases is through the preface of a truly great text of a previous era, Cooley and Lohnes (1971, p. v). They draw a distinction between mathematical statisticians whose intellect gave birth to the field of multivariate analysis, such as Hotelling, Bartlett, and Wilks, and those who chose to "concentrate much of their attention on methods of analyzing data in the sciences and of interpreting the results of statistical analysis .... (and) ... who are more interested in the sciences than in mathematics, among other characteristics."

I find the distinction between individuals who are temperamentally "mathematicians" (whom philosophy students might call "Platonists") and "scientists" ("Aristotelians") useful as long as it is not pushed to the point where one assumes "mathematicians" completely disdain data and "scientists" are never interested in contributing to the mathematical foundations of their discipline. I certainly feel more comfortable attempting to contribute in the "scientist" rather than the "mathematician" role.

As a consequence, this book is primarily written for individuals concerned with data analysis. However, as noted in Chapter 1, true expertise demands familiarity with both traditions.

One consequence of my bias is that even though I have a great love for data, I have long since learned not to worship a particular data set, i.e., I believe in sampling error and replication. I especially believe in Henry Kaiser's (1970) aphorism "It don't make no nevermind" about highly elaborate weighting schemes that more often than not prove less useful than simpler ones such as weighting variables equally. (Kaiser, by the way, shows the limitations of the "rule of thumb" distinction between Mathematician/Platonists and Scientist/Aristotelians; bright people do both as his numerous other contributions such as the varimax rotation and alpha factoring attest.) If you are unsure as to what I mean by "magical equations," pick up almost any scholarly journal containing path analyses and confirmatory factor analyses. Similarly, it should not be too difficult to locate a book in which the author attempts to use the force of copyright law to protect the weighting scheme used in an equation.

The major reason that I refer to Cooley and Lohnes (1971) as belonging to a prior generation is that it was written before the ascendancy of the major computer packages. I assume you will be using these packages. At one point in writing this book, I thought of offering a "translation" table to explain the printouts that are provided by the packages. The reason that I did not devote more space to the topic is the rate at which revisions of the packages make such information obsolete.

The one feature that I hope sets this book apart from the many other excellent books in the field is my use of the computer as a device to teach you about data structures. It is all too easy to see only the data analytic features of computer packages, as wonderful as they are. (Consider that in almost no time at all I can enter the coding to do all variants on a particular analysis that would have been prohibitive in terms of time when I was a student.) Much less apparent to the student is the way that a computer can *generate* data to conform to a model or deviate in specified ways. Scholars have long used Monte Carlo and related simulation approaches; I feel that it is sufficiently easy for students at this level, or even at a more introductory level, to perform simulations so that they should be part of all students' training.

The material in this book is designed to be covered in a standard one semester graduate course. It is assumed that a student has had a conventional first semester graduate class in statistics. I have, however, devoted a chapter to material that is largely a summary of this core material (Chapter 2). Of course, I have also tried to include useful information that would make the book valuable beyond the formal confines of the course (*lagniappe*, as one would say in the language of those to my Southeast).

Acknowledgments

I would like to thank Springer-Verlag for their faith in this project. Robert Widner's comments on various points of the text were most highly appreciated. Various ideas were outgrowths of conversations I had with various departmental colleagues, especially Jim Nairne, Jim Erickson, Jim Baerwaldt, Bill Ickes, Paul Paulus, Duane Martin, and the ophthalmologists at the Glaucoma Associates of Texas. I also am grateful to Melvin Pierce, Tom Kennedy, Ed Homko, Michael Griffin, and others at the University of Texas Academic Computer center, Rory Gresham of Seabrook Computers, and Sara Kapka of IBM for their technical assistance. The oblique, but nonetheless vital contributions of Emma Peel, Ferdinand LaMenthe, John B. Gillespie, John Coltrane, Charles C. Parker, Jr., Larson E. Whipsnade, Jonathan Steed, John Sheridan, and James Cullum and associates are also noted. Finally, the wisdom of a comment by my long-term friend and colleague, Professor Stanley

Coren of the University of British Columbia that "you never finish writing a book, they just take it away from you" is hereby duly noted.

Arlington, Texas   IRA H. BERNSTEIN
May 1987

Contents

CHAPTER 10   CLASSIFICATION METHODS—PART 3. INFERENTIAL CONSIDERATIONS IN THE MANOVA

1
Introduction and Preview

Chapter Overview

Chapter 1 contains six major topics:

I. MULTIVARIATE ANALYSIS: A BROAD DEFINITION—I begin by offering a very broad definition of multivariate analysis. The definition is: *an inquiry into the structure of interrelationships among multiple measures.*

II. MULTIVARIATE ANALYSIS: A NARROW DEFINITION—The broad definition is important because virtually all behavioral research deals with questions about structure. Unfortunately, it would subsume all of statistical analysis, making for quite a large textbook! Consequently, it is customary to define multivariate analysis in more limited terms: *the study of linear representations of relations among variables.* Contained within this narrow definition are several interrelated models that are discussed in later chapters: (1) *multiple regression* (Chapters 4 and 5), (2) *factor analysis* (Chapters 6 and 7), (3) *discriminant analysis, related classification techniques, and the multivariate analysis of variance and covariance* (Chapters 8–10), (4) *profile and canonical analysis* (Chapter 11), and (5) *analysis of scales* (Chapter 12).

III. SOME IMPORTANT THEMES—Models like factor analysis and multiple regression used to infer structure are all too often looked upon as if they were separate, unrelated procedures. In reality, certain themes recur regardless of the specific analytic procedure: (1) *equations that are the by-product of a particular analysis should be meaningful;* (2) *cutoffs need to be established defining "how high is high" and "how low is low" when one develops a prediction equation;* (3) *questions of statistical significance often arise;* (4) *outliers can render otherwise elegant analyses meaningless or, worse, highly misleading;* (5) *multivariate investigation should be guided by theory;* and (6) *particular problems are likely to arise when relations among individual items, as opposed to multi-item scales, are the unit of analysis.*

IV. THE ROLE OF COMPUTERS IN MULTIVARIATE ANALYSIS—A generation ago, many analyses that were conceived of were not practicable. The availability of computers and sophisticated computer packages now make such analyses routine. The increasing role of the personal computer is also noted.

V. CHOOSING A COMPUTER PACKAGE—There are several important computer packages now on the market. Some of the pros and cons of the three most popular ones—SAS, SPSSX, and BMDP—are discussed.

VI. PROBLEMS IN THE USE OF COMPUTER PACKAGES— Knowing how to use a computer package is important to multivariate analysis, but it is not sufficient. Four necessary ingredients to a successful analysis are considered: (1) *substantive knowledge of the research topic*; (2) *computer knowledge, including knowledge of the package*; (3) *empirical experience with various kinds of data*; and (4) *formal knowledge of the analytic procedures.*

This textbook is written for those who need to analyze complex behavioral data, whether in field settings such as clinical and social psychology, in applied settings like nursing and marketing research, or in experimental settings like learning and perception. Although I cannot escape some degree of formality, I am writing for students whose primary interests lie more in empirical phenomena as opposed to rigorous mathematical statistics.

Although I very much appreciate why examples related to your specific interests are important, I hope I can "wean" you from examples limited to your own content area as the textbook topics progress. One of the things you should note is that if you are a clinical psychology student working with personality test data, you will have problems that are abstractly *identical* to a market researcher working on a consumer survey. One of the reasons that I find quantitative applications so rewarding is that I can work in a variety of areas, as long as I have someone to provide me with a background of the underlying empirical issue or have that background myself. At any one time, I can and have been working on the issue of selecting police officers, studying patients attitudes toward health care, looking at choices of financial institutions, and evaluating different forms of eye surgery. What I learned in one setting applied to all. I hope you can share the enjoyment that I have been experiencing.

One of the decisions that any author of a quantitative textbook needs to confront is how to choose examples. Conceptually, it should not matter if examples come from clinical psychology, marketing, or visual psychophysics; yet it does matter to most students. What I will do, therefore, is to pick my examples to illustrate the relevance of the various multivariate models in different settings.

Multivariate Analysis: A Broad Definition

As with most topics, it is useful to try to define what is meant by the term "multivariate analysis" before proceeding too far into its details. In the broadest and most literal sense, it means *an inquiry into the structure of interrelationships among multiple measures.* To illustrate what is meant by structure, consider one of the teacher evaluation forms you probably have filled out in the past. Questions that are commonly asked are: (1) how interesting you found the course to be, (2) how much you learned; (3) how much you liked the textbook, and (4) your overall rating of the course. The instructions usually ask you to respond to each item independently. However, it is doubtful that anybody ever does that. Ratings of individual items are strongly influenced by the *halo* or overall view of the course and instructor. Your intuitions may be sufficient to convince you that your judgments reflect halo effects, but the analysis may be conducted more formally using methods I will discuss. You will find that there is in fact a thread (the halo) unifying all items, which will be reflected in relatively high correlations among items. (The halo may be so strong that the *same* textbook that is evaluated in *different* sections of the *same* course can receive quite *different* ratings, depending on your halo of the instructor.)

The fact that the ratings are not independent or uncorrelated suggests that they possess a structure, but this realization alone is not sufficient to tell one what that structure is. Consider each of the following as a *hypothesis*. First, it is possible that all of the different items responded to by students within a given class simply reflect the fact that students vary in the extent to which they like (or dislike) the instructor. That is, *one* number is sufficient to describe their attitudes. *Summing* or *averaging* (statistically, it does not make any difference, because once you know the sum and the number of items, you can derive the average) the items gives a composite score that conveys *all* of the information contained in the individual items. One could argue that a one-item survey would do just as well, although I will show in Chapter 12 that a one-item survey will generally be less *reliable* (statistically noisier) than the result of averaging several related items.

Conversely, although the items in general may relate to one another, their relationships may vary in some systematic manner. For example, items dealing with *liking* of the instructor (whether in a "happiness" or in a professional sense) tend to group together in terms of their relationship, and items dealing with the *clarity* of the instructor's presentation and *amount* of material presented in lecture tend to form a separate, although perhaps related, grouping. If this particular hypothesis or any other that involves more than one grouping of variables is true, then a single index, like the sum, will discard some important information. With sufficient imagination, hypotheses involving three or even more groupings can also be formulated. One of the important things to do is see how *data* can help decide among competing hypotheses.

The point that multiple ratings of the same object cannot usually be viewed as independent has another important aspect to it. As one learns about psychology as a science, often one is first taught that behavioral experiments should be conducted with the stimulus environment constant save for one variable, the *independent* variable. The independent variable is then systematically manipulated to determine its effect upon some specific criterial behavior, the *dependent* variable. You should be familiar by now with the use of the *simple analysis of variance (ANOVA)* to determine whether differences in the independent variable affect the means of the dependent variable to an extent greater than chance.

It is quite possible, though, that you have gone beyond the simple ANOVA to the next most simple design—a *two-way factorial* design. A two-way factorial design involves manipulating two independent variables simultaneously and independently of one another. If so, you have probably learned that an important new concept applies here that does not apply in the simple ANOVA situation, namely, that of *interaction*. Thus, you might find that a particular treatment is more effective than no treatment in one condition, but the reverse is true in another condition.

For example, you might find that it is harder to learn verbal material when practice is concentrated (massed) than when it is distributed so that performance following one 2-hour practice session is worse than performance following eight 15-minute practice sessions when the material to be learned is easy, but the opposite is true when the material is more difficult. In other words, the effects of massed versus distributed practice are contingent upon the difficulty of the material. An interaction implies that the effects of two or more independent variables are related to one another.

Had two investigators performed the massed-versus-distributed learning experiment separately, one with easy material and the other with hard material, they would have gotten into a needless (and perhaps even endless) dispute about the *validity* of one another's results. Both are in fact correct within their own narrowly defined contexts. Thus, multivariate analyses, which include the two-way factorial and higher-order ANOVAs, allow one to explore the generality of findings affecting an individual variable.

Although my example of a relationship dealt with the interaction between two independent variables, I can use multivariate analysis to study the effects of a given independent variable upon two or more *dependent* variables. For example, mild food deprivation (the independent variable) often makes experimental animals (1) leave the start area of a runway to obtain food more quickly as well as (2) run down the runway more rapidly. It is possible that the two effects of food deprivation occur independently of one another: some animals leave the start box more quickly when food deprived, others run down the runway faster, others do both, and still others do neither. This interpretation is quite different from saying that the two effects both occur within the same animal. Consequently, it is quite common to study the structural relations among a series of dependent variables in order to see if their effects are correlated within a particular group of subjects.

Another important example is that perceptual systems have evolved to take advantage of the many naturally occurring interrelations that exist in the environment. Experiments that force the underlying events to be independent require one to conduct things differently than in an otherwise identical setting where the variables have their natural degree of relationship. Egon Brunswik

(1956), who had a great intellectual influence on my approach to psychology, stressed the importance of studying behavior in a natural environment.

Here is a simple example that illustrates Brunswik's approach. Suppose you were trying to estimate how far away a given object was, such as an oncoming automobile on a misty day. The automobile provides you with information or cues as to its distance. Two of the cues furnished are the size and clarity of the image it casts on your eyes. If the car is relatively far away, it will cast a small image that will appear to be blurred owing to the mist. An important facet of the situation is that there is a correlation between the two cues—a car that casts a large image generally appears to be clear and a car that casts a small image generally appears blurred.

The accuracy of human subjects' distance judgments has been studied for many years in the laboratory. Perhaps the most common strategy used is the so-called *systematic* design. In the present case, one would attempt to separate the effects of the two cues by eliminating their naturally occurring correlation. The design would require four equally probable stimulus combinations: (1) large–clear, (2) large–unclear, (3) small–clear, and (4) small–unclear, and not just the more probable combinations of (1) and (4). A systematic design is useful when you are interested in looking at the isolated roles of the two cues.

Brunswik's strategy is the so-called *representative* design, because it attempts to represent the natural correlation between the two cues by sampling from naturally occurring stimulus situations. A representative design is not as good as a systematic design if one's goal is simply to specify how individual distance cues are used. However, a representative design is much better for studying perception as a global process. Human performance in a representative design is often amazingly accurate. What is sometimes considered a visual "illusion" in the context of a systematic design is simply the consequence of an unlikely combination of cues. People in the Brunswikian tradition therefore consider it very important to study the correlational structure of stimuli.

One reason to present a "broad" definition of multivariate analysis before narrowing it down is to cite the existence of a very important set of structural models and procedures that in some ways are an alternative to the "classical" multivariate models I will consider—namely, *multidimensional scaling (MDS)*. MDS has certain similarities to factor analysis, but it differs in two ways. One is that MDS makes much less restrictive assumptions about the underlying measurement scales than the classical approach. In the classical approach, one assumes that the underlying measures form an *interval scale* (possess a true unit of measurement). In MDS, however, one can, as an example, derive an interval data structure from rank–order data.

MDS also allows one to examine two forms of structural relationships—those based on relative *similarity* among variables and those based on relative *dominance* (preference) of one variable over the other variables. Classical multivariate procedures consider only similarity relations because they are based on correlational measures, which are measures of similarity and not dominance. Similarity measures differ in at least one significant way from dominance (preference) measures—the former are inherently *symmetric* whereas the latter are inherently *asymmetric*. That is, if stimulus A is very similar to stimulus B, then stimulus B is by definition also similar to stimulus A. The correlation between A and B is the same as the correlation between B and A. On the other hand, if stimulus A is dominant over (preferred to) stimulus B, then stimulus B does *not* dominate stimulus A, by definition. The distinction between dominance and similarity is important because many studies inherently involve dominance, not similarity, relationships such as the "taste tests" commonly employed in marketing research. I will not consider MDS further, although the concepts considered here will form a useful foundation. Kruskal and Wish (1978) provide a useful introduction to MDS.

To conclude a discussion of the "broad" definition of multivariate analysis, the Gestalt tradition in psychology stresses that the "whole is different from the sum of its parts." The reason is that the whole contains the *interrelations* among the parts as well as the parts themselves.

Multivariate Analysis: A Narrow Definition

If I were to explore the preceding broad definition in greater depth, I would be writing a book that would cover virtually all topics in advanced statistics. It would make for one long semester! As a consequence, practical considerations require a more restricted but still highly useful definition of multivariate analysis: *the study of linear representations of relationships among variables.*

Linear relations are important because of their simplicity. If variable Y depends on another variable X, the simplest possible relation between the two is that of a straight line—$Y = BX + A$. Only two quantities, B and A, are needed to specify the relation between them, and X can be entered into the relation directly without having to manipulate it. By contrast, the *quadratic* relationship, $Y = CX^2 + BX + A$, forces one to determine up to three terms (A, B, and C), and X has to be squared along the way. The only simpler way to describe Y is through the expression $Y = A$, which means that Y does not depend on X at all.

In some cases, the straight line relation is *exact*. One example is the formula $F = \frac{9}{5}C + 32$, where F is temperature in degrees of Fahrenheit and C is temperature in degrees of Celsius (centigrade). In statistics one is usually interested in deriving *approximations* from observation and experimentation. One seldom, if ever, finds *exact* relationships. A straight line is still the simplest way to describe the relationship. That is why such an extensive mathematics of linear relations has evolved.

In multivariate applications, a given variable Y may depend on several X variables, not just one. For example, a customer's willingness to purchase a particular item of merchandise may depend on his or her financial state at the time, the attractiveness of the newspaper advertising, the time of the year (is it near Christmas?), what one has heard from ones friends, etc. Consequently,

I will talk about variables $X_1, X_2, \ldots, X_n$. The term "X_i" will denote any given member of the set X. Y will be termed a *criterion* when it depends on one or more X_i variables and the X_i variables will be called *predictors* (sometimes, I will also be referring to situations with more than one criterion, which will be designated $Y_1, Y_2, \ldots, Y_m$).

The generalization of a linear relation to the case of multiple predictors involves the concept of a *linear combination*, which is an equation of the form illustrated in Eq. (1-1). Equations of this form are used to estimate the criterion Y from the set of predictors (three in the equation). Sometimes, as in component analysis (Chapter 6), I will not be "predicting" Y from the X_i. Instead, I will be describing a relation exactly, just as I did in the case of my example involving the conversion of temperature from degrees of Fahrenheit to degrees of Celsius.

$$Y = .270X_1 + .317X_2 + .153X_3 + 1.17 \qquad (1\text{-}1)$$

Equation (1-1) is used to estimate Y by multiplying each of the weights (.270, .317, .153) by an individual's scores and then adding in the constant term (1.17). The resulting value on the corresponding predictor (Y') is a best guess of each individual's criterion score, in a sense to be described. The individual predictors might respectively represent high school grade point average (GPA), Scholastic Aptitude Test (SAT) Verbal score, and SAT Quantitative score. The criterion might be predicted is college GPA.

Very powerful techniques have evolved to form linear representations of data. As will be seen in the Chapter 2, such models can be used in a wide variety of circumstances and can even handle nonlinear relations. (Do not worry about being limited to linear relations—although you cannot do things like multiply X_1 and X_2 directly, there are ways to incorporate nonlinear relations indirectly.)

The prediction example illustrates but one of the applications of the general linear model—*multiple regression*—discussed in Chapters 4 and 5. Multiple regression forms a linear combination of predictors to best predict a continuous criterion. The theme appears in Chapters 8 through 10, where the linear combination is used to predict group membership and thereby classify individuals whose membership is unknown and to make inferential statements. The topics that are considered include *discriminant analysis, classification models, multivariate analysis of variance (MANOVA), and multivariate analysis of covariance (MANCOVA)*. In Chapter 11, one further step is taken, *canonical analysis*. In canonical analysis, linear combinations from one group of variables are related to linear combinations derived from another group of variables.

Factor analysis, discussed in Chapters 6 and 7, differs from the preceding in a very important respect: It forms linear combinations in order to obtain criterion variables that are *internal* to a set of measures. The concept of internal prediction is illustrated by one specific type of factor analysis, the method of principal components, which derives linear combinations that account for the most variance shared by a set of measures. By contrast, confirmatory factor analysis forms linear combinations to test substantive definitions of which measures "go together."

Correlations (more specifically *Pearson product–moment correlations*) are measures of linear similarity that are based on certain geometric and algebraic assumptions considered in the Chapter 2. They play a fundamental role in multivariate analysis. The weights used in linear combinations are typically derived from correlations, although the correlations and the weights are numerically different and conceptually distinct. Moreover, after forming weights as in Eq. 1-1, one typically determines how closely related the actual and predicted criterion values are—the *multiple correlation*.

Some Important Themes

Obtaining Meaningful Relations

Expressions such as Eq. 1-1 can be very imposing because they may contain numerous predictors, and the weights can be carried out to many apparently significant decimal places. However, the particular results you obtain, while optimal for a given sample, are only one of many plausible outcomes. If your primary interest is in formulating a prediction equation, many alternative equations are simpler yet predict just as well in new samples. For example, you may find that simply taking four predictors from a larger set of possible predictors and adding them, without differential weighting, correlates just as well with the criterion using data from a *new* sample as the complete equation based on the first sample. Users of multivariate techniques should seek to provide the most coherent and sensible results, not the most quasiprecise. Your computer printout can quite easily inspire awe and paralysis or, conversely, false pride at the wonders of modern computer gimmicks. Unfortunately, any slight change in the composition of your sample will cause one set of awe-inspiring numbers to be replaced by a new and very different set of awe-inspiring numbers. In order to best serve your interests, be prepared to spend considerable time simplifying your initial prediction equation after obtaining it.

I have previously noted that the "whole is different from the sum of its parts" because the whole contains the structure of interrelations among the parts. Knowledge of structure often allows data analyses to be simplified radically. In the example I gave involving the initial latency and running speeds of experimental animals tested under different levels of mild food deprivation, I indicated that it was important to determine the correlation between the latency and speed measures. If the two measures were highly correlated so that those animals that left the start area most quickly also ran most rapidly, the two variables could be effectively reduced to a single *construct*, perhaps termed "response strength." The redundancy of the two independent variables would not be apparent were you to limit yourself to univariate analyses of the two variables taken separately. The unifying power that potentially arises from the use of multivariate methods comes at a price, however. I will frequently note that there are many ways for a multivariate analysis to go awry if you are not completely familiar with the details of the analysis. Consequently, it is equally true that a series of univariate analyses will be more meaningful than a badly done multivariate analysis.

Selecting Cutoffs

Much of multivariate analysis concerns choosing weights for the X_i predictors. A satisfactory linear combination of predictors defines a "blend" or "mix" of variables, which is often equally weighted. This combination reduces a multivariate problem to a univariate one. Choosing a proper blend is perhaps the most widely discussed topic in multivariate analysis. However, there is often an equally important and separate problem of deciding where upon the resulting *decision axis* to place the *cutoff* or *criterion* needed for selection. For example, you may use data from former students at a particular university and decide that high school GPA be weighted twice as heavily as SAT scores. The issue of determining a minimum admission score on the resulting linear combination for admission is a totally separate question.

Questions of Statistical Inference

Statistical inference was a very important topic in your previous statistics courses. In particular, you have probably become quite concerned with the most common (but not the only) form of statistical inference—answering the question "is an observed difference statistically significant?" Anyone trained in statistics must be familiar with how to decide whether two or more group means, variances, or other statistics differ more than can be accounted for on the basis of purely random (chance) factors, specifically, sampling error.

Another part of your training is recognizing the existence of statistically real but spurious effects due to confoundings, a situation often referred to as the *third variable problem*. Well-designed experiments, as opposed to field studies, are the most effective way to rule out third variable effects. At the same time, field studies often are the best way to evaluate a particular problem because you can study naturally occurring phenomena.

One often must determine how important a relation is. One problem in defining importance is its dependence on context and perspective. A variable that accounts for a certain amount of variance may be highly important to one setting but irrelevant to another. Even in a given setting, different theoretical positions on the substantive issues can lead to very opposite interpretations about what is commonly termed "practical significance."

I will devote considerable space to assessing strengths of relationships, often called the *psychometric* rather than *inferential* tradition in statistics. In the long run, the two traditions are more complementary than antagonistic, but they are different. Specifically, many settings, most commonly experiments, of necessity involve gathering less data (using fewer subjects) than one would like. In "small-sample" situations, chance can play a very strong role. However, there are a great many settings, such as surveys, where the data gathering costs are much less and large amounts of data can be collected. Hence, the third variable problem and determination of strength of relationships are far more important considerations. Maintain the flexibility of thought needed to separate the considerations involved in "large-sample" and "small-sample" research. (The terms are in quotes to denote the somewhat arbitrary dividing line between the two.) Specifically, note that any correlation larger than .10 will be statistically significant with a sample of 500 or more, even though it only represents a 1% overlap in the variances of the two variables involved.

Multivariate analysis presents a problem in statistical inference that you probably did not encounter in your previous courses. Consider doing a simple ANOVA. Regardless of how group means differ, the familiar F ratio is the test most able to demonstrate the significance of group differences, i.e., it is the most powerful test for any form of univariate difference in group means. Use of the F test assumes that error within groups is normally distributed, equal in magnitude, and independent among groups. Even when the assumptions do not hold, you will probably not be led seriously astray. In short, there is only one natural test of univariate group mean differences; you do not have to worry about choosing among alternatives.

The situation is quite different in the MANOVA, which evaluates the effects of one or more independent variables on multiple dependent variables. The inferential test that is most powerful when the dependent variables correlate highly among themselves is not necessarily the most powerful when they do not. Consequently, attention must be directed to choice among several possible inferential tests in the MANOVA.

Outliers

Outliers are observations that do not belong to the population from which the remaining observations have been sampled. One often can detect certain observations that do not fit merely by looking at the raw data. You certainly do not need much training to recognize that a body temperature of 989 degrees is some form of error in acquisition, data entry, or the like. Intuitively, you would feel like not using that particular observation, and you would be perfectly right in so doing (although, like most people, you would probably feel a bit guilty about it). Clearly, as problems become more complex or if the observation were not so clearly out of range, detection becomes more difficult. More subtle outlying may exist, such as in correlational problems. Consider the following pairs of numbers: (2, 5), (4, 7), (1, 4), (6, 9), (8, 11), (3, 6), (2, 5), and (7, 4). As you can see, the second member of each pair is three more than the first in all cases save the last. The last case could well be an error in data entry.

Yet, the individual members of that erroneous pair each fall well within the range of correct values. Detecting the outlying pair is relatively easy in this example because the relation is otherwise perfect, a situation rarely found in practical problems.

Outliers play more of a role in disturbing multivariate analyses than univariate analyses because measures like correlations are inherently more sensitive to the problem of outliers than are measures like means. I will discuss ways to identify outliers in Chapter 5. Much current statistical research involves finding measures that are less sensitive to outliers or *robust estimation*. I will not deal with the topic further, however, since the appropriate techniques and references are just becoming available. Hoaglin, Mosteller, and Tukey (1983) provide an important introduction to the topic. Mosteller and Tukey (1977) is another useful source. Unfortunately, their discussions are limited to the simpler problems of outliers in univariate and bivariate situations.

The main point for you to remember is the old "GIGO" adage (garbage in, garbage out) will be more applicable as you get more heavily involved in multivariate analysis. Simply "dumping and running" with a large data base is not likely to prove profitable. An important part of your job is to see if the data under analysis are really descriptive of the situation. There is a corollary to the traditional meaning of "GIGO" that one encounters when dealing with sophisticated (or at least convincing) multivariate analysts—"GIGO" may translate into "garbage in, gospel out." Methods of multivariate analysis afford one the *potential* of being able to capture the essence of very complicated situations, but potentiality is not actuality. The methods can fail, at least in part, for several reasons. Nothing, however, limits their utility more than analysis of the "wrong" data.

The Importance of Theory

There is an important distinction between what are called *exploratory* and *confirmatory* procedures in multivariate analysis. The difference is that the former make minimal assumptions about the organization of the data and use *mathematical* criteria to explore the potential structure of the data. The latter, by contrast, employ *substantive* criteria that you supply and are designed to see how well your hypothesized organization fits the data. The exploratory/confirmatory distinction is actually more of a continuum. Your act of choosing variables to be included in an analysis should be regarded as a theory that you are testing. Moreover, different procedures allow you to test progressively more highly specified statements.

Stepwise multiple regression is a very popular exploratory procedure. The procedure involves the specification of a set of variables that *might* be included in the ultimate equation. However, the *procedure* chooses the variables using any of several *statistically* derived criteria, independently of theory. For example, the algorithm might begin by choosing a predictor that is most highly related to the criterion. If a significance test were to reveal that the correlation is significant, it might next look for a variable which, when added to the first, would increase the multiple correlation maximally. If the increase were significant, it would proceed to find another variable which, when added to the first two, would again increase the multiple correlation maximally, etc. The process stops when the increment becomes nonsignificant.

The most popular forms of factor analysis are also exploratory. For example, the method of principal components chooses the linear combination that accounts for the most available variance among a set of variables. Both stepwise regression and exploratory factor analysis involve choosing variables independently of what you as an investigator feel are the underlying relations.

In contrast, variables might be entered in what is known as *simultaneous* fashion in multiple regression. That is, you can specify that you want a particular set of variables entered and determine optimal weights for the set, thereby controlling what variables are entered. Another confirmatory procedure is to enter the variables *hierarchically* by specifying successive sets of variables to be entered. The analysis determines how much predictive power later sets *add* to earlier sets.[1] Finally, one may use *prior weightings* to define both the variables and their weights, most probably making them equal. In factor analysis, there are several procedures to see how well specified sets of relations among the variables describe the overall structure of the data.

A simple example illustrates the different ways of developing a linear composite using multiple regression. Assume that you have high school GPA, SAT-Verbal, SAT-Quantitative, and judgments made by an admissions committee for a group of students who have just completed their freshman year at college. You are interested in using the four variables to predict their freshman GPA. Stepwise selection chooses the predictors on the basis of normative data. The algorithm might include anywhere from none to all four of the variables in the regression equation. By contrast, simultaneous selection include all four variables in the equation, regardless of whether they are needed. There are several possible hierarchical strategies. One is to determine first if high school GPA predicts college GPA by itself. Assuming it does, the next step would be to see if the two SAT measures add to the prediction possible from high school GPA alone. Finally, one would determine if the committee's judgment adds to the prediction possible from high school GPA and the two SAT scores. The theory (and it is one, despite not being very elaborate) is that all students will have a high school GPA, so that information might just as well be looked at first. The next question is therefore whether it is worth having the students take the SAT, and the final question is whether the effort, time, and expense for both faculty and prospective students required in interviewing pays off in adding prediction. Finally, one could simply

---

[1] Some authors use the term "stepwise" to denote any means of building a linear combination by successively adding in variables and do not distinguish between selection on statistical grounds versus selection based on theory. Others make the same distinction that I make.

average the four measures (or perhaps just the first three) using some suitable correction for the differences in unit of measurement for high school GPA and SAT without attempting to weight them differentially.

Speaking simply from the standpoint of writing a computer program, exploratory procedures are often more intellectually challenging to develop than their confirmatory counterparts. There are some very important exceptions, such as Jöreskog's LISREL program (Jöreskog, 1969; Jöreskog & Sorbom, 1986), which is a confirmatory program reflecting a massive intellectual undertaking. Exploratory data analysis is in fact a distinct area of statistical inquiry of considerable complexity. In contrast, a more basic confirmatory program such as one simply designed to produce the regression equation and multiple correlation for a specific set of predictors is very easy to write.

As a researcher whose primary interest is empirical matters, I feel rather differently about the role of the most highly exploratory techniques—they are no substitute for thought. Always try to be aware of the theories guiding your work even if they are limited to why you consider certain variables to be important. There is no measurement without theory. Organize your analyses to test some of the your theoretical notions. Many people expect multivariate analyses to provide novel findings. Even if they are not disappointed in their initial study, they often become so later when their results fail to replicate. There is often unwarranted cynicism about multivariate analysis in general. No statistical wizardry can substitute for what you know about the phenomena you are studying. The techniques can and should serve your substantive hypotheses instead the converse.

I am not saying that you should never use exploratory techniques. They have a most legitimate place. They are most likely to prove useful when you wish to select some variables from a larger set and have equal interest in all variables in that larger set. Questionnaire construction often involves a set of items that you are "indifferent" about. Moreover, some confirmatory programs, such as those used in factor analysis, may be difficult to use and obtain. The situation exists because factor analysis historically evolved primarily as an exploratory tool. The point is to limit the circumstances under which you engage in "blind" data exploration as much as possible. Typically, exploration is appropriate at the early stages of investigation when interest centers in identifying the most important variables. Once some (not necessarily all) of the variables are identified, consider using confirmatory analyses to test structural hypotheses.

Problems Peculiar to the Analysis of Scales

A particular class of problems that is neglected in most standard textbooks on multivariate analysis, although found in books on psychometric theory, deals with how to make up *scales*, i.e., a collection of individual *items*. An individual item often tells one very little about the person responding, but a properly constructed scale can tell one a great deal.

I have devoted Chapter 12 to scale construction for two major reasons. The first is that students from a variety of disciplines need to know how to construct scales. However, it is often difficult for them to fit a formal course in psychometric theory into their curriculum. Courses like the present are an alternative place to consider scale construction. The second reason is that several problems emerge when multivariate analyses are conducted at the item as opposed to scale level (Bernstein & Eveland, 1982; Bernstein & Garbin, 1985a).

The Role of Computers in Multivariate Analysis

The importance of computers in multivariate analysis has long been accepted. One reason is that computers are as nearly perfect as any device can be at performing the iterative operations needed to solve many statistical problems.

As programming sophistication advanced, many people took a *systems* point of view to develop packages designed to solve a variety of multivariate problems. A systems design is possible because a few, very basic operations (which I will talk about more in Chapter 3) underlie nearly all analyses. Some packages date back at least 20 years. Some packages became quite popular and available in nearly the same form in many different computer installations. The packages were a godsend when people moved from one place to another, because they did not have to learn a new system from scratch to solve old problems.

Computer packages have all but eliminated the long hours spent in laborious and often uninformative (if not actually erroneous) computation. However, they have created at least two new problems. The first problem is that a student has to learn the conventions of the package's language. Once a particular package is learned so that you can solve one problem, such as multiple regression, it is easy to solve related problems such as factor analysis. However, an involved process of getting introduced to computers in general and the specific package still is necessary. The increasing computer literacy has minimized but not eliminated this problem. The second problem is the truly enormous volumes of thoroughly confusing output that can be generated by means of a few simple commands.

There used to be little text material to tie computer languages to the underlying statistical theory. Students often spent time reading articles devoted to teaching the very hand calculations that the computer packages were designed to eliminate instead of clarifying the underlying nature of the analysis. It was often difficult for students to see what actually went on generally, since they necessarily had to pay attention to computational details.

About 10–15 years ago, an important pair of books appeared that were intended to teach multivariate analysis to graduate students in psychology and related areas (Cooley & Lohnes, 1971; Overall & Klett, 1972). They were the first generation of textbooks to use computer programs as teaching devices. However, they suffered from their reliance upon FORTRAN as a computer language, which requires much more skill than the computer packages now in common use. This strategy was understandable when computer packages were in their infancy and were not supported by all university computer centers.

In subsequent years, several excellent texts have appeared that stress the use of computer packages as learning tools. Pedhazur's (1982) marvelous textbook not only provides a good theoretical grounding in the mathematics of multiple regression, but also does a superb job teaching students how to translate mathematics into the language of computer packages.

Using a computer to learn multivariate analysis allows an *inductive, empirically oriented* approach, which I prefer. Other authors, such as Timm (1975) and Morrison (1976) illustrate a more *deductive, mathematically oriented* approach. I am not saying that one is necessarily better than the other. The approach an author takes reflects that author's bias and interests. Different students will appreciate and learn more from one approach than from the other. The general approaches are only incompatible in so far as a graduate student's time is limited, which is always a real problem. My particular concern is that the analysis of real data has numerous problems that are not brought up in mathematically oriented textbooks. Nonetheless, I strongly encourage you to delve more deeply into the roots of multivariate analysis at some later point beyond the introduction I can provide in the next two chapters.

Multivariate Analysis and the Personal Computer

When I first started writing this book, personal computers played a very limited role in advanced statistical analysis. It was taken for granted that any complicated statistical analysis would be done on a mainframe computer. Since 1985, personal computer versions of every major package have started becoming available. In general, these versions are more restricted than their mainframe counterparts, but the limitations often do not pose a real problem. If you are just starting to work with data bases, you may wish to work through your university computer center and add a statistical computer package of your choice later. The cost of the statistical software is not major, but using the mainframe version first allows you to learn about the system at essentially no cost on your part.

If you do own a personal computer, one step you can and should take, if you have not done so yet, is to obtain a communication package such as CROSSTALK to send and receive data from your personal computer to the mainframe. The communication package that I use was developed at the university where I teach and is sold at a nominal fee. If you remain in a setting where you have access to a mainframe, the computer center can offer two services that are likely to be useful even after you obtain a multivariate analysis package for your personal computer: (1) It probably has a device, like an optical scanner, that allows you to enter data far more efficiently than you could with the personal computer's own input devices, and (2) it serves as a repository for your files. Both of these services are very important.

Although mass input devices like optical scanners are also available for personal computers, they are relatively expensive and not nearly as efficient as those found with mainframes. The average user of a personal computer simply does not have the needs for mass input that a researcher working with multivariate analysis does. This situation is likely to continue. Indeed, most academic computer centers have better devices for mass input than commercial computer companies.

It is difficult to overemphasize the role a computer center plays as a repository (backup) for your valuable files, because it is difficult to say enough about backing up files. I am a fairly compulsive person, but I cannot match the precautions taken by the computer center at my university! Of course, you will want to keep your own backups, but the added safety of a duplicate tape file at your computer center cannot be overestimated.

Perhaps the most obvious difference between mainframes and personal computers is that the mainframes are currently much faster. Well over 90% of the jobs I run on the mainframe require 15 seconds or less of actual computer time. A 15-second mainframe job will currently take several minutes for a personal computer to execute. However, I do not consider the difference to be the major one separating the two approaches in the long run. The reason is that although the efficiency of both is increasing at a rapid rate, the practical consequences of an increase in personal computer efficiency is much more significant. It is quite probable that a 15-second mainframe job will take 10 seconds or less within the next few years. That increase in speed will certainly be appreciated.

However, the practical effect of an increase in the efficiency of mainframes will be far less noticeable than an increase in the efficiency of personal computers. Consider the impact of a decrease from 15 to 5 seconds on the mainframe relative to a decrease in personal computer time from 1 minute to even 30 seconds, which is also quite likely to occur in the very near future. Your major problem on the mainframe will continue to be getting access, which depends on the number of other users, and the real time for computation, which includes the time shared with concurrent users as well as the access time. Multivariate statistical packages demand considerable mainframe resources and, at least at my university computer center, are deliberately placed at a disadvantage in scheduling so that running a statistical analysis actually takes much longer in real time than a job requiring the same amount of computer time.

Another significant development that is likely to affect personal computers in the very near future, perhaps by the time this book is printed, is increased *multitasking*, i.e., performing two or more functions at the same time. If you have an IBM or IBM compatible personal computer that uses MS-DOS as an operating system, you are probably aware that you can print a file while you are performing some other function such as making statistical computations. The printing "steals" time between keystrokes and other operations. However, you cannot be intercorrelating a set of variables at the same time that you are writing a report with the current version of MS-DOS. This situation is quite likely to change, further minimizing the advantages of the mainframe.

If you are fairly new to the use of computers, my advice is that you spend at least some time with your computer center personnel (with the added caution that you look at them as *computing* and not *statistical* resource people). The time will be well spent even if you reduce your mainframe needs to mass input and file storage, because the knowledge and skills needed for a mainframe and a personal computer are more similar than they are different.

Choosing a Computer Package

If you are using a large mainframe computer to solve multivariate problems, it is highly probable that you will be using one of three major packages: *Statistical Analysis System* (SAS, 1985), the *Statistical Package for the Social Sciences* (SPSSX, 1986), and the *Biomedical Computer Programs: P-Series* (BMDP, 1983). All three have greatly democratized statistical analyses by allowing them to be done by people with relatively little formal training, and have fostered the evolution of newer techniques. The two most heavily used procedures, factor analysis and multiple regression, have evolved the most.

Originally, the three packages had a very distinctive flavor. SPSSX was oriented toward the social sciences; SAS was most closely tied to basic statistics, but was heavily slanted to problems in agriculture and economics; and BMDP was oriented to biomedical applications, as its name indicates. They have greatly broadened their appeal recently, in part motivated by commercial demands which have blurred differences among them. I will talk a bit more about their current differences shortly, but the similarities among them are probably more important to consider first.

Consider a problem such as, without using a computer, predicting improvement in psychotherapy from the 14 major clinical scales of the MMPI based on data from, say, 500 patients. This multiple regression problem is, in abstract form, typical of many. Old age would long have caught up with you by the time you solved the problem by hand calculation. Of at least as much importance is that you would be ill inclined to explore alternative prediction models, say, deleting one or more of the 14 scales to see if those to-be-deleted scale or scales are important to prediction. While the recomputation necessary to explore alternative solutions is minor compared to that involved in solving the original problem, it is certainly not trivial. However, it *is* trivial in terms of the code one needs to add to a program written in BMDP, SAS, or SPSSX once the initial file is defined.

The similar functions to which SPSSX, BMDP, and SAS are used naturally invite comparisons among them. There are several major differences, but any of the major packages can perform most of the popular analyses. Unfortunately, none can perform some highly useful techniques such as oblique multiple groups factor analysis (an important type of confirmatory factor analysis). Your "choice" may in fact be dictated by your instructor, the computer center at your university, etc., and it is probably just as well. The one thing I would suggest is to stick to one of the packages until you have learned it well before trying another. As you will discover there are an infinite number of ways that you can make an error in writing a program and, in many cases, erroneous results may appear to be correct. Knowing how to debug programs efficiently and how to avoid common errors comes only with practice.

If you do have a choice as to package or are curious as to the major differences among them, the following points may prove useful. SPSSX had the early lead in number of users. The earlier editions of its manual were clearly the most useful for learning both the analytic techniques and the details of the language. In that sense, it assumed less statistical knowledge than BMDP or SAS. Unfortunately, that manual was rendered obsolete by the new version of SPSS (SPSSX), and its new manual has little general didactic value. I also find many of SPSSX's printouts for simpler procedures such as crosstabulations to be the clearest. However, their printouts associated with more complex procedures are not necessarily the best. Its RELIABILITY program for item analysis has no current parallel in SAS.

One complaint I have with SPSSX is that it tries to do too much for the beginner. Many beginning users, particularly those who do not explore the effects of changing default options, come away thinking that there is only one way to perform a particular analysis.

SPSSX was introduced to meet the competition (primarily SAS) that allowed sophisticated users to develop their own programs in a modified matrix notation. The SPSSX matrix language is still in the process of implementation and debugging. Also available as a part of SPSSX in some computer installations is Jöreskog's LISREL program, a highly sophisticated program that can be used to test various multivariate hypotheses. I will talk a bit about LISREL in Chapter 6.

BMDP has an extremely wide variety of programs that are especially useful in the analysis of experimental, as opposed to field, data. However, I feel its documentation is clearly the poorest of the three major packages. A second weak point is that it is least likely to be available on disk (a situation true at the Academic Computing Center of the University of Texas at Arlington, where I teach). Lack of disk access is very inconvenient as users need to wait for the tape to be mounted on each run, causing turnaround time to be long.

SAS has probably evolved the most rapidly and is probably the language of choice for statistical users who had not already become fluent in one of the other packages, as I had. It was the first of the three packages to allow users to write their own routines in matrix notation. Its manual has improved tremendously over the years, and I prefer its defaults. SAS is also extremely flexible in the way that output from one procedure to be used as input to another, which can be a most time-saving feature.

Regardless of which package you use, you should learn how to save system files, which all three allow. Your initial run will usually consist of raw data, program instructions that tell how the data are to be read, descriptive names for the variables, "missing values" (codes which denote that the values of certain variables are to be disregarded for particular cases), and new variables that the program may generate (such as the sum of two or more variables that have been individually read in). Saving information on a system file allows a few simple commands to retrieve the system file and replaces the initial data and program. Moreover, an SPSSX system file can be read in SAS (but not the reverse in the current version of SPSSX). System files are an extremely efficient way to analyze data, especially if you have to use punched cards or tape as opposed to data entry from a terminal.

The point of my discussion is to illustrate just a bit of the incredible impact of the computer and computer packages and to emphasize their evolution. I do not want to extoll the virtues of the old days, when analysts were analysts and *really* learned factor analysis, multiple regression, and the like by doing it by hand, any more than I want to lie about how bad winters were when I was young. I really did not learn that much after getting the kind of headache that old-fashioned mechanical calculators gave you following a not-too-long period of time. Until the computer came along, the division between those people knowledgeable as to the substantive aspects of a problem and people who were technically sophisticated but substantively ignorant was all too great. The situation is still somewhat true (after all, it does take a fair amount of effort to learn about the computer system you are using, then learn the details of the package, etc.), but it has become less of a problem with the growth of well-conceived packages.

Problems in the Use of Computer Packages

I would like to point out two related problems. One is the frequent tendency to confuse knowledge of the *syntax* and *semantics* of a language, i.e., knowing how to get a problem to run correctly, with knowledge of its *pragmatics*, i.e., how to best answer the underlying empirical questions. It is the job of the computer center staff to address the former, not the latter. Secondly, performing an extremely complex analysis has been made quite easy, especially after the basic data file has been created. As little as one line of code can generate pages and pages of printout. Unfortunately, it is now extremely easy for people to obtain results that are mainly, if not totally, spurious, because they do not know the details of their analysis.

The guides provided by the publishers of the packages do not and cannot provide the information that a text can about the pragmatics of analysis. Package developers follow generally accepted guidelines in choosing defaults.

However, you will lose much, if not all, of the value of a package by slavishly following the defaults. One can learn a great deal about the intricacies of a technique by "playing around" with the various options. Indeed, "playing around" is a must.

In short, the ability to solve practical problems of a complex nature requires you to bring together four things:

1. *substantive* knowledge of the area of interest as to what theories exist, what previous data have been brought to bear on the topic, etc.;
2. *computer* knowledge of how to get analyses done in a manner empirically relevant to the problem;
3. *empirical experience* with various kinds of data bases; and
4. *formal* knowledge of the techniques in a mathematical sense.

I do not suggest that you have to be equally and deeply versed in each area. I am not going to be very formal in a mathematical sense and do not feel I have to be. However, I strongly urge you eventually to get at least minimal training in each of the four areas. I particularly urge you to become sufficiently proficient so that the problem dictates the method and not the reverse.

I am hopeful that you will become sufficiently involved in multivariate analysis to study its formal bases. I hope to minimize the number of what I call "SPSSX analysts" (or "SAS analysts" or "BMDP analysts" or, for that matter "all available package" analysts) within empirical disciplines. The term describes people who are virtuosos at the level of semantics and syntax of computer languages but ignorant of the pragmatics. Of course, no insult is intended to the packages themselves nor to the people whose job it is to develop and implement them.

The Importance of Matrix Procedures

SAS has had a procedure called "PROC MATRIX" for some time, and SPSSX is introducing a parallel procedure. (As this book is being completed, SAS is in the process of revising its matrix procedure under the name of 'PROC IML.") Matrix procedures allow the user to specify multivariate computations that may not be part of any specific procedure. For example, suppose you have generated what is called a *data matrix* named "X" with NR rows specifying people and NC columns specifying variables. You could use SAS PROC CORR or other related procedures to determine the correlations among the variables. However, you can write your own program in PROC MATRIX. The following key steps produce a correlation matrix, symbolized "R":

$$COV = (X'^*X - X(+,)'^*X(+,) \# /NR) \# /(NR - 1.);$$

$$RSD = HALF(INV(DIAG(COV)));$$

$$R = RSD^*COV^*RSD;$$

It is not important that you know what the code means. The point is that it took me only three statements to obtain the desired result.[2] If you have previously tried to write a program in BASIC, FORTRAN, PASCAL, or similar languages, you should have a special appreciation for the simplicity of these calculations because these latter languages require you to perform countless "bookkeeping" operations like initializing variables, which you do not have to do in PROC MATRIX.

The particular application I originally wrote the above code for was to compute what will be introduced in Chapter 12 as *coefficient alpha*, a statistic that defines the reliability of a scale. Despite the many virtues of SAS, it does not have a reliability procedure as does SPSSX. However, knowing PROC MATRIX allows me to overcome this limitation.

It is not necessary for you to know PROC MATRIX to use this book. However, once you have mastered the materials of Chapter 3, you will be prepared to exploit most of the features of PROC MATRIX. You can then write routines to perform analyses discussed in later chapters and learn the logic of the methods very directly. You will discover that most analyses require but a relatively few procedure statements once the relevant data matrix or matrices are defined.

Having completed the introduction, I will move on to an examination of some basic statistical concepts. Most will be at least somewhat familiar, but I will introduce some concepts, such as partial correlation, which you may have heard of but never dealt directly with, and introduce some others that are even less familiar. One important set of concepts are: *total*, *between-group*, and *within-group* correlations.

---

[2] The program actually can be written in one step. I used three because I needed the output of the first step, "*COV*," which is the *variance–covariance matrix* to be introduced in Chapter 2, when I originally wrote the program.

2
Some Basic Statistical Concepts

Chapter Overview

Chapter 2 contains three major topics:

I. UNIVARIATE DATA ANALYSIS—Several topics contained in most basic statistics texts are discussed: (1) the concept of a frequency distribution, (2) the normal distribution in both its general and standard forms, (3) the distinction between parameters and statistics, (4) measures of location, (5) measures of variability, (6) the concept of estimation, (7) the special case of binary data and the binomial distribution, and (8) data transformations.

II. BIVARIATE DATA ANALYSIS—Basic concepts in correlation and regression are reviewed. The specific topics are: (1) characteristics of bivariate relationships, (2) bivariate normality, (3) measures of bivariate relation, (4) range restriction, (5) Pearson measures of relationship, (6) non-Pearson measures of relationship, (6) the sampling error of a correlation, (7) the Z' transformation, (8) linear regression, (9) the geometry of regression, (10) the concept of a residual, (11) the concept of a standard error, and (12) why the term "regression" is appropriate.

III. STATISTICAL CONTROL: A FIRST LOOK AT MULTIVARIATE RELATIONS—I will conclude this chapter with material that is very likely to be new to you: (1) partial and part correlation, (2) statistical versus experimental control, (3) multiple partialling, and (4) within-group, between-group, and total correlations.

Chapter 2 is concerned with three broad topics: (1) characteristics of an individual variable or *univariate analysis*, (2) characteristics of the relation between pairs of variables while ignoring the effects of other variables or *bivariate analysis*, and (3) characteristics of the relation between pairs of variables that simultaneously considers additional variables or *statistical control*. You have probably been exposed to most of the essentials of the first two topics in prior courses, since they deal with the fundamentals of descriptive statistics, simple correlation, and linear regression. I will assume that you at least know what terms like mean, standard deviation, and correlation denote. In order to avoid duplication of material covered in introductory textbooks, I will simply highlight such material. If it has been a while since you had your basic statistics course, you might wish to review these subjects. Do not worry too much about the material on statistical inference, since it will be covered later. The third topic includes the concept of partial correlation and some other important concepts related to it such as within-group, between-group, and total correlations, which may be new to most of you.

Univariate Data Analysis

Frequency Distributions

A useful way to describe a variable is in terms of its *frequency distribution*, which represents how often a particular value of a given variable occurs. If I designate the variable as X and its frequency as Y, the relation may be symbolized in the form of Eq. (2-1):

$$Y = F(X) \tag{2-1}$$

Normal Distributions

The most important frequency distribution is the normal or Gaussian distribution, defined by Eq. (2-2):

$$Y = \{1/[s(2\pi)^{1/2}]\} \exp\{-.5[(X - \bar{X})/s]^2\} \tag{2-2}$$

where π is the constant 3.1416... and exp is the constant 2.71828... (the base of natural logarithms). Note that only two parameters, $\bar{X}$ and s (its mean and standard deviation), are free to vary. Specifying both, then, completely specifies the distribution. You will frequently see references like: "The distribution is Normal (100, 15)" or even "The distribution is N(100, 15)," which is shorthand for "The distribution is normal in form with a mean of 100 and a standard deviation of 15."

Standard Normal Distributions

If the mean of a normal distribution is set to 0, and its standard deviation is set to 1, the result is a *standard normal distribution*, which may be symbolized as "Normal(0, 1)." Its formula is given by Eq. (2-3):

$$Y = [1/(2\pi)^{1/2}] \exp(-z^2/2) \tag{2-3}$$

Traditionally, "z" is used instead of "x" to denote a variable in standard normal form. If the original distribution is normal, the standard form can be obtained by subtracting a raw score from its mean, then dividing by the standard deviation: $z = (X - \bar{X})/s$. However, the symbol "z" is also often used to denote a variable that is not normally distributed but which is transformed to a mean of .0 and standard deviation of 1, using the above equation. Such a variable would be called "standardized" or "in standard form," but would not be normal. A *z* score derived from a normal distribution is referred to by the somewhat paradoxical term *normal deviate*. Appendix A contains a table of the probabilities associated with *z* scores derived from a normal distribution.

Normal distributions are important because they are often useful as models or representations of the *random error* that is a part of behavioral data. Most familiar inferential tests assume normality. However, data that many people believe are or should be normally distributed, such as observed test scores, are in fact not nor should they necessarily be normally distributed because they are strongly influenced by some *systematic* factors.

Normality is a consequence of the *central limit theorem*, which is basic to the study of random error. The central limit theorem may be described as follows. Suppose you have a distribution of arbitrary shape, called a *parent distribution*. Let μ and σ denote its mean and standard deviation. (Greek letters are used to distinguish these quantities from sample data; see the subsequent section on *parameters* if you are not already familiar with this distinction.) Now, form successive random samples of individual observations from the parent distribution. (A random sample is one in which each member of the population has an equal opportunity to be selected.) The successive samples form a distribution of their own, called a *sampling distribution of size 1*, in the present example (since the individual observations in this sampling distribution are based on single observations drawn from the parent distribution). The sampling distribution will match the parent distribution in shape and will have the same mean and standard deviation (μ and σ, respectively).

Repeat the same sampling process but now choose a *pair* of observations in each random sample, independently of each other. As before, repeat the process of sampling many times. Plot the average of the two observations that are obtained from each sample to form a *sampling distribution of size 2*. The shape of the distribution will differ from the shape of the parent distribution. It will be more peaked—that is, more of the observations will be close to μ and fewer will be at the extremes or tails—because it is less likely (by the factor of a square compared to the case of a single observation) that you will get two extremely low or two extremely high observations as compared to a single low or a single high observation in one sample. The mean of the distribution will still be μ but the standard deviation will be $\sigma/2^{1/2}$. The standard deviation of the sampling distribution of a mean is known as the *standard error of the mean*.

Now, keep repeating the process by obtaining successive samples of size 3, 4, . . . , so that you obtain sampling distributions of size 3, 4, ... In each case, the mean of the sampling distribution will equal the mean of the parent distribution (μ), but the successive standard deviations will be $\sigma/3^{1/2}$, $\sigma/4^{1/2}$, $\sigma/N^{1/2}$, where N is the sample size, and *the successive sampling distributions obtained from progressively larger-sized samples will approximate the normal distribution more and more.* At some point, the sampling distribution will be indistinguishable from a normal distribution. How many observations are needed per sample to achieve normality depends somewhat on the shape of the parent distribution, but sampling distributions based on 12 or more observations per sample are fairly normal and those based on 30 or more can usually be treated as normal. Keep in mind that the observations within the sample must be *independent of (uncorrelated with) each other.*

Because many scores, especially those derived from a multi-item scale, are based on averages of many items (or sums, as a distribution of sums will have the same shape as a distribution of averages), they meet the central limit theorem in part. However, it is not likely that the items are independent of each other. Items are included on a test precisely because they *are not* independent of each other. They are there because they measure a common construct, such as knowledge of material in a given course, general cognitive ability, anxiety, or attitudes toward a given product. Although you may be adding several components (items) to obtain a total score, you will not necessarily be adding *independent* components. If, in fact, the components (items) are independent, you have made up a poor test—the items do not measure anything in common (see Chapter 12).

Another important condition giving rise to a variable that will be normally distributed occurs when you form that variable by adding variables that are themselves normally distributed. It does not matter whether the individual normally distributed variables are sampled independently of each other, nor does the number of observations being added matter. The normality of sums of normally distributed variables is a very important concept in advanced statistical theory.

As a consequence of the interdependency among items, distributions based on test scores that are defined by adding over items will be more platykurtic (flatter) than the normal distribution. In addition, if most of the items have a low probability of being scored "correct" (answered in the keyed direction), the distribution will be positively skewed, thus lacking the normal distribution's symmetry. The reverse will hold if most of the items have a high probability of being scored "correct"; the distribution will be negatively skewed.

The reason that I used test scores in my example of nonnormality was to illustrate a point that is frequently misunderstood. In actuality, distributions of obtained scores will often be approximately normal so as not to cause severe problems in most cases when normality must be assumed. Normality is usually assumed for inferential tests of significance, but it is not required for most purely descriptive statistics. Moreover, the assumption that is critical to most inferential tests is that the *sampling error* of statistics like the mean be normally distributed, not the *individual observations* on which they are based. Furthermore, symmetric distributions are not always desirable. For example, the individual scales on the Minnesota Multiphasic Personality Inventory (MMPI), which is widely used to diagnose emotional maladjustment, produce scores that are quite positively skewed. Intended skew like this is appropriate because there is usually more interest in making discriminations among people who score high on a given scale than those who score low when the high end is the one denoting maladjustment.

Parameters and Statistics

When a distribution is viewed as an entity to itself and not as a subset of some larger body of data (actual or potential), properties that describe it, such as the mean, median, variance, and standard deviation, are called *parameters*. Corresponding properties of data sampled from this distribution are called *statistics*. An important area within mathematical statistics is concerned with problems of *estimation* of a parent distribution's parameters based on sample statistics. It is common for books on statistics to use Greek letters to symbolize parameters and English letters to symbolize statistics. I will use English letters when the distinction between statistics and parameters is not important to discussion.

Locational Parameters and Statistics

The first thing that one usually wishes to know about a distribution is its location (central tendency or "typicalness"). Measures of location include various types of mean, median, and mode. If a distribution is reasonably symmetric, the ordinary arithmetic mean (which I will simply call the *mean*) is generally preferred for descriptive purposes since it tends to be relatively stable across samples, i.e., is more *efficient* (the meaning of which will be explained shortly), than other descriptive indices like the median. The median, conversely, is preferred when distributions are highly asymmetric. There are in fact a whole class of compromise measures called *trimmed* means that are obtained by deleting the first and last K observations rank ordered in terms of magnitude. The median is indeed the limiting case of a trimmed mean since all but the middle one or two observations are trimmed.

Practically all multivariate analyses are based on the mean as a measure of location. Thus, even though many applications of multivariate analysis do not require normality, results obtained from highly skewed distributions can be misleading for the same reasons that they are in the univariate case. If nine people have zero income and the tenth earns a million dollars a year, the mean salary for these 10 persons of $100,000/year does not really describe anyone's income as well as the median of $0 does. To repeat the point made in Chapter 1, *artifacts that cause problems in univariate analysis cause even worse problems in multivariate analysis.*

Measures of Variability

As in the case of describing the location of a distribution, there are several ways to describe its variability (spread). The variability of distributions is at least as important as is location. In some procedures, specifically factor analysis, variability is the major point of interest and location is usually irrelevant. Variability measures answer the question of "how typical is typical." The most frequently used measure of variability is the *variance* defined as:

$$s^2 = \frac{\sum x^2}{N} \tag{2-4a}$$

$$s^2 = \frac{N \sum X^2 - (\sum X)^2}{N^2} \tag{2-4b}$$

Equation (2-4a) is the definitional formula and (2-4b) is a computational formula. I will follow the common convention of using lower case symbols ("x") to denote a *deviation score* (also known as a *centered* score), which is obtained by subtracting a raw score (written in upper case) from the mean of the distribution, i.e., $x = (X - \bar{X})$. The numerator of both equations defines the *sum of squares*, which plays an important role in statistical theory. The square root of the variance is the *standard deviation*.

You probably were taught that the more accepted formula for the variance uses $N - 1$ in the denominator instead of N. I will be using N in most cases for two reasons. First, the quantity $N - 1$, or *degrees of freedom* (*df*—the number of original observations that are not *constrained by the requirements of estimation*), is used instead of N to eliminate *bias* in the estimation of the population variance. That is, using $N - 1$ can be shown to produce estimates that are neither too high nor too low in the long run. However, it can also be shown that N produces the most *likely* (most probable) estimate of the variance in a normal (or nearly normal) distribution, an equally desirable property. Second, the practical difference between $N - 1$ and N in samples of the size I will discuss in this book is negligible. I will make exceptions where it is necessary to use the *df* in the formula for the variance.

A Note on Estimation

The difference between using N and $N - 1$ to estimate a variance provides an opportunity to discuss some of the problems of statistical estimation. The general problem may be stated as how to "best" estimate a parameter from sample data. Many statisticians are interested in general definitions of "best" and the strategies and formulas needed to obtain such estimates in various situations. The problems have proven difficult.

Statisticians recognize four basic properties of sample statistics:

1. *Bias*—A statistic is *biased* if its average value over repeated *random* samplings differs from the true value of the parameter being estimated. Conversely, if its average value is equal to the value of the parameter being estimated, it is said to be *unbiased.* The sample mean is an unbiased estimate of the population mean because the mean of all possible sample

means equals the population mean. An individual sample mean may and probably will differ from the population mean, but not *systematically*, if the sampling is random. As I noted previously, dividing the sum of squares by N instead of $N - 1$ to estimate the variance of a population yields a biased estimate because it will be systematically too low by a factor of $(N - 1)/N$.

2. *Efficiency*—The efficiency of a statistic is the relative lack of variability in its values across samples. Efficiency (actually "inefficiency") is defined as the variance of the sampling distribution of the statistic in question. If it is reasonable to assume that a particular distribution is symmetric, you can then use either the sample *mean* or the sample *median* to estimate the population mean. Both can be shown to be unbiased. However, the variance of a sampling distribution of means is about 25% smaller (more efficient) than a sampling distribution of medians.

3. *Consistency*—A statistic is consistent if any bias it might have approaches zero as the sample size increases. Thus, dividing the sum of squares by N instead of the *df* produces a consistent estimate of the sample variance. The bias approaches zero as sample size increases because the ratio of N to $N - 1$ approaches 1.

4. *Sufficiency*—A statistic is sufficient if it provides all the information possible about the parameter. For example, once you have added a series of scores and divided by N to obtain a sample mean, no further information can help you to estimate the population mean better, e.g., knowing the sample standard deviation will not help you predict the population mean.

Bias and efficiency are much more important considerations than consistency and sufficiency in most applications of statistical theory.

There are several estimation techniques that are applicable to a variety of parameters. For example, there are *least squares* procedures to estimate the mean, variance, lines of best fit, etc. Other techniques include *minimum chi-square* and, especially, *maximum likelihood*. All are based on minimizing a mathematical definition of error or, alternatively, maximizing a definition of goodness of fit. As it turns out, there is no "best" way of estimation that is both unbiased and most efficient in all situations. In addition, most earlier strategies considered only sampling error and not the effects of outliers.

The major concern of early statisticians was to avoid bias. Least squares procedures, which minimize the squared difference between the expected value of the statistic and the parameter, were the first to emerge because they are unbiased. Moreover, they have the useful property of not requiring assumptions about the form of the underlying distribution in most (but not all) applications. Specifically, *least squares estimates usually do not assume normality*.

On the other hand, most statisticians' interest in recent years has shifted toward maximizing *efficiency*. *Maximum likelihood* methods have become popular as a consequence. This procedure chooses the value of the parameter that is most *probable* given the data. Maximum likelihood estimators tend to be slightly biased but more efficient than least squares estimators of the same parameters. However, the former require assumptions about the underlying distribution, typically that of normality, which the latter do not require.

Dividing the sum of squares by N rather than $N - 1$ provides a maximum likelihood estimate of the variance if the data are sampled from a normal distribution. Suppose you obtain a series of sums of squares by sampling from a normal population. If you divide each sum of squares by N, the resulting variance estimates will vary less among themselves than if you divide each sum of squares by $N - 1$.

In some cases both the least squares and the maximum likelihood estimators are the same. Using the sample mean to estimate the population mean is a very common example.

Binary Data and the Binomial Distribution

I will now change topics to discuss a form of data that is very important in the analysis of scales based on individual items—*binary* data. Distributions based on binary (dichotomous or two-valued) data are extremely common. Test items are often constructed in agree–disagree, correct–incorrect, or yes–no fashion. In other cases, such as the MMPI, the response alternatives contain a "cannot say" or "neutral" category that makes the items, in principle, not binary. If, however, few people actually use the neutral category, the data can also be considered to be binary.

In a special case, called the *binomial distribution*, a series of items (or other forms of data derived from binary responses) can be considered independent of each other (passing or failing one item provides no information about passing or failing any other item, where "passing" and "failing" are used in a general sense of "agreeing with the scorer's key") *and* the probability of passing any one item is the same as the probability of passing any other. In that case, successive items define what is known in statistics as a series of *Bernoulli trials*.

Assume for a moment that items are answered independently. If that is indeed the case, the probability of passing any one item can be expressed as p, and the complementary probability of failing that item, which equals $1 - p$, can be expressed as q. It can be shown that the *proportion* of total items passed will also equal p and the *number* of items passed will equal Np, where N is the number of independent trials. Depending on the situation, "items" can be the number of items on the test, *or* it can be the number of people responding to a given item. The variance associated with proportion of items passed is pq, and the variance associated with the number of items passed is Npq.

To illustrate, assume that the probability of passing any one item on a 50-item test is .7. One would expect 70% of the items to be passed, which represents an average score of 35 items ($50 \times .7$). Similarly, the variances will be .21 ($.7 \times .3$) for the proportion of items or 10.5 for the number of items ($50 \times .7 \times .3$). The standard deviation of the total score will be $(10.5)^{1/2} = 3.2$.

If the lesser of Np and Nq is small, say, less than 5, the binomial distribution is quite nonnormal, but it tends toward normality if both Np and Nq exceed

5. As p increases from .0 to 1., and q correspondingly decreases from 1. to .0, the distribution goes from being positively skewed, to symmetric (at $p = .5$), to negatively skewed. Consequently, data that are based on a small number of independent events with extreme values of p (either very high or very low) can be quite nonnormal.

Ordinarily, test data such as questionnaires do not fit the binomial distribution, because both the assumptions of constant probability and independence are not met. First, some people are consistently smarter (more liberal, better adjusted, etc.) than others across items. Also, some items are harder than others. Moreover, items are chosen for scales precisely because they measure the same trait, and thus are not independent.

One reason the binomial distribution is important is that its variance (Npq) is a lower limit of the variance of a test based on binary data, since it describes the variance of a random set of items. In other words, suppose you constructed a 10-item test and each item had a p value of .5. Suppose the test were as bad as it could be, consisting of totally unrelated items. The total score would be derived from pooling unrelated entities, "apples" and "oranges" in almost a literal sense. Even so, total test scores will still vary over subjects. The magnitude of the variance will 2.5 ($Npq = 10 \times .5 \times .5$).

The test you actually construct will consist of items that are related to each other. Even if each item's p is .5, a person who gets item 1 correct, for example, will have a greater than .5 probability of getting item 2 correct, etc. A direct consequence is that the actual variance of subjects will be greater than 2.5 items. The *reliability* of a test (the consistency with which the items measure a given trait) is indexed in part by the extent to which the variance of subjects' scores exceeds the baseline set by the binomial variance of unrelated items (see Chapter 12).

The binomial distribution has another important property. Suppose that the *lesser* of the quantities Np and Nq is 5 or more so that the binomial distribution can be approximated by the normal distribution. There will still be an important difference between the two distributions. The binomial distribution is *discrete*. That is, the number of correct responses can only take on a limited number of distinct values, the integers 0 to N. In contrast, normal distributions are *continuous*. The quantity z can assume any value. The use of the normal distribution to approximate the binomial distribution is discussed in standard introductory tests such as Hays (1981).

Data Transformation

I will shift topics again to consider the important process of transforming scores from one unit of measurement or *metric* to another. Such data transformations are of two types. A *linear transformation* merely changes the mean and standard deviation to a more convenient or familiar unit. Equation (2-5) provides the general form of a linear transformation:

TABLE 2-1. Some commonly occurring transformations

Name	$\bar{X}$	s
z	0.0	1.0
SAT, GRE	500.0	100.0
(McCall) T-Score	50.0	10.0
(Deviation) IQ	100.0	15.0
Sten	5.5	2.0
Normal Curve Equivalents	50.0	21.1
Stanine	5.0	2.0
U.S. Employment Service Tests	100.0	20.0

$$Y = \frac{s_y}{s_x}(X - \bar{X}) + \bar{Y} \tag{2-5}$$

where, X, $\bar{X}$, and s_x denote the raw score, the mean, and the standard deviation of the original distribution, respectively. Conversely, let Y, $\bar{Y}$, and s_y denote the corresponding transformed score, its mean, and its standard deviation.

Linear transformations do not alter the *shape* of the distribution. In contrast, a *nonlinear* or *area* transformation *does* change the shape of a distribution. One common purpose of such transformations is to make a distribution more normal. The following steps are used to perform a normal curve transformation. First, find the proportion of cases falling at or below the midpoint of each class interval, i.e., determine the *cumulative probability distribution*. Then, determine the z score that corresponds to each cumulative probability (proportion) using a table of the normal curve. The resulting scores will have a mean of 0 and a standard deviation of 1. Equation (2-5) may be used to convert them to those having a more desirable mean and standard deviation. Hays (1981, Chapter 5), along with most authors of introductory texts, discuss linear transformations with relevant examples.

Certain transformations (combinations of means and standard deviations) appear commonly enough to deserve special designation and are presented in Table 2-1. In each case, the underlying data are normalized. However, scaled MMPI scores, for example, are presented as "T-Scores," since the scores are scaled to a mean of 50 and a standard deviation of 10, but they are usually not normalized.

Bivariate Data Analysis

Characteristics of Bivariate Relationships

Bivariate data analysis considers the relations among pairs of variables. A *scatterplot* is a good way to represent bivariate data. Figure 2-1 contains three

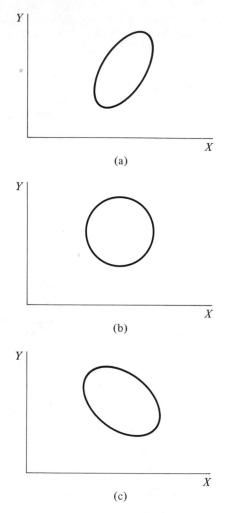

FIGURE 2-1. Scatterplots representing (a) positive, (b) zero, and (c) negative correlations.

scatterplots. One (2-1a) denotes a *positive* linear relation, such as between the tendency to complain about one's health as indexed by an MMPI scale and the number of job days per year lost through sickness. Figure 2-1b describes the *absence* of a linear relation (as is true of all too many of my studies), and Fig. 2-1c describes a *negative* linear relation, as might exist between ratings of the perceived honesty of individuals and ratings of liking them.

The general shape or *envelope* of points in a scatterplot will be *elliptical* if each of the two variables tends toward normality. The ratio of the length of the longer (major) axis of the ellipse to the shorter one is an index of the strength of the relationship between the two variables. When the relationship is perfect, the shorter (minor) axis of the ellipse degenerates to a length of zero. When there is no relation between the two variables, as in Fig. 2-1b, the two axes of the ellipse are of equal length. If the major axis of the ellipse slants up to the right, the relation between the two variables is positive (direct); if the major axis of the ellipse slants down to the right, the relation is negative (indirect). This assumes that values of X increase from the left and values of Y increase from the bottom.

The two axes of the ellipse define what are known as the _principal components_ of the space in which the points fall. Principal components play a major role in multivariate analysis. When the two variables are standardized, they always slope at 45 degrees and 135 degrees, but their orientations depend on the units of measurement when the data are plotted as raw scores. *As important as the principal components are, do not confuse them with more commonly encountered and perhaps more important regression lines, which are used to predict one variable from others.* The concept of regression line will be discussed later in this chapter. Among several differences to be discussed, regression lines slope at different angles depending on the strength of relationship between the two variables in question.

[handwritten margin note: the line you get when r=1]

Bivariate Normality

The observations in most scatterplots tend to be concentrated at the point representing the average of the two variables or *centroid*. The *density* of the points falls off in all directions from the centroid. There is a formal probability model for a two-dimensional space derived from two variables that are each normally distributed. Equation (2-6) gives the probability density (height) at a given two-dimensional region when two variables (z_x and z_y) are standardized (the formula for nonstandardized variables is quite cumbersome). The function is known as a *bivariate normal distribution*:

$$Y = \frac{\exp\{-[z_x^2 + z_y^2 - 2rz_xz_y]/[2(1 - r^2)]\}}{[2\pi(1 - r^2)]} \qquad (2\text{-}6)$$

The bivariate case requires the *covariance* of X and Y, $\text{COV}(X, Y)$, discussed below. When X and Y are in standard score form, $\text{COV}(X, Y)$ becomes the correlation between X and Y, as in Eq. (2-6). If the covariance term is large compared to the standard deviations of the two variables, the envelope will form an elongated ellipse. If the covariance term is small, the envelope will be more nearly circular.

In order to visualize the two-dimensional relationship better, consider what the distribution of Y scores would look like if you *ignored* the X scores, and vice versa. In each of the three cases illustrated in Fig. 2-1, both X and Y are distributed normally, which will occur commonly but not universally. Now, imagine drawing straight lines at different angles with respect to X and Y. The lines correspond to different "mixes" or linear combinations of X and Y. In each case, you will obtain distributions that are approximately normal but with standard deviations that depend on the orientation of the axis. Observations will vary most along the axis defined by the longer of the two principal axes of the ellipse. The concept can be extended to joint distributions of three or more variables. While it can be considered algebraically, as in Chapter 6, it cannot be readily visualized. Figure 2-2 illustrates some distributions of different linear combinations of X and Y derived from the data of Fig. 2-1a.

In addition to looking at the distributions for X alone and Y alone, called *marginal distributions*, and their linear combinations, it is often important to look at the distribution of values of Y for a specified value of X or the reverse, called *conditional distributions*. X needs not be quantitative when Y is conditional upon X.

The conditional distribution of Y will be more homogeneous than the original (marginal) distribution of Y if X and Y are linearly related. Thus, scores on a scale measuring depression will vary less among a group of depressed psychotherapy patients than for patients in general. The result is very important to regression analysis since it implies how knowing something about X reduces your uncertainty about Y and vice versa.

In all of the cases depicted in Figs. 2-1 and 2-2, changes in Y are linear with changes in X and vice versa. (This is so even in Fig. 2-1b where X and Y are unrelated.) This so-called *linearity of regression* will always hold when X and Y have a bivariate normal relationship, although it may also arise when X and Y possess some other form of relationship. Thus, bivariate normality is *sufficient*, but not *necessary*, for linearity of regression. Linearity of regression is very important within multivariate methods.

Figure 2-3 illustrates the envelop of some *nonlinear* regressions. Figure 2-3a is a *nonmonotonic* relation, which might arise under the following circumstances. Suppose X is how long it has been since an animal was last fed and Y is how long it takes that animal to run to a spot containing food. Animals that have been fed recently will probably be in no hurry to run to the food. At the other end, animals that have been deprived of food long enough to be starved will be unable to run because of their debilitated physical condition. Somewhere along the food deprivation continuum, there will be a point at which animals will run most rapidly.

Note that the variances in Fig. 2-3a for a conditional Y distribution are also quite different as X varies, which is known as *heteroscedasticity*. If the variances were roughly the same (which could be even though the relation is nonmonotonic), the result would be termed *homoscedasticity*. Nonlinearity of regression and heteroscedasticity are totally independent concepts in that both, either, or neither can occur. Nonetheless, they often arise from the same empirical factors. Conversely, when the assumptions of bivariate normality are met, regressions will be both linear and homoscedastic.

In Fig. 2-3b a second form of nonlinearity is illustrated. Assume that X is a measure of intelligence and Y is a measure of proficiency in a difficult graduate program. Below a certain point or *threshold* on the intelligence

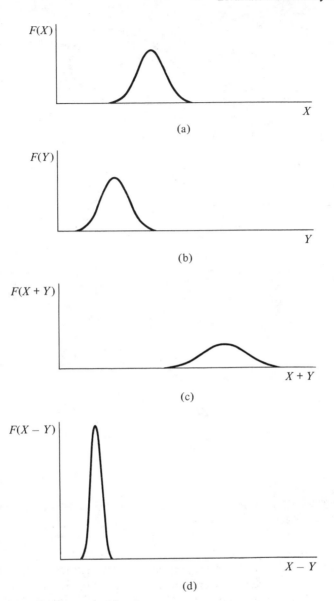

FIGURE 2-2. Frequency distributions of: (a) X alone, (b) Y alone, (c) $X + Y$, and (d) $X - Y$ when X and Y are positively correlated, normally distributed variables with equal variance.

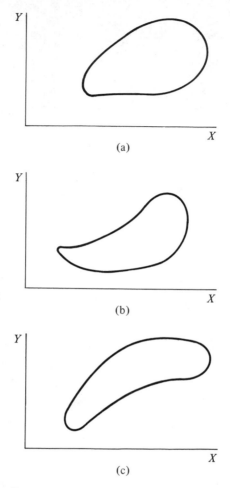

FIGURE 2-3. Some nonlinear relations: (a) heteroscedasticity (heterogeneity of variance), (b) a threshold effect, and (c) a ceiling effect.

continuum, there is no difference in proficiency as all students will do relatively poorly. Above the threshold there is a fairly strong positive relation. A threshold effect can occur at the other end—below a certain point on the X continuum, there is a relation between X and Y, but Y becomes independent of X at higher levels. The relation between visual acuity (X) and ability to operate an automobile (Y) is a good example of a threshold relationship.

In the two preceding examples, the nonlinearity may be assumed to be inherent in the underlying variables. Conversely, it can arise from deficiencies in the definitions of the variables. For example, assume that in a given group there are no threshold problems to affect the relation between intelligence and performance. Suppose, though, that you made the performance test too easy so that large numbers of people got perfect scores on that test. Your results might look like those portrayed in Fig. 2-3c, where the nonlinearity and heteroscedasticity are both due to the presence of an *artificial* "ceiling effect" on the Y measure. A ceiling effect could affect the bivariate relationship in precisely the same manner were it due to a restriction on the top score that is obtainable on the intelligence measure, X. The converse type of effect involves the same problems; a test that is too hard so that people are piled up at the low end is called a "floor effect," naturally enough.

Nonlinear data transformations are often used when two physically obtained variables are related in a nonlinear manner and one wishes to use methods of linear correlation. *There is no requirement that the variables that were physically obtained be the same ones that are analyzed.* If X and Y are known to be related in a nonlinear fashion but X can be transformed into X', which will be linearly related to Y, it is perfectly proper to study the linear relation between X' and Y rather than between X and Y. Once you have determined the strength of the linear relation between X' and Y, you can utilize the results to make statements about the relation between X and Y by transforming backward. For example, in sensory psychophysics, the relation between a physical measure of energy, say the luminance of a light source, is known to relate to judgments of intensity (apparent brightness) by a power law of the form indicated by

$$Y = aX^b + c \qquad (2\text{-}7)$$

where Y represents brightness (the psychological measure), X represents luminance (the physical measure), and a, b, and c are constants. The constant b is the critical one. Stevens (1950) found it equal to about .35. The constants a and c are used basically for scaling purposes, although c is of interest in other contexts. It defines the *energy threshold*, i.e., the minimal physical energy needed to evoke a psychological response.

In the example involving luminance and brightness, the relation between the original X and Y measures is *monotonic* even though it is not *linear*. That is, as X increases, Y also increases, although the amount of change in Y per unit change in X varies. (This would not happen, by definition, if the relation were linear.) One possible approach to relations that are montonic and reasonably linear is simply to use the raw measures, since the effects of mild nonlinearities upon statistics like correlation coefficients are relatively minor compared to the effects of the random "noise" (sampling or measurement error).

Even when the relation is nonmonotonic, a properly chosen transformation can be applied. For the relation between food deprivation and running time, a quadratic function of the form $Y = (X - c)^2 + d$, where c and d are constants, may explain the relation quite well.

Linear transformations are most meaningful when the raw data are reasonably homoscedastic. When heteroscedasticity arises from a floor or ceiling effect, one should simply think about rerunning the study with a better measure or measures. To say that one should not waste one's time with elaborate manipulations of poorly collected data is merely to restate the adage that one cannot make a silk purse out of a sow's ear.

Measures of Bivariate Relation

There are a variety of formulas that can be used to describe the *correlation* or joint relation between a pair of variables. By far the most important is a family of formulas that illustrates the extent to which the relationship between a pair of variables can be described by a *linear* (straight line) relationship. The full name of the coefficient used to index this relationship is the *Pearson product–moment correlation coefficient*, conventionally symbolized as r. When it is important to distinguish between the statistic and the parameter, the symbol "ρ" is the most common symbol for the latter. I will simply use the word "correlation" to describe r, even though technically the word "correlation" denotes a more general set of formulas.

Equations (2-8) are equivalent formulas that can be used to compute the correlation between two variables X and Y. (Whenever it is necessary to specify which pair of variables are being correlated, subscripts will be used; however, subscripting will not be used if context makes the variables involved in the correlation clear.)

$$r = \frac{\sum z_x z_y}{N}$$

$$= \frac{1}{N} \frac{\sum [(X - \bar{X})(Y - \bar{Y})]}{s_x s_y} \tag{2-8a}$$

$$r = \frac{\text{COV}(X, Y)}{s_x s_y} \tag{2-8b}$$

$$r = \frac{(N \sum XY - \sum X \sum Y)}{\{[N \sum X^2 - (\sum X)^2][N \sum Y^2 - (\sum Y)^2]\}^{1/2}} \tag{2-8c}$$

Equation (2-8a) illustrates why the term "product–moment" is used in the full identification of r. Products of z scores, which are related to the mathematical concept of a *moment* (defined as deviations from the mean, which z scores incorporate) are used in the computation of r. The formula also tells us that a correlation is a kind of average, as many other concepts in statistics are. The computation involves calculating a set of terms (products of z scores), summing them, and then dividing by the number of subjects. In addition, you can see why the largest positive value of r is 1. No relation is stronger than the case where each and every $z_y = z_x$. If that is the case, Eq. (2-8a) reduces to $r = (1/N) \sum (z_y z_x) = (1/N) \sum (z^2)$. The latter term is simply the variance of a set of z scores, which is 1. Similar logic can illustrate why the lower bound of r is -1.

Equation (2-8b) involves the concept of a covariance, which I mentioned earlier. It may be computed by means of Eq. (2-9):

$$COV(X, Y) = \frac{\sum xy}{N}$$

$$= \frac{\sum (X - \bar{X})(Y - \bar{Y})}{N} \qquad (2\text{-}9a)$$

$$COV(X, Y) = \frac{N \sum XY - \sum X \sum Y}{N^2} \qquad (2\text{-}9b)$$

The covariance is an *absolute* measure of the joint variation of two variables; it is like a variance of a single variable except that instead of squaring an individual *deviation score* (a raw score minus its mean), one computes products of pairs of deviation scores. The covariance is rarely presented as a statistic by itself, but it does play a considerable role in statistical theory. In the present case, one may say that a correlation equals the *covariance divided by the geometric mean of the variances*, since the *geometric mean* of a pair of numbers equals the square root of their product. Conceptually, the correlation is simply the joint variation of a pair of variables relative to the individual variation.

The unit of measurement of the covariance is the product of the individual dimensions. Thus, if height and weight are being correlated, the joint dimensionality might be, for examples, foot-pounds or meter-kilograms. Since the individual dimensions are represented in the denominator, r is dimensionless, which is why it is referred to as a *coefficient*.

Equation (2-8c) is not terribly instructive, but it is useful if you have to analyze the data without the benefit of a computer package, since it is the easiest formula to use in hand calculations.

Many more formulas that are algebraically equivalent could be presented.

Range Restriction

A constant, which has a standard deviation of .0, cannot correlate with a variable, because the zero in the denominator of correlation equations makes the ratios involved undefined. An important extension of this fact is the concept of *range restriction*, where any factor that causes the variance of X and/or Y to diminish, will also diminish their correlation. Many experimental artifacts found in the psychology literature arise from failure to take range restriction into account.

One commonly occurring example arises in test validation. Often, a test is first used to select people for certain positions, and the results of that test are then correlated with a proficiency measure among those so selected. For example, one might use the SAT to admit students to college and then correlate their SAT scores with their college GPAs. One should expect the correlation to be quite low because students who have been admitted are more homogeneous in the trait measured by the SAT (academic ability) than applicants in general. The correlation has been range restricted because SAT scores are used as both a selection and a prediction device. The obtained correlation is much lower than the correlation that would have been obtained had applicants been admitted *randomly*.

Pearson Correlation Formulas in Special Cases

Under certain special conditions, Pearson r may be calculated by means of simplified formulas that are useful in hand calculation. For example, suppose the X and Y variables are in the form of ranks. Then, r may be computed by means of

$$\rho = \frac{1 - 6\sum d^2}{N^3 - N} \tag{2-10}$$

This equation was originally developed by Spearman and is generally known as *Spearman's rho* (ρ), $\sum d^2$ is the sum of the squared differences between X ranks and Y ranks.

Sometimes, one may wish to compute the correlation between two variables; one is continuous and the other is binary (dichotomous). Equation (2-11) may be used to compute this so-called *point biserial correlation*:

$$r_{pb} = \frac{(\bar{X}_1 - \bar{X}_2)(pq)^{1/2}}{s} \tag{2-11}$$

In this equation, $\bar{X}_1$ and $\bar{X}_2$ are the means for the two distributions, s is the standard deviation based on the entire distribution, and p and q are the proportion of cases in the two distributions, $p + q = 1$.

Finally, one may wish to correlate one dichotomous variable with a second dichotomous variable. The index of correlation between two dichotomous variables is termed ϕ, the *phi coefficient*:

$$\phi = \frac{ac - bd}{[(a + b)(a + c)(b + c)(b + d)]^{1/2}} \tag{2-12}$$

"a" is the frequency of cases coded "1" on both variables, "b" is the frequency of cases coded "1" on the X variable and "0" on the Y variable, "c" is the frequency of cases coded "0" on the X variable and "1" on the Y variable, and "d" is the frequency of cases coded "0" on both variables.

Although all three formulas have special names, all are basically formulas for a Pearson correlation coefficient. You may verify this yourself by correlating some arbitrary set of binary data using Eq. (2-8) and then using Eqs. (2-10)–(2-12). Because of the identity, Spearman rho values, point biserial, and phi coefficients may be used in any application where Pearson's r formula is used, such as multiple regression and factor analysis.

Non-Pearson Estimates of Pearson Correlations

Often, either or both variables in a correlation are binary and, therefore, are not normally distributed. One may wish to estimate what the correlation between the two variables would be if both were normally distributed and, therefore, continuous. Measures of this type are known as "non-Pearson estimates of Pearson correlations" because they do *not* follow the same mathematical logic of a Pearson correlation, but, instead, try to estimate what a Pearson correlation would be if certain conditions held.

One such estimate is known as the *tetrachoric* correlation. Its formula will not be presented here because of its complexity. The measure assumes that a variable with $p = .5$ represents data from a normal distribution cut at the mean, one with a p of .84 represents data from a normal distribution cut one standard deviation above the mean, etc. Tetrachoric r attempts to compensate for the information that is presumably lost through the dichtomization process. Consequently, a tetrachoric r will always be larger than the Pearson r (phi coefficient) obtained from the same set of data.

Likewise, suppose one of the two variables was continuous and normally distributed, but the other variable was binary. The *biserial* correlation estimates what the correlation would be if the dichotomized variable were actually normally distributed. A biserial r may be obtained from a point biserial r [itself defined in Eq. (2-11)]:

$$r_{bis} = \frac{r_{pb}}{h} \tag{2-13}$$

h is the ordinate or height of the normal curve corresponding to p, the percentage of cases in one of the distributions—which one is chosen does not matter because of the symmetry of the normal curve. The height may be obtained from Eq. (2-2) or from the table presented in Appendix A.

Note that the only difference between Eq. (9-14) and that for the point biserial correlation [Eq. (2-11)] is a division by h, the ordinate of the normal curve at the "cut" point in the binary distribution.

Tetrachoric and biserial correlations are not Pearson correlations. Their use in multivariate correlation procedures can very easily lead to bizarre outcomes, for reasons I will consider later. I am not saying never use them (I never like to say never), but be especially careful when values of p are very close to 0 or to 1, since the resulting tetrachoric and biserial correlations will be highly unstable because of such things as sampling error.

The Eta-Square Measure

You may have already been introduced to *eta square* (η^2) or *correlation ratio* statistic when you studied the simple ANOVA. The η^2 is defined as the ratio of the between-group sum of squares to the total sum of squares. It is a *nonlinear* measure of correlation. It may be compared to r^2 to determine the amount of nonlinearity in the relation between X and Y. To the extent that η^2 and r^2 are similar, the two variables may be assumed linearly related. There are other measures of strength of a nonlinear relation.

Phi Coefficients with Unequal Probabilities

A phi coefficient is limited in its magnitude by the similarity of the two p values (probabilities that X and Y will be answered in the keyed direction). If the p values are different, X and Y cannot correlate perfectly because all people coded as "1" on X cannot be coded as "1" on Y and all people coded as "0" on X cannot be coded as "0" on Y, simultaneously. Several authors (e.g., Bernstein & Eveland, 1982; Gorsuch, 1983) have shown how the limitation upon ϕ affects multivariate analyses.

Items on a questionnaire dealing with a common theme will tend to be positively correlated. However, some items naturally evoke more positive response (are easier, have larger p) than others. Thus, people with emotional problems tend to answer more items in the clinically pathological direction on a personality inventory than people with fewer emotional problems. (The tests would not be valid if no such difference existed.) However, items differ in their probability of evoking a pathological response. The net effect is for those items with similar p values to correlate more highly with each other than items with different p values even though all items are measuring the same construct. Changes in the wording of items that affect p (as in changing "sometimes" to "rarely," etc.) can affect the correlation among items considerably (and, in a very fundamental sense, spuriously). The role of p values is quite important in such topics as the item-level factor analysis and is another way in which range restriction affects correlations.

Sampling Error of a Correlation

If X and Y are unrelated in a given population, and each is normally distributed, successive samples of size N will have an average correlation of .0. The standard error of the correlation will be equal to $1/(N-1)^{1/2}$. Consequently, the sampling error of a correlation possesses the same square-root relation between sample size and precision found elsewhere in statistics, such as in the standard error of a mean. This important relation shows that when the sample size is 100, the approximate 95% confidence limits of r range from $+.20$ to $-.20$, or one-fifth the entire range of possible outcomes.

The preceding relation can be used to see if an obtained correlation differs significantly from .0. If it is necessary to see whether a correlation differs significantly from some nonzero value, the problem is a shade more complicated. To pick an extreme example, if the true population value is .95, sampling error can produce a value of r that is only .05 units above the true value but can produce a value that is 1.95 units below, albeit with rapidly diminishing probability.

The Z' Transformation

Fisher (1921) first recognized the inherent skewness of distributions of sample correlations when the population correlation is nonzero. He developed the Z'

transformation to normalize sampling distributions of correlations. The transformation of r to Z' is given by

$$Z' = .5\ln[(1 + r)/(1 - r)] \qquad (2\text{-}14)$$

Values of Z' sampled from a given bivariate population will be normally distributed regardless of the correlation within that population. The standard error of Z', unlike that of r, is $(N - 3)^{1/2}$. Thus, one may test the significance of a difference between a sample correlation and a proposed population correlation by converting the sample value and the expected population value to their respective Z' values. Next, the difference is divided by $(N - 3)^{1/2}$. The result can be evaluated by means of a table of z values. Thus, a two-tailed test with a .05 alpha level requires a result greater (in absolute value) than 1.96.

Linear Regression

Linear regression involves determining a straight line that best describes the relation between X and Y. Unlike correlational analysis, one of the variables in a regression analysis must be designated as a predictor (independent variable) and the other as a criterion (dependent variable). It makes a big difference which is which; the regression of X upon Y is different from the regression of Y upon X. Thus, correlation involves a *symmetric relation* between X and Y, whereas regression involves an *asymmetric relation* between X and Y, even though regression and correlation are usually discussed in the same general context. Specifically, regression analysis assumes that the relation between the criterion and the predictor is imperfect because the criterion, and only the criterion, contains error. The correlation, by contrast, does not assign the imperfection (error) to either of the variables involved.

The Geometry of Regression

Figure 2-4 illustrates the problem of attempting to determine a straight line that best describes the relation between X and Y. Because the lack of perfect relation is attributed to error contained in the criterion (Y), the deviation between the line under consideration and a given (X, Y) point used for illustration is drawn *vertically*. A vertical deviation will exist for each and every point in the set. This basic information will be used to choose the "best line," in some sense.

Most commonly (but not always), the definition of "in some sense" is "least squares." That is, one usually seeks to position the regression line so that the average *squared* deviation between predicted and observed values measured along the Y axis is as small as possible. Least squares is not the only criterion that can be used to obtain estimates of regression parameters. Long (1983a) provides an elementary introduction to the use of maximum likelihood estimation, and Marascuilo and Levin (1983) illustrate the use of minimum chi-square with a dichotomous criterion. However, the method of least squares is useful over a wide range of situations.

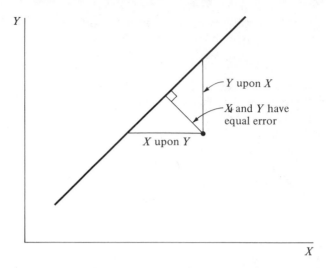

FIGURE 2-4. The geometry of a line of best fit. *Note*: To regress Y upon X, thereby treating X as error-free, the squared *vertical* distances are minimized; to regress X upon Y, thereby treating Y as error-free, the squared *horizontal* distances are minimized; but when one views X and Y as containing equal amounts of error, the squared *perpendicular* distances from points to the line are minimized.

It is natural to ask what would result if the deviations were computed and their squares minimized *horizontally*, instead of vertically. In that case, one would be treating the Y data as infallible and the X data as containing error. The result provides the regression of X upon Y. Still a third possibility is to measure and minimize the squared deviations *perpendicular* to the line of best fit. This criterion implies that the error between X and Y should be shared equally. The resulting line of best is the first *principal component* introduced previously as the major axis of the scatterplot's envelope. Gaito (1965) illustrates situations where it is appropriate to use the first principal component as a line of best fit.

The regression line is extremely simple to describe if X and Y are in z-score form; the Y-intercept is .0 and the slope is r. Equation (2-15a) describes the slope of the regression line for standardize variables:

$$\beta_{y \cdot x} = r \tag{2-15a}$$

$$b_{y \cdot x} = \frac{r s_y}{s_x} \tag{2-15b}$$

$$b_{y \cdot x} = \frac{\text{COV}(X, Y)}{s_x^2} \tag{2-15c}$$

where z_y is the predicted value of Y in z-score form, r is the correlation between X and Y, and z_x is the value of the predictor (X) in z-score form. Thus, the

Pearson correlation, r, has a geometric interpretation as the slope of the line of best fit in predicting Y from X. Hays (1981) contains a demonstration of the important proof that $r = \beta$. (The proof requires the differential calculus and will not be presented here.) Note that the asymmetrical nature of linear regression forces the slope ($\beta_{y \cdot x}$) to be identified by an appropriate subscript. The symbol denotes the regression of Y upon X. Its value will be different, in general, from $\beta_{x \cdot y}$. The former is read as "the slope in regressing Y upon X," and the latter is read as "the slope in regressing X upon Y."

I will return to a discussion of the assumptions that underlie linear regression in Chapter 4 when I extend discussion to the use of multiple predictors (multiple regression).

Raw-Score Formulas for the Slope

Equations (2-15b) and (2-15c) are *raw-score* formulas for the slope. Each has an interpretation that is useful in understanding regression. The former simply corrects the z-score formula for differences in the units used to measure X and Y. The latter illustrates that the expected rate of change in Y is the extent to which X and Y jointly vary relative to the extent to which X alone varies.

Raw-Score Formulas for the Intercept

It can be shown that the least square regression line passes through the centroid, i.e., the point $(\bar{X}, \bar{Y})$. Knowing the slope of any straight line and any one point on that line is sufficient to determine the equation for that line. Consequently, the formula for the intercept (the "a" term in "$Y = bX + a$") in raw score form is given by

$$a_{y \cdot x} = \bar{Y} - b_{y \cdot x} \bar{X} \tag{2-16}$$

The intercept of the regression line in standard-score form will always be .0. The result emerges because the centroid is $(.0, .0)$, and, therefore, it is both the X-intercept and the Y-intercept.

It is common to refer to the z-score parameter by the Greek letter beta (β), hence the term "beta weight" is one you will frequently encounter. For simple linear regression with standard scores, one could just as well use the symbol "r," since that is what β equals. However, the determination of values of β is much more complex when there is more than one predictor (multiple regression). Consequently, there is the general need to denote weights derived from z scores, using the Greek letter β, versus weights derived from raw scores, using the English letter b.

Residuals

The difference between a score predicted from a regression equation and the obtained (actual) score is known as the *residual*. Residuals may be expressed in z-score form or in raw-score form. The z-score definition is given by

Eqs. (2-17a), and the raw score definition is given by Eqs. (2-17b):

$$\hat{z}_y = z_y - z'_y$$

$$= z_y - r_{xy}z_x$$

$$= z_y - \beta_{y \cdot x}z_x \qquad (2\text{-}17a)$$

$$\hat{Y} = Y - Y'$$

$$= Y - (b_{y \cdot x}X + a) \qquad (2\text{-}17b)$$

If the data are bivariate normal and if there are no other systematic influences upon Y, the residuals will be normally distributed. Even when X and Y are not bivariate normal and Y is influenced by other variables, residuals will be independent of the linear effects of X. Geometrically, residuals are simply the *vertical* distances from the observation to its projection on the regression line.

A given obtained z score, z_y, can therefore be viewed as consisting of two independent parts. One part, the *predicted score* (z'_y) is perfectly related to z_x and equals rz_x. The other, or *residual* $(\hat{z}_y)$, is linearly independent of X and equals $z_y - rz_x$. Because the predicted score and the residual are independent of one another, the two components may be squared and summed as in the analysis of variance. The total variance of z_y is 1., by definition, and may be partitioned into a systematic component, the variance of z'_y, called the *coefficient of determination*, which is equal to r^2, and a residual component, the variance of $\hat{z}_y$, called the *coefficient of nondetermination*, which is equal to $1 - r^2$.

The Standard Error of Estimate

The standard deviation of the residuals is known as the *standard error of estimate* and is symbolized by $s_{y \cdot x}$. Its computation is given by Eq. (2-18a). The standard error of estimate may be estimated more simply by Eq. (2-18c) when the data are bivariate normal. Equations (2-18b) and (2-18d) are corresponding raw-score forms.

$$s_{y \cdot x} = [\sum(z_y - z'_y)^2/(N - 2)]^{1/2} \qquad \text{(z-score form)} \qquad (2\text{-}18a)$$

$$s_{y \cdot x} = [\sum(Y - Y')^2/(N - 2)]^{1/2} \qquad \text{(raw-score form)} \qquad (2\text{-}18b)$$

$$s_{y \cdot x} = (1 - r^2)^{1/2} \qquad \text{(z-score form)} \qquad (2\text{-}18c)$$

$$s_{y \cdot x} = s_y(1 - r^2)^{1/2} \qquad \text{(raw-score form)} \qquad (2\text{-}18d)$$

The $s_{y \cdot x}$ is a *conditional* standard deviation that describes the spread of Y scores *given that you know an X value with which it is associated*. In contrast, the standard deviation (s) is an *unconditional* measure that describes the spread of Y scores *in the absence of any knowledge about X*. For example, assume that the standard deviation of freshman GPAs at a given university is .4. That is a measure of the spread of grades, *assuming you knew nothing relevant about the students*.

Suppose you knew that a student did well in high school, having a GPA of 3.5. Assume high school and college freshmen GPAs are positively correlated, as the two, in fact, are to an extent that varies among colleges. Students with a high school GPA of 3.5 will be more homogeneous as a group than the freshman class taken as a whole. Students who get better grades in high school will also tend to get better grades in college, but my point concerns their relative *homogeneity* and not their relative *superiority*. The $s_{y \cdot x}$ estimates the variability of students with a 3.5 (or any other) high school GPA. The larger $s_{y \cdot x}$ is, the less informative X (high school GPA) is about Y (freshman GPA).

I use the *df* to compute the standard error because I am computing a least squares *estimate* of the conditional standard deviation. Two, rather than the one degree of freedom, which is typically used to estimate an ordinary standard deviation, are lost since both a slope and an intercept need to be estimated. My estimate may or may not be equally accurate at all levels of the predictor (X). It might be that students with extremely low (or high) high school GPAs have larger (or smaller) conditional standard deviations in their freshman GPAs than students who have average high school GPAs. Consequently, the $s_{y \cdot x}$ obtained from Eq. (2-18) may be an underestimate or overestimate of the true $s_{y \cdot x}$ for a given value of X.

The quantity $(1 - r^2)^{1/2}$ in z-score form describes the relative reduction in uncertainty about Y produced by the knowledge of X. It denotes that a correlation of .3, which is large enough to be statistically significant in virtually any correlational study and which I have seen psychologists get excited about (sometimes including myself, I confess), reduces one's uncertainty about Y by only 5%. A correlation of .6, which prompts some to start writing Nobel Prize acceptance speeches, provides a reduction of only about 20%. Finally, a correlation of .9, which leads some researchers to request a burial place at Westminster Abbey, only reduces the uncertainty by a little over half (56%)!

I am not saying this reduction is of trivial importance. Even a small reduction as to the uncertainty of the future performance of a group of job applicants can translate into a huge financial savings for a company and be fairer to applicants than a poorer prediction scheme. However, you have no doubt been taught many times the difference between statistical and practical significance. My point is a slight variant on that same theme—apparently large values of r do not reduce uncertainty about outcomes nearly as much as one's intuition might suggest.

In sum, the coefficient of nondetermination is the square of the standard error of measurement and thus describes the residual variance in Y given knowledge of X. In a like manner, the coefficient of determination represents the variance in predicted scores, i.e., $r^2 = s_{y'}^2$.

This statement, however, is *not* necessarily equivalent to the statement that r^2 of the variance in Y is *shared* with X and vice versa. To employ r^2 as a definition of *shared* variance implies that the regression model holds. In this case *all* variation in X would, in fact, be shared with Y, although part $(1 - r^2)$ of Y's variance would not be shared with X. Figure 2-5 illustrates the two extreme cases in which all variation in X is contained in Y and the proportion

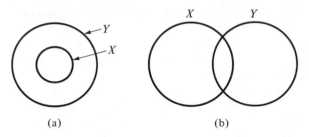

FIGURE 2-5. Situations in which: (a) all variation in X is contained in Y and (b) X and Y each contain unique variance.

of nonshared (*unique*) variance in X is the same as the proportion of nonshared variance in Y.

Suppose, however, that the regression model did not hold in that X and Y each contained a unique source of variance, perhaps measurement error, as well as a source of variance in common. This situation is as consistent with the correlation model as the preceding case in which all X variance is incorporated in Y. The estimate of shared variance depends on the relative magnitudes of the two unique sources. If these two sources are equal, r rather than r^2 would describe the proportion of variance in Y that it shares with X and vice versa (Ozer, 1985). However, when you have digested the contents of Chapters 6 and 7, you should read a commentary on Ozer's paper by Steiger and Ward (1987).

Why the Term "Regression"?

Using the term "regression" has a bit of psychoanalytic aura to it, so a word on its derivation is in order. A useful starting point is the everyday observation that when things seem at their worst, you have no place to go but up. A more formal statement is that because $z'_y = r z_x$, a predicted z_y value (z'_y) will always be closer to zero than the z_x value upon which it is based.

Generalizing to the raw-score case, a predicted score will always be closer to its mean than will the predictor score to its mean as long as the relation between the predictor and the criterion is imperfect. In the special case of $r = .0$, the predicted score will be the mean. Thus, predicted scores "move toward" or "regress toward" the mean.

The concept of regression applies to *predicted* scores. It does not speak to *individually obtained* scores. If a particular person obtains a z score of $+.5$ on a predictor X that has a correlation of .3 with the criterion Y, that person's predicted Y score is .15 (.5 × .3). That individual has some probability of obtaining any given Y score, including those that were larger than the original X score of .5. However, if the assumptions of regresion are met and the average Y score is obtained for all individuals obtaining an X score of .5, their average Y score will be .15.

TABLE 2-2. Relations among quantities in regression analysis

Statistic	Variable[a]			
	z_x	z_y	z'_y	$\hat{z}_y$
Mean	0	0	0	0
Variance	1	1	r^2	$1 - r^2$
Standard Deviation	1	1	r	$(1 - r^2)^{1/2}$
r with z_x	1	r	1	0
r with z_y	r	1	r	$(1 - r^2)^{1/2}$
r with z'_y	1	r	1	0

[a] r is the correlation between X and Y.

The *statistical* process of regression is relevant to a variety of phenomena that seem to require some *substantive* explanation. For example, consider initial improvement in psychotherapy (to choose an example that is bound to offend some). People's mood fluctuates from day to day. It is reasonable to assume that a person is most likely to enter therapy when that person is feeling very bad. Assume I can measure the person's mood. Call the person's initial mood "X" and the mood at the start of therapy "Y." Since "X" and "Y" are not perfectly correlated but both are probably negative in value, one may predict that virtually anything would cause "Y" to increase (become less negative). Thus, therapists have an initial, built-in, statistical success factor.

Similarly, in a great deal of medical research, investigators use patients who do not respond to conventional therapy. Results are termed "encouraging" if the people do better, e.g., live longer than "expected" (a usually ill-defined term). Sports fans often hear of outstanding "prospects" who perform less well in the major leagues than they did in the minor leagues. Substantive explanations are offered like "he couldn't stand the pressure" or "the bright lights got to him." Since major and minor league performances are imperfectly related, people selected because they perform well in the minor leagues would be expected to be closer to the average in the major leagues.

A Summary of Some Basic Relations

Table 2-2 (adapted from Nunnally, 1978, p. 129). summarizes some of the relations among the original z score for X and Y, the predicted z score, and the residual.

Statistical Control: A First Look at Multivariate Relations

Partial and Part Correlation

Partial and part (also called semipartial) correlations fall technically outside of bivariate analysis because both involve at least three variables. However,

I will present them here because the topic is closely tied to the concept of residuals.

A *partial* correlation is the correlation between two variables holding a third variable constant. I will refer the two variables being correlated as X and Y, as before, and designate the third (*covariate* or *control*) variable as W. A correlation between the full (unadjusted) values of two variables is called a *zero-order correlation*. Partial correlations take on special importance in my discussion of statistical versus experimental control later in the chapter.

The partial correlation, $r_{xy \cdot w}$, is the simple correlation between z_x and z_y, the residuals of X and Y, after each has been predicted from W. In other words, one correlates scores of the form $z_y - r_{wy}z_w$ with scores of the form $z_x - r_{wx}z_w$. However, it is not necessary to actually compute the individual residuals in order to compute a partial correlation. Instead, the covariance of the residuals is, by definition

$$(1/N)\sum(z_x - r_{wx}z_w)(z_y - r_{wy}z_w)$$

but the expression can be shown to reduce to

$$r_{xy} - r_{wx}r_{wy}$$

and the respective variances, from Table 2-2, are

$$1 - r_{wx}^2 \quad \text{and} \quad 1 - r_{wy}^2$$

Hence, applying formulas (2-8b), which define a correlation as the ratio of a covariance to the geometric mean of variances (product of standard deviations) yields

$$r_{xy \cdot w} = \frac{r_{xy} - r_{wx}r_{wy}}{[(1 - r_{wx}^2)(1 - r_{wy}^2)]^{1/2}} \tag{2-19}$$

An important point may be inferred from Eq. (2-19). If X and Y correlate in *opposite* directions with the covariate W but positively with each other (as in the example), the partial correlation $r_{xy \cdot w}$, will usually be *stronger* (*larger in absolute magnitude*) than the zero-order correlation r_{xy}. Removing W eliminates a source of variation or influence upon X and Y that operates upon them in different directions to reduce their observed relationship.

Conversely, if both X and Y correlate with W in the *same* direction, the partial correlation will usually be *weaker* (*smaller in absolute magnitude*) than the zero-order correlation. Partialling removes a common influence that is working to strengthen the observed relationship. The word "usually" is a qualifier because if *both X and Y are* uncorrelated with W, the zero-order, partial, and both part correlations (a concept to be explained subsequently) will be the same. The reverse is true if X and Y are negatively correlated with each other.

Correlations with the covariate affect the partial correlation in two distinct ways. First, the *covariance* of the residuals will differ from the covariance of the original scores. Second, the *variances* of the residuals will be less than the variances of the original scores. The latter is true as long as at least one variable involved in the partial correlation correlates above zero with the covariate. In a practical sense, partialling will make little difference if both correlations with the covariate are small (less than about .3).

A *part* correlation is similar to a partial correlation except that the covariate is removed from only one of the two variables. Thus, one finds the part correlation between X and Y by removing the effects of W from Y or from X, but not both. The results will differ from one another, as well as from the partial correlation and simple correlation, sometimes substantially. The covariance between X and the Y residuals and between Y and the X residuals is identical to the covariance between X residuals and Y residuals. However, the standard deviations are different since only one of the two variables involved is a residual. Thus, the complete formula for the part correlation between X and Y removing W from Y but not X is given by Eq. (2-20a) and the formula for the part correlation between X and Y removing W from X but not Y is given by Eq. (2-20b):

$$r_{x(y-w)} = \frac{r_{xy} - r_{wx}r_{wy}}{[(1 - r_{wy}^2)]^{1/2}} \tag{2-20a}$$

$$r_{x(w-y)} = \frac{r_{wx} - r_{xy}r_{wy}}{[(1 - r_{wy}^2)]^{1/2}} \tag{2-20b}$$

The absolute value of a part correlation can never be greater than the corresponding partial correlation. Both have the same numerator. However, the denominator of the part correlation contains only one variable that has been adjusted for W, whereas the denominator of the partial correlation contains two variables that have both been adjusted for W. The part correlation thus contains one term that is less than 1 and another that equals 1.; the partial correlation contains the same term that is less than 1., *but the second term is also less than 1.* Hence, the denominator of the part correlation will always be at least as large, and usually larger, than the denominator of the partial correlation, causing the overall ratio (correlation) to be smaller.

Partial correlations are of inherent interest in a variety of situations. For example, a college admissions office may be interested in looking at the relation between college grade point average (GPA) and Scholastic Aptitude Test (SAT) scores *adjusting both measures for high school GPA.* The purpose of the analysis is to see if the SAT provides any information about college performance (aids in predicting college GPA) *above and beyond the information contained in high school GPA.* The SAT may or may not provide additional information about college grades *even though SAT scores are correlated with college GPA.* If the correlation between SAT and college GPA is small after adjustment for high school GPA, there would be little or no reason to use the SAT as a predictor. Part correlations, on the other hand, are rarely used in similar situations. They are of lesser interest because one is rarely concerned with the effects of adjusting only one of the variables. However, part correlations do play an important role in multiple regression and factor analytic theory.

For my first example, suppose that the correlation between college GPA and SAT scores is .3, the correlation between high school GPA and SAT is .4, and the correlation between high school and college GPA is .7. Applying Eq. (2-20) to obtain the correlation between SAT and college GPA, adjusting for high school GPA yields the following results:

$$r = \frac{[.3 - (.4)(.7)]}{[(1. - .4^2)(1. - .7^2)]^{1/2}}$$

$$= \frac{.3 - .28}{[(1. - .16)(1. - .49)]^{1/2}}$$

$$= \frac{.02}{[(.84)(.51)]^{1/2}}$$

$$= \frac{.02}{[.4284]^{1/2}}$$

$$= \frac{.02}{.65}$$

$$= .03$$

In other words, once a moderate zero-order relation between college GPA and SAT scores ($r = .3$) is corrected for high school GPA, college GPA and SAT scores are essentially unrelated ($r = .03$). Using the preceding correlations, the SAT provides essentially no added information that could not be determined from high school GPA alone. Consequently, there is no reason to use it.

For a second example, assume that the correlation between college GPA and SAT scores is .6, the correlation between high school grades and SAT is .2, and the correlation between high school and college GPA is .4. Adjusting the new correlation between SAT scores and college GPA for high school GPA would leave a correlation of .58, which most would agree is sufficiently large to justify its continued use.

The partial correlation in the first example was so low (.03) that the two part correlations and the partial correlation are numerically indistinguishable from one another. I will therefore use the second example to illustrate how part correlations are calculated. The quantity $(.6 - .2 \times .4)/(1 - .2^2)^{1/2} = .52/(.96)^{1/2} = .52/.98 = .53$ is the outcome of removing the effects of high school GPA from SAT scores but not from college GPA. Conversely, the quantity $(.6 - .2 \times .4)/(1 - .4^2)^{1/2} = .52/(.84)^{1/2} = .52/.92 = .56$ is the outcome of removing high school GPA from college GPA but not from SAT scores. Note how both part correlations are smaller in absolute value than the partial correlation (.58).

Statistical versus Experimental Control

Partial correlations can be used for *statistical* control. In the previous examples, I illustrated how the correlation between SAT scores (an ability measure) and college GPA (a performance measure) was affected when high school GPA (a second performance measure) was held constant. However, I did not *actually* hold students' high school GPA constant. Suppose I had obtained the necessary three measures from a very large group of students. I could limit my study to those individuals whose high school GPAs were in a narrow range. In theory, the correlation between college GPA and SAT for students selected on the basis of their high school GPA (a *zero-order correlation* since there would not be any *statistical* control) should be the same as the partial correlation obtained when I used all of the students and corrected their high school SAT scores statistically.

Partial correlations obtained through statistical control are often quite different from zero-order correlations obtained through experimental control. The correlation might well depend on the particular high school GPA level that I chose. If I chose a group of students who all performed poorly in high school, that group might obtain uniformly low college GPAs. Range restriction would produce a very low correlation between college GPA and SAT. At the other extreme, suppose I chose a group of students who all did well in high school. Some students might be of limited academic ability who nevertheless succeeded in high school by working very hard. Others would be of true superior academic ability. Assuming that the SAT is a good index of academic ability and that more academic ability is required in college than in high school, the correlation between SAT and college GPA could be substantial in a group of students who did well in high school. The correlation between SAT scores and college GPA with *experimentally controlled* high school GPA might be similar to the *statistically controlled* correlation only for a limited range of high school GPAs.

It is usually preferable to control a third variable experimentally at several levels so that one can see if it interacts with the magnitude of correlation. I am not saying that experimental control is always possible or that statistical control always produces meaningless results. Rather, the same general principles that hold throughout science hold here—multiple studies with different methods that lead to converging results are preferable to "one-shot" studies (See Garner, Hake, & Eriksen, 1957 for a brilliant discussion of the need for *converging operations*, multiple but independent definitions of the effect that you wish to study.)

Multiple Partialling

Multiple variables can be statistically controlled for in the same study. Thus, one may partial out age, gender, or any other variable of interest in addition to high school GPA. The concept remains the same, one obtained residuals (which are now obtained from earlier residuals instead of raw scores), determines their variance and covariance and computes a correlation based on the principles involved in Eq. (2-20).

The *order* in which partialling of variables occurs does not affect the final outcome. Thus, it does not matter if one partials out high school GPA and then age or partials out age and then high school GPA. The final *second-order partial correlation* between SAT and college GPA with age and high school GPA controlled will be the same in both cases. Similar considerations apply to *higher-order partial and part correlations* with more than two covariates.

Within-Group, Between-Group, and Total Correlations

Within-group, between-group, and total correlations and related concepts (sums of squares and covariances) also deal with the effects of a third variable and play an extremely important role in advanced statistical analysis.

Consider the following example. Three groups of people from the same state are each asked how much they like the two U.S. senators from the state, both of whom are Democrats. They rate each senator on a 10-point scale with 10 being most favorable. One group consists of three Democrats; the second consists of four Independents, and the third consists of three Republicans. (The example is chosen to be kept simple and to show that the groups do not have to be the same size.) The results of this hypothetical opinion survey are shown in Table 2-3.

You may note the correlations between the ratings of the two senators is -1.0 within each of the three groups. Yet, if your were to disregard the fact that the 10 people fall into 3 groups, the correlation among the 10 measures is quite strongly positive ($r = .78$). Figure 2-6 contains the scatterplot. As you

TABLE 2-3. Hypothetical ratings of two U.S. senators (Senator A and Senator B) made by three groups of raters

		Rating	
Rater	Party	Senator A	Senator B
1	Democrat	10	8
2	Democrat	9	9
3	Democrat	8	10
4	Independent	7	4
5	Independent	6	5
6	Independent	5	6
7	Independent	4	7
8	Republican	3	1
9	Republican	2	2
10	Republican	1	3

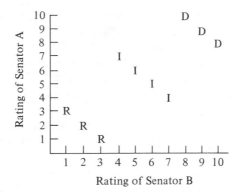

FIGURE 2-6. Scatterplots relating judgments of two hypothetical senators (D = judgments of Democrats, I = judgments of Independents, and R = judgments of Republicans).

can see, points with the same letter, such as R slant *downwards* to the right. However, the set of all 10 points slants *upwards* to the right.

To keep the example simple, I will assume the scatterplots from each group are *homogeneous* in the sense that the envelopes of the three groups have the same shape and would be perfectly overlapping if I were to "slide" the group centroids along the graph to a common location. Homogeneity implies that the correlations and standard deviations are the same in each of the three groups.

The average of the three individual correlations, weighted by their group size, is called the *pooled within-group correlation*. It is computed from pairs of scores expressed as deviations about the *group* means to which the scores belong. The process *adjusts* for groups mean differences. The *pooled within-group covariance* and some terms to be considered in Chapter 3 are defined analogously.

Conversely, the *total correlation* is obtained by *ignoring* group membership and expressing scores as deviations about the *grand* means. Again, a *total covariance* and related terms may be defined analogously.

The *between-group correlation* reflects the correlation of the three group means for Senator A (9, 5.5, and 2) and the corresponding means for Senator B (9, 5.5, and 2). The correlation in my example is 1., but it can take on any value. A between-group correlation *ignores* variation and covariation within-groups. A *between-group covariance* and other related terms may be defined in an analogous manner.

My discussion should evoke memories of the simple ANOVA. In fact, the concepts I am discussing are an extension of the ANOVA from the analysis of a scalar (single variable) to the analysis of a vector (set of variables, a pair in the present example).

The concepts I am discussing form the basis of discriminant analysis and the MANOVA (Chapters 8–10). However, they are very important in their own right. Suppose you have gathered data from people classified into various groups based upon relevant criteria, e.g., religion or gender. If you were to ignore the group variable and if the group mean differences are large, you will quite probably be confounding variability and covariability among *groups* with variability and covariability among *individuals* within-group.

One can have a strong relation in the total correlation matrix that reflects covariances among groups means that is absent within-group, or the reverse may hold. In general, between-group and within-group correlations can be positive, negative, or zero, independently of one another. In some contexts, the between-group correlation may be of major interest; in other contexts, the within-group correlation may be of major interest. The important thing is to avoid confounding them. Only when group mean differences are negligible can the total correlation be used to estimate the within-group correlation. One of the more important content issues is knowing which groups are most important.

I have now reached the point of the book where I am going to present the "building" blocks used in multivariate analysis—matrix theory. There will be a large number of relatively new terms. Recognize that your understanding of models to analyze data is greatly facilitated by your understanding how these blocks are put together.

3
Some Matrix Concepts

Chapter Overview

Chapter 3 contains five major topics:

I. BASIC DEFINITIONS—In contrast to a single number or *scalar*, a *matrix* is a rectangular array of numbers, and a *vector* is a single row or column of numbers. Some basic definitions used to describe different kinds of matrices and vectors and their properties are introduced: (1) the *data matrix* ($\mathbf{X}$), which usually contains scores for subjects (rows) on different variables (columns); (2) a z-score matrix ($\mathbf{Z}$), in which the columns (ordinarily) of $\mathbf{X}$ are transformed to z-scores (normalized); (3) a *square* matrix, which has as many columns as rows; (4) the *principal* or *major diagonal* of a square matrix that runs from the top left to the bottom right; (5) the *trace* of a matrix, which is the sum of the elements on the major diagonal of a square matrix; (6) a *symmetric* matrix, which is a square matrix where the element in the ith row and jth column equals the element in the jth row and ith column, such as a *correlation matrix*; (7) a *variance–covariance* matrix, which contains variances along the major diagonal and covariances off the major diagonal; (8) *diagonal* matrix, which is a matrix whose off-diagonal elements are all zero; (9) an *identity* matrix, which is a diagonal matrix whose diagonal elements are all 1's; (10) a *triangular* matrix, which is a square matrix whose elements above (or below) the diagonal are all zeros; (11) a *null* matrix, which consists of 0's only; (12) a matrix *transpose* of order $N \times M$ obtained by interchanging the rows and columns of an $M \times N$ matrix; and (13) *matrix equality*, which means each and every element in two matrices are numerically equal to one another. (It also implies that the two matrices have the same number of rows and columns.)

II. BASIC MATRIX OPERATIONS—Two matrices or vectors may be added or subtracted using rules that are equivalent to the rules used to add or subtract two scalars. The only restriction is that the two matrices have to contain the same number of columns and rows. However, there are several different types of matrix *multiplication*. Multiplying a matrix by a *scalar* is similar to multiplying two scalars. Unfortunately, the most common way to multiply one matrix by another *matrix*, which is called *dot multiplication*, is more complex and can only be performed under uncertain specific conditions. There is no exact equivalent of matrix division. However, one can compute the equivalent of the reciprocal of a scalar, called a matrix *inverse* under certain circumstances. Multiplying matrix **A** by the inverse of matrix $\mathbf{B}(\mathbf{B}^{-1})$ is therefore like dividing scalar *a* by scalar *b*. Only certain *square* matrices have an inverse. Matrices that have an inverse are known as *nonsingular* matrices. A nonsingular matrix has the property that all of its rows are *linearly independent* of one another, as are its columns. By contrast, one or more rows of a *singular* matrix (which need not be square) are *linear combinations* of other rows (or it could be that one or more columns are linear combinations of other columns). In applied work with matrices, it is also important to look at nonsingular matrices in which one or more rows is approximately but not exactly a linear combination of other rows, called an *ill-conditioned matrix*, which can be determined through inspection of the *determinant* of the matrix. Determining the *rank* of a matrix, which is the number of rows (or columns) which cannot be expressed as linear combinations of other rows (or columns) is essential to multivariate analysis. A *Gramian* matrix is obtained by multiplying a given matrix by its transpose. A correlation matrix with 1's in the diagonal is a very important example of a Gramian matrix. A Gramian matrix can be expressed as the product of a triangular matrix and the transpose of that triangular matrix through the very important process of *Cholesky decomposition*. This operation is the matrix equivalent of obtaining a square root. A final operation important in matrix theory is to *partition* a given matrix into *submatrices*.

III. AN APPLICATION OF MATRIX ALGEBRA—Some of basic matrix operations are illustrated in computing a correlation matrix.

IV. MORE ABOUT LINEAR COMBINATIONS—This brief but important section ties matrix theory to the concept of a linear combination. In particular, I will discuss how one can compute the variance of a linear combination and the covariance and correlation between two linear combinations of the same set of variables—basic operations in factor analysis.

V. EIGENVALUES AND EIGENVECTORS—One matrix operation, *eigenanalysis*, requires separate discussion, since it is a foundation of exploratory factor analytic methods. An eigenanalysis consists of obtaining the *eigenvectors* and *eigenvalues* of a square (but not necessarily symmetric) matrix. Eigenvectors were briefly introduced in Chapter 2 under the name principal components, which are the axes of the elliptical pattern typically descriptive of a scatterplot. The successive eigenvectors of a correlation matrix have the crucial property of explaining the maximum possible amount of variance, and their associated eigenvalues describe the amount of variance explained. This section describes some of the properties of eigenvectors and eigenvalues, both in the general case and in the special case of a symmetric matrix, and how they are obtained.

Much ground needs be covered, and this chapter is probably more difficult than any of the other chapters because it establishes the foundation for all remaining chapters. Once you master the material in this chapter, the remaining material follows in a logical and coherent pattern.

This chapter introduces some of the basic concepts in matrix algebra.

Once you fully understand the concepts that will be presented, you will understand the bases of multivariate analysis. A typical multivariate procedure such as multiple regression uses combinations of a relatively few matrix operations. The concepts may seem fairly strange to you at first. For example, when I ask you to multiply two numbers, you do not have to ask which number goes first—because ordinary or *scalar* multiplication, which uses single numbers, is *symmetric*—$2 \times 3 = 3 \times 2 = 6$. Matrix products are not usually symmetric. The matrix product **AB** can be quite different from the matrix product **BA** and either or both may not even be defined! Fortunately, differences between scalar and matrix algebra will become less strange with experience.

As I indicated in Chapter 1, you may eventually wish to take a formal course in matrix algebra; if you do, you will see that in many ways I just barely touch the surface. Even if you do not have the opportunity to take a formal course in matrix algebra, you may profit by the much more detailed treatment of the subject in texts like Horst (1963) or Searle (1966, 1971). Fortunately, many difficult aspects of matrix theory are not relevant to multivariate analysis since you will not have to deal with imaginary numbers, for example.

Matrix theory originated from a general need to solve systems of simultaneous equations. You probably have worked with problems like the following, where you need to determine the values of X and Y:

$$X + Y = 5$$

$$X - Y = 1$$

One way to solve for X and Y is to add the two equations, yielding $2X = 6$, eliminating Y in the process. The result is $X = 3$. Substituting 3 for X into either equation allows you to determine that $Y = 2$. Obviously, not all problems are this simple. You may have to add 5 times the first equation to 4 times the second; it may be easier to solve for Y first, and there may be many equations and unknowns. The consequence of the search for general methods to solve systems or sets of simultaneous equations led to the development of matrix theory. Matrix theory is particularly well suited for the computer, and many numerical analysts specialize in inventing more efficient ways to automate performance of basic matrix operations, for example, matrix inversion. Moreover, as statistics developed, it became clear that the solutions to basic questions like finding the parameters (beta weights) for regression equations and the like were merely special case of more fundamental matrix operations.

Basic Definitions

A *matrix* is simply a rectangular array of numbers. As an example, just imagine answers to five survey questions that are asked of 10 shoppers at a mall, questions such as "How much money do you spend at the mall on a weekly

TABLE 3-1. Hypothetical responses from 10 mall shoppers to five interview questions[a]

$$X = \begin{bmatrix} 4 & 4 & 4 & 5 & 7 \\ 7 & 5 & 6 & 6 & 4 \\ 3 & 3 & 5 & 4 & 4 \\ 4 & 4 & 5 & 7 & 8 \\ 4 & 4 & 2 & 4 & 2 \\ 6 & 4 & 5 & 5 & 4 \\ 2 & 2 & 1 & 2 & 3 \\ 4 & 7 & 5 & 3 & 5 \\ 5 & 4 & 6 & 5 & 6 \\ 3 & 4 & 2 & 2 & 2 \end{bmatrix} \quad Z = \begin{bmatrix} -.14 & .08 & -.06 & .43 & 1.24 \\ 1.90 & .70 & 1.06 & 1.04 & -.25 \\ -.81 & -.85 & .50 & -.18 & -.25 \\ -.14 & -.08 & .50 & 1.65 & 1.74 \\ -.14 & -.08 & -1.17 & -.18 & -1.24 \\ 1.22 & -.08 & .50 & .43 & -.25 \\ -1.49 & -1.63 & 1.73 & -1.41 & -.74 \\ -.14 & 2.25 & .50 & -.79 & .25 \\ .54 & -.08 & 1.06 & .43 & .74 \\ -.81 & -.08 & -1.17 & -1.41 & -1.24 \end{bmatrix}$$

[a] Raw data are on the left; transformations are on the right.

basis?" Because many different matrices will be encountered, it is important to identify the particular matrix as a *data* matrix and symbolize it is **X**. The left-hand side of Table 3-1 contains an **X** matrix. The actual data are simply random numbers chosen to fall along a 1 to 8 scale with equal probability, i.e., *uniform* random numbers. I built in a correlation among items by making each of the random numbers the sum of two other random numbers. One of the two numbers was chosen to be the *same* quantity for each person. Hence, all five variables share one term in common and another that is unique to each. This general procedure to produce correlated data will be used in many later chapters.

A general convention is to let the rows or *horizontal* elements of **X** represent subjects (respondents), and the columns or *vertical* elements represent variables (questionnaire items). By convention, a boldface capital letter is often used to identify the entire matrix, a convention I will follow. An individual element is identified by a lower case letter and a pair of subscripts. The first subscript identifies the row position of the element and the second identifies the column position. Thus, x_{23} identifies the element in the second row and third column of Table 3-1, which has the numerical value of 6. The physical array is usually enclosed in either brackets or large parentheses to identify it as a matrix. I will follow the former convention. The *order* of a matrix is defined by the number of rows and the number of columns. Thus, **X** is of order 10×5 or, more simply, **X** is a 10×5 matrix. If only a single value is given, the matrix is to be assumed a square matrix.

A *vector* is a matrix with but a single column or a single row of elements. It may be part of another matrix. For example, the answers to question 3 going down the 10 respondents form a 10-element *column* vector, and the answers given by respondent 8 going across the 5 questions form a five-element *row* vector. By convention, a column vector is symbolized by a lower case boldface letter but a row vector is symbolized by a lower case boldface letter and a prime ('), which allows it to be distinguished from a column vector. A single subscript is used to identify a given element in a vector. However, I will be presenting several examples involving only pairs of variables. In many cases, it is much simpler to call them "*X*" and "*Y*" (which many other texts do) than to identify them as "X_1" and "X_2" or the like. I will try to avoid complicated notation whenever possible.

Each column of a data matrix is often transformed to a mean of .0 and a standard deviation of 1.0 over subjects. That is, multivariate analyses are commonly based upon z-score transformations of a raw data matrix. Following convention, I will use the symbol **Z** to describe such matrices. The right-hand side of Table 3-1 contains the z-score transformation upon columns of **X**. You may wish to spot check the computations. The means across subjects for the five questions are 4.2, 4.1, 4.1, 4.3, and 4.5, and the standard deviations are 1.5, 1.3, 1.8, 1.6, and 2.0. (Your values will probably differ from mine since the calculations internal to the computer program I used carried the data to more decimal places than I gave you.)

Square Matrices

There is no inherent relation between the "height" (number of rows) and the "width" (number of columns) of most matrices, although a data matrix is usually "taller" than it is "wide" because there are usually more subjects than there are variables in most studies. Some particular matrices are inherently square. The matrix of intercorrelations among a set of variables is inherently square. It is common to refer to a matrix of intercorrelations of raw data by the symbol **R**. Table 3-2 is an example of a correlation matrix formed from the data in Table 3-1 by correlating across subjects, and it contains the correlation between responses to all possible pairs of items.

The *principal* or *major* diagonal of a square matrix consists of those elements running from the top left position to the bottom right. Their row position equals their column positions (the diagonal running from top right to bottom left is not important). The *trace* of a square matrix is the sum of its diagonal elements.

An **R** matrix has several important properties. One is that it is *symmetric* in that the element in the *i*th row and *j*th column (r_{ij}) must be the same as the element in the *j*th row and *i*th column (r_{ji}). In addition, its diagonal elements

TABLE 3-2. Intercorrelation
matrix based on the data of
Table 3-1

$$\mathbf{R} = \begin{bmatrix} 1.00 & 0.46 & 0.71 & 0.66 & 0.19 \\ 0.46 & 1.00 & 0.48 & 0.14 & 0.19 \\ 0.71 & 0.48 & 1.00 & 0.71 & 0.60 \\ 0.66 & 0.14 & 0.71 & 1.00 & 0.69 \\ 0.19 & 0.19 & 0.60 & 0.69 & 1.00 \end{bmatrix}$$

Table 3-3. Variance–covariance
matrix based on the data of
Table 3-1

$$\mathbf{C} = \begin{bmatrix} 2.18 & 0.87 & 1.87 & 1.60 & 0.56 \\ 0.87 & 1.66 & 1.10 & 0.30 & 0.50 \\ 1.87 & 1.10 & 3.21 & 2.07 & 2.17 \\ 1.60 & 0.30 & 2.07 & 2.68 & 2.28 \\ 0.56 & 0.50 & 2.17 & 2.28 & 4.06 \end{bmatrix}$$

usually will equal 1.0. Consequently, its trace will equal the number of variables and, therefore, the order of **R**. However, some applications, notably common factor analysis, involve numbers less than 1.0 in the diagonal positions, and certain forms of multiple regression may involve numbers greater than 1.0. When the diagonal elements are not 1.0, the trace will not equal the number of variables or the order.

A *variance–covariance* matrix is also symmetric. As its name indicates, it consists of variances of individual variables, which are located in the diagonal positions, and covariances between variables, which are located off the diagonal positions. Its trace equals the sum of the variances of individual variables, a quantity that appears in many psychometric analyses.

Table 3-3 contains the variance–covariance matrix (**C**) for the data of Table 3-1. The quantities in **C** may be obtained by dividing sums of squares ($\sum x_i^2$ terms) and sums of cross products ($\sum x_i x_j$ terms) either by N to obtain maximum likelihood estimates (assuming the underlying distributions are normal) or by $N - 1$ to obtain least squares estimates (without making the assumption about normality). I have used $N - 1$ in the present case.

A correlation matrix (**R**) may be derived from a variance-covariance matrix (**C**), but not the other way around. The correlation of items 1 and 2 is their covariance divided by the product of their standard deviations (Eq. 2-8b). Conversely, the covariance of items 1 and 2 is the standard deviation of item 1 times the standard deviation of item 2 times the correlation between the two items.

A *skew symmetric* matrix is one in which $y_{ij} = -y_{ji}$. Skew symmetric matrices have important applications to *rotation of axes* in factor analysis and the study of *preferences*.

A *diagonal* matrix is a special kind of symmetric matrix in which all elements off the diagonal equal .0. The following is a diagonal matrix (elements on the diagonal can also equal zero):

$$\begin{bmatrix} 2 & 0 \\ 0 & 4 \end{bmatrix}$$

If all of the diagonal elements of a diagonal matrix have the same value, the result is called a *scalar* matrix.

An *identity* matrix is a diagonal matrix in which all diagonal elements equal 1.0. The identity matrix plays the same role in matrix theory that unity plays in ordinary (scalar) algebra as an *identity operator* in *multiplication.* The name given to a matrix that consists of only zeros is a *null* matrix. It plays the same role as zero; it is an identity operator in *addition and subtraction.* (Fundamental matrix operations will be defined below.) The standard symbol used to denote an identity matrix is **I**. I will use the symbol **0** to denote a null matrix, but this notation is less standardized.

A *triangular* matrix is a special type of asymmetric matrix. An *upper* triangular matrix consists of zeroes below the main diagonal, and a *lower* triangular matrix consists of zeroes above the main diagonal. The following are upper and lower triangular matrices, respectively:

$$\begin{bmatrix} 2 & 3 & 7 \\ 0 & 3 & 4 \\ 0 & 0 & 8 \end{bmatrix} \qquad \begin{bmatrix} 6 & 0 & 0 \\ 1 & 3 & 0 \\ 5 & 4 & 6 \end{bmatrix}$$

Another important square but asymmetric matrix is of the following general form when it is of order 2:

$$\mathbf{T} = \begin{bmatrix} \cos x & -\sin x \\ \sin x & \cos x \end{bmatrix}$$

The matrix **T** provides an *orthonormal transformation* in analytic geometry. That is, its function is to take coordinates that are defined relative to one pair of axes and express the coordinates relative to a new pair of axes by a rigid (right-angled) rotation of the original axes. For example, suppose a point had coordinates of (.71, .71) with respect to one pair of axes. If a new pair of axes were obtained by rotating each of the first pair of axes by 45 degrees, the point would have a coordinate of 1.0 with respect to one of the new axes and .0 with respect to the other. Problems involving rotation of axes frequently appear within multivariate analysis, particularly factor analysis. This matrix is skew-symmetric for reasons inherent in the geometry of rotation.

The preceding orthonormal transformation produces a *rigid rotation.* Each of the two axes (or more, in more complex problems) is rotated by the same degree, just as if you had made the original pair of axes immobile with respect to one another by gluing them together and then turning them about their origin. If the rotation were 30 degrees, the transformation matrix would appear as

$$\begin{bmatrix} .87 & -.50 \\ .50 & .87 \end{bmatrix}$$

since the cosine of 30 degrees is .87 and the sine of 30 degrees is .50.

A transformation matrix is an example of an *orthonormal* matrix because it possesses two distinct properties: (1) *Geometric Orthogonality* ("right-angledness")—both axes are rotated by the same amount (a necessary condition for geometric orthogonality is that the sum of the products of each pair of rows or columns be zero); and (2) *Normality* ("unit length")—the new axes are the same length as the old ones. Property (2) is a consequence of the general relation $\cos^2 x + \sin^2 x = 1$. A necessary condition for normality is that the sum of the squares within each column be 1, which will be true even when the rotation is not orthogonal. The sum of squares within each row of a ortho-normal transformation matrix will also be 1, but this need not be the case when the transformation is not orthogonal. I will discuss subsequently the more general case in which one axis is rotated by a certain amount and a second axis is rotated by a different amount—*oblique* rotation.

A matrix may be orthogonal but not normal, as in the following:

$$\begin{bmatrix} 2 & 4 \\ -4 & 2 \end{bmatrix}$$

Conversely, the columns of a matrix may be normal, but the matrix need not be orthogonal, as in the following:

$$\begin{bmatrix} .71 & .50 \\ -.71 & .87 \end{bmatrix}$$

Such matrices are used to provide oblique transformations. (Note that the rows of an oblique transformation matrix are not orthogonal nor normal.)

Transposition

A matrix is *transposed* by reversing its rows and columns. The following pair of matrices are transposes of one another:

$$\mathbf{W} = \begin{bmatrix} 9 & 8 & 6 & 4 \\ 2 & 1 & 9 & 5 \end{bmatrix}; \quad \mathbf{W}' = \begin{bmatrix} 9 & 2 \\ 8 & 1 \\ 6 & 9 \\ 4 & 5 \end{bmatrix}$$

Note that the element in the second row and third column of the matrix on the left is the same as the element in the third row and second column of the matrix on the right. The prime is used to denote the transpose of a matrix. Any matrix may be transposed, square or not, although a symmetric matrix will be its own transpose. A row vector is the transpose of a column vector, hence the use of a prime to denote a row vector.

Matrix Equality

Two matrices are *equal* if and only if their corresponding elements are identical. Thus, $\mathbf{A} = \mathbf{B}$ means that each and every element in $\mathbf{A}$ is the same as each and every element in $\mathbf{B}$, which, in turn, implies they have the same order. Two matrices may be related to one another in ways other than equality, such as being transposes. Other important relations between matrices will be noted at various points.

Basic Matrix Operations

There are matrix operations corresponding to the fundamental scalar operations of addition, subtraction, multiplication, and division. The first two are quite similar, but the latter two are performed in a quite different manner.

Matrix Addition and Subtraction

Matrix *addition* and matrix *subtraction* generalize quite easily from the scalar case. Both addition and subtraction are simply done element by element. There is one requirement, however—the two matrices must be of the same order. Although any pair of scalars have a sum and a difference, *two matrices will have a sum and a difference if and only if they have the same order.*

Thus, if **A** and **B** are matrices

$$\mathbf{A} = \begin{bmatrix} 5 & 2 & 4 \\ 3 & 5 & 1 \\ 4 & -1 & 3 \end{bmatrix}, \qquad \mathbf{B} = \begin{bmatrix} 6 & 1 & 8 \\ 7 & 7 & 3 \\ 1 & 1 & 0 \end{bmatrix}$$

their sum, **C**, and their difference, **D**, are as follows:

$$\mathbf{C} = \begin{bmatrix} 11 = 5 + 6 & 3 = 2 + 1 & 12 = 4 + 8 \\ 10 = 3 + 7 & 12 = 5 + 7 & 4 = 1 + 3 \\ 5 = 4 + 1 & 0 = -1 + 1 & 3 = 3 + 0 \end{bmatrix},$$

$$\mathbf{D} = \begin{bmatrix} -1 = 5 - 6 & 1 = 2 - 1 & -4 = 4 - 8 \\ -4 = 3 - 7 & -2 = 5 - 7 & -2 = 1 - 3 \\ 3 = 4 - 1 & -2 = -1 - 1 & 3 = 3 - 0 \end{bmatrix}$$

Addition and subtraction of vectors is merely a special case in which there is only 1 row or column. Addition or subtraction is still performed element by element and two row vectors must have the same number of elements.

Both the *associative* and the *commutative* laws of addition and subtraction hold for their matrix counterparts. The associative law states that the grouping of the matrices does not affect the outcome. Thus if one is told to add matrices **A** and **B** and subtract matrix **C**, **A** and **B** may be added first and **C** subtracted from their sum, $(\mathbf{A} + \mathbf{B}) - \mathbf{C}$, or **C** may be subtracted from **B** and the result added to **A**, $\mathbf{A} + (\mathbf{B} - \mathbf{C})$. The commutative law states that the order of addition and subtraction is also immaterial. Thus, **C** may be subtracted from **A** and added to **B**, $(\mathbf{A} - \mathbf{C}) + \mathbf{B}$, or **C** may be subtracted from **B** and added to **A**, $(\mathbf{B} - \mathbf{C}) + \mathbf{A}$.

Matrix Multiplication

Unlike its scalar counterpart, there are several different forms of *multiplication* involving matrices. I will be concerned with the two most important general forms, the multiplication of a matrix by a *scalar* and the multiplication of a matrix by a *matrix*. Multiplying a scalar by a vector obeys the same rules as multiplying a scalar by a matrix, and multiplying a vector by a vector obeys the same rules as multiplying a matrix by a matrix.

Multiplication of a matrix by a scalar, like the addition and subtraction of a pair of matrices, is a fairly simple generalization of the ordinary multiplication of a pair of scalars—one simply multiplies each and every matrix element by the scalar to produce the new matrix. The new matrix will have the same order as the original matrix. Thus, if one wishes to multiply the matrix C, above, by a scalar, k, whose value is 2.0. The result, kC, is

$$kC = \begin{bmatrix} 22 = 11 \times 2 & 6 = 3 \times 2 & 24 = 12 \times 2 \\ 20 = 10 \times 2 & 24 = 12 \times 2 & 8 = 4 \times 2 \\ 10 = 5 \times 2 & 0 = 0 \times 2 & 6 = 3 \times 2 \end{bmatrix}$$

Multiplying a scalar by a vector is just a special case. You still multiply every element of the vector by the scalar. Thus, if you multiply the vector $(2, 1)$ by 3, the result is $(6, 3)$.

Multiplication of two matrices is more complex and counterintuitive. There are actually several types of multiplication referred to in advanced matrix theory. However, only one type is of interest to multivariate analysis. It is commonly referred to as *dot* multiplication. When I used the term "multiplication" of matrices, assume dot multiplication.

As I mentioned at the beginning of the chapter, not all pairs of matrices can be multiplied and the order in which a pair of matrices is multiplied is crucial to the result. The left-hand member of a matrix product (A in the expression AB), is called the *prefactor* and the right-hand term (B) is called the *postfactor*. The expression "multiply A into B (or A by B)" implies this particular left to right order, AB. Thus, one would say that B is *premultiplied* by A, or that A is *postmultiplied* by B.

In order for multiplication to be defined, a very basic condition has to be met: *the number of columns in the prefactor must equal the number of rows in the postfactor*, a property known as *conformability*. I will refer to the number of columns of the prefactor (and, consequently, the number of rows of the postfactor) of conformable matrices as the *common dimension*. The product matrix will have the same number of rows as the prefactor and the same number of columns as the postfactor. Thus if the prefactor is three rows by five columns (order of 3×5) and the postfactor is five rows by two columns (order of 5×2), their product is defined: the number of columns in the prefactor (5) equals the number of rows in the postfactor (5). The product will have 3 rows $\times$ 2 columns (order of 3×2).

The actual multiplication follows what is commonly termed the *row by column* rule. The element in the ith row and jth column of the product matrix will be the sum of cross products of the ith row vector of the prefactor and the jth column vector of the postfactor. If the prefactor is symbolized as **A**, with a_{ik} being an arbitrary element, the postfactor is symbolized as **B**, with b_{kj} being an arbitrary element, and the resultant matrix is symbolized as **C**, with c_{ij} being an arbitrary element, Eq. (3-1) describes dot multiplication in summation notation:

$$c_{ij} = \sum a_{ik}b_{kj} \tag{3-1}$$

For a simple example, consider the following matrices:

$$A = \begin{bmatrix} 5 & 2 & 4 \\ 3 & 5 & 1 \\ 4 & -1 & 3 \end{bmatrix}; \quad B = \begin{bmatrix} 6 & 1 & 8 \\ 7 & 7 & 3 \\ 1 & 1 & 0 \end{bmatrix}$$

The element in the first row and first column of the product, $C = AB$, is the sum of cross products of the first row vector of **A** (the numbers 5, 2 and 4) and the first column vector of **B** (the numbers 6, 7 and 1). Application of Eq. (3-1) produces $(5 \times 6) + (2 \times 7) + (4 \times 1) = 48$. The remainder of $C = AB$ is:

$$C = AB = \begin{bmatrix} 48=5\times6+2\times7+4\times1 & 23=5\times1+2\times7+4\times1 & 46=5\times8+2\times3+4\times0 \\ 54=3\times6+5\times7+1\times1 & 39=3\times1+5\times7+1\times1 & 39=3\times8+5\times3+1\times0 \\ 20=4\times6-1\times7+3\times1 & 0=4\times1-1\times7+3\times1 & 29=4\times8-1\times3+3\times0 \end{bmatrix}$$

Although you probably will never have to multiply two very large matrices by hand, because that is what computers are there for, you will find it useful to practice multiplying simple matrices to get a feel for the general process required with larger matrices.

Several things can happen in matrix multiplication that do not happen in scalar multiplication. For example, the product of two nonzero scalars cannot be zero. This is not necessarily the case in matrix multiplication! Consider the following pair of matrices, and verify their product is a null matrix:

$$A = \begin{bmatrix} 1 & 1 \\ 2 & 2 \end{bmatrix}, \quad B = \begin{bmatrix} 1 & 4 \\ -1 & -4 \end{bmatrix}$$

Also, the *commutative* law does not hold for matrix multiplication even though it does hold in both scalar multiplication and matrix addition. Thus, the product of matrices **ABC** will not generally equal the product of **ACB**, which, in fact, may not even be defined. The common dimension of **A** and **B** bears no relation to the common dimension of **B** and **C**. Thus, **A** and **C** or **C** and **B** may not be conformable. As a rule, products must be performed in the order dictated by the equation.

There are, fortunately, several properties of matrix multiplication that are the same as their counterparts in scalar multiplication. The *associative* law holds; in forming the matrix product **ABC**, the product of **A** and **B** may be computed first and used as the prefactor for **C** or the product of **B** and **C** may be computed first and used as the postfactor for **A**.

Also, the *distributive* law holds in both scalar and matrix multiplication. Thus, **AB** + **AC** = **A**(**B** + **C**), and you can algebraically factor out matrix **A**. However, you cannot factor **A** if it is a prefactor in one product and a postfactor in the other—**AB** + **CA** is not the same as **AB** + **AC**. Only the latter equals **A**(**B** + **C**).

Two scalars that have a product of 1.0 are said to be *reciprocals* of one another, e.g., 2 and .5. There are analogous situations in matrix multiplication. In one, the two matrices generate an identity matrix regardless of the order in which they are multiplied. For example,

$$A = \begin{bmatrix} 2 & 1 \\ 1 & 2 \end{bmatrix}, \quad B = \begin{bmatrix} .67 & -.33 \\ -.33 & .67 \end{bmatrix}$$

B is said to be the *inverse* of **A** and is symbolized by A^{-1}. Alternatively, **A** could just as well be said to be the inverse of **B** and symbolized as B^{-1}. You might wish to verify that both **AB** and **BA** equal an identity matrix (**I**) within rounding error. Only certain matrices may have an inverse—the matrix must be square (though not necessarily symmetric); but being square is not sufficient. Obtaining inverses is one of the most basic operations in matrix theory, and it will be treated as a special topic.

An orthonormal matrix has the interesting property that its transpose is also its inverse. You can use the matrix **T** given previously to verify this relationship if you know elementary geometry.

Sometimes **AB** forms an identity matrix but **BA** does not. Consider the following pair of matrices:

$$G = \begin{bmatrix} -1.00 & -1.33 & 1.00 \\ 3.00 & 3.67 & -2.00 \end{bmatrix}; \quad H = \begin{bmatrix} 2 & 1 \\ 0 & 0 \\ 3 & 1 \end{bmatrix}$$

GH is an identity matrix of order 2, but **HG** (which is of order 3) is not an identity matrix. **G** is called the *left-hand pseudoinverse* or *generalized inverse* of **H**, and **H** is called the *right-hand pseudoinverse* or *generalized inverse* of **G**.

Correlation Matrices and Matrix Multiplication

If you wished to go from the z scores of Table 3-1 to the correlations of Table 3-2, you could just multiply the corresponding elements in pairs of columns, add, and divide by either $N = 10$ or $N - 1 = 9$, depending on how you had defined the standard deviations. The process would be repeated for the 10 (5 × 4/2) distinct pairs of columns.

The computation of a correlation matrix may be stated in more general terms. The matrix operation $Z'Z$ sums squared values of z over subjects ($\sum z_i^2$

in summation notation) when the row of $\mathbf{Z}'$ is the same as the column of $\mathbf{Z}$ and sums of cross products ($\sum z_i z_j$ in summation notation) when they are different. Next, scalar multiplication by $1/N$ produces unities on the diagonal, since the sum of a set of z scores squared divided by N is 1.0, and correlations on the off diagonals, since $r_{ij} = (1/N)\sum z_i z_j$. In short, the entire process of forming $\mathbf{R}$ may simply be summarized as $(1/N)(\mathbf{Z}'\mathbf{Z})$.

Partitioned Matrices and Their Multiplication

Sometimes it is convenient to think of a matrix as being composed of other matrices or *submatrices*. Suppose you interviewed a number of people about their attitudes toward purchase of various automobiles. Your interview might consist of, say, five questions of a demographic nature, such as income, and a series of 15 questions devoted to evaluating a particular automobile.

You might wish to obtain the 20×20 item intercorrelation matrix. The matrix has an important structure. One 5×5 submatrix will contain the intercorrelations among the demographic variables. I will use the symbol $\mathbf{W}(d)$ to describe the intercorrelations *within* demographic variables. Similarly, there will be a 15×15 submatrix of intercorrelations within the automobile preference ratings, $\mathbf{W}(a)$. Finally, there will be a pair of matrices containing correlations *between* variables in the two sets that will be transposes of one another; I will call them $\mathbf{B}$ and $\mathbf{B}'$, respectively. One 5×15 matrix, $\mathbf{B}$, will contain correlations such as that between income as a row variable and ratings of Porches as the column variable; the other 15×5 matrix, $\mathbf{B}'$, will contain the same correlation between ratings of Porches as the row variable and income as the column variable. Instead of talking about a 20×20 matrix containing correlations of individual items, one can talk of a *supermatrix* with the following structure:

$$\begin{bmatrix} \mathbf{W}(d) & \mathbf{B} \\ \mathbf{B}' & \mathbf{W}(a) \end{bmatrix}$$

Partitioning makes the organization of the data clearer.

Some Rules and Theorems Involved in Matrix Algebra

Many theorems greatly simplify the algebra needed for matrix operations. Assume in all cases the matrices involved are conformable.

1. The transpose of the product of two matrices equals the product of the transposes taken in reverse order:

$$(\mathbf{AB})' = \mathbf{B}'\mathbf{A}$$

2. The inverse of the product of two matrices equals the product of the inverses taken in reverse order:

$$(\mathbf{AB})^{-1} = \mathbf{B}^{-1}\mathbf{A}^{-1}$$

3. Premultiplying an arbitrary matrix by a diagonal matrix multiplies all elements of the ith row of that arbitrary matrix (postfactor) by the ith value of the diagonal matrix. Thus, the matrix **D** multiplies all values in the first row of the postfactor (**E**) by 2 and all values in the second row of the postfactor by 3:

$$\mathbf{D} = \begin{bmatrix} 2 & 0 \\ 0 & 3 \end{bmatrix}, \quad \mathbf{E} = \begin{bmatrix} 7 & 2 \\ 1 & 4 \end{bmatrix}, \quad \mathbf{DE} = \begin{bmatrix} 14 & 4 \\ 3 & 12 \end{bmatrix}$$

4. Postmultiplying an arbitrary matrix by a diagonal matrix multiplies all elements of the ith column of that arbitrary matrix (prefactor) by the ith value of the diagonal matrix. Thus, the matrix **D** multiplies all values in the first column of the prefactor (**E**) by 2 and all values in the second column of the prefactor by 3:

$$\mathbf{D} = \begin{bmatrix} 2 & 0 \\ 0 & 3 \end{bmatrix}, \quad \mathbf{E} = \begin{bmatrix} 7 & 2 \\ 1 & 4 \end{bmatrix}, \quad \mathbf{ED} = \begin{bmatrix} 14 & 6 \\ 2 & 12 \end{bmatrix}$$

(Note that the diagonal elements of **DE** and **ED** in the two examples are identical; only the off-diagonal elements are different.)

5. If **w** and **v** are vectors, the result of the operation $\mathbf{w}'\mathbf{v} = \mathbf{v}'\mathbf{w}$, both of which are called the *scalar* (*inner*) *product* of the vectors, is a scalar. Recognize the difference between the expression $\mathbf{w}'\mathbf{v}$ and the alternative *outer product*, of the form $\mathbf{w}'\mathbf{v}$, which is a matrix. Thus:

$$\mathbf{w} = \begin{bmatrix} 2 \\ 1 \\ 3 \end{bmatrix}, \quad \mathbf{v} = \begin{bmatrix} 4 \\ 0 \\ 1 \end{bmatrix}, \quad \mathbf{w}'\mathbf{v} = \mathbf{v}'\mathbf{w} = 11, \quad \mathbf{wv}' = \begin{bmatrix} 8 & 0 & 2 \\ 4 & 0 & 1 \\ 12 & 0 & 3 \end{bmatrix}$$

Products of Symmetric Matrices

Perhaps surprisingly, the product of two symmetric matrices is usually not symmetric. If a matrix is symmetric, then $\mathbf{A}' = \mathbf{A}$. Hence, **AB** will equal $\mathbf{A}'\mathbf{B}'$, which will equal $(\mathbf{BA})'$ by rule 1. However, $(\mathbf{BA})'$ is not necessarily the same as **BA**. To illustrate:

$$\begin{matrix} \mathbf{A} & \mathbf{B} & \mathbf{AB} \end{matrix}$$
$$\begin{bmatrix} 3 & 1 & 2 \\ 1 & 4 & 3 \\ 2 & 3 & 1 \end{bmatrix} \begin{bmatrix} 2 & 0 & 7 \\ 0 & 2 & 4 \\ 7 & 4 & 1 \end{bmatrix} = \begin{bmatrix} 20 & 10 & 27 \\ 23 & 20 & 26 \\ 11 & 10 & 27 \end{bmatrix}$$

I have left a demonstration that the product **BA** is also not symmetric as an exercise for you.

The asymmetry of the product of two symmetric matrices slightly complicates discriminant analysis (Chapter 8).

More about Vector Products

The square root of the scalar (inner) product of a vector with itself $(v'v)$ is the *length* of the vector. The length of the vector $v = (3, 4)$ is $[(3 \times 3) + (4 \times 4)]^{1/2} = [9 + 16]^{1/2} = 25^{1/2} = 5$. (When a vector has only two elements, think of each element as the side of a right triangle and the length of the vector as the length of the hypotenuse of the right triangle.) If the length is 1.0, the vector is said to be *normal* or of *unit length*. The vector $v = (.50, .87)$ is normal because $v'v = (.50 \times .50) + (.87 \times .87) = .25 + .75 = 1.0$, and the square root of 1.0 is 1.0. You may yourself verify that the vector $(.707, -.707)$ is also normal.

It is often necessary to normalize a nonnormal vector by finding a scalar constant to "shrink" or "stretch" it as needed. The needed constant is the reciprocal square root of the scalar product $1/(v'v)^{1/2}$.

A related concept is that if w and v are both normal, their scalar product $w'v$ (or $v'w$) defines the *cosine* of the angle between them. If they are not normal, their inner product may be divided by their lengths to obtain the desire cosine:

$$\text{cosine}(w, v) = \frac{w'v}{[(w'w)(v'v)]^{1/2}} \qquad (\text{or } v'w) \qquad (3\text{-}2)$$

There is a fundamental equivalence between Eq. (3-2) and Eq. (2-8b), which defines the Pearson product–moment correlation. A set of scores is indeed a vector, and the correlation between two such sets of scores is, in fact, mathematically equivalent to the cosine of the angle between them. If they are uncorrelated, the result is equivalent to vector products like $(1, 0)$ and $(0, 1)$ or $(.707, .707)$ and $(.707, -.707)$. A cosine (correlation) of .0 implies a right angle (orthogonal) relation between the pair of vectors. That is why uncorrelated vectors are called "orthogonal."

You may wonder why the apparently complex definition of dot multiplication is used so frequently. The answer is that for all the apparent complexity, dot multiplication leads to some very desirable results. Matrix theory as an algebraic system emerged through the work of various 19th century mathematicians, notably Sylvester and Kronecker, and was applied to statistical analysis by early 20th century statisticians like Fisher, Hoetelling, and Thurstone. In its general form, it is used to solve systems of linear equations. These linear equations often involve the linear combinations that are basic to multivariate analysis.

Exponentiation

There is a matrix analog to raising a number to a power. However, it is not simply multiplying a matrix by itself, since only square matrices are conformable with themselves. Rather, one may square a matrix X by premultiplying it by its transpose. That is, the relation $Y = X'X$ is defined for any matrix, square or not, and, by analog to scalar algebra, **Y** may be thought of as the "square" of **X**. By extension, one may also talk about raising **X** to any integral power.

In the same sense, the matrix **X** may also be said to be the "square root" of **Y**, since **X** is the quantity that, when "multiplied by itself" (actually, its transpose, to conform to the rules of matrix multiplication), produces **Y**. Finding a *triangular* matrix **X** having the property $X'X = Y$, where **Y** is symmetric, is known as a *Cholesky decomposition*. A Cholesky decomposition plays an important role in discriminant analysis and canonical analysis, among other places. I mention it here so that you will recognize it as the matrix equivalent of finding a square root when you encounter it, such as in Chapter 8.

There are important differences, however, between the square root of a scalar and the square root of a matrix. Every positive number has a square root that is unique except for sign. Thus, the square root of 4 has an absolute value of 2, but it could be $+2$ or -2. Not all matrices have square root matrices comprised of real elements. At the very least, a matrix must be square and symmetric. A very important class of matrices do have square roots and therefore can be expressed in the form $Y = X'X$. They are called *Gramian* matrices. If the relation $Y = X'X$ holds, the relation $Y = WW'$ will also hold by letting $W = X'$. *Consequently, a Gramian matrix can be expressed as the product of a matrix and its transpose.* A correlation matrix with unities on its diagonal is a Gramian matrix

Another very important fact is that if a matrix has a square root, i.e., is Gramian, it has infinitely many. For example, you should be able to verify that (within rounding error):

$$\begin{bmatrix} 2 & 1 \\ 3 & 2 \end{bmatrix}\begin{bmatrix} 2 & 3 \\ 1 & 2 \end{bmatrix} = \begin{bmatrix} 2.22 & -.22 \\ 3.60 & .08 \end{bmatrix}\begin{bmatrix} 2.22 & 3.60 \\ -.22 & -.08 \end{bmatrix} = \begin{bmatrix} 5 & 8 \\ 8 & 13 \end{bmatrix}$$

As will be seen in discussion of factor analysis, one of the basic equations may be stated as: $R = BB'$ (Eq. 6-3). The square root of **R** obtained from a Cholesky decomposition satisfies this equation. However, an infinite number of other matrices, which are not triangular in form, are also acceptable. In fact, one rarely uses the triangular square root of **R** as a factor solution, for reasons to be discussed.

Determinants

The *determinant* is an important property of a square matrix. (It is not defined for nonsquare matrices.) In a 2×2 matrix, it equals the product of the diagonal entries minus the product of the remaining two entries $(x_{11}x_{22} - x_{12}x_{21})$. The determinant of the first of the preceding matrices is therefore $2 \times 2 - 3 \times 1$ or 1.

The other matrices in the example also have determinants of 1.0 within rounding error—$[2.22 \times .08 - (-.22 \times 3.60)]$ and $(13 \times 5 - 8 \times 8)$. *The* determinant of the product of two matrices equals the product of the two matrices' determinants. In the present case, $1 \times 1 = 1$.

It is useful to be able to calculate the determinant, $|X|$, of a 3×3 matrix, X. Equation (3-3) provides one formula:

$$|X| = (x_{11}x_{22}x_{33} + x_{21}x_{32}x_{13} + x_{31}x_{12}x_{23})$$
$$- (x_{31}x_{22}x_{13} + x_{21}x_{12}x_{33} + x_{11}x_{32}x_{23}) \qquad (3\text{-}3)$$

To illustrate, let X be defined as follows:

$$X = \begin{bmatrix} 1 & 2 & 4 \\ 0 & 3 & 1 \\ 2 & -1 & 2 \end{bmatrix}$$

Then

$$|X| = 1 \times [(3 \times 2) - (-1 \times 1)) - 0 \times ((2 \times 2) - (-1 \times 4)) + 2((2 \times 1)$$
$$- (3 \times 4)]$$
$$= 1 \times (6 + 1) - 0 \times (4 + 4) + 2 \times (2 - 12)$$
$$= (1 \times 7) - (0 \times 8) + (2 \times -10)$$
$$= 7 - 0 - 20$$
$$= -13.00.$$

I will not be concerned with calculation of higher-order determinants.

Matrix Singularity and Linear Dependency

Matrices that have a determinant of zero are called *singular* matrices, and matrices that have a nonzero determinant are called *nonsingular* matrices. Only nonsingular matrices have an inverse. One or more rows (columns) of a singular matrix are *linearly dependent* on one or more of the remaining rows (columns). Consequently, if one multiplies certain rows (columns) by a suitable constant and adds the products, the resultant will equal one or more of the remaining rows (columns). For example, if you multiply the first row of the following 2×2 matrix by -2, it will equal the second row; you can also multiply the second row by $-.5$ to produce the first row:

$$\begin{bmatrix} 2 & -3 \\ -4 & 6 \end{bmatrix}$$

Alternatively, you can multiply the first column by -1.5 and obtain the second column or multiply the second column by $-2/3$ and obtain the first column. The determinant of the matrix $[(2 \times 6) - (-4 \times -3)]$ is $.0$. Larger matrices may require you to multiply one row (or column) by one constant, a second row (or column) by a second constant, etc.

An important theorem states that the number of linearly independent *rows* of a matrix equals the number of linearly independent *columns.* If a matrix is asymmetric, it is possible for its rows to be linearly independent and its columns linearly dependent (if it has more columns than rows) or vice versa.

Linear dependence does not imply any *particular* set of columns or rows is uniquely independent. To say that row 3 equals the sum of rows 1 and 2 does mean that a dependency exists. However, one could just as well say row 2 equals the difference between rows 1 and 3 or row 1 equals the difference between rows 2 and 3. The concept of dependency means that a *properly chosen* set of rows (columns) called a *basis* can be used to derive the remaining rows (columns). However, the basis of a set of vectors is not unique as different sets of vectors can serve as a basis. Because a basis is not unique, the result of a factor analysis is not unique.

If a matrix is formed from real data, it is almost impossible for an exact linear dependency to exist, save for one situation that is usually the result of an unintentional mistake made by a beginning data analyst. A dependency will arise if one places both individual items and their sum or average in the same data matrix. The sum is, by definition, linearly dependent on the individual items; hence, it is redundant. Variants on this basic error include incorporating the difference between two scores as well as the original scores.

A real data matrix may be approximately but not exactly singular, which implies the measures are highly interrelated. A high degree of intercorrelation, or *multicollinearity*, is often found among items within a scale or scales on a personality test. Multicollinearity produces highly unstable results in operations like factor analysis or multiple regression, meaning slight differences due to sampling error or even rounding can lead to substantially different results.

All major computer packages have routines to detect an exact linear combination, but they do less well in spotting the multicollinearity arising from such things as the high correlations among scales on some personality tests (Bernstein, Schoenfeld, & Costello, 1982). It is quite easy for users to miss a near-singularity in such *ill-conditioned* matrices.

You can see whether a correlation or variance–covariance matrix is ill-conditioned by looking at its determinant. The maximum value of the determinant of **R** (the most commonly inspected square matrix) is the number of measures, implying the measures are mutually uncorrelated and **R** is therefore an identity matrix. Theoretically, the minimum value is .0 (singularity).

An ordinary matrix cannot have a negative determinant because its largest values are on the main diagonal. It is difficult to define "ill-conditioned" exactly; however, a value of .1 for the determinant of **R** is suggestive.

Matrix Rank

The *rank* of a matrix is its number of linearly independent rows (or columns, since they will be equal). Another way of putting it is that the rank equals the *highest-order nonzero determinant.*[1] In other words, if at least one $M \times M$ determinant obtained from a matrix of order N (larger than M) is not zero, and all $(M + 1) \times (M + 1)$ determinants are zero, the matrix has rank M.

The rank of a null matrix is zero because all scalar values, hence all first-order determinants, are zero. If a matrix is *uniform* in the sense that all entries have the same value, all of its 2×2 determinants will be zero even if the matrix is not a null matrix. The rank of a uniform but nonnull matrix is 1, as is also the case when all rows (columns) are multiples of one another. If at least one 2×2 determinant is not zero, the rank is *at least* two, etc. A matrix of *full rank* is one whose *order* equals its *rank*.

Matrix "Division"

Division is not defined in matrix algebra in the sense one can meaningfully write an expression like $\mathbf{Y} = \mathbf{A}/\mathbf{B}$. However, one can accomplish the intended effect by postmultiplying $\mathbf{A}$ by an inverse (if it exists), since the expression $\mathbf{Y} = \mathbf{A}\mathbf{B}^{-1}$ is perfectly well defined. Pseudoinverses can also be used to "move" a matrix from one side of an equation to the other.

The Inverse of a 2 × 2 Matrix

If $|X|$ is the determinant of a 2×2 matrix $\mathbf{X}$, the inverse $(\mathbf{X}^{-1})$ is

$$\mathbf{X}^{-1} = \frac{1}{|\mathbf{X}|} \begin{bmatrix} x_{22} & -x_{12} \\ -x_{21} & x_{11} \end{bmatrix}$$

The inverse is therefore formed by reversing the signs of x_{12} and x_{21} and the positions of x_{11} and x_{22}. Each element is then multiplied by the reciprocal of the determinant of $\mathbf{X}$. If $|\mathbf{X}|$ is zero, the elements of $\mathbf{X}^{-1}$ are undefined, since it will involve division by zero. The requirement that a matrix must have a nonzero determinant to be inverted holds also for higher-order matrices and illustrates the relation between linear dependence (linear dependence means a determinant of zero) and singularity (singularity means noninvertability).

Inverses of Higher-Order Matrices

Some higher-order matrices have easily computed inverses. The identity matrix is the simplest, since it is its own inverse, just as unity is its own reciprocal:

---

[1] The order of a determinant is the order of the matrix from which it is derived. Thus, the determinant of a 3×3 matrix is called a "third-order determinant." This matrix will have several (nine to be exact) 2×2 submatrices, and a second-order determinant may be obtained from each. Finally, the matrix has nine scalars that define nine first-order determinants.

$$\mathbf{I} = \begin{bmatrix} 1 & 0 & 0 \\ 0 & 1 & 0 \\ 0 & 0 & 1 \end{bmatrix}; \quad \mathbf{I}^{-1} = \begin{bmatrix} 1 & 0 & 0 \\ 0 & 1 & 0 \\ 0 & 0 & 1 \end{bmatrix}$$

The inverse of a diagonal matrix is only slightly more complex. The off-diagonal elements of the inverse will all be zero and the diagonal elements will be the reciprocals of their counterparts in the original matrix:

$$\mathbf{D} = \begin{bmatrix} 1.0 & .0 & .0 \\ .0 & 2.0 & .0 \\ .0 & .0 & 0.5 \end{bmatrix}; \quad \mathbf{D}^{-1} = \begin{bmatrix} 1.0 & .0 & .0 \\ .0 & 0.5 & .0 \\ .0 & .0 & 2.0 \end{bmatrix}$$

An orthogonal matrix is also easy to invert because its transpose is also its inverse—$\mathbf{X}' = \mathbf{X}^{-1}$:

$$\mathbf{O} = \begin{bmatrix} .87 & -.50 \\ .50 & .87 \end{bmatrix}; \quad \mathbf{O}^{-1} = \begin{bmatrix} .87 & .50 \\ -.50 & .87 \end{bmatrix}$$

Certain specific inversion methods are possible when a matrix is symmetric. The *square-root* method is described in numerous sources (Harman, 1976; Overall & Klett, 1972). This algorithm is useful in the unlikely event that you need to invert a symmetric matrix by hand. (Much more efficient inversion routines exist for the computer.) The square-root method is of additional interest because it also provides a factoring of the matrix and uses a Cholesky decomposition. Most computer packages provide the inverse of a symmetric matrix as an optional output.

Recalculation of an Inverse Following Deletion of Variable(s)

Even though you will probably never have to calculate an inverse from scratch, you may wish to recalculate an inverse after you have deleted one or more variables. The process is comparatively straightforward. Notationally, I will call the deleted variable P and assume it is in the pth row (of $\mathbf{M}$) in $\mathbf{X}^{-1}$, whose elements are x^{ij}.[2] I will call the new inverse $\mathbf{X}_r^{-1}$ and its elements x_r^{ij}. If either i or j equals p (that is, if the row or column of the new inverse corresponds to the deleted variable), then ignore the element. Otherwise, use Eq. (3-4):

$$x_r^{ij} = x^{ij} - \frac{x^{ip}x^{jp}}{x^{pp}} \tag{3-4}$$

Equation (3-4) has considerable practical implication because you do not need to recompute the entire inverse. The procedure can be repeated as needed to delete additional variables such as when you desire to perform parallel analyses on subsets of variables. For example, one can form a regression

---

[2] The use of superscripts to denote elements of an inverse is a very common convention.

equation using all 14 commonly scored MMPI scales to predict a criterion. Then one can look at the effects of deleting various individual scales. The recomputation requires little programming effort or computer time.

Remember, Eq. (3-4) is used to *delete* a variable(s). You cannot go the other way and *add* variables without recomputing the entire inverse from scratch.

An Application of Matrix Algebra

I have previously discussed the very important matrix equation $\mathbf{R} = (1/N) \times (\mathbf{Z'Z})$ used to take a matrix of z scores within columns and produce a correlation matrix $(\mathbf{R})$. Now I will discuss the even more important operation of taking a matrix of *raw scores* and computing $\mathbf{R}$.

Let $\mathbf{X}$ be a data matrix with N subjects as rows and M variables as columns. For purposes of an example, I will use the data of Table 3-1. Also, let $\mathbf{1}$ denote an N-element column vector of 1's. called a *unit vector*. The unit vector in the present case is therefore

$$\begin{bmatrix} 1 \\ 1 \\ 1 \\ 1 \\ 1 \\ 1 \\ 1 \\ 1 \\ 1 \\ 1 \end{bmatrix}$$

Unit column vectors are commonly used in matrix theory as postfactors to add rows of other matrices, as will be done here. Their transposes (row vectors) are used in an analogous fashion as prefactors to add columns. The steps needed to obtain $\mathbf{R}$ from $\mathbf{X}$ are as follows:

1. Obtain the *uncorrected (raw) sum of products (Raw SP) matrix* $(\mathbf{X'X})$. The Raw SP matrix contains sums of squares (values of ΣX^2) on the diagonal and sums of cross products (values of ΣXY) off the diagonal. The numeric result is:

$$\begin{bmatrix} 196 & 180 & 189 & 195 & 194 \\ 180 & 183 & 178 & 179 & 189 \\ 189 & 178 & 197 & 195 & 204 \\ 195 & 179 & 195 & 209 & 214 \\ 194 & 189 & 204 & 214 & 239 \end{bmatrix}$$

Note that element $(1, 1)$ of the matrix (196) is the sum of the squared elements in the first column of $\mathbf{X}(4^2 + 7^2 + 3^2 + \cdots + 3^2)$ and elements $(1, 2)$ and $(2, 1)$

of the matrix (180, reflecting its symmetry) are the sum of the cross products of the first two columns of $\mathbf{X}$ [$(4 \times 4) + (5 \times 5) + (3 \times 3) + \cdots + (3 \times 4)$], etc.

2. Obtain a column vector of sums $(\mathbf{X'1})$ which contains the sums of the variables (values of $\sum X$). The vector equals

$$\begin{bmatrix} 42 \\ 41 \\ 41 \\ 43 \\ 45 \end{bmatrix}$$

The first element of the vector (42) is the sum of the elements in the first row of $\mathbf{X}$ ($4 + 7 + 3 + \cdots + 3$), etc.

3. Obtain the *corrected sum of products (Corrected SP) matrix through the operation* $[(\mathbf{X'X}) - (1/N)(\mathbf{X'1})(\mathbf{X'1})']$. The matrix contains corrected sums of squares (values of $\sum x^2$) on the diagonal and corrected sums of cross products (values of $\sum xy$) off the diagonal. The term being subtracted $[(1/N)(\mathbf{X'1}) \times (\mathbf{X'1})']$ is the *correction term* you have used previously in computing standard deviations, correlations, etc. Also note that it is the outer or matrix product of $\mathbf{X'1}$ and not the dot or scalar product. I will first present the correction term, which is

$$\begin{bmatrix} 176.4 & 172.2 & 172.2 & 180.6 & 189.0 \\ 172.2 & 168.1 & 168.1 & 176.3 & 184.5 \\ 172.2 & 168.1 & 168.1 & 176.3 & 184.5 \\ 180.6 & 176.3 & 176.3 & 184.9 & 193.5 \\ 189.0 & 184.5 & 184.5 & 193.5 & 202.5 \end{bmatrix}$$

Element $(1, 1)$ or (176.4) is the square of the summed elements in the first column of $\mathbf{X}$ (42^2) divided by 10. Likewise, elements $(1, 2)$ and $(2, 1)$ are the cross products of the sums of the first two columns of $\mathbf{X}$ (42×41) divided by 10. Note the matrix is symmetric. It is also the multivariate extension of the concept of a correction term used to obtain a sum of squares in elementary statistics.

Subtracting the correction term from the Raw SP matrix obtained in Step 1 yields the corrected SP matrix:

$$\begin{bmatrix} 19.6 & 7.8 & 16.8 & 14.4 & 5.0 \\ 7.8 & 4.9 & 9.9 & 2.7 & 4.5 \\ 16.8 & 9.9 & 28.9 & 18.7 & 19.5 \\ 14.4 & 2.7 & 18.7 & 24.1 & 20.5 \\ 5.0 & 4.5 & 19.5 & 20.5 & 36.5 \end{bmatrix}$$

4. Obtain the *variance–covariance matrix* (**C**) by multiplying the Corrected SP matrix by the scalar $1/N$ for maximum likelihood estimates or $1/(N - 1)$

for least squares estimates. Choice between the two will not affect the final correlation matrix as both the variance and the covariance will be divided by the same number, which will be cancelled out. In fact, if you do not need **C**, you may obtain **R** from the Corrected SP matrix. The matrix **C**, obtained with $1/(N-1)$, has already been presented in Table 3-3, so I will not present it here.

5. Form a diagonal *scaling matrix* of reciprocal standard deviations, **D**, from the square roots of the diagonals of **C**. I could have used the notation "-1" to point out that **D** is an inverse of a diagonal matrix of standard deviations, but did not do so to keep the notation simple. Since the matrix is diagonal, all off-diagonals will be .0. The resulting matrix is

$$
\begin{bmatrix}
0.6776 & 0.0000 & 0.0000 & 0.0000 & 0.0000 \\
0.0000 & 0.7772 & 0.0000 & 0.0000 & 0.0000 \\
0.0000 & 0.0000 & 0.5580 & 0.0000 & 0.0000 \\
0.0000 & 0.0000 & 0.0000 & 0.6111 & 0.0000 \\
0.0000 & 0.0000 & 0.0000 & 0.0000 & 0.4966
\end{bmatrix}
$$

Note that element $(1, 1)$ of **D** (.6776) is the reciprocal square root of element $(1, 1)$ of **C**: $(1/2.18)^{1/2}$.

6. Obtain **R** from the relation **D'CD**. Because **D**, like all diagonal matrices, is symmetric, it is its own transpose. One therefore does not really need the transpose symbol. However, it is a good practice to recognize the frequent sequence **A'BA**. It will produce a symmetric rescaling of **B** based on **A**.

You may feel the last two steps are a bit awkward notationally, and they are to a certain extent. What you really need to remember is to take the variance–covariance matrix and divide element c_{ij} by the square root of the product of c_{ii} and c_{jj} to conform to the definition of a correlation as a covariance divided by the product of the respective standard devitations. The final matrix, **R**, has already been presented as Table 3-2, so I will not present it again.

In general, learn to recognize the relations among the Raw SP matrix, the Corrected SP matrix, **C**, and, finally, **R**. The calculations may be applied to within-group, between-group, or total matrices (see Chapter 2). Although it is possible you will never perform the above calculations, the logic is important. In addition, you may find them useful in a matrix-based language like APL or SAS PROC MATRIX.

More about Linear Combinations

Equation (1-1) illustrates the most basic concept in multivariate analysis, a linear combination. In general, a linear combination is the sum of a series of terms, each of which is the product of a variable and a weighting constant. The weighting constants may be constrained in various ways, for example, to produce scores with unit variance, in which case the term "factor" may be used instead of "linear combination". Equation (3-5) is a generalization of the specific equation presented in (1-1):

$$Y = b_1 X_1 + b_2 X_2 + \cdots + b_m X_m + a \qquad (3\text{-}5)$$

The definition may appear quite limiting since it might seem to rule out useful relations like products of two or more variables $(X \times Y)$, powers of variables (X^2), or functions of variables like $\log(X)$, $\sin(X)$, etc. Because the various terms do not have to correspond to the variables you actually measured, the limitation is minimal. Thus, if X and Y are variables you have measured, W may denote their scalar product, V may denote X^2, etc. These derived measures can (and commonly are) be treated just like any other measures. That is, multivariate procedures like multiple regression do not know or care where a particular variable came from.

The Mean of a Linear Combination

Suppose means from a set of variables $(X_1, X_2, \ldots)$ are entered into a linear combination, and one wishes to find the mean of the linear combination, Y. The result is very simple—*the mean of the linear combination is the linear combination of the means* (one more example of some relative euphony in multivariate analysis): In the special case where all of the weights are unity, the mean of the sums is simply the sum of the means. Thus: if $Y = b_1 X_1 + b_2 X_2 + \cdots + b_m X_m$, then $\bar{Y} = b_1 \bar{X}_1 + b_2 \bar{X}_2 + \cdots + b_m \bar{X}_m$.

The Variance of a Linear Combination

Unfortunately, the situation is more complex in determining the variance of a linear combination. To illustrate, I will derive the variance of a linear combination of two variables, X and Y, each of which is given a unit weight. For simplicity, I will assume each variable has been scaled to zero mean, but not necessarily unit (or even equal) variance. It is not necessary to assume the variables are centered, but the proof is much simpler if it is assumed that they are. I will call the sum S.

First, by definition:

$$S = (X + Y)$$

By the definition of a variance

$$s_s^2 = (1/N) \sum (X + Y)^2$$

Squaring the term on the right yields

$$s_s^2 = (1/N) \sum (X^2 + Y^2 + 2XY)$$

Distributing the summation sign and the quantity $1/N$ yields

$$s_s^2 = (1/N) \sum X^2 + (1/N) \sum Y^2 + (2/N) \sum X \sum Y$$

Remember that the mean of the distribution of X and Y are both zero, the three terms on the right are, respectively, the variance of X, the variance of Y, and twice their covariance. It can be verified easily that the covariance of two variables equals their correlation times the product of their standard deviation. [See Eq. (2-8) and solve for the covariance instead of the correlation (r).] Equations (3-6) are the result:

$$s_s^2 = s_x^2 + s_y^2 + 2rs_xs_y \qquad (3\text{-}6a)$$

$$s_s^2 = s_x^2 + s_y^2 + 2\,\mathrm{COV}(X, Y) \qquad (3\text{-}6b)$$

Consequently, *the variance of the sum equals the sum of the variance plus two times the covariance.* The variance of the sum (s_s^2) will equal the sum of the variance $(s_x^2 + s_y^2)$ if and only if the variables are uncorrelated $(r_{xy} = 0)$. If the two variables are positively correlated, the variance of the sum will be greater than the sum of the variances, and if they are negatively correlated, the variance of the sum will be less than the sum of the variances. When the individual variances are equal, the variance of the sum can range from zero to four times the individual variances.

The covariance term is extremely important because it appears twice, and the outcome forms the basis of the theory of test reliability. The reliability of a scale is in part a function of the degree to which items are intercorrelated. Holding constant the variances of the individual items, their scoring, and their number, the result is the variance of a total score is very strongly determined by the individual item covariances and, consequently, so is the reliability. Thus, the more variance in a scale of a given number of items, the more reliable it is; this is an issue to be reconsidered in Chapter 12.

It is still possible to obtain the variance of a sum even if there are more than two variables and they are differentially weighted. Let $\mathbf{v}$ be a column vector of weights (which may contain negative values), and $\mathbf{C}$ be the variance–covariance matrix of the variables. Then Eq. (3-7) describes the variance of their sum in matrix form:

$$s_s^2 = \mathbf{v'Cv} \qquad (3\text{-}7)$$

A product of the form $\mathbf{v'Cv}$, where $\mathbf{v}$ is a vector of weights and $\mathbf{C}$ is a symmetric matrix, is called a *quadratic form.* The name is derived from its use in the solutions of quadratic equations.

In several applications, including factor analysis, the original vector of weights, $\mathbf{v}$, is divided by the standard deviation of Y. The resulting linear combinations will have a variance of 1.0. It should be distinguished from normalizing $\mathbf{v}$. To produce scores with unit variance, $\mathbf{v'Cv}$ must equal 1.0; to normalize $\mathbf{v}$, $\mathbf{v'v}$ must equal 1.0. Other constraints upon v are used in other settings.

Covariances between Linear Combination

Suppose $\mathbf{w}$ and $\mathbf{v}$ are two weighting vectors that are both applied to a set of variables whose variance–covariance matrix is $\mathbf{C}$. The covariance of the two resulting linear combinations is $\mathbf{w'Cv}$ or, equivalently, $\mathbf{v'Cw}$. Thus, Eq. (3-7) is a special case of a more general principle involving linear combinations.

The Correlation between Two Different Linear Combinations

Since $\mathbf{w'Cv}$ (or $\mathbf{v'Cw}$) is a covariance and $\mathbf{w'Cw}$ and $\mathbf{v'Cv}$ are variances, the former divided by the square root of the product of the latter is, by Eq. (2-8b), a correlation. Specifically, it is the correlation between the two linear combinations.

Another way to calculate the correlations among linear combinations is to enter the vectors $\mathbf{w}$ and $\mathbf{v}$ as *columns* of a matrix, which I will symbolize by $\mathbf{V}$. This device is especially useful if you have more than two sets of weights; it allows you to obtain the variances, covariances, and intercorrelations among the linear combinations simultaneously. The relation $\mathbf{V'CV}$ produces a variance–covariance matrix of the various linear combinations. Once you have obtained $\mathbf{V'CV}$, treat it the same as the relation $\mathbf{D'RD}$ as described steps 5 and 6 of the section "An application of matrix algebra." Although $\mathbf{C}$ is termed a variance–covariance matrix, it contains the variances and covariances among the *original variables*, not the variances and covariances of the resulting *linear combinations*.

It is of interest to look at the case in which two weight vectors are the sum and difference of two variables, X and Y, which have equal variance, but which can have any degree of correlation. It can be shown that their sum and their difference will be uncorrelated. Thus, even though the raw variables may be related, the pair of linear combinations will be unrelated. Finding the covariances among different linear combinations is very basic to factor analysis and other multivariate methods. The orthogonality of the sum and difference of two variables with equal variance can be verified by noting that the $\mathbf{V}$ matrix for the sum and difference will be of the following form:

$$\begin{bmatrix} 1 & 1 \\ 1 & -1 \end{bmatrix}$$

Because X and Y have equal variance, their variance–covariance matrix will have the following form:

$$\begin{bmatrix} \mathbf{A} & \mathbf{B} \\ \mathbf{B} & \mathbf{A} \end{bmatrix}$$

where $\mathbf{A}$ is the variance of each of the two variables and $\mathbf{B}$ is their covariance. Compute $\mathbf{V'CV}$ and note how the off-diagonals of the final product are .0.

Correlations between Linear Combinations and Matrix Notation

The correlations among two or more linear combinations may be stated more succinctly using matrix language. In the general case, $\mathbf{V'CV}$ will contain variances among the linear combinations described by $\mathbf{V}$ along the diagonal and covariances among pairs of linear combinations off the diagonal. Let the matrix $\mathbf{D}$ be a scaling matrix, as described in step 5 of "Using matrix operations to compute a correlation matrix from raw data." That is, it will contain the reciprocal standard deviations of $\mathbf{V'CV}$ (variances of the linear combinations).

Equation (3-8) produces the intercorrelations among the linear combinations. I have used the symbol "$\mathbf{C}_{Ic}$" to denote the result is a matrix of intercorrelations among linear combinations, in contrast to "$\mathbf{R}$," the matrix of correlations among the raw variables. However, the matrix is given different names in different applications. For example, it will be called a "factor correlation" matrix in Chapter 7 when I discuss oblique multiple groups factor analysis and be given the symbol "$\mathbf{\Phi}$". Recognize the *form* of Eq. (3-8) as a vehicle to convert covariances to correlations:

$$\mathbf{C}_{Ic} = \mathbf{D'V'CVD} \tag{3-8}$$

The "It Don't Make No Nevermind" Principle

Kaiser (1970, also see Wainer, 1976) chose the aforementioned nongrammatical introduction to make what is one of the more important points in this chapter. One of the more lucrative, but not to say the more statistically appropriate, uses of multivariate analysis is to construct what I will refer to as a "magic equation," such as one predicting job performance from personality test data, background information, and so on (or how to create an effective advertisement from certain demographic variables, etc.). In a great number of situations, the variables used as predictors are highly correlated (multicollinear).

The problem of multicollinearity in behavioral research does not arise from mathematical considerations any more than it would in nonbehavioral applications. Rather, consider some of the common sources of data. If you administer a personality test like the MMPI, you are obtaining scale scores that are related to one another by factors such as differences in the test-taker's level of adjustment, mood, test-taking attitudes, etc. Put more simply, if people are inclined to gripe on one item, they are going to gripe on a variety of others. (The problem of multicollinearity does not necessarily require that people gripe on *all* items!) Similarly, when you do a marketing survey in which you evaluate attitudes toward various products, there will be a "halo" arising from their general tendency to like or dislike those products, their willingness or reluctance to participate in the survey, etc.

Before I get into any of the specifics associated with any given technique like multiple regression, very different appearing equations can, under such circumstances, give rise to almost identical results—thus, the prinicple of "it don't make no nevermind", i.e., any apparent "magical" equation will hardly be unique when the predictors are highly (or even moderately) inter-correlated.[3]

For a very simple example, consider just two variables, X and Y, and assume their correlation is .9. Now, consider two linear combinations—X alone and Y alone. The two "combinations" (and they should be regarded as such, even though each is defined by only one of the two variables) can be represented by two orthogonal vectors, $(1, 0)$ and $(0, 1)$. Although the vectors of weights are orthogonal, the linear combinations they produce are not. Their covariance is

$$[1 \quad 0] \begin{bmatrix} 1.0 & .9 \\ .9 & 1.0 \end{bmatrix} \begin{bmatrix} 0 \\ 1 \end{bmatrix} = .9$$

The variance of the first linear combination is

$$[1 \quad 0] \begin{bmatrix} 1.0 & .9 \\ .9 & 1.0 \end{bmatrix} \begin{bmatrix} 1 \\ 0 \end{bmatrix} = 1.0$$

The variance of the second linear combination is

$$[0 \quad 1] \begin{bmatrix} 1.0 & .9 \\ .9 & 1.0 \end{bmatrix} \begin{bmatrix} 0 \\ 1 \end{bmatrix} = 1.0$$

Hence, their correlation is $.9/(1 \times 1)^{1/2}$ or .9. The magnitude actually is obvious since it merely equals the correlation between the observed variables. However, if you construct *any* linear combination in which both X and Y have positive weights, say $(.9, .1)$ and $(.1, .9)$, the correlation between the two linear combinations will be *at least* as high (.9), as you may verify. Thus, all linear combinations formed from multicollinear sets of variables will be highly correlated as long as the signs used are consistent, i.e., as long as one excludes from consideration vectors like $(-1.1, .9)$, which reflect a weighted *difference.* Weighted differences certainly lead to different results than weighted sums.

The conclusion, therefore, is that it "don't make no nevermind" because the effects of different weighted sums of positively correlated variables are often so highly correlated it will be impossible or nearly impossible to determine empirically which one is best, in the long run. This conclusion does not mean you should ignore the beta weights you get from procedures like multiple regression. There are many applications where they are quite meaningful and important to interpret. What I am saying is that you should place them in a broad context and consider simpler-to-use alternatives when you are using a linear combination as a *predictive* device, independently of theoretical considerations.

---

[3] Kaiser (1970) and Wainer (1976) were dealing with a slightly different, but related, issue. The principles are quite similar and Kaiser certainly deserves credit for introducing this term.

Eigenvalues and Eigenvectors

You may have seen printouts from factor analyses or other procedures that contain the mystifying terms "eigenvalue" and "eigenvector." Even the more English versions of these terms, "characteristic value," "characteristic vector," "invariant value," or "invariant vector" are not necessarily informative at a first glance. However, the basic concepts can be visualized rather simply. I will spend some time considering the case of two variables. At the same time, I will provide a linkage to the concept of a principal axis (a particular type of eigenvector), described in Chapter 2.

In Chapter 2 I mentioned that the principal components of a scatterplot were the major and minor axes of the elliptically shaped envelope of the scatterplot. The principal components are just another name for the eigenvectors. Figure 3-1 is a scatterplot with the eigenvectors drawn in to allow them to be visualized in a specific, two-dimensional space.

Of equal importance is that *the successive eigenvectors of a Gramian matrix such as* **C** *or* **R** *account for as much information in the matrix, e.g., account for as much of its variance, as is mathematically possible, and the associated eigenvalues (symbolized* λ*) describe how much information has been accounted for.* The result is basic to the logic of factor analysis. I will discuss the role of eigenvectors in accounting for variance in detail in Chapter 6.

I will make a brief comment on the eigenvectors here to give you a feel for their importance. Note that the observations are correlated if you look at them in respect to the measures, X and Y—most of the points are located in the top left and bottom right quadrants. Now, look at how the points fall with respect to the two principal axes (eigenvectors)—they form a pair of right angles, but observations are equally divided among the four quadrants they produce. In other words, the observations are orthogonal with respect to the

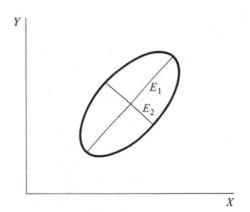

FIGURE 3-1. The two eigenvectors (E_1 and E_2) associated with X and Y when X and Y are positively correlated.

eigenvectors. Eigenanalysis, the collective name for the process of obtaining eigenvalues and eigenvectors, is the basic way one takes a set of correlated observations and creates a new set of uncorrelated variables from them. The resulting orthogonality is but part of the reason eigenanalysis is so important.

An eigenanalysis can be performed on any square matrix, but it is most commonly performed on symmetric matrices, particularly correlation matrices. In one important exception, applicable to MANOVA, discriminant analysis, and canonical analysis, the matrix subject to eigenanalysis is not symmetric. The complexities that emerge when the matrix is not symmetric will be discussed in Chapter 8.

The terms involved in an eigenanalysis are defined by Eq. (3-9), called the *Characteristic Equation*:

$$\mathbf{X}\mathbf{v} = c\mathbf{v} \qquad (3\text{-}9)$$

where $\mathbf{X}$ is any square matrix, $\mathbf{v}$ is an eigenvector, and c is an eigenvalue. One simple requirement is that the vector $\mathbf{v}$ not be null $(0, 0, \ldots, 0)$, since the outcome will be trivial.

Equation (3-9) is deceptively simple. Although $\mathbf{v}$ appears on both sides of the equation, it cannot be cancelled because $\mathbf{X}$ is a matrix and c is a scalar. It is, however, proper to state that $\mathbf{X}$ "acts" like the scalar c in terms of its effects upon $\mathbf{v}$. In other words, when $\mathbf{v}$ is multiplied into $\mathbf{X}$, $\mathbf{v}$ changes its length by a factor of c, but it does not change its direction—the multiplicative factor c affects each element of $\mathbf{v}$ equally. If a given vector is an eigenvector of a matrix, then any scalar multiple of that vector is also an eigenvector, e.g., if $(1, 1, 1)$ is an eigenvector of a particular matrix, then so are $(2, 2, 2)$, $(-1, -1, -1)$, $(2.4545, 2.4545, 2.4545)$, etc. It is therefore not proper strictly speaking to talk about "an" eigenvector in any unique sense unless a restriction is introduced, for example, that its length be set to 1.0 (normalized) or it produces scores of unit variance. Different restrictions are applied in different situations.

A Simple Eigenanalysis

Because some large matrices will be introduced later, I will use a simple, but asymmetric matrix, called $\mathbf{Y}$, for an example here:

$$Y = \begin{bmatrix} 1 & 16 \\ 4 & 1 \end{bmatrix}$$

It can be easily demonstrated that the vector $(1, 2)$ is an eigenvector of $\mathbf{Y}$. If I multiply the vector into $\mathbf{Y}$, the result is the vector $(9, 18)$ or nine times the original vector $(1, 2)$. Thus, the scalar 9, which is the eigenvalue, and the eigenvector $(1, 2)$ fulfill Characteristic Equation [(3-9)]:

$$\begin{bmatrix} 1 & 2 \end{bmatrix} \begin{bmatrix} 1 & 16 \\ 4 & 1 \end{bmatrix} = 9 \begin{bmatrix} 1 \\ 2 \end{bmatrix}$$

In addition, you may also verify the vector $(1, -2)$, with an associated eigenvalue of -7, is also an eigenvector, albeit a different eigenvector; multiplying $(1, -2)$ into $\mathbf{Y}$ produces the vector $(-7, 14)$. Actually, any vector of the form $(X, 2X)$ or $(X, -2X)$ will serve as an eigenvector. It is useful to normalize each of them, just for practice. The length of each, $(1, 2)$ and $(1, -2)$, is the square root of $1^2 + 2^2$ or 5, which equals 2.24. Thus, their normal forms are $(.45, .90)$ and $(.45, -90)$. The latter may also be written as $(-.45, .90)$.

A couple of additional relations are useful to note. The *trace* of $\mathbf{Y}$ $(1 + 1 = 2)$ equals the *sum* of the two eigenvalues $(9 + -7 = 2)$. Also, the *determinant* of $\mathbf{Y}$ $(1 \times 1 - 16 \times 4 = -63)$ equals the *product* of the two eigenvalues $(9 \times -7 = -63)$. These two equalities will always hold. However, it is possible to construct matrices where the eigenvalues are complex numbers, but the problem will not arise in the matrices you will have to analyze by hand. A third important point is that the number of nonzero eigenvalues (two in the example) is equal to the *rank* of the matrix. All three relations are very important, and I will state the first two formally as Eq. (3-10):

$$\sum \lambda_i = \text{Trace}(\mathbf{X})$$

$$= \sum X_{mm} \tag{3-10}$$

The process of obtaining eigenvectors and eigenvalues is easily demonstrated in small matrices. Rearranging the basic definition of Eq. (3-9) demonstrates that the eigenvalues may be found by solving for values of c in the following matrix:

$$\begin{vmatrix} x_{11} - c & x_{12} & x_{13} & x_{14} \\ x_{21} & x_{22} - c & x_{23} & x_{24} \\ x_{31} & x_{32} & x_{33} - c & x_{34} \\ x_{41} & x_{42} & x_{43} & x_{44} - c \end{vmatrix} = 0$$

In other words, eigenvalues are constants that, when subtracted from each of the diagonals, produce a new matrix with zero determinant. The constant, c, can be 0 if the original matrix is singular, but the outcome has been ruled out by definition. The important point is that nonzero values of c can be solutions even when the matrix is singular.

In the specific example

$$\begin{bmatrix} 1 - c & 16 \\ 4 & 1 - c \end{bmatrix} = 0$$

The resulting quadratic equation is $(1 - c)(1 - c) - 16 \times 4 = (1 - c)^2 - 64 = 0$. It can be shown that 9 and -7 are the two solutions (eigenvalues).

To find the eigenvector corresponding to 9, solve for X and Y as follows:

$$[X\ Y]\begin{bmatrix} 1 & 16 \\ 4 & 1 \end{bmatrix} = 9\begin{bmatrix} X \\ Y \end{bmatrix}$$

The result is a pair of equations

$$X + 4Y = 9X$$

$$16X + Y = 9Y$$

The two equations are redundant since both can be reduced to $Y = 2X$. If they were not, they would either provide unique X and Y values (an eigenvector whose length is uniquely defined), which has already been shown not to be the case, or inconsistent, so that there would be no solution. Hence, one can choose any pair of values of the form $(X, 2X)$ Using -7 instead of 9 provides the second eigenvector.

I have used the most straightforward method to perform an eigenanalysis upon a small matrix. However, this method is not practicable for larger matrices. The reason is simple. A 2×2 matrix requires the solution of a quadratic or second-order equation, i.e., $(1 - c)^2 - 64 = 0$. In general, the order of the equation to be solved is the same as the order of the matrix. Since it is common to analyze 20×20 (or larger) matrices, you definitely do not want to have to solve simultaneous equations with terms to the 20th power! Fortunately, you need not worry about complex calculations because other methods exist.

Eigenanalysis of Gramian Matrices

If the matrix is Gramian (the product of a matrix and its transpose, such as an SP, covariance, or correlation matrix), some important conditions hold. First, all of the eigenvalues will be positive or zero. Specifically, the number of nonzero eigenvectors will equal the rank of the matrix. Second, the eigenvectors will be mutually orthogonal. Thus, if $\mathbf{w}$ and $\mathbf{v}$ are any two of the eigenvectors (perhaps out of many others), then $\mathbf{w}'\mathbf{v} = \mathbf{v}'\mathbf{w} = 0$. Furthermore, one can perform an eigenanalysis of a Gramian matrix in a different and instructive manner, which I will discuss in Chapter 6. Common factor analysis is a relatively slight modification that involves reducing the values of the diagonal elements (making them less than 1.0 in a correlation matrix) to reduce the rank of the matrix.

Having completed a discussion of basic concepts, I will move on to introduce the first of the specific multivariate models—multiple regression. The reason it is discussed first is that it is more "tangible" than some other multivariate models, such as factor analysis. The concepts introduce in multiple regression fortunately generalize quite well to other models.

4
Multiple Regression and Correlation—
Part 1. Basic Concepts

Chapter Overview

Chapter 4 contains material related to the broadest of multivariate models, multiple regression:

I. ASSUMPTIONS UNDERLYING MULTIPLE REGRESSION— Multiple regression is concerned with weighting predictors optimally, usually in the least squares sense, in order to best predict an external criterion. Multiple correlation defines the strength of the resulting optimal weighting scheme. Three assumptions underlie all forms of the regression model: (1) the predictors are perfectly *reliable*; (2) the criterion consists of a *systematic* component that is perfectly related to the predictors and a *residual* component that is totally unrelated to the predictors; and (3) the residual is purely random error. In addition, the multiple regression model assumes that the predictors are linearly independent for the solution to be unique. Even if the predictors are linearly independent, a high degree of intercorrelation (multicollinearity) makes it difficult to differentiate various alternative solutions. The common model for multiple regression does not require normality for purposes of estimation but does require normality to perform inferential tests. As a result, the multivariate normal distribution is introduced. Some of the geometry of multiple regression is presented in this section.

II. BASIC GOALS OF REGRESSION ANALYSIS—Many different questions can arise in a multiple regression analysis. Some of the most important questions are: (1) What are the optimal weights? (2) What is the magnitude of the multiple correlation? (3) Is the multiple correlation significantly different from chance? (4) Are the contributions made by individual predictors greater than chance? (5) Which predictors are most important? (6) How can one derive the most useful predictive equation? Questions 1 and 2 involve *description*, whereas 3 and 4 involve *inference*. Collectively, the four questions deal with the *logic* of multiple regression. In contrast, questions 5 and 6 involve *understanding* the relations among the predictors, which concerns the *heuristics* of the regression analysis.

III. THE CASE OF TWO PREDICTORS—The simplest situation involves two predictors. Even though the two-predictor case may be subsumed within the more general situation, it is discussed in great detail. A visual example is given. Next, the concept of *suppressor* variable is introduced. Computational formulas are then given to illustrate the important difference between *simultaneous* and *successive* entry of predictors. The next topic considered is the problem of defining the *importance* of the various predictors. Finally, the *bias* in estimates of multiple regression is noted.

IV. THE CASE OF MORE THAN TWO PREDICTORS—The analysis and evaluation of a fixed set of predictors is considered, including the computations. *Multicollinearity* is a common problem due to redundancies (correlations) among the predictors. *Residual analysis* is also discussed.

V. INFERENTIAL TESTS—Several specific tests are described: (1) the multiple correlations (R) is .0, (2) individual weights are .0, and (3) an additional predictor or set of predictors does not improve prediction.

VI. EVALUATING ALTERNATIVE EQUATIONS—A regression equation should be *robust* (perform well in different situations), as *simple* as possible, and make *economical* use of predictors. Weights may be unstable because they were derived from too small a sample or because of multicollinearity. Some procedures useful in testing prediction equations are discussed: (1) *cross validation*, (2) *a priori* weights including equal weighting of some or all predictors, (3) *hierarchical* entry of groups of predictors, and (4) *principal components* (a topic considered in Chapter 6). The limitations of *stepwise* regression are noted, especially in regard to theory construction.

VII. EXAMPLE 1—PERFECT PREDICTION—Hypothetical data leading to a multiple correlation of 1.0 is generated and used to explain standard computer printout.

VIII. EXAMPLE 2—IMPERFECT PREDICTION PLUS A LOOK AT RESIDUALS—The first example is modified by deleting one of the predictors, which makes prediction imperfect ($R < 1.0$). Lack of perfect prediction produces *residuals* that need to be examined further.

IX. EXAMPLE 3—REAL PERSONALITY ASSESSMENT DATA—The final example involves real-life data concerned with how applicants to security guard positions at nuclear power plants differ from applicants to other positions at the plants.

X. ALTERNATIVE APPROACHES TO DATA AGGREGATION—Multiple regression allows a high score on one predictor to *compensate for a low score on another predictor*. Alternative *noncompensatory* models are introduced.

This chapter and Chapter 5 consider the broadest and most commonly used multivariate model—multiple regression. Beyond covering the assumptions underlying multiple regression, I will also discuss the general problem of aggregating data from several predictors, consider multiple regression and correlation with two predictors, and then examine multiple regression with several predictors. The next chapter will consider various extensions of the basic points covered in this chapter.

Assumptions Underlying Multiple Regression

A regression analysis fits data to a model, so it is important to understand its underlying assumptions. Mathematically, the model may be defined through an equation of the form indicated in Eq. (4-1a) when the predictors are in raw score form and in (4-1b) when the predictors are in z-score form.

$$Y = bX + a + e \qquad (4\text{-}1a)$$

$$z_y = \beta z_x + e \qquad (4\text{-}1b)$$

Both equations are a special case of Eq. (1-1), the difference being the inclusion of a random error term (e) as a part of the regression model. The assumptions are the same for both the raw-score and z-score cases. I will only discuss the raw-score case when the units of measurement must be taken into consideration.

All straight lines have an intercept parameter. In the raw-score case, the intercept must be estimated from the data; in the z-score case, the intercept parameter will always be .0, so it does not need to be estimated.

The assumptions of simple (bivariate) regression were discussed in Chapter 2 and may be briefly summaried as follows:

1. The predictor (z_x) contains no error, i.e., it is perfectly *reliable (repeatable)*, but it need not relate perfectly to the criterion (z_y), i.e., it may be only partially *valid*.
2. One component of z_y (z_y') relates perfectly to z_x, implying *linearity of regression*. Another component, the residual ($\hat{z}_y$), is totally independent of z_x.
3. The $\hat{z}_y$ is purely random error with a mean of .0. Consequently, its value associated with any one subject (observation) is independent of the value associated with any other subject. Moreover, its variance is the same for all values of z_x, implying *homoscedasticity (homogeneity of variance)*.

The same assumptions hold in multiple regression except that instead of one z_x to predict from, there are several, the z_{x_i}, and the assumptions hold for each of them. One more assumption must be added—the z_{x_i} are *linearly independent*.

Linear independence implies that one cannot derive a perfect multiple correlation in predicting any individual z_{x_i} from the remaining z_{x_i}. It follows that any two predictors are not perfectly correlated.

The assumption of linear independence is necessary to obtain a unique solution. In order to see why linearly dependence prevents a unique solution, consider the simple case of two predictors that are perfectly correlated, z_{x_1}

and z_{x_2}. The first could be used by itself to produce the relation $z'_y = r_{x_1y}z_{x_1}$. However, z_{x_2} could substituted for z_{x_1} because the two are perfectly correlated. For this matter, an infinity of linear combinations of the form $\beta^2 z_{x_1} + (1 - \beta^2)z_{x_2}$ could be used.

As I noted in Chapter 3, exact linear dependency normally does not occur, but close approximations often do. A unique solution is possible, but it will be very similar to other solutions. Consequently, *multicollinearity* is a potential problem to be considered in multiple regression that does not occur, by definition, in simple regression.

Multicollinearity affects *estimation* of regression weights from data. It is somewhat less of a problem when testing the predictive validity of weights derived from theoretical considerations. One extremely important example is to give the predictors equal weight in either raw or z-score form. Only the three weaker assumptions of simple regression need be met when weights are defined in advance (*a priori*) rather than estimated from the data. Moreover, if the problem is fundamentally one of bivariate correlation and not regression, assumption (1) requiring perfectly reliable predictors is not necessary since only the regression model requires predictors to be perfectly reliable. Perfect reliability is still assumed in multiple correlation because the correlation requires the estimation of weights, and the estimation of weights is a regression problem.

It is very important to understand the greater complexity involved in estimation relative to using *a priori* weights. The stability of weights that are estimated is affected by the *size* of the normative sample. In Chapter 2, the central limit theorem was introduced, and it was noted that the range of possible outcomes obtained from samples varying in size (the *sampling error*) decreased as a square-root function of the sample size, assuming that the observations are independent—large samples provide more *efficient* estimates than small samples. The increase in efficiency with increase in sample size also holds in multiple regression.

Estimating regression weights is also more complex than estimating means. Estimation of a mean ordinarily depends only on one set of data—individual observations, e.g., scores of individual students in a class are *sufficient* to estimate the class mean. Unfortunately, no one single set of data is sufficient to estimate regression weights. For example, suppose you wish to predict students' final examination scores from their scores on a pair of one-hour examinations. Your estimate of the first one-hour examination's weight depends on: (1) the correlation between the first one-hour examination and the final examination, (2) the correlation between the two one-hour examinations, and even (3) the correlation between the second one-hour examination and the final examination. Consequently, the correlation between the first one-hour examination and the final examination by itself is insufficient to determine how heavily the first one-hour examination should be weighted to predict the final examination.

Moreover, the estimate of the weight given the second one-hour examination uses the same basic information as the estimate of the weight given the first one-hour examination. Consequently, the two estimates are not *independent*.

When *a priori* weights are used, assumptions such as equal weighting *replace* estimation. I am not saying you should always avoid estimation. Your assumption about weighting may substitute one problem for another. For example, equal weighting may predict the final poorly because the second one-hour examination may be a vastly better indicator of the final. Individual differences on the first one-hour examination might relate to knowledge of the instructor's methods of testing, a factor that becomes less important as students get to know the instructor better.

The Multivariate Normal Distribution

In Chapter 2, I discussed a predictor Y that was a normally distributed function of a single predictor [Eqs. (2-2) and (2-3)] and a pair of predictors [Eq. (2-6)]. The concept of normality extended to the case of multiple predictors as Eq. (4-2):

$$f(\mathbf{x}) = (2\pi)^{-m/2} |\mathbf{C}|^{-1/2} \exp[-.5(\mathbf{x} - \boldsymbol{\mu})'\mathbf{C}^{-1}(\mathbf{x} - \boldsymbol{\mu})] \qquad (4\text{-}2)$$

where $\mathbf{x}$ is a vector of predictors, $\boldsymbol{\mu}$ is a vector of their means, $|\mathbf{C}|$ is the determinant of the variance–covariance matrix of the independent predictors, and m is the number of predictors. Thus, a variance–covariance *matrix* of relations among the predictors replaces the *scalar* correlation in the bivariate case. As in the univariate case, one can obtain a *standard normal* form in which $\boldsymbol{\mu}$ is a null vector of means and $\mathbf{R}$ is a correlation matrix.

In a univariate normal distribution, the probability that an outcome falls between two values of the predictor is the *area* between the two points. For example, the probability of obtaining a value between $+1.96$ and -1.96 standard deviation units is .95. With two independent predictors, the probability of an outcome between two values of each of the two independent predictors such as $+1.96$ and -1.96 is a *volume* in the three-dimensional space bounded by the height of the curve and the distances between pairs of points. Even though the probability of obtaining each outcome is .95, the joint probability cannot be determined unless one knows the correlation between the two events. With more than two predictors, the probability of obtaining an outcome between pairs of values for each of the independent predictors cannot be visualized since it is contained in a *hyperspace* of many dimensions. As in the bivariate case, one needs to know the correlations among the predictors to determine the probability of the joint outcome.

A Bit of the Geometry of Multiple Regression

Multiple regression, like bivariate regression, involves minimizing squared distances from points to a line, the least squares criterion, which gives rise to "magic" equations in some users' eyes. The distance is computed along axes in several dimensions, each one representing a predictor. The total distance from point to line is measured along all of the dimensions according to the *Pythagorean theorem*. With only two predictors and a criterion, the results may be described in a space of three dimensions. If W is the criterion and X and Y are the predictors, then one minimizes the average of the squared distances from the points to the line along the X dimension plus the corresponding distance along the Y dimension.

With three or more predictors, the definition of "distance" becomes more abstract, and it is useful if I define the dimensions as $X_1, X_2, \ldots, X_n$. Equation (4-3) defines the *general distance measure* as the square root of the sum of the squared differences between point and line; it has wide application:

$$D = (X_1^2 + X_2^2 + \cdots + X_n^2)^{1/2} \tag{4-3}$$

After you have determined a regression line, it is just another dimension or axis in the space. If one can predict better than chance, the regression line will never be completely orthogonal (at right angles) to all of the predictors. However, the regression line may be orthogonal to some predictors that do not contribute to prediction. Because the regression line is just another axis, you can use it to form a scatterplot relating predicted and obtained values. The problem, after the beta weights are determined, is simply a bivariate problem. All of the information in the individual predictors is now summarized by the prediction equation. The equation is sufficient, assuming that the assumptions of multiple regression are met. For example, in the previously discussed example of how to combine scores on two one-hour examinations to predict final examination scores, the linear combination of the first and second one-hour examinations replaces the individual scores on the two one-hour examinations.

Basic Goals of Regression Analysis

A surgeon must possess two types of skill. He or she must know how to perform a given type of operation, but, more importantly, must know when to perform it. The same holds true in statistical analysis. In multiple regression, you must know how to answer a series of questions in order to perform the analysis and interpret the results. With modern software packages, it is not too difficult to perform the analysis, and the package will take care of the logic necessary to answer a series of questions about the data. The questions fall in the following six categories:

1. What are the optimal regression weights in both standardized (β weight) and raw or unstandardized (b weight) forms.

2. What is the correlation between the linear combination defined by optimal weights and the criterion, the multiple correlation (symbolized R^1)?
3. Is the overall correlation significantly different from chance?
4. Are the contributions made by individual predictors greater than chance?
5. Which predictors are most important?
6. How to derive the most useful predictive equation?

Questions 1 and 2 involve *description,* whereas questions 3 and 4 involve *inference.* Collectively, the four questions concern the *logic* of the analysis. These issues may not be equally important to a given problem, e.g., you may only be interested in the magnitude and significance of R (questions 2 and 4), and not the beta weights or their significance (questions 1 and 3). The logic of multiple regression is complex. For example, many more steps are needed to compute a series of regression weights than to compute statistics like means or standard deviations. However, the computations necessary in regression analysis follow directly from the data, just as the computations in univariate analyses. If you follow the algorithm correctly, the correct answers follow; the computer package or your hand calculation contains the logic. Any of the questions you ask in 1, 2, 3 or 4 have one and only one correct answer.

Questions 5 and 6 are very different because they deal with *heuristics* or what *should* be done rather than *how* to do it. In essence, the broadest heuristic question is "Is multiple regression the best way for me to aswer the empirical questions I am facing?"

Unlike questions of logic, questions of heuristics do not have unequivocally "correct" answers. Some situations may be so clear that there is total agreement about what should be done. For example, your sample may be so biased or so plagued by outliers that everyone looking at it would agree that the data are not worth analyzing. Unfortunately, it is also probably true that no empirical means of sampling ever meets the mathematical definition of true "randomness" and that no (or at least few) data sets are without outliers. A particular point to keep in mind is that you will often be using rather unreliable predictors and thus violating the first assumption of regression. Consequently, there is a shade of gray in all situations.

My concern in this chapter is not with the "gloom and doom" of a data set that is garbage. I will assume that your data are potentially meaningful even though I will not necessarily assume that your sample is large enough to profit from least squares estimation. Some alternatives to least squares estimation will be considered later in the chapter so that you will be aware of alternative heuristic devices.

I will further assume that all predictors are *quantitative* in that they possess a meaningful unit of measure. In other words, they form at least an *interval*

---

[1] Note the difference between **R** as the symbol for a correlation matrix and R as the symbol for a multiple correlation.

scale. The requirement that predictors be quantitative will be dropped in Chapter 5 so that you can employ *categorical* (*nonquantitative*) predictors like sex, race, or religion.

The Case of Two Predictors

A Visual Example

The following visual example is possible when there are only two predictors. It will take advantage of the correspondence between cosines of angles (which can be visualized) and correlations that was discussed in Chapter 3. Take three toothpicks that are the same length but of different colors, say, red, blue, and green. The common length of the three toothpicks defines the *unit* of measurement.

Place the three toothpicks so that their tips are touching but have them come off at different angles and fasten them with chewing gum or clay. Relations will be a bit easier to see if all of the angles are acute. Orient them so that the blue and green ones are lying flat on the table and the red one points upward, but not straight up. Measure the angles among the toothpicks with a protractor. In this example, the red toothpick will serve as the criterion; the blue and green toothpicks will serve as the predictors.

Now, draw a straight line down from the tip of the red toothpick to the table top. The table top is the *space* of the two predictors. Mark the point at which the line intersects the table, and draw a line on the table from the origin (intersection of the toothpicks) to the point. The line is the *projection* of the red line onto the space. You can readily see that the distance must be shorter than the length of the red toothpick. The more the red toothpick points upward of the two predictors, the smaller the projection will be. The situation is illustrated in a bird's-eye view as Fig. 4-1.

You should see a relation between the distance from the origin of the three

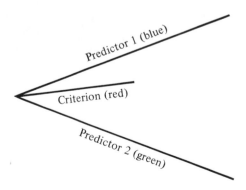

FIGURE 4-1. The geometry of multiple regression. *Note*: Assume that you are looking *down* from a distance and have one eye closed so that you cannot judge distance.

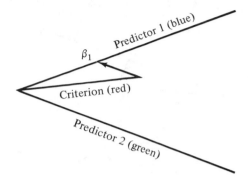

FIGURE 4-2. The geometry of beta weights. *Note*: Assume that you are looking *down* from a distance and have one eye closed so that you cannot judge distance.

toothpicks to the point of projection and a multiple correlation, for indeed there is. The length of the projection *is*, in fact, the multiple correlation.

I have made an additional construction in Fig. 4-2 onto the bird's-eye view of the situation by drawing a line on the table that is parallel to the blue toothpick, starting from the red toothpick's projection and ending at the green toothpick. The distance along the green toothpick is the *beta weight* (β) for the green toothpick. It describes the amount of change in the criterion (red toothpick) per unit change in a given predictor (the green toothpick), holding constant the other predictor (the blue toothpick). The beta weight for the blue toothpick can be found in an analogous fashion.

Now, construct a line from the tip of the red toothpick directly to the green toothpick rather than straight down onto the table. The line and the green toothpick will form a right angle. The distance from the tip of the green toothpick to the point of intersection is the *correlation* between the red and green toothpicks, since it is the cosine of their angle. The equivalence follows from the definition of a cosine as the length of the adjacent side of a right triangle (the projection onto the green toothpick) divided by the hypotenuse (the red toothpick itself) and the unit length of the toothpicks.

Note that the length of the projection onto the green toothpick cannot be longer than the length of the projection onto the table, although the two can be the same. Consequently, a multiple correlation must be at least as large as the largest zero-order or simple correlation between a predictor and the criterion, as illustrated in the bird's-eye view of Fig. 4-3.

Here are some additional demonstrations:

1. Make the red toothpick point straight up, perpendicular to the table. Regardless of the angle between the blue and green toothpicks, the projection of the red toothpick onto the table will be zero. Thus, for a multiple correlation to exceed zero, at least one predictor must correlate with the criterion.

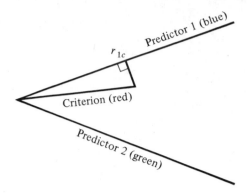

FIGURE 4-3. The geometry of a correlation. *Note*: Assume that you are looking *down* from a distance and have one eye closed so that you cannot judge distance.

2. Hold the angle between the red toothpick and the other two constant but spread the latter two further apart so that they go from being close to one another (correlated) to right-angled (independent). You can see that the advantage of the multiple correlation over the simple correlations will increase as the predictors become more independent of one another. The simple correlations will be termed *validities* in the discussion of multiple regression. Predictors are best combined when they are independent of one another but both highly correlated with the criterion, because then each of the predictors will contribute information independently. In fact, when the two predictors are at right angles to one another, a very important relation will hold. The projection of the red toothpick onto the space of the blue and green toothpicks (the table) will equal the square root of the sum of the squared projection of the red toothpick onto the blue toothpick and the squared projection of the red toothpick onto the green toothpick. Hence, the multiple correlation will equal the square root of the sum of the squared validities. Under any other condition, the multiple correlation will be smaller because of the redundancy of the predictors, a special case of the *Pythagorean* theorem.
3. Fix the angle between the blue toothpick and the red toothpick at 90 degrees but be sure that the other two angles are not right angles. You should be able to verify that the multiple correlation will still exceed the green tooth-pick's validity. That is, even though one predictor is unrelated to the criterion, it can still aid in prediction. Such a predictor is known as a *suppressor variable* because it serves to suppress irrelevant variance in the other predictor.

A Note on Suppressor Variables

A broader definition of a suppressor variable is one that (a) has zero validity but a nonzero beta weight, *or* (b) has a validity and a beta weight with opposite signs. The following is an example. Assume that a recorded SAT score is the last of several that a person might take. Assume further that (a) SAT scores are positively correlated with college GPA, (b) the number of times a person takes the SAT is positively correlated with the final SAT score, owing to practice, but (c) the number of times a student takes the SAT is *not* correlated with college GPA. Knowing only how often a student took the SAT would not help you predict GPA directly because of assumptions (c), but it would be useful indirectly because you could correct SAT scores for practice effects.

The suppressor relation in the above example is substantively meaningful, but it is often spurious. Most of the time you will simply see predictors that have low but significant positive validities and low but significant negative beta weights, or vice versa. Typically suppressor relations arise from multicollinearity and are a statistical annoyance (to put it mildly) rather than of theoretical interest.

Computational Formulas

It is very easy to compute the multiple correlation and beta weights by hand when there are only two predictors. If the criterion is called Y and the two predictors are called X_1 and X_2, the equation for R^2 is given by Eq. (4-4a). Formulas stated in terms of R^2 are easier to describe than corresponding formulas stated in terms of R. Remember to include a square-root operation at the end. The formulas for the beta weights, β_1 and β_2, are given by Eqs. (4-4b) and (4-4c):

$$R^2 = \frac{r_{x_1 \cdot y}^2 + r_{x_2 \cdot y}^2 - 2r_{x_1 \cdot y} r_{x_2 \cdot y} r_{x_1 \cdot x_2}}{1 - r_{x_1 \cdot x_2}^2} \tag{4-4a}$$

$$\beta_1 = \frac{r_{x_1 \cdot y} - r_{x_2 \cdot y} r_{x_1 \cdot x_2}}{1 - r_{x_1 \cdot x_2}^2} \tag{4-4b}$$

$$\beta_2 = \frac{r_{x_2 \cdot y} - r_{x_1 \cdot y} r_{x_1 \cdot x_2}}{1 - r_{x_1 \cdot x_2}^2} \tag{4-4c}$$

The following simple example illustrates the use of Eqs. (4-4). Suppose you want to know which stocks to invest in, and you get a financial analyst to predict the rate of growth of 100 stocks. You also compute the growth of the stocks in the previous six months. You then wait six months and correlate both the expert's judgment (predictor X_1) and the prior growth (predictor X_2) with the subsequent growth (criterion Y). Suppose the expert's validity is .60, the validity of prior growth is .50, and the expert's judgment and prior growth correlate .70 with one another.

Applying Eq. (4-4a) produces an R value of .61. Then, applying Eqs. (4-4b) and (4-4c) gives beta weights of .49 and .16, which means that the least squares equation to predict these 100 stocks is

$$z_y' = .49z_{x_1} + .16z_{x_2}$$

the term z_y' is the *predicted* growth in z-score form, not to be confused with the *actual* growth, z_y. The predicted and actual growths of each stock will be as similar as can be in a least squares sense, but they need not be very similar in their actual values if R is low.

Consequently, if one were to combine predictors z_{x_1} and z_{x_2} in an optimal manner, the result would correlate .61 with the criterion. However, if you were simply to use the expert's judgment alone, the correlation would be .60! The two models may be compared explicitly by obtaining the difference in R^2—the variance accounted for by the combination minus the variance accounted for by predictor z_{x_1} alone. The result is $.61^2 - .60^2$ or .0121. Thus, you can increase the variance accounted for by only 1% if you combine the information from two correlated predictors.

The example illustrates what often happens when information is combined from highly correlated predictors—you simply do not gain much. Suppose, however, that the two predictors were uncorrelated. In that case, R would be the square root of the sum of the squared individual correlations ($.6^2 + .5^2 =$ .61; $.61^{1/2} = .78$), and the beta weights will be the two respective validities (.6 and .5). The increment in variance accounted for ($.5^2$ or .25) will be large when the predictors are uncorrelated as they contribute independent information.

Raw-Score Formulas

It is more likely that you will work with raw scores rather than z scores. The raw-score b weight for a given predictor is simply its z-score beta weight multiplied by the ratio of the criterion's standard deviation to the predictor's standard deviation. The standard deviations act as a *scaling factor* to take the actual, and often arbitrary, units of measurement into account. If the particular predictor is identified as X_j, the relation between its beta weight (β_j) and its b weight (b_j) is given by Eq. (4-5):

$$b_{x_1} = \frac{s_y \beta_{x_1}}{s_{x_1}}$$

$$b_{x_2} = \frac{s_y \beta_{x_2}}{s_{x_2}} \qquad (4\text{-}5)$$

There will also be a constant, or Y-intercept term. The line of best fit will pass through the *centroid* because of features inherent in a least squares solution. Thus, if the predictors X_1 and X_2 are at their average, the predicted Y value will also be at its average, leading to Eq. (4-6):

$$a = \bar{Y} - (b_1 \bar{X}_1 + b_2 \bar{X}_2) \qquad (4\text{-}6)$$

Other Equations for R^2

Equation (4-4a) is but one of several equivalent ways to obtain R^2. It says, in effect, (1) add the respective r^2 values between the two predictors and the criterion (the squared validities), (2) subtract their redundancy, and (3) divide by the variance, again correcting for redundancy. This equation effectively corrects each predictor for the variance it shares with the other. Conversely, one could use the following:

$$R^2 = r_{y \cdot x_1}^2 + r_{y(x_2 - x_1)}^2 \tag{4-7}$$

In this equation I am (1) computing the variance shared by predictor X_1 and the criterion, ignoring predictor X_2; (2) computing the variance shared by criterion and X_2 after the variance X_2 shares with X_1 has been removed (the squared part correlation); and (3) adding the two r^2 values. One can reverse the roles of the two predictors to obtain

$$R^2 = r_{y \cdot x_2}^2 + r_{y(x_1 - x_2)}^2 \tag{4-8}$$

Equations (4-4a), (4-7), and (4-8) will all yield the same numerical value of R, but do so by different means. The first named adds the contributions of the predictors *simultaneously* while the latter two do it *successively*. I will make extensive use of the distinction between adding predictors simultaneously and successively in the construction of regression models. Also, the order in which you add in the predictors, i.e., X_1 before X_2 or vice versa, is extremely important, even though you will wind up with the same final value of R, because the predictive value of a predictor by itself (its validity) is different from its ability to *improve* upon the prediction afforded by other predictors.

Still another way to obtain R^2 is as the sum of the products of the beta weights and the validities:

$$R^2 = \beta_1 r_{y \cdot x_1} + \beta_2 r_{y \cdot x_2} \tag{4-9}$$

Equation (4-9) is applicable when the predictors are independent, because, then, the validities *are* the beta weights.

Regardless of which equation is used, *if two equations use the same sets of predictors, their beta weights will be identical within the limits of rounding error.* However, when the predictors are multicollinear, rather different *appearing* formulas can lead to *nearly* the same predicted criterion scores.

Determining the Relative Importance of the Two Predictors

Question 5 is concerned with determining the relative importance of the predictors. Unfortunately, no single measure can define predictor importance unequivocally, because it can be shown that the question itself is ambiguous. There are three broad indices of importance. The indices will lead to equivalent outcomes when there are only two predictors or if the predictors are orthogonal. In most other cases, they also will lead to highly similar results. However, Wilkinson (1975) has provided a very interesting numerical illustration in which one predictor was most important by one criterion, a second was most important by another criterion, and a third was most important by yet another criterion.

The three classes of indices are:

1. The variance shared by a predictor and the criterion, *ignoring* the other predictor. An appropriate index is the *squared validity* or squared simple correlation of the predictor and the criterion, although the absolute value of the validity will do just as well. Measures derived from validity information tell you which predictor is best when used *alone*.
2. The change in the criterion produced by unit change in predictor *adjusting for* changes produced by other predictors. Two relevant measures are the *beta weights* and the *b weights*. Beta weights have the advantage of correcting for scale differences among predictors, so that predictors in different units of measurement can be directly compared. However, *b* weights have a different advantage. Beta weights can very considerably across samples due to differential *range restriction*. However, range restriction reduces *both* the standard deviation of a predictor and its validity. The two effects will be somewhat offsetting, causing *b* weights to be more stable across samples.
3. The increase in prediction when the predictor is *added* to the prediction possible from the other predictor. A suitable measure is the value of R^2 (variance accounted for by *both* predictors) minus the squared validity of the other predictor (variance accounted for by the other predictor). This difference is called the *uniqueness*. In general, the uniqueness of a given predictor is defined as R^2 with all predictors included in the model (the full or *saturated* model) minus R^2 with the given predictor excluded from the model.

Bias in Multiple Correlation

Estimates of R, unlike estimates of r, are positively biased—the more predictors there are, the larger the expected value of R. Bias is present because the *sample* estimate of an individual predictor's validity will *not* be precisely .0 even if the *population* validity is .0. Individual sample validities will differ from .0 through sampling error, just like any other statistic. The standard deviation of r's sampling distribution is $1/(N-1)^{1/2}$ when the population correlation is .0. (See *Sampling error of a correlation* in Chapter 2.) Even though the *average* validity will be .0, the sampling error can be substantial in small samples. For example, roughly 5% of the correlations will be larger than .20 or smaller than $-.20$ in a sample as large as 400. Indeed, because the correlation is a continuous measure, the probability that the estimate will be *exactly* zero is .0. As long as the sample validity is not zero, the sample value of R will be larger than any of the sample validities (zero-order correlations). Similarly, adding a predictor to an existing set will always increase the sample estimate of R even when the new predictor is totally unrelated to both the criterion and the original set of predictors in the population.

The Case of More Than Two Predictors

I will now consider how least squares regression weights are obtained from a given set of predictors and how to obtain the multiple correlation from the set. I will assume that all predictors are to be incorporated in the regression equation in this section. I will discuss how to reduce the number of predictors later in the chapter. I will also discuss some related output that is generally a part of the computer printout, including information about multicollinearity. The section concludes with a consideration of *residuals*. Examination and analysis of residuals is an integral part of any regression analysis.

The easiest way to describe the computation of the vector of beta weights (β) and R^2 is through matrix theory. Both computations require (1) the inverse of the matrix of intercorrelations among predictors ($\mathbf{R}^{-1}$), and (2) the vector of validities (**v**). The equation for the beta weights is

$$\boldsymbol{\beta} = \mathbf{v}'\mathbf{R}^{-1}$$

$$= \mathbf{R}^{-1}\mathbf{v} \tag{4-10}$$

To help you remember a very basic equation, think of $\mathbf{R}^{-1}$ as a set of validities that have been corrected for the overlap or intercorrelations among the predictors. When the predictors are mutually orthogonal, $\mathbf{R}^{-1}$ will be an identity matrix and can be dropped from the equation.

The *b* weights can be obtained from the beta weights as in the two-predictor case by multiplying by the ratio of the criterion's standard deviation to the predictor's standard deviation. Likewise, the intercept is the criterion mean minus the sum of the predictor means multiplied by their respective *b* weights:

$$\mathbf{b} = \frac{s_y}{s_x}\boldsymbol{\beta} \tag{4-11}$$

Another way to get *b* weights is to obtain a matrix of predictors in raw-score form. Add an additional column of 1's to the matrix and call the result **X**. Now, obtain a vector of criterion scores, called **y**. The equation for the *b* weights is

$$\mathbf{b} = (\mathbf{X}'\mathbf{X})^{-1}\mathbf{y} \tag{4-12}$$

The vector **b** will contain the intercept as its first element, followed by the *b* weights, which is an outgrowth of the use of 1's in the first column of **X**.

The R^2 is most commonly obtained as a matrix extension of Eq. (4-9), i.e., as the square root of the sum of the beta weights times validities over all the predictors. The extension is described by

$$R^2 = \mathbf{v}'\mathbf{R}^{-1}\mathbf{v} \tag{4-13}$$

Equation (4-14) is commonly encountered. Because one can substitute the vector **b** for $\mathbf{R}^{-1}\mathbf{v}$, using Eq. (4-13), I can obtain R from the following:

$$R^2 = \boldsymbol{\beta}'\mathbf{v} \tag{4-14}$$

The vector product reduces to the statement that R^2 is the sum of the products of beta weights times validities, which I noted in the case of two predictors.

Checking for Multicollinearity

Inspection of the diagonal elements of $\mathbf{R}^{-1}$ (the r^{ii} values) is a basic way to look for multicollinearity. Specifically, the diagonal elements of $\mathbf{R}^{-1}$ can be used to obtain multiple correlations between individual predictors and the remaining predictors. Equation (4-15) shows how one can obtain the R^2 between the ith predictor and the remaining predictors from r^{ii}:

$$R^2 = 1 - 1/r^{*ii} \tag{4-15}$$

The *tolerance* of a predictor is the proportion of variance in that predictor that it does not share with the other predictor(s). It equals 1.0 minus the value of R^2 or $1/r^{ii}$. If one or more predictors have low tolerance (high R with the other predictors), they should be deleted, which is done automatically in most computer packages. Also, check the magnitude of the determinant of $\mathbf{R}^{-1}$, $|R^{-1}|$. If it is large, say > 10 (or, conversely, if $|R|$ is small, say $< .1$, since $|R| \times |R^{-1}| = 1$), your predictor set is multicollinear. One way to deal with the problem is to eliminate one or more redundant predictors. The redundant predictors will have large diagonal elements in $\mathbf{R}^{-1}$. Other ways to handle multicollinearity will be considered in the section devoted to Evaluating Alternative Equations.

Another Way to Obtain R^2

Yet another way to obtain R is to form a single matrix containing the intercorrelations among the M predictors and the criterion, with the criterion entered as the last row and column in the matrix. (The location is arbitrary, but placing the criterion last aids in communication.) Call the $(M + 1) \times (M + 1)$ matrix $\mathbf{R}^*$ to distinguish it from the $M \times M$ predictor intercorrelation matrix, $\mathbf{R}$. Now obtain $\mathbf{R}^{*-1}$. Applying Eq. (4-15) to $\mathbf{R}^{*-1}$ allows you to obtain R^2 as $1 - 1/r^{(M+1)(M+1)}$—one minus the reciprocal of the bottom diagonal element of the inverse [see Eq. (4.15)]. The method is particularly useful when you need to determine alternative values of R^2 obtained from deleting various predictors by hand. You would obtain $\mathbf{R}^*$ as a starting point. If you wished to delete predictor k, you would use Eq. (3-4) as described in the section *Recalculation of an Inverse Following the Deletion of a Predictor* of Chapter 3. Your new value of R can then be determined from the new value of $r^{(M+1)(M+1)}$.

Residuals

As in simple regression, the variance of z_y can be partitioned into the variance of the predicted scores (R^2) and the variance of the residuals ($1 - R^2$). The analogous partitioning of Y leads to a predicted score variance of $s_y^2 R^2$, and a residual variance of $s_y^2(1 - R^2)$.

Residuals are, by definition, independent of the *linear* effects of the predictors giving rise to them. However, they need not be random. They may even relate to the predictors in a nonlinear fashion. Residuals may be and often are very highly correlated with predictors that have not been included in the prediction equation.

Analysis of residuals is an important part of multiple regression. In order to make the analysis meaningful, I will discuss some of the considerations involved in the analysis of salary inequity and use sex as an example. The same considerations apply to race or any other possible bases of discrimination.

The goal of a salary inequity study is typically to determine whether lower female salaries reflect sex *per se*, and are therefore illegally discriminatory, or the effects of other predictors that are unrelated to sex (Hunter & Schmidt, 1976). One relevant predictor is length of job service—men have been employed at many jobs longer than women on average. If the inequity were to disappear following adjustment for length of service, the position of those claiming sex discrimination would be complicated although not necessarily untenable. Opponents of the salary policy would have to demonstrate that the difference in tenure was produced by the company's discriminatory policies, which takes the process a step away from the original issue. Conversely, if the inequity were to remain, the burden would shift to the company who would have to determine other possible confoundings in defense of its policies.

One approach to the problem is to choose predictors such as length of service and form a regression equation *ignoring* sex. Next, form a regression equation with the same predictors but *including* sex. The difference in R^2 between the two models defines the unique contribution of sex, above and beyond the other predictors included in the model. The magnitude and significance of the uniqueness are crucial to the issue at hand.

An alternative approach is to use one equation with sex included and examine the magnitude and significance of the beta weight for sex, i.e., the contribution of sex to the prediction of salary, holding other predictors constant. The information provided by the beta weight for sex and its uniqueness differs somewhat, but both are far more meaningful than the uncorrected sex difference or related statistics such as the simple (point-biserial) correlation between sex and salary.[2]

Regardless of whether there is evidence for a disparity and of how it is determined, the residuals after predicting salary from length of service need be examined, separated by sex and in the aggregate. All major computer packages provide simple ways to obtain and analyze residuals. An examina-

---

[2] Multiple regression, as a *statistical* model, assumes a particular *substantive* model: equal pay for equal work. An alternative has recently emerged: equal pay for *comparable* work, a situation in which multiple regression applies less clearly. Choice between the two substantive models is an *ethical* one in which statisticians play no "special" role.

tion of the residuals might suggest any of the following:

1. The residuals might be correlated with the criterion, implying you have *underspecified* the model by omitting relevant predictor(s). If so, correlating residuals with predictors not included in the model might help identify the omitted predictor(s). Suppose that one group of employees is predominantly male and is supervised by one individual and that a second group of employees is predominantly female, perform a similar job, but is supervised by a different supervisor. Now, assume that the former supervisor is more lenient in evaluating employees than the second, *consistently for both males and females.* Ignoring which supervisor rated the employees would cause all people in the first group to earn more than predicted and all people in the second group to earn less than predicted. The difference in composition of the two groups will produce an apparent sex difference. However, the difference will disappear when supervisor is included in the model.

2. Variance differences (heteroscedasticity) may exist apart from differences in means. Specifically, one may find that the female residuals are more homogeneous than the male residuals because of attempts to equate *mean* salaries by sex with inadequate attention given to evaluating individual differences. All females would "look alike."

3. Similarly, one may find skewness differences, which suggest a few unrepresentative observations, perhaps highly paid male outliers, produced the sex difference. Even if you are not investigating group residual differences, you should look to see if outliers share common properties that were not included in the original model. Determining common properties of outliers is an important way to improve a model's specification.

4. A predictor that *was* included in the model could correlate with the residuals because it is *nonlinearly* related to the criterion. Suppose an analysis were conducted in 1984, but the company had paid unusually high salaries to female recruits the previous year. Newer employees would still be paid less than employees with longer tenure, but the linear correction would not properly correct nonlinearity. The analysis could obscure sex differences present among older workers.

5. The magnitudes of the residuals may be related to their rank ordering within the data base, assuming the ordering is not arbitrary. The *Durbin–Watson* statistic (Neder & Wasserman, 1974) can be used to evaluate serial order effects. The predictor serving as the basis for ranking may be relevant but unspecified, or, if specified, may relate nonlinearly to the criterion.

Inferential Tests

Testing R

The most basic inferential question is whether R differs significantly from zero. Equations (4-16) provides appropriate F tests:

$$F = \frac{R^2/M}{(1 - R^2)/(N - M - 1)} \qquad (4\text{-}16a)$$

$$F = \frac{s_y^2 R^2/M}{s_y^2(1 - R^2)/(N - M - 1)} \qquad (4\text{-}16b)$$

Equations (4-16) are equivalent to the F tests you have previously calculated as the ratio of the mean square between groups to the mean square within groups even though it may appear different and more complex. The value of R^2 in Eq. (4-16a) is a sum of squares for the systematic portion of the data. Consequently, it describes the relative proportion of variance accounted for. In the language of Chapter 2, R^2 thus is a coefficient of determination. Dividing R^2 by the number of predictors (M) produces a mean square. The quantity M is the *degrees of freedom* (df) representing the number of constraints (requirements) you have placed upon the data through the process of estimation. Conversely, $1 - R^2$ is the sum of squares for error which, when divided by its df $(N - M - 1)$, gives the error mean square. The symbol "N" denotes the total number of subjects.

You will often see F derived from the equivalent form of Eq. (4-16b) with s_y^2 (the variance of the criterion) included in both the numerator and the denominator. The inclusion has no effect upon the final F ratio. Including s_y^2 scales sums of squares in the original measurement units rather than proportions. Equation (4-16b) will prove especially useful to the discussion of the ANOVA in the next chapter.

Testing Beta Weights

Tests can be performed on individual beta weights to see if they differ significantly from zero and, consequently, if their associated predictors are needed in the equation. One first computes the standard error of a beta weight from Eq. (4-17):

$$SE(\beta_j) = \left(\frac{r^{jj}(1 - R^2)}{N - M - 1}\right)^{1/2} \qquad (4\text{-}17)$$

where r^{ii} is the element of $\mathbf{R}^{-1}$ that corresponds to the ith beta weight. The standard error of a particular beta weight, β_i, may be divided into β_i itself to obtain t with $(N - M - 1)$ df:

$$t = \frac{\beta_j}{SE(\beta_j)} \qquad (4\text{-}18)$$

Beta weights may be evaluated using an equivalent F test. The standard error can also be used to draw confidence intervals about β_i. To obtain the standard error of the raw weights instead of the beta weights, multiply the standard error by the ratio of the standard deviation of the criterion to the standard deviation of the predictor. The computation is the same as the one used to obtain b weights from β weights.

Testing the Uniqueness of Predictors

It is common to inquire whether one or more predictors *adds* to the prediction possible with an existing group of predictors, i.e., if the uniqueness of a given predictor is significantly greater than .0. The issue in the two-predictor problem discussed earlier is if the Expert improves upon the prediction possible from the Prior Data alone. Let R_a and R_b be the values of R obtained with M_a and M_b predictors, where $M_b > M_a$ and N is the number of subjects.[3] In the example, M_a is 1 (Prior Data) and M_b is 2 (Expert plus Prior Data). The formula is given by:

$$F = \frac{(R_b^2 - R_a^2)/(M_b - M_a)}{(1 - R_b^2)/(N - M_b - 1)} \qquad (4\text{-}19)$$

(Some texts use a symbol to denote the *added* set of predictors. In that case, the equation will appear to be diferent, but will be equivalent.)

The quantity $R_b^2 - R_a^2$ is the uniqueness. The associated df is the number of *added* predictors $(M_b - M_a)$. The quantity $1 - R_b^2$ is the error variance and has $(N - M_b - 1)df$.

In many cases, one predictor will be added, i.e., $M_b - M_a = 1$. The question therefore becomes one of seeing if it is appropriate to add a particular predictor to the original model. Equation (4-20) may be used.

$$F = \frac{(R_b^2 - R_a^2)}{(1 - R_b^2)/(N - M_b - 1)} \qquad (4\text{-}20)$$

A predictor may add significantly to prediction yet have a nonsignificant beta weight because the error term used to test the *incremental effect* of a predictor is not the same as the error term used to test the beta weight.

Evaluating Alternative Equations

The heuristic distinction is often made between situations in which you wish to include a particular set of predictors for theoretical reasons and situations in which you wish to develop a prediction equation without regard to any theoretical considerations. The distinction is often blurred because most situations have at least some element of theory. Nonetheless, there are many clearly defined cases where one is vitally interested in the beta weights. The ANOVA to be discussed in the next chapter is a case in point, and it will be shown that tests of substantive effects are clearly linked to one or more beta

---

[3] Many books use a rather cumbersome system of subscripts which I prefer to avoid such as the symbol "$R_{y \cdot 12345678}$" to denote the multiple correlation between a criterion (Y) and a set of predictors (1, 2, 3, 4, 5, 6, 7, and 8). My notation refers to the two multiple correlations as "R_a" and "R_b", where "a" and "b" may designate sets of predictors.

weights. Conversely, there are many other situations in which the content of the prediction equation is not of theoretical interest. Equal weighting of high school GPA and SAT scores to predict college GPA, for example, may be quite satisfactory.

Regardless of where along the "theory versus empirical prediction" continuum your specific problem falls, there are three heuristic criteria that may be used to evaluate a proposed regression equation:

1. The equation should be *robust*, performing well in different populations.
2. The equation should be *simple* as to the number of predictors and their regression weights, especially if designed for hand application.
3. The equation should make *economical use of predictors*, especially when particular predictors are costly, e.g., expert judgments.

The principle of "It don't make no nevermind" mentioned in Chapter 3 suggests one alternative to least squares regression weights—equal weighting. Equal weighting is especially useful when the sample size is small. As I noted earlier, you do not need nearly as large a sample to evaluate the correlation between an equally weighted sum of predictors as you do to estimate the optimal weights.

Wilks (1938), Kaiser (1970), and Wainer (1976, 1978) have compared least squares beta weights to simpler alternatives in a variety of situations. Their results indicate that the actual beta weights seldom provide better prediction than simpler alternatives. For different points of view, see Laughlin (1978) and Pruzek and Frederick (1978). These authors discuss conditions under which least squares weights are more appropriate than simpler alternatives.

One variant on equal weighting is to replace some but not all predictors by their sum or average. For example, if you know that X_1, X_2, and X_3 intercorrelate highly but all are relatively independent of X_4, replace X_1, X_2, and X_3 with their sum. The problem is simplified from one involving four predictors to one involving only two.

A priori weights need not be equal. For example, suppose you found that high school GPA is a much better predictor of college GPA than SAT scores is. This finding provides you with justification to weight high school GPA twice as heavily as SAT scores. A particularly important case of *a priori* weighting occurs when you take regression weights that have been obtained from one sample and apply the weights to another sample, a procedure known as *cross validation*.

Cross Validation

The basic procedures in cross validation are to obtain a set of beta weights from one sample, which I will call Sample *A*. Next compute r^2 in a second sample, Sample *B*, using the weights obtained from Sample *A*. (I am using r^2 instead of R^2 to call attention to the point that r is in fact a simple correlation.) Also compute the value of R^2 in Sample *B* by using the optimal weights for that sample. The difference, $R^2 - r^2$, defines the *shrinkage*. The shrinkage tells you the extent to which your results capitalize on chance.

A test of whether R^2 is significantly greater than r^2 is presented below. The point for you to keep in mind is that the *arithmetic* difference between the two can often be quite large, yet not be *statistically* different.

Cross validation may be performed in several different ways. One is to take a very large sample, say 1000 or more cases, and split it into equal halves on some random basis, commonly odd- versus even-numbered cases. Shrinkage may be computed "in both directions" by estimating the reduction separately in the two groups, which is known as *double cross validation*. It is better to divide a small sample unequally, say in a 9 to 1 ratio, so that the equation of interest (the one in the larger group) will be more stable.

A distinction that I find useful is between cross validation based on groups that differ *randomly*, versus groups that differ *systematically*. An example of the latter would be to develop an equation on males and then apply it to females and vice versa. When groups vary randomly, shrinkage simply reflects sampling error; when groups vary systematically, shrinkage reflects both sampling error and the systematic differences between the two groups. An equation is said to be *robust* when it shows little shrinkage across samples that differ systematically.

Computing a Correlation from *a priori* Weights

The correlation between a linear combination produced by *a priori* weights and the criterion is given by

$$r^2 = \frac{(\mathbf{a'v})^2}{\mathbf{a'Ra}} \tag{4-21}$$

where $\mathbf{a}$ is the vector of *a priori* weights, and $\mathbf{v}$ is the vector of validities, as above.

When using *a priori* weights, you lose only one *df* since you are not *estimating* the weights. A correlation computed from *a priori* weights is a *simple* correlation and not a *multiple* correlation, despite the fact it uses multiple predictors. Conversely, you lose one *df per predictor* when weights are estimated.

Testing the Difference between R^2 and r^2 Derived from *a priori* Weights

You may test the significance of the difference between R^2 obtained from least squares weights and r^2 obtained from *a priori* weights (as obtained either on a theoretical basis or from another sample) using

$$F = \frac{(R^2 - r^2)/(M - 1)}{(1 - R^2)/(N - M - 1)} \tag{4-22}$$

Hierarchical Inclusion of Predictors

Another important alternative to obtaining the least squares weights for a fixed set of predictors is to enter subsets of the predictors in a theoretically determined order, i.e., *hierarchically*. Hierarchical inclusion means performing the analysis in stages, a process that underlies many of the topics considered in the next chapter. Entry may proceed in either a *forward* or a *backward* direction. Forward entry involves *adding* predictors from the null model ($Y' = $ a constant) to see if the successive groups of predictors improve upon the prediction possible from previously chosen groups of predictors. Thus, one first looks at predictor set A by itself, adds predictor set B to predictor set A, adds predictor set C to predictor set $A + B$, etc. The process terminates when a new set fails to add significantly to prediction. The backward approach is just the opposite. You start with the full or "saturated" model and delete theoretically chosen subsets of predictors to see if their deletion significantly *lowers* R^2, i.e., if the deleted predictors cause a significant reduction in prediction.

Equation (4-20)[4] can be used to test the significance of changes in R^2. All major multiple regression packages allow you to enter any predefined hierarchy very easily and print out results at each stage. I strongly urge you to employ a hierarchical approach if for no reason other than to get you to think about what goes into the equation and whether you need to add in certain predictors. Hierarchical entry is also known as *successive* entry. The groups of predictors are chosen on the basis of *theory*.

Stepwise Inclusion of Predictors

In stepwise regression, predictors are added in stages as in the aforementioned hierarchical method. The difference is that the selection of predictors is data-driven rather than theory-driven. There are several types of stepwise regression, such as the method of *forward* selection, which I discussed in Chapter 1.

In the simplest form of forward selection, the predictor with the highest validity is selected first. Next, the predictor with the highest squared part correlation, controlling for the first predictor but not the criterion (the predictor producing the largest increment in R^2) is added to the equation. At the third step, one looks for the predictor which has the largest squared part correlation with the criterion, holding constant the first two predictors. The process continues until all predictors that can significantly improve prediction are in the model.

The basic process is commonly modified in two ways. First, one also determines if a predictor that had been included in a prior step can be excluded

---

[4] Equation (4-20) is only appropriate if you have chosen the particular predictors in advance. It is not appropriate when searching for the "best predictors" in stepwise selection, discussed subsequently, since it will capitalize on chance.

because its ability to predict has been absorbed by newly entered predictors. Thus, Predictor A may predict the criterion better than Predictor B or C, but A may offer little added prediction once B and C are in the model. The issue is addressed by seeing whether R^2 using A, B, and C is significantly greater than R^2 using only B and C. Second, inferential tests determine if the predictor added at a given step improves prediction over the previous step significantly. If one reaches a point where adding the most unique predictor does not significantly raise R^2 and deleting the least unique predictor does not significantly lower it, the process stops because the desired simplification is presumably achieved.

One alternative form of selection is *backward* selection, in which one starts with the full model and then deletes predictors based on their part correlations with the criterion. Stepwise and hierarchical methods can be combined easily in most computer packages. Thus, one can enter is a set of predictors that have been chosen theoretically, search through another set, choosing only those that add to prediction, enter in another set chosen theoretically, etc.

Some authors are relatively positive toward stepwise selection (Draper & Smith, 1981); others are considerably more hesitant (Cooley & Lohnes, 1971; Pedhazur, 1982). I generally lean toward the latter point of view. Stepwise selection magnifies the role of chance many times over. Predictor A may be only slightly (and nonsignificantly) more valid than Predictor B. Even so, Predictor A may be included in model and Predictor B excluded. In a new sample, the reverse may hold; Predictor B may appear in the model and Predictor A may be excluded, again because of nonsignificant differences. One should *never* use stepwise selection to derive a regression equation and then attempt to interpret the beta weights or the predictors that were included in the model versus those that were excluded. Unfortunately, stepwise selection is often used to test substantive models.

Stepwise selection is appropriate in some situations in which a set of predictors is known to measure essentially the same thing. This is the condition Draper and Smith (1981) discuss. Your ultimate intent is to decide which predictors in the set to use, and you are theoretically indifferent about selection of predictors. You are willing to let the program dictate the selection.

A situation I encountered illustrates what I consider to be a legitimate use of stepwise selection. The problem was to predict visual acuity following eye surgery. Patients in the normative sample received an examination that included two physiological tests. Because the two physiological tests were costly, only one would probably be given to future patients unless each contributed uniquely to the final diagnosis. There was no theoretical basis for initially perferring one test over the other. Consequently, I used stepwise selection. Although the procedure did select only one of the tests, the R^2 obtained with the chosen test was only slightly greater than the R^2 obtained with the alternative. Neither R^2 was significantly poorer than the R^2 obtained using both tests. The chosen test seemed a "best bet" in a situation where differences were slight.

Other Ways to Handle Multicollinearity

Multicollinearity is easily rectified when it arises from one or more redundant predictors—simply delete the offending predictor or predictors from the analysis. Predictor(s) with low tolerance (or, equivalently, large values of r^{ii}) are likely candidates. Most programs detect inadequate tolerance of predictors automatically.

Another possibility is to use the first few *principal components* of the predictors instead of the predictors themselves. (See Chapter 8.) Successive principal components account for the most possible variance shared by the predictors. Using them "squeezes" the variance contained in a large set of intercorrelated predictors into a smaller, orthogonal set. The reliabilities of the first few principal components will generally be higher than that of the average predictor. Bernstein, Schoenfeld, and Costello (1982) provide an illustration of component regression.

In recent years, several investigators have worked with ways of "doctoring" an ill-conditioned predictor matrix to make its inverse more stable. The process is known as "ridge regression" when it involves adding a small quantity to the diagonal elements of **R** prior to inversion. Many numerical analysts support its use. Price (1977) and Darlington (1979) summarize its use, whereas Rozeboom (1979), Morris (1982), and Pagel and Lunneborg (1985) take a more critical view. Ridge regression is a reasonable strategy if a situation demands inclusion of highly correlated predictors. For example, sex and length of service are often highly correlated in salary inequity studies. Females entered professional jobs more recently than males. Both predictors need be included in the analysis because the goal of the analysis is in fact to separate sex from job seniority.

Comparing Alternative Equations

When comparing two or more regression equations, whether obtained from the same or different samples, one should *never* conclude that they differ just because the weights and/or predictors included in the equation "look" different. The basic test for similarity of regression equations is how highly correlated their predicted scored are (see pp. 81–83). Formally testing the similarity of two equations is especially important when the predictors are highly correlated because very different looking equations can produce very similar results. This point holds doubly when the equations are produced by stepwise selection, which is designed to accentuate apparent differences among predictors, by definition.

When two least squares equations have different numbers of predictors, the one having the greater number will typically produce larger values of R due to its aforementioned bias. The difference may not be significant. A distinction exists between cases in which the predictors in the smaller set are *nested* within the larger and when they are not. Nesting would occur when one model contains scales on a personality inventory, for example, and another model contains the same scales plus clinical judgment. The difference in R^2 values for nested sets of predictors can be tested using Eq. (4-19) or (4-20).

If each regression equation contains predictors that the other does not have, then they are not nested. If the models contain the same number of predictors, their associated values of R may be compared directly using Eq. (4-21). If one model has more predictors than the other, the model with the greater number of predictors will have an unfair advantage due to the bias inherent in R as the number of predictors increases (cf. p. 213). One way to compare the two models is to correct for the number of predictors. Equation (4-23) is perhaps the most popular correction formula:

$$R^{*2} = 1 - (1 - R^2)[(N - 1)/(N - M)] \qquad (4\text{-}23)$$

Equation (4-23) only provides an approximation. Moreover, R^{*2} can be negative, which is certainly anomalous; set R^{*2} to .0 when it is negative.

Many people expect each of a large number of predictors included in a regression equation to contribute to prediction. This is usually not the case; a few predictors usually account for nearly all the prediction possible in most settings. One possible exception arises when the predictors are relatively unreliable, as when they are items on a scale. Because of their unreliability, increasing the scale's length may improve prediction (but keep in mind the practical problem that longer scales take more time to complete). In addition, the effects of increasing a test's length obey the " law of diminishing return," as will be made explicit in Chapter 12. It is extremely rare for more than a few predictors to contribute uniquely to prediction when the predictors are relatively reliable.

Example 1—Perfect Prediction

The following hypothetical problem was constructed to illustrate what happens when three predictors predict the criterion perfectly ($R = 1$). Perfect prediction does not occur in the real world, of course, but there are circumstances in which prediction can be quite high. One situation I studied involved predicting academic salaries from one year to the next using the previous year's salary as one of the predictors. Salaries become highly predictable for two reasons. First, people who get large raises one year because they are productive also tend to be productive the following year. In addition, raises tend to be proportional to one's base salary. Consequently, higher-paid faculty tend to get raises that are larger in absolute magnitude than lower-paid

Example 1—Perfect Prediction   115

faculty. Values of R predicting one year's salary from the previous year's salary often exceeded .98.

I will refer to the three predictors of the present problem as X_1, X_2, and X_3. The predictors were independent and normally distributed $(0, 1)$. I simply had the computer package generate three independent normal deviates by means of three assignment statements.

The criterion Y was defined as $.5X_1 + .3X_2 + .2X_3$, using a fourth assignment statement in the program. The predictors in a sample observation were .34, -1.40, and $-.03$, and the associated criterion was $-.256$. You may wish to repeat my demonstration. Your results will be similar but not identical to mine because your random numbers will differ from mine due to sampling error. I generated a total of 1000 cases.

The results were as follows. The predictor means, $\bar{X}_1$, $\bar{X}_2$, and $\bar{X}_3$, were .037, $-.001$, and .029, and their standard deviations were 1.01, 1.035, and 1.029, respectively. The criterion mean, $\bar{Y}$, was .024, and its standard deviation was .623. All means are within sampling error of .0 and all standard deviations are within sampling error of 1.0.

Of more importance is the **R** matrix of intercorrelations among predictors:

$$\begin{bmatrix} 1.000 & -.003 & -.005 \\ -.003 & 1.000 & -.027 \\ -.005 & -.027 & 1.000 \end{bmatrix}$$

Its inverse $(\mathbf{R}^{-1})$ is, consequently,

$$\begin{bmatrix} 1.000 & .003 & .005 \\ .003 & 1.001 & .027 \\ .005 & .027 & 1.000 \end{bmatrix}$$

and the validity (**v**) vector of predictor–criterion correlations is

$$\begin{bmatrix} .807 \\ .487 \\ .313 \end{bmatrix}$$

You may verify that R is within rounding error of 1.0, so F is undefined. (the program actually generated a very large but finite number, reflecting computational imprecision.) The analysis has three df for regression (one per predictor), and 996 df for residual (the number of cases minus the number of predictors minus one).

The b weights were .5, .3, and .2—exactly the weights used to generate Y. The constant (intercept) is a very small number (effectively zero), and the beta weights were .81, .49, and .33. The beta weights are proportional to the b weights. The constant of proportionality is s_y because the predictors are standard scores but Y is not. Because R is 1.0, the standard errors of the b weights are negligible, and the weights themselves differ from .0 well beyond the .001 level.

Because the predictors are uncorrelated z scores, s_y^2 equals the sum of the predictors' squared b weights. Consequently, $.5^2 + .3^2 + .2^2$ or .38. The Y mean (.024) is the product of the predictor means times the weights $(.037 \times .5 - .001 \times .3 + .029 \times .2 = .024)$, a relation that does generally hold. Since the predictors are uncorrelated, the validites are also determinable as the square root of the ratio of the predictor's squared b weight (the variance shared by that predictor and the criterion) to the sum of the squared b weights (total shared variance). Thus, the correlation between X_1 and Y (.807) is the square root of the ratio of $.5^2$ to $.5^2 + .3^2 + .2^2 = .25/.38 = .66$ because the predictors are uncorrelated.

Example 2—Imperfect Prediction plus a Look at Residuals

I used exactly the same predictors in Example 2, except I excluded X_3 and let it represent error. Because X_3 is independent of X_1 and X_2, the data will still meet the formal assumptions of multiple regression. In addition, the data will also meet the normality assumptions necessary for inferential testing.

I used a different set of random numbers to generate the data from those used in the previous example, but you can closely approximate my results from the data given above, using Eq. (3-5) to recompute $\mathbf{R}^{-1}$ and the first two elements of $\mathbf{v}$.

The R is .95, R^2 is .8985, and R^{*2} is .8983. The standard error is .20047 or s_y times the square root of $1 - R^2$. The F ratio is 4412.84 (.8985/2.)/ $[(1 - .8985)/997]$ and therefore highly significant with 2 and 997 df. Thus, R and related terms are quite large but not at their maxima. Roughly 10% of the variance $[.2^2/(.5^2 + .3^2 + .2^2)] = .04/.38$ is now error, as can also be seen from computing the coefficient of nondetermination. The standard deviation of the residuals (standard error), which is s_y^2 (.629) times the square root of the coefficient of nondetermination $(.1015^{1/2} = .3186)$, is .2007 in raw-score units. The b and beta weights are the same as in the previous example. A unit change in X_1 still produces a .5 unit change in Y, holding X_2 constant, and a unit change in X_2 still produces a .8 unit change in Y, holding X_1 constant, because both X_1 and X_2 are independent of X_3.

I also computed predicted Y scores (Y') and residuals for each of the 1000 cases. The residual analysis provided new information. Because of the unbaised nature of estimation, the predicted score mean, the residual score mean, and the obtained score mean were all .0 ($z_y' = \hat{z}_y = z_y = .0$). The standard deviation of the predicted scores ($s_y \times R$) was .60, and the standard deviation of the residuals (standard error of estimate) or $s_y \times (1 - R^2)^{1/2}$ was .04. Predicted scores ranged from -2.04 to 1.58, and residuals ranged from $-.5735$ to .6591.

The 10 cases with the largest residuals were identified. Because of the way the data were generated, the outcome is due to pure chance so there was no point nor any way to identify their common property.

Example 3—Real Personality Assessment Data   117

Example 3—Real Personality Assessment Data

Between 1980 and 1982, I gathered personality test data (MMPI profiles) from applicants to either (a) security guard or (b) nonguard positions at nuclear power plants. The data will be used to see how the groups differ and how different they are. Discriminant analysis (Chapters 8–10) could also be used to the same ends. Regression and discriminant analysis produce equivalent equations when there are only two groups, but most discriminant analysis packages allow accuracy of classification to be assessed directly (see Chapter 9).

Groups were arbitrarily coded so that positive correlations, b weights, and beta weights arose when nonguard means exceeded guard means, and negative values arose when guard means exceeded nonguard means. Prediction was based on 14 standard MMPI scales. It is not important to know what the scales measure, but it is important to know that they are quite multicollinear.

The analysis is not concerned with literally "predicting" group membership— it is far simpler to find that out by asking the applicants. However, the logic is the same as a prediction problem, such as one that compares employees' job performance who were previously found satisfactory or unsatisfactory. Second, I have to assume the applicants were a random sample from a larger population. I tested applicants at only some power plants, so it takes faith (heuristic assumptions) that I request. The same faith is essential to a reading of the literature. Similarly, I did not randomly assign people to the two groups. It may be assumed that both self-selection of group and MMPI scores are correlated with several other predictors, although sex and age were not among them as I found from preliminary analysis. The study involved 3263 cases.

The R was .3190, R^2 was .1018, and R^{*2} was .0980. Because the sample was large, the relatively small multiple correlation was highly significant, with an F ratio of 26.30. This result is fairly unspectacular but typical.

I will not present the regression equation because it is complicated. Four scales failed to have significant beta weights, despite the large sample size, but one of them did correlate significantly with the criterion. This particular scale also correlates to a high degree with another MMPI scale. Hence, it has little to contribute beyond what that other scale contributes. No single scale correlated above .15 with the criterion. Only four scales had beta weights above .1, the largest of which was .26.

I used a cross validation design to test for shrinkage in the "magic" equation and to try out two simplified equations. One equation was based on the unweighted sum of the 14 scales, giving proper sign based on their validities. The other equation simply used the five best individual predictors based on the validity coefficient with sign determined in the same manner. The three equations were applied to a new sample of 464 cases.

The results were also typical of many real life applications. The correlation in the new sample using weights derived from the old sample shrunk to .2653. The figure actually was slightly lower than the value obtained using only the simple sum of the 14 predictors (.2655) and barely larger than the sum of the five "best" predictors (.2378).[5] of the original data base.

I could have chosen an example with a stronger or more dramatic relation, but I wanted to give you a feel for what is really a very common situation. I think that the average person tends to think that personality differences between occupations are fairly strong. I do not deny that differences do exist. Many are artifacts of uncontrolled predictors. Those that are not artifactual typically are subtle. Of course, sharp differences can be found when you take very extreme groups, say closed ward psychiatric patients and normals. Moreover, similar findings (lack of one predictor sufficient for prediction, shrinkage, simpler equations working as well as "magic" least squares solution) also arise even when relations are strong. Indeed, the major difference between my example and many others is my large data base.

Alternative Approaches to Data Aggregation

Multiple regression is but one of several ways to combine information for decision-making purposes. In order to consider others, imagine the problem of using (a) high school GPA and (b) SAT scores for college admissions. Assume that all measures have been standardized to means of .0 and standard deviations of 1.0, so that differences in the units of measurement (grades being on a 4-point system in some cases and not in others, SAT scores ranging from 400 to 1600, etc.) can be ignored.

Several strategies might occur to aggregate high school GPA and SAT scores even if you knew nothing about least squares regression. One is to allow high school GPA and SAT scores to *compensate* for one another. You would accept a low GPA applicant if the SAT were high or vice versa. An alternative is to use one of two possible *noncompensatory* decision rules for admission. One is a *conjunctive* rule requiring students to have a high GPA *and* a high SAT. The other is a disjunctive rule allowing students to enter with a sufficient GPA *or* SAT.[6]

Figure 4-4 is a scatterplot of some hypothetical college applicants. The scatterplot shows a moderately strong positive correlation between the pre-

---

[5] For those familiar with the MMPI, the following interpretion of the results (the five "best" predictors) may be of added interest. Applicants for security guard positions seem slightly (a) more inclined to try to "beat the test" (higher L), (b) less inclined to use more sophisticated defenses (lower K), (c) less inclined to complain about their health when under stress (lower Hy), and (d) more pessimistic and withdrawn (higher D and Si, respectively) than applicants for nonguard positions.

[6] If the criteria for *admission* are conjunctive, then the criteria for *rejection* are disjunctive—an applicant is rejected if he or she fails to meet the cutoff on one predictor regardless of the score on the other predictor. Conversely, if the criteria for *admission* are disjunctive, then the criteria for *rejection* are conjunctive, since a person must fail both high school GPA and the SAT cutoffs to be rejected.

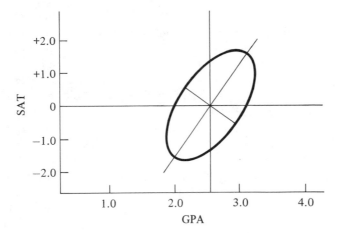

FIGURE 4-4. Scatterplot representing consequences of different decision rules. *Note*: Under the parameters given in text for the *conjunctive model, only those people falling in the top right quadrant will be accepted.* Similarly, under the parameters give for the *disjunctive model, only those people falling in the bottom left quadrant will be rejected.* The line that slopes upwards to the right represents a *compensatory* model in which SAT and GPA are equally weighted in z-score units. The line which slopes downward to the right that is perpendicular to this line is the cutoff obtained by requiring the equivalent of average performance on the SAT and an average GPA. All people falling above the latter line are accepted; all falling below it are rejected. For purposes of example, both GPA and SAT are assumed to be measured in z-score units.

dictors, as one would expect, to make it more plausible. The diagonal line represents the simplest form of compensatory rule—the standard scores for the two predictors are added, without any differential weighting. If the sum exceeds zero, the person is accepted; otherwise the person is rejected. Anyone falling above the line that slants at a 45 degree angle will be accepted under this rule.

Now consider the vertical and horizontal lines that are respectively drawn at the points corresponding to a z score of zero for high school GPA and SAT. The lines divide the space into four zones. If the lines are used as cutoffs to define passing versus failing on the two predictors, then the zones correspond to (a) meeting neither high school GPA nor SAT criteria (bottom/left), (b) meeting the high school GPA criterion but not the SAT criterion (bottom/right), (c) meeting the SAT criterion but not the high school GPA criterion (top/left), and (d) meeting both criteria (top right). Only those people in zone (d) will be accepted under a conjunctive rule, but anyone in zones (b), (c), or (d) will be accepted under the disjunctive rule.

It might appear that the conjunctive rule is the most rigorous, the compensatory rule intermediate, and the disjunctive role the most lenient. However, any outcome is possible if different cutoffs are used. The criterion lines can be moved downward to accept students with below average GPA and SAT scores under a conjunctive rule and moved upward to accept students only with above average scores under a disjunctive rule. The two predictors may be weighted unequally under the compensatory rule and the line slanted at any angle (reflecting the ratio of the weights). As a result, the same total number of students can be admitted under each rule, but the resulting student populations would be somewhat different.

The compensatory, conjunctive, and disjunctive rules are the only *pure* rules of interest, but they can be mixed. For example, applicants might have to meet some preliminary cutoff such as a GPA sufficient for graduation before being eligible for inclusion in the compensatory equation. When there are more than two predictors, mixtures of noncompensatory rules such as meeting two of three criteria can be employed. In sum, data aggregation involves four basic considerations: (a) the form of rule (compensatory, conjunctive, disjunctive), (b) the predictor(s), (c) the weightings in the compensatory case, and (d) the cutoffs in the noncompensatory cases.

All three types of rules are perfectly logical, but the compensatory rule leads to the simplest mathematics through multiple regression. The procedures to obtain the parameters needed for noncompensatory models are beyond the scope of the text. Chapter 8 considers how to choose cutoffs defining acceptance versus rejection.

When you have the need for a more extensive treatment of multiple regression, there are several excellent sources. Two that have already been cited are Pedhazur (1982) and Draper and Smith (1981). Yet another is Cohen and Cohen (1975). I am now ready to deal with nonquantitative (categorical) predictors. In the course of doing so, I will provide a very important linkage between multiple regression and the analysis of variance.

5
Multiple Regression and Correlation—
Part 2. Advanced Applications

Chapter Overview

Chapter 5 addresses advanced applications of the basic multiple regression model. Most of this chapter is devoted to the use of multiple regression in performing the analysis of variance (ANOVA). *Be prepared; I will introduce the topic from a very different approach than you have probably been taught.* The way it is taught here and in many other multivariate texts uses multiple regression, not the approach generally called "partitioning of sums of squares." The results are identical to the way it is taught in basic statistics and experimental design courses, but use of multiple regression greatly simplifies many computations, especially those arising when the number of subjects in the various groups differs (the *unequal-N* case). One reason the ANOVA is not taught as a special case of multiple regression in undergraduate statistics courses is that it would be too difficult to cover basic material on multiple regression like that in Chapter 4 first. Teaching the ANOVA as a special case of multiple regression has the advantage of illustrating the way computer packages operate, since the packages do not use the methods you were taught as an undergraduate.

    I. NONQUANTITATIVE VARIABLES—Nonquantiative (categorical) variables may be used in multiple regression by breaking them down into a series of variables that individually can be assumed to have a true unit of measurement. There are actually infinite ways one can take the original variable with K categories and form $K - 1$ derived variables. All will produce the same correlations with a criterion and lead to the same F ratio in hypothesis testing. Three particular methods are popular because the resulting regression equations possess useful properties: (1) *dummy coding*, (2) *effect coding*, and (3) *orthogonal coding*.

    II. THE SIMPLE ANALYSIS OF VARIANCE (ANOVA)—The process of forming $K - 1$ derived variables from a categorical variable is the basis of the ANOVA from the multiple regression perspective. The linkage is made explicit and some important distinctions found are introduced. One distinction is between a *fixed* and a *random* effect. This section concludes with a numerical example.

III. MULTIPLE COMPARISONS—Issues relevant to making specific comparisons among groups are considered, and related procedures discussed. Three important issues are (1) orthogonal versus nonorthogonal contrasts, (b) planned versus unplanned comparisons, and (c) individual versus groupwise alpha levels in hypothesis testing.

IV. THE TWO-WAY ANOVA—The use of the ANOVA when two variables are factorially manipulated is presented. A central issue is how to use multiple regression to test an *interaction*. The problem posed by unequal-N is discussed. Finally, a device useful in graphing group means is presented.

V. EVALUATION OF QUANTITATIVE RELATIONSHIPS—When an independent variable is quantitative, it is possible to go beyond demonstrating that there is a functional relationship between the independent variable and the dependent variable. The situation allows you to perform *trend tests*. In most cases, interest will center on what are known as *polynomial functions*, which are of the form $Y = a + b_1 X^1 + b_2 X^2 + b_3 X^3 + \cdots + b_n X^n$. Interest will usually focus on the case of *linear* relationships where the highest algebraic power is 1. The general strategy of curve fitting is also discussed.

VI. THE ANALYSIS OF COVARIANCE (ANCOVA)—The analysis of covariance is shown simply to be a special case of multiple regression. A *covariate* is a variable used to reduce error variance in the criterion. From the standpoint of multiple regression, it is simply a variable that is entered hierarchically before the variables of interest (*treatment* variables). The purpose of the ANCOVA is to reduce individual differences in the criterion, which constitutes experimental error in most ANOVA designs, through *statistical* control.

VII. REPEATED MEASURES, BLOCKED AND MATCHED DESIGNS—Use of multiple regression for other commonly employed designs is considered. The designs examined in this section are intended to reduce error in the criterion, just like the ANCOVA is. However, the three all employ *experimental* control.

VIII. HIGHER-ORDER DESIGNS—Finally, some of the general principles involved when there are several independent variables are presented.

I will begin this chapter with a discussion of how to employ categorical variables, such as religion, in multiple regression. The resulting procedures lead to the analysis of variance (ANOVA) and analysis of covariance (ANCOVA).

Regression methods are also often used to infer causal relationships (*path analysis*). Path analysis will not be discussed until Chapter 7 because it requires concepts that are closely related to other topics considered at that point, such as tests of correlational structure.

Nonquantitative Variables

In the previous chapter, measures were assumed to have a true unit of measurement, i.e., the measurement forms an *interval* scale. Consider the following: You are interested in studying the effects of various drugs on behavior. Clearly, drug type is a variable, but, without further information about the specific drugs, you cannot say it has a true unit of measurement. It is a *nominal* variable. You may code four drugs as "*1*", "*2*", "*3*", and "*4*", but you have no reason to assert that Drug "*2*" is halfway between Drug "*1*" and Drug "*3*", an important property of true interval variables. Indeed, it is completely arbitrary which drug you label as "*1*". Some variables are *ordinal*, so the rank order properties of numbers can be used, i.e., if Category "*2*" is greater than Category "*1*", Category "*3*" will be greater than Category "*2*". Academic ranks (Instructor, Assistant Professor, Associate Professor, Professor) are ordinal (at least that is what I tell my family and friends).

Although codes for nominal and ordinal variables like "*1*", "*2*", etc., cannot be used *directly* in multiple regression, these codes can be used *indirectly*. The trick is to turn one nonquantitative variable into several quantitative variables. The specific trick is to take the original variable consisting of K categories and form $K - 1$ new, quantitative variables. The process can actually be done in an infinite number of ways, but three specific strategies called *dummy coding*, *effect coding*, and *orthogonal coding* are most useful. The three strategies will all lead to the same values of R^2 and associated sums of squares, but their regression equations and their interpretations are different. Also, their specific properties will depend on whether or not the number of observations in each category is the same or not (equal-N versus unequal-N), as discussed in Pedhazur (1982, pp. 274–332).

To be specific, suppose you are planning to study the effects of four drugs named "*A*", "*B*", "*C*", and "*D*" upon a measure of activity. Assume that the first three are stimulants, so you have reason to believe they will increase bodily activity. Drug "*D*" is a neutral substance or placebo.

Dummy Coding

Dummy coding compares each specific group against a reference group. Tactically, one group is given a code of "*1*" and all other groups a code of "*0*" for each of the $K - 1$ dummy variables that you derive from the original variable. The first dummy variable defines whether or not a subject is assigned to the first group; the second dummy variable defines whether or not a subject is assigned to the second group, etc. Different groups are coded "*1*" in the different variables, but one group, preferably the control group if it exists, is coded "*0*" on all variables and thereby serves as a point of reference. Table 5-1 contains one possible set of dummy codes. Group "*D*" serves as the

TABLE 5-1. Dummy, effect, and orthogonal codings for four drugs[a]

				Coding					
	Dummy			Effect			Orthogonal		
Drug	X_1	X_2	X_3	X_4	X_5	X_6	X_7	X_8	X_9
A	1	0	0	1	0	0	1	1	1
B	0	1	0	0	1	0	1	−1	−1
C	0	0	1	0	0	1	−1	1	−1
D	0	0	0	−1	−1	−1	−1	−1	1

[a] The orthogonal codes presented above assume that the number of subjects in each group is the same (equal-N).

reference group, which is the most reasonable choice because subjects in that group receive a placebo.

The meanings of the three dummy variables, which I will designated as X_1, X_2, and X_3, can be very simply described. Variable X_1 is "Did I give the subject Drug A"; variable X_2 is "Did I give the subject Drug B"; and variable X_3 is "Did I give the subject Drug C". I do not need to have a fourth variable to code Drug D, since if I did not give a subject Drug A, B, or C and, consequently, variables X_1, X_2, and X_3 are all zero, I know that the subject was given Drug D by default. Thus, a subject given Drug A is represented by a vector of predictors $(1, 0, 0)$ and subjects in other groups are represented by other appropriate vectors: $(0, 1, 0)$, $(0, 0, 1)$, and $(0, 0, 0)$ for Drugs B, C, and D, respectively.

If the overall R^2 value relating the dummy codes to the criterion is significantly greater than zero, it can be assumed that the four groups differ significantly, which will be expanded upon below as part of general discussion of the ANOVA. The point of interest here is the meaning of the resulting raw-score regression equation:

$$Y_i = a + b_1 X_1 + b_2 X_2 + b_3 X_3 + e_i \qquad (5\text{-}1)$$

The intercept parameter (a) is the mean of the control group (the group assigned a code of 0 on all predictors) and *each regression weight (b_i) is the mean differences between that group and Group D (the control group).* Hence, *the test of significance of each regression weight is a test of whether the group associated with that dummy code differs from the control group,* a most useful property, as I will later illustrate. In addition, *neither the coding strategy nor the interpretation of the regression equation depends upon equal-N.*

Effect Coding

The strategy of effect coding is to compare the mean of each group against the grand mean. Tactically, the difference between dummy coding and effect coding is that the control group is assigned a code of −1 instead of 0, as may be seen in Table 5-1. The resulting raw-score equation [Eq. (5-2)] now has some slightly different properties; The variables X_4, X_5, and X_6 denote the effect codes:

$$Y_i = a + b_4 X_4 + b_5 X_5 + b_6 X_6 + e_i \tag{5-2}$$

With *equal-N, the intercept of the regression equation is the mean of all observations and each regression weight is the difference between the mean of the group coded "1" on that variable and the grand mean,* termed the *treatment effect* for that group, hence the name "effect coding." Consequently, the "*a*" term is different from the "*a*" term of Eq. (5-1). The concept of a treatment effect is very important to the ANOVA.[1] With *unequal-N, the regression weights are less informative. The intercept is the unweighted mean*[2] of the group means, and the regression weights are deviations *from the unweighted grand mean. Consequently, significance tests of the regression weights in either case are concerned with whether or not a given group mean differs from the unweighted grand mean.*

Whether or not deviations from the unweighted mean are of interest depend on how meaningful the unweighted mean is. It is usually not meaningful when sample size differences reflect inherent differences in the population. For example, suppose a political scientist constructed a sample with 270 people registered as Democrats, 210 people registered as Republicans, 120 people who were not registered within either party but who had voted, and 400 people who had not voted, in order to study income and other differences as a function of political affiliation. The group sizes were based on recent election figures in the city where the study was conducted. In other words, the investigator had determined that 27% of the city was Democratic, 21% Republican, 12% Independents but voters, and 40% nonvoters. The weighted mean income of the groups is the average income of individuals in the sample. The weighted mean is the best estimate of the city's mean income given random sampling. The unweighted mean (mean of the four group means) does not correspond to the mean of any well-defined group and treats four groups that are inherently unequal in size as if they were equal.

Sometimes, an unweighted mean may be more meaningful than a weighted mean. Suppose an experimenter wished to compare each of four treatment

---

[1] It is very tempting to think of the placebo as having "no effect," which is true in the conventional use of the term. However, the treatment effect for the placebo will *not* in general be zero when the group means are different, because the mean of the placebo group will usually not equal the grand mean.

[2] Assume you have one person in Group A who gets a score of 0, one person in Group B who gets a score of 2, and two people in Group C who both get scores of 5. The group means are thus 0, 1, and 5. The *weighted* mean takes into account the different number of people in each group and is $(1 \times 0 + 1 \times 1 + 2 \times 5)/4 = 11/4 = 2.75$. The weighted mean equals the mean of the *individual* observations. In contrast, the *unweighted* mean is simply the mean of the three group means, *ignoring* differences in size. Hence, it is $(0 + 1 + 5)/3 = 6/3 = 2$.

groups against a common control group. Because the control group is used in every comparison and the individual treatments are used only once, it is reasonable to make the sample size of the control group larger than any of the individual treatment groups. The weighted mean reflects the greater size of the control group. However, the greater size simply reflects an experimenter's decision. The five group sizes would be equal if an unlimited number of subjects could be run. The unweighted mean estimates the grand mean of the five equally sized groups, so the regression weight derived from orthogonal coding would be highly informative.

Orthogonal Coding

Orthogonal coding compares one linear combination of groups with a second linear combination of groups. The two linear combinations may be, and often are, chosen on the basis of theoretical considerations. Normally, one equally weighted set of groups is compared with a second equally weighted set of groups. The tactic is based on the concept of a *comparison* or set of coefficients in which the sum of the coefficients times the number of subjects in the group adds to zero:

$$c_1 N_1 + c_2 N_2 + \cdots + c_k N_k = 0 \tag{5-3}$$

The coefficients (c_i) thus add to zero with equal-N. As you can see from Table 5-1, I contrasted Drugs A and B with Drugs C and D to produce variable X_7. Then, I contrasted Drugs A and C with Drugs B and D to produce variable X_8. Finally, I contrasted Drugs A and D with Drugs B and C to produce variable X_9. Three separate and orthogonal tests result.

Contrasts are *orthogonal* (*independent*) when the following condition is met:

$$c_{11} c_{12} N_1 + c_{21} c_{22} N_2 + \cdots + c_{k1} c_{k2} N_k = 0 \tag{5-4}$$

c_{11} is the coefficient for the first group and first contrast, c_{12} is the coefficient for the first group and second contrast, etc.

The contrasts described in Table 5-1 for orthogonal coding will, in fact, be orthogonal with equal-N. The effect codes will also form contrasts, but the contrasts will not be orthogonal, but the dummy codes do not form contrasts at all since the sum of their coefficients is not zero. Specifically, the predictor intercorrelation matrix ($\mathbf{R}$) derived from orthogonal coding that is used to obtain R^2 will be an identify matrix so that the contributions of the squared validities will be additive. As was previously noted, the R^2 values are proportional to the sums of squares associated with each of the effect, the constant of proportionality being s_y^2. Note that there is no way you could form an additional contrast that will be orthogonal to the three contrasts already formed. However, you could set up other groups of three contrasts in an infinite number of ways. You are not limited to values of $+1$, -1, and 0. As a general rule, if there are K groups, you can form an infinite number of sets of contrasts, each containing $K - 1$ orthogonal contrasts.

One interpretation of a significant b_7 effect in orthogonal coding is the property Drugs A and B had in common differed from the property Drugs C and D had in common. The interpretation is more specific than simply concluding the four groups differ. However, b_7 could also be significant if B, C, and D were equal but differed from A. Consequently, the validity of any conclusion depends on how the contrasts are formed, the pattern of each group's means, and the results of other contrasts.

I formed the X_9 codes for each group by multiplying the respective X_7 and X_8 codes together. I will term a contrast formed by multiplying other pairs of contrasts an *interaction code*, which is why the interaction of two variables, X and Y, is referred to as the "X *times* Y" interaction.

The interpretation of the regression equation obtained from orthogonal coding is the same for both equal-N and unequal-N. *The intercept parameter is the weighted mean and each b weight is the magnitude of the corresponding contrast. Consequently, the significance of the regression weight denotes that the means of the two linear combinations are different. Hence, it tells us that the two sets of group means are different.* With equal-N, the intercept parameters obtained from orthogonal coding will be the same as the intercept parameter obtained from effect coding because the weighted mean and unweighted mean will be the same.

The regression equation using orthogonal coding is given by Eq. (5-5); its "a" term is different from the "a" terms of Eqs. (5-1) and (5-2):

$$Y_i = a + b_7 X_7 + b_8 X_8 + b_9 X_9 + e_i \qquad (5\text{-}5)$$

The Simple Analysis of Variance (ANOVA)

Because the simple ANOVA is usually discussed in more basic statistics texts, I will omit many details. You may find sources such as Hays (1981), Keppel (1982), or Kirk (1968) useful in presenting a conventional treatment. Winer (1971) and Scheffé (1959) are standard sources for more advanced topics.

I will assume the existance of K groups, and N_j subjects in the jth group. (Note: the symbol N without subscripts denotes the total number of subjects.) Each subject is assumed to be tested in one, and only one, of the conditions.

The null hypothesis may be phrased in several ways: (1) observations in the K groups were all sampled from the same population, (2) the K group means are equal, and (3) the treatment effects for the K groups are all zero. In a very general sense, it is possible to think of (1) as being different from (2) or (3). For example, suppose the K population means were the same, but the variances were different. However, the formal ANOVA model *assumes* equal variance as a deduction from basic premises. The definition of a treatment effect as a deviation from the grand mean makes (2) and (3) equivalent.

Fixed Effects versus Random Effects

In most cases, the way values of the independent variable is determined by your specific interest in them. In a *fixed effects* model the levels of each variable chosen for study (*sample* of levels) are identical to the levels of study you could have chosen (*population* of levels). The issue is whether *mean* differences exist among groups. For example, should you fail to find a difference among the four drugs, you cannot extend your conclusion to any other drug because a new drug that has not been included in your study might have different effects.

In contrast, suppose you were interested in seeing whether different brands of aspirin found in drug stores across the country are equally effective (to keep the example parallel). In principle, all brands contain the same active ingredient, but different manufacturers bind the tables differently and may also differ in their quality control. Assume there are too many brands to be studied all at once and that you are not specifically interested in comparing advertised brands with generic aspirin, etc. Your interest is simply in seeing how much variation there is among brands (specifically, whether or not there is any), so you decide to sample four brands at random from an exhaustive list of brands.

Random sampling from among brands illustrates a *random effect*. The sample of drugs (brands) chosen for the study is but a small fraction of the *population* of drugs you could have studied but, in most cases, did not. The estimated variation in drug means can be applied to brands that were available but not included due to "the luck of the draw." Failure to find mean differences among the four drugs studied therefore applies to the excluded brands. A design in which all effects are random is often referred to as the *components of variance model*.

There must be *at least one* random effect in the experiment for it to have any generality. If the study were conducted with *drugs* as a fixed effect, the *subjects* within the groups should still be chosen randomly. Hence, your conclusions about the specific drugs would generalize to the larger population of potential consumers.

The F test used to decide whether the groups differ is the same, regardless of whether the treatment effect (brands) is a fixed or a random effect in the simple ANOVA. However, the error term used in the F test of more complex designs depends on which variables are fixed and which are random. All treatment effects to be discussed will be fixed, but subjects will be random. Previously mentioned texts considered other cases.

The Simple ANOVA as a Formal Model

When you perform a simple ANOVA you are doing more than simply looking for mean differences among the groups. You are fitting data to a model that may be described in either "short form" as Eq. (5-6a) or in equivalent "long form" as Eq. (5-6b); the latter is included because it can easily be placed within the context of the general linear model:

$$Y_{ij} = a + b_j + e_{ij} \tag{5-6a}$$

$$Y_{ij} = a + b_1 X_1 + b_2 X_2 + \cdots + e_{ij} \tag{5-6b}$$

The symbol "Y_{ij}" denotes the observed score for the ith person in the jth group. The index i ranges from 1 to N_j, and the index j ranges from 1 to K. The intercept parameter (a) is a quantity that is the same for all subjects, so that it is termed the *universal effect*. The magnitude of a changes if you change the units of measurement, so it is normally of little interest. By contrast, the symbol "b_j" in Eq. (5-6a) will have the same value for individuals within a group but may differ for different groups. Hence, it is a property of the group and called the *group effect* as a consequence. Finally, the term "e_{ij}" in Eq. (5-6a) is a property of individual subjects. In theory, e_{ij} does not depend on the group a subject is assigned to and is known as the *error effect*.

The individual terms "X_1", "X_2",... "X_k" in long form Eq. (5-6b) are dummy variables and are "1" if a subject belongs to that group and "0" if the subject belongs to a different group. The long form illustrates how the ANOVA model defines an observation as the sum of (1) an intercept (a), (2) the sum of constants ("b_1", etc.) times predictors ("X_1", etc.), and (3) error (e_{ij}) just like any other raw-score regression equation [Eq. (4-1a)]. The short form follows directly from the long form. If a subject is in group "j", only that dummy code is not zero. In addition, X_j is "1", so it need not be written in the product, leaving only b_j and two other terms (a and e_{ij}).

The ANOVA, like any other application of multiple regression, requires parameter estimation. There is a bit of a problem in doing so. The data provide only N observable events, but one needs to estimate N values of e_{ij}, K values of b_j, and one value of a, or, in other words, there are $K + 1$ more parameters than observables. In order to make the parameters estimable (1) the b_j values are commonly restricted to sum to zero, which introduces one constraint, and (2) the e_{ij} values are normally restricted to sum to zero in each group, which introduces K additional constraints. These constraints allow N parameters to be estimated from N observables. Note that constraint (1) is considerably weaker than constraint (2). The former is just a mathematical convenience. The latter says that "error cancels out within groups." The assumption is reasonable when subject assignment is random, but the ANOVA is often used in situations where the subject assignment is not random, and, therefore, this assumption is often violated.

Conventional treatments of the ANOVA in basic statistics texts do not involve the computation of correlations. Therefore, the ANOVA's relation to multiple regression is not apparent.

An important part of conventional treatments of the ANOVA is a demonstration that the variance among group means (mean square between groups) estimates the variance of the e_{ij} values in the population plus a term derived from the variance of the b_j values, whereas the variance of subjects within groups (mean square within groups) estimates the variance of the e_{ij} terms alone. Consequently, the ratio of the two mean squares has an F distribution with K and $N - K - 1$ df when the null hypothesis is true. Another test is possible with 1 and $N - K - 1$ df to determine if the universal effect (a) differs significantly from .0. The test is usually of no interest. Criterion measures usually only possess interval and not ratio properties. The zero point is

TABLE 5-2. Hypothetical
data for the four drug
groups of Table 5-1
(conventional data layout)

| | Group | | |
A	B	C	D
113	107	93	68
117	111	87	64
111	111	99	74
116	108	104	75
125	101	100	52

therefore arbitrary, and the measures may be rescaled to any other mean value, including zero.

In Table 5-2, I have made up some activity data for the drug study as follows. I arbitrarily made the population grand mean (a) equal to 100 and the population group means for Drugs A, B, C, and D equal to 120, 110, 105, and 65, respectively. Hence, the corresponding treatment effects are 20, 10, 5, and -35. I then selected e_{ij} values from a table of random normal deviates (numbers obtained at random from a normal distribution with mean of .0 and standard deviation of 1.0), rounded them off to one decimal place, and multiplied by 10. The data layout is as presented in conventional treatments of the ANOVA. You can derive the random numbers by subtraction, e.g., the first subject in Drug group A had a value of -7 added to the 120 value of its population group mean to produce the final score of 113. The value of -7 is the *true* value of e_{11}.

If you computed ANOVA terms in the conventional manner, you would obtain the group sums (582, 538, 483, and 333). The grand sum is therefore 1936. The grand sum of scores squared $(\sum Y^2)$ is 195,176.

Consequently, the *total sum of squares, SS(T)*, is

$$195176 - (1936)^2/20 = 7771.20$$

The *between-group sum of squares, SS(B)*, is

$$(582^2 + 538^2 + 483^2 + 333^2)/5 - 1936^2/20. = 7064.40$$

The *within-group sum of squares, SS(W)*, is

$$7771.20 - 7064.40 = 706.80$$

The *total degrees of freedom, df(T)*, is one less than the total number of observations or 19. Similarly, the *between-group degrees of freedom, df(B)*, is one less than the number of groups of 3. Finally, the *within-group degrees of freedom, df(W)*, is the total number of observations less the number of groups or $df(T) - df(B)$; it equals 16.

The mean squares are the corresponding sums of squares divided by their respective *df*. However, only two mean squares are needed for the *F*-ratio. The *between-group mean square, MS(B)*, is

$$7771.20/3 = 2354.80$$

and the *within-group mean square, MS(W)*, is

$$706.80/16 = 44.18$$

Finally, the *F* ratio is

$$2354.80/44.18 = 53.30$$

The *F* ratio is significant beyond the .01 level with 3 and 16 *df*; hence, one may conclude that the drugs operate differentially.

Before relating the results to regression analysis, note the effects of sampling error. The data are unlike any you will gather, because I told you where the numbers come from. You can see that the grand sample mean is 96.8 and not 100.0. Similary, the mean of Group *A* is 582/5 or 116.4, not 120, so that its treatment effect is 19.6, not 20. The remaining sample means (107.6, 96.6, and 66.6) and associated treatment effects (10.8, −.2, and −30.2) also contain sampling error. Note, however, that the four sample estimates of the treatment effects add up to .0, just as the four population parameters do.

Results of Regression ANOVAs

Table 5-3 contains the same data in a layout that illustrates how multiple regression can be applied to the data. My example uses dummy coding. Hence, each observation (Y_{ij}) has associated with it three predictors, X_1, X_2, and X_3. The arrangement you would need for effect and orthogonal coding would be similar. For example, the X_4, X_5, and X_6 predictors are identical to X_1, X_2, and X_3 for the first 15 observations in effect coding. All you would have to do is to convert the three "0" predictors to "−1" for the last five observations.

I ran all three regressions, and I suggest you do the same thing for practice. The $SS(T)$ equals $N − 1$ times s_y^2, for reasons previously noted. The $SS(B)$ equals $N − 1$ times s_y^2 times R^2, reflecting only the *systematic* portion of the data or *coefficient of determination*. Finally, the $SS(W)$ equals $(N − 1)$ times s_y^2 times $(1.0 − R^2)$, reflecting the *random* portion of the data or *coefficient of nondetermination*, as discussed in Chapters 2 and 4.

The *df*, *MS*, and *F* ratio are calculated exactly as above. In fact, it may be easier to think of *df(B)* as the *number of predictor variables* rather than one less than the number of groups.

The regression equation using dummy codes is:

$$Y' = 49.80X_1 + 41.00X_2 + 30.00X_3 + 66.60$$

Similarly, the regression equation using effect codes is

$$Y' = 19.60X_4 + 10.80X_5 − .20X_6 + 96.80$$

TABLE 5-3. Hypothetical
data for the four drug
groups of Table 5-1 (layout
for dummy coding)

X_1	X_2	X_3	Y
1	0	0	113
1	0	0	117
1	0	0	111
1	0	0	116
1	0	0	125
0	1	0	107
0	1	0	111
0	1	0	111
0	1	0	108
0	1	0	101
0	0	1	93
0	0	1	87
0	0	1	99
0	0	1	104
0	0	1	100
0	0	0	68
0	0	0	64
0	0	0	74
0	0	0	75
0	0	0	52

Finally, the regression equation using orthogonal codes is

$$Y' = 15.20X_7 + 9.70X_8 - 5.30X_9 + 96.80$$

Note that the dummy code intercept (66.6) is the mean of group D (the control group) and b_1, b_2, and b_3 (49.80, 41.0, and 30.0) are the mean differences between Groups A, B, and C, respectively, and Group D. All three of the regression weights differ significantly from zero ($p < .01$), implying that each of the drugs differ from the placebo. Dummy coding is quite useful in any situation where each of several group means needs to be compared to a control group mean. (See, however, the subsequent section entitled "Multiple Comparisons.")

The effect parameters are the parameters of Eq. (5-2), except for the parameter associated with the control group, which may be obtained by subtraction $0 - (19.60 + 10.80 - .20)$ or 30.2, since all four treatment effects add to zero. Tests on individual regression weights test whether a given group differs significantly from the grand mean. Groups A, B and D, but not C differed from the grand mean, but the results are not of great interest because the grand mean is not a meaningful statistic here. Hence, the fact that the regression weights for effect coding are ANOVA parameters is of limited use in this example (and in most practical applications) because the ANOVA parameters themselves do not describe useful features of the data.

The orthogonal code parameters are parameters for the corresponding contrasts. All three regression weights are significantly different from zero. The significance of b_7 could imply that whatever Drugs A and B might have in common sets them apart as a unit from Drugs C and D. However, the fact that the b_9 effect is also significant makes other interpretations possible. For example, examination of Table 5-2 suggests that Drugs A, B, and C simply reflect diminishing stimulant affects relative to the placebo, Drug D. The pattern of means is the same as would occur if diminishing amounts of the *same* drug were used instead of *different drugs*. If you multiply b_7 by 4 (the number of groups), you obtain the sum of the A plus B means minus the C plus D means. I will discuss the significance of the b_8 and the b_9 effects later in the chapter.

Intercorrelate the three sets of predictors, i.e., intercorrelate X_1, X_2, and X_3; intercorrelate X_4, X_5, and X_6; and intercorrelate X_7, X_8, and X_9. Note that the three dummy codes (X_1, X_2, and X_3) correlate $-.33$; the three effect codes (X_4, X_5, and X_6) correlate .50, but the three orthogonal codes (X_7, X_8, and X_9) are uncorrelated, which reflects the mutual independence implied in the name "orthogonal." Orthogonal codes produce the usual sources of variation (sums of squares) in the ANOVA. Dummy and effect codes do not.

Multiple Comparisons

The discussion of significance tests for regression weights and correlations among predictors leads to the topic of multiple comparisons, which deals with making more specific statements about how the group means differ. The topic is broad, and I will again refer you to the sources I cited earlier about the ANOVA for more detailed treatment. Many alternatives tailored to specific needs exist. I will limit my discussion to (1) the distinction between *orthogonal* (*independent*) and *nonorthogonal* (*nonindependent*) comparisons, (2) the distinction between *planned* (*a priori*) and *unplanned* (*a posteriori* or ad hoc) comparisons, and (3) alpha levels in *individual* tests versus alpha levels in *groupwise* tests.

Orthogonal versus Nonorthogonal Contrasts

Equation (5-4) defined orthogonal contrasts, and the preceding results attest to the resulting lack of correlation among the predictors. In Chapter 4, I noted that R^2 equals the sum of the squared zero-order correlations and the zero-order correlations are the beta weights when the predictors are orthogonal. The three orthogonal codes correlate .771, .492, and .269 with the criterion. The sum of their squares is .909. The previously stated F ratio (53.31) is equal to $(.909/3.)/[(1. - .909)/16.]$.

The substantive import is that the three orthogonal comparisons are independent in the sense that the outcome of one tells one nothing about the outcome of the other. In contrast, the results of the three dummy or effect codes are nonorthogonal. Different authors feel differently about the importance of orthogonality. This property is generally more important when making contrasts that are not planned in advance (*a posteriori* or ad hoc contrasts), as discussed subsequently. I personally feel that planned contrasts need not be orthogonal; go ahead and use nonorthogonal comparisons if there is good reason to do so, but make sure to inform the reader that the comparisons are not orthogonal.

Planned versus Unplanned Comparisons

Another distinction is between a comparison decided upon in advance, without first looking at the data (though perhaps and justifiably by looking at *related* data) versus comparisons that came to mind after looking at the overall results. The distinction is important because of the greater role that chance plays in unplanned comparisons relative to planned comparisons.

Thus, suppose you were specifically interested in the difference between Drug *A* and Drug *D*, prior to running the experiment. The fact that other drugs were included in the study is really not material to the value of the test statistic needed to establish statistical significance (its *critical value*). The level of alpha *in this particular comparison* is unaffected.

A contrast has the property of comparing a set of one or more groups with a second set of one or more groups. Normally, groups within each set are given an equal weight. For example, if you had an equal number of Catholic, Protestant, and Jewish respondents to a questionnarie, you might wish to contrast Christian and Jewish opinions. Weights of .5, .5, and −1 (or, equivalently, −1, −1, and 2, etc.) would be used. Your second orthogonal comparison would then have to be Catholic versus Protestant, which involves weights of 1, −1, and 0.

Chance can play a greater role in unplanned comparisons. Suppose you picked two numbers at random. Their range (difference) will be some specific value. Now, pick a third number. The number will either (1) fall between the two or (2) fall outside the two. If (1) holds, the estimated range based on the first pair of numbers will be unaffected, but if (2) holds, the estimated range will increase. *Adding the third number can only increase and not decrease your estimated range.* Consequently, the estimated range will tend to increase with the number of observations.

The range of group means will therefore tend to increase as the number of groups increases even when there are no real group mean differences. If you only look at means of extreme groups and do not correct for the number of groups, it is easy to be led astray. Winer (1971) contains an excellent discussion of how to correct for the number of groups. Virtually all textbooks in experimental design present Scheffe's (1959) procedure to correct for the number of comparisons. Dunnett's (1955, 1964) procedure for comparing experimental groups to a single control group is also useful. Perhaps the best strategy when one encounters an unexpected finding is to report the unplanned comparison but replicate the effect in a second study. When the comparison is made the second time, it becomes a planned comparison.

Individual Alpha Levels versus Groupwise Alpha Levels

There is a second reason that you are more likely to conclude falsely that two group means differ as the number of groups increases—you will be making more comparisons than you would with fewer groups. Suppose you compare 15 different drugs against a placebo. Each is found to differ significantly from the control at the .05 level. The probability that a given *individual* result would occur by chance is 1 in 20. However, the probability that *at least one* of the effects is due to chance is much higher (actually slightly above .5). The relation between the groupwise alpha level or probability of *at least one* false rejection of the null hypothesis, $p(g)$, as a function of the individual (nominal) alpha level used for each comparison, $p(i)$, and the number of such comparisons, NC, is given by

$$p(g) = 1 - [1 - p(i)]^{NC} \tag{5-7}$$

The number NC is *not* necessarily the number of groups. It can be quite large. For example, if you have K groups and look at all possible pairs of differences, NC will be $K \times (K - 1)/2$. I previously limited comparisons to those involving a specific drug versus the placebo. As a result, NC was the number of nonplacebo drugs.

Several procedures have been suggested to compensate for the increased likelihood of a type I error following a series of individual comparisons. Most procedures involve reducing the alpha level of the individual comparisons. One approach that is both straightforward and well grounded in statistical theory involves what is known as Bonferroni inequalities (Feller, 1957; Hays, 1981). The adjustment is simply to divide the individual alpha levels by the number of comparisons. Thus, assume you are interested in making a total of 10 comparisons at the conventional .05 level. Simply use an alpha level of .005. One difficulty is that conventional statistical tables may not contain critical values for the resulting alpha level. Some *post hoc* procedures like Duncan's multiple range test correct for the alpha level to begin with.

I apologize for being a nudge,[3] but the safest way to guard against type I errors is to try to replicate your findings.

Evaluation of Quantitative Relations

Thus far, the independent variable has only been assumed to have nominal properties; specifically, the variable "drug type" consists of four arbitrarily chosen chemical substances. Suppose, however, that the independent variable

---

[3] For those who are not fluent in Yiddish, the word "nag" will probably suffice.

is interval or ratio is character, such as drug dosage, so that different amounts of a single drug are given to different subjects. The placebo would be a special case in which the dosage is zero. The precise quantitative relation between dosage and behavior is often of interest. Tests concerned with evaluating quantitative relations are known as *trend tests*.

There is no limit to the variety of possible quantitative relations that may be of interest. However, a large number, perhaps the majority you will encounter, belong to an important class known as *polynomial functions*. The appropriate model is given in Eq. (5-8). In the example, the model includes all possible relationships of the form drug dosage, (drug dosage)^2, (drug dosage)^3, etc., times appropriate weighting coefficients, plus random error (the equation is given in z-score form; the analogous raw score form would contain an additional intercept parameter):

$$Y_i = b_1 X^1 + b_2 X^2 + b_3 X^3 + e_i \qquad (5\text{-}8)$$

I am going to discuss two somewhat different procedures to perform trend tests. Method I is very general. It can be used with unequal-N and when the levels of the independent variable are unequally spaced. The major liability of Method I is that the specific b_j terms are not independent.

Method II employs a very elegant procedure called *orthogonal polynomials*. It is a type of orthogonal contrast; hence, it has the advantage of producing additive components to test for linear, quadratic, cubic, etc., components. The disadvantage is that it is more difficult to use when spacings or group sizes are unequal.

Method I

Suppose that your four dosages were 0, 1, 3, and 9 units of a particular drug. (I used unequal spacings for generality—equal spacings would probably be used in the real study.) Furthermore, suppose you have already obtained $SS(B)$ from a simple ANOVA. The $SS(B)$ subsumes all group mean variation and uses $K = 3$ predictors.

Assume that you are interested in whether there is both a linear and a quadratic trend. *Let predictor X_1* simply be the numerical value of the predictor (its *dosage*) and let predictor X_2 be the square of its value. That is, subjects in the four groups will have predictors assigned to them as $(0, 0)$, $(1, 1)$, $(3, 9)$, and $(9, 81)$, respectively.

The first thing you would do is to see if the value of R^2 using *only X_1* $[R^2(X_1)]$ is significantly greater than zero. If it is, then at least part of the overall relation is linear. The result of multiplying R^2 by $N - 1$ times the criterion's variance (s_y^2) is the sum of squares associated for the linear component or trend, $SS(Lin)$. The test has one df, since only one parameter is estimated—the slope of the linear relation (b_1) referred to in Eq. (5-8).

You test the linear effect by obtaining its corresponding mean square. (Since it has only one df, the sum of squares and mean square are equal.) The mean square is then divided by $MS(W)$ to provide an F ratio.

The difference between $SS(B)$ and $SS(Lin)$ is the *residual* sum of squares with respect to the linear trend, which I will call $SS(Res_1)$. It has two df, the difference between the df in $SS(B)$ or three, in the present example, and $SS(Lin)$, which will always be one. If it is not significant, you can assume that a linear relation is sufficient to account for the overall relation and stop.

If the residual is significant, compute a new value of R^2 with X_1 and X_2, denoted $R^2(X_1, X_2)$ to see whether or not the result is significantly greater than $R^2(X_1)$, i.e., whether X_2 *adds to* the prediction possible from X_1 alone. The quantity $(N - 1)s_y^2[R^2(X_1, X_2) - R^2(X_1)]$ is the sum of squares associated with the quadratic trend, $SS(Quad)$. *Note that you cannot evaluate X_2 alone using Method I.*

The reason that you must test the increment provided by X_2 to X_1 and not X_2 alone is that the two predictors are correlated. In fact, if you correlate the vector (0, 1, 3, and 9) with the vector (0, 1, 9, and 81), the result is the correlation that would obtain with equal-N, which equals .98. Notice that this is nothing other than a special case of the multicollinearity problem.

Assuming that a test for incremental effects of X_2 is significant, you can obtain a second residual sum of squares, $SS(Res_2)$, which has one df in the example. You cannot proceed further with only four groups as the sum of squares for the linear component and the residuals totally account for $SS(B)$. You could test additional residuals with more groups, although there is rarely a need to go beyond the linear and quadratic terms.

In addition to inferential tests, I would recommend that you also *describe* the percentage of $SS(B)$ accounted for by the linear relation, which is simply $SS(Lin)/SS(B)$. The percentage of between-group variance accounted for by the quadratic component is $SS(Quad)/SS(B)$.

Testing the linear trend first, then the quadratic trend, then the cubic trend, etc., illustrates a hierarchical approach. The linear component is tested first because it is the simplest way groups may differ. The slope parameter is sufficient to explain linear relationships. If the linear change is sufficient to explain the group differences, one should stop. If not, one should try the next simplest function, a quadratic trend, which requires two parameters, etc. Seeking the least complex function to explain the data is one specific instance of the *law of parsimony* in science.

A perhaps more controversial technique is to test an *ordinal* variable for linearity to see how well treating it as a series of equally spaced points on an interval scale will fit the data. For example, I was once involved in a regression analysis of faculty members' salaries where one variable was the four ranks previously mentioned. The ranks were not intended to be equally spaced, but nearly all of the variance accounted for by dummy codes was also accounted for by assuming linearity. Assuming the ranks were equally spaced allowed me to express rank as a single variable instead of a series of dummy codes. Pearson product-moment correlations are usually not seriously affected by mild nonlinearities as long as the relation is monotonic.[4]

Method II

Method II relies upon a series of orthogonal contrasts derived from fitting independent or orthogonal functions to the data. The contrasts are presented in Appendix C, assuming equal-N and equality of spacing of the independent variable. Gaito (1965) generalizes the procedure to situations involving unequal-N or unequal spacing. He also describes other details useful in curve fitting.

In order to use the table of Appendix C, assume that the spacings are 0, 2, 4, and 6 units and sample sizes are equal. Replace these actual spacing values with the tabled values. The coefficients in the table may be used to form a series of orthogonal contrasts. Note that the predictors in Method I are neither orthogonal, since X_1 and X_2 are correlated, nor are they contrasts by the definition of Eq. (5-4), since neither $0 + 1 + 3 + 9$ nor $0 + 1 + 9 + 81$ adds up to zero. However, the coefficients for the linear trend $(-3, -1, 1, 3)$ and the quadratic trend $(-1, 1, 1, -1)$ individually sum to zero and the sum of their cross products is zero. Likewise, the coefficients for the cubic trend $(-1, 3, -3, 1)$ form a third contrast that is orthogonal to the previous two. The contrasts account for independent portions of $SS(B)$.

Obtaining coefficients for linear trend with equal sample sizes but unequal spacing is fairly simple. Simply express the coefficients as deviations from the mean of the independent variable. Thus, suppose you had five levels of drug dosage (0, 1, 5, 7, and 17, for some perverse reason). The mean is $6[(0 + 1 + 5 + 7 + 17)/5]$ so the coefficients are $-6, -5, -1, 1,$ and 11.

The Two-Way ANOVA

Just so I will have a little different example and can relate to students of market research, consider the following problem. You are consulting to a large chain of record stores. The stores desire to evaluate an advertising campaign. Record store executives would like to determine the relative effectiveness of two different advertising formats designed to appear in newspapers, which I will symbolize as a_1 and a_2, and three different television commercials, which I will symbolize as b_1, b_2, and b_3. You have access to which combination of advertisements appears for which store. For simplicity, assume that the advertisements that are designed to affect one store do not affect another store. However, you do not have to assume that the physical sizes, volumes of

---

[4] As a statistician, I was delighted for the simplification. As a Professor, I was most disheartened.

business, or other features of the stores are equal. Factors like previous sales and size of the stores will, however, be considered later in discussion of the ANCOVA. Consequently, assume discussion is limited to a series of cities in the 100,000 to 200,000 size, of which there may be many.

Likewise, assume that there is in fact a vast array of stores so that you are sampling from a larger population, for purposes of example. "Stores" are serving the same role as "subjects" in most examples as a random effect so that your results may generalize. By contrast, the six possible advertising strategies (two newspaper ads by three TV ads) are combinations of two fixed effects, newspaper ad (A) and TV ad (B).

The six different treatments clearly have a two-dimensional structure, type of newspaper ad and type of TV ad. There are in fact three separate questions one can explore: (1) does the type of newspaper advertisement used affect sales, (2) does the type of TV advertisement used affect sales, and (3) are the effects of newspaper and TV ads independent of one another or do they interact? The last question deals with whether mean differences among types of newspaper ads change as the type of TV ad changes and vice versa, i.e., whether or not the two variables *interact*.

The three issues, just like the single issue disussed previously relative to the simple ANOVA, may be stated in terms of the parameters of a linear model, which is stated in "short form" as Eq. (5-9a) and in "long form" as Eq. (5-9b):

$$Y_{ijk} = a + a_j + b_k + ab_{jk} + e_{ijk} \tag{5-9a}$$

$$Y_{ijk} = a + a_1 X_1 + a_2 X_2 + \cdots + a_j X_j + b_1 W_1 + b_2 W_2$$
$$+ \cdots + b_k X_k + ab_{11} X_1 W_1 + ab_{12} X_1 W_2 + \cdots$$
$$+ ab_{jk} X_j W_k + e_{ijk} \tag{5-9b}$$

A constant term (a) is part of both equations and represents the same universal effect discussed in the simple ANOVA. The major difference is that there are now three sets of terms describing treatment effects, not just one.

One set of terms is identified as a_j in the short form and $a_1 X_1 + a_2 X_2 + \cdots + a_j X_j$ in the long form. This defines the treatment effect for a. The terms $a_1, a_2, \ldots, a_j$ denote parameters to be estimated, and the terms $X_1, X_2, \ldots, X_j$ denote dummy variables, as in the simple ANOVA. Since there are only two levels of a in the example, there really are only two terms, $a_1 X_1$ and $a_2 X_2$, but I want to indicate the possibility of more in other cases. (Note that the presence of a subscript distinguishes A's treatment parameters from the unsubscripted universal effect.)

The second set of terms identified as b_k in the short form and $b_1 W_1 + b_2 W_2 + \cdots + b_k W_k$ in the long form defines the B effect. The terms $b_1, b_2, \ldots, b_k$ denote parameters and $W_1, W_2, \ldots, W_j$ denote dummy variables. Because there are three levels of B, the long form description of the effect is specifically $b_1 W_1 + b_2 W_2 + b_3 W_3$.

The final set of terms identified as AB_{jk} in the short form and $ab_{11} X_1 W_1 +$

TABLE 5-4. Effect codes for a 2×3 factorial ANOVA

		Code				
Newspaper	TV	α_1	β_1	β_2	$\alpha\beta_{11}$	$\alpha\beta_{12}$
a_1	b_1	1	1	0	1	0
a_1	b_2	1	0	1	0	1
a_1	b_3	1	-1	-1	-1	-1
a_2	b_1	-1	1	0	-1	0
a_2	b_2	-1	0	1	0	-1
a_2	b_3	-1	-1	-1	1	1

$ab_{12} X_2 W_2 + \cdots + ab_{jk}$ in the long form code the interaction. Since there are six combinations of levels of A and B, the sum contains six terms of the form $ab_{jk} X_j W_k$.

Finally, e_{ijk} is the error term and corresponds to e_{ij} in the simple ANOVA. The reason the error term contains three instead of two subscripts is that the individual must be identified as to (1) location within group (the "i" subscript), (2) level of A (the "j" subscript, $=1$ or 2) and (3) level of B (the "k" subscript, $=1, 2,$ or 3).

In order to make the model estimable, it is assumed (1) $a_1 + a_2 = 0$, (2) $b_1 + b_2 + b_3 = 0$, (3) $ab_{11} + ab_{12} + ab_{13} + ab_{21} + ab_{22} + ab_{23} = 0$, (4) $ab_{11} + ab_{12} + ab_{13} = 0$, (5) $ab_{21} + ab_{22} + ab_{23} = 0$, (6) $ab_{11} + ab_{21} = 0$, (7) $ab_{12} + ab_{22} = 0$, (8) $ab_{13} + ab_{23} = 0$, and (9) $\sum e_{ijk} = 0$. Assumption (1) means only a_1 (or a_2, but not both) needs be estimated. Assumption (2) means that only b_1 and b_2 need be estimated, and assumptions (3) to (8) mean that only ab_{11} and ab_{12} need be estimated. The "bottom line" is that five regression weights plus a universal effect are sufficient to estimate the six group means. The null hypothesis for effect A is that a_1 (and, consequently, a_2) $= 0$; the alternative is that $a_1 = 0$. The forms of the null hypotheses for effect B and the interaction are analogous: the null hypothesis for effect B is the $b_1 = b_2 = 0$, and the null hypothesis for the interaction is that $ab_{11} = ab_{12} = 0$.

The six groups may now be identified with appropriate codes to estimate the five regression weights, and the results are presented in Table 5-4 using dummy codes, although effect or orthogonal coding could suffice. The term α_1 identifies the level of A as a dummy code. It replaces the two codes, X_1 and X_2, because of the first scaling assumption. Likewise, β_1 and β_2 replace the three codes $W_1, W_2,$ and W_3, because of the second scaling assumption. Finally, $\alpha\beta_{11}$ and $\alpha\beta_{12}$ replace the series of terms $X_1 W_1, X_1 W_2, X_1 W_3, X_2 W_1, X_2 W_2,$ and $X_2 W_3$ because of scaling assumptions (3) to (8). If the renaming of the codes seems confusing, just keep in mind that all I am doing is using a series of five codes to identify the six groups. One defines the A effect, two define the B effect, and two define the interaction.

The first dummy variable (α_1) simply identifies which newspaper ad was used; likewise, the next two dummy variables (β_2 and β_3) identify the TV ad. The final two ($\alpha\beta_{11}$ and $\alpha\beta_{12}$) code the interaction. *Note that I obtained the*

TABLE 5-5. Hypothetical data for the
two-way ANOVA of Table 5-4[a]

α_1	β_1	β_2	$\alpha\beta_{11}$	$\alpha\beta_{12}$	Y
1	1	0	1	0	57
1	1	0	1	0	70
1	1	0	1	0	56
1	1	0	1	0	73
1	1	0	1	0	67
1	1	0	1	0	78
1	0	1	0	1	28*
1	0	1	0	1	17*
1	0	1	0	1	19*
1	0	1	0	1	10
1	0	1	0	1	14
1	0	1	0	1	32
1	−1	−1	−1	−1	43*
1	−1	−1	−1	−1	40*
1	−1	−1	−1	−1	47
1	−1	−1	−1	−1	50
1	−1	−1	−1	−1	61
1	−1	−1	−1	−1	63
−1	1	0	−1	0	50*
−1	1	0	−1	0	62
−1	1	0	−1	0	52
−1	1	0	−1	0	71
−1	1	0	−1	0	64
−1	1	0	−1	0	68
−1	0	1	0	−1	7*
−1	0	1	0	−1	15*
−1	0	1	0	−1	8*
−1	0	1	0	−1	10*
−1	0	1	0	−1	18
−1	0	1	0	−1	11
−1	−1	−1	1	1	36
−1	−1	−1	1	1	30
−1	−1	−1	1	1	15
−1	−1	−1	1	1	15
−1	−1	−1	1	1	22
−1	−1	−1	1	1	10

[a] The dependent variable represents sales in thousands of dollars. All cases were included in the equal-N analysis; those cases denoted by an asterisk were deleted in the unequal-N analysis.

$\alpha\beta_{11}$ code for each group by multiplying the α_1 code and the β_1 code. Also note that I obtained the $\alpha\beta_{12}$ code by multiplying the α_1 code and the β_2 code. That illustrates the meaning of an interaction code.

Table 5-5 contains some hypothetical data for the study which I have arrayed in a manner similar to Table 5-3. In conventional treatments of two-way ANOVA, a format based on Table 5-2 would be used. The newspaper ad dimension would be represented as "columns" and the TV ad dimension as "rows" or vice versa. Instead, Table 5-5 represents each store as a line of data with its associated effect code predictors (α_1, β_1, β_2, $\alpha\beta_{11}$, and $\alpha\beta_{12}$) and criterion values (Y).

In order to incorporate the problem of unequal-N into the discussion, I have analyzed the data in two ways. First, I included all 36 cases so that you could see the results of an equal-N design with six cases per group. Next, I redid the analysis, eliminating those cases indicated by an asterisk. The unequal-N case is often referred to as the *nonorthogonal ANOVA* in the literature.

Only one regression equation, incoporating all parameters, was needed to test the main effect in the simple ANOVA. In the present case, several need be discussed. I have adopted the following convention. I will refer to predictors by the name of their set. Thus, the predictor α_1 belongs to set A, the two predictors β_1 and β_2 belong to set B, and the two predictors $\alpha\beta_{11}$ and $\alpha\beta_{12}$ belong to set AB. Consequently, $R^2(\alpha, \alpha\beta)$ refers to the squared multiple correlation using α_1, $\alpha\beta_{11}$, and $\alpha\beta_{12}$ as predictors of Y.

The main effect of A (newspaper ad) denotes the prediction of Y possible from the α codes alone. The prediction is most obviously given as (1) $R^2(\alpha)$, but it may also be defined in three other ways: (2) $R^2(\alpha, \beta) - R^2(\beta)$, (3) $R^2(\alpha, \alpha\beta) - R^2(\alpha\beta)$, and (4) $R^2(\alpha, \beta, \alpha\beta) - R^2(\beta, \alpha\beta)$. Definition (1) *ignores* the B effect and the interaction; definition (2) *adjusts for* the B effect but *ignores* the interaction; definition (3) *ignores* the B effect but *adjusts for* the interaction, and definition (4) *adjusts for* the B effect and the interaction. *The four definitions provide the same value of R^2 for all effects when either effect or orthogonal coding is used and there is equal-N.*[5] (Dummy coding will lead to the same R^2 values for the main effects but a different value for the interaction.) *Consequently, the sums of squares, mean squares, and F ratios will be the same. However, the terms are not equal with unequal-N.* I will discuss the consequences of the lack of equivalence and consider the problem of which definition to choose when I present the unequal-N analysis. The four definitions exist in analogous form for the B (TV) effect and the AB interaction.

Equal-N Analysis

Table 5-6 contains R^2 values for the various predictor sets. The $SS(T)$ equals the total degrees of freedom (35) times s_y^2 (546.25) or 19118.70. Multiplying by R^2 in Table 5-6 provides the same sums of squares that would

---

[5] With equal-N, the correlation between variables derived from different sets, e.g., α_1 and $\alpha\beta_{12}$ will be zero for both effect and orthogonal codes. The correlation between variables within the same set, e.g., β_1 and β_2, will be zero for orthogonal, but not effect, coding. The main effect dummy codes will be orthogonal with respect to each other, but not with respect to the interaction. Orthogonality allows the four definitions to yield the same result. With unequal-N, orthogonality does not generally hold for any of the coding schemes.

TABLE 5-6. Values of R-square for the
two-way ANOVA of Table 5-5

Predictors	Equal-N	Unequal-N
$\alpha, \beta, \alpha\beta$	.8883	.8855
α, β	.8359	.7870
$\alpha, \alpha\beta$	.1514	.2566
$\beta, \alpha\beta$	.7893	.8085
α	.0000	.1156
β	.7369	.6823
$\alpha\beta$	.0524	.1956

TABLE 5-7. Results of ANOVA of data in Table 5-4
(equal-N analysis)[a]

Source	SS	df	MS	F
A (newspaper ad)	1892.25	1	1892.25	26.58
B (TV ad)	14088.50	2	7044.25	98.95
AB (interaction)	1002.17	2	501.08	7.03
Error	2135.83	30	71.19	
Total	19118.70	35		

[a] All effects are significant beyond the .01 level.

result by the conventional partitioning of sums of squares method. Thus, $R^2(a)$ (.0990) is equivalent to $SS(A)$ for the newspaper ad effect of 1892.25 (19118.70 × .0990 = 1892.25). The error term is the residual after the saturated model (a, b, ab) is used. Hence, the error sum of squares is 2135.83 or $(1. - .8883) \times 19118.70$. Table 5-7 contains the complete ANOVA table.

Consequently, the four definitions of the A effect yield the same value of R^2 and, hence, the same sum of squares: .0990 = .8359 − .7369 = .1514 − .0524 = .8883 − .7893. The R^2 and sums of squares are also equal in the B effect and the AB interaction. All three effects are highly significant.

Unequal-N Analysis

There were only 26 cases included in the unequal-N analysis and s_y^2 was 553.90. Consequently, the total sum of squares is 13847.54. The error or total sum of squares times $1 - R^2(\alpha, \beta, \alpha\beta)$, is 1585.28 and $MS(W)$ is 79.26 with 20 df.

Before considering the ANOVA, you need examine Table 5-6 and note the lack of equivalence of the four definitions of the A effect. As can be seen in Table 5-6, definition (1) leads to a sum of squares for A of .1156 × 13847.54 or 1600.78 and an F ratio of 20.19. Definitions (2), (3), and (4) lead to F ratios of 18.46, 10.65, and 13.45. Consequently, the F ratios vary over a range of nearly 2 to 1. All four F-ratios are significant in the example, but need not be so in general.

It is natural to ask "which F ratio is the one to use?" You should *not* look at all of them and pick the largest. All have a meaning, but their meanings differ. Definition (4) is in a sense the most "pure" definition and (1) is the least "pure" because the B effect and the AB interaction were removed from (4) but remain in (1). The differnece between the two definitions is a function of the imbalance of the group sizes. However, what A shares with B or AB might "belong" to A in some cases so the "purity" of definition (4) may be irrelevant.

One strategy (Applebaum & Cramer, 1974) is to look at the interaction using definition (4), i.e., adjusting it for the main effects. If the interaction is significant, do not even test the main effects, since the interaction implies that the A effect depends on the B effect and vice versa. (In the present case, the effectiveness of a TV ad does, in fact, depend on the newspaper ad with which it is coupled.) Instead, look at the *simple effects*. That is, look at the differences among TV ads associated with newspaper ad 1 and the differences among TV ads associated with newspaper ad 2. The simple effects model is discussed below. You could also look differences between the two newspaper ads, separately for each of the three TV ads. Note that there is evidence for an interaction, but the interaction is *order preserving* in that regardless of type of newspaper ad, TV ad 1 is most effective and TV ad 2 is least effective. Hence, as a practical matter, the main effect of TV ad will not lead you to a different substantive conclusion than the two simple effects will.

Perhaps you learned that it was difficult to perform a two-way ANOVA with unequal-N. There is actually no computational difference when the analysis uses regression methods. The problem is clearly one of interpretation— choice of definition. You can see why equal-N designs are preferable whenever possible.[6]

In essence, the problem is one of defining what you mean by the effects. It is reasonable to ignore nonsignificant interactions. If AB were nonsignificant, the situations would be reduced to (1) and (2). Definitions (1) and (3) will be similar as will (2) and (4). When two main effects are significant and there is an inherent lack of independence of group sizes, as is true of race and income, both definitions (1) and (2) have meaning but the meaning is different. Definition (1) asks what the existing race and income differences are. Definition (2) asks what one difference, say race, would be *if* the other difference (income) did not exist. Although it is hypothetical, it is also of interest.

You are probably used to seeing the sums of squares for the various effects and error add to the total sum of squares. Additivity may or may not occur with unequal-N. Table 5-8 contains the results of four models. For compactness, I have only presented the sums of squares and final F- ratio. The row marked "Sum" is the sum of the sum of squares for A, B, and error. The first

---

[6] The notion of equal-N applies to both the *populations* from which subjects are drawn as well as the specific *samples*. If you were studying nonexperimental variables that are unequally distributed, like race or income, you would *not* resolve the problem of unequal-N by choosing samples of the same size.

TABLE 5-8. Results of alternative ANOVAs for data in Table 5-4 (unequal-N analysis)[a]

	Model							
	Hierarchical		Main Effect		Unadjusted		Type II	
Source	SS	F	SS	F	SS	F	SS	F
A	1600.62	20.19	1449.39	20.19	1600.62	20.19	1066.16	13.45
B	9297.23	58.65	9297.23	58.65	9448.46	59.91	8708.99	54.94
AB	1364.41	8.61	1364.41	8.61	2708.61	17.09	1364.41	8.61
Error	1585.28		1585.28		1585.28		1585.28	
Total	13847.54		13847.54		13847.54		13847.54	
Sum	13847.54		13696.31		15342.97		12724.83	

[a] The sum equals the sums of the sum of squares for A, B, AB, and error.

(*Hierarchical* or *Type I*) model uses the unadjusted sum of squares for A, adjusts the B effect for A, and adjusts AB for A and B. The next or *Main Effects* model adjusts the main effects for each other but not the interaction. The interaction is adjusted for the main effects. The third or *Unadjusted* model uses unadjusted sums of squares for all effects. Finally, the *Type II* model adjusts all effects for every other effect. Other models are possible. The roles of A and B could be reversed in the Hierarchical model, for example. Labels used for the various models will differ considerably from textbook to textbook. The point to keep in mind is that all models will produce *identical* results when there is equal-N.

If there is unequal-N, the sums of squares for the various effects will equal the total sum of squares only in the Hierarchical model. The Unadjusted model effects add to more than the total because the variance shared by two effects appears within both effects. Conversely, the Type II model effects do not add to the total because all overlapping variance is eliminated. Because the error term is the same in all models, the Unadjusted model will produce larger F ratios than the Type II model, in general. Hence, the Type II procedure is the most conservative. Researchers are probably most used to additivity from their experience with the equal-N case and would therefore prefer a Hierarchical model, but most people who work with unequal-N analyses consider additivity to be only a minor advantage.

Fitting Parallel Lines

Dummy code parameters are particularly useful in graphing results because you may construct parallel lines describing the various main effects given the absence of an interaction. You can therefore see group differences reflective of main effects more clearly.

Panel A of Fig. 5-1 contains a bar graph of the obtained (actual) sales figures. A bar graph is used because neither independent variable (the three TV ads and the two newspaper ads) is quantitative. The data are based on the equal-N data, but the logic would be the same for the unequal-N data.

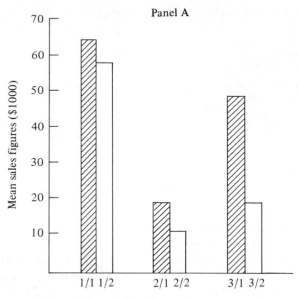

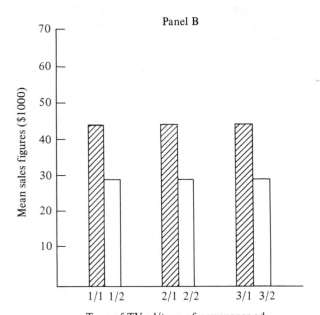

FIGURE 5-1. Mean sales figures from hypothetical market research study Panel A—obtained means. Panel B—predicted means for a model containing only a effect for type of newspaper ad. Panel C—predicted means for a model containing only a main effect for type of TV ad. Panel D—predicted means for a model containing main effects for both newpaper and TV ads.

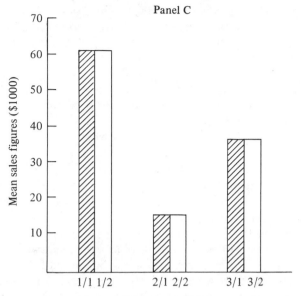

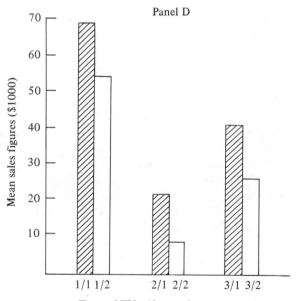

The dummy code equation for a model in which only type of newspaper ad is represented assumes that type of TV ad has no effect. The equation is $Y' = 14.50X_1 + 31.33$. The bar graph in Panel B of Fig. 5-1 contains the predicted means. The Y' are 45.83 for the three cases in which newspaper ad 1 was used—since $a_1 = 1$, $Y' = 14.50 + 31.33$. Similarly, $Y' = 31.33$ for the three cases in which newspaper ad 2 was used—since $X_2 = 0$, $Y' = 0 + 31.33$. Panels A and B are dissimilar because type of TV ad has a very strong effect upon mean sales.

The dummy code equation for a model in which only the TV ad variable is represented, which is the converse of the previous model, assumes that type of newspaper ad has no effect. The equation is $Y' = 28.00W_1 - 20.25W_2 + 36.00$. The predicted mean for the two cells in which TV ad 1 appears is obtained by setting W_1 to 1 and W_2 to 0. The result is $Y' = 64$. The corresponding prediction for the two cells in which TV ad 2 is used is obtained by setting W_1 to 0 and W_2 to 1. The result is $Y' = 15.75$. The predicted mean for the two cases in which TV ad 3 is used is obtained by setting both W_1 and W_2 to 0. The result is $Y' = 36$. The results are contained in Panel C of Fig. 5-1. Panel C resembles Panel A more closely than Panel B resembles Panel A because the effect of TV ad is stronger than the effect of newspaper ad, but the results are still disparate because the latter effect is statistically significant and not of trivial magnitude.

A third model is one in which both type of newspaper ad and type of TV ad, but not their interaction, are represented. The model is $Y' = 14.50X_1 + 28.00W_1 - 20.25W_2 + 28.75$. Note that the weights for X_1, W_1, and W_2 appearing together in the equation are the same as they were previously, where they appeared separately. Letting $X_1 = W_1 = 1$ and $W_2 = 0$ provides the predicted mean for the combination of TV ad 1 and newspaper ad 1 ($Y' = 14.50 + 28.00 + 28.75 = 71.25$). Letting $X_1 = W_2 = 1$ and $W_1 = 0$ provides the predicted mean for the combination of TV ad 1 and newspaper ad 2 ($Y' = 14.50 - 20.25 + 28.75 = 23.00$), and letting $X_1 = 1$ and $W_1 = W_2 = 0$ provides the predicted mean for the combination of TV ad 1 and newspaper ad 3 ($Y' = 14.50 + 28.75 = 43.25$). The corresponding predicted means for the three newspaper ads in conjunction with TV ad 2 are $Y' = 28.00 + 28.75 = 56.75$, $Y' = -20.25 + 28.75 = 8.5$, and $Y' = 28.75$. The latter three means are exactly 14.50 less than their counterparts with TV ad 1, which is the value of a_1. The predicted means are portrayed in Panel D of Fig. 5-1. These means are closer to the obtained means of Panel A than either the Panel B or Panel C means are, but they differ systematically because the omitted interaction terms are in fact significant.

Simple Effect Models

Although the partitioning of the six cells into an A effect, a B effect, and an AB interaction is the most commonly taught ANOVA and would be appropriate in the present context, it is not the only way possible. For

Table 5-9. Effect codes for a simple effects ANOVA

Newspaper	TV	\multicolumn{5}{c}{Code}
		α_1	c_1	c_2	d_1	d_2
a_1	b_1	1	1	0	0	0
a_1	b_2	1	0	1	0	0
a_1	b_3	1	-1	-1	0	0
a_2	b_1	-1	0	0	1	0
a_2	b_2	-1	0	0	0	1
a_2	b_3	-1	0	0	-1	-1

example, one might choose to ask the following three questions: (1) Do the two newspaper ads differ (as above)? (2) Do the three TV ads differ when the first newspaper ad is used? (3) Do the three TV ads differ when the second newspaper ad is used? Effect (1) is identical to the preceding A effect. Effects (2) and (3), each of which have two df, are called *simple effects*.

It is unfortunate that the main effects model is nearly always presented because substantive hypotheses are often stated as simple effects. For example, suppose you propose that one group of subjects vary over trials but that a second group will not. The test is a very straightforward evaluation of the two simple effects. However, what is normally done is quite cumbersome. The two main effects and the interaction are evaluated. If the interaction is significant, one then tests the simple effects. However, if the purpose of the study was to look at the simple effects, the simple effects should be obtained and tested directly. The interaction tells you very little because it could be significant if both groups varied over trials but by different amounts or in different directions.

As a rule, you should calculate the error terms for the two simple effects separately and use the pooled error term only if the separate estimates are quite similar. You should also report a difference in magnitude of error for the simple effects. For example, suppose you are interested in the simple effects of two groups, X and Y, over trials, but that subjects within the X groups are more variable than subjects within the Y groups. The pooled error term will be an average of the two variances. When you use the pooled error term, you will underestimate the experimental error affecting the X groups and over-estimate the experimental error affecting the Y groups.

Table 5-9 describes an appropriate effect coding. Predictors c_1 and c_2 code the differences in TV ads for newspaper ad 1, and predictors d_1 and d_2 do the same for newspaper ad 2.

Note that the two nested effects are not independent of the α_1 predictor. The appropriate way to obtain the nested effects is to adjust them for the main effect of A.

You could also construct a simple effect model by looking at the differences between the two newspaper ads separately for each TV ad. The model would have a main effect of TV ad with two *df* and three simple effects, each with one *df*. In short, there are many ways to partition the groups; do not automatically assume that the main effect model is the best one.

The Analysis of Covariance (ANCOVA)

Differences among subjects within groups are error in the simple ANOVA because individual differences are not correlated with the predictors. However, variation within groups need not be random. Perhaps the most active subject in each group (the last subject in group *A*, for example) would also be most active even in the absence of a drug effect. A *covariate* is normally a continuous variable that correlates with the criterion within groups, but does not correlate with the predictors.[7] This so-called *baseline* activity measures obtained before drugs are administered are a potential covariate that can be used to adjust the criterion scores. Instead of asking whether the group means differ *ignoring* individual differences, one now asks if the group means differ *adjusting for* individual differences. The analysis consists of adjusting *Y* for the covariate as the first step in a hierarchy. The second step is to use dummy, effect, or orthogonal codes as predictors, just as was done in the simple ANOVA. The only difference is that the dummy or other codes are now tested for their *incremental* effects following adjustment for the covariate.

The model for the ANCOVA in "short form" is given by

$$Y_{ij} = a + b_j + b_c + e_{ij} \tag{5-10}$$

The terms Y_{ij}, a_i, b_j, and e_{ij} have the same meaning as defined in Eq. (5-5a). However, only the Y_{ij} and *A* values will be the same when an ANOVA and an ANCOVA are applied to the same set of data. In addition, the b_j estimates will be slightly different. The e_{ij} values will be more homogeneous (vary less) in the ANCOVA because of the *covariance term*, b_c. This term describes the slope of the regression line predicting the criterion from the covariate times the deviation of the covariate score from its group mean. In essence, the model states that the e_{ij} terms in the ANOVA can be decomposed into two parts. One part is predictable from the covariate and the other is its residual. Only the latter is treated as error.

The model contains one more testable parameter, b_c, the slope of the regression line relating the covariate to the predictor. It should be, and usually is, quite significantly different from zero. If it is not so, the covariate was poorly

---

[7] In an experiment, the principle of random assignment will normally guarantee that most covariates of interest will be uncorrelated with the predictors. Problems arise in nonexperimental settings because of nonrandom assignment. A weaker requirement is often substituted—that the covariate has no *causal effect* on the treatment variable(s). Unfortunately, asserting lack of causality is more difficult to evaluate than asserting lack of correlation.

TABLE 5-10. Covariate
(baseline) data for the four
drug groups of Table 5-1
(conventional data layout)

| | Group | | |
A	B	C	D
64	67	63	71
68	68	56	63
63	69	65	72
64	68	68	74
72	62	69	56

chosen. One df is required for estimation, which comes from the original error df in the ANOVA. Thus, the effects in the ANCOVA with K groups and a total of N subjects are (a) the treatment effect ($df = K - 1$, as before), (b) the slope of the regression line predicting the criterion from the covariate ($df = 1$), (c) error ($df = N - K - 1$), and (d) total ($df = N - 1$).

Table 5-10 contains a series of baseline scores designed to illustrate the ANCOVA.

The sum of squares associated with the covariate (X) is 367.02. The sum of squares for the Drug effect, adjusted for the covariate, is 7344.02. As $SS(T)$ remains at 7771.20, the residual or error is 60.16. The corresponding mean squares for the covariate, Drug effect, and error are 367.02, 2448.01, and 4.01. The covariate effect is highly significant, with an F ratio of 91.56 (the df are 1 and 15). Thus, the covariate is indeed related to the criterion. Of more importance is the F ratio for the Drug effect, which is 610.48 with 3 and 15 df. The drug effect is much larger and the error is much smaller here than in the simple ANOVA because the covariate removed a source of systematic variance, general activity level, from the error term. The result demonstrates the power of the ANCOVA (reflecting, in part, my selection of the covariate).

Effects of the ANCOVA on the Treatment Sum of Squares

The treatment sum of squares in the ANCOVA is slightly larger (7344.02) than the treatment sum of squares in the simple ANOVA (7064.40) because the *adjusted* group means vary slightly more than the *unadjusted means*, but the difference should be purely random. Proper application of the ANCOVA will lead to as many decreases in $SS(B)$ as increases. The change arises because adjustment of within-group variation influences both the estimates of $SS(B)$ and $SS(W)$ even when the population means are equal.

There should not, in general, be a correlation between group criterion means and group covariate means. Indeed, if the principle of random assignment was used, the covariate means should differ only by chance. Some researchers assume that the ANCOVA is a device to equate groups for preexisting differences. *This use is not proper*! Its only proper use is as a device to minimize *within-group* variation.

Equation (5-11) can be used to obtain criterion means (Y_j^*) that have been adjusted for the covariates. These adjusted means are a function of the unadjusted means (Y_j), the slope parameter (b_c), and the deviation of the covariate mean for that group from the grand mean of the covariates (x_j).

$$Y_{ij} = Y_j - b_c X_j \qquad (5\text{-}11)$$

Using Dummy Codes to Plot Group Means

I have plotted the data from my example as Fig. 5-2 with separate symbols used to identify the four groups.

The group slopes are similar. The covariate by treatment interaction is used to test the slope differences for significance. The predictors are obtained by

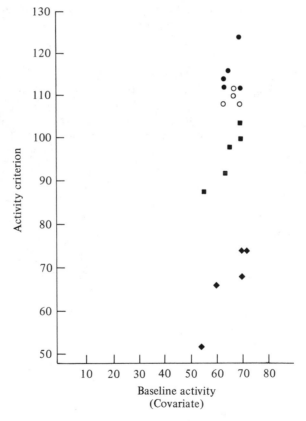

FIGURE 5-2. Scatterplot depicting the relation of criterion scores to the covariate. Filled circles (·) denote Drug *A*; open circles (o) denote Drug *B*; filled squares (■) denote Drug *C*; and diamonds (♦) denote Drug *D*.

multiplying the covariate and main effect predictors. Because the interaction effect is not independent of the treatment effect and interaction, it should be adjusted for the two effects. This test requires a new error term based on the residual after the covariate, main effect, and interaction are removed.

Slope differences present a problem only when they are substantial, e.g., the slope of one group is positive and the slope of another group is negative. When N is large, the power of the test can easily produce a significant but meaningless effect, perhaps because of slight nonlinearities. You should test the effect, but if the composite slope is visually similar to the individual slopes, go ahead and use the pooled slope estimate.

An alternative procedure when slope differences are large is the *separate slopes* model. As its name indicates, the model fits each group with its own regression line. Although this procedure is straightforward, it has several ramifications. One is that the underlying model changes to the form illustrated by Eq. (5-12), which may be compared to the "classic" covariance model of Eq. (5-10); The symbol "b_{cj}" denotes the separate group slopes:

$$Y_{ij} = a + b_j + b_{cj} + e_{ij} \qquad (5\text{-}12)$$

The separate slopes model requires that K slopes rather than one slope be estimated. The consequent loss of $(K - 1)df$ in estimation has little impact when N is large, but it can pose problems when N is small. The interpretive problem is more serious; both the mean differences and the slope differences need to be explained. I recommend the use of the separate slopes model only as a last resort.

It is possible to use more than one covariate, to use noncontinuous covariates (such as a dummy code for sex), and to apply the model to higher-order designs. These procedures follows the principles already discussed.

Repeated Measures, Blocked and Matched Designs

I have considered one design in which individual differences constitute the error term (the ANOVA) and a second design, which provides *statistical* control over individual differences (the ANCOVA). I will now consider two more designs that provide *experimental* control: (a) the *repeated measures* or *within-subjects* design and (b) the *blocked* design. I will also discuss an alternative means of statistical control, the *matched* design.

In a repeated measures design, the same subject receives all levels of the independent variable, e.g., administering each drug to every subject. This experimental procedure requires you to run the study so that the drug effects completely wear off between administrations, i.e., there is no *carryover* effects. The order of administering the drugs to subjects should also be varied. Using the same order of administration prevents you from separating order effects from drug effects. You could not tell whether Drug A (assuming it was given first) had its particular effects because of its pharmacological properties or because of its order in the series. Order can be evaluated apart from drug when it is manipulated in certain ways. A particularly elegant model is called a *Latin square design* (Winer, 1971) in which each condition follows every other condition an equal number of times. I will, however, ignore order effects in discussion.

A randomized block design assigns different subjects to the various treatments, as in the ANOVA. Unlike the ANOVA, however, subjects are rank ordered on a blocking variable, which acts like a covariate. Indeed, a baseline measure would be an appropriate blocking variable in the present case. Then, subjects are grouped into M blocks of K subjects each ($KM = N$), based on the ranking. One subject within each block is assigned at random to each treatment condition. Thus, the four most active subjects in the present case would be identified on the basis of their baseline measures. One would be given Drug A, one Drug B, etc., at random.

ANCOVA and randomized block designs are used much less frequently than are repeated measures designs, because a repeated measure design involves fewer total subjects (M in the present case rather than MK). However, repeated measures designs suffer from problems of carryover effects. The assumption that error is uncorrelated is unlikely to be met since the design employs measures obtained from the same subjects. However, if the more relaxed assumption that error correlations are *homogeneous* is met, no serious problems will arise using coventional alpha levels.

The model for both the repeated measures and randomized block design is the same and is given by

$$Y_{ij} = a + b_j + s_i + bs_{ij} \tag{5-13}$$

This model is actually the same as that used in the two-way factorial cases, except that subjects or blocks (symbolized as S_j) represent the second dimension. The treatment by subjects or treatment by blocks interaction (BS_{ij}) constitutes the remaining source of variance. However, there is no way to obtain e_{ij} directly, as there is only one measure for each combination of subject and drug. Also, subjects or blocks are a random, not a fixed, effect.

The strategy of analyzing the data is basically the same (indeed a shade simpler) than in the two-way factorial design. First, generate the codes for the treatment effect. Next, generate codes for subjects as if subjects were a separate treatment. Third, generate the treatment by subjects interaction. If you correct all effects for each other, then the coding does not matter, but if you dummy code subjects, be sure to correct the main effect for the interaction, since the interaction will not be independent of the main effect. You will thus have three sources of variation: treatments, subjects, and the interaction (treatments by subjects) that have $K - 1$, $M - 1$, and $(K - 1)(M - 1)$ df, respectively. The appropriate F ratio for the treatment effect is $MS(B)$ divided by the mean square for the interaction. In other words, error is no longer simply individual differences. Instead, it is individual differences in response to the treatments.

The reason for using the interaction as an error term is as follows. The obtained mean square for any treatment effect reflects any actual group mean differences in the population, but it also reflects *random errors of measurement*. Were you to test a subject twice in the same condition, you would not obtain identical criterion scores, and variation due to measurement error contributes to group mean differences.

There is one more influence on group means in a repeated measures design: sampling error associated with *differential response to the treatments among subjects*. Potentially, treatment effects may vary among subjects, e.g., one subject may respond more to treatment *A* than treatment *B*; a second may react in the reverse manner; and a third may respond equally to all treatments. Your sample means are a function of the kinds of subjects you sampled. In sum, the estimated treatment effect reflects (1) variation due to the treatment, (2) variation due to measurement error, and (3) variation due to the individual differences in response to the treatment in a given sample.

Your interest is in seeing if source (1) is greater than zero. A proper test is the ratio of the mean square for the treatment effect to a source of variation that just consists of sources (2) and (3). The treatment by subjects interaction fills the bill perfectly—by definition, it measures individual differences in response to the treatment and, like any source of variation, will be influenced by measurement error.

The mean square associated with sample variation among subjects is influenced by just two factors: population differences among subjects (some subjects get high scores on all measures; others get low scores on all measures) and measurement error. *Unlike the treatment effect, the subject effect is not influenced by individual differences in response to treatment if treatments are a fixed effect. By the definition of a fixed effect, treatments are not sampled—the entire population of treatments of interest is included in the study.*

A minor problem is that the repeated measures and blocked designs contain no source that estimates only measurement error, so there is no proper error term to test the subject effect. In most situations, an *F* ratio is formed by dividing the subjects effect by the interaction. The interaction will be large if individual differences in response to the treatment exist, because any such interaction affects the denominator but not the numerator. The test is said to be *negatively* biased in that it *underestimates* the true population mean differences. Values of *F* for subjects are systematically too low. Consequently, you are less likely to conclude that a difference is significant than you should. If the *F* ratio is not significant, you do not know whether subjects truly did not differ on the variable or the negative bias in the error term is responsible for the lack of significance.

The fact that tests of the subjects effect is negatively bias is usually not major in a practical sense. The subjects effect is nearly always of minor interest compared to the treatment effect. In addition, overall variation among subjects is usually so large that it overcomes the negative bias. Nonetheless, the topic is important because it introduces the theory of how to choose a proper error term in more complex designs.

Repeated measures and blocked designs provide experimental control over individual differences is that the control is exerted *prior* to data collection. Suppose you had noted a characteristic of subjects that related to the criterion *after* the data had been gathered (which might well be the baseline measure but shame, shame if you did not consider it in advance). You can then *match* subjects with the variable in question. You then incorporate the matching variable as one level of a two-way factorial design. Because the number of subjects in each cell will probably be unequal, the ANOVA will be nonorthogonal.

Because of the *statistical* nature of matching, there will be an interpretive problem if the matching variable and the treatment variable interact strongly. A strong interaction means that the treatment effect depends on whatever determined the matching. For example, if subjects were matched on a baseline activity measure in a drug study, the interaction might force you to qualify your overall statements about the effects of the drugs. You might find that two or more drugs differentially affect behavior only among subjects that were active to begin with, but do not affect those subjects who were initially nonreactive. The qualification arising from the matching variable × treatment interaction is but a special case of the point that all interactions force qualifications in statements made about main effects.

Higher-Order Designs

Independent variables (predictors) can vary along three or more dimensions. You can employ more than one covariate, and independent group manipulation of treatments can be mixed with repeated measures or blocked variables. Cell sizes can vary and, in some cases, cells themselves can be missing. The principles governing coding are the same, but the problems increase geometrically, especially with unequal-N designs.

The general strategy is the same. Covariates are removed before treatment effects. Main effects are coded as in previous examples. First-order interactions are then coded by multiplying pairs of main effect codes. Second-order interactions are then coded by multiplying first-order interaction codes by main effect codes.

Such higher-order designs gain considerable efficiency and generality as you can study how an effect depends on more than one independent variable. However, by doing so, you also pay a price. Designs with more than three independent variables become extremely difficult to interpret, especially when there are higher-order interactions present and cell sizes are unequal.

Having considered multiple regression in some detail, I will now turn to factor analysis, where the "criteria" are actually the observed variables and the "predictors" are linear combinations of the observed variables that are chosen because they are more parsimonious than the original variables. The first situation considered, which occupies the entire next chapter, is *exploratory* factor analysis. All exploratory forms of factor analysis involve linear combinations defined on the basis of mathematical (atheoretical) considerations.

6
Exploratory Factor Analysis

Chapter Overview

Factor analysis may be viewed as a set of models for transforming a group of variables into a simpler and more useful form. In essence, linear combinations are formed from variables, and the resulting linear combinations are used to "predict" the original variables. The reason for using this apparently circular process is that a small number of linear combinations, which define a new set of variables, may be able to describe all or nearly all of the meaning of the larger set of original variables.

There are many forms of factor analysis. One basic distinction, discussed in Chapter 1, is that between *exploratory* and *confirmatory*[1] factor analysis. In exploratory factor analysis, the linear combinations are formed in such a way as to satisfy some *mathematical* (*nonsubstantive*) criteria, such as explaining the highest percentage of variance inherent in the original set of variables. The researchers's major task is to interpret the meaning of the factors so obtained. In confirmatory factor analysis, the linear combinations are formed to satisfy some *substantive* criteria implicitly or explicitly suggested by a theory. Here, the goal of the inquiry is to see if the defined factors fit the data well. The present chapter is focused on exploratory factor analysis; confirmatory factor analysis will be covered in Chapter 7. This chapter is divided into eight parts.

I. THE BASIC FACTOR ANALYTIC MODEL—All factor analytic models contain a *factor equation* that relates an observable *raw-score matrix* to the product of two new matrices that are not directly observable: (a) the *pattern matrix*, which contains beta weights to predict variables from factors, and (b) the *factor score matrix*, which contains scores for each subject on each factor. A *classic* or *common factor model* contains two additional matrices, namely, the pattern and factor score matrices for *unique factors*. These unique

---

[1] My definition of confirmatory factor analysis follows from Nunnally's (1978) point of view. Those who work within the LISREL tradition discussed in the next chapter adopt a more restricted definition.

factors, in essence, represent random or measurement error. On the other hand, a *component model* does not contain an explicit concept of measurement error.

Using simple algebra, one can derive a *covariance equation* from the factor equation. The covariance equation defines the observed *correlation* or *variance–covariance* matrix as the product of the aforementioned pattern matrix and the *factor correlation matrix*, which describes the correlations among the factors. The factor correlation matrix is an *identity matrix* in an *orthogonal* solution. When the factor correlation matrix is not an identify matrix, the result is known as an *oblique* solution. The covariance equation contains one more term in the common factor model, the *uniqueness matrix*, which contains the error variance for each variable. An infinite number of pairs of pattern and factor score matrices provide mathematically equivalent solutions to the factor equation. Similarly, an infinite number of pairs of pattern and factor correlation matrices provide mathematically equivalent solutions to the covariance equation. Consequently, *no factor analytic solution is unique.* This is termed *the first form of factor indeterminacy.*

II. COMMON USES OF FACTOR ANALYSIS—There is no such thing as "a" factor analysis of a set of data. One reason there are alternative strategies is that factor analyses may be used for different purposes. Some of the major functions of factor analysis are (1) *orthogonalization* of a set of variables, (2) *reduction* in the size of a set of variables, (3) *dimensional analysis* of latent dimensions, (4) generation of *factor scores*, and (5) *statistical control.*

III. AN OVERVIEW OF THE EXPLORATORY FACTORING PROCESS—In this brief section, four steps common to nearly all factor analyses are described: (1) *entering the data*, (2) forming the *correlation matrix*, (3) obtaining the *unrotated (principal component)* solution, and (4) *rotating* factors to a *secondary solution*, which is normally the final product of interest.

IV. PRINCIPAL COMPONENTS—Even though a principal component (PC) solution is usually an interim result, it is very important to understand it. A simulated problem is presented in which the solution is shown to depend on an eigenanalysis (Chapter 2) of the correlation or variance–covariance matrix. Specifically, the principal components are demonstrated to be eigenvectors, and the variance they account for are their associated eigenvalues. Among the most important properties of a PC solution is the fact that the first, second, third, ..., PC account for the most available variance, both individually and collectively.

One reason a principal component solution is important is that its results commonly determine the number of factors retained in the rotation. Some of the major criteria for deciding on the number of factors are discussed. Although the most common criterion for determining the number of factors is the number of eigenvalues greater than 1.0, it is not the only criterion, and others may be more suitable in different situations. In particular, what is known as the *Scree* criterion may be a better alternative in item-level factoring.

Various matrices derivable from the basic matrices contained in the factor and covariance equations are introduced here. Perhaps the most important of these is the matrix containing correlations between variables and factors—the *structure matrix*.

V. FACTOR DEFINITION AND ROTATION—Some distinctions among different kinds of factors are introduced: (1) a *general factor* on which all variables in the set load (contain a substantial beta weight); (2) a *group* factor on which some, but not all, variables load; (3) a *singlet* factor on which only one variable loads (other variables may have *small* loadings on it); (4) a *unipolar* factor (which may be a general or a group factor) on which all variables either load in the same direction, i.e., are all positive or all negative, or do not load at all; and (5) a *bipolar* factor (which may also be a general or a group factor), which some variables load positively and others load negatively. *Factor definition* refers to the identification of the properties common to a group of variables that load on a particular factor.

The reason these distinctions are important is that there exist an infinite set of factors which provide totally equivalent representation of the data (the first form of factor indeterminacy). Put in another way, various factor solutions are *mathematically* equivalent. However, not all solutions have equal *psychological* utility. Different schools of thought on this issue will be discussed. The popular view is Thurstone's (1947) *simple structure*, in which a general factor is undesirable. Holzinger (Holzinger & Swineford, 1937), on the other hand, emphasized the importance of a general factor in his writings.

Alternate, equivalent solutions can relate to each other through the concept of *rotation*. Principles of rotation are introduced with emphasis given to *orthogonal* rotation. *Graphic* representations of rotations are quite useful and more so before the invention of computers. Most rotation now is done *analytically*, i.e., to satisfy one of several possible *mathematical* criteria. The logic of the two most popular methods of analytic rotation—*quartimax* and, especially, *varimax*, is covered. This section concludes with a discussion of *oblique* rotations.

VI. THE COMMON FACTOR MODEL—Many investigators prefer the common factor model to the component model. One reason that was noted earlier is that the common factor model contains an explicit concept of measurement error; the component model does not. A second reason is that a given number of common factors will reproduce the original correlation matrix better than the same number of components. From a computational standpoint, the common factor model operates upon a correlation matrix with numbers less than unity in the diagonal (termed *communalities*), whereas the component models operate upon a correlation matrix with unities in the diagonal. Unfortunately, several methods have been suggested to define communalities, but there is no general agreement upon the "best" method. Three general approaches to the communality problem are (1) *formal definition*, e.g., using the reliability coefficient to define the communality; (2) *direct estimation*, which is used by LISREL and related programs; and (3) communalities as a *by-product* of other operations. For example, one method, known as *Alpha*

(Kaiser & Caffey, 1965) determines the most reliable factors in a sense to be discussed in Chapter 12. The communalities emerge once the set of factors is defined.

VII. AN EXAMPLE OF THE COMMON FACTOR MODEL—The simulated example used for the component problem is modified slightly here to demonstrate a common factor solution.

Among the complexities of the common factor model noted in this section is that common factors are not completely specified by the variables, i.e., the multiple correlation between variables and a given factor is usually less than one—a fact that gives rise to what will be termed *the second form of factor indeterminacy.*

VIII. FACTOR SCORES—In most factor analytic work, it is not necessary to compute the scores individual subjects obtained on each factor (factor scores). Hence, the *factor score matrix*, which transforms variables into factors, is of minor interest. However, situations do arise in which factor scores are needed. The component model allows *exact* factor scores to be obtained that completely fit the data in the original sample; the common factor model does not because of the second form of factor indeterminacy. However, this comparative shortcoming of the common factor model is minor because when a component model obtained from one sample is applied to a new sample, its factor scores will not fit the model exactly because of sampling error. In this section, I cover (1) procedures to obtain component scores, (2) procedures to obtain common factor scores, and (3) criteria to evaluate the alternative procedures. It is noted that in a great many applications, *approximating* the factor score weight matrix from *salient variables* (those variables loading most highly upon a factor) will prove satisfactory although their properties should be evaluated.

The more abstract topic of factor analysis will now be considered. The previous two chapters dealt with how one set of variables could be used to predict a criterion. Predictors and criteria are all rather tangible entities and distinct from each other conceptually; you can easily visualize a set of drugs, on the one hand, and an activity measure, on the other hand. Factor analysis is more like regression analysis than it is different—one set of variables is used to predict another set of variables. However, in factor analysis, the "predictors" are linear combinations of the "criteria" and vice versa. This may sound like it goes around in circles. In order to show you that this is not the case, I will devote some space to defining the various goals of factor analysis. First, though, we will present the basic model common to all forms and applications of factor analysis.

In reading both this chapter and the next one, keep in mind that one use of factor analysis (and, for that matter, any time you derive linear combinations, which includes virtually the entire field of multivariate analysis) is to pool what different measures have in common to obtain a "purer" measure of a construct. In that sense, you are performing what Garner, Hake, and

Eriksen (1957) termed *converging operations*. That is, the individual variables defining a factor "converge" or meet together to define a construct.

The Basic Factor Analytic Model

The Factor Equation

The basic model for factor analysis is given by Eq. (6-1a) in a form designed to show you the similarities between it and previous uses of the general linear model. Equation (6-1b) defines factor analysis in a more compact matrix form. Both equations define the *factor equation*:

$$x_{ij} = f_{i\mathrm{I}}b_{j\mathrm{I}} + f_{i\mathrm{II}}b_{j\mathrm{II}} + \cdots + f_{ip}b_{jp} \quad [+ f_{iu}b_{ju}] \tag{6-1a}$$

$$\mathbf{X} = \mathbf{FB'} + \mathbf{F}_u\mathbf{B}_u' \tag{6-1b}$$

The Raw-Score Matrix

The symbol x_{ij} in Eq. (6-1a) denotes an observed score (element of $\mathbf{X}$). Most commonly, the first subscript denotes subjects, varying from 1 to N, and the second denotes the number of variables that have been obtained, varying from 1 to K. Usually, N is much greater than K. However, some applications of factor analysis reverse the role of subjects and variables or even study a single subject for whom multiple measures are obtained on different occasions. Thus, $\mathbf{X}$ is simply a data matrix as the term was introduced in Chapter 3 and is so identified in the basic relation, Eq. (6-1b).

The factor analytic model does not require raw scores to be scaled in any particular form. By convention (and in many computer programs, exclusively) each column of $\mathbf{X}$ is scaled to a mean of .0 and a standard deviation of 1.0, so that it is a $\mathbf{Z}$ matrix in the sense of Chapter 3. Assume this is the case unless told otherwise.

Factor Scores and the Factor Score Matrix

The individual elements identified in Eq. (6-1a) as $f_{i\mathrm{I}}, f_{i\mathrm{II}}, \ldots$, are the *factor scores* for subject i across the various factors. (Roman numerals traditionally identify the various factors.) Factor scores are analogous to predictor scores in multiple regression. The main difference is that factor scores are defined on unobservable or *latent* variables, which is another name for factors. The matrix of factor scores is denoted F in Eq. (6-1b) with subjects as rows and factors as columns. Factor scores are conventionally scaled to a mean of .0 and a standard deviation of 1.0, i.e., as z scores.

Pattern Elements and the Pattern Matrix

The individual elements identified in Eq. (6-1a) as $b_{j\mathrm{I}}, b_{j\mathrm{II}}, \ldots$, for measure j are called *pattern elements* for factors I, II, ... Even though I will not use the

Greek symbol to describe these elements, they are in actuality beta weights. However, instead of relating one observed variable to another observed variable, pattern elements relate factors (latent variables) to observed variables. The collection of pattern elements forms the *pattern matrix* (**B**) whose transpose appears in Eq. (6-1b). The **B** matrix has variables as rows and factors as columns. Its transpose is used in the equation to conform to the rules of matrix algebra. The **B** matrix and matrices closely related to it are the most important products of most factor analyses because they are the primary means of telling one what a set of factors are measuring.

Error Scores and Error Loadings

The final term in Eq. (6-1a) is the product of two quantities that arise from a series of special factors called *unique factors*. There is one unique factor for each variable in the model. The loading of each variable on its "own" unique factor is given by b_{ju}, *and all other variables are usually assumed to have loadings of .0 on that factor.*

The subject's factor score on each unique factor, f_{iuj}, has the same properties as do the factor scores for the other factors. *Moreover, scores on a given unique factor are assumed to be uncorrelated with scores on any other factors, unique or not.* The matrix of pattern elements, B_u in Eq. (6-1b), is therefore a diagonal matrix.

Brackets are placed around the b_{ju} and f_{iu} terms and their matrix counterparts because their inclusion is optional. Including the terms produces the *classical* or *common factor model*. The nonunique factors are known as *common factors*. Excluding the terms produces the *component model*.

Some people reserve the term "factor" for the common factor model. Others use it to cover both models, as will be done in this book. The unique factors are the factor analytic counterpart of error in the regression model. The common factor model has some definite benefits but also introduces certain complications. Lack of an explicit concept of error in the component model is often regarded as a very serious drawback, but it need not always be so.

In certain recent formulations of the common factor model (e.g., Jöreskog, 1974; Jöreskog & Sörbom, 1986), unique factors can correlate with other unique factors to represent correlated error but cannot correlate with the common factors themselves.

The Covariance Equation

There is a second form of the factor model given by Eq. (6-2); it is derivable from Eq. (6-1b) and is called the *covariance equation*:

$$\mathbf{R} = \mathbf{B\Phi B'} + [\mathbf{U}] \tag{6-2}$$

The left-hand side consists of a matrix, **R**, whose precise properties depend on the original scaling of **X**. **R** may be a variance–covariance matrix (hence, the name of the equation), in which case **C** would replace **R**. Assuming that the columns of **X** are z scores, **R** contains the correlations among the observed variables off the diagonal. In a common factor model, the diagonal elements contain numbers less than 1.0 called *communalities*, which represent the *common factor variance* of each variable, i.e., the proportion of variance that is treated as systematic. The communalities in a component model are unities because the model treats *all* variance as if it was systematic.

The matrix **B** is the pattern matrix of Eq. (6-1b). The matrix **Φ** contains correlations among the factors and is called the *factor correlation matrix*. The matrix **U** contains the variance of the unique factors and is called the *uniqueness matrix*. It is a diagonal matrix by virtue of the assumed independence of the unique factors and is omitted in a component model.[2]

The First Form of Factor Indeterminacy

Neither **B** nor **F** is unique to a given set of data in the sense that an infinite number of pairs of such matrices will reproduce the data *exactly* as well. All, however, will be related to each other by a suitable transformation in the sense described in Chapter 3. The reason is the same as the reason you cannot give a unique answer to the question: "I am thinking of two numbers whose product is 8. What are the two numbers?" You can provide *an* answer, such as 1 and 8 or 4 and 2. You cannot provide *the* answer, since you do not have enough information to define the result uniquely. *Unless constraints are introduced, there are an infinite number of mathematically equivalent ways to factor a matrix. Therefore, there are infinite sets of factors that will reproduce* **R** *equally well.* This is known as the first form of factor indeterminacy. However, alternative solutions will not be equally meaningful by psychological criteria.

The "=" sign as used in both of the preceding equations does not literally mean "equals" in most applications. If you were to apply Eq. (6-2) to factor analytic results, you would find that it would not repreduce the individual correlations perfectly, although it would be "close" (typically, in the least squares sense). The similarity of the *reproduced* correlations to the *obtained* correlations can be used to evaluate the fit of the model. Many textbooks use different symbols for these two matrices, but I will try to keep the number of different matrices used to a minimum.

---

[2] Equation (6-1b) leads fairly simply to Eq. (6-2). The proof is most easily stated for a component model, but also holds for the common factor model. Premultiply both sides of Eq. (6-1b) and divide by number of subjects, N: $(1/N)\mathbf{X'X} = (1/N)(\mathbf{FB'})'(\mathbf{FB'})$. The term $(\mathbf{X'X})$ contains sums of squared z scores on its diagonal and sums of products of z scores off the diagonal under conventional scaling. Dividing by N produces the correlations. Hence, the left-hand side is a correlation matrix. The right-hand side can be rewritten as $(1/N)(\mathbf{BF'})(\mathbf{FB'})$ because the transpose of a product $(\mathbf{FB'})'$ is the product of the transposes in reverse order and because $(\mathbf{B'})'$ is **B**. Since the columns of **F** (hence, the rows of $\mathbf{F'}$) are z scores, $(1/N)(\mathbf{F'F})$ is a correlation matrix, but of factor scores, not the raw scores in $\mathbf{R} = (1/N)(\mathbf{X'X})$.

An Important Special Case

The definition of $\mathbf{F}$ does not require factor scores to be independent of each other (uncorrelated), i.e., for $\mathbf{\Phi} = (1/N)(\mathbf{F'F})$ to be an identity matrix. When factor scores are uncorrelated, the result is termed an *orthogonal solution* and Eq. (6-2) can be reduced to a simple form, often termed the "fundamental equation of factor analysis." Solutions in which factors are not orthogonal and are hence correlated are known as *oblique*. In an oblique soltion, $\mathbf{\Phi}$ is not an identity matrix:

$$\mathbf{R} = \mathbf{BB'} + [\mathbf{U}] \qquad \text{(orthogonal factors)} \qquad (6\text{-}3)$$

Using different notation, it was noted in Chapter 3 that when a matrix $\mathbf{A}$ had the property that $\mathbf{A'A} = \mathbf{R}$, $\mathbf{A}$ was the (nonunique) square root of $\mathbf{R}$. If each element of a matrix of z scores ($\mathbf{Z}$) is divided by the square root of N, it can easily be shown that the resulting matrix is a square root of $\mathbf{R}$. Orthogonal factor analysis of a correlation matrix can be thought of as the search for other matrices that are also the square roots of $\mathbf{R}$. In that same section of Chapter 3, I also noted that if the square root matrix was triangular, the result was called a "Cholesky decomposition." Before computers, the "square root method," which involves a Cholesky decomposition of $\mathbf{R}$, was a popular method of factoring. The point to keep in mind is that an orthogonal pattern matrix is a "square root" of a raw SP (sum of products), corrected SP, covariance, or correlation matrix.

Up to now, a number of different matrices have been discussed:

$\mathbf{R}$ = the correlation matrix
$\mathbf{B}$ = the pattern matrix (beta weights to predict variables from factors)
$\mathbf{F}$ = the factor score matrix (scores of subjects on factors)
$\mathbf{B}_u$ = the pattern matrix for unique factors (common factor model)
$\mathbf{F}_u$ = the factor score matrix for unique factors (common factor model)
$\mathbf{\Phi}$ = the factor correlation matrix (an identify matrix, $\mathbf{I}$, for orthogonal solutions)

There will be a few more matrices to consider, although they will involve quantities derivable from the above. Before presenting any more, however, I will turn to a consideration of common uses of factor analysis.

Common Uses of Factor Analysis

There are several fundamental distinctions made regarding the types of models that are formulated accordingly to Eq. (6-1) or, equivalently, Eq. (6-2). I feel that the distinction between *exploratory* and *confirmatory* factor analysis is the most important one. In the former, factors are defined in such a way as to meet certain mathematical considerations, without regard to any theory. The resulting factors are then named based on the variables that correlate

most strongly with them and thereby contribute most heavily to their definition. In the latter, factors are defined according to the specification of a
substantive theory. Interest here is directed toward seeing how well the data
fit the proposed theory. Most students in the past learned only exploratory
methods, but they then used these methods to examine the underlying structure of a set of data for which an underlying theory really existed. I believe
this approach to be wrong. Recently, Jöreskog's LISREL program (Jöreskog
& Sörbom, 1986) has become a popular tool for confirmatory factor analysis.
It is an important step forward, although I personally favor a much older
confirmatory method known as *oblique multiple groups* for certain types of
problems because of its simplicity.

I will be exclusively concerned with traditional methods of exploratory
analysis in this chapter. These methods are important in their own right
because there are certainly many instances in which you will have little or no
idea of the structure of your data before you collect them. Moreover, my
discussion will also allow me to introduce some concepts that are also useful
in confirmatory factor analysis. However, to perhaps overstate a point: *do not
use exploratory factor analysis if you are testing a proposed organization of the
data, such as one which says which variables "go together" to form factors.
Under such circumstances, confirmatory methods offer a more direct approach.*

Gorsuch (1983, p. 374)[3] describes four broad uses of exploratory factor
analysis. Although he notes the four specific uses stated below, his discussion
will be modified somewhat.

Orthogonalization

Orthogonalization involves replacing a set of correlated variables with a new
set of mutually uncorrelated variables called factors. Although factors are
linear combinations of other variables, they can also be thought of as variables
in their own right. The new variables (factors) will not necessarily be mutually
uncorrelated when they are applied to a new sample, but their intercorrelations will generally be low if the original and the new samples are similar in
composition. The *full component* model, in which the entire set of variables is
replaced by a like number of components, can be used to examine stability
across samples.

---

[3] Among the major reference works solely devoted to factor analysis, I consider
Gorsuch's (1983) to be the best at concisely describing the overall role of factor analysis
in behavioral research. His work was largely stimulated by Raymond Cattell, whose
many works are seminal to those interested in factor analysis as a tool in personality
research. Cattell (1957, 1966) is the best starting place. Cattell (1978) is another source.
Harman (1976) and Mulaik (1972) are also excellent texts with the former quite good
at showing calculational steps. Most factor analytic studies, particularly those conducted prior to 1950, were to studies of cognitive abilities (intelligence). Certain
attitudes about factoring developed from those studies, particularly from the work of
Thurstone (cf. Thurstone, 1947). These attitudes have been carried over into other
areas, particularly the study of personality where the attitudes may be less applicable.

Reduction in the Number of Variables

One may choose to *reduce the size of a set of variables*. In general, one needs as many components as there are variables to reproduce all the information contained in the original set of variables. However, the information contained in the original set of variables can often be *approximated* by a much smaller number of components. Sometimes, this approximation is perfectly adequate. When that is the case, one can adopt the *truncated component* model, which uses only the most important components for estimation purposes. Some refer to truncated components as a "cheap" form of common factor analysis. However, the logic of truncated components is not unreasonable. The common factor model attempts to decide what is *shared* among variables versus what is *unique* to individual variables. A truncated component solution attempts to decide what is *important* versus what is *trivial*.

Bernstein, Schoenfeld, and Costello (1982) used truncated components of the MMPI's 14 major scales as predictors in multiple regression. These authors were concerned with predicting various performance measures from police cadets' MMPI profiles. This is an excellent example of data which produce a multicollinear correlation matrix because of the interrelations among the subscales. It was found that five components accounted for most of the predictive variance in performance and only excluded little (but, in one case, some) information important to prediction. Thus, a truncated component model was applied that greatly simplified the task of prediction.

Dimensional Analysis

A third use of exploratory factor analysis is *dimensional analysis*, which allows one to make statements such as "k factors contain *all* the variance that the p variables share with each other or can share with other variables, the remaining variance being error." A common factor model is more appropriate for dimensional analysis because the factor analysis is primarily being used as a theoretical tool to decide what is systematic and what is random. Dimensional analysis can also involve forming *higher-order factors*. If the derived factors are oblique, their correlation matrix, Φ, can be further factored using the same general methods as those used to factor the original correlation matrix, $\mathbf{R}$ itself, to obtain "factors of factors." The process produces a *hierarchy* of factors. The process can also be repeated, but the idea of a "hierarchy of a hierarchy of factors" has not proven fruitful thus far, perhaps understandably.

Determination of Factor Scores

Exploratory factor analysis may be used to obtain individual *factor scores* ($\mathbf{F}$). Actually, for all the seemingly mystical aspects of factor analysis, practically every time you take a test, what you receive are, in essence, factor scores. Suppose your instructor scores one point for each item you get correct on a multiple choice or true–false test. Your score is the sum of the number of items you answer correctly; hence, it is a linear combination with equal weighting. Were all students' scores rescaled in the form of z scores, the result is what is called the *first centroid factor*. (Centroid factor analysis, which involves forming successive equally weighted sums, was an early form of factor analysis.) If, in contrast, you take an essay test with different weights for different questions, the resulting z scores would no longer be derived from the first centroid, since the weighting is unequal, but they would still be factor scores.

The weights that are used to obtain factor scores from raw scores, such as responses to individual items, form yet another matrix called the *factor score weight matrix*, which will be denoted by the symbol "**W**." The factor score weight has the same physical layout as the pattern matrix, **B**, and the structure matrix, **S**, defined subsequently (variables in rows; factors in columns), but its content is quite different from both matrices. The factor score weight matrix is used to estimate *factors* as linear combinations of *variables*. **W** is read *columnwise* (*factorwise*) and the weights are used to compute factor scores. In contrast, **B** is read *rowwise* (*variablewise*) and is used to estimate *variables* from *factors*. All three matrices are related, but in a complex manner that depends on whether one has chosen a component or a common factor model. Regardless of the model chosen, the elements of both **W** and **B** should be thought of as beta (regression) weights. However, in **W**, the predictors are variables and the criteria are factors, whereas in **B**, the converse is true.

Gorsuch (1983) also notes how the properties of orthogonal solutions can be used for a fifth purpose, that of *statistical control*. For example, suppose that one factor is age. (It is quite possible for a factor to be defined in terms of a single observed variable.) All factors orthogonal to that factor are, by definition, independent of the linear effects of age. In general, orthogonal factoring is logically equivalent to a hierarchical or successive solution in multiple regression, a device also used for statistical control, as previously noted. (Similarly, oblique solutions may be viewed as a type of simultaneous multiple regression.)

Clearly, factor analysis can be employed for many different purposes. Because the goals of data analysis are quite varied, different factor analytic methods are appropriate for different situations. This fact has three implications: (1) there is no such thing as "the" factor analysis of a data set, (2) you need to get a feel for the variety of strategies that are possible, and (3) you need to get a feel for what happens when you instruct the computer to override the defaults built into whichever package you used. Several specific techniques of factor analysis will be discussed here and in the Chapter 7. Factor analysis routines in the major packages perform the same type of analysis on all factors. This is not necessary! You may use different factoring methods for different factors, a procedure known as *ad lib factoring*.

An Overview of the Exploratory Factoring Process

If you used different packages to factor a set of data, the results would differ slightly because there are differences in defaults and strategy. One common approach will be presented, which is essentially the default procedure used by SPSSX, but there are numerous variations. The overview will also allow some additional concepts to be introduced. Don't worry if some terms do not make too much sense to you at this moment, because they will be discussed at the appropriate time. A component analysis will be presented first, because it is simpler than a common factor analysis. The basic steps in a component factor analysis are as follows:

1. The raw data are entered.
2. The correlation matrix (**R**) is obtained from the raw data.
3. An *initial* (*primary*) principal component (PC) solution is obtained, which is orthogonal. If you request an oblique solution, it will be provided at the next step. The major purpose of step (3) is to control the number of factors retained in step (4), although you can set that number yourself.
4. A *rotated* (*secondary*) solution is obtained from the PC solution in step (3). When you talk about "the" factor solution, you are normally talking about the results obtained from step (4). Note, however, that an exploratory factor analysis normally includes *at least* two distinct (although related) solutions, initial and rotated.

Principal Components

The initial PC solution possesses some very important properties. I have simulated some data for you, which will allow me to discuss these properties in tangible terms. I first generated two numbers, F_I and F_{II}, which are "factor scores" on 500 "subjects." (A more formal symbolizing of the two factor scores would also include the subscript "i" to denote that they vary across subjects.) I then constructed six "variables," X_1 to X_6, as linear combinations of F_I and F_{II}. Assume the first three were tests devised, respectively, by investigators named Tinkers, Evers, and Chance to assess verbal fluency by three different methods. Likewise, assume that the last three were tests devised, respectively, with different methods by investigators named Larry, Curly, and Moe to measure numerical ability. The model is

$$X_1 = .96F_I + .28F_{II}$$

$$X_2 = .95F_I + .31F_{II}$$

$$X_3 = .98F_I + .20F_{II}$$

$$X_4 = .31F_I + .95F_{II}$$

$$X_5 = .28F_I + .96F_{II}$$

$$X_6 = .20F_I + .98F_{II} \tag{6-4}$$

A typical observation consists of factor scores (F_I and F_{II}) of $-.147$ and -1.002. The "observed" scores, X_1 to X_6, are $-.422$, $-.451$, $-.345$, $-.999$, -1.004, and -1.01, respectively. The observed scores are slightly different from real data because they contain no error. However, because the scores contain no error, they fit a component model perfectly. *Do not assume, however, that the coefficients in Eqs. (6-4) are going to appear as part of the PC solution; the same observed quantities could have been produced by an infinite number of different pairs of components, which reflects the "first form of factor indeterminacy."*

If there were no sampling error, you could determine the actual correlations among the variables from knowledge of the weights given by Eq. (6-4). Each variable will have a standard deviation of 1.0 within sampling error because (a) the two underlying components, F_I and F_{II}, are independently distributed with unit variance; hence, the variance of the sum will be the sum of the variance by Eq. (3-7); and (b) multiplying each score by a constant, k, changes the variance of that variable by a factor of k^2. Thus, the variance of $.96F_I$ will be $.96^2$ or $.92$ and the variance of $.28F_{II}$ will be $.28^2$ or $.08$, so their sum, the variance of X_1, will be 1.0. You may verify that the squares of the coefficients for each of the remaining observables adds to 1.0. The covariance is the sum of the cross products of the weights: $(.96 \times .31) + (.28 \times 95)$ or $.564$, which will also be their correlation since the variables are in standardized form.

Table 6-1 contains the correlations among the six overt "variables." Note that the actual value of r_{14} is $.604$ rather than $.564$ because of sampling error.

First, note that X_1, X_2, and X_3 are defined in terms of a relatively large weight on F_I and a small weight on F_{II}. The remaining three variables, X_4, X_5, and X_6, are defined in a converse manner. Also note that the correlations among the first three measures are at least $.99$, so that the three variables form a cluster. Likewise, the high correlations among variables X_4 to X_6 suggest they form a second cluster. However, the correlations between members of *different* clusters, such as X_1 and X_4 are lower, ranging from $.444$ to $.630$. If you had no knowledge of the way in which the data were generated, you would probably "see" two factors in the data, and you would be correct.

A less obvious feature of the data is that they form a correlation matrix of rank 2. That is, only two of the rows and columns of Table 6-1 are linearly

TABLE 6-1. Intercorrelations among six hypothetical error-free variables

	X_1	X_2	X_3	X_4	X_5	X_6
X_1	1.000	0.999	0.996	0.604	0.581	0.517
X_2	.999	1.000	0.993	0.630	0.607	0.544
X_3	.996	0.993	1.000	0.536	0.511	0.444
X_4	.604	0.630	0.536	1.000	0.999	0.994
X_5	.581	0.607	0.511	0.999	1.000	0.997
X_6	.517	0.544	0.444	0.994	0.997	1.000

independent. It is useful for you to figure out at least one way of deriving the rows or columns from each other. Don't worry if it does not come out exactly, since there will be rounding error. *The fact that* **R** *is of rank two is a consequence of the fact that each observed number is a linear function of two and only two different underlying numbers.*

The PCs of a correlation matrix are obtained from an eigenanalysis of that matrix, as the term was used in Chapter 3.[4] In a like manner, PCs may be obtained from a variance–covariance, corrected SP, or uncorrected SP matrix through eigenanalysis. *Because all of these matrices can be expressed in the general form* $(1/N)\mathbf{X'X}$, i.e., as the product of a matrix and its transpose, they are Gramian as defined in Chapter 3. Consequently, the eigenanalysis will have those properties discussed in the section entitled "Eigenanalysis of Gramian Matrices" in that chapter. In order to appreciate the properties of a PC solution, it is necessary to consider eigenanalysis in more depth than was given in Chapter 3. I will first discuss the solution obtained from the six hypothetical variables and then discuss how it was obtained.

The Eigenvectors and Eigenvalues of a Gramian Matrix

The SAS routine I used to obtain the PCs for the data in Table 6-1 produces normalized eigenvectors (eigenvectors whose sum of squared elements is 1.0) and eigenvalues. The first eigenvalue (λ_1) is 4.654, the second (λ_2) is 1.346, and all remaining eigenvalues are .0. The fact that only two eigenvalues are nonzero is a consequence of the fact that the matrix is of rank 2. The normalized eigenvector associated with the first eigenvalue is (.412, .419, .393, .418, .412, and .395). The normalized eigenvector associated with the second eigenvalue is (.457, .429, .530, $-.432$, $-.458$, and $-.524$).

It is instructive to note that if you multiply the first eigenvector (treating it as a row vector) into **R**, each resulting element will be 4.654 times its corresponding element in the input vector. The result satisfies the definitions of eigenvalues and eigenvectors contained in Eq. (3-9). Performing the same operation with the second eigenvector produces an output vector that equals 1.346 times the input. The sum of 4.654 and 1.346 is the trace of **R** $(1 + 1 + 1 + 1 + 1 + 1 = 6)$ as noted in Eq. (3-10). The product of all six eigenvalues is .0, since four have a value of .0; consequently, the determinant of **R** is .0, reflecting its singularity.

The normalized eigenvectors are not, however, factors, since they do not produce factor scores of unit variance. That is, if **v** denotes an eigenvector, $\mathbf{v'Rv}$ must equal 1.0 for proper scaling. Normalized eigenvectors have a very different property, that is, $\mathbf{v'v} = 1.0$ (see pp. 63–64). Rescaling normalized eigenvectors to produce factors is very simple, however. To obtain factors, *all*

---

[4] Eigenvalues are also called "characteristic values," "characteristic roots," "latent roots," and "invariant roots." Likewise, eigenvectors are called "characteristic vectors," "latent vectors," and "invariant vectors."

TABLE 6-2. PC and varimax solutions for the data of
Table 6-1

	PC_I	PC_{II}	V_I	V_{II}	h^2
X_1	.889	.457	.306	.952	1.000
X_2	.903	.429	.336	.942	1.000
X_3	.848	.530	.225	.974	1.000
X_4	.902	−.432	.943	.331	1.000
X_5	.889	−.458	.952	.304	1.000
X_6	.851	−.524	.973	.230	1.000
% Variance	.776	.224	.500	.500	1.000

one needs do is multiply the normalized eigenvector by the square root of its corresponding eigenvalue; the two square roots are 2.16 and 1.16. The first pair of columns of Table 6-2 contains the PC factors, which you may derive yourself from the preceding normalized eigenvectors and the square roots of the eigenvalues.

The columns labeled PC_I and PC_{II} contain the pattern weights relating each factor to the respective row variable. The row corresponding to X_1 implies that $X_1 = .889F_I + .457F_{II}$. A PC solution is always an orthogonal solution; hence, PC_I and PC_{II} are uncorrelated. *The beta weights for X_1 are also the correlations between X_1 and the two factors.* The name given to the matrix containing *correlations* between variables and factors is the *structure matrix. In an orthogonal solution, the pattern and structure matrices are identical. Often the term "loading matrix" is used instead. In an oblique solution, one must obtain separate pattern and structure matrices. The term "loading" is ambiguous in that case and should not be used without further specification.*

The pattern (structure, loading) matrix for the PC solution has some further interesting properties. In Chapter 4, it was noted that the R^2 between an orthogonal set of predictors and the criterion is the sum of the squared beta weights (or, equivalently, correlations). In factor analysis, the squared multiple correlations are termed "communality estimates," and the symbol h^2 is used to denote them instead R^2. The last column of Table 6-2 contains the h^2 values, which are 1.0 in all cases. *The h^2 values are 1.0 because only two factors are needed to define any of the variables, whether or not these factors are PCs. These two factors will reproduce the variables perfectly and produce h^2 values of 1.0 for all six variables.*

The term "varimax" and the columns marked "V_I" and "V_{II}" refer to a rotated solution and will be discussed subsequently.

Now, square and sum the loadings going *down* the first *column* and divide by N (6), obtaining $(.889^2 + .903^2 + \cdots + .851^2)/6$. The resulting average of the squared structure elements is the *proportion of total variance* accounted for by PC_I (.776) and is presented in column 1 of the last row. It represents the average R^2 between variables and component I. It literally means that the first factor accounts for a little more than three-quarters of the total variance.

No other factor can account for more variance than the first PC in the sample. Also note that the magnitude of the first eigenvalue (4.654) divided by N (6) yields the same estimate of variance accounted for. *The eigenvalues of a PC solution describe the total variance accounted for; when divided by the number of variables, they define the proportion of total variance accounted for.* Doing the same for PC_{II} leads to a value of .224.

Nunnally (1978) summarizes some important properties of a PC solution:

1. *Each factor maximizes the variance explained.* This has three important implications: (a) The sum of squared loadings going down a column is as large as possible, (b) the residual matrix for a given number of factors (explained subsequently) is as small as possible, and (c) the first PC explains more variance in **X** than any other linear combination of the original variables.
2. *Any group of successive PCs explains at least as much variance as any like number of components obtained by any other method.*
3. *The sum of the squared loadings for a PC equals the eigenvalue of that PC.*
4. *All eigenvalues of a PC solution will be zero or greater when Pearson product-moment correlations have been used to define* **R**.
5. *The number of nonzero eigenvalues* (two in the present case) *equals the number of factors underlying the data.* In most real applications, all eigenvalues will be greater than zero, however, unless a redundancy has been built into the data by including a variable that is linearly dependent on some other variables.
6. *The sum of the eigenvalues equals the sum of the diagonal elements of* **R** (its trace) which, in turn, equals the number of variables.
7. *PCs are mutually orthogonal.*
8. *The factor scores produced by a PC solution are also uncorrelated.* This lack of correlation among factor scores holds true in all orthogonal component solutions, not just a PC solution.
9. *The sum of squared cross products of the factor pattern (the off-diagonal elements of* **B'B**) *are .0.*

When **R** has what is known as *positive manifold* in the sense that all correlations among the original set of variables are positive, as is true here, the solution has another property. Loadings on the first factor will all be positive. On all remaining factors, half of the loadings will be positive and half will be negative, creating what is called a *bipolar* factor (see subsequent *Types of Factors* section.) Furthermore, because the sum of cross products on any pair of factors is .0, half of the loadings that were positive on any one PC will be negative on any other PC and vice versa (except for the first PC).

A Note on the Orthogonality of PCs

Although a formal proof of the mutual orthogonality of eigenvectors is complex, a graphical demonstration is useful. Reexamine Fig. 3-1, which contains the envelope of a scatterplot for two variables, z_x and z_y, which are in z-score form for convenience (see p. 85). The relation between the two variables is fairly strong; hence, observations are concentrated in the upper right and bottom left quadrants relative to the upper left and bottom right quadrants. Note, though, that the major axis of the ellipse (which corresponds to the first PC) and the minor axis of the ellipse (which corresponds to the second PC) divide the observations in the scatterplot into four areas of equal size. In other words, the observations are uncorrelated when the two PCs are used as coordinate axes instead of the original variables, z_x and z_y.

How an Eigenanalysis Is Performed

An example of an eigenanalysis on a matrix of rank 2 was presented in Chapter 3. The eigenvalues and eigenvectors could be obtained directly, but this is not generally possible with larger matrices.

With large matrices, the eigenanalysis requires *iterative* methods. Although you will never have to do one by hand, it is instructive to look at one way to perform the analysis.

1. In the simplest but not the most efficient method, one begins with an arbitrarily chosen nonzero vector, which will be called v_{in}. It will have as many elements as there are variables to be factored. Assume that it is normalized, i.e., $v'_{in}v_{in} = 1.0$.
2. Form the product $v_{in}R$. Determine the ratio of the length of v_{in} to $v_{in}R$ and call the result λ. Call the *normalized* vector product v_{out}. Compare v_{in} and v_{out}. If the two are equal within tolerance, i.e., if the corresponding elements are sufficiently similar in magnitude, go to step (4).
3. Replace v_{in} with v_{out} and repeat step (2).
4. The vector v_{in} or; equivalently, v_{out}, is the eigenvector and λ is its associated eigenvalue.
5. Form a *residual variance–covariance matrix* by subtracting $\lambda v_{in}v'_{in}$ (the *outer* or *matrix* product of the eigenvector times the scalar eigenvalue) from R. This process *partials (adjusts)* R for the linear combination represented by PC_1. Its rank will be one less than the rank of R. As with any variance–covariance matrix, it may be converted to a *residual correlation matrix* by dividing each off-diagonal element by the square root of its corresponding diagonal entries.

After the first eigenvalue, its associated eigenvector, and the residual matrix are obtained, the process is repeated to obtain successive factors. *The fact of successive partialling is what makes PC factors orthogonal. Any strategy that defines a factor, partials out that factor, forms a new factor, partials out that new factor, etc., will produce orthogonal factors.*

It is useful to look at the structure of a PC solution symbolically. Let V be a matrix whose columns are the normalized eigenvectors of R, and let Λ be a diagonal matrix of eigenvalues. Equations (6-5) describe the relations:

$$R = V'\Lambda V$$

$$= (V\Lambda^{1/2})'(V\Lambda^{1/2}) \tag{6-5}$$

In other words, any correlation matrix can be expressed as the product of eigenvalues and associated eigenvectors. The eigenvalues, in turn, describe the variance explained by each factor.

Determining How Many Components to Retain

The next step in the analysis is to decide how many factors are needed in the rotated solution. This is true whether one remains within the component framework or adopts a common factor model. Several rules have been proposed:

1. *Choose only those eigenvectors whose associated eigenvalues are 1.0 or greater.* The Kaiser–Guttman (Guttman, 1954; Kaiser, 1960, 1970) "$\lambda > 1$" criterion is historically the most widely used rule to determine the number of factors to keep. It says, in essence, "deem a component to be important if, and only if, it accounts for at least as much variance as an individual variable does." Following this rule, the resulting number of factors does not depend on the number of subjects but it is influenced by the number of variables. For example, when you factor six variables, as in the above example, a factor must account for at least one-sixth the total variance to be "important." (Note, the term "significant" is not being used because of its inferential connotations, which do not apply here.) If, however, you were factoring 100 variables, a factor would only have to account for 1% of the total variance to be considered "important." Note that considerable "juggling" of the constants of Eq. (6-4) had to be done in order to obtain two components with eigenvalues greater than 1.0 even though the data actually did consist of two underlying factors.
2. *Infer the number of factors from the relations among successive eigenvalues.* This inference is usually made graphically by presenting eigenvalues along the Y axis and their serial positions along the X axis. It is known as a *scree plot*, after the geological term for the rubble at the bottom of a cliff (Cattell, 1966). The goal is to separate the overall curve into two functions with the early eigenvalues representing "important" factors and the later ones "unimportant" factors.
3. *Employ a significance test.* Bartlett (1950) has developed a chi-square tests to determine (a) if a correlation matrix with unity diagonals differs significantly from an identity matrix, and (b) if a residual matrix differs significantly from a null matrix *following* extraction of one or more PCs. Their respective equations are

$$\chi^2 = -[N - 1 - (2k + 5)/5]\ln|R| \tag{6-6}$$

$$df = k(k - 1)/2$$

$$\chi^2 = -[N - 1 - (2k + 5)/6 - 2p/3]\ln(c), \tag{6-7}$$

where

$$c = \frac{|\mathbf{R}|}{\prod \lambda_i [(k - \sum \lambda_i)/(k - p)]^{k-p}}$$

and

$$df = (k - p - 1)(k - p - 2)/2$$

N is the number of subjects; k is the number of variables, $\mathbf{R}$ is the correlation matrix; f is the number of factors; $\prod \lambda_i$ is the product of the eigenvalues, and $\sum \lambda_i$ is the sum of the eigenvalues. These formulas correct for both number of subjects and number of components. However, with large samples, a matrix containing trivial residual variance can still differ from a null matrix, resulting in the extraction of trivial factors.

4. *Examine the residual correlations.* Look at the residual *correlation* matrix. If these residuals are all small (as a rule, less than .3 in absolute value) and there is no apparent pattern, then stop. (Do not use the residual *covariance* matrix; its numbers are misleadingly small because the residual variances will also be small.)
5. *Use the variance explained as a criterion.* Choose some value, such as 90% of the total variance, to determine how many factors are in the data.

There is nothing magical about any of the preceding criteria. If you have certain reasons to consider a particular number of factors, use that number, especially when you are comparing your results to those obtained from a prior study. The number of factors extracted has a profound effect upon the subsequent step of rotation to a final solution. A prior study may have decided upon three factors, perhaps because the fourth eigenvalue was .9999. If your fourth eigenvalue is 1.00001 and you decide to keep four factors, you may conclude that your factor structure is different from those previously obtained with the same measures when the difference might just be sampling error (or perhaps even rounding error by the different algorithms used by various packages). Look at solutions with more and fewer factors to see what you gain and what you lose in the process. Better yet (and reflecting a real bias I have), consider a confirmatory factoring procedure as discussed in Chapter 7; if you have a theory which specifies how these variables should be organized, test the factor structure implied by that theory directly.

Other Initial Component Solutions

Although PCs are very important, they are not the only type of components. I have already noted two others that were quite popular in the days before computers made eigenanalysis rather simple. One is the *centroid* method, based on successive equally weighted sums, and the other is the *square root* (*solid staircase,*[5] *diagonal, pivotal condensation*) method, which is simply a

---

[5] So named because its pattern matrix looks like a "staircase," with all entries above the diagonal equal to .0.

Cholesky decomposition of **R**. The variances accounted for by successive centroid factors are often very similar to the variances accounted for by successive PCs, because there usually is little difference between the equal weighting of the centroid method and the differential (optimal) weighting of the PC solution (assuming variables are properly signed), another illustration that, often, "it don't make no nevermind." The square root method is also useful as a technique to obtain partial correlations (Nunnally, 1978).

Factor Definition and Rotation

Despite their many useful mathematical properties, PCs and related direct solutions usually do not provide the most useful way to describe data. The original solution is usually *rotated* to make it more interpretable.[6]

A suitable rotation can accomplish two objectives. One is that the resulting factor will fall "closer" to relevant variables in a geometric sense to be illustrated below. This allows the investigator to separate those variables that "belong" to the factor from those that do not. In contrast, correlations between individual variables and a given factor tend to be relatively homogeneous (except possibly for sign), so that the factor is not clearly defined by any particular group of variables. In addition, successive PCs explain maximal amounts of variance that remains, by definition. Consequently, they are of unequal importance. Rotated factors can be more nearly equal in the variance they explain and are thus of more nearly equal importance.

In order to appreciate the process of rotation more fully, familiarization with distinctions among various types of factors is useful.

1. A *general* factor is one on which all variables included in the data set have high loadings.
2. A *group* factor is one on which at least two but less than all variables have high loadings.
3. A *singlet* factor is one on which one and only variable has a high loading. It is somewhat like a *unique* factor in common factor analysis. However, a singlet factor may arise in a component solution and loadings of other variables are not constrained to be *exactly* zero, whereas unique factors are by-product of the common factor model and loadings of other variables are constrained to be .0.
4. A *unipolar* factor is a group or general factor on which all variables load in

---

[6] The MMPI is somewhat of an exception to be discussed in the Chapter 7. The first PC of the MMPI's 14 scales is very closely related to what is called "profile elevation" by users of that test—the tendency to endorse items that psychiatrically impaired individuals also endorse. Likewise, the second PC is closely related to the test taking attitudes of the respondent—whether they are trying to project a favorable or unfavorable self-image, and the third PC is closely related to what may be called optimism versus pessimism.

the *same* direction. Usually, the loadings are all positive. (If all loadings are negative, all signs may be reversed, a process known as *reflection*.) The first PC in Table 6-2 is a unipolar factor.

5. A *bipolar* factor is a factor on which at least one variable has a substantial positive loading and at least one other variable has a substantial negative loading. The second PC in Table 6-2 is a bipolar factor.

"Loadings" of variables may be defined in terms of either pattern elements (beta weights) or structure elements (correlations), which will be numerically the same in an orthogonal solution. One reason to use the structure matrix for interpretation, regardless of whether the solution is orthogonal or oblique, is that it is less affected by sampling error than the pattern matrix. The issue is the same as was discussed in Chapters 4 and 5 relative to the instability of regression weights. A point in favor of using the pattern matrix is that the weighting of each factor in predicting the variable adjusts for the remaining factors.

A structure weight of .3 in absolute magnitude indicates a 10% overlap in variance between variable and factor. This .3 value is a commonly used cutoff to define variables that are important to the definition of a factor (*salients*). The choice of .3 as a cutoff is just a rule of thumb. It may also be used if a decision is to be based on the pattern matrix but it is a common practice to use a higher cutoff when the variance accounted for by that factor is high.

Factor Definition

For all the mathematical elegance of factor analysis, it is of little use to the empirically oriented researcher unless the emerging factors are psychologically interpretable. As a matter of fact, the most difficult problem in exploratory factor analysis is to define the resulting factors. There are several considerations involved in defining factors, some of which have much to do with personal philosophy, preference, and context in the sense that different factor solutions for the same set of data can each be meaningful. Many data sets can be factored to preserve a general factor or to distribute general factor variance among several group factors, simply by choice of different rotation methods. The choice of different rotation methods arises because of the inherent ambiguity of the definition of a factor structure. A related issue is whether to allow factors to be correlated or require them to be orthogonal.

Whether or not to retain a general factor is a historical issue. Spearman (1904) reflected the British philosophical tradition by believing in the unity of mental processes. He reasoned that if a single factor did underlie cognitive ability, intercorrelations among relevant ability tests should possess a particular structure—each test should measure one and only one trait (general intelligence or "*g*") plus random error. One important implication of Spearman's model is that *if all systematic variance is contained in a general factor, then a matrix of intercorrelations will be of rank one once measurement error is removed.*

Thurstone's (cf. Thurstone, 1947) work, among others, makes it clear that more than one factor is needed to explain variation in cognitive ability. Once a general factor is removed from the data, group factors remain, reflecting systematic relationships among subsets of variables. However, the consequences of the need for group factors raised various issues. One issue was whether or not group factors should be orthogonal to each other. A second issue reflected a dispute between Karl Holzinger and L.L. Thurstone about the role of "*g*".

Holzinger and Swineford (1937) attempted to work within the Spearman tradition. He preferred solutions in which a "*g*" factor plus some group factors resulted. His approach to factoring provides what is called a *bifactor* pattern. On the other hand, Thurstone (1947) represented a contrasting philosophical tradition, which views the mind in terms of multiple "faculties" or loosely related cognitive abilities. This view led him to rotate in such as way as to minimize "*g*".

Three things are important to note about the preceding brief discussion of a very complex issue. One is that the Thurstonian tradition has dominated American psychology. A second is that a great deal of work with factor analysis has nothing to do with measures of cognitive ability. Thurstone's view may not be applicable in those areas. Therefore, the blind acceptance of default rotations may inadvertently bias individuals toward the Thurstone tradition. The third is that rather than being an argument against factor analysis, which is one point of view over the Spearman–Holzinger versus Thurstone dispute, one could argue that factor analysis demonstrates how different perspectives can each be valuable and that certain issues are not resolvable empirically.

Simple Structure

The dominant approach to exploratory factoring is the goal of achieving what Thurstone (1947) termed *simple structure*. Simple structure implies five general properties:

1. Each variable should have a loading that is nearly zero on at least one factor.
2. Each factor should contain more than one variable whose loadings are nearly .0.
3. Given any pair of factors, A and B, some variables should load on A but not on B and others should load on B but not on A.
4. For any pair of factors, A and B, many variables should not load on either A or B.
5. For any pair of factors, A and B, only a few variables should load on both A and B.

Normally, simple structure requires factors to be correlated.

Many situations dictate that data be described in terms of a series of group factors, making simple structure important. However, many other situations dictate the retention of a general factor.

PC versus Simple Structure

Clearly, the PC solution for our six hypothetical tests does not meet the criteria for simple structure. Each variable loads on both PCs; hence, only one of Thurstone's conditions for simple structure (5) holds. The example is typical of many real-world situations, especially those leading to correlation matrices with positive manifold.

In any situation where R has positive manifold like the present, PC_I measures what all the tests have in common. Specifically, and by definition, PC_I maximizes the sum of squared factor loadings. Hence, it provides one definition of "g." The definition of tests does depend on which tests were sampled, however.

The PC_{II} is a bipolar factor, as it will always be the case when there is positive manifold, which contrasts what the Tinkers, Evers, and Chance tests have in common versus what the Larry, Curly, and Moe tests have in common.

One argument for simple structure is that it is useful to know what a factor measures and what that factor does *not* measure. Also, bipolar factors of cognitive abilities are not easiest things to conceptualize. In the present case, positive factor scores on PC_{II} mean that the person is more verbal than quantitative, and negative factor scores mean that the person is more quantitative than verbal. Hence, PC_{II} does not describe a unitary type of intelligence. It describes the *difference* between two kinds of intelligence. In some settings, however, such as personality assessment, bipolar factors can describe meaningful and unitary traits like introversion-extroversion.

Another problem is that, by definition, successive PCs account for maximal amounts of residual variance. Consequently, the average factor loadings will become progressively smaller (compare the individual loadings of PC_I and PC_{II}), and it is progressively more difficult to find salient variables on successive factors, whether or not there is positive manifold. Mathematically, it is quite possible for a component to meet a conventional criterion for "importance" and be a singlet factor. When that happens, one will have difficulty in finding what specific property of a given variable made that factor important, since it probably will also load on another factor. Even worse, the factor may meet statistical criteria for "importance" but contain only trivial loadings.

The factor structure of the hypothetical test data may be simply described by noting that it contains a verbal ability group factor and a numerical ability group factor. This interpretation simplifies discussion of the factors, but is perhaps test understood from a geometric standpoint.

Graphic Representation

Figure 6-1a contains the PC solution. All I have done is to use the loadings on PC_I as the abcissa (X coordinate) and the loadings on PC_{II} as the ordinate (Y coordinate). Were the solution to demand three or more factors, it would become difficult to visualize the results in a single graph. The standard practice is to look at a series of graphs each containing a pair of factors.

Even though Fig. 6-1 contains no new information, it makes the "group-ings" of X_1, X_2, and X_3 and of X_4, X_5, and X_6 more apparent to the eye. The graph also illustrates why the utility of an unrotated PC solution is limited. Note how the X and Y axes "float free" of the six variables in that none of the points are located near either axis. *A factor is most easily interpreted when points denoting variables fall near the axis that represents the factor.*

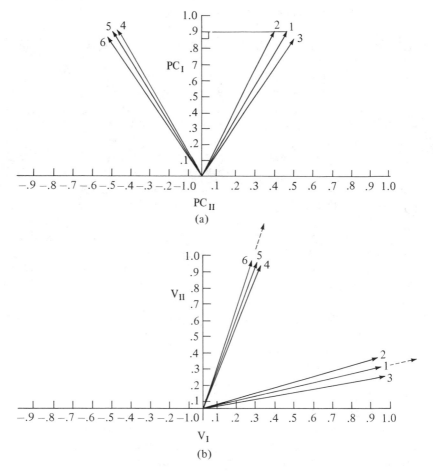

FIGURE 6-1. Factor structures corresponding to Table 6-2: (a) Principal component solution; (b) varimax rotation.

Figure 6-1b contains the points redrawn relative to a different pair of axes. These points were determined by a specific means of rotation called *varimax*. I will discuss the varimax rotation in more detail later in this chapter. However, I could have obtained similar results graphically. I located a new axis, which I called V_1, roughly 45 degrees from the old X axis, PC_I. (Conventionally, the angle of rotation, symbolized θ for the general case, is measured *from* the original axis *to* the new axis, in the *counterclockwise* direction.) In order to maintain orthogonality, I also obtained a second axis (V_{II}) by rotating the original Y axis (PC_{II}) by 45 degrees. Physically rotating one of the two panels should convince you that the relations *among* the points are unchanged, only the *axes* that provide a frame of reference are changed.

Clearly, the points fall closer to the new axes (V_I and V_{II}) than to the original axes (the PCs). Tests X_1, X_2, and X_3 now fall very close to the V_{II} axis, and tests X_4, X_5, and X_6 fall very close to the V_I axis. V_I thus can be thought of as a relatively pure measure of numerical ability, and V_{II} can be thought of as a relatively pure measure of verbal ability. You might choose to argue that an even better solution is represented by the dashed lines that actually pass through the clumps of points. To do so is to argue for an oblique solution. Experienced factor analysts might prefer an oblique solution to an orthogonal solution in this case. The properties of an oblique rotation will be considered later in this chapter.

Both graphs contain other important features. Draw lines from the origin to each of the points. Note that the lines (*vectors*, since they describe line segments) are all of unit length. This is because I chose a *component* solution that treats all of the variance contained in each variable as systematic, and employed standardized variables. Had I chosen a common factor solution, the length of the vectors would have been less than one because only a portion of each variable's variance would have entered into the analysis.

The more general outcome with orthogonal factors is that the length of each vector with respect to a given pair of factors is the square root of the sum of the two squared factor loadings. The result follows from the Pythagorean theorem, Eq. (4-3). The total length of the vectors in a component solution, taking all factors into account, is 1.0. It is more complicated to describe a vector's length when factors are oblique.

Now, note the line drawn from the point corresponding to X_1 to the PC_I axis. The point of intersection with the axis is called its *projection*. The line connecting point and projection will also be parallel to the Y axis. If the vector is of unit length, as it is here, the length of the projection will equal the cosine of the angle between that vector and the PC_I axis. Because the cosine between two angles is equivalent to the correlation between two standardized variables (cf. Chapter 3), the projection represents the loading of that variable on PC_I. Similarly, the projection of the point onto the PC_{II} axis represents the loading of X_1 on PC_{II}.

As noted in Chapter 3, a rigid (orthogonal) rotation can be represented mathematically by an *orthonormal transformation matrix* of the form:

$$\begin{bmatrix} \cos(x) & -\sin(x) \\ \sin(x) & \cos(x) \end{bmatrix}$$

If I refer to the matrix as **T**, the matrix product **BT** takes a set of loadings relative to one coordinate system (here, but not necessarily, a set of PCs) and expresses the relations among the varibles relative to a new coordinate system (here, but not necessarily, a varimax rotation). The new pattern (**B*** = **BT**) will preserve all the relations among the variables present in the original pattern matrix but can present the information in a more useful manner.

Analytic Orthogonal Rotation

In order to transform **B** orthogonally into **B***, all one needs is a suitable rotation angle, θ, for all pairs of axes. Choice of rotation angle was made visually before the computer era. Rotations are now usually performed to satisfy one of several possible mathematical criterion. Numerous criteria exist. However, *varimax* (Kaiser, 1958) is clearly the most popular one, primarily because it most closely approximates orthogonal simple structure. Varimax rotation has largely replaced an earlier analytic solution, *quartimax* (Ferguson, 1954) even though there are situations where thought would dictate that the latter is preferable. Generally speaking, varimax tends to represent the goals of the Thurstonian tradition, and quartimax tends to represent the goals of the Spearman–Holzinger tradition.

I will describe quartimax first because it is somewhat simpler. The goal of a quartimax rotation is to make the loadings on each *row* (that is, for each *variable*) of the pattern matrix as large (close to 1.0) or as small (close to .0) as possible in absolute value. The purpose is to maximize the variance of squared factor loadings in a rowwise manner. Since a variance involves squaring terms and the terms being squared are themselves squares (of factor loadings), one works with fourth powers, hence the prefix "quarti."

The logic used by Ferguson (1954) and others working at about the same time (Carroll, 1953; Neuhaus & Wrigley, 1954) is most elegant. They noted that since the sum of squared factor loadings across rows is invariant:

$$h^2 = \sum b^2$$

This equality holds for all variables individually and, therefore, collectively. One may square both sides of the equation, leading to a sum of h^4 values on the left-hand side of the equation. The right-hand side consists of two types of expressions. One is the sum of fourth powers of b (b^4). The other consists of cross products of b^2 values for a given variable on pairs of factors. The result is nothing other than an expansion of $(X + Y)^2$ into $X^2 + Y^2 + 2XY$. The first two terms (X^2 and Y^2) represent the b^4 terms and $2XY$ corresponds to crossproducts of b^2 terms for different factors.

In quartimax, the b^4 terms are maximized, which is equivalent to minimizing the squared cross-product terms, as the two terms add to a constant.

Maximizing b^4 accomplishes the objective of making the absolute values of loadings across rows as large or as small as possible.

For any pair of factors, the angle needed to achieve the quartimax criterion can be readily determined through calculus. Because it is complex and already available in all major statistical packages, I will refer you to Harman (1976, pp. 285–286) for details.

When more than two factors are rotated, the following procedure must be used. Factors I and II are rotated through an angle of θ degrees determined by the quartimax criterion. Rotation yields two new factors, which will be called I' and II'. The process is repeated for all possible pairs of factors, forming a *cycle* of rotation. Whenever the results obtained from two successive cycles differ little, the process terminates, just like any other iterative operation, e.g., eigenanalysis.

The objective of quartimax is to simplify *rows*. It can, and frequently does, lead to a solution where each variable loads maximally on the same factor, producing a general factor. The Thurstonian tradition regards a general factor as undesirable, but it need not be so if the remaining factors are well defined. *Varimax* was developed to minimize the role of general factors and is therefore closer to Thurstone's idea. In its original form, varimax simply consisted of applying the logic of quartimax to *columns* (*factors*) instead of *rows* (*variables*). This original form typically gave rise to results that were highly similar to those obtained from quartimax. Kaiser's (1958) ingenious "trick" was to *normalize* the loadings of pairs of factors before rotation. It leads to an angle of rotation that is also difficult to describe here (interested readers should consult Harman, 1976, pp. 291–292). To appreciate the difference between the original version of varimax and normalized varimax, consider (a) rotating PC_I and PC_{II} by forming a rotation angle to maximize the variance of the b^2 values on each of the two columns versus (b) forming the angle with the normalized eigenvectors and rescaling the rotating factors to unit length. The results will not be the same and the latter, in fact, leads to solutions that more closely approximate simple structure as well as more nearly "even out" factor variances. In the present case, the quartimax solution, which was not presented, was essentially identical to the varimax which is given in Table 6-2 and presented graphically in Fig. 6-1b.

One important thing to remember about varimax rotation is that *it should not be used when theoretical considerations dictate a general factor* (Gorsuch, 1966, 1983), since it tends to destroy that factor. Even so, if the data are *overwhelmingly* dominated by "*g*," implying the variables are highly intercorrelated and thus individually quite reliable, the general factor will remain following a varimax rotation. One of the most inappropriate, yet common, uses of factor analysis is as follows. Investigator A proposes that a scale measures a single factor. Investigator B uses a liberal rule to decide upon the number of factors, uses a varimax rotation and then "shows" that there are multiple factors. But the varimax rotation method is specifically designed to eliminate the single-factor structure proposed by Investigator A, which it might well do since intercorrelations among *items* tend not to be very high because of their unreliability.[7] If the situation dictates a Holzinger bifactor solution and you wish to maintain factor orthogonality, leave the first factor as is and rotate all subsequent factors to varimax. The first factor will thus be a general factor and the remaining factors will have the requisite group structure. Unfortunately, this is difficult to accomplish using standard packages, since they apply the same criterion to all factors.

Oblique Rotations

Using the data of Fig. 6-1, one might choose to place axes as close to each of the two groups of points as possible, sacrificing their orthogonality. The resulting factor structure can now be better described by their salient variables. However, by doing so, other complications may arise.

For one thing, the factor pattern is no longer the same as the structure for the same reason that beta weights and zero-order correlations in multiple regression are not the same when the predictors are highly correlated.

In order to deal with correlated factors, I need consider some properties of them as a system of axes. Figure 6-2 contains two points, A and B, which are located within a pair of oblique axes, O_I and O_{II}.

Consider point A. The line drawn *perpendicularly* to O_I is the *structure* weight (correlation between the variable and the factor). I will designate the structure weight for variable i on factor j as "s_{ij}." Now, consider the other line drawn *parallel* to O_{II}. The distance from the origin to the intersection is the pattern element. I will maintain the notation b_{ij} to describe the pattern weight for variable i on factor j. It literally means the beta weight in predicting variable i from factor j. Pattern weights can exceed 1.0; structure weights cannot. Finally, note the equivalence of the geometry illustrated here to Figs. 4-2 and 4-3.

The relation between the pattern matrix $\mathbf{B}$ and the structure matrix $\mathbf{S}$ is mediated by the factor intercorrelation matrix, $\mathbf{\Phi}$, as given in

$$\mathbf{B} = \mathbf{S}\mathbf{\Phi}^{-1}$$

$$\mathbf{S} = \mathbf{B}\mathbf{\Phi} \tag{6-8}$$

---

[7] I will return to another problem associated with analyzing items in Chapter 12. The number of factors is related to the heterogeneity of the correlations among the individual items. Individual items can be poorly correlated because they are measuring different things. However, the items can also correlate poorly even though they measure the same thing because their distributions differ in shape. The former reflects *content* as a basis for factor structure, the latter reflects *statistical* bases. If I asked you "Do you eat ice cream at least twice a day?," I would be measuring the same thing as if I had asked you if you eat it at least once a month, yet the proportion of "yes" answers on the two questions would clearly be different, which may lead the two questions to load on different factors. *Difficulty* factors (a term derived from the abilities literature) are factors in which loadings reflect similarity of response distribution rather than similarity of content. Consequently, such factors are essentially artifacts.

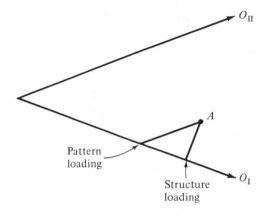

FIGURE 6-2. Graphical determination of a structure element and a pattern element.

Because the factors are correlated, h^2 (the multiple correlation between factors and a given variable) is no longer the sum of the squared factor loadings. (As noted previously, the term "loading" is ambiguous for oblique factors.) Instead, it is the sum of the products of the pattern elements and their corresponding structure elements over factors, i.e., $h_j^2 = \sum b_{jk}^* s_{jk}$, where j denotes the variable and k is an index for factors, paralleling Eq. (4-14). The matrix product $\mathbf{BS}'$ contains the h^2 values of the individual variables in its diagonal and the estimated correlations among the variables off the diagonals. *Do not attempt to compute h^2 values by summing the squares of factor loadings across factors when the solution is oblique. Likewise, do not attempt to obtain the total variance by adding the individual factor variances.*

The rather different matrix product $\mathbf{B}'\mathbf{S}$ is also useful. It contains factor variances in its diagonal and covariances among the factors off the diagonals. The variance accounted for by an individual factor may be obtained just as in the orthogonal case.

It is very easy to be fooled by an oblique solution in exploratory factor analysis. Consequently, it should not be used until you first become very familiar with orthogonal solutions. Normally, people interpret the pattern elements rather than the structure elements. Pattern elements reflect only the *direct* contribution of a factor to a variable and not the *total* contribution, which is indexed by S. With very high factor correlations, it is quite possible for a variable to be "explained" by one factor, since it can have a high b weight for that factor and a low b weight for all other factors. However, its s weight can be large on all factors.

Reference Vectors

Although oblique rotations to simple structure could be done visually, Thurstone (1947) developed a procedure based on the concept of *reference vectors*.

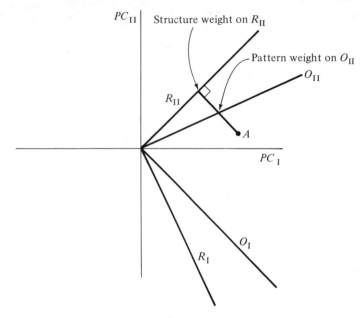

FIGURE 6-3. Principal components (PC_I and PC_{II}), oblique rotations (O_I and O_{II}), and reference vectors (R_I and R_{II}).

Because hand rotation is seldom performed nowadays, reference vectors are rarely used for their original purpose, but the vectors have some interesting properties. Figure 6-3 contains a pair of such vectors.

Suppose O_I and O_{II} are a pair of oblique factors. Now, choose an axis that is orthogonal to O_{II} (and any other axes except O_I). The axis is the reference vector for O_I, R_I. The reference vector for O_{II}, R_{II}, can be constructed in a like manner. (Do not confuse R_I and R_{II} with the correlation matrix **R**.) I have included a point (A) on the graph. Note that its *structure weights* on R_{II} are proportional to its pattern weights on O_{II}. By this construction, the reference structure weights contain correlations between a variable and a factor (the reference vector) *partialling out all original factors* (O_I in the example), save one. Pattern weights on the original factor are proportional to reference structure weights. Consequently, pattern weights index partial correlations for the same reason that beta weights describe the change in criterion per unit change in the predictor, holding all other predictors constant.[8] Reference vectors are part of the oblique rotation output in SAS and some other packages.

---

[8] In order to obtain the reference structure matrix, S_r, form the matrix product **B'RB**. Its diagonals contain the variances of the linear combinations of **B** as applied to **X**, another instance of Eq. (3-8). Form a diagonal matrix that contains the reciprocals of the variances and call the matrix **K**. Then, $S_r = \mathbf{KB}$.

Analytic Oblique Rotation

A bewildering number of analytic oblique rotations have been developed. As a result, I will not attempt to review them all here. As usual, Gorsuch's (1983) section on this topic is quite lucid. One important point to keep in mind is that many such rotation methods contain a parameter that allows you to control the degree of correlation among factors. The reason is that several procedures compromise between one criterion that produces highly correlated factors and a second criterion that produces nearly orthogonal factors. The parameter determines the extent to which one criterion is weighted relative to the other(s). If you wish to use an oblique exploratory rotation, you need to go on a bit of a "fishing expedition" with several values of the parameter. Factor patterns with highly correlated factors can look quite pretty, but such factors will be highly redundant, by definition.

As was noted in the orthogonal case, one may wish to leave the first PC unrotated as a measure of "g" and rotate the remaining PCs obliquely. The first factor, i.e., PC_I, will be orthogonal to all remaining factors, but the latter will be correlated among themselves, producing a *correlated* or *oblique bifactor solution*. Unfortunately, bifactor solutions are difficult to obtain directly with existing packages.

The Common Factor Model

Considerable space has been devoted to the component model which many investigators support, at least to some extent (e.g., Bernstein & Eveland, 1982; Bernstein & Garbin, 1985a, 1985b; Nunnally, 1978; Schoenemann & Wang, 1972). However, most researchers working in the field probably prefer a common factor model, although nothing was wasted in discussing the component model because most concepts covered earlier are also applicable to the common factor model. One reason for the greater popularity of the common factor model is that the component model does not contain a concept of error, and it is clear that some of the observed variance is nothing but garbage. Random error is granted an explicit status in a common factor model through the concept of *error variance*, which reflects the *unreliability* of the individual measures being factored. (See Chapter 12 for a detailed discussion of test reliability.) A second reason is that a variable may measure something quite systematically, but what it is measuring may be totally unrelated to what the other variables are measuring.[9] Systematic variance in a variable that is not shared with other variables in the set is known as *specific variance*. Error and specific variance jointly and independently form the *unique variance* in the common factor model. One goal of common factor analysis is to separate

---

[9] If you are familiar with the relations among the MMPI's 14 standard scales, you might recognize Scales ? and 5 (Mf or masculinity–femininity) as being relatively independent of the remaining major scales.

unique variance from common factor variance and prevent the former from affecting the factor structure.

Operationally, the common factor model involves a matrix whose diagonal elements (values of r_{ii}) are less than 1.0. One consequence is that the rank of the matrix will be reduced; hence, a given number of common factors will approximate the obtained correlations better than a like number of components. However, the gain in fit may be offset in part by the need to estimate the r_{ii} (communality) terms. The communalities need be distinguished from the *communality estimates* (h^2 values obtained from the diagonals of **BS'**). Although communalities and communality estimates will usually be very similar, the two need not be identical. *From the user's standpoint, the most important feature of the common factor model is that it weights variables unequally; the component model ordinarily weights all variables equally, whether or not a given variable has anything in common with the other variables being investigated.*

One issue relevant to the common factor model, which some view as a problem, is that good arguments can be made for somewhat different communalities. In general, all common factor models employ an eigenanalysis of a matrix with communalities in the diagonal to obtain a primary solution. The same rotational concepts may then be applied to common factors as to a PC solution.

The term *principal axis* (PA) is used generically to describe an eigenvector of a correlation matrix containing communalities. In many cases, more specific names like "alpha factor" are used to describe specific ways that communalities estimates are determined. The more specific name would be preferred in that context.

An important consideration is that common factor analysis involves relations among *inferred* linear combinations. That is, common factors cannot be observed precisely in the data in the sense that components can be. Common factors are not simple linear transformations of observable variables, as will be shown, because they are not completely *determined*. In a great many situations, your interest may be limited to relations among observable variables, in which case a component model would be preferable.

There are three general ways to define communalities. One is by a formal, theoretically based definition. The second is by a direct estimation process. The third is to define them as a by-product of the operations defining other statistics, specifically the factor pattern (B).

The following are examples of the first approach:

1. Communalities (values of r_{ii}) can be defined as the total amount of *systematic* variation. This definition assumes that *specific* variance is, in principle, zero. In other words, if a variable measures something systematically, another variable could be found that would correlate perfectly with that variable. Conversely, all unique variance (lack of communality) is assumed

to arise from random error (unreliability). Using the *reliability coefficient* (Chapter 12) as the communality follows from this definition. Empirically, common factors obtained using reliabilities as communalities will be quite similar to PCs unless one or more of the measures are extremely unreliable. The communalities obtain using reliability coefficients will generally turn *larger* than the communality estimates (values of h^2).

2. Conversely, one can use *squared multiple correlations* (SMCs) between a given variable and all other variables in the set as communalities. As noted in Chapter 4, the SMCs may be obtained as 1.0 minus the reciprocals of the corresponding elements of $\mathbf{R}^{-1}$, i.e., $1.0 - 1/r^{ii}$. Using SMCs as communalities limits analysis to that variance a given variable actually shares with other variables in the data set. Consequently, variance not shared with the specific set of variables is treated as unique. Common factors derived from SMCs will differ more from components than common factors derived from reliabilities because the SMCs will always be smaller than the reliabilities. In addition, the communalities will generally be *smaller* than the communality estimates.

3. An attempt can be made to *equate* the communalities, r_{ii}, to the communality estimates, h^2, by *iteration*. The analysis usually begins with SMCs, as in (2), as initial values. These SMCs are then compared to the resulting h^2 values. If the two sets of values agree within tolerance (which is unlikely), the process stops. Otherwise, the h^2 values replace the SMCs as the communalities. The matrix is then refactored and the communalities (initial h^2 values) are again compared with the resulting communality estimates. The process stops at convergence or after a preset number of iterations. When the process does converge, which need not occur, the communalities *equal* the communality estimates, by definition. This method is very widely used.

4. *Image* analysis is an extension of method (2). The image of a given variable is the portion of variance of that variable that is predictable from the other variables in the set, i.e., $1 - 1/r^{ii}$ for variable i. Instead of factoring the observed correlations, the correlations among the images are factored, as implied by the name of the procedure (Guttman, 1953). Although images could be obtained directly by generating scores for each variable using the other variables as predictors, intercorrelating the scores, and factoring the resulting matrix, the actual computations follow from an extremely ingenious algorithm.

Examples of direct estimation include:

1. Various formulations of the *exploratory maximum likelihood* model (Jöreskog, 1967; Rao, 1955). These models provide maximum likelihood estimates of all parameters, i.e., $\mathbf{B}$, $\mathbf{\Phi}$, and $\mathbf{U}$. Consequently, r_{ii} will be as similar to h^2 as the fit provided by the given number of factors allows.

2. *Generalized least squares* (Bentler & Bonnett 1980; Browne 1974) is an alternative criterion to maximum likelihood estimation and produces very

similar estimates of relevant factor analytic matrices. Unlike the ordinary forms of least squares estimation previously considered, generalized least squares assumes that the variables are normally distributed.

3. A third method of estimation, *unweighted least squares*, which is an option in Jöreskog and Sörbom's (1986) LISREL program discussed in Chapter 7, can be used without normality assumptions. In some ways, this method is like a component solution because each variable contributes equally to the estimation process. In contrast, variables that, on average, correlate more highly with the other variables in the set are given greater emphasis in maximum likelihood and generalized least squares estimations. Note that it was the need to weight variables differentially that originally led to the development of the common factor model. As a rule, unweighted least squares estimates differ more from maximum likelihood or generalized least squares estimates than the latter two differ from one another.

Some computer programs, such as the Multiple Indicator Linear Structural Models (MILS) (Schoenberg, 1982) and, especially, LISREL (Jöreskog & Sörbom, 1986), allow the user to specify the fitting criterion. In general, all three methods are iterative and need not converge to a solution. The maximum likelihood and generalized least squares procedures, in particular, allow various powerful inferential tests to be made. *Inferential tests may or may not be important as nearly all will prove significant in a large sample.* I will return to this topic in Chapter 7.

Examples of approaches that provide communality estimates as a by-product include:

1. Choosing factors to maximize their reliability—the *alpha* method (Kaiser & Caffey, 1965).
2. Choosing factors to minimize the average squared difference between an observed correlation and the correlations estimated from the factor analytic model (Harman & Jones, 1966). Estimated correlations may be obtained from the matrix product $\mathbf{B'\Phi B} = \mathbf{BS'} = \mathbf{SB'}$. The index of fit, which the model minimizes, is called the *root mean square* (RMS) error. The particular approach is known as *minres*.

An Example of the Common Factor Model

The example that I have chosen to illustrate the common factor model is based on the previous hypothetical test data with two basic changes. First, I added in 10% specific variance to each of the six designated tests by taking .33 ($.10^{1/2}$) times a normal deviate that is generated separately for each of the six tests. In addition, a seventh variable, uncorrelated with the six others, was added. This variable was simply an independent normal deviate, denoted the "Byitself" test. From the data, it is impossible to tell the extent to which the

"Byitself" contains specific variance versus measurement error. The equations defining the tests are

$$X_1 = .96F_I + .28F_{II} + .33F_{1u}$$

$$X_2 = .95F_I + .31F_{II} + .33F_{2u}$$

$$X_3 = .98F_I + .20F_{II} + .33F_{3u}$$

$$X_4 = .31F_I + .95F_{II} + .33F_{4u}$$

$$X_5 = .28F_I + .96F_{II} + .33F_{5u}$$

$$X_6 = .20F_I + .98F_{II} + .33F_{6u}$$

$$X_7 = \qquad\qquad\qquad 1.00F_{7u} \qquad\qquad (6\text{-}9)$$

These equations define a correlation matrix, presented in Table 6-3.

Comparing the results to those obtained with the hypothetical error-free data presented in Table 6-1, you will note that the correlations here are lower, because adding in 10% random error reduces (*attenuates*) the correlations by that amount. Also note that the Byitself test is uncorrelated with the original battery of six tests, within sampling error.

A preliminary component analysis revealed that the first three eigenvalues were 4.219, 1.395, and .988, accounting for 60.3%, 19.9%, and 14.1% of the *total* variance. The fourth eigenvalue was .113, accounting for only 1.6% of the total variance. According to the Kaiser–Guttman "$\lambda > 1$" criterion, a two-factor solution would be accepted, since the third eigenvalue was less than 1.0. Whenever an eigenvalue is as close to 1.0 as the third eigenvalue (.988) is in the present case, I strongly suggest you look at the the results of including versus excluding the corresponding factor, instead of slavishly adhering to the criterion. In actuality, the third PC was a singlet factor defined by the Byitself test (X_7). Consequently, there was no reason to retain it.

The effects of adding a third PA differ from the effects of adding a third PC. The third PC does not affect the loadings of the first two components. Hence, the factor variances and other statistics associated with PC_I and PC_{II} are unaffected. The reason is that the same diagonal elements (1.0) are used in the

TABLE 6-3. Intercorrelations among seven hypothetical variables containing error

	X_1	X_2	X_3	X_4	X_5	X_6	X_7
X_1	1.000	.901	.902	.513	.477	.443	−.008
X_2	.901	1.000	.898	.536	.519	.480	−.009
X_3	.902	.898	1.000	.462	.432	.395	.020
X_4	.513	.536	.462	1.000	.894	.902	−.056
X_5	.477	.519	.432	.894	1.000	.893	−.043
X_6	.443	.480	.395	.902	.893	1.000	−.059
X_7	−.008	−.009	.020	−.056	−.043	−.059	1.000

TABLE 6-4. PA and varimax solutions for the data of
Table 6-3

	PC_I	PC_{II}	V_I	V_{II}	h^2
X_1	.883	.457	.178	.933	.902
X_2	.852	.417	.220	.922	.899
X_3	.804	.510	.119	.945	.907
X_4	.847	−.432	.872	.378	.904
X_5	.824	−.452	.873	.348	.884
X_6	.808	−.501	.901	.304	.905
X_7	−.031	−.059	−.065	.014	.004
% Variance	.588	.184	.348	.425	.772.

different component solutions. However, adding PA_{III} increases the communalities of all the variables, which, in turn, redefines PA_I and PA_{II}. Consequently, the first PA in a two-factor solution will be slightly different from the
first PA in a three-factor solution of that same data, etc. In the data to be
presented, communalities were defined as SMCs followed by iteration. Table
6-4 contains both the unrotated (PA) and varimax solutions.

The following may be inferred from the table:

1. The PA structure of the six original variables is quite similar to the PC
   solution presented previously. However, the loadings are slightly smaller,
   a characteristic of common factor solutions, since only a portion of the total
   variance is being treated as systematic and analyzed.
2. The varimax rotation of the PA solution for the six original variables is also
   similar to the varimax rotation of the PC solution. (You may need to reverse
   the two factors from the printout, as I did, to facilitate comparison.)
3. The Byitself test (X_7) has essentially no loading on either factor in both the
   PA and varimax solutions. Consequently, its h^2 value is essentially .0.

A Second Form of Factor Indeterminacy

Components are *completely* determined by the original variables, which
means that if *variables* are used to predict a given *component*, the resulting
value of R^2 will be 1.0. The R^2 value for the ith component may be obtained
from the ith column vector of $\mathbf{B}$, $\boldsymbol{\beta}_i$, as $\boldsymbol{\beta}_i' \mathbf{R}^{-1} \boldsymbol{\beta}_i$.

The same formula may be applied to common factors, but the resulting
values of R^2 will be less than 1.0. The present two PAs have R^2 values of .976
and .929, whereas the two rotated factors have R^2 values of .958 and .947.
Typically, R^2 values of PAs are more disparate from each other than R^2 values
of rotated factors. In the present case, all R^2 values were high enough for the
factors to be well defined. Some later PAs may be poorly defined (have low
R^2 values) and therefore should be excluded. The R^2 values will typically
parallel the variances accounted for, but they are not identical in form or
substance.

I also ran a PC solution using all seven variables that actually led to nearly identical loadings. Two differences are important to note. The first two PCs accounted for more of the *total* variance (80.2% versus 77.2%) than two PAs. However, the two PAs accounted for essentially all (99.97%) of the *common factor* variance. The *total variance* accounted for by two PCs is the sum of their eigenvalues (4.219 + 1.395 = 5.614) divided by the number of variables (7). The total variance accounted for by the two PAs is the analogous sum of their two eigenvalues (2.971 + 2.436 = 5.407) divided by the number of variables (7). However, the *common factor variance* accounted for by the two PAs is the sum of their eigenvalues (5.407) divided by the sum of all the eigenvalues or, equivalently, the sum of the communalities (5.409). In addition, the RMS error (the square root of the average squared discrepancy between obtained correlations and those predicted from **BB'**) was lower in the common factor solution than in the component solution (.005 versus .039). However, keep in mind that better fit is gained at the expense of having to estimate seven communalities.

In sum, the results were like many you will encounter in that the common factor model led to rather similar results to the component model. The two solutions will be similar when either (a) most variables are highly inter-correlated, as was true here, or (b) there are a large number of variables (20 or more).

Factor Scores

You will not need factor scores in most studies. If you do, however, you will need a factor score weight (**W**) matrix to transform raw scores to factor scores.

A weight matrix (**W**) may be defined in one of three basic ways (Horn, 1965): (1) *"Exact"* solutions, which are only possible with components (the reason for the quotes will be made clear shortly); (2) *estimation,* which is used with common factors; and (3) *approximation,* which is appropriate to either components or common factors.

"Exact" Procedures

Factor score weights are obtained for a component solution by solving Eq. (6-1b) for the matrix of factor scores (**F**). When there are as many components as there are variables and no linear dependencies exist among the variables, the pattern matrix (**B**), and, therefore, **B'** will be of full rank. Consequently, $\mathbf{B}'^{-1}$ will exist. Multiplying both sides of the equation by $\mathbf{B}'^{-1}$ leads to $\mathbf{F} = \mathbf{XB}'^{-1}$. *In other words, the rows of* $\mathbf{B}'^{-1}$, *and, as a consequence, the columns of* $\mathbf{B}^{-1}$, *provide the desired* **W** *matrix since they transform raw scores into factor scores.*

Usually, however, the full set of components are not retained nor desired. **B** will therefore not be a square matrix and will not possess a true inverse.

The desired matrix is therefore the right-hand pseudoinverse, $\mathbf{B}(\mathbf{B'B})^{-1}$. As it is customary to present $\mathbf{W}$ with variables as rows and factors as columns, the pseudoinverse is usually transposed.

The factor score weight matrix derived from a PC solution is quite simple to obtain. The relation is

$$\mathbf{W} = \mathbf{V'}\lambda^{-1} \tag{6-10}$$

Equation (6-10) is very similar to Eq. (6-5). To obtain a *pattern* (**B**) matrix from PCs, one *multiplies* normalized eigenvectors by the square root of their associated eigenvalues; to obtain a *factor score weight* (**W**) matrix from PCs, one *divides* normalized eigenvectors by the square root of their associated eigenvalues.

The above procedures are called "exact" because they will produce an $\mathbf{F}$ matrix having the properties of the model *for that set of data*. However, the procedures are also subject to sampling error just as any other quantity is, so that the precision you get from using the $\mathbf{W}$ matrix output from a computer package is more apparent than real. At the same time, it is often convenient to use the $\mathbf{W}$ matrix, as it has already been calculated.

Estimation Procedures

A consequence of the second form of factor indeterminacy discussed previously and the subsequent lack of perfect multiple correlation between variables and any given factor is that there exist an infinite number of sets of factor scores that can fit the data equally well. Consequently, the "true" factor scores are unknowable. Perhaps the most common way to define $\mathbf{W}$ is through the relation $\mathbf{R}^{-1}\mathbf{S}$. This definition reveals a relationship between how regression weights were obtained in Eq. (4-10) and how factor score weights are derived.[10]

Although *common factors* may be orthogonal, *estimates* of factor scores may not be, particularly when the regression method is used. One consequence of the second form of factor indeterminacy is that matrices describing relations among *factors*, i.e., **B**, $\mathbf{\Phi}$, **S**, etc., have corresponding, but not identical, counterparts that describe relations among *factor scores*. Likewise, factor scores need not be perfectly correlated with the factors they presumably measure and may actually be correlated with factors they are not intended to measure. The lack of correspondence will not be a major problem in a clearly defined solution in which the R^2 values that predict factors from variables is high.

In theory, it is not possible to achieve all the goals desired of common factor scores. Mulaik (1972), Harman (1976), and Gorsuch (1983) discuss the various methods possible. Most of the methods lead to rather complex and uninstruc-

---

[10] The result is just a special case of Eq. (4-13). Structure elements may be viewed as correlations between variables (predictors) and factors (criteria). $\mathbf{R}^{-1}$ may therefore be viewed as the inverse of a predictor intercorrelation matrix.

tive equations, so they will not be presented here. Many computer packages allow alternative ways to generate factor scores. In practice, if a factor is well defined, in the sense that its R^2 with the predictor variables is large, different estimation methods will agree highly with each other.

Estimation procedures generally *do not* produce scores with unit variance. Their variance will ordinarily be the R^2 between the factor and variables.

Approximation Procedures

The many similarities between factor analysis and multiple regression lead to similar considerations in the definition of a factor score. In general, weights that are much simpler than those obtained from an exact or estimation process will suffice. Weight the salient variables on each factor equally. Standardize the resulting sums, if desired (which usually is unnecessary), to conform to scaling assumptions. The most important thing to keep in mind is to *examine the properties of the derived variables empirically*.

In other words, if you wished to define factor scores for the two factors above, simply define one as $X_1 + X_2 + X_3$ and the other as $X_4 + X_5 + X_6$, but be sure to compute their correlation. The properties of the two sums may be explored further using the method of confirmatory factor analysis to be considered in Chapter 7.

The basic concepts of exploratory factor analysis have now been introduced. Perhaps the most important point was how different goals dictate different factoring methods. Starting with principal component analysis, I discussed how rotations often made the results more readily interpreted. I then showed how a common factor model might be used to minimize the role played by variables that had little in common with other variables in the set being factored. The chapter concluded with a discussion of the different ways factor scores could be obtained when they are needed.

In Chapter 7, I will deal with concepts related to *confirmatory* factor analysis. Part of my discussion deals with the essential topic of replication— how you can determine the similarity of two sets of factors. Another deals with how you can evaluate the properties of proposed factors and not simply depend on those generated by satisfying certain mathematical criteria. A final part of the next chapter deals with the controversial topic of how causality may be inferred from correlational data—path analysis.

Addendum: Constructing Correlation Matrices with a Desired Factor Structure

You may wish to generate a series of measures that produce a specified factor structure. The following SAS DATA step was used to construct the seven measures used in the common factor analysis:

```
DATA;
RETAIN SEED1 SEED2 1984 ERR1–ERR7 1984
DO I = 1 TO 500;
F1 = RANNOR (SEED1);
F2 = RANNOR (SEED2);
E1 = RANNOR (ERR1);
E2 = RANNOR (ERR2);
E3 = RANNOR (ERR3);
E4 = RANNOR (ERR4);
E5 = RANNOR (ERR5);
E6 = RANNOR (ERR6);
E7 = RANNOR (ERR7);
X1 = .96 * F1 + .28 * F2 + .33 * E1;
X2 = .95 * F1 + .31 * F2 + .33 * E2;
X3 = .98 * F1 + .20 * F2 + .33 * E3;
X4 = .31 * F1 + .95 * F2 + .33 * E4;
X5 = .28 * F1 + .96 * F2 + .33 * E5;
X6 = .20 * F1 + .98 * F2 + .33 * E6;
X7 = E7;
OUTPUT;
END;
```

Note: The program simply consists of a loop that is executed 500 times. The variables F1 and F2 are common factor scores that are the same for each of the seven observed variables (X1 to X7). The variables E1 to E7 are error scores that are unique to their respective observed variables. The common factor scores and the error scores are all sampled independently from standard normal distributions using the SAS random number generating (RANNOR) function. The RETAIN statement sets a random number "seed" which allows the sequence of random numbers to be reproduced. Changing the "seed" to a different number provides a new, independent replication sample. The quantities .96, .28, ..., are the weights used to define the factor scores. Note that the sums of the squared weights for each observed variable are 1.0 in all cases, e.g., $.96^2 + .28^2 + .33^2 = .95^2 + .31^2 + .33^2 = 1.0$. Because F1, F2, and each of the error scores are independent, each of the observed variables will also be in standard normal form. The principle may readily be extended to any number of variables and any number of factors. Simply make sure that the sums of squared coefficients for each variable adds to 1.0. Note that if, in addition, the coefficients for the error scores are .0, the data will fit a component model.

The same computations may be programmed in SPSSX as follows:

```
INPUT PROGRAM
LOOP #I = 1 TO 500
SET SEED = 987654321
COMPUTE F1 = NORMAL (1)
```

```
COMPUTE  F2 = NORMAL (1)
COMPUTE  E1 = NORMAL (1)
COMPUTE  E2 = NORMAL (1)
COMPUTE  E3 = NORMAL (1)
COMPUTE  E4 = NORMAL (1)
COMPUTE  E5 = NORMAL (1)
COMPUTE  E6 = NORMAL (1)
COMPUTE  E7 = NORMAL (1)
COMPUTE  X1 = .96 * F1 + .28 * F2 + .33 * E1
COMPUTE  X2 = .95 * F1 + .31 * F2 + .33 * E2
COMPUTE  X3 = .98 * F1 + .20 * F2 + .33 * E3
COMPUTE  X4 = .31 * F1 + .95 * F2 + .33 * E4
COMPUTE  X5 = .28 * F1 + .96 * F2 + .33 * E5
COMPUTE  X6 = .20 * F1 + .98 * F2 + .33 * E6
COMPUTE  X7 = E7
END CASE
END LOOP
END FILE
END INPUT PROGRAM
PEARSON CORR X1 TO X7
STATISTICS ALL
LIST VARIABLE = X1 TO X7
```

7
Confirmatory Factor Analysis

Chapter Overview

As a general topic, confirmatory factor analysis refers to the examination of properties of linear combinations that have been defined in advance. This chapter surveys several situations in which such *a priori* linear combinations are likely to be found. Specifically, six major topics are discussed.

    I. COMPARING FACTOR STRUCTURES—Factor analyses are too often conducted in isolation from prior studies employing the same or similar variables. A very important class of procedures deals with how one can compare two set of factor analytic results in a formal manner. Perhaps the two most common errors in relating results to one another are to conclude that (a) additional factors are needed when, in fact, the original factor structure will explain the data equally well and (b) two factor solutions that *look* different are in fact different. The most basic way to decide how similar two factors are is to correlate scores the two factors generate within a sample. When variables are highly intercorrelated, quite different appearing linear combinations can lead to very similar results. Moreover, even though two or more factors derived from one set of factor weights may individually not relate very highly to two or more factors derived from a second set of factor weights, the overall similarity of the two sets of weights may be high if the two sets are rotations of one another.

    Traditionally, five specific cases may be defined that deal with the general issue of factor similarity: (1) alternate solutions derived from the same data may be compared, (2) alternate solutions obtained from the same subjects but on different variables may be compared, (3) alternate solutions with the same variables but on different subjects may be compared when the matrix information from both solutions is available, (4) alternate solutions with the same variables but on different subjects may be compared when the matrix information from neither solution is available, and (5) two sets of factors may be matched to make them as similar as possible.

    II. OBLIQUE MULTIPLE GROUPS TESTS OF WEAK STRUC-

TURE—I define a test of a weak structure as one that is limited to specifying which variables "go together." If one wishes to test that two groups of items form separate subscales within a larger scale and do not wish to test any stronger statements such as that the pattern elements for each group of items on a given subscale are the same, he or she is testing a "weak substantive model." There are several ways to test a weak model. One is the method of oblique multiple groups (OMG), which defines a factor as the sum of a set of variables that are (usually) weighted equally. The OMG method is very simple to use, and a simulated example is presented.

III. LISREL TESTS OF WEAK SUBSTANTIVE MODELS—LISREL is a general approach to building linear models that has become extremely popular in the past 10 years. This approach involves the simultaneous estimation of parameters in several matrices, including the pattern (**B**), factor correlation (Φ), and uniqueness (**U**) matrices of a factor model. Basic concepts about LISREL will be introduced, which include (1) the difference among *free*, *constrained*, and *fixed parameters*; (2) *specification*, or defining the basic relations in the substantive model; (3) *fitting functions*, which define the goodness of fit measure to be maximized; (4) *identification*, which determines whether the obtained sets of estimates are unique; and, (5) *assessment of fit* or evaluation of the results.

IV. LISREL TESTS OF STRONG SUBSTANTIVE MODELS—Sometimes, one may wish to evaluate more specific propositions about the structural relations among a set of variables such as that the variables all load equally on a factor, which I call a *strong* substantive model. LISREL-type approaches are uniquely suited to test of such models. A very important distinction is between a *nested* model (one which can be viewed as a "special case" of another model) and a *nonnested* model, which is not a "special case of another model." Two specific strong substantive models are presented—the *parallel test model*, which assumes that variables loading on a given factor have equal pattern weights and error variances, and the *tau equivalent model*, which assumes that the variables have equal pattern weights but might have unequal error variances.

V. CAUSAL MODELS AND PATH ANALYSIS—Although terminology varies somewhat, causal modeling refers to the use of correlational data to infer causation and path analysis refers to the specific application of regression models. In both cases, the questions that are asked are of the form: "Does variable A affect variable B directly or is the entire influence of A upon B mediated by a third variable, C?" In applying path analysis, one must make certain assumptions about which variables affect other variables, which variables do not affect other variables, and the direction of causation. Strengths of causal relationships are defined as regression weights, known in the context of path analysis as *path coefficients* if they are standardized and *path regression coefficients* if they are not standardized. The process of deciding upon possible causal paths involves two considerations covered in the section devoted to confirmatory factor analysis: *specification* and *identification*. Typically, path analytic models are *recursive*, which implies that if A causes B then B cannot cause A, but *nonrecursive models*, which allow mutual causation, may also be tested. An important aspect of specification is to assert which variables are *exogenous* (caused by sources outside the model) and which are *endogenous* (caused, at least in part, by variables within the model). An important part of the result is the decomposition of the observed correlations. Specifically, an observed correlation between two variables reflect (1) *direct* effects of one variable on another, (2) *indirect* effects of one variable upon another as mediated through other variables, (3) *unanalyzed* effects due to correlated causes, and (4) *spurious* effects produced by one variable that influences the correlation between two other variables. The sum of the direct and indirect effects upon a particular variable is known as the *total* effect, and the sum of the unanalyzed and spurious effects are known as the *noncausal* effect. Three examples of path analyses are discussed.

VI. CAUSAL MODELS AND LISREL—Causal modeling often uses observable variables, but it may also use latent variables, i.e., common factors. In particular, the LISREL program may be viewed as (1) a confirmatory factor analytic program for a set of exogenous variables, (2) a confirmatory factor analytic program for a set of endogenous variables, and (3) a structural program that links the two sets of derived factors by means of path coefficients.

The material in Chapter 6 can be viewed as a starting point to explore the structure of a set of interrelations. As knowledge grows about the structure of the measures, more detailed hypotheses may be formulated. The purpose of this chapter is to consider the strategies involved in testing hypotheses about factor structures.

I will first discuss how one may compare the similarity of two or more sets of factors. This situation is likely to arise when two or more factor analytic studies have been done using the same or similar variables and you wish to determine how similar the resulting sets of factors are. I will next turn to testing of formal hypotheses where the implications of the distinction between *weak models* and *strong models* will be discussed.

A weak model is one which only asserts that certain groups of variables "go together." The data from Chapter 6 serve as an example. Suppose one were to either rerun the study or, before the initial data collection, postulate that texts X_1 to X_3 (the Tinkers, Evers, and Chance tests) measured one trait and tests X_4 to X_6 (the Larry, Curly, and Moe tests) measured a different trait (test X_7, the Byitself test, will not be considered here). Furthermore, suppose that the investigator was not overly interested in whether the measures contributed differentially or equally to the definition of the trait or whether they differed in unique variance. He or she would be testing a weak model.

In order to understand the concept of a weak model more fully, consider what outcomes might falsify (run counter to) the asserted relation. One possibility is that the data contain no structure, so that the intercorrelation matrix is "spherical," i.e., does not differ significantly from an identify matrix. That possibility was considered in Chapter 6 as Bartlett's test [Eqs. (6-6) and (6-7)].

Although you might wish to include Bartlett's sphericity tests for complete-
ness, you will probably find that at least some variables are correlated with
each other if your data base is even of modest size. It is much more likely for
you to find that some other grouping better describes the data, e.g., X_1, X_3,
and X_5 form one group and X_2, X_4, and X_6 form another.

In contrast, a strong model deals with quantitative relationships among
variables that form proposed factors. One such possible strong model is that
X_1, X_2, and X_3 are actually *parallel forms* of the *same* test. Parallel forms have
(a) identical factor loadings in the sense that their pattern elements are the
same and (b) identical uniquenesses. Another posssibility is that the tests are
tau-equivalent: condition (a), but not (b) is met. Strong models essentially
assume underlying weak models—one would not test for parallelism in a set
of measures unless one had a reasonable basis for assuming they "go together"
in the first place.

The distinction between weak and strong models is my own invention. The
whole topic of confirmatory factor analysis is presently in a state of rapid
evolution. Actually, factor analysis began as a tool to test a particular substantive model, Spearman's "g" model of intelligence. Consequently, the first
formal factor analytic model proposed actually was confirmatory in nature.
However, until quite recently, the major emphasis was upon refinements of
exploratory methods. One important exception, which forms an integral part
of the chapter, is the *Oblique Multiple Groups* (*OMG*) method. This method
was developed nearly simultaneously by Holzinger (1944; also cf. Guttman,
1953), who did conceive of it as a hypothesis testing (confirmatory) technique,
and Thurstone (1945) who viewed it more as another exploratory device. Some
authors, such as Stewart (1981), consider OMG to have been rendered obsolete
by Jöreskog's LISREL model (1969, 1974; Jöreskog & Sörbom, 1986), which,
along with its variants (Bentler, 1980; Schoenberg, 1982) represents an important advancement.[1] I personally do not feel OMG is obsolete. Indeed, I feel
that OMG is actually better suited to test weak models. Many authors, such
as Long (1983a, 1983b) consider confirmatory factor analysis to be part of the
LISREL model. Others, such as Nunnally (1978) and Gorsuch (1983) consider
the LISREL model to be just one of several approaches to confirmatory factor
analysis. I will follow the latter tradition.

One problem in teaching LISREL is that even though it is a part of the
common factor tradition, its notation and terminology tend to be different
from that used historically. For example, traditional factor analysts refer to
"factors," which are defined in terms of variables (or "measures" or "items").
Users of LISREL refer to "constructs," which are defined in terms of "indicators." Differences like this tend to make LISREL appear more revolu-

---

[1] The term "LISREL" denotes two related but separable concepts. First, it is an
abstract mathematical model also known as the *analysis of covariance structures*. It is
also a specific computer program, which may be constrasted with other computer
programs performing the same types of analyses, e.g., MILS (Schoenberg, 1982).

tionary and less evolutionary than it really is. In order to improve the linkage between your textbook and the LISREL literature, traditional terminology will be used wherever possible and "translational" information will be provided at the end of the chapter after the full LISREL model is stated.

As I noted previously, I will also consider approaches to the study of causal relations (path analysis). Path analysis is one of the many models that can be incorporated within LISREL, although it can also be performed by using ordinary regression techniques.

Comparing Factor Structures

I will first consider the problem of determining how similar two groups of factors are. This problem takes several forms. Before considering each, I will state a basic unifying principles: *Sets of factors are equivalent to the extent that they or their corresponding factor scores correlate highly.* The correlation between a pair of components equals the correlation between their corresponding factor scores, but the two correlations are not the same in the common factor model. The corelation between common factor scores is a joint function of the correlation between corresponding factors and the particular estimation procedure that gives rise to them.

This definition means that you should *not* conclude that two factor solutions are the same or different simply by inspecting their respective loadings. You cannot simply correlate the pattern weights because this operation is not sensitive to the correlational structure within R. As previously noted, two linear combinations can appear to be quite different from one another yet correlate very highly if the underlying variables that give rise to them are highly intercorrelated, a situation which is at least modestly probable in many applications. Basically, what you should do is to correlate linear combinations the way the topic was discussed in Chapter 3.

Similarity of Individual Factors versus Similarity of the Overall Solution

One of the considerations underlying studies of factorial similarity is whether you are concerned with the similarity of *individual* factors or similarity of the *overall solution* in your particular application. For example, suppose Investigator A had proposed a two-factor solution for a given set of variables and Investigator B had proposed a different two-factor solution for the same set of data. One could obtain the correlations among the two pairs of factors. These two pairs of factors produce six correlations. Four involve a correlation between one of Investigator A's factors and one of Investigator B's factors, e.g., the correlation between Investigator A's first factor and Investigator B's first factor. The remaining two are the correlation between Investigator A's first and second factor and between Investigator B's first and second factor.

The similarity of Investigator A's first factor to Investigator B's first factor may be defined by the corresponding correlation, ignoring the remaining five correlations. However, many situations demand that you consider the overall similarity of the two proposed factor structures. If that is the case, all six correlations must be taken into account.

Consider the following possible outcome. You discover that (1) Investigator A's first factor correlates .71 with Investigator B's first factor and .71 with Investigator B's second factor, (2) Investigator A's second factor correlates .71 with Investigator B's first factor and $-.71$ with Investigator B's second factor, (3) Investigator A's two factors are orthogonal to one another, and (4) Investigator B's two factors are orthogonal to one another. It can be shown that while Investigator A's two factors and Investigator B's two factors are individually somewhat dissimilar, their sums and differences are the same. Put in other terms, the two sets of factors are *equivalent* in the sense that one set can be *rotated* into the other (in the present case by a 45 degree orthogonal transformation matrix), just as a PC and a varimax solution could.[2] Discussion in this section will be limited to the problem of the similarity of individual factors. A subsequent section devoted to factor matching will consider the overall similarity of two different sets of factors. Readers interested in this topic may find further information in Gorsuch (1983) and Harman (1976).

Case I—Comparing Alternate Solutions Derived from the Same Data

The problem is to compare two solutions that were obtained from the same data, specifically the same $\mathbf{R}$ matrix. In the simplest case, a direct rotation from PC or PA to secondary solution, the transformation matrix is generally provided by the package, at least as an option. The element in the ith row and jth column describes the correlation between factor i in the original solution and factor j in the rotated solution.

In other situations, you may wish to correlate factor scores obtained from two different procedures, say, a PC and a PA, or perhaps a formal estimation and a salient weight approximation. Let $\mathbf{W}_a$ and $\mathbf{W}_b$ denote the respective factor score weight matrices. It does not matter how $\mathbf{W}_a$ and $\mathbf{W}_b$ were derived, i.e., "exactly," through estimation, or through approximation, or even if the two were scaled to produce scores with unit variance (which might not be the case if a common factor model was used, depending on the estimation procedure). Let two diagonal matrices, $\mathbf{D}_a$ and $\mathbf{D}_b$, contain the reciprocals of the standard deviations of the two sets of factors.[3] The $\mathbf{D}_a$ is obtained by first computing the matrix product $\mathbf{W}_a'\mathbf{R}\mathbf{W}_a$. The diagonals of the matrix contain

---

[2] When there are just two factors, the two sets can be referred to as *coplanar* in the sense of both describing the same plane.

[3] Unfortunately, there is no ideal symbol for the scaling matrix. Were I to refer to it as $\mathbf{S}^{-1}$, to remind you that its diagonals contain reciprocals of standard deviations, it would be easily confused with the structure matrix.

the standard deviations of the linear combinations. (The off diagonals contain their covariances, which are not presently needed.) Then, $\mathbf{D}_a$ is obtained from the square roots of the reciprocals of the diagonal elements of $\mathbf{W}_a'\mathbf{R}\mathbf{W}_a$. The other scaling matrix, $\mathbf{D}_b$, is formed analogously from $\mathbf{W}_b$. Then, the two *scaling* matrices, $\mathbf{D}_a$ and $\mathbf{D}_b$, the two weight matrices, $\mathbf{W}_a$ and $\mathbf{W}_b$, and R are used to form correlations between the A and B sets according to

$$\mathbf{R}_{ab} = \mathbf{D}_a'\mathbf{W}_a'\mathbf{R}\mathbf{W}_b\mathbf{D}_b \qquad (7\text{-}1)$$

There are three things to note about Eq. (7-1). One is that even though two sets of factor scores are being correlated, it is not necessary to generate the actual scores from each individual. The second point is that the resulting matrix of factor correlations, $\mathbf{R}_{ab}$, is *not* symmetric; the correlation between factor scores i of set A and factor scores j of set B is not the same as the correlation between factor scores j of set A and factor scores i of set B. *Logically*, the two correlations are based on independently derived sets of weights. Indeed, the number of factors comprising set A need not even be the same as the number of factors comprising set B. If the two sets contain different numbers of factors, then $\mathbf{R}_{ab}$ will not be a square matrix so that $\mathbf{R}_{ij}$ may exist but $\mathbf{R}_{ji}$ may not.

You may wish to correlate a set of *factors* with a set of *factor scores* in order to evaluate how well the factor scores were estimated. The relationship is given by Eq. (7-2), which specifies the correlation between the set of factors A, as given by its structure matrix, $\mathbf{S}_a$, and the set of factor scores B, as given by its $\mathbf{W}_b$, and $\mathbf{D}_b$ matrices:

$$\mathbf{R}_{ab} = \mathbf{S}_a'\mathbf{R}\mathbf{W}_b\mathbf{D}_b \qquad (7\text{-}2)$$

This procedure is extremely useful in determining how well a particular method of estimating or approximating factor scores succeeds in its effort. A low correlation between a factor and a set of factor scores suggests that the trait has not been measured well. In a component analysis, any given factor will correlate perfectly with "exact" factor scores in the original sample, so application of the equation in that case would simply be an exercise to aid understanding of factor analytic methods. However, Eq. (7-2) could be meaningfully applied to data from a *new* sample. Under these conditions, you may wish to compare the "exact" (actually, least squares estimates) weights with simpler (e.g., equal) weights in order to see how much you gain with unequal weighting. As noted in Chapter 2, this is particularly useful when your original variables are highly intercorrelated.

Finally, one may wish to correlate one set of *factors* and a second set of *factors*. This correlation is given by

$$\mathbf{R}_{ab} = \mathbf{S}_a'\mathbf{R}\mathbf{S}_b \qquad (7\text{-}3)$$

$\mathbf{S}_a$ and $\mathbf{S}_b$ are the structure matrices for the respective factors.

The purpose of this procedure is to determine how closely related two traits are. This method does not assume any particular method of obtaining factor scores. Indeed, it does not rely on the existence of factor scores at all. Instead, it is concerned with the correlation (similarity) of factors as abstract entities.

Case II—Comparing Solutions Obtained from the Same Subjects but on Different Variables

In many situations, the data gathered from each subject can naturally be viewed as falling into two different sets. For example, suppose one were to obtain a set of k_a demographic measures and then obtain a second set of k_b attitudinal measures from a group of subjects. One could factor the entire set of $k_a + k_b$ measures. However, it is more likely that one would want to obtain one set of demographic factors from the first set of variables and a second set of attitudinal factors from the second set of variables instead of a group of factors that combine both types of variables. An interesting question would then involve how highly correlated are the various demographic factor scores and the various attitudinal factor scores.

Conceptually, a simple way to correlate the two sets of factors is to generate factor scores for each set of factors and intercorrelate the resulting factor scores. This approach is proper in defining the correlation between factor scores. However, it is not necessary to actually generate the individual factor scores, which involves large data matrices. A computationally simpler approach to obtaining the correlation between factor scores is given by

$$\mathbf{R}_{ab} = \mathbf{S}'_a \mathbf{R}_{ab} \mathbf{S}_b \qquad (7\text{-}4)$$

The major difference between Eq. (7-4) and its Case I counterpart, Eq. (7-1), is that $\mathbf{R}_{ab}$ contains correlations between the two sets of variables. The matrix is not necessarily square nor symmetric. Element r_{ii}, if it exists, is the correlation between variable i in set A and variable i in set B, which need not have anything in common.

Formulas analogous to (7-2) and (7-3) can be developed if one wishes to correlate factors in one domain, such as demographic, with factor scores in another, such as attitudinal, or if one wished to correlate factors with factors. It is far more likely that you would be interested in correlating the respective factors. For example, investigators commonly correlate a demographic factor such as socioeconomic status with an attitudinal factor such as liberalism–conservatism. It is much less likely that you would want to correlate socio-economic status factor scores with liberalism–conservatism factor scores, since any lack of correlation confounds the separability of the traits themselves with the properties of the particular factor score estimation procedure. Normally, Eq. (7-2) is limited to correlating factors with scores derived from those particular factors as a methodological check on the determination of the factor scores. Remember that one of the complications in the common factor model is that the correlation between factors is not the same as the correlation between corresponding factor scores. Also, the distinction between factors and factors scores is blurred in the likely event that factor scores are approximated from salient variables rather than estimated from an explicit **W** matrix.

Case III—Comparing Solutions with the Same Variables but on Different Individuals; Matrix Information Available

Suppose one had conducted a study using a particular set of variables on one group of individuals and had then repeated the study on a second group of individuals. Assume that their respective scaling matrices (**D**), factor score weight matrices (**W**), and correlation matrices (**R**) are available. There are two different reasons you might wish to compare the two resulting solutions. First, there may be no systematic difference between the samples, e.g., they may be randomly split halves of a larger sample. The basic issue would then be one of *replication*. If, conversely, there is a systematic difference, such as in gender, then the fundamental issue is one of *invariance* or *robustness*. Properly speaking, the latter involves both replication and invariance, since differences between the two groups reflect both sampling error and systematic differences which can be difficult to disentangle with small sample sizes. In both cases, you are performing the factor analytic equivalent of a double cross validation as discussed in Chapter 4.

Let $\mathbf{D}_a$, $\mathbf{W}_a$, and $\mathbf{R}_a$ denote the scaling, factor score weight, and corelation matrices for one group and $\mathbf{D}_b$, $\mathbf{W}_b$, and $\mathbf{R}_b$ denote the corresponding matrices in the other group. Regardless of whether the group differences are random or systematic, the similarity of the two sets of factor scores within set A is given by Eq. (7-5a); the similarity of factor scores within set B is given by Eq. (7-5b).

Equations (7-5a) and (7-5b) are really the same, but both are included to denote the importance of defining factor similarity within each sample. Because a double cross validation design is used, you will have two sets of results. The symbols "$R_{ab \cdot a}$" and "$R_{ab \cdot b}$" can be read as "the correlation matrices for the factor scores within Sample A" and "the correlation matrices for the factor scores within Sample B," respectively. The two sets of results are unlikely to differ radically in the real world, but they could.

$$\mathbf{R}_{ab \cdot a} = \mathbf{S}_a' \mathbf{R}_a \mathbf{S}_b \qquad (7\text{-}5a)$$

$$\mathbf{R}_{ab \cdot b} = \mathbf{S}_a' \mathbf{R}_b \mathbf{S}_b \qquad (7\text{-}5b)$$

The situation becomes a bit more complex when comparisons are to be made among more than two groups. One approach is to consider all possible pairs of groups, but this may involve a large number of comparisons. Kaiser, Hunka, and Bianchini (1971) suggest forming the *pooled within-group correlation matrix* as described in Chapter 2. The factors derived from this matrix are then correlated with the factors derived from the individual matrices. Their approach reduces the number of comparisons from $P(P - 1)/2$ to P, where P is the number of groups. However, some similarity between the two sets of factors will be built in since each group contributes to the pooled correlation matrix.

Case IV—Comparing Solutions with the Same Variables but Different Individuals; Matrix Information Unavailable

Suppose two sets of factors may have been obtained, but the information contained in $\mathbf{W}$ and $\mathbf{R}$ is not available. However, assume that the respective pattern matrices, $\mathbf{B}_a$ and $\mathbf{B}_b$, are available. *The coefficient of congruence* as developed by Burt (1948), Tucker (1951), and Wrigley and Neuhaus (1955) is one way to describe the similarity between the two sets of factors. Let $\mathbf{b}_{ia}$ denote the vector of weights for factor i from pattern matrix $\mathbf{B}_a$, and let $\mathbf{b}_{jb}$ denote the corresponding vector of weights for factor j from pattern matrix $\mathbf{B}_b$. Equation (7-6) denotes the resulting index:

$$c = \frac{b_{ia}b_{jb}}{(b_{ia}^2)^{1/2}(b_{jb}^2)^{1/2}} \tag{7-6}$$

Equation (7-6) resembles the formula for a correlation given by Eq. (2-8b) in that the numerator involves the sum of cross products, much like a co-variance term, and the denominator resembles the product of two sums of squares. However, it is not generally interpretable as a correlation. One important exception occurs when the $\mathbf{b}_{ia}$ and $\mathbf{b}_{jb}$ vectors were derived from standardized components. In that case, the coefficient of congruence equals the factor correlation.

Case V—Factor Matching

Factor matching deals with a related, but distinct, problem. I have thus far considered only the correlations among *fixed* factors or factor scores. I will now consider the question of how to *transform* each of two sets of factors to make them as similar to each other as possible. One procedure was developed by Cliff (1966) and is discussed at length in Harman (1976, pp. 347–352). Cliff's procedure rotates one set of factors, *maintaining their angular relations*, until it is maximally similar to a second set. The procedure is the simplest of a larger set of factor matching methods that also includes *Procrustes* (Browne, 1967, 1972a, 1972b; Hurley & Cattell, 1962), which "shrinks" some factors and "stretches" other factors to maximize the fit even further.

Cliff's general strategy is as follows. Let $\mathbf{B}_a$ and $\mathbf{B}_b$ denote two pattern matrices derived from the same $\mathbf{R}$ matrix. These two pattern matrices do not have to contain the same number of factors. Suppose one takes $\mathbf{B}_a$ and applies a transformation matrix, $\mathbf{T}_a$, to it. The matrix product $\mathbf{B}_a\mathbf{T}_a$ will produce a new pattern matrix, $\mathbf{B}_a^*$. Now do the same thing with $\mathbf{B}_b$. That is, find a second transformation matrix, T_b, to produce B_b^*. What is needed are the two T matrices to be chosen in such a way that the columns of B_a^* and B_b^* will be maximally similar to each other. (Unlike the original pair of **B** matrices, the two **B*** matrices will possess the same number of factors.)

$$L = (B_a' B_b)(B_b' B_a) \tag{7-7a}$$

$$M = (B_b' B_a)(B_a' B_b) \tag{7-7b}$$

Transformation matrix T_a is obtained as follows. Compute the matrix product defined in Eq. (7-7a), denoted as matrix **L**. The eigenvectors of **L**, represented as columns, constitute T_a. Specifically, the column associated with the largest eigenvalue represents the dimension of greatest similarity between the two factors, the column associated with the second largest eigenvalue represents the dimension of next largest similarity independently of the first, etc. Matrix **M** is defined analogously, and its eigenvectors produce T_b.

Even though the factor matching procedure transforms each of the original pattern matrices to maximum similarity with one another, the two factors may not be very similar in an absolute sense. One should apply the coefficient of congruence, Eq. (7-6), to corresponding pairs of factors in order to determine the absolute degree of similarity.

Factor matching is useful in allowing one to recognize that the overall *structure* of two solutions can be quite similar even if individual factors are somewhat dissimilar. For example, suppose that one solution produced two factors, A and B, and that another solution produced two factors of the form $C = (A + B)$ and $D = (A - B)$. It can be shown that the individual correlations between pairs of factors from the two studies, such as A and C, will be .7071 in absolute magnitude (B and D will correlate $-.7071$). A and C will correlate as highly as B and C. However, the major point is that a suitable (45 degrees in the example) rotation of either solution relative to the other will bring the two into complete congruence.

The following example may help elucidate the role of factor matching. Suppose that a test of maladjustment like the MMPI contains two factors: (1) actual maladjustment and (2) willingness to present a favorable versus unfavorable self-image (which, in fact, the MMPI measures, among other things, cf. Bernstein & Garbin, 1985b). Now suppose that a group of psychiatric outpatients vary quite widely in degree of maladjustment relative to their variation in self-image, but that the converse is true of a group of people being tested for employment related purposes, e.g., police applicants. The first PC obtained from the therapy patients will reflect maladjustment more than it will self-image, and the converse will be true of the first PC obtained from the job applicants. As a result, the second PC obtained from the outpatients will tend to reflect self-image, and the second PC obtained from applicants will tend to reflect maladjustment. Factor matching allows one to determine the similarities of the overall structure by adjusting for the differences in variance on the maladjustment and self-image factors.

Oblique Multiple Groups Tests of Weak Structure

I will now turn to a test of weak models. For example's sake, I will consider the question posed at the beginning of the chapter as to whether the Tinkers, Evers, and Chance tests "go together" to form a meaningful "numerical abilities" factor and the Larry, Curly, and Moe tests "go together" to form a meaningful "verbal abilities" factor. Assume that I have concluded that test X_7 of the last chapter, the Byitself test, is not of interest in the context of the other six tests. Hence, the six tests are administered to a *new* group of subjects. The equations defining the underlying variables, which, of course, are not knowable in reality, were given in Eqs. (6-4) as a device to generate correlation matrices. I will use the equations containing random error for realism's sake. The **R** matrix in the new sample differs slightly from the original, as may be seen in Table 7-1.

Earlier in the chapter, I mentioned two different approaches to test of weak structure, OMG and LISREL. The Procrustes method, discussed earlier, is a third general alternative, but it does not have any particular advantages over either OMG or LISREL.

Basic Approach

In order to answer the question as to whether certain variables "go together," one needs to have some definition of the term. First, note that by definition any linear combination of variables qualifies as a factor (as long as it is standardized, a trivial restriction). However, a given factor or group of factors is not necessarily as good as any other factor or group of factors. A factor is considered "good" *to the extent that it helps account for the variance of individual variables and/or the correlations among variables.* The first criterion is the variance accounted for, and the second is the RMS error discussed in Chapter 6. The two lead to equivalent results in a component solution, but they can differ in a common factor solution.

TABLE 7-1. Intercorrelations among six hypothetical tests containing error[a]

	X_1	X_2	X_3	X_4	X_5	X_6
X_1	1.000	.898	.895	.489	.470	.406
X_2	.898	1.000	.890	.526	.504	.443
X_3	.895	.890	1.000	.431	.404	.336
X_4	.489	.526	.431	1.000	.905	.907
X_5	.470	.504	.404	.905	1.000	.893
X_6	.406	.443	.336	.907	.893	1.000

[a]Correlations are based on the same equations that led to the data of Table 6-3 but differ because of "sampling error" (differences in the random number seeds).

In OMG, factors are defined *directly* according to properties ascribed to them by the model. In the present example, consider the two *equally* weighted sums.[4] The two linear combinations are $Y_I = X_1 + X_2 + X_3$ and $Y_{II} = X_4 + X_5 + X_6$. Standardizing Y_I and Y_{II} produces the desired factors, F_I and F_{II}. Either a component or a common factor model may be used. A component model is assumed in most of the discussion.

Evaluating the Substantive Model

Before presenting details of how to calculate an OMG solution, I will first discuss some of the general considerations in evaluating the substantive model you are testing. My points are simply intended as guidelines because the context in which you are using factor analysis (or any other technique) will be quite important. My discussion generally applies to LISREL too.

The first criterion is that the model should *fit the data* in an overall sense. I will use the percentage of variance accounted for to define overall fit because of its greater familiarity. RMS error is a useful alternative.

Many times you will see investigators refer to the fit of a solution (exploratory as well as confirmatory) in absolute terms. For example, the investigator might report that "two factors accounted for 81.3% of the total variance." However, the value needs be placed within an appropriate context for you to decide how well it really supports the model under investigation.

By definition, the most variance that F_I and F_{II} or any other pair of factors can jointly account for is the sum of the variance accounted for by the first two PCs, PC_I and PC_{II} (the upper limit of fit). It is quite unlikely (for all intents and purposes, impossible) for F_I and F_{II} to describe the data as well as PC_I and PC_{II} *in the sample from which the PCs were obtained*, as the latter, by definition, are optimal for the specific data set. Hence, one basic question is *how close* the defined factors come to the upper limit of fit.

Among the various things that cannot be stated exactly is "how close is close" and "how far is far." If PC_I and PC_{II} account for little variance, then F_I and F_{II} will account for even less. All leftover variance in a component solution is considered systematic, but it may not be meaningful. Residual variation may reflect various statistical artifacts. One can look at the residual

---

[4] The reason equal weights are used to define most substantive models is that there usually is no theoretical reason for differential weighting. If there were, one would be testing a strong model. The logic of how one *specifies* (defines) a particular weak model in OMG is slightly different from that employed in LISREL. Also, in the present example, I am defining equally weighted sums of z scores. It would be just as proper to test the model with equally weighted *raw scores*. Specification may be accomplished either by applying the operations to be discussed upon the variance–covariance matrix or by using the reciprocal standard deviations of the variables as weighting factors. The results of a z-score and a raw-score analysis (which is one way to conduct an *item analysis* as discussed in Chapter 12) are normally very similar unless the raw scores differ quite widely in their variances.

correlations for evidence of unaccounted for meaningful relations. I will distinguish between *useful* and *nonuseful* models on the basis of their ability to reproduce the variance explained by a like number of PCs. However, even if a model is *useful* in the sense of accounting for variance, it may not be *complete* in the sense of accounting for *all* meaningful relations. You may wish to add factors to the original substantive model by incorporating results derived from examination of *residual* variation.

Many correlation matrices, especially those derived from item interrelations, are extremely noisy and the average correlation among items tends to be low. Consequently, factor variance will be spread among several PCs. The structure is known as *diffuse* in that case. The converse case in which a few PCs account for all or nearly all of the variance is known as a *concentrated* structure (a concept discussed at length in Chapter 8). Consider the possibility that the data structure may be so diffuse that no meaningful test of any proposed factor structure is possible. Perhaps your guess that a factor structure even existed was incorrect.

An additional consideration is that the fit should be better than any *alternative* representations of the data. To say that X_1, X_2, and X_3 form one factor and X_4, X_5, and X_6 form another is to assert that the two factors are better way of grouping the data than alternatives. There are in fact two different types of alternatives you should examine. One is a model with *fewer factors*. One example, suitable to the present case as well as most you will encounter, is a single factor based on the equally weighted sum of all variable, i.e., $X_1 + X_2 + X_3 + X_4 + X_5 + X_6$, called a *single centroid model*. Given that the goal of any form of scientific explanation is *parsimony*, one should not make arbitrary distinctions among variables, thereby forming unnecessary factors.

It is also important to compare *alternative groupings containing the same number of factors*. Certain alternative groupings may arise from competing theories of how the variables should be organized. It is obviously important to evaluate such proposed organizations, if they exist. Research is typically more fruitful when different theories can be compared than when only one is available for acceptance or rejection. At the same time, simply looking at arbitrarily defined groupings can be valuable. There are situations in which any groupings of variables into a given number of factors produces nearly equivalent fit. When that is the case, the proposed model is not "special" in the sense of fitting better. When a proposed model fits no better than a model based on arbitrary assignment of variables to factors, a simpler model (one with fewer factors) will suffice.

Bernstein and Garbin (1985a) termed the difference in fit between a PC model and one based on arbitrary assignment of variables to a given number of factors as the *window* for that number of factors. It describes how much "space" there is for the proposed substantive model to fit. If it is very small, *any* model with that number of factors will fit about as well as the proposed model. Consequently, no single model can be thought of as especially appropriate to the data. A model derived from arbitrary assignment of variables to factors can fit as well as a proposed model either when the data contain a poor structure *or* the wrong number of factors have been proposed.

In addition to overall fit, one should look at the composition of the factors as given in the pattern and structure matrices to see if the loadings "make sense." In general, a variable will have a somewhat spurious loading on a factor to which it is assigned simply because it enters into the definition of that factor. However, it is still possible for a variable to load more highly on another factor (cf. Bernstein, Lin, & McClellan, 1983). Also, even though a variable is not assigned to a given factor, it can still correlate with that factor if it correlates with variables which define that factor. If the correlation does not make sense, consider revising the theory that gave rise to the substantive model.

The most important thing to keep in mind is that you should not expect one number to allow you to accept or reject a substantive model. Successful evaluation demands looking at the data from a variety of perspectives.

Alternative Models

In the course of performing an OMG analysis, you will probably need to examine the fit of several models, at least implicitly. These models fall into three categories. The first is (are) the substantive model(s) you are testing. In the present case, the substantive model is that tests X_1, X_2, and X_3 form one factor and that X_4, X_5, and X_6 form a second factor. The model is based on the theory that verbal and quantitative skills are separable.

The second class of models is used to estimate an *upper* limit of fit given the intercorrelations among these tests and the number of proposed factors. It has already been noted that the upper limit for the particular *sample* is obtainable from a PC solution. Normally you do not need to perform a separate OMG analysis in order to determine how much variance a given number of PCs (two in the present case, since the substantive model proposes two factors) accounts for as the information will be contained in the PC (exploratory) factor solution. You may find the following of use as a learning device. Perform a PC analysis and obtain the factor score weight (**W**) matrix for the specified number of factors. Use that as input to the OMG solution employing the methods discussed subsequently, and you will find it will reproduce the original PC solution. One result will be that the PCs are uncorrelated. You can therefore see if you are using the OMG program correctly.

Part of the difference in fit between the PC solution and the substantive solution is that the PC solution capitalizes upon chance. You can get an approximate idea of how much is due to chance by performing a kind of double cross validation, related to what was discussed both in Chapter 4 and in determining the similarity of factors, Case III. Split the cases into odd and even halves. Take the factor score weights (**W** matrix) from the odd-numbered cases and apply it to the **R** matrix obtained from the even-numbered cases.

The difference in fit between the OMG solution and the PCs of the even-numbered cases defines the shrinkage within the even-numbered data set. By applying the factor score weights from the even-numbered cases to the **R** matrix of the odd numbered cases, the shrinkage in the odd-numbered data set can also be computed. The two estimates can be averaged. Keep in mind that each of the two estimates reflects samples half as large as the original, so that this procedure tends to overestimate the contribution of chance to the difference between the substantive and PC models slightly.

As was also noted in context of determining factorial similarity, Case III, you may wish to compare systematically different samples to study the invariance (robustness) of the PC solution. Simply apply the PC factor score weights from that other sample to the data of major interest. Note that in all cases involving PC factor score weights, you are employing differential weightings. The differential weights are not really an exception to the point made previously, that weak substantive models usually imply equal weighting because none of the PC models are substantive.

The final class of models is used to define a *lower* limit of fit (baseline), which is important in showing that the substantive model in question is not simply one of several models that fit the data equally well (implying there are too many factors for the data). In scale-level analyses, a lower limit may be obtained from a model in which variables are assigned to factors in an arbitrary manner, which Bernstein and Eveland (1982) called a *pseudo-factor model*. Assignment should be as *independent* of the substantive model as possible. For example, one pair of pseudo-factors consists of assigning tests X_1, X_3, and X_5 to one factor and X_2, X_4, and X_6 to the second factor. Note that this assignment is not completely independent of the substantive assignment. This is because the number of tests defining each substantive factor is odd. Consequently, these tests cannot be divided equally and assigned to separate pseudo-factors. Also note that other pairs of pseudo-factors can be obtained such as assigning X_1, X_2, and X_4 to one pseudo-factor and X_3, X_5, and X_6 to the second. Evaluating more than one pseudo-factor model is useful in estimating the range of outcomes that can be formed by arbitrary groupings.

In most cases, you will probably be computing the single centroid model obtained from weighting all variables equally on one factor. *It is not meaningful to compare a centroid model to one that contains multiple factors. The model with more factors will almost invariably fit better for the same reason (bias) that a multiple correlation is going to be larger than any simple (zero-order) correlation and one based on more predictors will be larger than one based on fewer predictors as discussed in Chapters 4 and 5. Instead, simply consider that if the substantive model fails to fit better than a pseudo-factor model; a model with fewer factors such as a single centroid may be warranted.*

If you are testing a model with more than two factors, things can get more complicated. For example, you may suspect that proposed Factor I separable from proposed Factors II and III, but the latter two are not separable from one another using criteria discussed below. A model against which you may compare the three proposed factors would leave Factor I as it is but would divide the remaining variables defining Factors II and III arbitrarily into two pseudo-factors.

When performing analyses at the item level, baselines formed by arbitrary groupings of items are often not sufficient. For reasons to be considered in Chapter 12, you may also need to look at baselines formed by assigning items on the basis of other characteristics, such as the similarity of their response distributions.

Performing the Actual OMG Analysis

The most fundamental concept to an OMG solution is a *raw hypothesis matrix* (H), which contains the information necessary to specify a particular model. Functionally, it is a factor-score weight (W) matrix, since it defines factors in terms of variables rather than a pattern (B) matrix that does the converge.

Table 7-2 contains two H matrices. One provides the above definition of F_I and F_{II} and is designated as H_s (the substantive hypothesis matrix). The second, H_p, illustrates a pseudo-factor model. I will now describe the steps involved in computing an OMG component solution.

Computational Steps

1. Obtain the matrix product $H'RH$. The product will contain the variances of the linear combinations defined by H in its diagonals and the covariances off the diagonals.
2. Form a diagonal scaling matrix, D, from the reciprocals of the square roots of the diagonal elements of $H'RH$. As was true of scaling matrices discussed earlier, this step provides information needed to transform the linear combinations defined by H which have arbitrary variance, into factors that have unit variance.
3. Obtain the *structure matrix*, $S = RHD$. The inclusion of the scaling matrix, D, is to make the specific units used for each column of H unimportant. Had you assigned a "2" instead of a "1" to define the variables assigned

TABLE 7-2. Substantive (H_s) and pseudo-factor (H_p) OMG hypothesis matrices

Variable	H_s		H_p	
X_1	1	0	1	0
X_2	1	0	0	1
X_3	1	0	1	0
X_4	0	1	0	1
X_5	0	1	1	0
X_6	0	1	0	1

to proposed factors, $\mathbf{D}$ would change proportionately. Consequently, $\mathbf{S}$ would not be affected.

4. Obtain the *factor correlation matrix*, $\boldsymbol{\Phi} = \mathbf{D}'\mathbf{H}'\mathbf{RHD}$. As implied by the name of this matrix, the factors will be correlated. Hence, $\boldsymbol{\Phi}$ will be an identity matrix and, in fact, will be very important to the interpretation of the solution. Specifically, if two or more factors are very highly correlated, the traits they represent will be difficult to separate, and you might wish to combine the factors into one. It is also important to specify $\mathbf{H}$ so that $\boldsymbol{\Phi}$ is nonsingular because $\boldsymbol{\Phi}^{-1}$ is needed in subsequent steps and will not exist if $\boldsymbol{\Phi}$ is singular. For example, if two columns of $\mathbf{H}$ are multiples of one another, the resulting factors will be perfectly correlated and $\boldsymbol{\Phi}$ will be singular. This situation is not likely to arise in component solutions unless you did something like include a series of variables and their sum in the same analysis.

5. Obtain the *pattern matrix*, from Eq. (6-8) as $\mathbf{B} = \mathbf{S}\boldsymbol{\Phi}^{-1}$.

6. Compute the *estimated correlation matrix*, $\mathbf{R}^* = \mathbf{SB}' = \mathbf{BS}'$, which contains the correlations estimated by the model as off diagonals. The diagonal elements of $\mathbf{R}^*$ are equally important, since they are h^2 values for the individual variables. Because the solution is oblique, you cannot compute h^2 values by adding the squared structure elements over factors.

7. Compute the *variance accounted for* as the average of the h^2 values obtained in (6).

8. Compute the *individual factor variances* as the diagonal entries of $\mathbf{S}'\mathbf{S}$ divided by the number of variables. Because the solution is oblique, the trace of $\mathbf{S}'\mathbf{S}$ will exceed the percentage of variance accounted for.

9. Compute the *residual correlation matrix*. Begin first by computing $(\mathbf{R} - \mathbf{R}^*)$, which is the residual *variance–covariance matrix*. It is a variance–covariance matrix rather than a correlation matrix because it contains the residual variance in $\mathbf{R}$ once the relations defined by the model as reflected in $\mathbf{R}^*$ are subtracted out. Because the solution may exhaust most of the variance, its off-diagonal elements will generally be small. Small residuals may falsely lead you into believing that there is little systematic variance left. To avoid this problem, convert the entries, which are covariances, to correlations by means of the procedures that were previously discussed—form a diagonal scaling matrix $(\mathbf{D})$ from the reciprocal square roots of $(\mathbf{R} - \mathbf{R}^*)$, and then pre- and postmultiply $(\mathbf{R} - \mathbf{R}^*)$ by $\mathbf{D}$. Also, obtain the square root of the average squared value of the off-diagonal elements of $(\mathbf{R} - \mathbf{R}^*)$ divided by the number of such terms. This defines the RMS error. The RMS error can be used as an alternative index of fit in place of the percentage of variance accounted for (average value of h^2), but people are generally more familiar with the variance accounted for as a statistic. The two statistics generally lead to similar results; hence, it is usually not necessary to present both. Models that account for large amounts of variance also leave small RMS errors.

10. Optionally, you may wish to compute the *reference vectors* that contain

the correlation between variables and factors with other factors partialled out. The reference vectors are simply rescalings of the columns of **B**. The scaling factors are the reciprocal square roots of the diagonal elements of **B'RB**. As with parallel operations, pre- and postmultiply **B** by the resulting scaling matrix.

OMG Common Factor Solutions

As in exploratory factor analysis, one may insert communality estimates in the diagonals of **R** to produce a common factor solution, which estimates among hypothetical error-free variables rather than the observed linear combinations. There are three major consequences.

One is that a "Heywood case" (h^2 value > 1.0) may arise. A Heywood case implies that more than 100% of a variable's variance has been explained, which is a *nonsequitor*. Heywood cases also arise in exploratory factor analysis and are signs that the communality estimates are too low. If you are analyzing scales (sums of items), I suggest you use their reliability coefficient (see Chapter 12 for its definition) as the communality estimate. Using reliabilities would probably, but not definitely, prevent a Heywood case.

Second, the estimate of the upper and lower limits of fit should be based on a hypothesis matrix applied to the *reduced* **R** matrix with communalities in the diagonal instead of the *original* **R** matrix with unities in the diagonal. Thus, a suitable upper limit is a PA solution with the same communality estimates.

The third problem, however, is in defining a lower limit. As a practical matter, even the worst substantive model will account for at least some variance. The only exceptions are when you add variables with a perfect negative correlation or subtract variables with a perfect positive correlation. To put things simply, if you knew anything at all about your data, you wouldn't do anything that dumb. However, it is quite likely that a pseudo-factor solution for a lower limit will not be possible for the following reason. In a component solution, two distinct linear combinations, e.g., $X_1 + X_3 + X_5$ and $X_2 + X_4 + X_6$ will not correlate perfectly even though the two only differ by random assignment of variables to factors. Hence, **Φ** will be nonsingular. A common factor solution, however, is designed to eliminate random error. Consequently, the two linear combinations, *expressed as common factors*, will have a perfect or nearly perfect correlation, making **Φ** singular or at least quite unstable.

A Numerical Example

Table 7-3 contains results of an OMG component solution of the data contained in Table 7-1. The table contains the structure matrix (**S**), the values of h^2 for individual variables, the pattern matrix (**B**) for the substantive solution implies by $\mathbf{H}_s$, the percentage of variance accounted for by the two

TABLE 7-3. Structure matrix, h^2 values and pattern matrix
for the substantive hypothesis matrix ($\mathbf{H}_s$)—OMG solution

	Structure		Pattern		
	F_I	F_{II}	F_I	F_{II}	h^2
X_1	.966	.471	.956	.012	.932
X_2	.964	.508	.935	.064	.932
X_3	.963	.404	.998	−.072	.931
X_4	.500	.970	.047	.947	.942
X_5	.477	.965	.020	.955	.932
X_6	.410	.966	−.067	.998	.936
% Variance	.572	.575			.934

factors both individually and collectively derived from the substantive solution ($\mathbf{H}_s$). Not shown in the table is the factor correlation (one off-diagonal element of $\mathbf{\Phi}$), which is .478.

The first two PCs accounted for .934 of the total variance, which is the mathematical upper limit. The two OMG factors, F_I and F_{II}, account for essentially equal amounts of variance as individual factors (.572 and .575). The sum of the two factor variances (1.147) is greater than the total variance accounted for (.934) because the two factors are not independent. The fit is therefore excellent, since it falls within rounding error of the ceiling imposed by the first two PCs. Clearly, correcting for shrinkage would not add any useful information. However, the proposed factors are moderately correlated.

Table 7-3 also provides an opportunity to examine an oblique solution in detail. In particular, note the differences between the structure and pattern loadings. For example, X_1 correlates .966 with F_I and .471 with F_{II}. Thus, while X_1 is highly correlated with the Numerical Ability factor, it also is moderately correlated with the Verbal Ability factor because the two factors are related. The pattern loadings also mean X_1 can be expressed as .956 times the Numerical Ability factor plus .012 times the Verbal Ability factor. Thus, if numerical ability is held constant, there is essentially no *direct* relation between verbal ability and scores on X_1. The results also indicate that .932 (.966 × .956 + .471 × .012) of the variance in X_1 is accounted for by the joint contributions of the two factors.

Figure 7-1 contains the solution graphically.

Table 7-4 contains the pseudofactor solution derived from $\mathbf{H}_p$ (the correlation between the two pseudofactors, P_I and P_{II}, is .867). Note that although $\mathbf{H}_p$ fits more poorly than $\mathbf{H}_s$ (.867 vs. .934), its absolute fit is sufficiently high to suggest that it would be appropriate had you not known the factors were formed arbitrarily. The fit is good because of the positive manifold of Table 7-1. *Any scheme that assigns "proper" (all positive) signs to the variables will account for a substantial amount of variance, even though the fit will be poorer than a "correct" specification by a substantive model. The result is yet another*

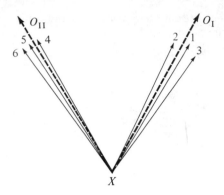

FIGURE 7-1. OMG structure corresponding to Table 7-1.

TABLE 7-4. Structure matrix, h^2 values, and pattern matrix for the pseudofactor hypothesis matrix ($\mathbf{H}_s$)—OMG solution

| | Structure | | Pattern | | |
	P_I	P_{II}	P_I	P_{II}	h^2
X_1	.925	.690	1.309	−.443	.905
X_2	.896	.757	.961	−.074	.805
X_3	.899	.638	1.385	−.562	.887
X_4	.714	.936	−.387	1.272	.914
X_5	.639	.904	−.137	1.005	.899
X_6	.654	.656	−.573	1.400	.867
% Variance	.515	.655			.867

variant on the theme stated as "It don't make no nevermind" when variables are highly intercorrelated.

As noted, there are other criteria that need be considered, and the present results illustrate their importance. First, the correlation between the two pseudofactors is much larger than that of the substantive model. Also, note how the structure and pattern are in fact more consistent with $\mathbf{H}_s$ than $\mathbf{H}_p$. Despite the fact that X_1 and X_5 were assigned to the same pseudofactor, the former correlates more highly with P_I, and the latter correlates more highly with P_{II}. The solution has "moved" from the proposed, but incorrect, solution toward a more correct grouping, an often overlooked advantage of OMG. Unfortunately, LISREL solutions do not "move."

For applications of OMG to "real" data, see Bernstein and Garbin (1985a, 1985b), Bernstein, Garbin, and McClellan (1983), Bernstein, Lin, and McClellan (1982), Bernstein and Eveland (1982), Bernstein, Teng, an Garbin (1986), and Garbin and Bernstein (1984).

LISREL Tests of Weak Substantive Models

In OMG, a substantive model was embodied within a single **H** matrix, which defined the properties of the factors. In LISREL, the substantive model is defined directly from the three basic factor matrices of Eq. (6-2), **B**, **Φ**, and **U**, through a process called *specification*. This very basic difference between OMG and LISREL should be understood. In OMG, the general properties of **H** (a type of **W** matrix) are defined by the user and **B**, **Φ** and **U** are obtained as by-products; in LISREL, the general properties of **B**, **Φ**, and **U** are defined by the user and **W** is effectively an incidental by-product.

The LISREL computer program then obtains a "best" estimate of a solution for each element in **B**, **Φ**, and **U** using the sample data and limits defined by the user. The limits are essentially restrictions on the possible estimates. When LISREL was originally developed, the term "best" meant "maximum like-lihood estimate," and much discussion was devoted to the difference between it and the traditional least squares methods such as the one employed by OMG. However, as different LISREL programs developed, various defini-tions of "best" were used, e.g., generalized least squares (which differs from traditional least square, cf. Browne, 1974), but these typically led to rather similar results as maximum likelihood. The definition of "best" is *not* a major difference between LISREL and OMG.

As with any problem in statistical estimation, the term "best" is relative to the user's assumptions about the data. Once the solution is obtained, one must decide whether the "best" solution warrants tentative adoption of the sub-stantive model. Before considering the process of evaluation, I will consider how a weak theory is specified.

Specification of Weak Models

The general process that is applicable to both weak and strong models of specification involves making a decision about each term in **B**, **Φ**, and **U**. Each element in each matrix constitutes an unknown population value or parameter. The model may make no statement about the possible values the parameter may assume. In that case, the element is known as a *free parameter*. Alter-natively, the model may limit the element to a specific value called a *fixed parameter* (*constant*). A third, intermediate, option is that the possible values the element may assume are limited to a certain range of values. Hence, the element is called a *constrained parameter*. Although any form of limiting is mathematically conceivable, normally one is only concerned with *equality*. That is, one can instruct a LISREL program that one element (called a *follower*) is to be numerically equal to another element (called a *leader*).

The present substantive model, which involves six tests and two factors, may be used to illustrate the basic concepts. It is desired to have X_1, X_2, and X_3 define factor I (F_I). Because a weak substantive model is being tested, no statement about their relative contribution needs to be made, so the loadings of the three tests on F_I are specified as free parameters in the **B** matrix. One does not want X_4, X_5, and X_6 to enter into the definition of F_I. Hence, their pattern loadings are all fixed at zero on F_I. The converse specification is used for F_{II}. The pattern loadings of X_4, X_5, and X_6 of F_{II} are free parameters, and the pattern loadings of X_1, X_2, and X_3 are fixed at .0. In sum, **B** is a 6×2 matrix with six free parameters (b_{1I}, b_{2I}, b_{3I}, b_{4II}, b_{5II}, and b_{6II}) and six parameters fixed at .0 (b_{1II}, b_{2II}, b_{3II}, b_{4I}, b_{5I}, and b_{6I}). Φ is a 2×2 factor correlation matrix whose diagonal elements must be fixed at 1.0, since a factor correlates perfectly with itself. Because a weak model makes no statement about the factor correlation, the correlation between the factors $\phi_{I \cdot II}$ (and, of course, $\phi_{I \cdot II}$, but LISREL programs recognize the symmetry of Φ so $\phi_{I \cdot II}$ is not considered in specification) is a free parameter.

Specification of **U** poses an instructive problem. Conceptually, if a component solution is desired, **U** would be a null matrix (all parameters fixed at .0), and if a common factor solution is desired, **U** would be a diagonal matrix of free parameters (all diagonal elements free and all off-diagonal elements fixed at .0). A component solution may or may not provide meaningful results. Depending on the computer program you employ, you may have to fix the diagonal elements at a very small value (say, .0001) for historic reasons. LISREL evolved from the common factor tradition (another point of contrast between it and OMG); hence, people who developed LISREL-type computer programs did not necessarily provide for component solutions.

I will always assume a weak specification in which elements of **B** are either free parameters (if the variables given by the row belongs to the hypothesized factor) or fixed at zero (if the variable given by the row does not belong to the hypothesized factor), the diagonal elements of Φ are fixed at 1 and the off-diagonal elements are free parameters, and **U** is either a null (component model) or a diagonal matrix of free parameters (common factor model). In the next section, which is devoted to strong substantive models, I will consider alternative specifications including the use of constrained parameters.

It is important to recognize the magnitude of intellectual contribution that LISREL makes. One facet of this is the complexity of the numerical estimation required; for K variables and P hypothesized factors, the data will provide $K(K - 1)/2$ known values. In general applications, there will be KP elements in **B**, $P(P - 1)/2$ elements in Φ, and as many as $K(K - 1)/2$ elements in **U**. Each individual free parameter and each group of constrained parameters must be estimated. The full LISREL model is even more general, since it incorporates both confirmatory factor analysis and causal modeling. There should be no small wonder why LISREL demands so much in the way of computer resources and why it is more difficult to use than OMG. Although it is far more flexible than OMG, LISREL's additional flexibility is not necessarily advantageous in testing weak substantive models, which arise far more often than any other application of confirmatory factor analysis. Conversely, LISREL is essential for tests of strong substantive models and causal modeling.

Estimation

The basic process of estimation starts with preliminary estimates of the unknown parameters, which are either supplied by the program or the user. Having a feel for what the estimates might be, which comes with experience, can reduce the time needed for solution tremendously. Treating the present example in component terms, there are seven parameters to be estimated, six elements of **B** and the one off-diagonal element of Φ. Treating it in common factor terms adds six more terms (the diagonals of **U**). In more complex programs, the number of parameters to be estimated can be far greater.[5]

The specific estimation process involves minimizing what is called a *fitting function*. Equation (7-8) is the fitting function for a maximum likelihood solution. The **R** is the obtained correlation matrix, **R*** is the estimated correlation matrix using Eq. (7-2) and the particular parameter set, and Q is the number of parameters to be estimated, which equals the sum of the number of free parameters and groups of constrained parameters (seven, all free); the symbol "tr" denotes the trace of the product matrix and "ln" means natural logarithm:

$$F(\mathbf{R}, \mathbf{R}^*) = \text{tr}(\mathbf{RR}^{*-1}) + \ln(\mathbf{R}^*) - \ln(\mathbf{R}) + Q \qquad (7\text{-}8)$$

Although the expression is formidable, there is really only one basic thing you need to know: the better a set of estimates fit the data, the closer **R** and **R*** will be, and, as a consequence, the smaller $F(\mathbf{R}, \mathbf{R}^*)$ will be. Just think of $F(\mathbf{R}, \mathbf{R}^*)$ as a form of RMS error that is used to describe how well a set of estimates reproduce the observed correlations.

Simply by way of contrast, Eq. (7-9) describes *unweighted least squares* estimation. It basically serves to maximize the variance accounted for, giving equal weight to all variables (as in a component model). Unweighted least squares solutions usually differ more from maximum likelihood and generalized least squares solutions than the latter two differ from one another:

$$F(\mathbf{R}, \mathbf{R}^*) = \text{tr}[\mathbf{R} - \mathbf{R}^*] \qquad (7\text{-}9)$$

Similarly, Eq. (7-10) is the formula for *generalized least squares*. It differs from Eq. (7-9) in that (1) it, like Eq. (7-8), assumes multivariate normality and (2) it weights variables according to their R^2 values with other variables (communalities) rather than equally:

$$F(\mathbf{R}, \mathbf{R}) = \text{tr}[(\mathbf{R} - \mathbf{R}^*)\mathbf{R}^{-1}] \qquad (7\text{-}10)$$

---

[5] Various results, e.g., estimates of Φ, may be described in terms of variance–covariance matrices instead of correlation matrices. My discussion will assume that results have been standardized so that correlation matrices will be output.

The estimation process terminates when the appropriate fitting function [Eq. (7-8) in the present example] is at an apparent minimum.[6]

Identification

A model is *identified* if the resulting estimates are unique. For example, the total number of parameters estimated (Q) cannot exceed the number of known values, $K(K-1)/2$, for the same reason that one cannot uniquely solve the equation $X + Y = 2$. However, having more knows than unknowns is not sufficient for identification. A model may not be identified even if Q is smaller than known values. The details of identification are complex and I will simply refer you to standard references (Jöreskog & Sörbom, 1986; Kmenta, 1971; Long, 1983a, 1983b). It can be shown that the present model is identified.

Assessment of Fit

The criteria discussed previously in regard to OMG can be applied to LISREL, although the particular LISREL program may not provide all information directly. For example, Schoenberg's (1982) *Multiple Indicator Linear Structural Models* (*MILS*) program will provide **B** and **Φ** but not **S**, which may, however, be derived from Eq. (7-8). There are a variety of other indicators that are unique to LISREL. Some, like the OMG tests, are descriptive, and others are inferential. Because of the earlier point that inferential tests derived from large samples have little meaning, since every test becomes significant, discussion will be limited to descriptive measures.[7]

One class of measures is derived from the absolute magnitude of the fitting function. One example is the *Modified Tucker–Lewis coefficient*, Eq. (7-11a). A second, and increasingly popular, measure is Jöreskog and Sörbom's (1986) *Goodness of Fit Index* (*GFI*), Eq. (7-11b). A third measure is Jöreskog and Sörbom's (1986) *Adjusted Goodness of Fit Index* (*AGFI*), Eq. (7-11c), which adjusts the GFI for the number of degrees of freedom in the model. Yet another

---

[6] One problem with any form of numerical estimation is that it is often impossible or at least quite difficult to test all possible values of the unknown estimates. A necessary (but, unfortunately, not sufficient) condition for a minimum to occur is that a change in any of the parameters causes the fitting function to increase. A "local minimum" or best solution for a particular region of values but not for all possible values may occur.

[7] Some view inferential tests as the basic reason for preferring LISREL over OMG. Several important figures, most noticeably Jöreskog himself (cf. Jöreskog, 1974; Jöreskog & Sörbom, 1986) and Bentler and Bonnett (1980) downplay the importance of inferential tests. Moreover, OMG allows for certain inferential tests, since the defined factors do not capitalize on chance. For example, one can test whether a structure element is significantly different from zero in the same way an ordinary correlation is tested. The standard error of a correlation is $1/(N-1)^{1/2}$. Consequently, any correlation larger in absolute magnitude than .197 will be significant in a sample as small as 100 subjects.

commonly used index is Bentler and Bonnett's (1980) *Normed Fit Index (NFI)*, Eq. (7-11d):

$$I = \frac{F(l) - F(o)}{F(l) - F(u)} \tag{7-11a}$$

$$GFI = 1 - \text{tr}(\mathbf{R}^{*-1}\mathbf{R} - \mathbf{I})^2/\text{tr}(\mathbf{R}^{*-1}\mathbf{R}^2) \tag{7-11b}$$

$$AGFI = 1 - [K(K + 1)/2df](1 - GFI) \tag{7-11c}$$

$$NFI = 1 - F(o)/F(l) \tag{7-11d}$$

In Eq. (7-11a) $F(l)$ is the lower limit of fit imposed by a model with no structure, i.e., a model with a null **B** matrix. It may be derived from either a maximum likelihood or a generalized least squares solution. $F(o)$ is the obtained value of the fitting function, and $F(u)$ is the upper limit imposed by an unconstrained solution, with all relevant parameters specified as free. In other words, the Modified Tucker–Lewis coefficient describes the relative distance of the obtained model from *mathematically* defined upper and lower limits. The measure contrasts with the more *empirically* defined limits discussed in reference to OMG. However, the denominator of Eq. (7-11a) is similar to the concept of a "window" discussed above. The symbols "$\mathbf{R}^*$", "$\mathbf{R}$" and "$\mathbf{I}$" in Eq. (7-11b) respectively denote the correlation (or variance–covariance) matrix generated by the LISREL model, the obtained correlation (or variance–covariance) matrix, and an identity matrix. The symbols "K" and "df" in Eq. (7-11c) are the number of variables and number of degrees of freedom, respectively. Finally, the meaning of $F(o)$ and $F(l)$ in Eq. (7-11d) is the same as in Eq. (7-11a).

In addition to statistics like the Modified Tucker–Lewis coefficient that apply to the model as a whole, there are statistics that help identify which particular parameters may be misspecified, e.g., whether it was proper to fix a factor correlation at .0 instead of allowing it to assume some nonzero value. The *partial derivative* of a given parameter describes how the overall fitting function changes with small changes in that parameter. If the value is large, there is evidence of a misspecification. One problem with LISREL compared to OMG is that a misspecified solution does not "move" to the correct solution. If a particular free parameter, particularly an element of **B**, is of small magnitude, there is evidence that it does not belong to that factor. However, you cannot easily tell whether it belongs to another factor or, like X_7 (the Byitself test) of the previous chapter, it does not belong to any of the factors at all. An inference can be made by respecifying, but the process can become a "fishing expedition" to make the model fit one way or the other, which is hardly confirmatory at all.

Numerical Examples

Table 7-5 contains the results of a LISREL component test of the hypothesis that X_1, X_2, and X_3 form one factor and X_4, X_5, and X_6 form a second factor

TABLE 7-5. Structure matrix, h^2 values, and pattern
matrix for the substantive hypothesis matrix
($\mathbf{H}_s$)—LISREL solution

	Structure		Pattern		
	F_{I}	F_{II}	F_{I}	F_{II}	h^2
X_1	.966	.462	.966	.000	.933
X_2	.964	.461	.964	.000	.929
X_3	.963	.460	.963	.000	.927
X_4	.463	.970	.000	.970	.940
X_5	.462	.966	.000	.966	.930
X_6	.462	.966	.000	.966	.932
% Variance	.572	.573			.932

that parallels the OMG solution. The results are almost identical to those presented in Table 7-3. Note that pattern loadings on the "wrong" factors are exactly zero, though. In addition, the factor correlation is identical within rounding error to the OMG factor correlation, .478. In principle, they may differ, however, since the LISREL correlation is derived from differentially weighted variables but the OMG correlation is derived from equally weighted variables. The component pseudofactor solution will not be presented, since it is nearly identical to its OMG counterpart. In other words, weighting variables *equally* on a **W** matrix with an *unweighted least square* (OMG) solution, provides nearly identical estimates of the pattern and structure elements as well as the factor correlation obtained by weighting variables *optimally* on a **B** matrix with a *maximum likelihood* (LISREL) solution, in terms of *traditional measures of fit*. Gorsuch (1983) cites an unpublished paper by Gerbring and Hunter (1980) which further illustrates the similarity of the two approaches.

However, the LISREL component solutions fared rather badly according its own measures of fit as opposed to traditional measures. In fact, the fit was even worse than would be obtained from a model that contained no structure, i.e., all variance is unique, $F(l)$. The data were actually constructed to fit the LISREL model quite well. Thus, measures derived from the fitting function, such as the Modified Tucker–Lewis coefficient, can be quite misleading when obtained from a component solution because the measures are highly sensitive to the communalities within the **R** matrix. *I strongly emphasize the applicability of a component model in at least some situations such as when you are interested in properties of observable measures.* LISREL estimates are quite proper, but the model(s) should be evaluated using traditional measures of fit such as the percentage of variance accounted for. At the same time, I should note that I am in a minority; LISREL measures of fit, particularly the GFI, are currently quite popular. If you do employ more traditional measures of fit, pseudofactor and other alternative models such as response probability models can place the fit of the substantive model in proper context.

I also obtained LISREL common factor solutions, which are generally more in accord with the LISREL tradition. The substantive and pseudofactor models accounted for .898 and .689 of the variance, respectively. The figures are each slightly smaller than their component counterpart because the total variance (the trace of $\mathbf{R}$) is also smaller. The structure, pattern, and h^2 values were also somewhat smaller. The RMS error was also lower—which reflects the basic ability of a common factor solution to reproduce $\mathbf{R}$ better than a component model with the same number of factors (although, as noted, at the expense of having to estimate an additional K parameters). The substantive factor correlation also increased slightly to .505, reflecting *attenuation*, discussed in Chapter 12 in detail. Basically, attenuation describes the fact that the correlation between estimates of error-free variables (common factors) will be greater than the correlation between similar quantities containing random error. The Modified Tucker–Lewis coefficients were .984 and .562, reflecting the good fit of the substantive model and poor fit of the pseudofactor model, respectively. Thus, LISREL indices now lead to appropriate results.

LISREL Tests of Strong Substantive Models

I have been mildly critical of LISREL because I do not believe that it is superior to OMG when one wishes to test a weak model, especially when a component model is appropriate. Now, attention will be directed toward tests of strong models and LISREL will have its chance to shine.

I hope you can accept that X_1 to X_3 "go together" as do X_4 to X_6 (because the data were constructed that way). I will now proceed to test three alternative models that will illustrate LISREL's beauty. Thus far, minimal restrictions have been placed on $\mathbf{B}$ and $\mathbf{U}$ beyond those necessary to identify the variables loading on the two factors. I will now test the consequences of (1) constraining all six nonzero elements of $\mathbf{B}$ to equality with each other, (2) constraining all the nonzero elements of $\mathbf{U}$ to equality with each other, and (3) constraining the nonzero elements of $\mathbf{B}$ with each other and the nonzero elements of $\mathbf{U}$ to equality with each other. Other models could be tested, for example, $b_{1\text{I}}$, $b_{2\text{I}}$, and $b_{3\text{I}}$ could be constrained to equality with each other and $b_{4\text{II}}$, $b_{5\text{II}}$, and $b_{6\text{II}}$ could be constrained to equality with each other but the two sets of b weights could be allowed to differ, etc.

One purpose of this inquiry is to see how much information is lost when a set of numbers that could be very similar to each other are forced to be equal. For example, Model (1) can be viewed as a special case of the original weak common factor model. The difference between the two models would be that six elements of $\mathbf{B}$ can vary in the original weak model, but the elements are constrained to equality in Model (1). Model (2) is another special case of the original weak common factor model. The difference is that the six diagonal elements of $\mathbf{U}$ were originally allowed to vary but now must be equal. Finally, Model (3) can be viewed as a third special case in which one set of elements in **B** and another set of elements in **U** were originally allowed to vary but are now constrained to equality. Model (3) can also be viewed as a special case of Model (1). In both models, six elements of **B** are constrained to equality, six elements of **B** are fixed at .0, and the factor correlation is a free parameter. The only difference is that the diagonal elements of **U** are constrained to equality in Model (3) but are allowed to vary freely in Model (1). Likewise, Model (1) is also a special case of Model (2) in which the only difference is in the specification of **U**. By way of contrast, Model (3) is not a special case of Model (2) nor is Model (2) a special case of Model (3). In Model (2) the elements of **B** are constrained and the elements of **U** are allowed to vary freely, whereas in Model (3) the elements of **B** are allowed to vary freely and the elements of **U** are constrained.

The technical term for a "special case" is a *nested model*, a very basic concept in LISREL. To say that a model such as Model (1) is nested in another model such as the original weak model means that the nested model is derivable from the original weak model by restricting a suitable set of parameters in the original weak model, e.g., by requiring all elements of **B** that originally could vary freely (b_{1I}, b_{1II}, b_{3I}, b_{4II}, b_{5II}, and b_{6II}) to be equal. Among the many types of nesting that are common besides the examples shown is the constraining of one or more factor correlations to 1.0, which is a very useful device to determine if the factors are separable. The main point to keep in mind when one model is nested in another is that *the nested model will fit more poorly and its degradation in fit is specific to the nesting parameters*. The nesting can involve elements in **B**, **Φ**, **U**, or any combination of them and can involve comparing fixed parameters with free parameters, fixed parameters with constrained parameters, or constrained parameters with free parameters. However, in order for the comparison to be useful, the two models that are contrasted should differ in meaningful ways.

The Modified Tucker–Lewis coefficients were .984 (which is the same as in the original weak model), .981, and .981 for Models (1), (2), and (3), respectively. The upper and lower limits, $F(u)$ and $F(l)$ are the same in all cases as well as in the original weak model because all models are based on the same correlation matrix and contain the same number of factors. Other indices, e.g., the GFI, reveal the same pattern. The fact that the original weak model and Model (1) fit equally well within rounding error means that nothing is sacrificed if the six nonzero pattern weights are all assumed equal. The weights actually do differ slightly, as Eq. (7-1) shows, but the differences are functionally trivial. Assuming that the uniquenesses but not the pattern weights differ [Model (2)] produces a marginal decrease in fit (.003). In fact, the uniquenesses were actually equal in the population, so the difference in fit is due to chance. Finally, Model (3) fits within rounding error of Model (2) and differs from Model (1) by .003. The small differences between Model (3) and Models (2) and (1) is the result of similarity of Models (2), (1) and the original weak model, since Model (3) simply combines the constraints of Models (2) and (1).

There are two particular strong models that are of special interest in many

LISREL applications, the *parallel test model* and the *tau-equivalent model*. A set of measures is parallel if their pattern elements are all equal and their uniquenesses are also equal. Each of a set of parallel measures may be thought of as an alternative version of the other and thus interchangeable. However, just because two or more measures are parallel, it does not mean that only one is needed. Because the measures contain independent error, their sum or average will be more reliable than any measure by itself.

Model (3) is actually a special case of a parallel test model in which all elements in **B** are constrained to equality. Had I wished to examine the parallel test model specifically, I would have constrained b_{11}, b_{21}, and b_{31} to equal each other; b_{4II}, b_{5II}, and b_{6II} to equal each other; u_{11}, u_{22}, and u_{33} to equal each other; and, finally, u_{44}, u_{55}, and u_{66} to equal each other. This would test a model in which the first three measures were parallel to each other and the last three measures were parallel to each other. Since the even more highly restricted model in which all nonzero **B** elements were equal to each other and all diagonal elements of **U** were equal to each other fit well, the model that assumes two parallel tests would have also fit well.

In the *tau-equivalent model*, relevant measures have the same **B** elements, but possibly different **U** elements. A set of parallel measures will also be tau-equivalent. Tau-equivalent measures may be thought of as measuring the same trait but with (possibly) different reliabilities.

The average of a set of tau-equivalent measures will generally be more reliable than any individual measure, as was the case with parallel measures, but it is quite possible for one or more of the measures to be relatively unreliable. In that case, the unreliable measure(s) should not be included in the composite. Even if a set of measures are not even tau equivalent, they may be fruitfully summed. Tau-equivalence, while useful, is not a necessary condition for doing so.

Many times, two alternative models will not be nested forms of each other, i.e., one cannot derive one from the other by simply restricting one or more parameters. For example, the original weak and pseudofactor models are not nested. Nesting is an important mathematical property, but its absence should not keep you from exploring the substantive models. Don't let the mathematics of the situation dictate your empirical issues.

Causal Models and Path Analysis

You have frequently heard the statement that "correlation does not prove causation." If variables A and B are correlated, it is possible that A causes B, B causes A, or both A and B are caused by a third variable C.

For purposes of general discussion, *causal modeling* refers to any approach to the inference of causation from correlational types of data. It may involve relations among observables (variables or indicators in LISREL terminology) or factors (constructs). Although notation is not precise, I will restrict the term *path analysis* to the use of multiple regression to infer causal relations among observed variables. Path analysis was first developed by Sewell Wright (cf. Wright, 1934). His influence has historically been much stronger in educational psychology, sociology, and economics than in psychology, in large part due to the stronger experimental tradition in the latter that has tended to divorce users of correlations from experiments, as Cronbach (1957) correctly noted. However, path analytic concepts have been incorporated in experimental psychology, most noticeably by Dulany (1962) and Eriksen (1960). My discussion of this topic will be fairly brief. Interested readers are referred to Pedhazur (1982) for a slightly more detailed introduction and, for that matter, on any other details of the topic of regression. Further sources include Blalock (1971) and Duncan (1975), the latter being a very basic source. Heise (1975) is useful for its mathematical rigor; Kenny's (1979) general treatment of causal modeling is also excellent.[8]

Fundamental Path Analytic Concepts

Assume for purposes of discussion that you have studied a large number of people. You have information about (a) their parents' socioeconomic status (SES), (b) their SAT scores, and (c) their income. The most general statement of the relations among the three variables may be stated in terms of a series of individual equations, Eq. (7-12a), or in a matrix form, Eq. (7-12b):

$$z_a = p_{aa}z_a + p_{ab}z_b + p_{ac}z_c + e_a$$

$$z_b = p_{ba}z_a + p_{bb}z_b + p_{bc}z_c + e_b$$

$$z_c = p_{ca}z_a + p_{cb}z_b + p_{cc}z_c + e_c \qquad (7\text{-}12a)$$

$$\mathbf{z} = \mathbf{Pz} + e \qquad (7\text{-}12b)$$

Here is what the expressions mean. Each symbol of the form "z_i" is, as usual, a z score associated with a given observed variable. Each symbol of the form "p_{ji}" or *path coefficient* describes how strongly variable i is caused (influenced, determined) by variable j. Each symbol of the form "e_i" is an error term that denotes the difference between an observed score, z_i, and an expected score based upon the variables that cause it. If the data were treated as raw scores, the path coefficients would be termed *path regression coefficients*.

---

[8] The present topics are rather controversial. I must confess that I am personally less involved in path analysis than in other areas of multivariate analysis because I have some difficulties with the concept, reflecting my background and training in *experimental* psychology, where one studies causation by the manipulation of relevant variables. Even people whose background is more purely correlational than mine, such as Pedhazur (1982), are concerned about the faddish and ill-conceived nature of much of the work. However, let's accept the utility of correlational approaches to the study of causation for purposes of discussion. In addition, recognize that philosophers struggled over the meaning of "cause" long before formal causal models were developed.

Without any theory, there would be nine path coefficients and three error terms, yielding 12 unknown parameters to be estimated from only three observable measures—the three correlations among SES, SAT, and income. As you might suspect, there are too many unknowns for a unique solution. A successful path analysis involves making a sufficient number of reasonable assumptions to *restrict* the number of unknown parameters. I will therefore assume (a) a variable does not cause itself[9] and (b) causation only works forward in time. Both should appear reasonable—whatever you are at 50 is a possible effect, but definitely not a cause, of what your parents did to you as a child. A great simplification of the equations is now possible as shown in Eq. (7-13):

$$z_a = e_a$$

$$z_b = p_{ba}z_a + e_b$$

$$z_c = p_{ca}z_a + p_{cb}z_b + e_c \qquad (7\text{-}13)$$

The model is now *identified*. There are only three path coefficients present—p_{ba}, p_{ca}, and p. Depending on the number of restrictions, the model might be *just-identified* (with as many path coefficients as observables) or it may be *over-identified* (with fewer path coefficients than observables).

The model has the further property that if p_{ij} is allowed to differ from zero, meaning that j can cause i, then p_{ji} must be zero, meaning that i cannot cause j. It is therefore said to be *recursive*. In a *nonrecursive model*, causal influences operate in both directions. Nonrecursive models generally require much more complex methods of analysis, such as LISREL, than recursive ones. Two things to note about a recursive model are that (1) the equations can be arranged so that the matrix P in Eq. (7-12b) will be triangular and (2) possible paths go in only one direction.

Figure 7-2 contains a series of *path diagrams* graphically illustrating some possible causal relationships among parents' SES, SAT, and income. In particular, Fig. 7-2a illustrates the most general case where all three causal effects are operative. Suppose, however, that there is no effect of your parents' SES upon income save what is mediated by academic ability, at least as indexed by SAT. In that case, $p_{ca} = 0$ and the result can be diagrammed as Fig. 7-2b.

An alternative is that your parents' SES influences income, there is also a separate influence of SAT upon income, but SES does not affect SAT. Consequently, $p_{ba} = 0$, and the relation is given in Fig. 7-2c. For cynics, a third

---

[9] The rather standard assumption that p_{ii} is always zero eliminates what you may be noted as a problem in Eq. (7-12b)—the sumbol "z" appearing on both sides of the equal sign. The point is that part of the equation involving $p_{ji}z_i$ on the right drops out of the definition of z_i on the left. In fact, many sources write matrix equations for causal models in a different form to eliminate this problem. In so doing, another problem arises. In Eq. (7-12b), a positive sign given any element in P denotes a positive influence. When the equation is given an alternative definition, positive elements in the resulting matrix denote inverse influences and vice versa.

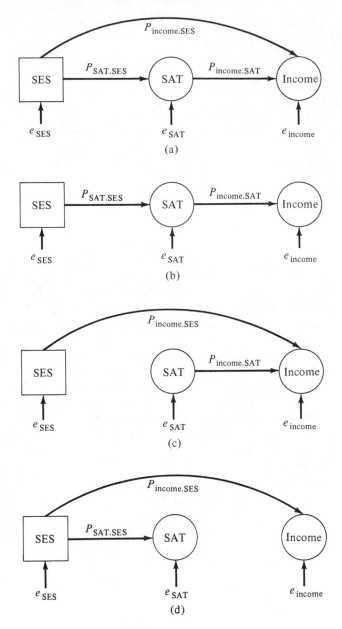

FIGURE 7-2. Possible path diagrams illustrating different causal relations among SAT, SES, and income: (a) three causal influences; (b) SAT causes income; (c) SES causes income; (d) SES causes both SAT and income.

possibility is that "its not what you know but who you know." This possibility would imply: (1) SES causes income ($p_{ca} \neq 0$) but (2) SAT does *not* cause income ($p_{cb} = 0$). The relation is diagrammed as Fig. 7-2d. Pairs or even all three path coefficients could be zero, which have not been diagrammed.

In each model, SES is assumed to be completely determined by influences outside of the model. SES is known as an *exogenous variable*. On the other hand, SAT and income are potentially influenced by a variable or variables in the model (SAT by SES and income by SAT and SES). Hence, the two illustrate *endogenous variables*. A model may have more than one exogenous variable, and the exogenous variables need not be independent of each other. However, a model must contain at least one endogenous variable. Otherwise, there would be no variables to be causally affected by the exogenous variable(s). One possible notation is to use squares to denote exogenous variables and circles to denote endogenous variables, which I have done.

Thus far, I have done quite a bit, but I haven't told you what the path coefficients specifically are or how you can obtain them. I hope you guessed that they are beta weights, because that is exactly what they are. Wright (1934) defined a path coefficient as the change in dependent variable (effect) relative to the change in independent variable (cause), holding constant all other independent variables (causes). In order to solve for the parameters of Eq. (7-13), all one has to do is to perform a series of regression analyses. There is, however, one further assumption that must be made: each residual (e_i) term must not be correlated with variables that precede it in the moel. Thus, if the model allows variable a to cause variable b, the correlation between e_b and z_a must be zero. The assumption follows from the basic definition of error—were e_b to correlate with z_a, e_b would be sensitive to something that is systematic about a.

Example I: One Exogenous and Two Endogenous Variables

The above example is a very simple one to deal with because one does not have the problem of disentangling correlated exogenous causes, such as race and parental income. As was also noted in Chapter 4, it is relatively easy to compute beta weights when there are only two predictors. For purposes of example, I will assume that $r_{ab} = r_{ac} = .6$, but $r_{bc} = .36$.

Because z_a is exogenous, it cannot be caused by any variable in the model. Hence, it has no path coefficients leading to it. In turn, z_b can only be caused by z_a. Its path coefficient p_{ba} is therefore beta weight, $b_{b \cdot a}$, which equals r_{ab} or .60. Finally, z_c can potentially be caused by z_a and z_b. Its corresponding path coefficients, p_{ca} and p_{bc}, are the beta weights obtained by predicting z_c from z_a and z_b, which may be determined from Eq. (4-4b). First, p_{ba} is $b_{c \cdot a}$, which is $(.6 - .6 \times .36)/(1. - .6^2)$ or .60. On the other hand, the path coefficient p_{ca} is $(.36 - .6 \times .6)/(1 - .6^2)$ or .0.

The error (e_i) terms are the standard deviations of the residuals, which equal $(1. - R_a^2)^{1/2}$. The values of R^2 associated with variables a, b, and c are .0

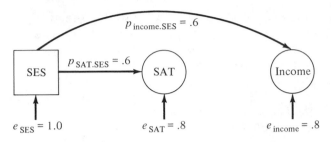

FIGURE 7-3. Path analysis with one exogenous and two endogenous variables.

(variable a, being exogenous, has no predictors associated with it), .36, and .36, respectively, as may be derived from Eq. (4-4a) or any equivalent formula for R^2. Hence, the error terms are 1.0, .8, and .8. Consequently, the variables in the model do not describe causal relations of the present data very well. Moreover, the fact that $p_{bc} = b_{c \cdot b}$ means that there is no causal effect of SAT upon income for the hypothetical data—the cynic's hypothesis is unfortunately confirmed (though, to repeat, the data are hypothetical). Figure 7-3 describes the outcome graphically.

I have now completely specified all of the terms in the model, Hence, the parameters will completely reconstruct the observed correlations. Do *not* assume, however, that the underlying substantive model is supported because you can reproduce the observed correlations. By definition, any just-identified model can reproduce all of the correlations. If I were to make causal assumptions in precisely the reverse manner by assuming that income determines parents' SES by retroactively altering what your parents were, the model would fit just as well. Over-identified models do not necessarily reproduce the observed correlations. Deviations between expected and obtained correlations can be of diagnostic value. The point to remember is that models proceding from very different assumptions about causality may all fit the same set of data equally well.

A just-identified model is therefore of limited value because it is very difficult to detect what is wrong with that particular model, i.e., to *falsify* it. In general, you should strive to develop models which have the fewest number of free parameters (path coefficients in the present case) relative to the number of known values (correlations) to eliminate weak causal linkages. Treating weak causal linkages as if they were zero is generally a suitable procedure even when these weak linkages are known to be nonzero, since weak causal linkages can be eliminated from the model without affecting estimates of stronger linkages. The "convenient fiction" that two variables having no causal linkages may be of value in identifying problems of a more major nature. If paths leading to a variable are all weak but paths leading from that variable are strong, treat that variable as exogenous to save the estimation of several parameters. Similarly, if all path coefficients leading to and from the variable are of small magnitude, eliminate that variable from the model. Moreover, adding in new variables can be of use as long as they do not enter into causal linkages with all other variables. (The new variables would create as many new parameters to be estimated as the number of data points they provide.) In sum, just-identified models are basically only of value in the earliest phases of inquiry.

In the more complex models that are usually employed for path analysis, the process of comparing estimated and observed correlations can be quite complex. One approach is to use LISREL, which will be considered in the next major section.

Example II: Two Exogenous and One Endogenous Variables

In the above example, it is *asserted*, on the basis of *theoretical* consideration, that parent's SES *caused* SAT scores, at least in part, which led me to treat SES scores as exogenous. Suppose that I viewed both SAT and SES as exogenous. Consequently, I would be treating both as if determined by unknown events beyond the scope of the substantive model.

This new assumption has two major effects. It leads to a new set of equations, Eq. (7-14), in which the equation for z_b is altered by the elimination of a path coefficient, p_{ba}, that was present in Eq. (7-13):

$$z_a = e_a$$

$$z_b = e_b$$

$$z_c = p_{ca}z_a + p_{cb}z_b + e_c \qquad (7\text{-}14)$$

The second implication Eq. 7-14 is that the model now contains only two unknowns to be estimated from the three known correlations (whose values will be assumed to be unchanged). By changing the assumptions slightly, the original justidentified model now becomes an over-identified model. This change illustrates the point made earlier of how treating a weakly determined variable as if it were exogenous can minimize the number of parameters to be estimated.

Figure 7-4 contains the resultant path diagram. Note that the path coefficient from SES to income (p_{ca}) is not changed, because the equation describing income remains the same. However, there is no longer a path connecting SES to SAT, since there is no longer a basis for assuming causal linkages between them. Instead, I connect the two by means of a bidirectional arrow to denote their lack of independence. The process of computing beta weights corrects for any lack of independence.

Looking at SAT in two different ways is more than a textbook exercise. You need to recognize how concepts are presented in different theories and then look at the consequences of the different assumptions.

Example III: One Exogenous and Two Endogenous Variables

In order to both minimize cynicism as well as illustrate some of the other possible outcomes, I will restate the problem but change the correlations so that all relevant paths are present. I increased the correlation between SAT and income to .7. The resulting path diagram is presented as Figure 7-5.

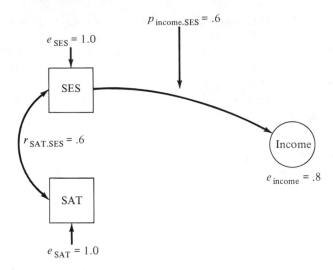

FIGURE 7-4. A path analysis with two exogenous and one endogenous variables.

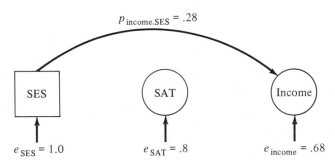

FIGURE 7-5. A second path analysis with one exogenous and two endogenous variables.

With $r_{cb} = r_{ca}r_{ba}$ in the first example, the path from b to c was eliminated, which will always be the case when a path coefficient from b to c equals the product of the path coefficients from a to c and from a to b. Since $r_{cb} > r_{ca}r_{ba}$, a path from b to c now exists, so that what you know now becomes more important than who your parents knew (were $r_{cb} < r_{ca}r_{ba}$, the causal link between SAT and income would be negative, which is unrealistic, I hope). In addition, e_c decreases and income is now more strongly determined by SES and SAT because of the change in correlation.

Decomposing Observed Correlations

Path analysis may be used to decompose correlations into four components: (1) *direct* effects, (2) *indirect* effects, (3) *unanalyzed* effects, and (4) *spurious* effects. The sum of the direct and indirect effects upon a particular variable is known as the *total* effect, and the sum of the unanalyzed and spurious effects are known as the *noncausal* effect.

The direct effect of a variable is the easiest to explain, since it is smply the path coefficient, and, hence, the beta weight. When SAT was treated as an endogenous variable, p_{ba} was .6; hence, the direct effect of SES upon Sat was also .6. Similarly, the direct effect of SAT upon income was .0 in the first two models and .53 in the last model. A direct effect of variable x upon variable y implies that a change in x is sufficient to cause a change in y.

Indirect effects arise because a variable can mediate the relation between other variables. For example, assume that there is no direct relation between SES and income but (1) SAT scores are higher in more affluent families because those families cultivate a more positive attitude toward academics and (2) income and SAT scores are positively related because entry into higher paying positions demands those cognitive skills indexed by the SAT. As a result, SAT scores will mediate a relationship between SES and income. In general, the extent to which variable y mediates an indirect relation between variables x and z is given as the product of p_{xy} and p_{yz}. In the present case, the indirect effect of SES upon income as mediated by SAT equals .6 × .0 or .0 in the first two examples and .6 × .53 or .318 in the third example. The indirect relation has an important property. If one were to hold the mediating variable (SAT scores) constant, there would be no relation between SES and income, i.e., the partial correlation, $r_{ac \cdot b} = 0$. This relation says that without the beneficial effects of parental SES upon SAT scores, there would be no correlation between SES and income; SES alone is insufficient to determine income.

The total effect, by definition, is the sum of these two types of determinants. There will only be one direct effect of variable x upon variable y, but there can be many indirect effects and the number of indirect effects increases geometrically with the number of other variables in the model if the other variables are allowed to mediate x and y. For example, suppose a model contains x as an exogenous variable and y, w, and z as endogenous variables with w and z each having paths between x and y. Potentially, three distinct indirect paths exist in a recursive model: (1) x influences w which influences y, (2) x influences z which influences y, and (3) x influences w which influences z which influences y (or x influences z which influences w which influences x, but not both). In a nonrecursive model, both indirect paths subsumed by (3) could arise.

The total effect of variable x upon variable y will equal the correlation between the two variables, r_{xy}. The relation can be derived formally, but I will not attempt to do so. The relation is illustrated in the third equation of both Eqs. (7-13) and (7-14).

Whenever two variables are caused by a third variable that appears earlier in the chain, the correlation between the two variables (their total effect) will reflect both the inherent causal relation between them (the direct effect) and the *spurious effect* of third variable(s). Consider r_{bc} in the third model (.70). The difference between this correlation and the path coefficient (.53) is .17. This difference reflects the causal effects of SES (variable *a*) upon both of them. Note that the product of p_{ca} (.28) and p_{ba} (.60) equals the difference (.17).

Finally, an *unanalyzed* effect arises from correlated exogenous factors. In the third model, the direct effect of SES upon income ($p_{ca} = .28$) is considerably less than the total effect of SES upon income ($r_{ac} = .60$). The difference (.32) cannot unequivocally be associated with (a) SES acting directly upon income versus (b) a third variable (SAT) acting upon both SAT and SES.

Causal Models and LISREL

A Formal Separation of Exogenous and Endogenous Variables

I introduced matrix equation (7-12a) before making the distinction between endogenous and exogenous variables simply as a teaching device. Now that I have covered the distinction, I am going to rewrite the equation. Note that it relates an observed score to a linear combination of predictor scores, weighted by path coefficients plus error.

The symbol "**B**" denotes the matrix of path coefficients obtained from exogenous variables, and the symbol "**Γ**" denotes the matrix of path coefficients derived from endogenous variables. In addition, "**η**" denotes the vector of latent exogenous variables (factor scores derived from independent variables), denotes the vector of latent endogenous variables (factor scores derived from dependent variables), and ζ denotes the vector of residual error. The relatively unfamiliar lower case Greek symbols are standard LISREL notation.

The resulting *structural equation* is given as Eq. (7-15a):

$$\mathbf{\eta} = \mathbf{B\eta} + \mathbf{\Gamma\xi} + \zeta \tag{7-15a}$$

$$\mathbf{x} = \lambda_x\mathbf{\eta} + \varepsilon \tag{7-15b}$$

$$\mathbf{y} = \lambda_y\mathbf{\xi} + \delta \tag{7-15c}$$

The structural model does not contain a direct reference to observable quantities. This is made through a pair of *measurement* equations. Equation (7-15b) is the measurement equation for the exogenous variables, and Eq. (7-15c) is the measurement equation for the endogenous variables. The two matrices "λ_x" and "λ_y" are simply pattern (**B**) matrices in the sense of Eq. (6-1b). As noted in the preceeding paragraph, **η** and **ξ** are factor scores. Likewise, ε and δ represent error. In other words, Eqs. (7-15a) and (7-15b) are nothing other than the basic measurement equation of traditional factor analysis, using a different notation. One other essential point to LISREL, developed subsequently, is the same process of matrix multiplication that led from measurement equations (6-1) to *covariance equation* (6-2).

The previous discussion of causal models dealt only with observable variables to keep the discussion as simple as possible. LISREL is used to evaluate causal relations among latent variables. The principles involved simply combine the previous discussion of LISREL's confirmatory factor model with the general discussion of path analysis. Basically, one makes a decision as to whether each variable is a free parameter, a constrained parameter, or a constant. Providing the resulting model is identified, unknown parameters (elements of the various matrices presented previously, e.g., **B** and Γ may be estimated.

A given value of β_{ij} and its counterpart, β_{ji}, may be both assume nonzero values in the **B** matrix. Hence, LISREL can solve nonrecursive as well as recursive models. In general, though, nonrecursive models are considerably more difficult to interpret than recursive models. All LISREL can do is to provide parameters; it won't tell you very much about how much substance there is to the model.

In addition, a LISREL analysis can proceed from raw data, an uncorrected SP matrix, a corrected SP matrix, a variance–covariance matrix, or a correlation matrix. The observabled variables consist of a set of exogenous indicators (variables) and a set of endogenous indicators.[10] Specification of the full model involves defining the three parts of Eqs. (7-15). Potentially, this might involve a total of nine matrices, three per step. However, not all problems require specification of all three equations; many important cases are simply special cases of the general model and do not require full specification. For example, a confirmatory factor analysis only involves Eq. (7-15b).

The Confirmatory Factor Model for Exogenous Variables

Relations among the observed exogenous variables (**x**) produce a variance–covariance matrix (correlation matrix for purposes of present discussion) symbolized Σ_{xx}. This matrix provides the basic data to estimate λ_x). The exogenous latent variables ξ will generally be correlated. Their intercorrelations are contained in a matrix denoted "Φ." Finally, there is a matrix containing correlations among the unique exogenous factors (correlations among error terms), denoted "Θ_δ." As previously noted, Θ_δ need not be a diagonal matrix, unlike its counterpart in classical factor analysis.

The Confirmatory Factor Model for Endogenous Variables

Relations among the observed endogenous variables (**y**) parallel those among the observed exogenous variables. Their intercorrelations produce a variance–covariance (correlation) matrix symbolized Σ_{yy}, which is used to estimate λ_y. The intercorrelations among the endogenous latent variables (η) are contained in a matrix denoted Ψ. The error correlations are contained in a matrix denoted "Θ_ε."

---

[10] I will now shift to LISREL notation, parenthetically indicating traditional usage of words and symbolism where necessary.

The Structural Model

The relevant data are the above latent variables and the correlations between exogenous and endogenous variables Σ_{xy},[11] the three matrices that are specified are the path coefficients within the endogenous set (**B**), the path coefficients from exogenous variables to endogenous variables (**Γ**), and a matrix describing relations between error terms in the two sets $\Theta_{\varepsilon\delta}$. $\Theta_{\varepsilon\delta}$ may or may not be implemented in a particular program. MILS does allow you to specify it, but the current version of LISREL does not, i.e., it is assumed to be a null matrix. Normally, one assumes that exogenous and endogenous error are uncorrelated. (Indeed, both Θ_{δ} and Θ_{ε} are perhaps most commonly specified as diagonal matrices, which assumes uncorrelated error.) However, circumstances may arise where it is desirable to assume interdependencies among error terms such as when one set of measures are obtained at one point in time, inducing one set of incidental temporal factors, and the remainder are obtained at another point in time, inducing a second set of temporal factors. Consequently, correlations among variables observed at a given time, which may be either endogenous or exogenous, may be partially spurious. By specifying that Θ_{δ} and Θ_{ε} are not diagonal and that $\Theta_{\varepsilon\delta}$ is not null, correlated error may be modeled. Of course, modeling correlated error increases the risk that the model may be improperly identified.

Selected portions of the full model may be used as necessary. For example, by specifying that λ_x and Σ_y are identity matrices and the corresponding error matrices are null, path models can be constructed among observables.

The model that results from a LISREL solution can look quite elegant or bizarre as a function of the user's conceptual ability. Keep in mind that its successful use requires, at a minimum, that you have three very distinct kinds of substantive knowledge as to how your variables interrelate, corresponding to the three separate phases of the model. If one or more models is nonsense, the overall results will also be nonsense. Typically, the initial model needs to be respecified in light of the data. The process of respecification, however, can often lead to much capitalization upon chance.

MacCallum (1986) has recently provided an extensive discussion of considerations leading to a successful respecification using computer simulations. Most appropriately, but perhaps not surprisingly, he concludes that the most successful respecification searches arise when (1) the model that was initially proposed provides a good first approximation, (2) the search goes beyond simply obtaining parameter estimates that fit well, (3) respecifications are

---

[11] The complete observed variance–covariance matrix, Σ, is a good example of a partitioned matrix. The conventional layout is with the endogenous variables at the top left and the exogenous variables at the bottom right. Hence, the top-left partition consists of correlations within the set of endogenous variables (Σ_{yy}), the bottom right partition consists of correlations within the set of exogenous variables (Σ_{xx}), and the two remaining quadrants, which are transposes of one another, consist of correlations between an exogenous and an endogenous variable, Σ_{xy} and Σ_{yx}.

based on well-defined substantive considerations, and (4) a large sample is used. Keep open as an option the approach of working with the three phases separately before attempting to put them together. Specifically, look at the results of the two confirmatory factor analyses first and explore alternative factor structures. When you are satisfied with the results, look next to the causal model.

In sum, I have discussed confirmatory factor analysis, which deals with tests of properties of linear combinations that have been defined in advance. The chapter began with a consideration of how to relate results from factor analytic studies to each other so that you can see if the results replicate. I then dealt with how to test "weak" substantive models, which propose that certain variables "go together." Two methods were discussed, OMG and LISREL. It was noted that LISREL's primary advantage over OMG was in testing "strong" substantive models—tests of more specific properties such as whether sets of variables have identical factor structures in the population. The topic of path analysis, which deals with making causal inferences from correlation data was then examined. Consideration of the full LISREL model, which ties together confirmatory factor analysis and path analysis, concluded the chapter.

I will now change areas of discourse and deal with problems of how to classify observations. This is a very broad and extensive topic that requires three chapters. Chapter 8 contains material that has much in common with multiple regression, since it deals with forming optimal linear combinations of variables to predict a criterion. The difference is that the criterion in multiple regression varies along one dimension only and is usually continuous, whereas the criterion in what is known as *discriminant analysis* is group membership, which is usually discrete and there is no requirement that it vary along one dimension only.

Addendum: A Program to Obtain Oblique Multiple Groups Solutions

Most of this chapter deals with oblique multiple groups (OMG) factor analysis and LISREL. Knowledge of proper application of LISREL to test what are referred to in the chapters as "strong" theories is, in effect, a course in itself. However, tests of "weak" theories by means of OMG are a great deal simpler. Unfortunately, no package currently offers an OMG procedure. Consequently, I have provided the following program, written in SAS PROC MATRIX, which may be used, assuming SAS is implemented at your computer institution. It optionally allows information to be entered as raw data, as a correlation matrix, or as an SAS data set. Note the comments, defined by a "*" in the first column. Also note that modifications may be needed when SAS PROC IML replaces PROC MATRIX.

```
OPTION NOCENTER;
TITLE 'TEST OF OMG WITH TWO UNCORRELATED FACTORS';
DATA C;
INPUT C1-C2 H1;
```

* C1 CAN TAKE ON ONE OF THREE VALUES.
  C1 = 0 MEANS THAT;
* THE DATA TO BE ANALYZED IN DATA STEP A BELOW ARE IN
  RAW SCORE FORM,;
* C1 = 1 MEANS THAT THE DATA IN STEP A ARE IN THE;
* FORM OF A CORRELATION MATRIX, AND;
* C1 = 2 MEANS THAT THE DATA IN STEP A ARE A SAS
  TYPE = CORR DATA SET;
* C2 IS THE NUMBER OF CASES;
* "H1" DEFINES THE NUMBER OF FACTORS IN THE
  HYPOTHESIS TO BE TESTED.;
* MORE THAN ONE HYPOTHESIS MAY BE TESTED IN
  A SINGLE RUN. E.G.,;
* "H1-H3" WOULD DENOTE THAT THREE HYPOTHESES ARE
  TO BE TESTED.;
* THE VALUE OF;
* H1 IS THE NUMBER OF FACTORS IN THAT HYPOTHESIS, ETC.;
* THE SAMPLE DATA ARE CORRELATIONS (C1 = 1),
  THERE ARE 500 CASES;
* (C2 = 500),;
* AND THE HYPOTHESIS INVOLVES TWO FACTORS (H1 = 2);

```
CARDS ;
1  500  2
;
DATA A;
INPUT X1-X12;
```

* THE STATEMENT "X1-X12" IMPLIES THAT THERE ARE
  12 VARIABLES. DATA;
* STEP A WOULD BE MODIFIED AS NEEDED WITH
  APPROPRIATE FORMAT;
* STATEMENTS, ETC., AS IN ANY OTHER DATA STEP.;
* THE DATA FOLLOW THE "CARDS" STATEMENT,
  AS IN ANY SAS DATA STEP;

```
CARDS;
 1.000 .418 .362 .438 .444 .461 .013 .003 .019 .055 .035 .050
 .418 1.000 .407 .467 .475 .473 -.065 .013 -.053 -.021 -.023 -.017
 .362 .407 1.000 .485 .443 .448 -.061 -.010 -.065 -.043 -.041 -.022
 .438 .467 .485 1.000 .559 .543 -.100 -.002 -.060 -.019 -.037 -.033
 .444 .475 .443 .559 1.000 .550 -.077 .003 -.021 -.062 -.011 -.045
 .461 .473 .448 .543 .550 1.000 -.054 -.036 -.049 -.034 -.034 -.026
 .013 -.065 -.061 -.100 -.077 -.054 1.000 .620 .576 .691 .693 .699
```

```
.003 .013 −.010 −.002 .003 −.036 .620 1.000 .578 .679 .713 .696
.019 −.053 −.065 −.060 −.021 −.049 .576 .578 1.000 .643 .670 .662
.055 −.021 −.043 −.019 −.062 −.034 .691 .679 .643 1.000 .761 .783
.035 −.023 −.041 −.037 −.011 −.034 .693 .713 .670 .761 1.000 .782
.050 −.017 −.022 −.033 −.045 −.026 .699 .696 .662 .783 .782 1.000
;
DATA HYP;
INPUT V1−V12;
* INSERT THE HYPOTHESIS MATRICES HERE: NOTE THAT
   THEY ARE;
* READ AS TRANSPOSES, I.E., VARIABLES ARE ROWS.
   CONSEQUENTLY,;
* "V1−V12" SHOULD BE CHANGED TO REFLECT THE NUMBER
   OF VARIABLES.;
* THE SUM OF THE VALUES ASSOCIATED WITH "H1−H2" OR
   THE EQUIVALENT;
* DETERMINES THE NUMBER OF LINES OF INPUT DATA
   TO BE READ;
* THE DATA FOLLOW THE "CARDS" STATEMENT,
   AS IN ANY SAS DATA STEP;
CARDS;
 −.03917 −.11975 −.13497 −.14697 −.13886 −.14205 .82976 .82061
 .79361 .88088 .89188 .89267
 .69259 .71232 .68324 .77612 .77194 .77150 .05184 .13247 .07593
 .11632 .12215. 12559
;
PROC MATRIX;
FETCH CHECK DATA = C ;
FETCH X DATA = A;
IF CHECK(1, 1) = 0 THEN DO ; *  DOES 'CHECK' HOLD X OR
   CORR MATRIX ? ;
SUM = X(+,);
XPX = X'*X − (SUM'*SUM)#/NROW(X);
S = 1#/SQRT(DIAG(XPX));
CORR = S*XPX*S;
 END;
ELSE CORR = X ;
NOTE CORRELATION MATRIX;
PRINT CORR;
Y = EIGVAL (CORR);
NOTE EIGENVAUES OF CORRELATION MATRIX ;
   PRINT Y ;
PCT = Y#/Y(+,);
CPCT = PCT;
DO INDEX = 2 TO NROW(CORR);
```

```
CPCT(INDEX, 1) = CPCT(INDEX, 1) + CPCT(INDEX − 1, 1);
END;
FETCH HY DATA = HYP;
* THIS LOOPS OVER THE DIFFERENT HYPS ;
NH = NCOL(CHECK) − 2 ;
HHYP = CHECK(1, NCOL(CHECK) − NH + 1:NCOL(CHECK) ) ;
LR = 0 ;
DO NHYP = 1 TO NH ;
PAGE ;
  FR = LR + 1 ;
  LR = LR + HHYP(1, NHYP) ;
 H = HY(FR:LR , )' ;
FCOV = H'*CORR*H;
SCALE = 1#/SQRT(DIAG(FCOV));
RFACT = SCALE'*FCOV*SCALE;
STRUCT = CORR*H*SCALE;
PATTERN = STRUCT*INV(RFACT) ;
HSQ = DIAG(PATTERN*STRUCT');
DO I = 1 TO NROW(CORR) ; HSQ(I, 1) = HSQ(I, I) ; END ;
HHSQ = HSQ( , 1) ;
FVAR = DIAG(STRUCT'*STRUCT)#/NROW(STRUCT) ;
TVAR = HHSQ(+, 1)   #/NROW(CORR) ;
DO I = 1 TO NCOL(STRUCT); FVAR(I, 1) = FVAR(I, I) ; END ;
HFVAR = FVAR( , 1) // TVAR ;
HPCT = PCT(1:NCOL(STRUCT) , ) ; HPCT = HPCT // HPCT(+, 1) ;
HCPCT = CPCT(1:NCOL(STRUCT), ) ;
HCPCT = HCPCT // HPCT(NCOL(STRUCT) + 1, 1) ;
STRTHSQ = STRUCT || HHSQ ;
FCTVAR = HFVAR' // HPCT' // HCPCT' ;
CHSQ = 'H**2' ;
RFVAR = 'OMG FVAR' 'PC FVAR' 'PC CUM' ;
NOTE HYPOTHESIS MATRIX;
PRINT H;
NOTE FACTOR STRUCTURE AND H**2 ;
IF CHECK(1, 3) = 1 THEN;
  PRINT STRTHSQ ;
 ELSE PRINT STRTHSQ ;
NOTE FACTOR VARIANCES (OMG AND PC);
  PRINT FCTVAR ROWNAME = RFVAR ;
NOTE FACTOR INTERCORRELATIONS ;
  PRINT RFACT ;
NOTE FACTOR PATTERN ;
IF CHECK(1, 3) = 1 THEN;
  PRINT PATTERN ;
```

ELSE PRINT PATTERN ;
END ;

If you type in the program correctly, it should produce the following output:

CORRELATION MATRIX

CORR	COL1	COL2	COL3	COL4	COL5	COL6
	COL7	COL8	COL9	COL10	COL11	COL12
ROW1	1	0.418	0.362	0.438	0.444	0.461
	0.013	0.003	0.019	0.055	0.035	0.05
ROW2	0.418	1	0.407	0.467	0.475	0.473
	−0.065	0.013	−0.053	−0.021	−0.023	−0.017
ROW3	0.362	0.407	1	0.485	0.443	0.448
	−0.061	−0.01	−0.065	−0.043	−0.041	−0.022
ROW4	0.438	0.467	0.485	1	0.559	0.543
	−0.1	−0.002	−0.06	−0.019	−0.037	−0.33
ROW5	0.444	0.475	0.443	0.559	1	0.55
	−0.077	0.003	−0.021	−0.062	−0.011	−0.045
ROW6	0.461	0.473	0.448	0.543	0.55	1
	−0.054	−0.036	−0.049	−0.034	−0.034	−0.026
ROW7	0.013	−0.065	−0.061	−0.1	−0.077	−0.054
	1	0.62	0.576	0.691	0.693	0.699
ROW8	0.003	0.013	−0.01	−0.002	0.003	−0.036
	0.62	1	0.578	0.679	0.713	0.696
ROW9	0.019	−0.053	−0.065	−0.06	−0.021	−0.049
	0.576	0.578	1	0.643	0.67	0.662
ROW1	0.055	−0.021	−0.043	−0.019	−0.062	−0.034
	0.691	0.679	0.643	1	0.761	0.783
ROW1	0.035	−0.023	−0.041	−0.037	−0.011	−0.034
	0.693	0.713	0.67	0.761	1	0.782
ROW1	0.05	−0.017	−0.022	−0.033	−0.045	−0.026
	0.699	0.696	0.662	0.783	0.782	1

EIGENVAUES OF CORRELATION MATRIX

Y	COL1
ROW1	4.45214
ROW2	3.31521
ROW3	0.649535
ROW4	0.578973
ROW5	0.565521
ROW6	0.469832
ROW7	0.456243
ROW8	0.421484
ROW9	0.353634

ROW10	0.300294
ROW11	0.228091
ROW12	0.20904

HYPOTHESIS MATRIX

H	COL1	COL2
ROW1	−0.03917	0.69259
ROW2	−0.11975	0.71232
ROW3	−0.13497	0.68324
ROW4	−0.14697	0.77612
ROW5	−0.13886	0.77194
ROW6	−0.14205	0.7715
ROW7	0.82976	0.05184
ROW8	0.82061	0.13247
ROW9	0.79361	0.07593
ROW10	0.88088	0.11632
ROW11	0.89188	0.12215
ROW12	0.89267	0.12559

FACTOR STRUCTURE AND H**2

STRTHSQ	COL1	COL2	COL3
ROW1	−0.0397364	0.692161	0.480688
ROW2	−0.119532	0.711881	0.521131
ROW3	−0.134455	0.683179	0.484886
ROW4	−0.146329	0.775859	0.623461
ROW5	−0.138291	0.771697	0.614728
ROW6	−0.141483	0.771059	0.614638
ROW7	0.829651	0.0521151	0.691002
ROW8	0.8204	0.132517	0.690529
ROW9	0.793475	0.0761508	0.635353
ROW10	0.880585	0.116729	0.788974
ROW11	0.891597	0.122583	0.809883
ROW12	0.892351	0.126032	0.812083

FACTOR VARIANCES (OMG AND PC)

FCTVAR	COL1	COL2	COL3
OMG FVAR	0.371012	0.276268	0.64728
PC FVAR	0.371012	0.276268	0.64728
PC CUM	0.371012	0.64728	0.64728

FACTOR INTERCORRELATIONS

RFACT	COL1	COL2
ROW1	1	0.000403565
ROW2	0.000403565	1

FACTOR PATTERN

PATTERN	COL1	COL2
ROW1	−0.0400157	0.692177
ROW2	−0.11982	0.711929
ROW3	−0.13473	0.683234

ROW4	−0.146642	0.775918
ROW5	−0.138603	0.771753
ROW6	−0.141794	0.771116
ROW7	0.82963	0.0517803
ROW8	0.820346	0.132186
ROW9	0.793444	0.0758306
ROW10	0.880538	0.116374
ROW11	0.891547	0.122224
ROW12	0.8923	0.125672

I have used the factor pattern from the data of Problem 5, Chapter 6 as input. A component factor pattern has the property that it will reproduce itself as output if it is used as a hypothesis matrix.

8
Classification Methods—Part 1. Forming Discriminant Axes

Chapter Overview

Chapter 8 is the first of three chapters devoted to classification. The material covered in this chapter deals largely with the process of combining two or more predictors to best discriminate among two or more groups—*discriminant analysis*. This chapter is divided into three main sections.

I. DISCRIMINANT ANALYSIS WITH TWO GROUPS AND TWO PREDICTORS—The simplest case is covered first by considering problems in which an observation defined by its score on two measures is to be assigned to one of two groups. The fundamental problem of classification is defined in its most basic terms: the need to maximize variance between groups relative to variance within groups. The necessary *discriminant weights*, which provide the optimal linear combination of the two measures (predictors), may be obtained by several different methods, all of which lead to equivalent outcomes. The various methods are useful for different purposes. The most general method requires a *Cholesky decomposition* and an *eigenanalysis*, as the terms were discussed in Chapter 3.

II. DISCRIMINANT ANALYSIS WITH TWO PREDICTORS AND THREE GROUPS—In general, adding additional groups means that group mean difference might be *diffused* along two or more dimensions versus *concentrated* along one dimension, a very important distinction. All solutions in the two-group case are concentrated, by default, as they must fall along a single dimension.

III. DISCRIMINANT ANALYSIS—THE GENERAL CASE—The final section deals with some strategies for use in the general case. One that is particularly important is to perform a component analysis upon the *pooled within-group correlation matrix*. The importance of *hypothesis testing* is stressed, along with *confirmatory factor analysis*. Finally, *stepwise discriminant analysis* is discussed.

The present chapter and the next two all deal with one of the "bread and butter" problems of applied multivariate analysis, classification of individuals into two or more discrete groups on the basis of multiple predictors. The result is a linear combination of the predictors called a *discriminant function* or *discriminant axis*. A score derived from such a discriminant function is termed a *discriminant score*, and the name given the procedure as a whole is, accordingly, termed a *discriminant analysis*. Discriminant analysis tells one how to pool information optimally for purposes of classification. I will first deal with the details of forming discriminant axes.

Discriminant axes allow classification decisions to be made such as the assignment of a person to a given group if the individual gets a high discriminant score and a different group if the individual gets a low score. At that point, one confronts the issue of "how high is high." This issue involves the selection of a suitable *cutoff* (or cutoffs when there are more than two groups), the focus of Chapter 9. Another issue is to decide whether the classification scheme performs better than chance (statistical inference), which will be considered in Chapter 10.

Discriminant Analysis with Two Groups and Two Predictors

Assume there are two types of employees at a large company: (1) sales personnel who tend to be slightly more verbal than numeric in their intellectual abilities and (2) technical staff who are just the reverse. The data consist of the Tinkers test of verbal proficiency and the Larry test of numeric ability. I simulated the data of 1000 people, using the first and fourth equations from Eq. (6-9). The first 500 were "Sales people" and designated as Group S. I added .2 units to each of their Tinkers (X_1) scores so that the scores were normally distributed (.2, 1). Their score on the Larry (X_4) test were left intact and were normally distributed (0, 1). I then did the converse for the "Technical people," Group T. That is, I left their Tinkers scores alone but added .2 units to their Larry scores so that the two distributions are also normal, (0, 1) and (.2, 1), respectively.

A basic issue is how the two measures can be combined so as to discriminate optimally between the two groups. One possible application would be as a selection device for future employees.

Suppose I were to classify people on the basis of their Tinkers test alone, utilizing the .2 unit population mean difference, ignoring scores on the Larry test. One way to index the effectiveness of this procedure is to compute the F ratio between the two groups, which was 14.52 and highly significant. Conversely, I might use the Larry test alone and ignore the Tinkers test. The result is a nonsignificant F ratio of 3.13 for the set of random numbers chosen.[1]

---

[1] The example allows me to make another point about sampling error. In actuality, there are *population* mean differences of the same magnitude (.2 units) for both variables. Hence, the failure to obtain a significant difference with the Larry test is a type II error. Different sets of random numbers that I simulated produced different patterns of significance even with the relatively large sample size and nontrivial mean difference. Of course, you would not know about the population mean differences in a real application.

A more general procedure is to use different linear combinations of the two tests—differentially weighted sums and differences. For example, simply add the two scores equally. The unweighted sum can be subject to an F test just like individual scores. The result was an even lower F ratio (1.30) because of the way scores are defined. Any sum cancels out the inherent pattern of the data (a high score on the Tinkers test and a low score on the Larry test being associated with sales people and the converse being associated with technical people) needed for discriminating the groups.

On the other hand, *difference* scores obtained from the two tests help discrimination. For example, the unweighted difference $X_1 - X_4$ led to an F ratio of 34.22. Moreover, the value of F may further be increased in magnitude by considering *weighted* differences.

The F ratio is equivalent to a number of other measures that can be used to describe the effectiveness of a particular set of weights in discrimination. For example, since there were only two groups, I could have maximized t instead of F. Because t^2 equals F, maximizing one of these statistics would maximize the other. A third possibility is to maximize the point–biserial correlation between the two groups and the linear combination of X_1 and X_4. However, any weighting that maximizes F can also be shown to maximize the point–biserial correlation. As it turns out, the linear combination that leads to the best discrimination by maximizing F will also be the best linear combination using any of a number of other criteria of "best."

Because one can seek to maximize F even when there are more than two groups, it serves as a very useful definition of best. Consequently, the goal of discriminant analysis may be stated in terms of finding the linear combination that *maximizes the variance between groups relative to the variance within groups*. Note that maximizing the between-group variance is equivalent to maximizing group mean differences (assuming that the dependent variables have been standardized). The result may be seen in the numerators of the formulas for F, which is the variance between groups, and t, which is the group mean difference.

In sum, I know that using an unweighted difference between X_1 and X_4 is better than using either one alone. I haven't yet told you how to find the *optimal* weights, which I will shortly. Before I do, I want to show you the situation graphically.

Graphic Representation

Figure 8-1 describes the situation graphically. There are scatterplots representing the envelopes of groups S and T. As you can see, the scatterplots overlap in the two dimensions of X_1 and X_4, but are nonetheless distinct.

There are also four pairs of overlapping distributions. The one designated "X_1 alone" at the bottom can perhaps be visualized better if you imagine looking at the two scatterplots from below. It reflects the mean difference on test X_1 alone. The one marked "X_4 alone" at the left is precisely the converse.

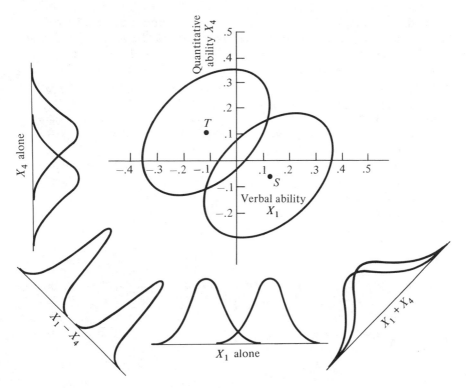

FIGURE 8-1. Scatterplots of sales and techical people on measures of verbal ability (horizontal axis) and quantitative ability (vertical axis). The scatterplots for the within-group correlations are not drawn to scale. (They are too small and do not indicate the actual overlap that is present.) They are inserted simply to indicate the positive correlation between verbal and quantitative ability of the relationships.

It describes what you would see were to look at the two distributions by sighting along the X_1 axis.

The one marked "$X_1 + X_4$" at the bottom right of the figure is what would obtain by using the sum. Note that there is practically no mean separation; hence, the variation between groups is very small. In addition, the two distributions are each more variable than X_1 alone or X_4 alone because $X_1 + X_4$ is the sum of two positively correlated variables. Twice the covariance of the two is combined with the individual variance terms of X_1 and X_4 in producing the variance of their sum as noted in Eq. (3-7).

Finally, the one marked "$X_1 - X_4$" at the bottom left represents the consequences of using the difference between the two tests. Note that there is greater mean separation (greater variance between groups) and less variability within each of the two groups as compared to either X_1 or X_4 alone.

I drew the four pairs of distributions away from the two scatterplots so that the picture would not be cluttered. The distributions could also have been drawn at the origin. Imagine a line placed through the origin. Now, slowly rotated the line through 180 degrees. For any given orientation, I would be able to describe the separation between the two groups in terms of an F ratio. Any one orientation is a *decision axis*, because it could be used to make decisions about classification, regardless of whether or not it is the *best* (*optimal*) one. There is one particular orientation of the decision axis that is best in terms of maximizing F. Since sample size remains constant as the axis is rotated, changes in F reflect two and only two quantities: (1) variability between group means on the composite variable and (2) variability within groups on the composite.

When I show you the calculations, you will see that the optimal orientation is near the one designating the unweighted difference in this example. The particular orientation of a decisional axis that maximizes between-group differences relative to within-group differences is the *discriminant function*.

One Way to Obtain Discriminant Weights

With only two groups, the desired weighting can be obtained by using dummy codes (or any other pair of distinct numbers) as criterion scores in multiple regression. The equivalence of discriminant analysis and multiple regression in the two-group case holds even when there are more than two predictor variables. The application of multiple regression to the discrimination between two groups is just a special case in which the criterion is a dichotomy, and I, in fact used a dichotomous criterion for the last example of Chapter 4. Unfortunately, the general algorithm for discriminant analysis is different from that of multiple regression. Moreover, most discriminant analysis algorithms provide other useful results besides the discriminant weights. It is of importance, however, to know that the best linear combination to *predict* class membership is also the best linear combination to *classify* cases so two obviously related concepts do not require different solutions. This equivalence holds despite differences in the mathematical goals of the two statistical models. Multiple regression minimizes the average squared discrepancy between obtained and predicted scores, and discriminant analysis maximizes variability between groups relative to variability within groups.

I suggest you try analyzing a set of data like the preceding one using both a discriminant analysis and a multiple regression routine. It is quite possible that the two equations you obtain may look different because of a difference in scaling which, in turn, reflects an assumption that is necessary for multiple regression but not necessary for discriminant analysis. The relevant assumption is that multiple regression requires a predicted score to fall as close as possible (in a least squares sense) to the obtained score. This assumption constrains the variance of predicted scores to $s_y^2 R^2$. However, the "blend" or relative contribution of the predictors will be the same in multiple regression and discriminant analysis so that the two sets of scores they produce will be perfectly correlated.

Because discriminant analysis uses a different criterion, any equation of the form $Y' = k(b_1 X_1 - b_4 X_4)$ will have the same utility (as is also true of many applications of multiple regression, since the scale of measurement is not necessarily important). Discriminant scores are usually scaled in one of two ways: (1) the *total* (overall) set of discriminant scores has a variance of 1.0 or (2) the average variance *within groups* is 1.0. I will emphasize the latter, within-group normalization, since it is the more common.

Another Way to Obtain Discriminant Weights

What is often referred to as the "classic solution" for the two-group case, elegantly derived by R.A. Fisher, who is responsible for much of modern multivariate theory, is given in Eq. (8-1a) to provide raw or unstandardized score (b) weights and in Eq. (8-1b) to provide standardized (β) weights:

$$\mathbf{b} = \mathbf{W}^{-1}\mathbf{d} \tag{8-1a}$$

$$\beta = \mathbf{R}_w^{-1}\mathbf{d} \tag{8-1b}$$

The vector of desired b weights, **b**, is the product of the inverse of the pooled within-group variance–covariance matrix ($\mathbf{W}^{-1}$) and the vector of group mean differences (**d**). The vector may also be written as ($\bar{\mathbf{x}}_S - \bar{\mathbf{x}}_T$), the vector difference between the centroids of groups S and T. Its two elements are $\bar{X}_1$ and $\bar{X}_4$. The vector of desired β weights, β, is the same except **d** is defined in terms of z-score differences and the inverse of the within-group correlation matrix ($\mathbf{R}_w^{-1}$) is used in place of the inverse of the pooled-within group variance–covariance matrix ($\mathbf{W}^{-1}$).

The concepts of within-group variance and covariance were discussed in Chapter 2, along with the important related concepts of between-group and total variance and covariance. The within-group variance and covariance are obtained by adding values of $\sum x_1^2$, $\sum x_4^2$, and $\sum x_1 x_4$ for the two groups and dividing by the number of subjects within each of the two groups. The matrix $\mathbf{W}^{-1}$ serves to correct the mean differences for the correlation between the two predictors. The solution merely provides the relative weights. You would get mathematically equivalent results by using the inverse of the within-group *correlation* matrix or the inverse of the *pooled within-group corrected sum-of-products (SP)* matrix.

The term "unstandardized" varies somewhat in meaning from program to program. In some cases, such as SAS, the predictor scores are treated as deviations from the grand mean, in which case the constant term (a) is zero. Equation (8-1a) is in deviation score form. Other statistical packages define discriminant functions in terms of raw scores and the constant term is therefore needed. The calculation of the constant follows the logic of Chapter 4 so that a is the sum of the cross products of the predictor means times their associated b weights. Hence, $a = \sum b_i X_i$. This computation adjusts the discriminant scores to a mean of zero.

Computation

It is useful to employ Eq. (8-1) to illustrate basic computations even though this equation can only be used when there are two groups. Computations presented later for the general case share a number of steps with this equation.

The raw data consist of a matrix, $\mathbf{X}$, which contains k predictors (two in the present case) as columns. Let g denote the number of groups (also two in the present case) and N denote the number of subjects (and, consequently, the number of rows of $\mathbf{X}$). Also, let the number of subjects in group j equal N_j so that $N_1 + N_2 + \cdots + N_g = N$. Now, imagine that $\mathbf{X}$ is partitioned by rows but not columns so that the first N_1 rows contain data for subjects in the first group (group S in the present case), the next N_2 rows represent the subjects in the second group (group T in the present case), etc. Table 8-1 contains data for a sample of cases (10 per group). However, the computations presented below involve the full data set.

Based on the logic set forth in Chapter 2, the computational steps are as follows:

1. The basic quantities are (a) the sums of each variable, (b) the sums of each variable squared, (c) the sums of cross products of each pair of variables, and (d) the number of observations. In all cases, the quantities will be obtained separately for each group and as a total across groups. In the present example, there will be two sums, respectively involving X_1 and X_4. Consequently, there

TABLE 8-1. Hypothetical raw data for a two-group, two-predictor discriminant problem

Subject	Group	X_1	X_4
1	S	−.9422	−.4695
2	S	−.5325	−1.5059
3	S	1.4435	2.2564
4	S	−.4650	−1.5879
5	S	1.5097	1.0420
6	S	.2259	−1.5755
7	S	−1.3979	−.8981
8	S	2.0077	.1095
9	S	.3502	−.6840
10	S	.3286	.8879
1	T	−.0276	−.4176
2	T	.2160	−.4605
3	T	.4894	.3192
4	T	−.0760	.6415
5	T	−.8761	−.8283
6	T	−.6340	.3490
7	T	−1.0413	−1.1337
8	T	1.0951	.8423
9	T	.8032	.2443
10	T	−1.1252	−1.2684

will also be two sums of squared observations and one sum of cross products. The number of observations within each group is 500; consequently, the total number of observations is 1000. The remaining quantities, (a)–(c), are as follows:

	Group S	Group T	Total
$\sum X_1$	142.18	14.23	156.42
$\sum X_4$	26.92	86.88	113.80
$\sum X_1^2$	599.97	564.56	1164.52
$\sum X_4^2$	570.19	595.48	1165.67
$\sum X_1 X_4$	322.32	309.92	632.24

Most packages do not make the above data directly available. You will not need them except to follow subsequent steps.

2. Obtain the *total corrected sum-of-products matrix* ($\mathbf{SP}_t$) which contains sums of squares ($\sum x^2$ values) in its diagonal and corrected sums of cross products ($\sum xy$ values) off the diagonals. The rows and columns of $\mathbf{SP}_t$ are the predictors (X_1 and X_4). Since sums of squares equal $\sum X^2 - (\sum X)^2/N$ and sums of cross products equal $\sum XY - (\sum X \sum Y)/N$, the result is:

$$\mathbf{SP}_t = \begin{bmatrix} 1164.62 - 156.42^2/1000 & 632.24 - 156.42 \times 113.80/1000 \\ 632.24 - 156.42 \times 113.80/1000 & 1165.67 - 113.80^2/1000 \end{bmatrix}$$

$$= \begin{bmatrix} 1140.15 & 614.44 \\ 614.44 & 1152.72 \end{bmatrix}$$

Each cell of $\mathbf{SP}_t$ has $N - 1 = 1000 - 1$ or 999 df (df_t) because the cell mean has to be estimated.

3. Obtain the *individual within-group corrected sum-of-products* matrices ($\mathbf{SP}_{wi}$). The $\mathbf{SP}_{wi}$ are analogous to $\mathbf{SP}_t$ but come from individual groups (S and T in the present case). Hence, the matrix for group S is

$$\mathbf{SP}_{wS} = \begin{bmatrix} 599.97 - 142.18^2/500 & 322.32 - 142.18 \times 26.92/500 \\ 322.32 - 142.18 \times 26.92/500 & 570.19 - 26.92^2/500 \end{bmatrix}$$

$$= \begin{bmatrix} 559.54 & 314.67 \\ 314.67 & 568.74 \end{bmatrix}$$

Similarly, the matrix for group T is

$$\mathbf{SP}_{wT} = \begin{bmatrix} 564.56 - 14.23^2/500 & 309.92 - 14.23 \times 86.88/500 \\ 309.92 - 14.23 \times 86.88/500 & 595.48 - 86.88^2/500 \end{bmatrix}$$

$$= \begin{bmatrix} 564.15 & 307.45 \\ 307.45 & 580.38 \end{bmatrix}$$

Each cell of both matrices has $N_j - 1 = 500 - 1$ or 499 df (df_{wi}) because each cell mean has to be estimated.

4. Obtain the *pooled within-group corrected sum-of-products matrix* $(\mathbf{SP}_w)$ by adding (pooling) the individual within-group corrected sum-of-products matrices $(\mathbf{SP}_{wi})$. Hence, $\mathbf{SP}_w = \sum \mathbf{SP}_{wi}$, where the index of summation, i, denotes the various groups. The result is

$$
\mathbf{SP}_w = \begin{bmatrix} 559.54 & 314.67 \\ 314.67 & 568.74 \end{bmatrix} + \begin{bmatrix} 564.15 & 307.45 \\ 307.45 & 580.38 \end{bmatrix} = \begin{bmatrix} 1123.69 & 622.12 \\ 622.12 & 1149.12 \end{bmatrix}
$$

Each cell of $\mathbf{SP}_w$ contains $N - g = 1000 - 2$ or 998 df (df_w), where g is the number of groups. The df_w is the sum of the df in the individual matrices.

5. Obtain the *between-group corrected sum-of-products matrix* $(\mathbf{SP}_b)$ as the difference between the total corrected sum-of-products matrix and the pooled within-group corrected sum-of-products matrix, $\mathbf{SP}_b = \mathbf{SP}_t - \mathbf{SP}_w$. The result is

$$
\mathbf{SP}_b = \begin{bmatrix} 1140.06 & 614.44 \\ 614.44 & 1152.72 \end{bmatrix} - \begin{bmatrix} 1123.69 & 622.12 \\ 622.12 & 1149.13 \end{bmatrix} = \begin{bmatrix} 16.37 & -7.68 \\ -7.68 & 3.60 \end{bmatrix}
$$

Each cell of $\mathbf{SP}_b$ has $g - 1 = 2 - 1$ or 1 df (df_b). Note that df_b equals the difference in df for $\mathbf{SP}_t$ and $\mathbf{SP}_w$: $(N - 1) - (N - g)$. Also note that the diagonals of $\mathbf{SP}_t$, $\mathbf{SP}_w$, and $\mathbf{SP}_b$ contain sums of squares which allow one to perform ANOVA on the individual predictors, X_1 and X_4.

6. Obtain the *total* $(\mathbf{T})$, *within* $(\mathbf{W})$, *and between* $(\mathbf{B})$ *variance–covariance matrices* by dividing the SP matrices by their associated df:

$$
\mathbf{T} = \begin{bmatrix} 1140.06/999 & 614.44/999 \\ 614.44/999 & 1152.72/999 \end{bmatrix} = \begin{bmatrix} 1.14 & .61 \\ .61 & 1.15 \end{bmatrix}
$$

$$
\mathbf{W} = \begin{bmatrix} 1123.69/998 & 622.12/998 \\ 622.12/998 & 1149.13/998 \end{bmatrix} = \begin{bmatrix} 1.13 & .62 \\ .62 & 1.15 \end{bmatrix}
$$

$$
\mathbf{B} = \begin{bmatrix} 16.37/1 & -7.67/1 \\ -7.67/1 & 3.59/1 \end{bmatrix} = \begin{bmatrix} 16.37 & -7.67 \\ -7.67 & 3.59 \end{bmatrix}
$$

In the absence of sampling error, the diagonals of $\mathbf{W}$ would be 1.0 in my example, since I added a constant for each group to sets of z scores. Computing $\mathbf{W}$ eliminates the group constant. In other words, the variance of X_1 and X_4 averaged across groups is 1.0 in the absence of sampling error. Also compute $\mathbf{W}^{-1}$ (see Chapter 3):

$$
\mathbf{W}^{-1} = \begin{bmatrix} 1.27 & -.68 \\ -.68 & 1.24 \end{bmatrix}
$$

7. Use the methods of Chapter 3, to obtain *correlation matrices* from the variance–covariance matrices separately for $\mathbf{T}$, $\mathbf{W}$, and $\mathbf{B}$. The results are total, within-group, and between-group correlation matrices, denoted as $\mathbf{R}_t$, $\mathbf{R}_w$, and $\mathbf{R}_b$, respectively. The diagonals of all three matrices will be 1.0, of course. The

off-diagonal elements of $\mathbf{R}_t$, $\mathbf{R}_w$, and $\mathbf{R}_b$ are .54, .55 and -1.0, respectively. The total correlation confounds two effects: (1) positive covariance between X_1 and X_4 among subjects within each group and (2) negative covariance between the two group means produced by the fact that X_1 is larger in group S than in group T but X_4 is larger in group T than in group S. The large number of subjects coupled with the relatively small mean differences mean that $\mathbf{R}_t$ was primarily influenced by $\mathbf{R}_w$ rather than $\mathbf{R}_b$, but the converse could also hold. $\mathbf{R}_t$ is usually not very informative but $\mathbf{R}_w$ and $\mathbf{R}_b$ usually are. Furthermore, with two groups, the between-group correlation must be 1.0, -1.0, or .0 (the last can only occur in the highly unlikely event that the two groups centroids are identical), since it is a correlation based on only two points. Consequently, $\mathbf{R}_b$ will be of rank 1.

8. Obtain the *group means* from the group sums. The X_1 means were .28 and .02, and the X_4 means were .05 and .17 for groups S and T, respectively. The difference vector of Eq. (8-1) is therefore $(.26, -.12)$. In the absence of sampling error, the difference vector should be $(.20, -.20)$. Sampling error therefore exaggerated the X_1 mean difference and attenuated the X_4 mean difference.

9. Obtain the b weights and/or the β weights. Applying Eq. (8-1a) yields b weights $(.41, -.32)$ and applying Eq. (8-1b) yields β weights of $(.46, -.37)$, although you would have to invert $\mathbf{R}_w$ yourself from the data given to compute the latter.

10. Although the b and β weights obtained in (8) are often perfectly adequate, it is more common to rescale them. Perhaps the most commonly used rescaling method is to make the pooled within-group standard deviation 1.0. The b weights derived from the classic solution produce the following variance:

$$\mathbf{b'Wb} = [.407 \quad -.324] \times \begin{bmatrix} 1.126 & .623 \\ .623 & 1.151 \end{bmatrix} \times \begin{bmatrix} .407 \\ -.324 \end{bmatrix} = .14$$

Dividing each element of the original vector $\mathbf{b}$ by the square root of .14 (the standard deviation) produces the new discriminant vector $(-1.08, .86)$. This vector appears in SAS printout under the heading "Raw Canonical coefficients." Similarly, when I applied the β weights from the classical solution to the pooled within-group correlation matrix, its variance was .16. Dividing by the square root of .16 produces $(-1.15, .92)$, identified as the "Standardized canonical coefficient" in SAS. Had I used the total matrices instead of the pooled within-group matrices, I would have obtained a set of discriminant weights that are standardized to a total variance of 1.0 instead of a within-group variance of 1.0. Because the present mean differences are small, within-standardized and total-standardized weights are similar.

11. Obtain the *group means on the discriminant function* by multiplying the group means on the predictors by the discriminant weights. The Group S mean is $.28 \times -1.08 + .02 \times .86$ or $-.28$. The mean is negative because salesmen are more verbal than quantitative and the verbal measure (X_1) has been assigned a negative weight. Conversely, the group T mean on the dis-

criminant function is .09, reflecting the quantitative nature of the technical staff and the positive weight given to the quantitative measure (X_4). It is instructive to look at the standardized means. The grand means for X_1 and X_4 are .16 and .1, which are obtainable from the grand sums (e.g., $X_1 = 156.42/1000$) above or as the average of the two groups means (e.g., $X_1 = [.28 + .08]/2$), since the sample sizes are equal. The within-group standard deviations, obtainable as the square roots of the diagonal elements of W, are 1.06 and 1.07. Standardizing the group S means to the within-group standard deviation produces $(.28 - .16)/1.06$ or .12 and $(.05 - .11)/1.07$ or $-.06$. Applying these means to the standardized discriminant weights produces $[(.12 \times -1.15) + (-.06 \times .92)]$ or $-.19$. *When the sample sizes are equal and there are only two groups, both the means of the individual predictors and the mean of the discriminant function will be complementary.* Hence, the group T means on X_1, X_4, and the discriminant function are $-.12$, .06, and .19, respectively.

A Third Way to Obtain Discriminant Weights

The most general way to obtain discriminant weights, which can be used when there are more than two groups, is through eigenanalysis. Specifically, raw score (unstandardized) weights may be obtained from the eigenvectors of $\mathbf{W}^{-1}\mathbf{B}$ (which some books describe in equivalent form as $\mathbf{B}\mathbf{W}^{-1}$) and z-score ($\beta$) weights may be obtained from the eigenvectors of $\mathbf{R}_w^{-1}\mathbf{R}_b$, where $\mathbf{R}_w^{-1}$ is the inverse of the pooled within-group correlation matrix and $\mathbf{R}_b$ is the between-group correlation matrix. In both cases, the operations of multiplying by the inverse of a correlation matrix parallel the computation of regression weights. An inverse obtained from variation within groups, "corrects" relations among group means for the redundancy among the predictors.

The eigenanalysis involves the product of symmetric matrices. As noted in Chapter 3, the product is not usually symmetric. It causes a minor difficulty if you are planning to develop your own programs in SAS matrix language because SAS eigenanalysis routines requires that matrices be symmetric. However, the problem can be solved rather easily. The solution involves using the square root inverse of $\mathbf{W}$ ($\mathbf{W}^{-1/2}$), where $\mathbf{W}^{-1/2\prime}\mathbf{W}^{-1/2} = \mathbf{W}^{-1}$. The technique was described in Chapter 3 as a *Cholesky decomposition* of $\mathbf{W}^{-1}$. In other words, you use one simple computer routine to compute $\mathbf{W}^{-1}$ and a second routine to perform the Cholesky decomposition, which yields $\mathbf{W}^{-1/2}$. I will define $\mathbf{W}^{-1/2}$ in such a way that it is an *upper* triangular matrix, i.e., all entries *below* the diagonal are .0; consequently, $\mathbf{W}^{-1/2\prime}$ is a *lower* triangular matrix. The "HALF" operation in SAS PROC MATRIX produces an upper triangle. Some sources, e.g., Overall and Klett (1972), define the triangular matrices in the opposite manner. By appropriately adjusting formulas, either one can be made to produce the correct results.

Next, compute the product of $\mathbf{W}^{-1/2\prime}\mathbf{B}\mathbf{W}^{-1/2}$, which will be symmetric and, as a consequence, amenable to standard eigenanalysis routines. The discriminant function coefficients are obtained by *premultiplying* the eigenvectors of $\mathbf{W}^{-1/2\prime}\mathbf{B}\mathbf{W}^{-1/2}$ (expressed as *columns*) by $\mathbf{W}^{-1/2\prime}$, i.e., the *lower* triangular matrix. The eigenvalues of $\mathbf{W}^{-1/2\prime}\mathbf{B}\mathbf{W}^{-1/2}$ and $\mathbf{W}^{-1}\mathbf{B}$ would be identical if the latter could be extracted directly.

Eigenanalysis of $\mathbf{W}^{-1}\mathbf{B}$ versus Eigenanalysis of $\mathbf{SP}_w^{-1}\mathbf{SP}_b$

Conceptually, a discriminant analysis involves the eigenanalysis of the product matrix $\mathbf{W}^{-1}\mathbf{B}$, following the general role that eigenanalysis plays in maximizing various quantities (the F ratio here). $\mathbf{W}$ and $\mathbf{B}$ both contain mean squares (variances and covariances), so that functions of $\mathbf{W}^{-1}\mathbf{B}$ contain F ratios. Moreover, the diagonals of $\mathbf{W}^{-1}\mathbf{B}$ represent F ratios for the individual variables. *However, the F ratios are not the F ratios one would obtain from simple ANOVA based on raw scores. The F ratios are partial F ratios reflecting ANOVA based on adjusted measures. Inversion serves to partial relations among measures.* The matrix information can yield unadjusted F ratios by *scalar* division. Thus, the conventional (unadjusted) F ratio for measure X_1 is b_{11}/w_{11}.

Normally, discriminant weights are functions of SP matrices ($\mathbf{SP}_w$ and $\mathbf{SP}_b$), through the relation $\mathbf{SP}_w^{-1}\mathbf{SP}_b$ (actually $\mathbf{SP}_w^{-1/2\prime}\mathbf{SP}_b\mathbf{SP}_w^{-1/2}$, using Cholesky decomposition, as discussed previously). The eigenvalues of $\mathbf{SP}_w^{-1}\mathbf{SP}_b$ differ from the eigenvalues of $\mathbf{W}^{-1}\mathbf{B}$. The eigenvalues of an SP matrix (in this case $\mathbf{SP}_w^{-1}\mathbf{SP}_b$) equal the eigenvalues of the corresponding variance–covariance matrix times df_b/df_w. As df_b is normally smaller than df_w, the eigenvalues obtained from a given SP matrix will be smaller than the eigenvalues obtained from the corresponding variance–covariance matrix. *All future references I make to eigenvalues in discriminant analysis will refer to quantities derived from SP matrices.* Because the SP and variance–covariance matrices are related by *scalar* multiplication, their eigenvectors will be identical. Both will differ, though, from those obtained from corresponding correlation matrices because a correlation matrix is obtained from a variance–covariance matrix by *matrix* multiplication.

The fact that the between-group correlation will be either 1 or -1 with two groups means that $\mathbf{R}_b$ and any related matrix like $\mathbf{B}$ will have a rank of 1 when there are only two groups. The product matrices, $\mathbf{W}^{-1}\mathbf{B}$ and $\mathbf{R}_w^{-1}\mathbf{R}_b$, are also limited to rank 1.

Strength of Relation

The multiple correlation between X_1 and X_4 as joint predictors of the dummy or other binary code for group membership is quite important to a discriminant analysis, since it tells how strong the relation between the predictors and group membership is. The correlation may be calculated separately, but it is easier to compute it from the eigenvalue of $\mathbf{SP}_w^{-1}\mathbf{SP}_b$ (λ), using

$$R = [\lambda/(1 + \lambda)]^{1/2} \qquad (8\text{-}2)$$

The term "multiple" correlation does not appear on the printout of most computer packages on discriminant analysis. Instead, the term used is "canonical" correlation. More generally, *canonical correlations represent the strongest possible relation between a linear combination of the predictors, on the one hand, and a linear combination of dummy codes for groups on the other. Hence, it is the correlation involving two sets of optimized β weights, not merely one as is true of multiple correlation.* I will discuss the properties of canonical correlations further in Chapter 11. For now, just consider it simply as an extension of the concept of a multiple correlation that is applicable when you have two or more predictors and three or more groups.

Discriminant Scores, Discriminant Means, and the Mahalanobis Distance Measure

Discriminant scores are obtained just like any other linear combination—multiply the observed scores by the corresponding discriminant weights. Naturally, b weights are applied to raw scores, and β weights are applied to z scores, one more application of Eq. (3-5).

The mean discriminant score for a given group j ($\bar{X}_{dj}$) may be obtained by summing individual discriminant scores within the group and dividing by the number of subjects. However, if the vector of group raw score means for that group, $\mathbf{X}_j$, is available, Eq. (8-3) may be used to obtain $\bar{X}_{dj}$:

$$\bar{X}_{dj} = \mathbf{X}'_j \mathbf{b} \tag{8-3}$$

If the two groups are of equal size, the two means will add up to zero. Otherwise, the product of group sizes (N_j) times the groups means will add to zero. In the present case, the means are $+.189$ and $-.189$; hence, the two groups are .378 units apart. This group mean difference in standard scores is called the *Mahalanobis distance measure*. Some computer programs report the squared distance, $.378^2$ or .143., symbolized as "d^2." Do not confuse the distance measure (d) with the vector of mean differences (**d**).

The Mahalanobis distance between two groups is a function of (1) mean differences on individual predictors and (2) the correlational structure of the predictors. The former is indexed by the **d** vector of Eq. (8-1) and the latter by the within-group correlation matrix, $\mathbf{R}_w$, and within-group variance–covariance matrix, **W**. Clearly, the larger the mean differences are with respect to X_1 and X_4, holding their correlation constant, the more different the two groups are, hence the greater the distance. Conversely, a given mean difference needs to be considered in the light of the covariance structure.

Although d^2 is easily computed from the mean discriminant scores, it may also be computed from

$$d^2 = \mathbf{d}'\mathbf{W}^{-1}\mathbf{d}$$

$$= (\mathbf{X}_S - \mathbf{X}_T)'\mathbf{W}^{-1}(\mathbf{X}_S - \mathbf{X}_T) \tag{8-4}$$

This formula illustrates how the inverse of a matrix of covariances or correlations can be used to correct for intercorrelations among the predictors. Note that if the predictors are orthogonal, the equation reduces to $\mathbf{d'd}$, the vector analogue of squaring. The result would then be the sum of the squared deviations on the individual predictors, which is the way a general Pythagorean distance is obtained.

The Discriminant Structure

Discriminant weights are analogous to factor-score weights in that both are used to obtain a composite measure from a set of observed measures. Just as one may obtain the factor structure in factor analysis, i.e., correlations between the composite and individual variables, so may one obtain the *discriminant structure*, i.e., the correlations between the discriminant axis and the individual predictors. There are actually three different such structures, one each for the total, within-group, and between-group correlation matrices, although in the two-group case, the latter will be either 1 or -1. The three structures are obtained from Eqs. (8-5a), (8-5b), and (8-5c), respectively:

$$\mathbf{S}_t = \mathbf{R}_t\boldsymbol{\beta} \tag{8-5a}$$

$$\mathbf{S}_w = \mathbf{R}_w\boldsymbol{\beta} \tag{8-5b}$$

$$\mathbf{S}_b = \mathbf{R}_b\boldsymbol{\beta} \tag{8-5c}$$

The total and within-group structures are as follows:

$$\mathbf{S}_t = \begin{bmatrix} 1.000 & .536 \\ .536 & 1.000 \end{bmatrix}\begin{bmatrix} -1.149 \\ .921 \end{bmatrix} = \begin{bmatrix} -.644 \\ .300 \end{bmatrix}$$

$$\mathbf{S}_w = \begin{bmatrix} 1.000 & .547 \\ .547 & 1.000 \end{bmatrix}\begin{bmatrix} -1.149 \\ .921 \end{bmatrix} = \begin{bmatrix} -.638 \\ .296 \end{bmatrix}$$

The two structures are quite similar for the same reason that $\mathbf{SP}_w$ strongly determines $\mathbf{SP}_t$—the number of subjects within groups is so much larger than the number of groups. The related considerations that $\mathbf{SP}_t$ confounds the effects of $\mathbf{SP}_w$ and $\mathbf{SP}_b$ also suggests that $\mathbf{SP}_w$ will be more informative than $\mathbf{SP}_t$ when the two SP matrices are discrepant. Both structures indicate that predictor X_1 is more important to group discrimination than X_4. Also, the fact that the correlation between X_1 and the discriminant function is negative whereas the correlation between X_4 and the discriminant function is positive further illustrates that a weighted *difference* between the two predictors is needed for optimal discrimination.

Interpreting a Discriminant Axis

With only two groups, the process of determining what accounts for group differences is relatively simple. One would look at the discriminant axis and, preferably, the structures as well to determine the salients (those predictors correlating most highly with the discriminant axis). The process is essentially the same as in naming factors. In the present case, the data were constructed to reflect the plausible difference between people who were high in verbal ability and low in numerical ability versus the converse pattern. Problems encountered in real-world situations, especially those containing three or more groups and variables, usually pose a more complex problem of interpretation.

There are other statistics that are of interest to the analysis, but many are of limited interest in the two-group case. Adding a third group allows one to deal with nearly all issues in the general case so I will now turn to that topic.

Discriminant Analysis with Two Predictors and Three Groups

The statistical and conceptual issues present when there are only two groups are relatively simple in most cases. The most basic question is usually whether the two groups differ in the population—Are groups S and T the same in the sense of having coincident centroids or are the two groups different? If the latter is true, two additional questions should be asked. First, how do the two groups differ—Is the between-group correlation positive, negative, or zero? The second question concerns the nature of the within-group correlation —is it positive, negative, or zero?

I will now add a third group of executives as group E. With three groups, it is possible that (1) all three centroids will be coincident, (2) two centroids will be coincident but different from the third one, or (3) all three centroids may differ. The first situation might arise if people were assigned to jobs in the company that were independent of whatever X_1 and X_4 measured (the assignments need not be totally random). The second situation might arise if executives were recruited from sales people but not technical people or vice versa. It could also arise if people looked for the same things in sales people and executives which was different from what was needed in technical people.

The most instructive case arises when all three groups are different. Figure 8-2 contains some centroids illustrating how differences might arise. The centroids have been derived from simulations that I will discuss subsequently.

In Fig. 8-2a, group E is the most verbal (highest scores on X_1) but the least quantitative (lowest scores on X_4). All group differences can be effectively summarized by one discriminant function (dimension of variation), which runs from the top left (high quantitative ability but low verbal ability) to the bottom right (high verbal ability but low quantitative ability). The group mean differences are *concentrated* along a single dimension. The structure would still be concentrated if the rank orderings of the three groups were different (perhaps in reality the executives were intermediate to the two groups in the two skills) or of the discriminant function sloped from bottom left to top right (the *group* means on the predictors correlated positively).

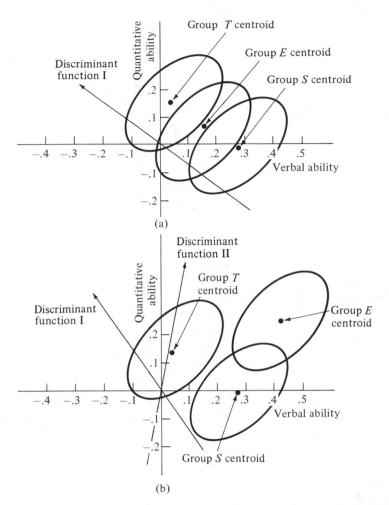

FIGURE 8-2. Discriminant functions for sales, executive, and technical groups (verbal ability = horizontal axis and quantitative ability = vertical axis): (a) concentrated structure; (b) diffuse structure. The scatterplots for the within-group correlations are not drawn to scale. (They are too small and do not indicate the actual overlap that is present.) They are inserted simply to indicate the positive correlation between verbal and quantitative ability of the relationships.

In contrast, consider Fig. 8-2b. Here, the group differences do *not* fall along a single dimension. Instead, the differences form a triangular pattern. The executives have less numerical ability than technical people, but roughly the same verbal ability. Conversely, the executives have the same quantitative ability as the sales people, but less verbal ability. Differences among the groups are *diffuse*—spread among two or more dimensions. Consequently, one discriminant function cannot completely describe how the groups differ.

It is hoped that executives who read this chapter will not be offended by my choice of location for their centroid. Had I chosen to place them at the same level of quantitative ability as the technical people and the same level of verbal ability as the sales people, the structure would be just as diffuse (as well as perhaps offending both the technical and sales people who read this book).

Figure 8-2b also indicates that the difference between sales people and executives is strictly one of verbal ability. Were none of the differences to fall parallel to any of the axes, the structure would still be diffuse. Moreover, when there are more than two groups and two predictors, the relations among the groups would not necessarily fall within a single plane. Hence, it would be difficult to perceive with one single figure. *A discriminant structure is concentrated to the extent the centroids fall along a single line and one discriminant function captures the group differences; the structure is diffuse to the extent that the centroids do not fall along a straight line, so that more than one discriminant function is needed.*

Note that I used the term "concentrated" in Chapter 7 to describe the extent to which a single factor could account for relations among a set of variables and "diffuse" to describe the extent to which more than one factor is needed. I am in fact using the terms in the same general sense except that in factor analysis one looks at how *correlations* among variables are spread, and in discriminant analysis one looks at how *group centroids* are spread.

Type of structures (diffuse or concentrated) can affect one's choice of an inferential test, which is why I will discuss multivariate inferential testing in a separate chapter. You may note at least one hint at an inferential test, though. The multiple correlation you obtain from Eq. (8-2) can be evaluated for significance using the F test of Eq. (4-17) just like any other test of R^2. If the R^2 is significantly greater than .0, the group centroids differ in location.

Extracting Multiple Discriminant Axes

If there are three groups, the correlation between group means for the two predictors can be of any magnitude between $+1.0$ and -1.0. Consequently, **B** will normally be of full rank (2, since I am still assuming two predictors). In turn, $\mathbf{SP}_w^{-1}\mathbf{SP}_b$ will also be of rank 2, since the rank of a product matrix is the lesser of the ranks associated with the components of the product. There will therefore be two nonzero eigenvalues, λ_1 and λ_2, and two associated eigenvectors.

Because eigenvectors are extracted successively, the discriminant scores for different discriminant axes will be orthogonal just like successive PCs or other orthogonal components. Each group will have a mean score on each eigenvector. The number of *possible* discriminant functions corresponds to the number of eigenvectors, which will be the *lesser* of (a) the number of predictors and (b) the number of groups minus one. The number of *usable* discriminant functions may be and often is less than the number possible. Deciding how many are usable has an element of subjectivity. Using methods to be described in Chapter 9, you can use inferential criteria to decide how many of them are statistically significant. Inferential criteria are generally regarded as necessary but not sufficient because a discriminant function may contribute little to the discrimination of group differences and hence not be usable even though it is statistically significant. My examples therefore lead to a maximum of two discriminant functions.

The eigenvector associated with the larger eigenvalue (λ_1) maximizes the variance among the three groups relative to the within-group variance. Were I to draw a figure like 8-1 with three groups instead of only two, you would see that the F ratio for the three groups would still be maximized as it was with the two-group case.

The eigenvector associated with smaller eigenvalue (λ_2) will maximize the remaining variance among groups in the example, although in more complex applications, three or more discriminant axes may be obtainable. A small value of λ_2 implies that all subsequent values of λ will also be small, since successive values of λ represent maximum amounts of *remaining* variance.

Inferring Concentration from the Eigenanalysis

One measure of concentration is to divide the sum of λ_1 and λ_2 (or, equivalently, to divide the trace of $\mathbf{SP}_w^{-1}\mathbf{SP}_b$) into λ_1. If the group centroids are concentrated, then the resulting index of concentration will be 1.0. At the opposite extreme (maximum diffusion of structure), λ_1 and λ_2 will be equal, so that the ratio will be .5 (in the general case, the reciprocal of the number of possible discriminant functions). The eigenvalues of a discriminant solution will be proportional to the squared canonical correlation. Most computer programs report the squared canonical correlations but not the eigenvalues. Consequently, a slightly different, but useful, index of concentration can be obtained as the square of the largest canonical correlation divided by the sums of the squared canonical correlations. This quantity indexes the proportion of total variance that is systematically related to the predictors.

Numerical Examples

I will now turn to discussion of two possible outcomes. One is totally concentrated, within sampling error; the other is relatively diffuse. Both analyses contain the same groups (S and T) discussed in the two-group case. In the concentrated analysis, I added a group of 500 executives (group E) whose X_1 mean was .4 units and X_4 mean was $-.2$ units. Scores within group E were constrained in the same manner as scores in the two other groups. The outcome, with group E representing the highest verbal skills and the least quantitative skills, has been presented in Fig. 8-2a. The diffuse structure corresponds to Fig. 8-2b in that the group E population means were both zero on X_1 and X_4. The population means for the concentrated structure form a straight line, and the population means for the diffuse case form an isosceles triangle with group E equally distant from group S and group T.

The actual means for groups S, T, and E in the concentrated solution were .28, .03, and .40 for X_1 and .05, .17, and $-.25$ for X_4, respectively. The corresponding means in the diffuse solution were .28, .03, and .00 for X_1 and .05, .17 and $-.05$ for X_4. The group S and group T means are the same in both examples because I used the same set of random numbers.

I will present the concentrated solution in detail. The SP matrices are

$$\mathbf{SP}_t = \begin{bmatrix} 1726.86 & 875.56 \\ 875.57 & 1790.53 \end{bmatrix}$$

$$\mathbf{SP}_b = \begin{bmatrix} 36.30 & -37.11 \\ -37.11 & 47.08 \end{bmatrix}$$

$$\mathbf{SP}_w = \begin{bmatrix} 1690.55 & 912.67 \\ 912.67 & 1743.44 \end{bmatrix}$$

The SP matrices have 1499, 2, and 1497 df. Dividing the SP matrices by their corresponding df yields the $\mathbf{T}$, $\mathbf{W}$, and $\mathbf{B}$ matrices:

$$\mathbf{T} = \begin{bmatrix} 1.15 & .58 \\ .58 & 1.19 \end{bmatrix}$$

$$\mathbf{B} = \begin{bmatrix} 18.15 & -18.55 \\ -18.55 & 23.54 \end{bmatrix}$$

$$\mathbf{W} = \begin{bmatrix} 1.13 & .61 \\ .61 & 1.16 \end{bmatrix}$$

Hence, the total, within-group, and between-group correlations between X_1 and X_4 are .50, .53, and $-.98$, respectively. The within-group quantities are nearly identical to the previous example because the additional 500 cases that were generated had an identical structure to the previous 1000 cases except for their mean. The process of computing the various within-group SP, variance–covariance, and correlation terms adjusts for mean differences among the groups. The between-group data are also nearly identical because the correlation among the three group means is nearly -1.0 $[-18.55/(18.15 \times 23.54)^{1/2} = -.90]$, whereas it is exactly -1.0 in the two-group case. Consequently, the total data, being the sum of the two, are little different in this example as compared to the two-group example.

The eigenanalysis of the SP matrices begins with a calculation of $\mathbf{SP}_w^{-1}$:

$$\mathbf{SP}_w^{-1} = \begin{bmatrix} .0008 & -.0004 \\ -.0004 & .0008 \end{bmatrix}$$

As noted in Chapter 3, it can be easily verified that $\mathbf{SP}_w^{-1}\mathbf{SP}_b$ is asymmetric despite the fact that $\mathbf{SP}_w^{-1}$ and $\mathbf{SP}_b$ are each symmetric. The product is

$$\mathbf{SP}_w^{-1}\mathbf{SP}_b = \begin{bmatrix} .0459 & -.0509 \\ -.0453 & .0537 \end{bmatrix}$$

Instead, the square root inverse of $\mathbf{SP}_w$, $\mathbf{SP}_w^{-1/2}$, is needed, which is obtained from a Cholesky decomposition:

$$\mathbf{SP}_w^{-1/2} = \begin{bmatrix} .0287 & -.0150 \\ .0000 & .0239 \end{bmatrix}$$

The product matrix $\mathbf{SP}_w^{-1/2\prime}\mathbf{SP}_b\mathbf{SP}_w^{-1/2}$ may now be obtained; it is symmetric:

$$\mathbf{SP}_w^{-1/2\prime}\mathbf{SP}_b\mathbf{SP}_w^{-1/2} = \begin{bmatrix} .0726 & -.0425 \\ -.0425 & .0270 \end{bmatrix}$$

The eigenvalues of $\mathbf{SP}_w^{-1/2\prime}\mathbf{SP}_b\mathbf{SP}_w^{-1/2}$ are .0980 and .0016. Note that their sum $(.0980 + .0016 = .0996)$ equals the trace of both $\mathbf{SP}_w^{-1}\mathbf{SP}_b$ $(.0459 + .0537)$ and $\mathbf{SP}_w^{-1/2\prime}\mathbf{SP}_b\mathbf{SP}_w^{-1/2}$ $(.0726 + .0270)$.

The degree of concentration is given by the ratio of λ_1 (.0980) to the sum of λ_1 and λ_2 $(.0980 + .0016)$ or .9839. It means that 98.4% of the total variance among the three centroids can be accounted for by the first discriminant function and hence by one straight line.

The associated canonical correlations are also useful. Applying Eq. (8-2) produces values of .299 $[.0980/(1 + .0980)]^{1/2}$ and .040 $[.0016/(1 + .0016)]^{1/2}$, which tells one that only .089 $(.299^2)$ of the *total* variance is associated with the first discriminant function. An even smaller amount, .001 $(.039^2)$, is associated with the second discriminant function. Collectively, the two functions account for .091 of the total variance. The canonical correlations place the concentration statistics in context. Jointly, the concentration statistic and canonical correlations mean that most of the variation in scores occurs among subjects within the three groups, but the variation that is associated with group membership is summarized by a straight line relation among the groups.

When you had proceeded far enough in the analysis to see that the number of usable discriminant functions (one in the present example) is less than the number possible (two, in the present example), you should rerun the analysis limiting the number of discriminant functions. Some of the outputs will be slightly affected by the presence of discriminant functions you are not using even if the discriminant function is not statistically significant. Future references to the second discriminant function of the concentrated example are purely for instructive purposes.

The eigenvectors of $\mathbf{SP}_w^{-1/2\prime}\mathbf{SP}_b\mathbf{SP}_w^{-1/2}$ are $(-.8582, .5133)$ and $(.5133, .8582)$. Note that the sum of their cross products is .0 because they are the eigenvectors of a symmetric matrix. However, discriminant analysis requires the eigenvectors of $\mathbf{SP}_w^{-1}\mathbf{SP}_b$, which are obtained by premultiplying each of the two eigenvectors of $\mathbf{SP}_w^{-1/2\prime}\mathbf{SP}_b\mathbf{SP}_w^{-1/2}$ (expressed as column vectors) by $\mathbf{SP}_w^{-1/2}$. The resulting eigenvectors are $(-.0246, .0252)$ and $(.0147, .0128)$. The sum of their cross products is not .0 because $\mathbf{SP}_w^{-1}\mathbf{SP}_b$ is not symmetric.

These computations may be visualized more readily by forming a matrix from the eigenvectors of $\mathbf{SP}_w^{-1/2\prime}\mathbf{SP}_b\mathbf{SP}_w^{-1/2}$. When this matrix of eigenvectors is premultiplied by $SP_w^{-1/2}$, the columns of the resultant are the eigenvectors of $SP_w^{-1}SP_b$:

$$\begin{bmatrix} .0287 & .0000 \\ -.0150 & .0239 \end{bmatrix} \times \begin{bmatrix} -.8582 & .5133 \\ .5133 & .8582 \end{bmatrix} = \begin{bmatrix} -.0246 & .0147 \\ .0252 & .0128 \end{bmatrix}$$

I have already shown you how eigenvectors may be rescaled to more convenient form, so I will not repeat the calculations. Similarly, the extreme concentration of the data makes the second discriminant function unnecessary. Scaling the first discriminant function to unit variance *within* groups yields the vector $(-1.023, 1.065)$ in z-score (β weight) units and $(-.953, .974)$ in raw score (b weight) units. Within groups, X_1 and X_4 correlate $-.454$ and .513 with the first discriminant function, which defines the within-group structure. The total structure was nearly identical. The two predictors, X_1 and X_4, respectively correlated .471 and .531 with the discriminant axis. All of these indicate that the first discriminant function has essentially the same properties that it had in the two-group case: the unweighted difference between X_1 and X_4.

Both the within-group and total structures are quite different from the between-group structure. The within-group correlations between both X_1 and X_4 and the second discriminant function are substantial (.891 and .858) as are the total correlations (.882 and .875). These high correlations might falsely suggest that the second discriminant function is measuring something systematic when in fact it is not. The *between-group* structure provides the relevant data as to how strongly X_1 and X_4 predict group membership—the correlations between the respective groups means and the discriminant axis are .243 and .209.

The means for group S (normalized within-group) on X_1 and X_4 are .044 and .056. Multiplying the means by the corresponding discriminant weights $(-1.023$ and $1.065)$ produces a mean discriminant score of .015 for the first discriminant axis. The means for group T and X_1 and X_4 are $-.197$ and .167, so their mean discriminant score is .375. Finally, the means for group E are .153 and $-.223$ and their mean discriminant score is $-.390$. Note that the three mean discriminant scores (.015, .375, and $-.390$) add up to zero, because the groups' sizes are equal. The three discriminant score means illustrate that group S is roughly intermediate to groups E and T within sampling error. The way the discriminant axis is defined, high discriminant scores imply large scores on X_4 (quantitative ability) and low scores on X_1 (verbal ability). The direction of the axis is an arbitrary by-product of the algorithm. The scale could be reversed (X is reflected) to reverse its meaning. You are free to reflect an axis if it helps interpretation.

Applying the Mahalanobis distance formula, Eq. (8-4), now requires subscripts to identity which pairs of groups are involved, since distances may be obtained for all possible pairs of groups and there are three such pairs in the present example. I will use the general terms "d_{ij}^2" and "d_{ij}" to denoted the squared distances and distances, respectively, for groups i and j. Applying Eq. (8-4) to groups S and T leads to a value of .138 for d_{ST}^2 and a distance of .371. Note that the distance is slightly greater than the distance between the two groups measured along the first discriminant function (.376 − .014 or .362) because the Mahalanobis measure effectively uses the distances along all discriminant functions. The distance between the two groups on the second discriminant axis is .086. One may use the distance measure of Eq. (4-3) to combine the differences along both axes. The result is $(.362^2 + .086^2)^{1/2}$, which does equal .371. The additivity of the Mahalanobis d^2 measures follows from the concept of a generalized Pythagorean distance.

The two remaining squared distance measures, d_{SE}^2 and d_{TE}^2, are .171 and .586, which correspond to distances of .413 and .766, respectively. The corresponding distances measured along the discriminant axis are .405 and .766. Note that the Mahalanobis distance from group S to group T plus the distance from S to E (.371 + .413 = .784) is essentially the same as the distance from T to E (.766). This equality is a consequence of the linear nature of the three group mean differences. In general, the *indirect* distance between two groups, such as S and E, as measured from a third group (group T), which is the sum of the two distances, d_{ST} and d_{SE}, will always be at least as great as the *direct* distance, d_{SE}. The result is a deduction from the very important *Cauchy–Schwarz* (*triangle*) theorem (Kemeny, Mirkil, Snell, & Thompson, 1959), which states that the sum of the distances along any two sides of a triangle is at least as large as the remaining side. In particular, *if the direct distance between two groups and the indirect distance through a third group are similar, then the differences among the three groups are concentrated along a single dimension.*

The $\mathbf{T}$, $\mathbf{W}$, and $\mathbf{B}$ matrices for the diffuse solution are as follows:

$$\mathbf{T} = \begin{bmatrix} 1.14 & .61 \\ .61 & 1.17 \end{bmatrix}$$

$$\mathbf{W} = \begin{bmatrix} 1.13 & .61 \\ .61 & 1.16 \end{bmatrix}$$

$$\mathbf{B} = \begin{bmatrix} 12.22 & .34 \\ .34 & 6.12 \end{bmatrix}$$

Hence, the total, within-group, and between-group correlations between X_1 and X_4 are .53, .53, and .04, respectively. The within-group variance–covariance matrix, and, hence, the within-group correlation between X_1 and X_4, are identical to their counterparts obtained in the concentrated case, which reflects the fact that the within-group structure was in fact the same in both the concentrated and diffuse simulations. The most important difference in the two solutions is that the between-group correlation is essentially zero. The total statistics did not change much because 1497 of the 1499 df were derived from within-group data; hence, the between-group data had only a minor influence.

As in the concentrated case, $\mathbf{SP}_w^{-1}\mathbf{SP}_b$ is of rank 2, and will therefore have two eigenvalues and eigenvectors. The two eigenvalues are .023 and .006. Consequently, 79.3% of the between-group variance is accounted for by the first discriminant function instead of .958 in the concentrated case. The associated canonical correlations are .151 and .078, which are both significant. Collectively, the two functions account for .029 of the total variance. This sum is less than it was in the concentrated case (.091), because I happened to make the groups mean differences smaller in generating the diffuse simulation.

The two associated eigenvectors are $(-.029, .020)$ and $(.007, .020)$. The vector of discriminant weights for the first function is $(-1.155, .848)$, and the vector of discriminant weights for the second function is $(.280, .826)$. The corresponding raw score vectors are $(-1.080, .784)$ and $(.262, .763)$. The within-group structure of X_1 and X_4 is $(-.698, .236)$ for the first function and $(.716, .972)$ for the second. The total structure was highly similar. The between-group structure was $(-.886, .429)$ for the first function and $(.464, .903)$ for the second. Thus, the major dimension of discrimination is still the difference between X_1 and X_4, but X_1 is weighted slightly more heavily. The second dimension of discrimination, which does contribute to differentiating the groups apart, is the sum of the two with X_4 given slightly heavier weighting. Although the analysis will not be presented, very similar results hold when equal weights are applied to the data.

The mean discriminant scores for groups S, T, and E on the first discriminant function are $-.199$, $.171$, and $.028$. Hence, the first dimension contrasts salesman at the negative pole and technical people at the positive pole with executives roughly in the middle. Because the sample sizes are equal, the three means add to zero. The discriminant means on the second function are $.042$, $.069$, and -1.09 (which, of course, also add to zero within rounding error) for groups S, T, and E. The second function thus contrasts sales people *and* technical people with executives. The smaller range of mean differences reflects the lesser variance accounted for by this second function.

The Mahalanobis distance measures are also instructive—d_{ST} was .371, d_{SE} was .273 and d_{TE} was .227. The distances are smaller than their counterparts in the concentrated example because the group separations are smaller. More importantly, note that any given direct distance is fairly dissimilar from its indirect distance, e.g., the indirect distance from group S to group T via group E is $.273 + .227$ or $.500$, as compared to the direct distance of .371. The dissimilarity is a consequence of the diffusion. I could have diffused the group means further by having them fall along an equilateral and not merely an isosceles triangle, but the two-dimensional differences here are sufficiently great to illustrate the point. Also note that the proportion of systematic variance is slightly greater in this example than in the previous example. I could have made them equal or even larger in the concentrated case by choice of mean differences; the concentrated versus diffuse distinction is totally independent of the overall systematicity.

Depiction of Group Differences in the Diffuse Example

Note that the two axes of the diffuse solution graphically presented in Fig. 8-2b do *not* cross at right angles, despite the independence of their factor scores. *The discriminant axes are not geometrically orthogonal since $z_1'z_2$ is not zero, where z_1 and z_2 are the two discriminant functions. The axes may be said to be statistically orthogonal as $z_i'Wz_j$ and $z_i'Tz_j$ are both zero.*

In contrast, the principal components and orthogonal rotations discussed in Chapter 6 are both geometrically and statistically orthogonal. The eigenvectors of any *symmetric* matrix such as a correlation matrix will be both geometrically and statistically orthogonal, but the eigenvectors of an *asymmetric* matrix such as $SP_w^{-1}SP_b$ will be statistically but not geometrically orthogonal.

Statistical orthogonality is the more important property. Because of it, I can make use of an alternative means of description portrayed in Fig. 8-3. I have drawn the discriminant axes at right angles because the functions are statistically orthogonal. Each group is represented by its discriminant function mean for the diffuse case. I could have done the same thing in the concentrated solution, but the centroids would simply be points along a straight line.

Figure 8-3 allows the previous interpretation of group differences to be

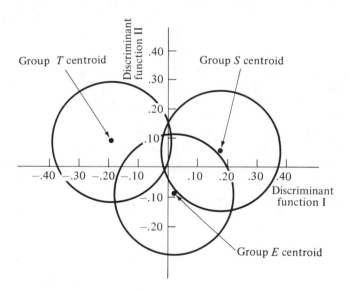

FIGURE 8-3. Discriminant functions for sales, executive, and technical groups; discriminant function I = horizontal axis and discriminant function II = vertical axis— diffuse solution. The scatterplots for the within-group correlations are not drawn to scale. (They are too small and do not indicate the actual overlap that is present.) They are inserted simply to indicate the orthogonality of the two discriminant scores.

visualized, i.e., that the first dimension contrasts groups T and S with group E in the middle, whereas the second dimension contrasts groups T and S, on the one hand, with Group E on the other hand. I have also drawn the group envelopes as circles to remind you that the two sets of discriminant scores are uncorrelated.

I will treat the problem of classification in more detail in the Chapter 9, but there is a useful point to be gleaned from the differences in the two axes. The first furnishes useful information about all three groups. If a person gets a large negative score, that person resembles a sales person. If a person gets a large positive score, that person resembles a technical person. However, if a person's score is near zero, he or she resembles an executive.

By contrast, a positive score on the second discriminant axis means the individual could be like a sales person or a technical person, although a negative score would connote that the person is like an executive. The first discriminant axis separated all three groups, but you will encounter situations where two or more groups are quite similar with respect to the first discriminant axis, and it will be the second or later discriminant axis that allow decisions to be made among groups which are similar on the first axis. The situation might occur were two of the groups to be fairly similar but both quite different from the third, and if the basis for the difference between the first two groups is different from their difference with the third. Were the latter condition not met, the structure would be concentrated and there would be no basis to choose between the first two groups, which sometimes occurs in real world situation.

Figure 8-3 by itself is not very informative as to what constitutes the discriminant axes in that it does not contain the information in Fig. 8-2 about the structure. Overall and Klett (1972) have suggested a modification, which I find quite useful, called the "insertion of *measurement vectors*." Figure 8-4 illustrates the use of measurement vectors.

The direction of the measurement vectors is obtained from the *between-group* structures, which are $-.886$ and $.429$ for X_1 ad X_4, respectively, with the first discriminant axis. The angles of the vectors are 152 and 65 degrees, respectively. The vector for X_1 will therefore point away (to the negative pole) but the vector for X_4 will point toward the positive pole. The *lengths* of the vectors are proportional to the magnitude of the correlation (between-group structure) times the ratio of between-group variance to within-group variance. Thus, the relative length of the X_1 vector is $.889 \times (12.22/1.13)$ or 9.61 (any arithmatic sign that may arise is immaterial and can be omitted), and the relative length of the X_4 vector is $.429 \times (6.12/1.16)$ or 2.26. The absolute lengths are not important; what is important is that the X_1 vector is 4.15 $(9.61/2.26)$ times as important as the X_4 vector. The absolute lengths would be unnecessarily long relative to the mean differences to fit in a compact manner on the graph. The corresponding vectors for the second discriminant function have an orientation of 62 degrees and relative length of 5.05 for X_1

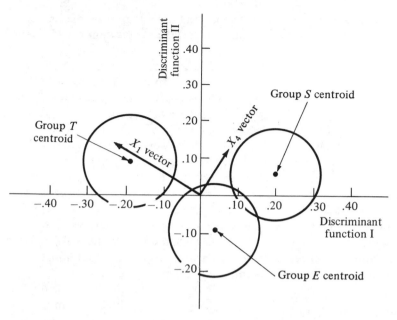

F<small>IGURE</small> 8-4. Discriminant functions for sales, executive, and technical groups, measurement vectors inserted—diffuse solution. The scatterplots for the within-group correlations are not drawn to scale. (They are too small and do not indicate the actual overlap that is present.) They are inserted simply to indicate the orthogonality of the two discriminant scores.

and an orientation of 25 degrees and relative length of 4.76 for X_4. These have not been drawn to keep the figure simple.

Varimax Rotation

The two discriminant axes may be rotated to the varimax (or, in principle, any other) criterion, which will level the discriminatory capacity of the individual axes. Rotation will produce a transformation matrix, new vectors, and associated structures. The rotation may or may not facilitate interpretation. *A varimax rotation should not be used with a concentrated structure, since it exaggerates the role of minor and perhaps statistically insignificant dimensions of variation.*

Use of Prior Weights

As with any application involving a linear combination, simplified weights (e.g., unit weights) often produce nearly the same results as optimal weights. I specifically used the following three sets of weights: (1) the simple (unweighted) sum for the concentrated case, (2) the pair of predictors $2X_1 - X_4$ and $X_1 + 2X_4$ for the diffuse case, and (3) the simple sum and difference for the diffuse case.

Simplified weights may be viewed as an acceptable substitute for optimal weights when there is little difference in the canonical correlations they produce. A subsidiary criterion is that the pairs of predictors be relatively orthogonal, since the optimal weights will produce orthogonal discriminant scores.

If you had data from a second sample available, you could cross validate both the original (optimal) and simplified weights. *It is quite possible that simplified weights discriminate better than the original weights in the new sample.*

Simply applying the simplified weights to the original data produced squared canonical correlations that were identical to three decimal places with the optimal (least squares) weights in all three cases. I was personally surprised to note that the equal weights applied to the diffuse data were more nearly orthogonal to one another ($r_w = -.018$) than were the unequal weights ($r_w = .34$). Score one more for "It don't make no nevermind," although, as in all prior statements, the issue is empirical.

Heteroscedasticity

The procedure that I use to generate the data ensured that the scatterplots for the three groups were the same except for chance. That is, I *made* the data conform to the linear model by making group differences additive with respect to within-group variability. Events occurring in the real world can be quite different.

Heteroscedasticity, which in the multivariate case denotes group differences in covariance as well as the variance of individual variables, can conceivably arise from two distinct processes. First, there could be group differences in variance on one or more predictors. Second, there could be group differences in covariance or correlation.

In principle, the latter can arise because two variables have an intrinsic tendency to correlate differentially in different populations. Whenever one variable (that defining the difference between populations in this case) affects the correlation(s) among other variables, that variable is said to *moderate* the relationship(s). Usually, though, differences in the magnitude of correlations in different populations are artifacts of differences in variability, i.e., one group is more range restricted than the other. For example, MMPI Scale 2 indexes the tendency to endorse symptoms that are characteristic of depressed patients, and MMPI Scale 9 indexes the tendency to endorse symptoms related to excitability and impulsiveness that are characteristic of patients with manic tendencies. Both scales were originally scaled to standard deviations of 10.0 among normal volunteers. There is a modest negative correlation between the two scales.

If the MMPI is given to a group of patients seeking therapy, scores on both scales will be more variable than the scores obtained in the original normative sample, perhaps producing standard deviations of 12 or more instead of 10. The range of both traits is greater—there will be more people who are clinically depressed as well as more people who are manic in the psychiatric sample than in the original normative sample since these two mood disorders led some people to seek therapy in the first place.

Conversely, if one tests job applicants, e.g., people seeking employment in nuclear power plants as described in Chapter 4, their standard deviations will be much smaller, around 7 or 8 (cf. Bernstein & Garbin, 1985b, for relevant data). Applicants are not necessarily freer of these mental disorder than normative subjects (although I hope that the applicants are freer of problems than the psychotherapy patients). Rather, applicants are more reluctant to admit to statements denoting mood disorder than were people in the normative group, as the latter did not have job prospects riding on the outcome of their MMPI profiles.

These differences in test-taking attitude translate into differences in the magnitude of correlations within the various groups. Correlations derived from applicants are more range restricted and hence lower than the normative sample, and the normative sample is more range restricted than patients seeking therapy. The range restriction affects the overall factor structures.[2] In addition, *mean* differences between groups may translate into differences in correlations because of floor or ceiling effects.

I have discussed the importance of the individual variance–covariance matrices in detail because it is important to look at them. These individual matrices should be relatively similar if you are going to pool them. A pooled within-group matrix, like any average, should be based on comparable quantities. The same principle is involved as in looking at homogeneity of variance in univariate data to see if groups are equally variable. I am not saying that you should dispense with the analysis if the matrices are heterogeneous. You should, however, inform the reader when it occurs. I will discuss some of the consequences of heteroscedasticity upon classification in Chapter 9.

The determinants of the individual and pooled within-group matrices are a commonly used summary statistic to describe the overall variance of the observations in the dimensions defined by a set of predictors. The larger a group's determinant is, the more nearly uncorrelated the set of predictors are within that group. Based on the discussion of determinants in Chapter 3, if two or more variables correlate perfectly, the resulting correlation matrix is singular and will have a determinant of .0. The more the group determinants vary among themselves, the more the group correlational structures differ.

I have noted that the inferential test for homogeneity is reasonably powerful

---

[2] It is truly amazing to learn that there are numerous studies that compare factor structures in different populations and conclude they are different when in fact the true cause of this difference is range restriction.

so that heteroscedasticity is usually the rule, and not an exception, with large samples. If two variables correlate .30 in one sample and .35 in another, the difference can be statistically significant yet trivial—do not follow the outcomes of null hypothesis testing blindly.

Discriminant Analysis—The General Case

The general case provides a number of discriminant functions equal to the lesser of the number of groups minus one and the number of predictors. This general case really does not present any new conceptual problems. The major point to remember is that even though you may be satisfied with the results of your initial analysis of a data set, it is more likely that you will benefit from exploring additional solutions. You may succeed in eliminating unnecessary predictors and/or discriminant axes. The strategy of simplifying the content of a particular discriminant function is identical to that involved in naming and simplifying factors (cf. Chapter 6). Deciding whether to retain a particular discriminant axis is a choice that depends on the needs of the situation, the variance the discriminant accounts for, its level of statistical significance, and its meaningfulness.

Components as Discriminant Variables

If you have many predictors, you may find it useful to perform a component analysis upon the *within-group* correlation matrix first to evaluate its dimensionality. I have found component analysis quite useful in two very different projects—the analysis of ratings of nurses and hospital patients about various aspects of medical care (Buckles, 1982) and the morphology of various species of frogs (Ford, 1981). The former led to a clearly defined three-variable structure. The latter was even simpler—some frogs are bigger than other frogs—so that a host of specific measures derived from head size, claw size, etc., could be reduced to one. Despite the fact that the analysis based on raw data suggested numerous discriminant functions, an analysis based on a single (size) predictor will do just as well.

Hypothesis Testing

As with other aspects of multivariate analysis, I strongly encourage you to formulate hypotheses about which variables are relevant. Predictors can be added in stages to determine how much they contribute to classification criteria such as the canonical correlation or Mahalanobis distances. Again, one should not simply think in terms of incorporating as many predictors as possible without thought as to how predictors are structured, since it is typical for multiple predictors to be correlated and therefore highly redundant.

Confirmatory Factor Analysis

The use of components and substantive hypotheses can be readily combined. Form the within-group correlation matrix and use your knowledge about within-group structure to set up an OMG or LISREL confirmatory factoring. Remember, that unlike the previous discussion of confirmatory factor analysis, there are really two structures to consider—one involving the predictors and the other involving the group centroids.

Stepwise Discriminant Analysis

Discriminant analysis can be done in a stepwise (atheoretical) manner. Several different options are available in the various packages. For example, you can add variables to produce the maximum gain in distance or the maximum increment in squared canonical correlation, or using other inferential criteria. There clearly is one case in which nearly every investigator supports a stepwise approach. That situation is when you wish to select from a set of predictors and have no theoretical interest in which ones to choose. As I noted at many points in this book, statistical algorithms are no substitute for thought about the data structure. Huberty (1984) provides a useful discussion of problems that may arise from misuse of stepwise discriminant analysis and discusses a variety of topics relevant to classification.

I have now explored the issue of how to combine predictors to form a discriminant equation. As with nearly all topics discussed in this book, a multivariate problem has been effectively reduced to a univariate problem because the information relevant to a set of predictors can be summarized by the discriminant axis. In order to perform the actual classification, however, one or more *cutoffs* need be made on the axis to define the specific categories that are going to be used. That topic will be considered in Chapter 9.

My presentation of the process of classification will be a bit unusual since I am going to begin the next chapter with a topic that thus far has not been presented in other textbooks on multivariate analysis—*signal detection analysis*. Signal detection theory (Egan, 1975; Green & Swets, 1967) is a joint product of sensory psychophysics, communication theory, and statistical decision theory, which was introduced into psychology a little over 30 years ago (Tanner & Swets, 1954) and represents one formal approach to classification. The general idea behind relating discriminant analysis and signal detection theory was suggested by Hake and Rodwan (1966) in the context of their discussion of measurement in perception. They pointed out how discriminant analysis deals with the problem of combining multiple sources of information such as visual angle and apparent distance into a single dimension of apparent size and how signal detection theory deals with classifying observations into categories defined by the experimenter, e.g., "large" versus "small."

9
Classification Methods—Part 2. Methods of Assignment

Chapter Overview

The part of classification that I am now concerned with is how to classify an individual observation. In order to deal with some logical problems, I will first present *Bayesian* considerations about the *values* and *base rates* associated with a decision. The topic leads into *signal detection theory*, an area of decision making that ties together communication theory, statistics, econometrics, and psychophysics.

I. THE EQUAL VARIANCE GAUSSIAN MODEL—The simplest problem in signal detection involves a decision as to whether an observation was drawn from a *noise (n)* or a *signal plus noise (s)* distribution. Observations from each are assumed to be normally distributed with equal variance, i.e., the signal adds a constant to noise. The outcome of a given trial can either be a *hit* or a *false alarm*, depending on whether a subject says "Yes" and the observation is drawn from the *s* or the *n* distribution, respectively. Likewise, the outcome can either be a *correct rejection* or a *miss*, if the subjects says "No" and the observations is drawn from the *n* or the *s* distribution, respectively. The associated *rates* of the four outcomes, specifically, the *hit rate* and the *false alarm rate* are the basic data for analysis. By being more or less willing to say "Yes" versus "No," i.e., by varying the response *criterion*, a subject can trade hit rates and false alarms for correct rejections and misses. A *receiver (relative) operating characteristic (ROC) curve* depicts a subject's hit rate as a function of his or her false alarm rate under different criteria (degrees of willingness to say "yes" versus "no"). Under the equal variance assumptions, it can be shown that the normal deviate corresponding to the hit rate is a linear function of the normal deviate corresponding to the false alarm rate. Essential to the analysis is the concept of a *decision axis*, which contains the information used to make a decision. If the equal variance Gaussian model holds, it can be shown that the optimal strategy is to choose a value along the decision axis as a *cutoff* or *criterion*; an ideal decision maker should say "yes" if an observation falls above that cutoff and "no" if it falls below. The *likelihood ratio* (ratio of the probability of the observation given signal to the probability of the observation given noise) increases monotonically with the magnitude of the observation.

II. THE UNEQUAL VARIANCE GAUSSIAN MODEL—In the next most commonly studied signal detection paradigm, the signal contributes variance of its own to the *s* distribution. As a consequence, the *s* distribution is more variable than the *n* distribution. There are several consequences of unequal variance. One is that the ROC curve has a *slope* of less than 1.0 when hit rate and false alarm rate are both expressed as normal deviates. A more important consequence is that the simple cutoff rule used in the equal variance case becomes nonoptimal, if not totally inapplicable, depending on how radically the two variances differ because *the likelihood ratio is not longer a monotonic function of the decision variable.*

III. OTHER SIGNAL DETECTION MODELS—This section looks briefly at several other models used for binary classification. None has had the import of the two Gaussian models.

IV. STRATEGIES FOR INDIVIDUAL CLASSIFICATION—The signal detection models are useful in describing some very basic issues in classification. However, these models are limited to situations in which there are two states of nature (*s* and *n*) and the decision maker is limited to two alternative judgments ("Yes" and "No"). In this section, the problem is broadened to consider what happens when there are multiple states of nature and judgments. The basic data to evaluate decision making under such conditions are summarized in a *confusion matrix* that contains the joint frequency with which particular states of nature occurred and particular judgments were made. Likewise, *Bayes' theorem* is extended to incorporate multiple states.

V. ALTERNATIVE STRATEGIES—AN OVERVIEW—There are many ways to form a decision axis for purposes of classification. Before listing alternatives, it is important to ask certain questions about the data at hand: (1) Is the structure primarily concentrated or diffuse? (2) Are normal curve assumptions appropriate? (3) Is it important to incoporate base rates and/or values associated with different decisions? (4) Are the components of the decision variable, which may or may not be the raw predictors, highly inter-correlated or relatively independent. (5) Do groups vary to approximately the same extent on the decision variable or do they vary considerably (are they homoscedastic or heteroscedastic)? (6) Will classification be done by hand or by computer? (7) Is the metric used to classify observations a familiar one? Probabilities and *z* scores are examples of familiar metrics. However, familiarity of the metric is more important in some situations than in others.

VI. A NUMERICAL EXAMPLE—In order to make things tangible, I consider a practical problem in classifying an individual as (1) a normal applicant to a police department, (2) a patient in a pain clinic, or (3) a person seeking psychotherapy, based on the profiles of two MMPI scales (Hy and Pd). As one might expect, the three groups are quite different.

VII. CLASSIFICATION BASED ON SALIENT VARIABLES—One very simple strategy is to identify those particular variables that best discriminate and use these *salient* variables as predictors, without unnecessarily employing any complex multivariate procedures. Use of salient variables is illustrated in several settings. Some procedures assume that the salient variable is distributed *normally*, others do not make such an assumption. In addition, procedures exist for cases in which the variance of the salient variable is the same across groups (*homoscedasticity*) versus cases in which the variance differs (*heteroscedasticity*). Finally, analyses can be conducted with or without the incorporation of Bayesian variables. One important point is made relative to the use of Bayesian variables: *It is quite risky to incorporate information about values without incorporating information about base rates at the same time.*

VIII. DISCRIMINANT FUNCTIONS AND CLASSIFICATION—A second class of measures can be derived from the discriminant function that is quite useful when the group means are concentrated. As was true of methods involving salient variables, different models can (1) utilize or not utilize normal curve assumptions, (2) assume or not assume homoscedasticity, and (3) incorporate or ignore Bayesian information. The role of the χ^2 distribution is discussed when one desires to employ some, but not all, discriminant functions in classification.

IX. CLASSIFICATION BASED ON DISTANCE MEASURES—A third class of measures is based on the Mahalanobis distance from an unknown observation to each of several group centroids. As in the previous two sections, various forms of this procedure can be used in conjunction with assumptions about normality, homoscedasticity, and the use of Bayesian information.

This chapter concludes with a brief contrast of the procedures in the context of the questions raised in Section V.

I will now discuss how decisions about individual cases are made. There are several methods of classification. Some are better suited to concentrated structures; others are more useful with diffuse structures. Some allow you to incorporate *Bayesian* information about the probabilities of the various classes (*base rates*) and the consequences of correct and incorrect decisions (*values*), other procedures ignore Bayesian information. Some methods are better suited for hand calculation, and others require a computer. In short, there is a rich set of methods that can be used, and the purpose of this chapter is to explore those methods.

I will begin with a situation like the one described in the previous chapter in which there are only two groups. Hence, the structure is concentrated. I will initially assume that the distributions of the two groups are normal (Gaussian) with equal variance and that Bayesian considerations are not important. I will then consider problems of a progressively more complicated nature.

Material in this chapter comes from two general sources. One is known in psychology as *signal detection theory* (Green & Swets, 1967; Egan, 1975), in which the methods are applied to areas such as perception and memory. The topic originally dealt with the ability of subjects to detect a *signal* or systematic event, such as a tone, in the presence of random *noise*, such as "white noise" (a sound like a hissing tea kettle). The problem of detecting a signal embedded in noise is a very familiar one to students of psychophysics. However, the form of the problem is the same as that studied in any context where one must assign high "scores" to one category and low "scores" to another by developing a suitable definition of "how high is high." Historically, the symbols "*s*" and "*n*," respectively denoting "signal" and "noise," are widely used; my example will exploit this convention. The other source is the formal literature on discriminant analysis. The roots of both areas are the same, the statistical theory of decision making. However, some conventions and terminology differ.

The Equal Variance Gaussian Model

For purposes of example, assume that body temperatures are a constant for a given healthy individual, but vary slightly across individuals. Specifically, assume that the distribution over people is normal (98.6, .2). Now assume a particular form of influenza that elevates one's temperature exactly by .4 degrees. At issue is correctly diagnosing an individual as normal or sick from his or her temperature reading alone. Assume that people have no idea of their normal body temperature. Hence, a person with a reported temperature of 98.8 degrees can be (1) normal, but with a usual temperature that is .2 degrees higher than the average persons, or (2) sick, but with a usual temperature which is 98.4 degrees, or .2 degrees less than average.

The data imply that the distribution of body temperatures of sick people will be normal (99.0, .2). Their standard deviation will be the same as normals because of the assumed *constant* effect of the sickness. Adding a constant (.4) to each observation in a distribution shifts the mean of that distribution by that amount, but does not affect its variability, as noted in Eq. (2-7). Figure 9-1 describes the *probability* distributions. This figure is misleading in one important respect. It makes it appear as if the *frequencies* of normal people and sick people are the same because both distributions have the same area (1.0, as they are probability distributions). In actuality, far more people are well than are sick at any given time.

The decision axis, temperature, may be depicted in one of three general ways, among others (1) as raw scores in degrees Fahrenheit, (2) as z scores scaled so that the *lesser* of the two means (normals) is .0, or (3) as z scores scaled so that the *grand* mean equals .0. Scaling (2) is most common in signal detection theory, but scaling (3) is the rule for classification problems in discriminant analysis, a convention I will follow. The data are also scaled so

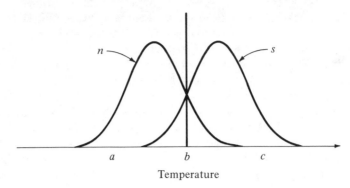

FIGURE 9-1. The equal variance Gaussian model of signal detection. The vertical line at b or criterion is located at $z_i = 0$ ($X_i = 99.0$). At any point below this particular criterion, such as a, it is more probable that a person is normal than sick. The ordinate to the n distribution is greater than the ordinate to the s distribution so the ratio or $l(z_i) < 1.0$. At any point above this criterion, such as c, it is more probable that the person is sick. The ordinate to the n distribution is smaller than the ordinate to the s distribution, so $l(z_i) > 1.0$. At the criterion (b), the two heights are equal so $l(z_i) = 1.0$. Temperature is a monotonic function of the likelihood ratio and therefore a proper decision variable in this case.

that the *within-group* standard deviations are 1.0, which is typical in both areas of application. (Paralleling the discussion of the previous chapter, the *total* standard deviation could be scaled to 1.0 instead, but I will not do so here.)

I have drawn a vertical line at the point where $z_i = 0$, the unweighted mean of 98.8 degrees, i.e., $(98.6 + 99.0)/2$. The symbol "X_i" will denote the value of the criterion in raw score units.

Decision Rules and Cutoff Rules

A *decision rule* is any rule that converts an observation into a decision. This definition even includes *random* rules. Of particular interest is any rule that places observations in one category if the observation falls above the cutoff and in the alternative category if the observation falls below the cutoff. This type of rule is known as a *single cutoff rule* or, more simply, a *cutoff* rule. Specifically, I will classify anyone with a temperature above 98.8 degrees as sick and anyone below 98.8 degrees as normal. (The precise cutoff will be changed at various points of discussion.) A cutoff rule is a decision rule, but a decision rule need not be a cutoff rule—there are situations (an example is considered in this chapter) in which a person should be classified as sick if their temperature is high *or* their temperature is low. (The reason this is not considered a cutoff rule is that the definition assumes a *single* cutoff.) A related point to keep in mind is that the rule a person uses to make *classifications* (judgments) need not be optimal in terms of *outcomes*—just because I classify someone as normal or sick does not imply that he or she is normal or sick in reality. Given the data, it can be shown that I will be correct more often than chance, but I may also make a substantial number of errors. I will defend the use of my particular decision rule later in the chapter.

There are four possible outcomes of any classification which jointly depend on whether (a) a given observation is greater than or equal to 0 versus less than 0 and (b) whether or not that observation was derived from a sick person (s) or a normal person (n). The terms "sick" and "normal" in my example were deliberately chosen so that their abbreviations correspond to the signal detection terms "signal" and "noise" as a way to help you to remember things.

When the observation consists of a temperature reading from a person who is in fact sick, the outcome is termed a *hit* if the person is correctly classified as sick or a *miss* (also called a *false negative*) if that sick person is incorrectly classified as normal. The *hit rate*, symbolized $p(Y/s)$, is the number of hits, divided by the number of s observations. Hence, it is a conditional probability. It is also the probability that an observation drawn from the s distribution exceeds 0 in my example, $p(z_i/s) > 0$, which is the area under the s distribution to the right of the cutoff, 0. The $p(Y/s) = p(z_i/s)$ can be determined from the data at hand. The grand mean is .2 units below the mean of the s distribution, which has a standard deviation of .2; hence, it is 1.0 z-score units below its mean. Elementary normal curve statistics reveal the area to be .84.

The *miss rate*, $p(N/s)$, is the complement of the hit rate. It is the probability that an s observation falls below 0 in the example, $p(z_i/s) < 0.$, which is the area under the s distribution to the left of the cutoff. Because of its complementary relation to the hit rate, it equals .16 in the example.

When the observation consists of a temperature reading from a person who is in fact normal, the outcome is termed a *false alarm* (also, a *false positive*) when that person is classified as sick and a *correct rejection* when that person is classified as normal. The *false alarm rate*, $p(Y/n)$, is the number of false alarms divided by the number of n observations. It is also the probability that an observation drawn from the n distribution equals or exceeds 0 in the example, $p(z_i/n) \geq 0$. which is the area under the n distribution to the right of the cutoff. The grand mean of the n distribution is 1.0 z-score units below the cutoff. Hence, the false alarm rate will be .16 in the present example.

Finally, the *correct rejection rate*, $p(N/n)$, is the complementary probability that an observation drawn from the n distribution is less than 0, $p(z_i/n) < 0.$, which equals .84 in the present example.

The relations among the four basic quantities may be visualized—first, the following matrix, which contains *joint* frequencies for the four outcomes. Thus, a = the number of times a person's temperature was elevated *and* they were *sick* in reality, b = the number of times a person's temperature was *not* elevated *and* they were *sick* in reality, c = the number of times a person's temperature was elevated *and* they were *normal* in reality, and d = the number of times a person's temperature was *not* elevated *and* they were *normal* in reality:

		Judgment	
		Yes Temperature elevated	No Temperature not elevated
R			
e			
a	Sick	a = Number of hits	b = Number of misses
l			
i	Normal	c = Number of false alarms	d = Number of correct rejections
t			
y			

Conditionalizing the probabilities by *rows* leads to the relevant rates:

		Judgment	
		Yes Temperature elevated	No Temperature not elevated
R			
e			
a	Sick	$a/(a + b)$ = Hit rate	$b/(a + b)$ = Miss rate
l			
i	Normal	$c/(c + d)$ = False Alarm rate	$d/(c + d)$ = Correct Rejection rate
t			
y			

Typically, only the hit rate and the false alarm rate are presented. You can determined the miss rate and the correct rejection rate from the hit rate and false alarm rate by subtraction. For example, the $p(N/s)$ is $1.0 - p(Y/s)$, since $a/(a + b) + b/(a + b) = 1.0$. Likewise, the $p(N/n)$ is $1.0 - p(Y/n)$, since $c/(c + d) + d/(c + d)$ also equals 1.0.

Other Properties

The height of a vertical line drawn to the s distribution at any given point along the decision axis yields the probability of obtaining that given temperature when a person is sick, $p(z_i/s)$. A vertical line drawn to the n distribution yields the corresponding probability of obtaining that given temperature when a person is normal, $p(z_i/n)$. The ratio of $p(z_i/s)$ to $p(z_i/n)$ is known as the *likelihood ratio*, $l(z_i)$.

The likelihood ratio has an extremely important property in the equal variance Gaussian model—it increases as z_i increases. That is, when z_i is low, both $p(z_i/s)$ and $p(z_i/n)$ are small, but $p(z_i/s)$ is much smaller than $p(z_i/n)$. It is unlikely that anyone's temperature is below 97 degrees, but if it is, that person is much more likely to be normal (relative to this strain of influenza).

As z_i increases, $p(z_i/s)$ and $p(z_i/n)$ both increase, but at different rates. Below the cutoff point $(z_i = 0)$, $p(z_i/n) > p(z_i/s)$, meaning that it is more probable a person is normal than sick in this range. The two probabilities also become progressively more equal. They become exactly equal at the cutoff of $z_i = 0$. Consequently, the likelihood ratio becomes 1.0.

The likelihood ratio increases and exceeds 1.0 for all values of z_i past the cutoff even though both $p(z_i/s)$ and $p(z_i/n)$ progressively decrease. Indeed, $l(z_i)$ increases without bounds.[1] Thus, the higher a person's temperature, the more likely it is that he or she is sick. Although $l(z_i)$ and z_i are not *linearly* related, they are *monotonically* related. Increases in z_i are never accompanied by decreases in $l(z_i)$. *A decision rule is considered proper if, and only if, the variable used by that rule increases monotonically with the likelihood ratio, that is, increasing values of the decision variable make it more probable that an observation belongs to the target (signal) group.* The z_i (or, for that matter, X_i) is a proper decision variable in the equal variance Gaussian model.

In sum, the equal variance Gaussian model has the property that several decision variables will lead to identical outcomes. Among other possibilities, I can diagnose people as sick if (1) their temperature is 98.8 degrees Fahrenheit or above, (2) their temperature is above 0. in z-score units, (3) $l(z_i)$ is 1.0 or greater, or (4) $p(s/z_i)$ is .5 or greater. Each rule will produce a hit rate, $p(Y/s)$, of .84 and a false alarm rate, $p(Y/n)$, of .16. Hence, the rule are *equivalent*, though not *identical* because the classifications are based upon different types of data.

Why a Cutoff Rule?

Green and Swets (1967, pp. 20–25) have demonstrated why cutoff rules like the ones chosen above are "best" in several senses of the word as long as one important condition is met—that the decision axis and likelihood of signal are monotonically related. In the present situation, one particular definition is most applicable—a cutoff rule will maximize the percentage of correct decisions. One will be correct 84% of the time, and no other strategy can do better. It can also be shown that a cutoff rule maximizes the hit rate for a given false alarm rate, which is not the same definition of "best."

Bayesian Considerations

The term "Bayesian considerations" includes two distinct concepts: (1) the *base rates* (also known as *prior probabilities* or *initial odds*) that a person is

---

[1] The fact that a likelihood ratio approaches infinity is mildly undesirable. A related index that tells us, relatively speaking, whether a given value of the decision variable is associated more strongly with being normal or sick is called the *posterior probability of signal*, $p(s/z_i)$. The $p(s/z_i)$ is the height of the curve for the s distribution divided by the sum of the heights of the s and n distributions. It also equals $l(z_i)/[1 + l(z_i)]$. Note that the posterior probability of signal is .5 at the cutoff, which means that at this particular temperature half of the cases will be sick and half will be normal.

sick versus normal and (2) the *values* or the rewards for hits and correct rejections relative to the penalties or costs for false alarms and misses.

I will use the following notation. The symbols $p(s)$ and $p(n)$ will respectively denote the probabilities that a person is sick versus normal. The ratio of $p(n)/p(s)$ describes the *odds favoring being normal*, which I will simply denote as "p." Describing the odds in this manner instead of in the converse manner as the odds favoring sickness is an expositional convenience.

Similarly, I will use the symbols $v(hit)$, $v(correct\ rejection)$, $v(false\ alarm)$, and $v(miss)$ to describe the *values* of the four possible outcomes of a given classification. Think of the outcomes in financial terms, so that the first two values are usually positive (rewards for being correct) and the latter two are usually negative (penalties for being wrong). Also, let $v(n)$, the value associated with judged normality, equal $v(correct\ rejection) + v(miss)$ and let $v(s)$, the value associated with judged sickness, equal $v(hit) + v(false\ alarm)$. The absolute values of $v(n)$ and $v(s)$ are not critical, but their ratio is. I will denote the ratio of $v(n)$ to $v(s)$ simply as v.

Why Bayesian Considerations Are Important

Assume that the particular form of flu under consideration in the present example is rare, so that $p(s)$ is extremely low.[2] Further assume that the consequences for correct and incorrect diagnoses are not extreme. Even if a person has a noticeably elevated temperature, it can be shown that it is still much more probable that the person is in fact normal. One fairly common error in classification is to overpredict rare events and, therefore, underpredict common events. As an example, get someone, preferably who has not read this paragraph, engage in a guessing game. Tell him or her that you are going to roll a pair of dice and that the task is to predict whether a "12" will apppear. This outcome has an actual probability of 1/36. However, you will probably find people predict the outcome "12" more often than 1/36 of the time.

If you have difficulty placing dollar values on decisional outcomes, do not think you are alone. It is not easy for, say, a physician to think in terms like "If I treat this person as if he or she was normal, my expected return in X. However, if I treat the person as sick, my expected return is Y ($Y > X). I will therefore assume that the person is sick." Many statisticians are still having trouble about the use of Bayesian considerations. Mathematical statisticians, in particular, do not like the inherent subjectivity associated with the process of assigning values. However, Bayesian concepts have been

---

[2] It is important that probabilities be defined *in the context under which decisions are to be made*. For example, suppose you are working at the health service of a university. The relevant probabilities are to be determined from past records at that health service, not the university at large. Perhaps only 10% of all students are sick at a given time. However, because students can diagnose themselves with some accuracy, more than 10% of those who come to the health service for treatment will be ill.

successfully applied in many areas such as marketing, medical diagnosis, and personnel selection. In defense of the procedure, you apply it every time you weigh pros and cons of deciding whether something is worth buying.

There is clearly import to getting you to think about the economic consequences of decisions if only in an approximate manner. For example, even with the limited_range of therapies for viral infections, the costs and benefits are usually not the same. Even suggesting that someone take a seemingly safe substance like aspirin when it will not help can have adverse effects. The differential economic consequences ("fuzzy" as they may be) obviously increase in situations where antibiotics or, in an even more extreme case, surgery, is an option. In short, there is no form of thereapy that is cost-free when inappropriately administered, nor is there any disease state, no matter how trivial, where there is no cost associated with the failure to classify (diagnose) it correctly.

The information contained in $p = p(n)/(s)$ and $v = v(n)/v(s)$ can be rather simply utilized. Use a cutoff of pv instead of 1.0 as a cutoff (in likelihood ratio units) when you have Bayesian information. (The standard symbol for the value of the cutoff is β, but the symbol does *not* have its familiar meaning of "beta weight.") In other words, when most people are normal, so that $p(n) > .5$ and/or the rewards that are associated with diagnosing illness exceed those for diagnosing sickness, *move the criterion upward so that you say "No" more often*. Likewise, when most people are sick so that $p(n) < .5$ and/or the costs associated with normality are less than those associated with sickness, *move the criterion downward so that you say "Yes" more often*. (The latter situation is obviously the more usual one.)

In general, the rule implies that if the values associated with the four outcomes are the same, your criterion should be at a likelihood ratio of p. Conversely, if $p(s) = p(n)$, your criterion should be at v.

Typically, it is useful to explore the consequences of using several values of β. However, the precise value defined by pv is known as the *maximum expected value* criterion. It is so named because if you follow it with the contingencies defined by p and v, you will maximize the financial return possible.[3]

Varying Base Rates

Computer packages performing discriminant analyses allow you to incorporate information about base rates, but their defaults tend to differ. Some use empirical frequencies, and others assume equality of prior odds. You can override the defaults. A point of irritation is that no current package allows you to "loop" through successive estimates in a single job step to see, for

---

[3] Do not think that you are committing a mortal (or even a venal) sin if you do not employ a maximum expected value criterion. Maximizing the expected value is but one reasonable definition of "best." See Atkinson (1963) for an alternative definition of "best."

example, the consequences of assuming base rate values of $p(n)$ equal to .25, .5, and .75, etc. You need run multiple jobs or job steps to obtain such estimates. When you nominally vary p, you are effectively varying v and p jointly.

Bayes' Theorem in Binary Classification

Bayes' theorem is concerned with obtaining the probability of a given state of nature (s and n) from data (z_i). In other words, you wish to determine $p(s/z_i)$ and $p(n/z_i)$. The data you have available are $p(s)$, $v(s)$, $p(z_i/s)$, $p(n)$, $v(n)$, and $p(z_i/n)$. The relevant relations are

$$p(s/z_i) = \frac{p(s)v(s)p(z_i/s)}{p(s)v(s)p(z_i/s) + p(n)v(n)p(z_i/n)} \tag{9-1a}$$

$$p(n/z_i) = \frac{p(n)v(n)p(z_i/n)}{p(s)v(s)p(z_i/s) + p(n)v(n)p(z_i/n)} \tag{9-1b}$$

The p and v parameters will drop out of the equation if they are 1.0. The decision rule is to pick the state associated with the larger of $p(s/z_i)$ and $p(n/z_i)$. The rule is logically equivalent to the use of maximum expected value. It is also a special case of the principle of *maximum likelihood*.

The relation between $p(s/z_i)$ and its inverse, $p(z_i/s)$, is complex because of the powerful mediating role that prior probabilities and values play. One of my favorite teaching examples is to take a case where $p(z_i/s)$ is relatively large (the probability that a profession basketball player is over 6' 6"), but $p(s)$ is small (not many people are professional basketball players). Consequently, the probability that a person is a professional basketball player given that he is over 6' 6" in height is essentially zero!

Receiver (Relative) Operating Characteristic (ROC) Curves

When the cutoff was set at $z_i = 0$, which corresponds to a likelihood ratio of 1 in the example, $p(Y/s)$ was .84 and $p(Y/n)$ was .16. Now, consider what happens to $p(Y/s)$ and $p(Y/n)$ as the criterion is set at different points, specifically from $z_i = -2.0$ to $+2.0$ in steps of .1 degree (98.4 degrees to 99.2 degrees). Table 9-1 contains the values of $p(Y/s)$ and $p(Y/n)$ and related statistics associated with different criteria, the z scores corresponding to $z(Y/s)$ and $z(Y/n)$, $p(z_i/s)$ and $p(z_i/n)$, and $l(z_i)$. The $l(z_i)$ will always correspond to a maximum expected value cutoff for appropriate combinations of p and v. For example, if $v = 1$ and $p(s)$ equals .88, the optimal criterion is a likelihood ratio of .12/.88, which equals a value of z_i of -1.0 and a raw score of 98.6.

A *receiver (relative) operating characteristic (ROC) curve is the set of outcomes derived from a given pair of distributions by varying the criterion*. The data may be plotted in two different ways. In Fig. 9-2a, hit rate is plotted as a function of false alarm rate, whereas in Fig. 9-2b, $z(Y/s)$ is plotted as a function of $z(Y/n)$. It is a convention that hit rate be plotted along the Y axis

TABLE 9-1. Alternative outcomes arising from different criteria—Equal variance case

z_i	X_i	$p(Y/s)$	$p(Y/n)$	$z(Y/s)$	$z(Y/n)$	$p(z_i/s)$	$p(z_i/n)$	$l(z_i)$
−2.0	98.4	.999	.841	3.00	1.00	.004	.242	.018
−1.5	98.5	.994	.691	2.50	.50	.018	.352	.049
−1.0	98.6	.977	.500	2.00	.00	.054	.399	.135
−.5	98.7	.933	.309	1.50	−.50	.130	.352	.368
.0	98.8	.841	.159	1.00	−1.00	.242	.242	1.000
.5	98.9	.691	.067	.50	−1.50	.352	.129	2.729
1.0	99.0	.500	.023	.00	−2.00	.399	.054	7.389
1.5	99.1	.308	.006	−.50	−2.50	.352	.018	19.556
2.0	99.2	.159	.001	−1.00	−3.00	.242	.004	55.000

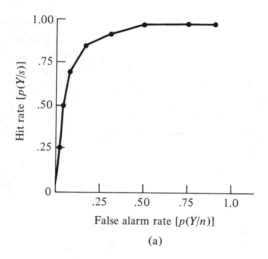

(a)

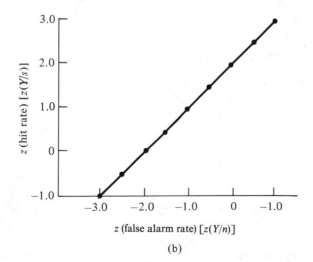

(b)

FIGURE 9-2. Receiver operating characteristic (ROC) curves for equal variances.

and false alarm rate along the X axis, regardless of whether probabilities or normal transformations are used (both are useful).

The positive diagonal running from bottom left to top right describes *chance* performance because each point along the line has the property that $p(Y/n) = p(Y/s)$. Consequently, the subject is saying "Yes" incorrectly (when n is present) as often as correctly (when s is present). Points along the positive diagonal describe differences in willingness to say "Yes" or *bias*.

In contrast, variation along the negative diagonal running from top left to bottom right describes differences in *accuracy* or *sensitivity*. Specifically, the point in Fig. 9-2a corresponding to $p(Y/s) = 1.0$ and $p(Y/n) = 0.$ at the top left, $(1.0, .0)$, is the best obtainable performance. By contrast, the point $(0., 1.0)$ is the worst obtainable performance. However, the latter event cannot occur by chance—a person who is wrong on every trial must know exactly as much as a person who is correct on every trial. Theodor and Mandelcord (1973) exploited this fact to demonstrate that a hysterically blind individual actually could see; the individual performed significantly *below* chance. The points in Fig. 9-2b that correspond to a hit rate of 1.0 and a false alarm rate of .0 or a hit rate of .0 and a false alarm rate of 1.0 cannot be presented because there are no z scores that correspond to probabilities of .0 or 1.0.

Note that the curve drawn in Fig. 9-2a is symmetric about the positive (chance) diagonal and that the curve drawn in Fig. 9-2b is a straight line with slope of 1.0. The symmetry of the first function and the unit slope of the second function are both consequences of the equal variance Gaussian model, although other pairs of distributions of lesser interest may also produce symmetric ROC curves. Moving the criterion from left to right in Fig. 9-1 corresponds to increasingly stricter criteria (lesser willingness to say "Yes"). The change in criterion corresponds to movement *down* the ROC curves of Figs. 9-2a and 9-2b from top to bottom. A more subtle point about Fig. 9-2a is that the *tangent* (slope or linear rate of change) to the curve at any point can be shown to equal $l(z_i)$ at that point.

Describing Accuracy of Classification (Sensitivity)

There is one essential point regarding performance in a binary classification task: *Both sensitivity and bias must be taken into account when evaluating a person's performance because $p(Y/s)$ and $p(Y/n)$ confound the two; hence, neither $p(Y/s)$ nor $p(Y/n)$ by itself is sufficient to describe performance.* The $p(Y/s)$ can be 1.0 because of flawless judgment. However, it can also occur simply because the subject always said "Yes."

The $p(Y/s)$ and $p(Y/n)$ can be combined in different ways to provide more meaningful measures of sensitivity and bias. If s and n distributions are each approximately normal and nearly equal in variance, a sensitivity measure known as "d'," given by Eq. (9-2), is applicable. It equals $+2.00$ in the example. As you may verify yourself from Table 9-1, the choice of cutoff (z_i) has no effect upon d', since $z(Y/s) - z(Y/n)$ is the same for all values of z_i. The d'

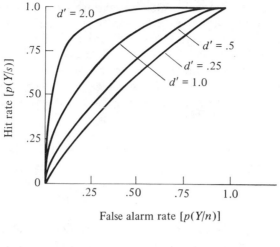

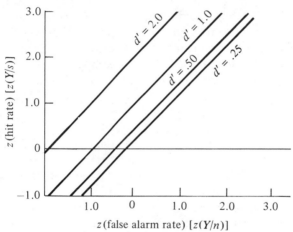

FIGURE 9-3. Receiver operating characteristic (ROC) curves for different d' values.

statistic is a measure of the distance between the mean of the s distribution and the mean of the n distribution using the standard deviation of the n distribution (and, by virtue of the assumption of equal variance, the s distribution as well) as a unit.

$$d' = z(Y/s) - z(Y/n) \tag{9-2}$$

Figures 9-3a and 9-3b contain ROC curves obtained with various values of d'. The former figure contains the data as a plot of $p(Y/s)$ versus $p(Y/n)$, and the latter figure contains the data as a plot of $z(Y/s)$ versus $z(Y/n)$.

Perhaps the most familiar measure of accuracy is simply the percentage of correct classifications. The percent measure is provided in most discriminant analysis routines. It is reasonable and straightforward *if pv* is closed to 1.0, but it can be quite misleading when most decisions are "yes" or most decisions are "no" as opposed to an equal balance of the two decisions. One particular situation that is of personal interest is the detection of dishonesty among employees and applicants using devices such as the polygraph or self-report inventories. Assume that the rate of dishonesty in the work force is 5%.[4] I once saw a particular lie-detection strategy correctly classify about 70% of the cases. What happened was that most of the 5% of employees who had committed dishonest acts were correctly identified. However, the false alarm rate was about 30%, which is not an atypical figure and indeed may be conservative (Lykken, 1979). Although the investigator was rather happy with the outcome, since it clearly surpassed the chance expectation of 50%, had the investigator classified *everybody* as honest, the "batting average" would climb to 95%!

You may object on the grounds that the "batting average" assumes that detecting an honest person has the same value as detecting a dishonest person. This objection is well taken even though "batting averages" are probably the most common index of performance. If you work for the company in question, it may be very important to catch a dishonest person. Even so, you cannot assume that false alarms are cost-free to the company because you reduce the pool of potential employees and may face frequent law suits. Consequently, you need to assess a decision maker's bias so that you can determine whether he or she is saying "Yes" and "No" in proportion to the values and base rates in the situation.

The value of $l(z_i)$ corresponding to the criterion is a useful index of bias, although X_i or z_i would also suffice. The index is referred to as "β" in the literature, but the term is also used to describe the optimal (maximum expected value) criterion as well as the empirical criterion.

Luce (1959, 1964; also see Shepard, 1958) proposed a model that employs a slightly different representation for random variation than the normal distribution, the *logistic* distribution. His model provides sensitivity and bias measures known as η and β, which are respectively defined in Eqs. (9-3a) and (9-3b):

$$\eta = \left[\frac{p(N/s)p(Y/n)}{p(Y/s)p(N/n)} \right]^{1/2} \tag{9-3a}$$

$$\beta = \left[\frac{p(N/s)p(N/n)}{p(Y/s)p(Y/n)} \right]^{1/2} \tag{9-3b}$$

---

[4] Trying to define "dishonesty" illustrates another and rather general problem. If one were to use a sufficiently lenient definition, which would include using a company's stationery for personal use, then $p(s) = 1.0$. There is obviously no point in trying to "predict" events that always or never happen. The figure of 5% represents my practical experience in being told the incidence of criminal acts. The percentage obviously varies from situation to situation, but is representative for example's sake.

Luce's two indices are *similarity measures*. The former measures the similarity of the stimulus categories (*s* and *n*), and the latter measures the similarity of the response categories (*Y* and *N*). Small values of η denote good performance, and small values of β denote a willingness to say "No." Consequently, their meaning is just the opposite of the more widely used d' and β measures. Luce's statistics are sometimes transformed to their negative natural logarithms in the literature, which converts them to *distance measures* describing the *log odds ratio*. The transformed measures have readily interpretable meanings— large values respectively denote good performance and a willingness to say "Yes."

The most popular current measure of accuracy is an index called A_z (Swets & Pickett, 1982). One first computes the perpendicular distance from the origin to the straight line ROC curve relating $z(Y/s)$ to $z(Y/n)$ and then converts the distance to a cumulative normal probability. The A_z is the proportion of the total area under the ROC curve that fits a normal curve model. Although the measure assumes normality, it appears to be fairly robust.

The *area under the obtained ROC curve* (cf. Egan, 1975, pp. 47–48, for a discussion of its calculation, which is cumbersome if done by hand) is a popular measure of sensitivity. Until the A_z measure became dominant, the obtained area was quite popular because it assumed neither normality nor equal variance. Consequently, it can be used when a nonparametric measure will suffice.

The obtained area also has another very useful property. Suppose, instead of presenting you with one person's temperature and asking you whether that person was sick or well (a *yes–no task*), you were shown *two* people's temperatures, one of whom is sick and the other is normal (a *two-alternative forced-choice task*). Your task is to determine which is which. The percentage of correct choices in a two-alternative forced-choice task is an appropriate sensitivity measure, unlike the yes–no case where it is highly sensitive to choice of criterion and thus confounds the information contained in d' and β. The percentage correct in a two-alternative forced-choice task will usually agree with the area under the ROC curve in a yes–no task.

The safest procedure is to provide $p(Y/s)$, $p(Y/n)$, and $p(s)$ so readers can derive statistics of their choosing. There exist many performance measures that reflect particular models. However, all can be derived from these three basic statistics.

The Unequal Variance Gaussian Model

Now assume the standard deviations of the two distributions are unequal. Either of the distributions can be made more variable. However, the *s* distribution is usually the more variable because variation in the *s* distribution contains the random variation of the *n* distribution *plus variation in s itself*. It was only for purposes of example that I assumed that all people in the previous

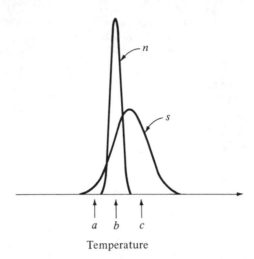

Temperature

FIGURE 9-4. The unequal variance Gaussian model of signal detection. At points a and c, it is more probable that a person is sick as opposed to normal because $l(z_i) > 1.0$. At point b, it is more likely that the person is normal, since $l(z_i) < 1.0$. Thus, temperature is not a monotonic function of likelihood ratio and therefore not a proper decision variable in this case.

example were equally sick. It is much more likely that some people get the flu become sicker than others. Holding their normal temperature constant, those who do get a worse case will run higher temperatures. Greater variability emerges more formally as a consequence of Eq. (3-6).[5]

Figure 9-4a contains a representative pair of distributions with unequal variance. Specifically, the distributions are drawn so that s has a standard deviation twice as large as n. Thus, s is normal (99.0, .4) and n is normal (98.6, .2).

The data giving rise to Table 9-2 parallel the data of Table 9-1 in form. Note that the term "z_i" is now ambiguous because, by definition, both groups cannot be normalized to the same standard deviation. I have normalized the data for the normals, which means that the patients' standard deviation will now become 2.0. This representation allows the relation between z_i and X_i to parallel that of Table 9-1.

There is a very important consequence of assuming the unequal variance model; *the likelihood ratio, $l(z_i)$, is no longer a monotonic function of the underlying decision axis, z_i. Hence, z_i (and X_i) is no longer a proper decision variable.* The likelihood of a person being sick with a very low temperature is

---

[5] I have neglected the covariance (correlation) term in the equation. It is possible but not probable that one's normal temperature and the severity of the flu might have a strong negative correlation (people with normally low body temperatures would be predisposed to getting sicker), which would allow s_s to be smaller than s_n.

TABLE 9-2. Alternative outcomes arising from different criteria—Unequal variance case

z_i	X_i	$p(Y/s)$	$p(Y/n)$	$z(Y/s)$	$z(Y/n)$	$p(z_i/s)$	$p(z_i/n)$	$l(z_i)$
-2.0	98.4	.933	.841	1.50	1.00	.130	.242	.537
-1.5	98.5	.894	.691	1.25	.50	.183	.352	.520
-1.0	98.6	.841	.500	1.00	.00	.242	.399	.606
$-.5$	98.7	.773	.309	.75	$-.50$	.301	.352	.855
.0	98.8	.691	.159	.50	-1.00	.352	.242	1.455
.5	98.9	.599	.067	.25	-1.50	.387	.129	3.000
1.0	99.0	.500	.023	.00	-2.00	.399	.054	7.389
1.5	99.1	.401	.006	$-.25$	-2.50	.387	.018	21.500
2.0	99.2	.309	.001	$-.50$	-3.00	.352	.004	88.000

actually greater than it is with slightly elevated temperature. Note specifically that $l(1.50) = .520$ is less than both $l(2.00) = .537$ and $l(1.00) = .606$. The sky will not fall when the disparity in standard deviations is slight, say less than 10%, but misleading results can occur with greater differences.

Unequal variance need not cause one to abandon a signal detection approach; rather, a different strategy is needed. By calculating $l(z_i)$ at several points along the decision axis, you can determine the region(s) that are most likely to contain signal, i.e., adopt multiple cutoffs.

In order to illustrate the effects of unequal variance, I have plotted the data of Table 9-2 in Fig. 9-5a, as a plot of $p(Y/s)$ versus $p(Y/n)$, and in Fig. 9-5b, as a plot of $z(Y/s)$ versus $z(Y/n)$.

Unequal variance has two major effects: (1) it produces an asymmetry or "bulge" in Fig. 9-5a and (b) it causes the slope to deviate from 1.0 in Fig. 9-5b. Specifically, *the slope of the unequal variance ROC curve equals s_n/s_s*. In the present case, $z(Y/s)$ will increase at half the rate of $z(Y/n)$, as may be seen in the relevant columns of Table 9-2.

The d' measure is not appropriate in the unequal variance case because the difference between $z(Y/s)$ and $z(Y/n)$ is no longer a constant but depends on the criterion chosen. Several alternative measures have been proposed. As previously noted, the A_z measure, which does not assume equality of variance, is perhaps the most popular one.

Other Signal Detection Models

Signal detection theory also deals with ROC curves generated by other various types of distributions, among other topics. Just for example's sake, Fig. 9-6 contains a pair of *exponential* distributions. These two distributions differ simply in terms of one parameter, called the "decay" parameter. As it turns out, they produce ROC curves that are identical in shape to unequal variance Gaussian models which require two parameters, the mean difference

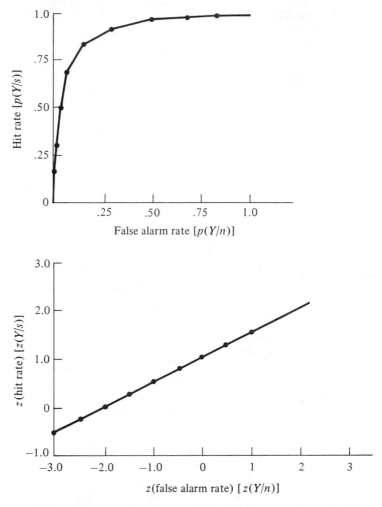

FIGURE 9-5. Receiver operating characteristic (ROC) curves for unequal variances.

between the s and the n distributions and the ratio of their standard deviations. A given pair of exponential distributions will produce an ROC curve identical to a pair of unequal variance Gaussian distributions, but the converse is not true—the ROC curve produced by a pair of unequal variance Gaussian distributions may not be obtainable from a pair of exponential distributions.

If you find the topic of interest, as I certainly do, consult the sources mentioned earlier, especially the recent interchange between Swets (1986a, 1986b) and Nelson (1986). One bit of consolation is that most of the special models will probably be of relatively little real-world application. When the decision axis is formed from a linear combinations like scales on a personality

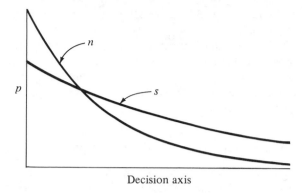

FIGURE 9-6. Exponential model of signal detection.

inventory, the central limit theorem will "push" the linear combination toward normality. Consequently, the data will almost invariably fit a Gaussian model though perhaps one in which the variances are unequal.

Strategies for Individual Classification

I will now broaden discussion to consider cases beyond binary classification and scalar dependent variables.

Describing Performance

The signal detection terminology needs to be modified when there are more than two groups into which an observation may potentially be classified. The outcomes are expressed in a K (number of categories) by K confusion matrix. I will assign the actual categories (states of nature) to rows and the decisions to columns, but you may see the converse representation used by other authors. It is conventional to conditionalize by states of nature as in the binary case. Thus, entry x_{ij} is the probability that a case is assigned to group i given that it really belongs to group j, $p(i/j)$.

Bayesian considerations, especially base rates, are still quite important. However, the most common performance measure is the percentage of correct decisions, despite its previously noted flaws. The reason the percent correct measure remains popular in the binary case is that many find signal detection analyses cumbersome. The point is reasonable when the stimulus categories occur with equal or nearly equal frequency, because the percentage of correct decisions is appropriate. However, failure to consider response bias has led many investigations astray. Unfortunately, there are no direct analogues of d' when there are multiple categories to be discriminated. Hence, one can employ Bayes' theorem, as will be shown, but one cannot use signal detection theory in a simple manner.

If the base rates are equal or nearly equal, it is meaningful to consider the range of possible classification outcomes as extending from $1/K$ to 1.0. However, if base rates vary widely a more meaningful frame of reference is what would obtain if everyone were assigned to the most probable category, just as in the binary case.

Bayesian Considerations with Multiple Groups

Bayes' theorem is readily generalized. Let X define the value of the predictor (*evidence*). Also, let $p(i/X)$ denote the probability that a person belongs to group i given the evidence X. The $p(i/X)$ is a function of $p(i)$, the base rate for group i, the net value associated with group i, $v(i)$, and $p(X/i)$, the probability of the evidence given membership in Group i. Equation (9-4) states the relation. The group index "j" is simply used as an index of summation in the denominator. The effects of p or v may be ignored by setting their values to equality. When both are eliminated, values of $p(i/X)$ will be proportional to $p(X/i)$:

$$p(i/X) = \frac{p(i)v(i)p(X/i)}{\sum p(j)v(j)p(X/j)} \qquad (9\text{-}4)$$

I will assume, for convenience, that both the base rates and values add to 1.0—$\sum p(j) = \sum v(j) = 1.0$. In many cases, values of $p(X/i)$ may be obtained from the normal curve. The $p(X/i)$ values are simply the ordinates of the normal curve at X. Values of $p(X/i)$ can also be obtained from other distributions in a like manner.

Base rates are normally expressed as probabilities, so the restriction that they add to 1.0 is straightforward. The parallel restriction on values requires a bit of discussion. Values are normally expressed in a *payoff matrix*, describing the economic consequences of states of nature and decisions. Assume actual outcomes are rows and the decisions are columns. The following is an example. Entries in the diagonal correspond to correct decisions. Note that there is no way to profit if the first outcome occurs.

Decision

		A	B	C
O				
u				
t	A	−5	−10	−15
c	B	3	5	1
o	C	6	1	10
m				
e				

The *net* values are the absolute value of the difference between losses for incorrect decisions and gains for correct decisions. The actual net values are therefore $20\,(-5 - (-10 + -15))$, $1\,(5 - (3 + 1))$, and $3\,(10 - (6 + 1))$. Now, all that needs be done is to divide the individual net values by their sum, yielding proportions of .83 $[20/(20 + 1 + 3)]$, .04 $[1/(20 + 1 + 3)]$, and .13 $[3/(20 + 1 + 3)]$.

If estimates of $p(X/i)$ are based on the normal or some other distributions, probability estimates become rather unstable in the tails. One strategy is to set a minimum value of $p(X/i)$ at some small level, say .01.

Alternative Strategies—An Overview

Assume that you have conducted a preliminary discriminant analysis. You know something about the structure of groups relative to the discriminating variables, particularly, how concentrated the means are. You now wish to use the information obtained from the analysis to classify individual observations. Several strategies can be used, which will generally lead to fairly similar outcomes, assuming Bayesian considerations are held constant. However, these strategies can lead to rather different outcomes in some situations, which is why it is important for you to become familiar with relevant alternatives. Before trying to decide which strategy is best, you need ask yourself several questions about the precise task at hand:

1. Is the structure primarily concentrated or diffuse?
2. Are normal curve assumptions appropriate?
3. Is it important to incorporate base rates and/or values?
4. Are the components of the decision variable, which may or may not be the raw predictors, highly intercorrelated or relatively independent?
5. Do group vary to approximately the same extent on the decision variable or do the groups vary considerably (are they homoscedastic or heteroscedastic)?
6. Will classification be done by hand or by computer?
7. Is it important that the classification variable be in a familiar metric like a probability or a z score? It is usually desirable, but not necessary that the metric be familiar.

I will return to these specific questions at the end of the chapter. One additional question has impact upon nearly all of the preceding issues and needs be considered first: Is the original calibration (normative) sample sufficiently large for me to assume that I have stable estimates of my parameters or was it relatively small? *Bad estimates of relevant parameters can lead to results that are worse than those obtained by treating parameters as equal.*

With a very large normative sample, distributions of the appropriate test statistic can be determined empirically, e.g., as percentiles. The methods required are no different than those discussed in elementary statistics texts so I will not present them here.

A Numerical Example

Calibration Study

I have used MMPI Scales Hy and Pd to classify subjects into one of three groups, based on normative data I had available: (1) *Pain patients* being seen for treatment of conditions such as lower back injuries (group P, $N = 127$), (2) *therapy patients* being seen as outpatients (group T, $N = 46$), and (3) *applicants* drawn from the same population of individuals seeking employment as police officers, security guards, and various positions at nuclear power plants as discussed in Chapter 4 (group A, $N = 138$). The various types of applicants were not differentiated for purposes of analysis. Although I had more applicant data available, I chose not to use them to make the problem similar to many you may encounter in real life.

For those unfamiliar with the MMPI, Scale Hy differentiates patients diagnosed as hysterics from normals. Hysterics tend to become sick when under stress and ignore danger in the environment. Scale Pd is designed to differentiate psychopaths from normals. People who are psychopathic report difficulties with their parents, seek excitement to relieve pathological boredom, tend to be angry and hostile, and are deficient in conscience. The content of the items on the two scales reflects relevant symptomatology.

The group P centroid, X_p, is (71.85, 60.15). The corresponding group T and group A centroids, X_t and X_a, are (63.71, 63.02) and (54.65, 56.82). Thus, the Hy means are approximately equally spaced. In contrast, group T has a slightly higher score on Pd than does group P, and both group means on Pd are considerably higher than that of group A. The means are therefore somewhat diffused. The grand (weighted group) means for Hy and Pd, which are 63.0 and 59.1, will be used at several points of discussion. Note that the means are *not* simply the average of the three group means because the groups are unequal in size.

The three within-group variance-covariance matrices, $\mathbf{W}_p$, $\mathbf{W}_t$, and $\mathbf{W}_a$, are as follows:

$$\mathbf{W}_p = \begin{bmatrix} 139.96 & 65.46 \\ 65.46 & 172.45 \end{bmatrix}$$

$$\mathbf{W}_t = \begin{bmatrix} 146.69 & 112.07 \\ 112.07 & 184.87 \end{bmatrix}$$

$$\mathbf{W}_a = \begin{bmatrix} 44.44 & 17.36 \\ 17.36 & 73.22 \end{bmatrix}$$

and the pooled variance–covariance matrix is:

$$\mathbf{W} = \begin{bmatrix} 98.46 & 50.88 \\ 50.88 & 130.12 \end{bmatrix}$$

Thus, the standard deviations for the Hy and Pd scales are 11.83 and 13.13 in group *P*, 12.11 and 13.59 in group *T*, and 6.66 and 8.55 in group *A*. The differences among centroids are large compared to the standard deviations. Classification should therefore generally be rather accurate.

The correlations between the Hy and Pd scales are .421, .680, and .304 within groups *P*, *T*, and *A*, respectively. An inferential test discussed in the next chapter indicated that the groups differed significantly in their variance–covariance structure. Specifically, group *A*'s structure differed from the two remaining groups, *P* and *T*, but the latter two did not differ from one another. The pattern of differences was reflected in the *natural logarithms (ln) of the determinants of the variance–covariance matrix*, an index of multivariate dispersion. The values were 9.896, 9.895, and 7.990 for groups *P*, *T*, and *A*. The smaller value associated with group *A* illustrates its relative homogeneity.

Group *A*'s homogeneity should not be surprising to those familiar with the MMPI—people applying for jobs are loathe to complain about their health. The fact that the correlation between the two scales is lowest among applicants is yet another example of range restriction. The pooled within-group standard deviations (9.92 and 11.40) and pooled within-group correlation (.449) are, as always, weighted averages of the standard deviations and correlations within individual groups. In the present case, the pooled quantities are not reflective of the individual groups.

Were the problem not simply for demonstration and were the data bases sufficiently large for me to feel comfortable about the individual estimates of the variance–covariance matrices, I probably would *not* pool the variance–covariance matrices if deciding between membership in group *A* versus the other groups were important, which it probably would be. With smaller sample sizes, I probably would pool because the greater stability of the pooled matrix is a significant point. Other experienced MMPI users might see the problem a bit differently. I will present analyses based on pooled and unpooled estimates for illustrative purposes.

The inverses of the individual and pooled within-groups variance–covariance matrices are as follows:

$$\mathbf{W}_p^{-1} = \begin{bmatrix} .0086 & -.0033 \\ -.0033 & .0070 \end{bmatrix}$$

$$\mathbf{W}_t^{-1} = \begin{bmatrix} .0126 & -.0077 \\ -.0077 & .0101 \end{bmatrix}$$

$$\mathbf{W}_a^{-1} = \begin{bmatrix} .0248 & -.0059 \\ -.0059 & .0150 \end{bmatrix}$$

$$\mathbf{W}^{-1} = \begin{bmatrix} .0127 & -.0049 \\ -.0049 & .0096 \end{bmatrix}$$

The between-group variance–covariance matrix (**B**) is

$$\mathbf{B} = \begin{bmatrix} 9785.71 & 1967.64 \\ 1967.64 & 781.52 \end{bmatrix}$$

Both discriminant functions were significant, supporting the initial observation that the structure of group means is diffuse. The canonical correlation between function I and group membership is .644. Its deviation score formula is $Y' = .111\text{Hy} - .029\text{Pd}$, and its standard score formula is $Y' = 1.413z_{\text{Hy}} - .350z_{\text{Pd}}$. The group P, T, and A means on function I are .952, $-.039$, and $-.863$. Thus, despite the diffusion, function I differentiates among all three groups, although it does not exhaust all systematic differences among the groups. Hy and Pd respectively correlate .953 and .157 with function I.

The canonical correlation of function II with group membership is .147. Its deviation score formula is $Y' = -.018\text{Hy} + .094\text{Pd}$, and its standard score formula is $Y' = -.225z_{\text{Hy}} + 1.084z_{\text{Pd}}$. The group P, T, and A means on function II are $-.058$, .354, and $-.064$, which means that function II only discriminates group T from groups P and A. Function I accounts for $.643^2/(.643^2 + .147^2)$ or nearly 94% of the variance among group centriods, and function II accounts for only 6%. Hence, the diffusion, though significant, is relatively slight. Hy and Pd respectively correlate .303 and .988 with function II.

It will be convenient at several points of discussion below to consider both the deviation (raw) and standard score weight matrices. I will identify the two matrices by the symbols $\mathbf{D}_d$ and $\mathbf{D}_s$, respectively. The matrices equal

$$\mathbf{D}_d = \begin{bmatrix} .111 & -.018 \\ -.018 & .094 \end{bmatrix}$$

and

$$\mathbf{D}_s = \begin{bmatrix} 1.413 & -.225 \\ -.350 & 1.084 \end{bmatrix}$$

I will also be referring to the coefficients associated with the individual functions, which are the *column vectors* of the two matrices. For example, I will designate $\mathbf{d}_{dI}$ as the first column vector of $\mathbf{D}_d$ (the elements .111 and $-.030$). My notation follows the convention of identifying factors by Roman numerals.

The Context of Classification

The sample observation I chose to illustrate the computations involved in classification was a male job applicant with scores of 51 on Hy and 57 on Pd. His scores are highly representative of group A.

At several points below, I will be considering the observation as (a) *deviations* from each of the three group means, (b) z score based on a *pooled* standard deviation over the three groups, and (c) z scores based on the *individual* standard deviations of the three groups. The measures may be summarized conveniently as matrices with the rows designating the group against which the observation is being compared and the columns representing the two predictors (Hy and Pd). I will designate the three matrices as $\mathbf{C}$, $\mathbf{Z}_p$, and $\mathbf{Z}_i$. I chose the symbol "$\mathbf{C}$" for the first matrix to denote that the scores are "centered" about the mean, which is an English terminology. You should find it relatively easy to remember what $\mathbf{Z}_p$ and $\mathbf{Z}_i$ denote. In order to derive the three matrices, place the observation vector as a series of *row vectors* three times (once for each of the three groups against which it is to be compared):

$$\begin{bmatrix} 51 & 57 \\ 51 & 57 \\ 51 & 57 \end{bmatrix}$$

The deviation score matrix ($\mathbf{C}$) is obtained by subtracting the matrix of group means from the grand mean:

$$\mathbf{C} = \begin{bmatrix} 51 & 57 \\ 51 & 57 \\ 51 & 57 \end{bmatrix} - \begin{bmatrix} 71.85 & 60.16 \\ 63.72 & 63.02 \\ 54.66 & 56.83 \end{bmatrix} = \begin{bmatrix} -20.85 & -3.16 \\ -12.72 & -6.02 \\ -3.66 & .17 \end{bmatrix}$$

The $\mathbf{Z}_p$ matrix is obtained from $\mathbf{C}$ by *scalar division*. Divide the first column by the pooled estimate of the standard deviation of Hy (9.92) and the second column by the pooled estimate of the standard deviation of Pd (11.41):

$$\mathbf{Z}_p = \begin{bmatrix} -20.85/9.92 & -3.16/11.41 \\ -12.72/9.92 & -6.02/11.41 \\ -3.66/9.92 & .17/11.41 \end{bmatrix} = \begin{bmatrix} -2.10 & -.28 \\ -1.28 & -.53 \\ -.37 & .01 \end{bmatrix}$$

$\mathbf{Z}_i$ is obtained in the same general manner as $\mathbf{Z}_p$ except that the individual standard deviations are used in place of the pooled values. Thus:

$$\mathbf{Z}_i = \begin{bmatrix} -20.85/11.83 & -3.16/13.13 \\ -12.72/12.11 & -6.02/13.59 \\ -3.66/6.66 & .17/8.56 \end{bmatrix} = \begin{bmatrix} -1.76 & -.24 \\ -1.05 & -.44 \\ -.55 & .02 \end{bmatrix}$$

As was true of the discriminant weights ($\mathbf{D}_d$ and $\mathbf{D}_r$), I will have occasion to refer to the individual *column* vectors of $\mathbf{C}$, $\mathbf{Z}_p$, and $\mathbf{Z}_i$. I will follow the same notation so that z_{p1} will equal the z scores derived from the pooled matrix for the first predictor (Hy), i.e., the values -2.10, -1.28, and $-.37$.

The "raw canonical coefficients" used in SAS and some other programs require that you enter the observation (51, 57) as a *deviation about the grand mean*. As the grand Hy and Pd means are 63.0 and 59.1, the observation has deviation scores of -12 (51 $-$ 63.0) and -2.1 (57 $-$ 59.1). Hence the discriminant score for function I is $(-12 \times .111) + (-2.1 \times -.030)$ or -1.089, and the discriminant score for function II is $(-12 \times .018) + (-2.1 \times -.094)$ or .195. The discriminant scores are standardized *within* groups. Because the group P, T, and A means on discriminant function I were .952, $-.039$, and

TABLE 9-3. Classification probabilities and alternative strategies

Method	Bayesian variable	Variance					
		Pooled			Individual		
		$p(P/X)$	$p(T/X)$	$p(A/X)$	$p(P/X)$	$p(T/X)$	$p(A/X)$
Hy alone	—	.074	.297	.629	.129	.350	.522
Hy alone	p	.033	.131	.836	.063	.171	.766
Hy alone	v	.075	.501	.424	.122	.550	.328
Hy alone	pv	.041	.271	.689	.073	.332	.594
Function I	—	.075	.341	.584	.131	.348	.521
Function I	p	.034	.157	.808	.064	.170	.765
Function I	v	.072	.551	.377	.124	.548	.328
Function I	pv	.041	.314	.645	.075	.331	.594
Both functions	—	.069	.390	.541	.136	.408	.456
Both functions	p	.033	.187	.780	.071	.213	.715
Both functions	v	.064	.602	.334	.122	.607	.271
Both functions	pv	.038	.361	.601	.079	.393	.528
Mahalanobis	—	.051	.272	.677	.116	.344	.539
Mahalanobis	p	.022	.116	.862	.056	.165	.779
Mahalanobis	v	.054	.474	.472	.111	.546	.343
Mahalanobis	pv	.028	.244	.728	.066	.324	.610

—.863, high scores indicate that the person resembles a pain patient, low scores indicate that the person resembles an applicant, and intermediate scores indicate that the person resembles a therapy patient. Similarly, high scores on discriminant function II are associated with being a therapy patient and low scores are associated with being either a pain patient or an applicant—this discriminant function does not discriminate between the latter two groups.

My notation will allow me to show you the many ways the data could be used to classify a test observation. Keep in mind that I am concerned with classifying a single observations. Depending on the particular method chosen, D_d, D_r, C, Z_p, Z_i, W^{-1}, and W_i^{-1} will appear in various combinations. The logic of classifying a group of cases follows quite simply from the discussion. Matrix notation can be cumbersome because C, Z_p, and Z_i are no longer two-dimensional (the groups being compared as rows vs. the predictor as columns). Individual subjects represent a third dimension or *slice*.

In order to illustrate the pros and cons of Bayesian considerations, I assumed that the subjects who took the MMPI were applicants to a police force. Pain and therapy patients usually do not apply to be police officers. Consequently, I assigned base rates of .2, .2, and .6 to groups P, T, and A, denoted as $p(p)$, $p(t)$, and $p(a)$. I assigned values to the three states, $v(p)$, $v(t)$, and $v(a)$, of .3, .5, and .2. You may disagree, and perhaps rightly so, about the values I chose, but some degree of subjectivity is unavoidable. Likewise, you may also correctly note that pain or therapy patients might well answer the MMPI differently when applying for a job than they actually did. Table 9-3 contains results of Bayesian analyses using several decision variables to do discussed.

Classification Based on Salient Variables

As situations dictate, one may chose one salient variable or use an equally weighted sum of variables (the principle of "it don't make no nevermind"), especially with a concentrated structure. Hy appears to qualify as a suitable salient variable, because it correlates .953 with function I and because function I can discriminate among the three groups.

Homoscedasticity Assumed

One procedure is to establish cutoff values on the Hy axis. Ignoring Bayesian considerations, one would be placed midway between the group P mean (71.85) and the group T mean (63.71) at a score of 68. A second cutoff would be placed at 59, midway between the group T mean and the group A mean (54.65). Scores above 68 would be classified as pain patients; scores between 59 and 68 would be classified as therapy patients; and scores below 59 would be classified as applicants. The sample observation would, in fact, be correctly classified. The cutoffs could be modified to incorporate Bayesian variables using the methods described earlier.

Two equivalent alternatives to the use of a raw score derived from a salient variable or variables are to assign the observation to the group with either the smallest deviation score or the smallest z score, using the pooled estimate, i.e., the group associated with the smallest element of $\mathbf{C}_1$ or $\mathbf{z}_{p1}$, respectively. The two methods will lead to the same conclusion because the two vectors will be proportional to one another. In the present case, the observation will be correctly assigned to group A because the associated elements (.17 and $-.01$) are the smallest. Values of z provide a familiar metric to judge similarity. Some observations may not fall near any of the reference groups. The observations might be outliers or perhaps suggest the need for additional reference groups.

Normality Assumed

Sophisticated methods of Bayesian classification can be employed using the *ordinates* of the normal curve corresponding to the elements of $\mathbf{z}_{p1}$ (-2.10, -1.28, and $-.37$). The ordinates are the probabilities of obtaining Hy as a chance deviation from each group centroid, assuming the underlying distributions are normal. In actuality, neither Hy nor Pd is normally distributed, but the deviation that a given value of Hy (X) was obtained given membership in groups P, T, and A based on the normal curve will be identified as $p(X/P)$, $p(X/T)$, and $p(X/A)$, respectively. The estimated probabilities are .044, .176, and .372.

The three probabilities could be used as a decision variable in the same way that C_1 or z_{pI} were used, but little would be gained as all three probabilities are monotonically related. A more important use for the $p(X/i)$ values is to obtain values of $p(i/X)$ using Eq. (9-4). The resulting values of $p(P/X)$, $p(T/X)$, and $p(A/X)$, respectively, are .074 = .044/(.044 + .1748 + .372), .297, and .630 when neither p nor v is taken into account. As noted earlier, values of $p(X/i)$ are proportional to values of $p(i/X)$ when the base rates and values associated with the various groups are equal. Consequently, nothing is gained by computing $p(i/X)$. The computations required to incorporate base rates are as follows: $p(P/X) = .033 = .2 \times .044/(.2 \times .044 + .2 \times .176 + .6 \times .372)$. Similarly, $p(T/X) = .131$, and $p(A/X) = .630$. Incorporating the base rates therefore increased the probability of a correct classification of X into group A.

The $p(P/X)$, $p(T/X)$, and $p(A/X)$ equal .075 = .3 × .044/(.3 × .044 + .5 × .176 + .2 × .372), .501, and .424, when value, but not base rates, are incorporated. *The outcome illustrates how heavily weighting an improbable event can lead to a misclassification despite the proximity of the observation to the correct category mean.* When base rates and probabilities are both included, the classification is again accurate. The respective probabilities for $p(P/X)$, $p(T/X)$, and $p(A/X)$ are .041 = .2 × .3 × .044/(.2 × .3 × .044 + .2 × .5 × .176 + .6 × .2 × .372), .270, and .689. The columns designated "Pooled" in Table 9-3 contain the values of $p(i/X)$, so that you may compare results of alternative strategies more readily. (The columns designated "Individual" refer to the method to be considered next.) I will not present the classification probabilities $[p(iX)]$ obtained from alternative procedures in text but simply refer to the table.

Despite the arbitrary nature of the present example, it is quite common for values and base rates to be inversely related. Usually, the most important things to detect are those that occur rarely. Consequently, one might consider whether to adjust for values and ignore base rates. Incorporating p and v led to nearly the same results as ignoring them, which is not always the case in real world applications.

Dealing with Heteroscedasticity

If the data are heteroscedastic, you should use z_{iI} (1.76, −1.05, and −.55) instead of z_{pI} to incorporate information about individual group variabilities. When you do this, you are saying that z_{pI} would represent an inappropriate pooling of variances and covariances which differ among the three groups to be classified. Classification may be based on the resulting z scores, leading to a correct choice. Conversely, the z scores may be converted to values of $p(z/i)$, allowing normal curve assumptions and Bayes' theorem to be used.

Assuming the data are heteroscedastic, the values of $p(X/P)$, $p(X/T)$, and $p(X/A)$ are .0848, .2299, and .3429, respectively. Using the individual standard deviations *increased* the similarity of the observation to groups P and T and *decreased* the similarity of the observation to group *A*, because of the latter's homogeneity, i.e., limited variability relative to the other two groups.

Discriminant Functions and Classification

Decisions are commonly based on discriminant scores obtained from applying the observation to the discriminant function. The process can produce several discriminant scores when there are multiple discriminant functions. I will begin my discussion assuming that you are using only a single function.

The classification process may be illustrated geometrically when there are only two predictors, which I have done in Fig. 9-7. All observations that fall along a line perpendicular to the discriminant axis have the same discriminant score, regardless of how far the predictors are from the discriminant, which may or may not be desirable. An observation located far from the discriminant axis is not really representative of any of the groups, but it would be lead to the same classification probability as an observation on the same perpendicular that was located near the discriminant axis. The outcome reflects the *compensatory* nature of a regression equation in the sense of Chapter 4. In the present example, discriminant scores on the first function are a weighted difference between the Hy and Pd. Hence, the same discriminant score can be achieved by suitably large values of Hy or small values of Pd.

One advantage of working with discriminant scores is that the scores are

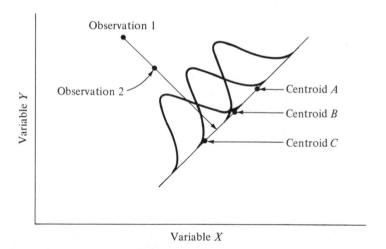

FIGURE 9-7. Geometry of classification based on discriminant functions. Observations 1 and 2 project to the same points on the discriminant function; therefore, they have the same discriminant scores on this function. Their classification probabilities will be the same. They are in fact indistinguishable as far as this classification model is concerned.

available as optional output from virtually every major discriminant analysis procedures, such as SAS PROC CANDISC.[6]

Homoscedasticity Assumed

It is possible to establish cutoffs along the discriminant axis as was done previously with the Hy axis alone. Thus, two cutoffs would be located at .45 and −.45. The first is midway between the mean discriminant scores for groups P and T (.95 and −.04, respectively), and the second is midway between the mean discriminant scores for groups T and A (−.04 and −.86, respectively). Test cases with discriminant scores above .45 would be assigned to group P; test cases with discriminant scores between .45 and −.45 would be assigned to group T, and test cases with discriminant scores below −.45 would be assigned to group A. The discriminant score associated with the test observation (1.269) would thus be correctly classified. The cutoffs can be modified to reflect Bayesian considerations, as was noted in the previous section.

Alternatively, the discriminant score can be expressed as a deviation from each of the three group mean discriminant scores (.953, −.034, and −.864). The resulting deviations are −2.04, −1.06, and −.22. As was true in the case of salient variables, the observation would be assigned to the group for which the absolute value of the deviation was smallest which is again (correctly) group A. Indeed, the results are very similar to those obtained with salient weights because the approximation in my example is a good one.

Normality Assumed

If normal curve assumptions are appropriate, the absolute values of the deviation scores (−2.04, −1.06, and −.22) may be transformed into estimated probabilities derived from the ordinates to the normal curve, as was done with the deviation on the Hy scale alone in the previous section. The deviations correspond to $p(X/P)$, $p(X/T)$, and $p(X/A)$ values of .050, .228, and .389. As one would expect on the basis of the similarity of the deviation scores on which they are based, the values of $p(X/i)$ are very similar to those obtained with the salient weights. The inverse probabilities, $p(i/X)$, are listed in Table 9-3, designated as "Function I."

---

[6] SAS PROC CANDISC performs what most people refer to as a "discriminant analysis," as the term was used in Chapters 8–10. It is, however, an acronym for "canonical discriminant analysis." On the other hand, SAS PROC DISCRIM does not actually perform a "discriminant analysis" in this sense, although that procedure can be used for classification. The latter classification methods employs the Mahalanobis d measure. This method will be considered in the next section.

Dealing with Heteroscedasticity

One deals with heterogeneous within-group variance–covariance matrices (W_i) by dividing the difference between the observation's location and each group centroid's location on the discriminant axis by the standard deviation of that group *as measured along the discriminant axis* instead of dividing by the pooled estimate that will always be 1.0. Because the pooled estimate of the standard deviation is 1.0, the differences in location are simply the discriminant score differences, which are -2.04, -1.06, and $-.22$ for groups P, T, and A, respectively.

Equation (3-7), then, is used to obtain the variance of a linear combination, and the standard deviation is obtained by taking the square root of the resulting variance. The variance of group P on discriminant axis I is therefore $d'_{dI} W_p d_{dI}$, where d_{dI} is simply the vector of raw discriminant weights for function I (.111 and $-.029$) and W_p is the within-group variance–covariance matrix for group P. The raw (deviation) score weights are used because W_p is not standardized. The resultant *will* be in z-score units. The variance is

$$[.111 \quad -.029] \times \begin{bmatrix} 139.96 & 65.46 \\ 65.46 & 172.45 \end{bmatrix} \times \begin{bmatrix} .111 \\ -.029 \end{bmatrix} = 1.4485$$

The standard deviation (s_p) is therefore $1.4485^{1/2}$ or 1.21. The standard deviations of groups T and A (s_t and s_a, respectively) are calculated analogously from W_t and W_a and are 1.11 and .71. Consequently, the differences between the observation (X) and each of the group centroids (P, T, and A, respectively) are $(X - P)/s_p = -2.04/1.21 = 1.69$, $(X - T)/s_t = -1.06/1.11$ or .95, and $(X - A)/s_a = -.22/.71 = -.31$. The observation is closer to group A than group P or group T, so it would again be correctly assigned. Group A's greater homogeneity makes the test case slightly more dissimilar to group A when individual, rather than pooled, variance estimates are used.

Using Multiple Discriminant Scores

If the group centroids are sufficiently diffuse so that more than one discriminant function is needed for optimum discrimination, one of the methods discussed in the next major section may be more appropriate. There are, however, ways in which the information contained in multiple discriminant scores (1.269 and .195) may be used. The procedure is generally most useful when you wish to use more than one but not all of the discriminant functions. One begins by obtaining the differences between the score on function II and each of the group centroids. The present differences are $(.195 - -.058)$ or .60, $(.195 - .354)$ or $-.18$, and $(.195 - -.064)$ or .60 for groups P, T, and A. Note that the test observation is closest to group T on function II, but function II is far less important to classification than is function I where the corresponding differences were -2.04, -1.06, and $-.22$. Consequently, do not use function II all by itself for classification purposes.

Normality and Multiple Discriminant Functions

The sums of the squared differences on the two functions may be interpreted as generalized (Mahalanobis) d^2 measures, which are $-2.04^2 + .60^2$ or 4.52, $-1.06^2 + .18^2$ or 1.16 and $-.22^2 + .60^2$ or .41. The square roots (2.13, 1.08, and .64) are the respective distances (d) between the observation and each of the group centroids *as measured in the two dimensions generated by both discriminant functions and not the single, optimal dimension (function I)*. Sums of squared deviations are Mahalanobis d^2 measures because of the orthogonality of successive discriminant functions. The observation is assigned to the group with the smallest d^2 measure, which is again group A.

The d^2 values have a useful property when the underlying scores can be assumed normally distributed. Because the d^2 values are sums of independently derived squared z scores, they can be viewed as samples from a *chi-square* distribution with df equal to the number of discriminant functions (two in the present example). Their associated probabilities can therefore be used as a decision variable. The general formula for the probability of a chi-square variable is given by Eq. (9-5). The symbol "$p(\chi^2, df)$" is the probability of obtaining that value of χ^2 (d^2), in group i. As before, the symbol "exp," denotes raising the number e (2.71828 ...) to the power indicated in the expression.

$$p(\chi^2, df/i) = \frac{(\chi^2)^{(df-2)/2} \exp(-\chi^2/2.)}{2^{(df/2)} \Gamma(df/2)} \tag{9-5}$$

The symbol "$\Gamma(df/2)$" denotes what is known as the *gamma function* with two degrees of freedom. I will not discuss the concept of a gamma function in detail. Suffice it to note that $\Gamma(df/2) = (df/2 - 1)!$ when df is even. Things are a bit more complex when df is an odd integer, so $df/2$ has a decimal remainder of .5. The formulas for even and odd df are presented explicitly in Eqs. (9-6a) and (9-6b), respectively. The quantity 1.77 is the square root of pi (3.14159 ...) and the expression that follows looks like a factorial in that one takes the successive product of $(df/2 - 1), (df/2 - 2)$, etc., as long as $(df/2 - i)$ is positive.

$$\Gamma(df/2) = (df/2 - 1)(df/2 - 2)... \qquad \text{(when } df \text{ is even)} \tag{9-6a}$$

$$\Gamma(df/2) = 1.77(df/2 - 1)(df/2 - 2)... \qquad \text{(for } df/2 - i > 0; \text{ when } df \text{ is odd)} \tag{9-6b}$$

When there are only two discriminant functions, $p(\chi^2, 2/i)$ reduces to the useful form of Eq. (9-7). Since all values of χ^2 considered in my example are based on 2 df, I will simplify my notation to "$p(\chi^2)$," "$p(\chi^2/i)$," etc.

$$p(\chi^2/i) = .5(-d^2/2.) \tag{9-7}$$

Thus, $p(\chi^2/P) = .5 \times \exp(-4.52/2.)$ or .052. The $p(\chi^2/T)$ and $p(\chi^2/A)$ are .294 and .408, respectively. The associated Bayesian probabilities are listed in the row designated "Both functions" of Table 9-3. The results again differ little from those presented earlier using other methods.

I have previously shown how to correct z-score differences on the first discriminant function for heteroscedasticity. The procedure was to compute each group's standard deviation along the function, which was divided into the deviation of the observation from the group centroid. The same operation may be performed using function II, which allows d^2 measures to be derived. The variance of group P on function II is $\mathbf{d}'_{dII}\mathbf{W}_p\mathbf{d}_{dII}$, which equals

$$[-.017 \quad .094] \times \begin{bmatrix} 139.96 & 65.46 \\ 65.46 & 172.45 \end{bmatrix} \times \begin{bmatrix} -.017 \\ .094 \end{bmatrix} = 1.3177$$

The variances of groups T and A on function II, obtained analogously, are 1.2712 and .5896. Hence, the three standard deviations are 1.15, 1.13, and .77. Dividing the standard deviations into the mean differences for each of the three groups produces .60/1.15 or .52, .18/1.13 or .16, and .60/.77 or .78.

The χ^2 scores for the sample values of d^2 are obtained by adding the squared z values for the two functions (recall that the deviations from the group centroids based on individual standard deviations were 1.69, .95, and .31 on function I). Thus, the χ^2 values for groups P, T, and A are $1.69^2 + .52^2 = 3.13$, $.95^2 + .16^2 = .93$, and $.31^2 + .78^2 = .351$. Equation (9-7) may be used to convert the χ^2 values to probabilities, which are .105, .314, and .351. The classification probabilities are listed in Table 9-3. The results are similar to the others presented, but the combined effects of using function II, where the observation was relatively close to the group T centroid, and group A's greater homogeneity make the various values of $p(A/X)$ somewhat smaller and $p(T/X)$ somewhat larger than in other comparisons.

Classification Based on Distance Measures

Some alternative methods use the *direct* distance between observations and group centroids rather than discriminant score differences, which involve projections upon discriminant axes. Direct distance measures are sensitive to the total distance of an observation from a centroid, unlike discriminant scores, which are only sensitive to the distance along the discriminant axis.

Figure 9-8 illustrates the basic geometry of direct classification. Although I have drawn the distance simply as a line connecting the observation and each of two group centroids, the differences are measured in slightly different ways by different approaches.

Simple Distance

The simplest decision variable for direct classification is the *root mean square* (*RMS*) difference between an observation and a group centroid. (The sum of squared differences between the observation and the group centroid may also be used since the two quantities are monotonically related.) This procedure ignores the covariance structure; hence, the decision variable has limited statistical properties. The results are not true Mahalanobis distances. A one

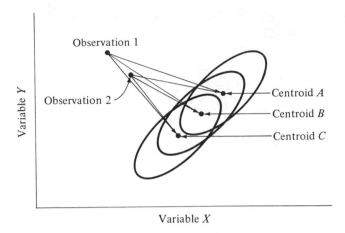

FIGURE 9-8. Geometry of direct classification. Observations 1 and 2 project are at different distances from each of the centroids; hence, they have different distance measures. Their classification probabilities will not be the same.

unit difference on each predictor is given the same meaning, i.e., that the predictors are assumed *commensurable*. Group differences in variance are ignored. The very simplicity of the method "keeps you out of trouble" when your estimates of the covariance structure are poor.[7]

The computations in the present example are as follows. The distance of the test observation $(51, 57)$ from the group P centroid $(71.85, 60.16)$ is $[(51 - 71.85)^2 + (57 - 60.15)^2]^{1/2} = [20.85^2 + 3.15^2]^{1/2} = 444.645^2 = 21.08$. Similar calculations lead to distances of 14.07 and 3.66 for groups T and A. The observation would thus be correctly assigned to group A.

Fisher's Classification Functions

One way to incorporate the covariance structure of predictors into classification is to obtain what Fisher originally referred to as "discriminant functions," a meaning now supplanted by the very different meaning of Chapter 8. The equations are now known as "Fisher's classification functions."

Fisher's classification functions are a series of regression equations used to predict group membership. The vector of b weights to predict membership in group i ($\mathbf{b}_i$) is given by Eq. (9-8a) for the pooled case. The scalar constant (a_i) used when base rates and values are ignored is given by Eq. (9-8b). The constant may be adjusted to provide a Bayesian analysis by the use of Eq. (9-8c).

---

[7] If the data are not in commensurable units, they may be made so by coverting them to z scores. Because the conversion is straightforward, I will not illustrate it. The T scores used to define the Hy and Pd scales in the example are also commensurable.

The term "$\bar{x}_i$" denotes the vector of predictor means for that group. Unlike distance measures, here *higher* scores are associated with group membership.

$$\mathbf{b}_i = \mathbf{W}^{-1}\bar{\mathbf{x}}_i \qquad (9\text{-}8a)$$

$$a_i = -.5\mathbf{b}_i'\bar{\mathbf{x}}_i \qquad (9\text{-}8b)$$

$$a_i = -.5\mathbf{b}_i'\bar{\mathbf{x}}_i + \ln[p(i)] + \ln[v(i)] \qquad (9\text{-}8c)$$

The classification function for group P (ignoring base rates and values for the moment) is obtained as follows:

$$\mathbf{b}_p = \begin{bmatrix} .013 & -.005 \\ -.005 & .010 \end{bmatrix} \times \begin{bmatrix} 71.85 \\ 60.15 \end{bmatrix} = \begin{bmatrix} .615 \\ .222 \end{bmatrix}$$

and

$$\mathbf{a}_p = -.5 \times [.615 \quad .222] \times \begin{bmatrix} 71.85 \\ 60.15 \end{bmatrix} = -28.74$$

Hence, $Y_p' = .615\text{Hy} + .222\text{Pd} - 28.77.$ and the score associated with the observation $(51, 57)$ is 15.25. The analogous equation for group T is $Y_t' = .497\text{Hy} + .290\text{Pd} - 24.98.$ with a score of 16.61, and the equation for group A is $Y_a' = .413\text{Hy} + .275\text{Pd} - 19.11$ with a score of 17.64. The observation is correctly classified to group A.

Adding $\ln(.2)$ or -1.609 to a_p and a_t and $\ln(.6)$ or $-.511$ to a_a allows base rate information to be incorporated in the decision process. The new constants are -30.379, -26.587, and -19.616, and the associated classification scores are 15.53, 16.04, and 16.81. Adding $\ln(.3)$ or -1.204, $\ln(.5)$ or $-.693$, and $\ln(.2)$ or -1.61 to the original a_p, a_t, and a_a constants incorporates values. The new constants are -29.974, -25.71, and 20.714, and the classification scores are 13.33, 15.35, and 15.20. Finally, adding $\ln(.2) + \ln(.3)$, i.e., $\ln(.6)$, or -2.813, $\ln(.2) + \ln(.5)$ or -2.303, and $\ln(.6) + \ln(.2)$ or -2.120 to the original constants incorporates both base rate and value information. The constants are -31.225, -27.280, and -21.225 and the classification scores are 11.716, 13.736, and 15.198. As is consistently the case, the observation is only misclassified when values are incorporated and base rates are ignored.

Individual rather than pooled variance–covariance matrices may be used when there is heteroscedasticity by using $\mathbf{W}_i^{-1}$ instead of $\mathbf{W}^{-1}$ in Eq. (9-8a).

Using individual matrices, the classification equations (ignoring base rates and values) are $Y_p' = .426\text{Hy} + .187\text{Pd} - 20.928$, $Y_t' = .324\text{Hy} + .144\text{Pd} - 14.875$, and $Y_a' = 1.021\text{Hy} + .534\text{Pd} - 43.088$. The classification scores are 11.45, 9.88, and 39.45. The difference between group A and groups T and A was so large that adding in the natural logs of p and v essentially had no effect.

Mahalanobis Distances

An alternative and largely equivalent strategy is to compute the Mahalanobis distances between a given observation and each of the group centroids.

SAS PROC DISCRIM uses Mahalanobis distance measures. Equation (9-9) contains the relevant equation for use with a pooled variance–covariance matrix. Except for notation, it is equivalent to Eq. (8-4). The only difference is that I am now concerned with the distance between an individual observation and a group centroid, whereas I was previously interested in the distance between two group centroids.

$$d_i^2 = \mathbf{d}_i'\mathbf{W}^{-1}\mathbf{d}_i$$

$$= (\mathbf{x} - \bar{\mathbf{x}}_i)'\mathbf{W}^{-1}(\mathbf{x} - \bar{\mathbf{x}}_i) \qquad (9\text{-}9)$$

The distance measures may be used in conjunction with Eq. (9-4) to perform a Bayesian analysis. The calculations involved in computing d^2 from the centroid of group P to the test observation, d_p^2, are as follows:

$$d_p^2 = [(51 - 71.85)(57 - 60.16)] \times \begin{bmatrix} .0127 & -.0050 \\ -.0050 & .0096 \end{bmatrix} \times \begin{bmatrix} (51 - 71.85) \\ (57 - 60.16) \end{bmatrix}$$

$$= [-20.85 - 3.15] \times \begin{bmatrix} .0127 & -.0050 \\ -.0050 & .0096 \end{bmatrix} \times \begin{bmatrix} 20.85 \\ -3.15 \end{bmatrix}$$

$$= 4.98$$

The corresponding values of d_t^2 and d_a^2 are 1.65 and .18. Hence d_p, d_t, and d_a are 2.23, 1.28, and .42. The test observation would therefore be correctly assigned on the basis of a minimum distance rule.

The d^2 values obtained here differ from the d^2 values obtained by combining discriminant scores, but they may also be converted to χ^2 probabilities for purposes of Bayesian analysis, using Eq. (9-7). The values of $p(\chi^2/P)$, $p(\chi^2/T)$, and $p(\chi^2/A)$ are .0415, .2195, and .4577. The classification probabilities are contained in the rows of Table 9-3 designated "Mahalanobis distance."

As with the other methods, individual variance–covariance matrices may be used to replace the pooled estimate when there is heteroscedasticity. The values of d_p^2, d_t^2, and d_a^2 are 3.41, 1.24, and .34. Hence, the associated d values are 1.85, 1.11, and .58; the $p(\chi^2/P)$, $p(\chi^2/T)$, and $p(\chi^2/A)$ values are .0908, .2689, and .4218. The associated classification probabilities are presented in Table 9-3.

A Summary of Strategic Considerations in Classification

The following basic models have been considered: (1) salient weights, (2) single discriminant function, (3) multiple discriminant functions, (4) simple distances, (5) Fisher's classification functions, and (6) Mahalanobis distances. In all cases except the simple distance model, either the pooled or the individual group variance estimates could be used. The salient weight, single discriminant function, multiple discriminant function, and Mahalanobis distance models allow normal curve or χ^2 assumptions to estimate probabilities of the test statistic given group membership, $p(X/i)$. The $p(X/i)$ values, in turn, readily permit a Bayesian analysis to determine $p(i/X)$. Despite all the procedures presented, I have not exhausted all possibilities. For example, Overall and Klett (1972) present a *pattern probability* model useful with categorical predictors.

I will now return to the seven questions posed in my overview of the topic. It should be clear that the most striking difference in results produced by the various methods was introduced by the addition of a Bayesian analysis. When the structure is more diffuse and there is greater heteroscedasticity, the results could be more varied. Under these conditions, the differences between use of one versus multiple discriminant functions and between pooled versus individual variance–covariance matrices will be more apparent. Consequently, experience with more than one method (although not necessarily all) is important. At the same time, note that the Fisher classification and Mahalanobis distance models (and, to a large extent, the multiple discriminant model) are inherently quite similar, though distinct. The major advantage of the Multiple discriminant model is that it allows distances to be derived from any number of discriminant functions.

1. In general, methods appropriate for a diffuse structure (simple distance, Fisher's classification functions, Mahalanobis distance, and the multiple discriminant model) can also be used when the structure is concentrated. By contrast, the remaining methods, which are designed for a concentrated structure, should not be used when the structure is in fact diffuse.

2. Whether or not normal curve assumptions fit the data usually must be determined empirically. All methods are reasonably tolerant of minor deviations, such as the minor skewness of Hy and Pd. In general, scores derived from sums of item responses will be sufficiently normal to be suitable (cf. Chapter 12, however), but quite misleading results can be obtained when the number of predictors is small and their distributions are highly skewed. Whether you should make normal curve assumptions depends on whether you plan to conduct a Bayesian analysis. There is no point in using a normal curve or χ^2 model if you are not planning to incorporate base rates, values, or both, in view of the monotonic relation between measures like z or d and associated values of $p(X/i)$.

3. Whether or not to conduct a Bayesian analysis depends on how good your estimates of the associated values and base rates are. To repeat, do not attempt such an analysis unless you have a good idea of the base rates.

4. Just as one should know whether the group (criterion, dependent variable) structure is diffuse or concentrated, one should also study the structure of the predictors (independent variables). The reason I presented the salient weight model first is to stress the importance of knowing what determines prediction. Highly intercorrelated predictors generally allow simplified classification procedures to be used.

5. Unpooled models demand larger normative bases than pooled ones. Remember that using bad estimates of the various parameters is worse than treating them as equal, just as was the case in (3).

6. A major advantage of the salient weight and simple distance models is that they lend themselves to hand calculation. To a certain extend, models based on discriminant scores or Mahalanobis distances contain a substantial degree of pseudoprecision even in relatively large samples. On the other hand, discriminant scores and/or Mahalanobis distances are readily available as intermediate outputs from most statistical packages.

7. The relative familiarity of a metric is neither a major nor a totally trivial issue. A minor advantage to the single discriminant function is that the decision variable can readily be presented as a familiar score without making major assumptions. The several models allowing $p(X/i)$ values to be estimated also offer a familiar metric but at the cost of stronger assumptions.

I have now completed the consideration of issues related to classification. I began with a consideration of some of the tradeoffs involved in using strict versus lenient criteria by discussing signal detection theory. Then, I considered a variety of strategies used for classification. Now, I am ready to consider the role that chance plays in classification in the next chapter.

10
Classification Methods—Part 3. Inferential Considerations in the MANOVA

Chapter Overview

I am going to conclude the general topic of classification and discrimination with a consideration of null hypothesis testing. Much of this chapter deals with the *multivariate analysis of variance (MANOVA)* and related themes. I have mentioned earlier at several points of the text that testing a multivariate hypothesis of centroid (vector, profile) differences is more complex than testing a univariate hypothesis of mean (location) difference. The basic point to remember is that an inferential test that is the most powerful for detecting a difference when centroids are concentrated is not necessarily the most powerful test for detecting a difference when centroids were diffuse. The general strategy is to treat all unknown differences in structure as if they are diffuse.

I. THE TWO-GROUP MANOVA AND HOTELLING'S T^2—The topic of null hypothesis testing is introduced through a two-group example, where the structure is concentrated, by definition. A multivariate extention of the t test known as *Hotelling's T^2* is discussed. In addition to comparing the overall equality of two groups' mean vectors, I discuss methods appropriate to (1) making specific comparisons, (2) examining if all elements of a single group's mean vector are equal, and (3) determining if a single group's mean vector can be regarded as null. This section concludes with a comparison of the repeated measures ANOVA and the MANOVA.

II. TESTS OF VECTOR MEANS WITH MULTIPLE GROUPS— Four tests are in common use for evaluating centroid differences. One has been suggested for use with concentrated structures—*Roy's largest root*—but its mathematical foundations are relatively weak. Three other tests that are relatively similar to each other are particularly appropriate for use with diffuse structures and are also preferable for general use: (1) *Hotelling–Lawley trace*, (2) *Wilks' lambda*, and (3) the *Pillai–Bartlett trace*. A useful adaptation of Wilks' lambda allows for *sequential* testing of individual discriminant functions. Finally, Box's M test is introduced, which allows an investigator to examine the homogeneity of variance-covariance matrices.

III. THE SIMPLE MANOVA WITH MULTIPLE GROUPS—An example of the simple MANOVA is presented to illustrate the relevant tests.

IV. THE MULTIVARIATE MANOVA—The two-way ANOVA allows tests of main effects and interactions (or, alternatively, a main effect and nested effects) upon a scalar. The multivariate MANOVA allows analogous tests upon a vector (profile) of dependent variables. A computational example is presented.

V. THE MANCOVA—Back in Chapter 5, I noted that the ANCOVA was a special case of multiple regression in which the role of one variable (the covariate) was to reduce error variance. The analysis simply consisted of entering the covariate into the regression model before the variables representing the treatment effect (*hierarchically*). This principle is now extended to include the analysis of a vector of dependent variables. A numerical example is provided.

I will now discuss the role that chance plays in determining relations established by the methodology presented in Chapter 8. Previously, I deliberately ignored the issue of statistical significance by assuming that the data base was large enough to ignore the role of chance. Clearly, one does not always have a large data base and, in fact, the role of chance is magnified many times over when a study involves vector rather than scalar data.

Most of the chapter will be devoted to the multivariate analysis of variance (MANOVA) and related models such as the multivariate analysis of covariance (MANCOVA). The MANOVA and MANCOVA are multivariate extensions of the ANOVA and ANCOVA, respectively; the data are vectors rather than scalars. My discussion will follow from the basics of discriminant analysis as discussed in Chapter 8 and principles of null hypothesis testing in the ANOVA. *The MANOVA and discriminant analysis rely upon the same basic operations. The difference is simply one of emphasis as the MANOVA (and MANCOVA) emphasizes inferential questions and discriminant analysis emphasizes descriptive questions.* In other words, most issues in the MANOVA simply deal with variants upon the question as to whether the amount of group discrimination produced by a discriminant function exceeds chance.

You have probably learned how to test the significance of the difference between a pair of group mean scalars using the t distribution before you learned how to test the significance among multiple group means using the F distribution. There is an analogous way to test the significance of the difference between a pair of group mean vectors called *Hotelling's T^2*, it serves as a useful way to introduce the topic even though, like the t distribution, the former could also be abandoned in favor of some more general tests.

The Two-Group MANOVA and Hotelling's T^2

For purposes of example, assume that one wishes to test the physiological effects of caffeine. A group of volunteers who regularly drink coffee is recruited. Subjects are then randomly assigned to drink two cups of either a decaffeinated coffee (group D) or regular coffee (group C). It is assumed that regular coffee "speeds" up bodily activity, but the concept cannot be associated with any single indicator. Rather, three measures that one could reasonably assume to be responsive are obtained: (1) heart rate (X_1); (2) systolic blood pressure, which is the blood pressure during a contraction of the heart (X_2); and (3) diastolic blood pressure, which is the blood pressure during relaxation of the heart (X_3). Data are gathered from 20 people, 10 in each group. Note that a between-group design is being used. I will consider the equivalent of a repeated measures design later. The data were constructed so that each dependent variable loaded on the same, single factor. The loading of X_1 was .64. In other words, it could be expressed as $.64F + .77e_1$, where F is the common factor and e_1 is the measurement error of X_1 (note that $.64^2 + .77^2 = 1$). In a like manner, X_2 had a loading of .25 and X_3 had a loading of .56 on the common factor F. As a consequence, the measurement error associated with X_2 and X_3 (e_2 and e_3) is .97 and .83.

The (simulated) raw data are presented in Table 10-1 along with the group means and standard deviations for the two groups and the aggregate. The data, especially those for X_2, are yet another illustration of sampling error. They actually were constructed from populations of equal variance and the standardized (z score) differences for X_1, X_2, and X_3 were .8, .3, and .75. You may verify that $r_{12} = .20$, $r_{13} = .39$, and $r_{23} = .43$.

Suppose I had just given you the raw data and ask you to figure out a way to test the null hypothesis that the mean population vector for group D, μ_d, is the same as the mean population vector for group C, μ_c, or, equivalently, that the vector representing the mean population *difference* is a null vector, $(0, 0, 0)$. If you knew nothing about discriminant analysis and the MANOVA but did know multiple regression, you could obtain a value of R^2 "predicting" group membership from X_1, X_2, and X_3 and use R^2 to compute a value of F from Eq. (4-17). However, there are two differences between applications considered in Chapter 4 and the present application. One is that the logical status of predictor and criterion is reversed in that the "predictors" are actually a consequence of group membership. The other is that group membership is represented by a series of dummy codes or the equivalent rather than as a continuous, normally distributed variable (hence, the validities are actually point biserial correlations). Neither consideration is important because the correlation model on which the analysis is based does not require continuous variables, as was seen in Chapter 5, and the multiple regression model relating one set of variables to another single variable does not make any assumptions about which comes first in time.

Equation (4-17) can be applied to the data with P (the number of dependent variables) $= 3$ and $N - P - 1 = 20 - 3 - 1$ or 16 df, where $N = N_d + N_c$. The value of R^2 is .4347 and $F = (.4347 \times 16)/[(1. - .4347) \times 3] = 4.10$, which is significant beyond the .02 level. It confirms the existence of a treatment effect, so that it can be assumed that the mean population vector differs in the two groups. You can see that caffeine did speed up bodily processes. Note that the omnibus test does not tell you anything about which specific dependent

TABLE 10-1. Heart rates (X_1), systolic blood pressures (X_2), and diastolic blood pressures (X_3) for individuals drinking decaffeinated Coffee (group D) versus regular coffee (group C)[a]

Group	Observation	X_1	X_2	X_3
D	1	55	132	81
D	2	62	114	78
D	3	61	133	83
D	4	58	124	83
D	5	54	113	63
D	6	58	104	82
D	7	46	132	72
D	8	71	123	74
D	9	67	117	87
D	10	51	107	78
D	$\bar{X}$	58.4	11.9	78.1
D	s	7.4	10.4	6.9
C	1	66	120	86
C	2	68	104	89
C	3	51	92	74
C	4	55	108	84
C	5	81	110	83
C	6	83	123	89
C	7	70	109	78
C	8	70	137	95
C	9	77	115	81
C	10	68	159	89
C	$\bar{X}$	69.9	118.0	84.9
C	s	9.0	18.7	6.0
All	$\bar{X}$	64.1	118.9	81.5
All	$s*$	8.2	15.1	6.4

[a] Standard deviations are pooled within-groups.

variables were affected. I will discuss the process of looking for specific differences below, although one possibility is to perform separate t tests on the three individual measures. Keep in mind that a series of inferential tests increases the probability of type I errors (see Chapter 5).

Perhaps the most common use of the MANOVA is as an omnibus test of group differences when there are several dependent variables, prior to tests upon the individual dependent variables. This use of the MANOVA to control for type I error rate is somewhat like the use of the ANOVA to perform an omnibus test upon a set of groups prior to performing t tests or other comparisons on levels of independent variables. Unfortunately, use of the MANOVA is all too often limited to control over type I error rate. The MANOVA can provide considerable additional information that is not present in the individual tests. Specifically, the discriminant weights show you what the composition of the most discriminating variable is. Moreover, in studies containing multiple groups where there is the possibility of more than one significant discriminant equation, you can determine whether two measures which both vary significantly among groups do so for the same or different reasons.

The Formal MANOVA Model

The model for the simple MANOVA is an extension of the ANOVA [Eq. (5-6)]. In that earlier case, an observed score (scalar) was expressed as the sum of (1) the grand mean, (2) a deviation of the group mean from the grand mean (treatment effect), and (3) a deviation of the individual score from the group mean (error). The grand mean was subtracted from both sides of the equation, converting the observed score to a deviation score. The resulting deviation score was then shown equal to a treatment effect plus error. Squaring both sides produces the basic ANOVA equation: the total sum of squares equals the between-group sum of squares plus the within-group sum of squares. Dividing the sums of squares by their respective *df* leads to mean squares, and dividing the mean square between by the mean square within leads to the *F* ratio.

The MANOVA employs a vector of dependent variables instead of a scalar. However, the same basic mathematical steps are employed, producing the *total, groups (between),* and *within sum of product (SP) matrices,* $\mathbf{SP}_t$, $\mathbf{SP}_g$, and $\mathbf{SP}_w$. The SP matrices, when divided by their respective *df*, lead to the total, between-group, and within-group variance–covariance matrices, $\mathbf{T}$, $\mathbf{G}$, and $\mathbf{W}$. (I could have referred to $\mathbf{SP}_g$ and $\mathbf{G}$ as $\mathbf{SP}_b$ and $\mathbf{B}$, respectively, in order to be consistent with previous notation. But, by so doing, my later discussion of the multivariate MANOVA would become more difficult.) The matrix analogue of division leads to the product matrix $\mathbf{W}^{-1}\mathbf{G}$. Here a slight complication arises since the multivariate analogue of F turns out to be one of several possible functions of the matrix. Moreover, as was discussed in Chapter 8, it is simpler to define most test statistics in terms of the corresponding SP matrices, $\mathbf{SP}_w^{-1}\mathbf{SP}_g$. The difference will not be apparent until the multiple-group case is considered, since the calculations made for the two-group case do not use variance–covariance matrices. One terminological note is also useful here. Many sources refer to $\mathbf{SP}_g$ in the simpler ANOVA as the *hypothesis* SP matrix, $\mathbf{SP}_h$, and $\mathbf{SP}_w$ as the *error* SP matrix, $\mathbf{SP}_e$. The terminology is quite useful in going beyond the simple ANOVA, since there can possibly be several systematic sources of variance and error is not necessarily variance within-group. However, I will stick to the terms "group" and "within" for most of my discussion, since these terms are more familiar.

The basic null hypothesis of the scalar ANOVA can be stated in at least two equivalent forms: (1) that the group means are equal and (2) that the treatment effects are zero for all groups. More precise tests, either *a priori* or *a posteriori*, were discussed. The basic null hypothesis in the MANOVA is the vector analogue of the ANOVA null hypothesis, and more precise tests are also possible.

There is one important difference between the MANOVA and the ANOVA. If there are K groups being observed on P dependent variables, group differences can exist in the lesser of $K - 1$ and P different dimensions. I will symbolize the lesser of $K - 1$ and P as "S." This number of possible differences, S, corresponds to the maximum number of discriminant functions. In actuality, groups can differ along none of these dimensions if their centroids differ only by chance, or they could differ along all S dimensions. Hence, the process of testing the null hypothesis is quite a bit more complex. Fortunately, in the two-group case, which I will discuss first, S is 1, just like in the scalar case.

When you are performing a discriminant analysis with a large sample so that random error of sampling tends to play a minor role, normal curve assumptions are relatively unimportant. The qualifier "relatively" is necessary because even with large samples, data from highly skewed distributions can cause problems for the mundane reason that means can provide misleading results, as you were taught in elementary statistics. The MANOVA's inferential tests, unlike the descriptive indices in discriminant analysis, require observations to be drawn from a multivariate normal population. However, as a practical matter, unequal sample sizes do not cause a major problem unless the variance–covariance matrices are extremely heterogeneous.

Hotelling's T^2

Equations (10-1) illustrate one way to infer whether profiles (vectors) associated with two groups differ by more than chance. Equation (10-1a) contains the standard formula for t used to evaluate the difference between two (scalar) group means, X_1 and X_2, assuming heterogeneity of variance and consequent pooling of the two variance estimates. Let s denote this pooled estimate, and N_1 and N_2 denote the sample sizes of the two groups. Equation (10-1b) contains one slight modification upon this basic formula: the symbol "D" is used to denote the mean difference (i.e., $D = \bar{X}_1 - \bar{X}_2$).

$$t = \frac{\bar{X}_1 - \bar{X}_2}{[s^2(1/N_1 + 1/N_2)]^{1/2}} \qquad (10\text{-}1a)$$

$$t = \frac{D}{[s^2(1/N_1 + 1/N_2)]^{1/2}} \qquad (10\text{-}1b)$$

Now square both sides of the equation. The result, Eq. (10-2), can either be called t^2 or F, since they are equivalent. I have written the derivation in three steps to illustrate how an apparently awkward representation in the second and third steps can lead to a useful result:

$$t^2 = F = \frac{D^2}{s^2(1/N_1 + 1/N_2)}$$

$$= \frac{N_1 N_2 D^2}{(N_1 + N_2)s^2}$$

$$= \frac{N_1 N_2 D(s^2)^{-1} D}{(N_1 + N_2)} \qquad (10\text{-}2)$$

The second step takes advantage of the fact that $1/(1/N_1 + 1/N_2) = N_1 N_2/(N_1 + N_2)$. Then, I replaced D^2/s^2 with its equivalent representation $D(s^2)^{-1}D$.

The third statement lends itself quite simply to multivariate expression. The multivariate equivalent of a scalar difference is a vector difference, which I will call "$\mathbf{d}$" as I have stated previously. Similarly, I have already shown how the multivariate extension of a variance is a variance–covariance matrix—the pooled within-group variance–covariance matrix ($\mathbf{W}$). Once I have made the substitutions, the resulting formula yields Hotelling's T^2, given in Eq. (10-3a):

$$T^2 = \frac{N_1 N_2 \mathbf{d}' \mathbf{W}^{-1} \mathbf{d}}{N_1 + N_2} \qquad (10\text{-}3a)$$

$$T^2 = \frac{N_1 N_2 d^2}{N_1 + N_2} \qquad (10\text{-}3b)$$

Equation (10-3a) should look familiar, in part: that portion of the numerator which reads $\mathbf{d}' \mathbf{W}^{-1} \mathbf{d}$ is the formula for the d^2 measure, Eq. (8-4). The relation is presented explicitly as Eq. (10-3b).

Unfortunately, is it *not* always the case that $T^2 = F$, except when $P = 1$. However, T^2 may be converted to F by means of Eq. (10-4) with df of P and $N - P$, where $N = N_1 + N_2$. The relation is important because tables of T^2 are usually more difficult to obtain than tables of F, although they may be found in Timm (1975).

$$F = \frac{(N - P - 1)T^2}{P(N - 2)} \qquad (10\text{-}4)$$

The R^2 and T^2 are functions of one another as both are function of F. Equations (10-5) states the relation between the former two statistics:

$$R^2 = \frac{T^2}{N - 2 + T^2} \qquad (10\text{-}5a)$$

$$T^2 = \frac{R^2(N - 2)}{1 - R^2} \qquad (10\text{-}5b)$$

The values of R^2 and F that I presented above from the data of Table 10-1 were obtained from an SAS program. You may verify from the table that

$\mathbf{d} = (11.59, -1.94, 6.92)$. The matrix $\mathbf{W}$ is

$$\begin{bmatrix} 67.87 & 25.62 & 20.91 \\ 25.62 & 229.25 & 42.19 \\ 20.91 & 42.19 & 41.58 \end{bmatrix}$$

hence, $\mathbf{W}^{-1}$ is

$$\begin{bmatrix} .017 & .000 & -.008 \\ .000 & .005 & -.005 \\ -.008 & -.005 & .034 \end{bmatrix}$$

From Eq. (10-3a)

$$T^2 = \left[\frac{10 * 10}{10 + 10}\right] [11.59 \quad -1.94 \quad 6.92] \times \begin{bmatrix} .017 & .000 & -.008 \\ .000 & .005 & -.005 \\ -.008 & -.005 & .034 \end{bmatrix} \begin{bmatrix} 11.59 \\ -1.94 \\ 6.92 \end{bmatrix}$$

$$= 13.96$$

It may also be readily verified that d^2 is 2.79. Computation of F and R^2 is left as an exercise.

The following exercise may also prove useful. It may be verified that the vector of discriminant weights is $(.088, -.031, .086)$. Use these weights to derive a composite variable, i.e., let $Y = .088X_1 - .031X_2 + .086X_3$. Perform a t test comparing the two groups. The resulting value of $t = 3.73$, which when squared, equals the preceding F ratio within rounding error. However, if you were to use a conventional table of t to evaluate its significance, you would seriously exaggerate the significance level because you would ignore the fact that three parameters were estimated (i.e., the three discriminant weights). The df associated with the numerator of an F distribution corrects for the estimation process so that the comparison is proper. The resulting value of t is clearly larger than the values of t obtained from the individual predictors, which are 3.16, .32, and 2.29, respectively. The fact that sampling error caused the X_2 mean to be smaller in group C than in group D also meant that t was substantially larger than the corresponding value based on either the simpler sum or mean (ignoring differences in variance) or the sums or means divided by the corresponding standard deviations (correcting for differences in variance), which were 1.59 and 2.31, respectively.

A value of T^2 (or F) may be significant when no individual value of t is significant. The situation can arise if individual response measures load on the same factor(s) and the sample size is too small to overcome the error associated with individual variables but large enough for the composite to be sensitive to the common effects of the treatment on the individual variables. As a general rule, look at the value of t obtained from either a simple sum or sum-correcting-for-variance. Because the univariate t test based on equal weighting does not involve estimation of weighting parameters, and because it is also sensitive to what the measures have in common, t may be significant when T^2 is not.

Post Hoc Comparisons

Values of t or the corresponding values of F are commonly available as by-products of discriminant analyses or MANOVA. As I noted in Chapter 8, the ratio of g_{ii} to w_{ii} is the F ratio for the ith variable as would be obtained from ignoring the other variable (or, in the general case, variables). In contrast, diagonal element i of $\mathbf{W}^{-1}\mathbf{G}$ is the partial F ratio for variable i, reflecting how much that variable is affected by the treatment, holding constant the other variable or variables. Both measures have $df = 1$ and $N - 1$.

A more general approach is to form contrasts, in the same sense the term was used in Chapter 5. All that need be done is to form the contrast as a suitable set of weights to be applied to the $\mathbf{d}$ vector. The weights need not sum to zero, as was the case previously, because, as a given weight is applied to one group, its complement (negative) is applied to the other, in effect. As a result, the weights actually add to zero when both groups are taken into account.

The basic logic is rather simple. If the vector of coefficients is called $\mathbf{g}$, then $\mathbf{g}'\mathbf{d}$ is the difference in weighted means, and $\mathbf{g}'\mathbf{W}$ is the variance. The standard error of the mean is the square root of $\mathbf{g}'\mathbf{W}$ times $N_1 N_2/(N_1 + N_2)$. Dividing the difference in weighted means by the standard error yields the test statistic, t (the process may be set up to yield values of F). Equation (10-6) summarizes the relationship:

$$ t = \frac{N_1 N_2 \mathbf{g}'\mathbf{d}}{(N_1 + N_2)(\mathbf{g}'\mathbf{W})^{1/2}} \tag{10-6} $$

Application of Hotelling's T^2 to a Single Group

Hotelling's T^2 statistic is also applicable to situations involving a single group. One is to test the null hypothesis that the vector of group means is a null vector, i.e., $\mu = (0, 0, 0, \ldots)$. The situation could arise when you wish to test whether each of a series of individual measures is drawn from a population with mean of .0. When this test is used, it is very likely that you have obtained repeated measures.

Suppose, for example, that the data from Table 10-1 were obtained in a repeated measures design. Instead of randomly assigning subjects to group D or group C, suppose a subject had been tested once with the decaffeinated coffee and on a second occasion with regular coffee. Naturally, sound experimental design dictates that the order of testing be counterbalanced.

I will use the data of Table 10-1 to illustrate the analysis. The data are unrealistic because there is no correlation between a given observation in group D and the corresponding observation in group C, which would be expected when the same subject is tested twice. The resulting difference scores and vector of means ($\mathbf{d}$) are presented in Table 10-2. The dependent variables have been designated as D_1, D_2, and D_3, denoting them as *difference scores*.

The pooled within-group variance–covariance matrix ($\mathbf{W}$) is

TABLE 10-2. Data from Table 10-1
as difference scores in single group design

Observation	D_1	D_2	D_3
1	11	−12	5
2	6	−10	11
3	−10	−41	−9
4	8	−16	1
5	27	−3	20
6	25	19	7
7	24	−23	6
8	−1	14	21
9	10	−2	−6
10	17	52	11
$\bar{X}$	11.7	−2.2	6.7
s	11.9	25.7	9.8

$$\begin{bmatrix} 141.34 & 115.49 & 44.46 \\ 115.49 & 659.51 & 127.04 \\ 44.46 & 127.04 & 95.79 \end{bmatrix}$$

and its inverse $(\mathbf{W}^{-1})$ is

$$\begin{bmatrix} .009 & -.001 & -.003 \\ -.001 & .002 & -.003 \\ -.003 & -.002 & .015 \end{bmatrix}$$

In a one-sample case, the formulas for T^2 and F are slightly different and are presented, respectively, in Eqs. (10-7a) and (10-7b). The value of T^2 is 15.71. Hence, $F = 6.88$. It is tested with $df = (P - 1) = 2$ and $(N - P + 1) = 8$[1] and is significant beyond the .05 level. The results confirm a significant treatment effect; the three mean difference scores cannot all be assumed to be .0. It is equivalent to the test conducted above when the two groups were considered independent.

$$T^2 = N\mathbf{d'}\mathbf{W}^{-1}\mathbf{d}$$

$$= Nd^2 \tag{10-7a}$$

$$F = \frac{(N - P + 1)T^2}{(P - 1)(N - 1)} \tag{10-7b}$$

Testing for Equality of Means

One is often interested in the question of whether the elements of the population vector are equal, apart from the question of whether the elements are all zeros. In other words, the null hypothesis is that $\mathbf{d}$ is of the form $(c, c, c, \ldots)$.

The basic procedure is to obtain a series of $P - 1$ predictors from the

---

[1] Had there been only two predictors ($p = 2$), the situation would reduce to that of an ordinary t test for repeated measures. F would equal T^2, paralleling the case of two independent groups and one predictor.

TABLE 10-3. Data from Table
10-2 as difference scores relative
to heart rate measures

Observation	D_{2-1}	D_{3-1}
1	23	6
2	16	−5
3	31	−1
4	24	7
5	30	7
6	6	18
7	47	18
8	−15	−22
9	12	16
10	−35	6
$\bar{X}$	13.5	5.0
s	23.9	12.2

original set of P that would have zero mean if the null hypothesis were true. The test can be performed in several ways. One is to select one of the variables, say the Pth variable as a referent and subtract the score on that referent from each of the remaining variables in turn. The transformation may be expressed as $Y_{ij} = X_{ij} - X_{ip}$, where Y_{ij} is the ith new variable $(1 \le i \le P - 1)$ for subject j, X_{ij} is the ith original variable for subject j, and X_{ip} is the Pth original variable for subject j. There are only $P - 1$ variables remaining because a constraint has been introduced—the mean of the transformed variables must equal the complement of the mean of the pth original variable. Were all P measures to be included, $\mathbf{SP}_w$ would be singular. It does not matter which of the variables is chosen as the referent, although if one variable is a control measure, that variable would be preferred.

One would usually not ask if the means obtained from Table 10-2 were equal as the three measures are not expressed in common (commensurable) units. Suppose, however, that their units were commensurable and that one wished to use X_1 as the referent. The raw data are given in Table 10-3. I have identified the two dependent variables "D_{2-1}" and "D_{3-1}". denoting that the data were obtained by subtracting the systolic (D_2) and diastolic (D_3) pressures from the heart rate measures (D_1).[2] You may wish to use the data of Table 10-3 to test for equality of different pairs of measures.

The resulting value of T^2 is 3.82, which is also equal to F. It is not significant, which means that the null hypothesis that caffeine has the same effect upon all three indices cannot be rejected. Because of the way the data were constructed, the outcome is in fact a type II error, a situation that has previously been encountered.

---

[2] The computations resemble covariance adjustments, but they are not. You may verify that D_{2-1} is not independent of D_1 as it would be were there to be a true covariance adjustment.

There are alternative ways to test the null hypothesis that the elements of the difference vector are equal. One way is to subtract scores on the second variable from the first one and then subtract scores on the third variable from the second one, etc. Here, Y_i equals the ith original variable minus variable $i - 1$, $X_i - X_{i-1}$. Another way is to subtract the mean of all preceding variables from the original variable. Thus, $Y_2 = X_2 - X_1$, $Y_3 = X_3 - (1/2) \times (X_1 + X_2)$, $Y_4 = X_4 - (1/3)(X_1 + X_2 + X_3)$, etc. There is no Y_1 term.

Any of the above approaches, as well as the approach used to test for a null difference vector, may be used in conjunction with the methods to be presented to test mean differences among multiple groups.

Single Group MANOVA versus Repeated Measures ANOVA

Suppose the data from Table 10-2 consisted of p individual measures that were commensurable (unlike the data I gave you, where the difference scores do not share a common unit). If you wished to test the null hypothesis that the population means were equal, you could perform a repeated measures ANOVA instead of transforming the data to a form like that presented in Table 10-3 and performing a MANOVA. The results would *not* be identical, because they rest upon different assumptions. In the ANOVA, a repeated measure is treated as an *independent* variable. Moreover, the model normally assumes that all pairs of repeated measures are equally intercorrelated (an assumption that usually is not tested). The MANOVA treats the repeated measure as a *dependent* variable and does *not* assume equal intercorrelations. There often is good reason to doubt that repeated measures are equally intercorrelated. Suppose that the measures are derived from a series of trials (P) on a learning task. A moment's reflection should convince you that scores on the first trial should be more highly correlated with scores on the second trial than scores on the last (Pth) trial.

In general, the magnitude of correlations would be a monotonically decreasing function of the separation in time of the measures, known as a *simplex* (Foa, 1965; Wiggins, 1973). Since the MANOVA adjusts for any type of correlational structure, it appears to be statistically more sound. However, unequal intercorrelations still my cause problems when testing differences between specific pairs of groups or forming other contrasts. This is because the data used in the omnibus test, which is essentially an "average" correlation over all groups, may not describe the specific correlation between a given pair of groups. A point favoring the ANOVA is that readers of psychological journals are more familiar with it. O'Brien and Kaiser (1985) have recently discussed the problems of the repeated measures ANOVA and MANOVA.

Tests of Vector Means with Multiple Groups

Although one may wish to test the null hypotheses that group mean vectors are null or consist of equal elements when there are more than two groups, the issues and computational procedures are considerably more complex. No longer will a single test suffice in the sense that T^2 and F were equivalent (though not necessarily equal) as above. Moreover, you (or at least a computer package) normally perform an eigenanalysis.

The Fundamental Problem

I will briefly discuss what may be viewed as the fundamental problem of multivariate hypothesis testing: *test statistics that are maximally powerful for detecting a concentrated structure are not maximally powerful for detecting a diffuse structure, and vice versa.* In the two-group case, the centroids always fall along a single dimension so all structures are concentrated because two points (centroids) must fall along a straight line. When there are more than two groups, the group centroids need not fall along a straight line.

The inferential problem may be contrasted with the relative simplicity of scalar ANOVA. Suppose you have three groups. There are two extreme outcomes when the null hypothesis is false. On the one hand, the three group means can be spaced in an equal manner. For example, the group means can be 5, 10, and 15. If the group sizes (N_j) are all equal to some common value (N), the treatment sum of squares will equal $50N$. Conversely, two group means may both be equal yet differ from a third group. Specifically, let the three means equal 10, 10, and 18.66. The treatment sum of squares willl also equal $50N$. Consequently, the treatment mean squares will be the same, as will the F-ratio (assuming within-group variation is the same.) You do not need different test statistics to look for equally spaced differences versus a single group that differs from the remainders. Differences among the groups are confined to a single dimension, by definition. Olson (1974, 1976) has provided an excellent summaries of the many tests available to test multivariate structures.

Consider what happens with a totally concentrated structure, i.e., one in which the groups fall perfectly along a straight line in the space of the criteria. All of the group differences will be summarized by the first (largest) eigenvalue. Indeed, all of the remaining eigenvalues will be .0 since the group centroids will be identical once they have been adjusted for the first discriminant function. Hence, the first eigenvalue is sufficient to form the basis of a test statistic.

In contrast, assume that the group differences are similar, in the sense that the average Mahalanobis distances are similar, but that the groups do not fall along a straight line. Furthermore, assume the differences are maximally diffuse in the sense of being distributed among $G - 1$ dimensions, where G is the number of groups. None of the individual eigenvalues will be as large as the first eigenvalue of the preceding situation.

If, in contrast to both cases, the null hypothesis were true, **G** and $\mathbf{SP}_g$ would be as close to null matrices as sampling error would allow. Consequently, $\mathbf{W}^{-1}\mathbf{G}$ and $\mathbf{SP}_w^{-1}\mathbf{SP}_g$ will also be close to null so that all of the latter's eigenvalues will be close to .0. As a consequence, attempting to reject the null hypothesis involves looking for a single large eigenvalue when the structure is concentrated. That is a relatively well-defined problem. The diffuse case is more complicated, since there could be as few as two and as many as $G - 1$ large eigenvalues. Your test statistic thus needs to incorporate the information contained in the entire set of eigenvalues or their equivalent. In essence, significant group differences imply eigenvalues that vary widely from large to small; when no significant group differences exist, the eigenvalues will all be nearly equal in value and small.

Testing a Concentrated Structure

The basic test statistic used when an investigator is highly confident that the underlying structure is concentrated is known as *Roy's largest root* (Roy, 1953). It is defined in Eq. (10-8). There is no standard notation to describe the test statistic. The symbol λ_1 denotes the first eigenvalue of $\mathbf{SP}_w^{-1} \mathbf{SP}_g$. Note that some computer printouts (SAS in particular) simply give λ_1.

$$R^2 = \lambda_1/(1 + \lambda_1) \qquad (10\text{-}8)$$

If you go back and examine Eq. (8-2), you will note that it equals the value of R^2 relating dummy codes for groups to the criterion (actually, the canonical correlation). However, significance levels are normally established either by means of graphs prepared by Heck (1960) or tables, prepared by Pillai (1965).

Roy's largest root is the most powerful test for a concentrated structure, but it is also weaker than those to be discussed for a diffuse structure as well as being based on the weakest mathematical foundation. It is quite prone to type I errors when the variance–covariance matrices are heterogeneous. Perhaps most of the time, an investigator does not know whether the obtained structure will be diffuse or concentrated. Consequently, Roy's test should be reserved for those relatively few cases when you expect the structure to be concentrated from prior experience or theoretical interest in the first dimension of variation, i.e., the first discriminant function, dominates the situation so strongly that other dimensions are theoretically meaningless. In essence, if you do not know what type of structure to expect, use one of the alternatives for testing a diffuse structure that I will now turn to. Of course, whatever you do, do not simply choose a test statistic simply because it furnishes the most favorable results to your theoretical biases when meaningful alternative positions could exist.

Testing a Diffuse Structure

There are three common tests that are appropriate when the structure is known in advance to be diffuse or there is no basis for assuming that the structure is either diffuse or concentrated. The three test statistics are the *Hotelling–Lawley trace* (*T*, Lawley, 1938, 1939), *Wilks' lambda* (*U*, Wilks, 1932), and the *Pillai–Bartlett trace* (*V*, Pillai, 1955). All can be used to obtain more familiar statistics like χ^2 and F.

The Hotelling–Lawley statistic is simply the sum of the eigenvalues of $\mathbf{SP}_w^{-1}\mathbf{SP}_g$, Eq. (10-9a). Because the sum of the eigenvalues of a matrix equals the trace of that matrix, T may be also defined by Eq. (10-9b).

$$T = \sum \lambda_i \tag{10-9a}$$

$$T = \text{tr}(\mathbf{SP}_w^{-1}\mathbf{SP}_g) \tag{10-9b}$$

Pillai (1960) has provided tables of the exact distribution of T from which critical values can be obtained. It is common to transform T to χ^2 by means of Eq. (10-10a). The df are the product of r_g and r_w, the ranks of $\mathbf{SP}_g$ and $\mathbf{SP}_w$ (Morrison, 1976). T may also be used to estimate F from Eq. (10-10b). The relevant df for the numerator (df_n) and the denominator (df_d) are given by Eqs. (10-10c) and (10-10d), respectively, where "S" denotes the minimum of P and K and "M" is .5 times $(1.0 -$ the absolute value of the difference between P and $K)$. Computer packages will generally supply one, but not both, estimates along with its associated significance level. Although statisticians may argue about which is preferable, either should be adequate to most applications so that you will not need Pillai's (1960) exact tables.

$$\chi^2 = NT \tag{10-10a}$$

$$F = \frac{2[S(N + 1)]T}{[S^2(2m + S + 1)]} \tag{10-10b}$$

$$df_n = S(2m + S + 1) \tag{10-10c}$$

$$df_d = 2[S(N + 1)] \tag{10-10d}$$

Wilks' lambda (also commonly symbolized as Λ) is perhaps the most widely used test statistic of multivariate mean differences. It may either be defined through products of terms involving eigenvalues as in Eq. (10-11a) or as a ratio of determinants as in Eq. (10-11b). Because the determinant of a matrix also equals the product of the eigenvalues of that matrix, as noted in Eq. (3-10), it may also be expressed as in Eq. (10-11c). However, there are easier ways to obtain U. My point is simply to demonstrate that the three tests of diffuse structure can be expressed as traces of appropriate product matrices.

Unlike many other test statistics, *small* values of U are associated with significance. The U statistic may also be interpreted descriptively as the product of successive coefficients of nondetermination $(1. - R^2$ values obtained from each of the discriminant functions). It may also be interpreted as the normalized variance among group means. Perhaps the most important property of U is that it forms a likelihood ratio under conditions of multivariate normality—it reflects the probability of obtaining the sample mean vectors given that they equal the population mean vectors relative to the probability of obtaining the sample mean vectors given that the population mean vectors equal one another.

$$U = \prod [1/(1 + \lambda_i)] \tag{10-11a}$$

$$U = \frac{|\mathbf{SP}_w|}{|\mathbf{SP}_t|}$$

$$= \frac{|\mathbf{SP}_w|}{|\mathbf{SP}_w + \mathbf{SP}_g|} \tag{10-11b}$$

$$U = \mathrm{tr}(\mathbf{SP}_t^{-1}\mathbf{SP}_w) \tag{10-11c}$$

Rao (1951) developed an exact F test for U which is presented in Eq. (10-12a). The df_g and df_w used to test F are defined in Eqs. (10-12b) and (10-12c).

$$F = \frac{(1 - U^{1/2})P}{U^{1/2}[K(N_j - 1) + (K - P - 1)]} \tag{10-12a}$$

$$df_g = 2P \tag{10-12b}$$

$$df_w = 2(df_w + K - P - 1) \tag{10-12c}$$

Rao's procedure is an omnibus test. An alternative way to test the significance of U is through Bartlett's *sequential* χ^2 method. The test is a slightly inferior alternative to Rao's procedure. The logic is to test sequential residual matrices, using a series of statistics to be denoted as U_i. When i is 1, U is computed as in Eq. (10-11). However, when i is equal to or greater than 2, the product only includes the ith through last (denoted "S" as above) eigenvalues. Equation (10-13a) describes this procedure. The resulting value of U_i is transformed logarithmically to χ^2 by means of Eq. (10-13b). The df at each step are given in Eq. (10-13c).

$$U_i = \prod [1/(1 + \lambda_j)] \tag{10-13a}$$

$$\chi^2 = -[(N - 1) - .5(P + K + 1)]\ln(U_i) \tag{10-13b}$$

$$df = (P - i + 1)(K - i + 1) \tag{10-13c}$$

Thus, if the χ^2 value based upon U_1 is not significant, one stops. Conversely, if U_1 is significant, it can then be assumed that the original matrices contain systematic variation, the group centroids are not coincident, and the first discriminant function should be examined. If it is not, one stops. If U_2 leads to a significant χ^2 value (assuming U_1 also did), there is evidence for systematic residual variation after the groups are adjusted for the first discriminant function. Consequently, the second discriminant function should be examined. However, if the χ^2 associated with U_2 is not significant, retain only the first discriminant function. In general, if the χ^2 associated with U_{i+1} is not significant but the χ^2 associated with U_i is significant, limit further consideration to the first i discriminant functions and ignore the remaining $S - i$ possible functions (recognizing both that a discriminant function may be significant yet account for a trivial amount of variance in a large sample and that a potentially interesting discriminant function may be nonsignificant in a small, pilot sample).

It is also possible to use the F distribution to test successive roots (see Marascuilo & Levin, 1983, p. 213) but the χ^2 procedure is much simpler. The procedure is used in some packages, specifically SAS. On the other hand, SPSSX uses the sequential χ^2 approach. One may use Eq. (10-8) and obtain canonical correlations from the λ_i values. However, in general, these eigenvalues cannot be transformed to F in the simple manner of Eq. (4-17) save for the last one.

The final commonly used test statistic is the Pillai–Bartlett trace, V, which is defined by Eq. (10-14). It represents the sum of successive R^2 values. It may also be expressed as the sum of the eigenvalues of $\mathbf{SP}_t^{-1}\mathbf{SP}_g$, although this matrix product is normally not computed.

$$V = \frac{\lambda_i}{(1 + \lambda_i)} \qquad (10\text{-}14)$$

The approximation to F used with V is presented in Eq. (10-15). Tables of critical values of V based on its exact distribution are presented in Pillai (1960, developer of the procedure). It is increasingly common for computer packages to present values of V. When they do, they normally present significance levels so the tables are unnecessary. The V statistic has become popular because it appears to be more robust to violations of homogeneity and normality than alternative statistics, such as U. It therefore may be the test statistic of choice for small samples. With larger samples, T, U, and V become equivalent.

$$F = \frac{2NS1(S - V)}{(2MS + 1)V} \qquad (10\text{-}15)$$

Testing for Homogeneity of Covariance

Testing for homogeneity of covariance is the multivariate extension of testing for homogeneity of variance in the t-test or scalar ANOVA. At issue is whether different groups possess the same covariance structure.

Statistical analyses conducted prior to 1960 reported tests for homogeneity of variance in an almost ritualistic manner before reporting a t or an F test of a mean difference. Then, research by Box (1953), Norton (in Lindquist, 1953), and Boneau (1960) directed investigators away from this procedure. Their studies indicated that tests of homogeneity were only necessary when extreme violations, especially of skewness, occurred because F and, especially, t are highly robust statistics. Moreover, group differences in variance imply that the independent variable had an effect though perhaps not in the additive sense of a linear model. Hence, one hardly, if ever, tests for homogeneity of variance in scalar analyses. Perhaps these tests should be used more often when sample sizes are small and distribution shapes are quite different.

Multivariate (vector) tests are less robust than univariate (scalar) tests because of the many additional parameters to be estimated. Consequently, one should evaluate the homogeneity of the various within-group variance–

covariance matrices, $\mathbf{W}_i$. There are several ways to test the null hypothesis that a set of $\mathbf{W}_i$ are drawn from the same population. Box's (1950) M test, based upon groundwork laid down by Bartlett (1937), is the most popular of these tests.

The M statistic is defined in Eq. (10-16a). As noted previously, the determinant of a variance–covariance matrix is a summary measure of variance. The M statistic effectively compares variability of the individual measures, $[\mathbf{W}_i]$, to the average $[\mathbf{W}]$. Next, one computes a quantity called C as defined in Eq. (10-16b). M and C jointly produce a value of χ^2 using Eq. (10-16c), which is tested with the df stated in Eq. (10-16d). This procedure is further described in Timm (1975). Morrison (1976) notes that C may be simplified to Eq. (10-16e) when subgroup sizes are equal, i.e., when $N_i = N$ for all groups. The test is described in various forms in different sources, some of which are quite cumbersome. The form used by SAS, which quite admirably lists many of its formulas, is extremely awkward as it involves raising the determinants to the rather large powers. Also, some texts, such as Morrison (1976), use samples sizes instead of df in all steps, including the calculation of the variance–covariance matrices. Do not be surprised if the formulas look quite different. They really aren't in reality.

$$M = (N - K)\ln[\mathbf{W}] - \sum(N_i - 1)\ln[\mathbf{W}_i] \tag{10-16a}$$

$$C = \frac{(2P^2 + 3P - 1)}{6(P + 1)(K - 1)} \times \frac{1}{\sum(N_i - 1)} \times \frac{1}{\sum(N - K)} \tag{10-16b}$$

$$\chi^2 = (1 - C)M \tag{10-16c}$$

$$df = .5[P(P + 1)(K - 1)] \tag{10-16d}$$

$$C = \frac{(2P^2 + 3P - 1)(K + 1)}{6(P + 1)(K - 1)(KN)} \tag{10-16e}$$

When sample sizes are at least moderate, I find that the χ^2 value to be almost invariably significant. Look at the individual values of $[\mathbf{W}_i]$ in relation to $[\mathbf{W}]$ to see if the differences between these individual values and the composite are large. Statistically significant differences can easily arise from incidental sources of a trivial nature.

The Simple MANOVA with Multiple Groups

The major differences between the multiple-group MANOVA and the two-group case is that in the former all group differences cannot be summarized by a single number such as T^2. Instead, one must look for the possible existence of significant between-group variation on more than one dimension.

The example I will use parallels that of the two-group case with independent groups presented as Table 10-1. I simply added in a third type of coffee (in honor of the stuff that you and I have either drunk late in the evening or removed varnish with). I with label this group the high caffeine (H) group. I made the coffee increase X_1, X_2, and X_3 by .96, .36, and .9 standard score units. You may verify that each quantity is 20% greater than its group C counterpart. Hence, the structure in the population is totally concentrated. Moreover, the covariance structure within group H is the same as the other two groups, which I left unchanged (in the world of simulated data, experiments sometimes do replicate!) but, because the "subjects" were different, the error components were generated independently.

The data have the same form as the data presented in Table 10-1. Since there are now 45 (3 groups × 15 subjects) three-element vectors, I will not present the raw data. The vector of means for groups D, C, and H were (62.0, 121.0, and 76.9), (67.0, 123.0, 82.6), and (72.7, 121.1, 85.1).

SP and Variance–Covariance Matrices

The SP_g is

$$\begin{bmatrix} 853.70 & -.45 & 645.42 \\ -.45 & 38.00 & 36.98 \\ 645.42 & 36.98 & 524.60 \end{bmatrix}$$

and SP_w (pooled) is:

$$\begin{bmatrix} 2975.51 & 1209.71 & 1505.20 \\ 1209.71 & 4766.98 & 513.43 \\ 1505.20 & 513.43 & 2058.88 \end{bmatrix}$$

The sum of SP_g and SP_w, SP_t, will not be presented.

Scalar division by df_g ($K - 1 = 2$) yields G:

$$\begin{bmatrix} 426.85 & -.22 & 322.71 \\ -.22 & 19.00 & 18.49 \\ 322.71 & 18.49 & 262.30 \end{bmatrix}$$

and scalar division by df_w ($N - K = 42$) yields W:

$$\begin{bmatrix} 70.85 & 28.80 & 35.83 \\ 28.80 & 113.50 & 12.22 \\ 35.83 & 12.22 & 49.02 \end{bmatrix}$$

It is useful to look at the pooled within-group correlations, which are $r_{12} = 28.80/(70.85 \times 113.50)^{1/2}$ or .32, $r_{13} = 35.83/(70.85 \times 49.02)^{1/2}$ or .61, and $r_{13} = 12.22/(113.40 \times 49.02)^{1/2}$ or .16. X_1 is thus quite highly related to X_3 and weakly related to X_2, but X_2 and X_3 are essentially unrelated.

Since I presented the steps involved in forming a Cholesky decomposition of SP_w^{-1} and subsequent eigenanalysis in Chapter 8, I will not repeat them here. The most important part is the set of three eigenvalues which are .360, .038, and, because the product matrix is of rank 2, .000. The first eigenvalue accounts for 90.5% of the variance, attesting to the concentration of the structure. Also needed are the values of $|\mathbf{SP}_w|$ and $|\mathbf{SP}_t|$ (or $|\mathbf{SP}_w| + |\mathbf{SP}_g|$) which were 16,475,836,818 and 23,235,309,842.

Applying Roy's largest root criterion to λ_1 indicates that the R^2 was $.360/(1 + .360) = .26$, corresponding to an approximate F of 7.59 with df of 2 and 42. It is significant beyond the .01 level. The sum of the eigenvalues $(.360 + .038 = 3.98)$ or Hotelling–Lawley trace corresponds to an approximate F of 2.58 with 6 and 78 df and is significant beyond the .03 level. Wilks' U measure equals $16,475,836,818/23,235,309,842$ or .709. It corresponds to an F-ratio of 2.50 with 6 and 80 df and is also significant beyond the .03 level. Finally, the Pillai–Bartlett trace equals $[.360/(1 + .360) + .038/(1 + .038)]$ or .301. It corresponds to an approximate F of 2.42 with df of 6 and 82 and is significant beyond the .04 level.

The three groups therefore have different mean vectors. The significance levels obtained with the Hotelling–Lawley, Wilks, and Pillai–Bartlett statistics are very similar, although all three are more conservative than Roy's. The difference in significance levels reflects weaknesses inherent in the Roy statistic, in part (some computer packages do not provide significance levels for Roy's test).

An additional point is that group differences are highly concentrated. The R^2 values associated with the two discriminants are $.360/(1. + 3.60) = .265$ and $.038/(1. + .038) = .037$. (Note that the values are squares of canonical correlations and not multiple correlations, despite my use of "R^2" as a symbol.) Applying the sequential χ^2 test to the first discriminant function produces a value of U_1 that equals $[1./(1. + .360)][1./(1. + .038)] = (1. - .265) \times (1. - .037) = .70837$. The result is equivalent to a χ^2 value of $-[(60 - 1) - .5(3 + 3 + 1)]\ln(.70837)$ or 19.14. It has $[(3 - 1 + 1) \times (3 - 1 + 1)]$ df and is significant beyond the .05 level. Consequently, the first discriminant function is significant. U_2 is $1/(1. + 1.038) = (1 - .037)$ or .96339. It is equivalent to a χ^2 value of $[(60 - 1) - .5(3 + 3 + 1)]\ln(.96339)$ or 2.06. It has $(3 - 2 + 1) \times (3 - 2 + 1 = 4$ df and is not significant, implying the group centroids are identical once an adjustment for the first discriminant function is made.

Applying Box's M Test

The following are the steps involved in Box's M test. (An M test would actually be performed first; I present the results here for purposes of exposition.) The variance–covariance matrix for group D is

$$\begin{bmatrix} 23.22 & 7.71 & 12.13 \\ 7.71 & 66.26 & 16.90 \\ 12.13 & 16.90 & 39.87 \end{bmatrix}$$

The determinant is 4758.5. Similarly, the determinants of the variance–covariance matrices for groups C and H are 285,195 and 203,541. The determinant of the pooled variance–covariance matrix is 222,382. The corresponding natural logarithms are 10.7311, 12.5609, 12.2236 for the three individual variance–covariance matrices and 12.3121 for the pooled variance–covariance matrix. Box's M test [Eq. (10-16a)] is $42 \times 12.3121 - (14 \times 10.7311 + 14 \times 12.5609 + 14 \times 12.2236)$ or 19.8968. The quantity C [Eq. (10-16b)] is $(2 \times 3^2 + 3 \times 3 - 1)/[6 \times (3 + 1) \times (3 - 1)] \times \{1/14 + 1/14 + 1/14 - 1/42)$ or .1032.[3] Using Eq. (10-16c), $\chi^2 = M(1 - C) = 19.8698(1 - .1032)$ or 17.62. The df are given in Eq. (10-16d) and are $3 \times (3 + 1) \times (3 - 1)/2$ or 12. The χ^2 value is not significant. Thus, despite the smaller generalized variance of group D, the three variance–covariance matrices may be assumed drawn from a common population or, alternatively, the groups may be thought of as varying in location but not in the size and shape of their envelopes.

Specifying the Nature of the Group Differences

After it is determined that the three groups differ, it is important to look at the nature of the group differences more precisely. Two very basic things to do are to look at the dependent variables individually and to look at the composition of the discriminant axis. Many users of the MANOVA only look at the overall test as a starting point for a series of simple ANOVAs. If that is all you do, the only role the MANOVA plays is to protect against experiment-wise type I errors. You will not fully exploit the MANOVA's potentials. You can also make any form of prior or posterior group comparison that you would have in the simple ANOVA as discussed in Chapter 5. In most studies it is quite useful to look at the discriminant axis for the information that cannot be not found elsewhere. *A MANOVA is more than the sum of a series of separate ANOVAs.*

The F ratios may be obtained by dividing diagonal entries of G by the corresponding entries in W, as was noted in Chapter 8. The results are $g_{11}/w_{11} = 426.85/70.85 = 6.03$, $g_{22}/w_{22} = 19.00/113.50 = .17$, and $g_{33}/w_{33} = 262.30/49.02 = 5.35$. All have $df = 2$ and 42. Hence, the F ratios for X_1 and X_3 is significant beyond the .01 level, but the F ratio for X_2 is not. This means that in our hypothetical data, the three levels of caffeine differentially affect heart rate and systolic blood pressure, but not diastolic blood pressure. Of course, I have noted that there were population differences in all three measures. Our sample size was too small to detect what was present in fact for X_2.

Ratios of the form SP_{gi}/SP_{ti}, the ratios of the ith diagonal in SP_g to the ith diagonal in SP_t are eta-square correlations, which describe how much of the total sum of square is systematic. The ratios may be identified as "R-SQUARE" or the equivalent in some programs. The values are $853.70/3829.22$ or .22, $38.00/4804.98$ or .01 and $524.60/2583.48$ or .20 for X_1, X_2, and X_3, respectively.

In Chapter 8, I recommended looking at the diagonals of $G^{-1}W$, which are

---

[3] Since there is equal N, the actual calculations should be written as $M = 42 \times 12.3121 = 14 \times (10.7311 + 12.5609 + 12.2231)$ and $C = (2 \times 3^2 + 3 \times 3 - 1)/[6 \times (3 + 1) \times (3 - 1)] \times \{3/14 - 1/42\}$.

F ratios for the individual dependent variables following adjustment for each other. The diagonals are 5.00, .20, and 3.12, for X_1, X_2, and X_3, respectively. The same pattern of significance is obtained as in the unadjusted case. However, the F ratio for X_3 is much smaller following adjustment, reflecting the fact that X_1 and X_3 are the two most highly related variables. Because the relation between caffeine and X_1 was slightly stronger than the relation between caffeine and X_3, the former withstood the partialling process somewhat better.

One can perform contrasts of the form considered in the two-group case. The particular one chosen (the LSD test, a procedure designed to control for pairwise alpha rate) indicated that group H did not differ from group C, and group C did not differ from group D although group H was greater than group D on X_1. Group H did not differ from group C but both differed from group D on X_3.

The vector of discriminant weights, normalized to unit within-group variance, was (.013, $-.004$, and .009). The result is consistent with my previous point X_1 is slightly more discriminating than X_3, and both are considerably more discriminating than X_2. The mean locations on the discriminant axis for groups D, C, and H were $-.71$, .01, and .70. The equal spacing implies that when all information about caffeine's effects was pooled, the groups were quite equally spaced, a very convenient way to summarize the group differences.

I find it quite useful to analyze data by looking at both MANOVA and discriminant analysis output. The comparison of outputs is quite likely to be informative.

The Multivariate MANOVA

I will now extend the simple MANOVA just as I did the simple ANOVA by considering a pair of independent variables that are being jointly manipulated. Whereas you previously had sums of squares associated with the A effect, B effect and AB interaction in the interaction model and analogous terms in the main effects model, you now have variance–covariance matrices. As before, the analysis can be presented as a linear model although I will not present the formal equation.

I will spend most time on the interaction model, since it is more commonly used. The principle to keep in mind is that you have various effects associated with A, B, and AB. *Each can be looked at and interpreted just as in the simple ANOVA*, and that is how I will proceed.

Terminology and Basic Logic

I will denote the two independent variables as A and B. Assume that there are K_a levels of A and K_b levels of B. As before, P is the number of dependent variables. For purposes of discussion, assume the number of subjects within each group (N_j) is the same. The total number of subjects (N) will equal $K_a K_b n$.

The logic of analysis is to form SP matrices representing the total, group, and within sources of variation, as before. The "group" SP matrix refers to all $K_a K_b$ groups, and the "within" SP matrix is pools over groups. I will use the symbols $\mathbf{SP}_t$, $\mathbf{SP}_g$, and $\mathbf{SP}_w$ as before. The main point is that $\mathbf{SP}_g$ represents the joint effects of A, B, and the AB interaction exactly as its counterpart in the factorial ANOVA.

The basic operations are to compute $\mathbf{SP}_t$ and $\mathbf{SP}_w$ as before. Then, obtain $\mathbf{SP}_g$ by subtraction, which will consist of three additive components, the SP matrices for A, B, and their interaction, denoted as $\mathbf{SP}_A$, $\mathbf{SP}_B$, and $\mathbf{SP}_{AB}$.

The $\mathbf{SP}_A$ and $\mathbf{SP}_B$ matrices are computed in two basic ways. One way to compute $\mathbf{SP}_A$ is to ignore B and compute a "within" matrix from the K_a groups. $\mathbf{SP}_A$ is obtained by subtracting the "within" matrix from $\mathbf{SP}_t$. The "within" matrix is no longer needed—it is of no further value since it contains variation due to B and the interaction as well as true variability within-group (error), which is why I placed quotes around the term. The alternative is to compute $\mathbf{SP}_A$ directly as in the ANOVA. Construct a matrix of group sums, $\mathbf{S}$, with groups on rows and variables on columns. The dimensions of $\mathbf{S}$ are K_A by P. Let $\mathbf{1}$ be a unit vector of 1's, $(1, 1, 1, \ldots)$ of dimension K_A. The product $\mathbf{S}'\mathbf{S}$ yields the *uncorrected* sums of squares and cross products of the variables over the K_A groups. The correction term is $(1/N)[(\mathbf{S}'\mathbf{1})(\mathbf{1}'\mathbf{S})] = (1/N)[\mathbf{S}'\mathbf{1})(\mathbf{S}'\mathbf{1})']$. The difference between the uncorrected sums of squares and the correction term is $\mathbf{SP}_A$.

The $\mathbf{SP}_B$ can be formed in an analogous manner. The interaction SP matrix, $\mathbf{SP}_{AB}$, is formed by subtracting $\mathbf{SP}_A$ and $\mathbf{SP}_B$ from $\mathbf{SP}_g$. The relationship $\mathbf{SP}_{AB} = \mathbf{SP}_g - (\mathbf{SP}_A + \mathbf{SP}_B)$ is equivalent to its counterpart in the two-way ANOVA.

The df for the A, B, AB, groups, within, and total sources are the same as in the two-way ANOVA. I will symbolize the terms as df_A, df_B, df_{AB}, df_g, df_w, and df_t (although the various terms involving groups are not necessary beyond their role in calculation). The df equal $(K_A - 1)$, $(K_B - 1)$, $(K_A - 1)(K_B - 1)$, $K_A K_B - 1$, $K_A K_B (N - 1)$, and $N - 1$, respectively. The A effect is assessed through eigenanalysis of $\mathbf{SP}_w^{-1}\mathbf{SP}_A$ (including a Cholesky decomposition needed to make the product symmetric). As was true in the simple MANOVA, univariate tests may be made using the diagonal terms of the variance–covariance matrices, $\mathbf{W}$ and $\mathbf{A}$, where $\mathbf{A}$ equals $(1/df_A)\mathbf{SP}_A$. Specifically, one may test each unadjusted dependent variable using the ratios a_{ii}/w_{ii} and test each dependent variable, adjusting for all other dependent variables, using the diagonal elements of $\mathbf{W}^{-1}\mathbf{A}$. The B effect and the interaction are derived from eigenanalyses of $\mathbf{SP}_w^{-1}\mathbf{SP}_B$ and of $\mathbf{SP}_w^{-1}\mathbf{SP}_{AB}$.

Unequal sample sizes cause somewhat of a problem, especially when they are highly disparate. The problems are the same as discussed in Chapter 6. The SP matrices for the various treatment effects will differ depending on whether you adjust for or ignore other effects. You have the same options in dealing with SP matrices that you had in dealing with sums of squares in factorial ANOVA.

A Numerical Example

The simulated example is an extension of those considered previously, and the A effect consists of the same three types of coffee (decaffeinated, regular, and high caffeine). The B effect consists of number of cups of coffee. Half of the subjects received the same amount as before (two cups), and the remainder had four cups. The effect that I built into doubling the amount of coffee was a .5 unit increment in X_1, a 1.3 unit increment in X_2, and a .2 unit increment in X_3. In addition, I built in an interaction by assuming that there was a .3 unit decrement in X_1, a .6 unit decrement in X_2, and a .1 unit decrement in X_3 among subjects who had four cups of decaffeinated coffee. There were again 10 subjects per group. The pooled within-group standard deviations were 9.33, 13.71, and 7.38 for X_1, X_2, and X_3. The Box's M test indicated that the variance–covariance matrices were homogeneous across groups; hence, the standard deviations can be assumed equal across groups. The means are presented in Table 10-4.

The first steps of the analysis produce $\mathbf{SP}_t$, $\mathbf{SP}_g$, and $\mathbf{SP}_w$, which are

$$\mathbf{SP}_t = \begin{bmatrix} 9652.00 & 5288.77 & 5596.56 \\ 5288.77 & 21957.63 & 3132.65 \\ 5596.56 & 3132.65 & 5576.20 \end{bmatrix}$$

$$\mathbf{SP}_g = \begin{bmatrix} 2336.25 & 2589.92 & 1332.31 \\ 2589.92 & 5982.60 & 797.21 \\ 1332.31 & 797.21 & 996.11 \end{bmatrix}$$

$$\mathbf{SP}_w = \begin{bmatrix} 7315.75 & 2698.84 & 4264.25 \\ 2698.84 & 15974.98 & 2355.44 \\ 4264.25 & 2355.44 & 4580.09 \end{bmatrix}$$

The df_t, df_g, and df_w are 89, 5, and 84. Note that the pooled within-group variances are the diagonal elements of $\mathbf{SP}_w$ divided by df_w. You may also obtain the pooled within-group correlations from $\mathbf{SP}_w$. The correlation between X_1 and X_2 is .25; the correlation between X_1 and X_3 is .74; and the correlation between X_2 and X_3 is .27. This indicates that any variable that affects X_1 will probably also affect X_3, unless there is a severe departure from

TABLE 10-4. $\bar{X}_1$ (mean heart rate), $\bar{X}_2$ (mean systolic blood pressure), and $\bar{X}_3$ (mean diastolic blood pressure) as a function of type of coffee and amount of coffee consumed

Type of coffee	Number of cups of coffee					
	$\bar{X}_1$	$\bar{X}_2$	$\bar{X}_3$	$\bar{X}_1$	$\bar{X}_2$	$\bar{X}_3$
D	63.64	123.96	80.58	65.67	132.30	77.44
C	71.18	128.68	83.26	76.21	141.88	85.17
H	72.89	123.44	86.46	77.52	144.38	86.65

the assumption that the individual variance–covariance matrices are homogeneous. However, the effects of an independent variable on X_2 are relatively indepenent of the effects of that independent variables on X_1 or X_3 (the SAS PROC MANOVA which I used to analyze these data refers to within-group correlations as "partial correlation coefficients from the error matrix," which they are, in fact).

The A Effect

The $\mathbf{SP}_A$ matrix contains the effects of type of coffee. It equals:

$$\begin{bmatrix} 1954.20 & 1236.42 & 1301.71 \\ 1236.42 & 864.84 & 776.20 \\ 1301.76 & 776.20 & 894.29 \end{bmatrix}$$

The A effect is obtained from premultiplying $\mathbf{SP}_A$ by $\mathbf{SP}_w^{-1}$. It gives rise to eigenvalues of .280 and .021. The disparity in the two eigenvalues confirms that the group structure is concentrated, as intended. Pillai's trace was .240, $F(6, 166) = 3.77$, $p < .01$. The results of using Wilks' and Hotelling–Lawley's criteria are quite similar: $U = .765$, $F(6, 164) = 3.93$, $p < .01$, and $T = .302$, $F(6, 162) = 4.08$, $p < .01$. Roy's largest root was .280, leading to an approximate F ratio of 7.77. The test value is considerably larger than the others because the structure is so concentrated—it is sensitive to the large value of λ_1, by definition. A sequential χ^2 test further attests to the highly concentrated nature of the data.

The first eigenvector of $\mathbf{SP}_w^{-1}\mathbf{SP}_A$ was (.009, .001, and .003). The fact that the first element of the vector (which is proportional to its discriminant weight, and thereby adjusts for the correlational structure among the dependent variables) is so much larger than the second or third element implies that between-group variation is primarily due to group differences in X_1, heart rate. The unadjusted F ratios obtained from X_1, X_2, and X_3, i.e., values of $(\mathbf{SP}_{A11}/df_A)/(\mathbf{SP}_{w11}/df_w)$, were 11.22 $(p < .01)$, 2.27 (ns), and 8.20 $(p < .01)$, respectively. Thus, X_1 and X_3 both differ significantly among groups. The significant effect of A upon X_3 effect is not surprising given the correlation between it and X_1 $(r = .74)$, as noted above. A better idea of the significance of the *independent* effects of A upon the three dependent variables may be determined from the *adjusted* F ratios, i.e., diagonal elements of $(df_w/df_A) \times (\mathbf{SP}_A\mathbf{SP}_w^{-1})$, which were 6.08 $(p < .01)$, < 1 and 1.64 (both ns), for X_1, X_2, and X_3, respectively. Thus, the effects of A upon X_3 were nonsignificant once the within-group correlation between X_3 and X_1 was adjusted for.

Results obtained from t tests among the three groups, using the LSD method noted above, indicated that groups C and H did not differ from one another, but both differed from group D. In sum, the presence of caffeine elevated heart rate and, secondarily, systolic blood pressure, but the high and low amounts did not differ from each other.

The B Effect

The $\mathbf{SP}_B$ was

$$\begin{bmatrix} 342.08 & 1242.30 & -30.77 \\ 1242.30 & 4511.59 & -111.76 \\ -30.77 & -111.76 & 2.76 \end{bmatrix}$$

Eigenanalysis of $\mathbf{SP}_w^{-1}\mathbf{SP}_B$ led to an eigenvalue of .407 (with only two levels of B, the structure must be concentrated). The Pillai–Bartlett trace was 11.12, $F(3, 82) = 11.12$, $p < .01$.

Further analysis of the B effect illustrated some of the complications that arise with highly correlated dependent variables. The (only) eigenvector of $\mathbf{SP}_w^{-1}\mathbf{SP}_B$ was (.008, .007, and $-.012$). The fact that all three elements of the eigenvector are somewhat similar in absolute value (meaning that the discriminant weights are also similar) implies that the three dependent variables were similarly affected by the amount of coffee consumed following adjustment for one another's effects and that the direction of the change was negative for X_3. Interpretive problems arose when inferential criteria were applied. For example, the unadjusted F ratios for X_1, X_2, and X_3 were 3.93, 23.72, and < 1.00, respectively. Only the effect of B upon X_2 was significant by this criterion. The adjusted F ratios (4.11, 12.44, and < 1.00) were only slightly different though the effect of B upon X_1 now became significant as well as the effect of B upon X_2. Part of the complication arises from the fact that X_1 is positively correlated with B and X_3 is negatively correlated with B even though X_1 and X_3 are themselves positively correlated. This (unintended, in terms of the way the problem was originally constructed) outcome illustrates some of the difficulties in multivariate analysis. One appears safe in noting that increasing the amount of coffee consumed (the high level of B) increased systolic blood pressure, but the possible effects upon heart rate or diastolic blood pressure are difficult to interpret.

The AB Interaction

The $\mathbf{SP}_{AB}$ matrix is obtained as $\mathbf{SP}_g - (\mathbf{SP}_A + \mathbf{SP}_B)$. It equals

$$\begin{bmatrix} 39.95 & 111.20 & 61.37 \\ 111.20 & 606.22 & 132.77 \\ 61.37 & 132.77 & 99.06 \end{bmatrix}$$

The relevant eigenanalysis led to a Pillai trace of .06, which was not significant. Hence, no further tests were performed. I might add that if you feel interpreting scalar interactions is difficult, wait until you try to explain a vector interaction!

The lack of interaction in a MANOVA shares something in common with the lack of interaction in an ANOVA—it means that you do not have to qualify your interpretations about the main effects. This has a substantive interpretation in the present case (assuming the data were real). The lack of interaction implies that the effects of amount of coffee consumed were the same regardless of the type of coffee a subject consumed. Yet caffeine *per se* was shown to have an effect upon heart rate as compared to decaffeinated coffee (the *A* effect). The *A* effect and lack of *AB* interaction jointly imply that the effects of amount of coffee upon systolic blood pressure (*B* effect) are due to the *amount of fluid* rather than the *amount of caffeine*, since they arose whether or not the subject had consumed caffeine.

The MANCOVA

The MANCOVA is the multivariate extension of the ANCOVA. However, it is inherently more complicated than its scalar counterpart. Indeed, as will be demonstrated, it often will reflect problems associated with both the ANCOVA and the MANOVA, which is why it is rarely used fruitfully.

In the MANCOVA, there are one (which I will limit discussion to) or more covariates. The covariates are *continuous* measures whose effects upon the dependent variables are to be removed and tested first by application of Eq. (5-10). To simplify notation a bit, let X_1 and X_2 represent two dependent variables and C the covariate, ignoring group membership and subject identification. Least square methods allow one to infer b_{c1} and b_{c2}, the regression weights for the two dependent variables, adjusting for the covariate. The quantities $(X_1 - b_{c1} C)^2$ and $(X_2 - b_{c2} C)^2$, summed over subjects, represents the *adjusted* sums of squares for X_1 and X_2. Likewise, $(X_1 - b_{c1} C)(X_2 - b_{c2} C)$ is the adjusted sum of products. The resulting SP matrix, which I will denote $\mathbf{SP}_{adj}$, contains what is left over *following* adjustment. Subtracting $\mathbf{SP}_{adj}$ from the $\mathbf{SP}_t$ yields the SP matrix that reflects the adjustment (covariate), symbolized as $\mathbf{SP}_c$. Thus, $\mathbf{SP}_t = \mathbf{SP}_{adj} + \mathbf{SP}_c$, just as $\mathbf{SP}_t = \mathbf{SP}_w + \mathbf{SP}_g$. The two calculations are different, however. The covariance adjustment uses techniques discussed in Chapter 4 rather than the methods previously considered in this chapter and in Chapter 8. However, the principles involved are basically the same.

One must also consider interactions between the covariates and the treatment variable(s). As in the scalar case, the interactions deal with whether the slopes of the regression lines are the same for the different groups.

The third stage is to obtain the treatment SP matrix following adjustments for the covariate(s) and the interaction. The matrix is obtained from what is actually a second residual matrix, containing what is left over following adjustment for both the covariate and the interaction. I will not notate the matrix as it simply contains error (residual variance within-group). Thus, whereas the simple MANOVA can be expressed as $\mathbf{SP}_t = \mathbf{SP}_g + \mathbf{SP}_w$, the simple MANCOVA can be expressed as $\mathbf{SP}_t = \mathbf{SP}_c + \mathbf{SP}_{int} + \mathbf{SP}_g + \mathbf{SP}_{res}$, where the latter four terms are defined as the SP matrices for (a) the covariate,

(b) the covariate by groups interaction, adjusting for the main effect of the covariate, (c) the groups effects, adjusting for the covariate and the interaction, and (d) the residual. The df are $N - 1$ for total, df_t, 1 for the adjustment, df_a, $(K - 1)$ for groups, df_g, $(K - 1)$ for the interaction, df_i, and $N - K + 1$ for the residual, df_{res}.[4]

The final stage involves assessing the effects of the covariate through an eigenanalysis of $SP_{res}^{-1}SP_c$. The covariate effect should be highly significant. If it is not, the adjustment process has merely lost degrees of freedom—the assumed covariate has no relation to the dependent variables.

Numerical Example

The example parallels the three-group MANOVA discussed above with the addition of a covariate and the use of independent error (as usual). Assume the covariate is an initial heart rate measure. I made it slightly noisier than the X_1 measure with a loading of .49 on the single factor.[5]

The first SP matrix extracted represents the covariate, SP_c, which is

$$\begin{bmatrix} 1215.12 & 309.84 & 908.71 \\ 309.84 & 79.00 & 231.72 \\ 908.71 & 231.72 & 679.57 \end{bmatrix}$$

Next, one obtains SP_{int}, *correcting* for the effects of the covariate, which is

$$\begin{bmatrix} 746.80 & 87.71 & 382.48 \\ 87.71 & 27.45 & 49.37 \\ 382.48 & 49.37 & 157.05 \end{bmatrix}$$

Next, the SP_g, *correcting* for both the covariate and its interaction with groups, which is:

$$\begin{bmatrix} 324.23 & 249.74 & 66.10 \\ 249.74 & 277.23 & -60.82 \\ 66.10 & -60.82 & 160.58 \end{bmatrix}$$

The SP_t is:

$$\begin{bmatrix} 4234.01 & 652.05 & 2517.35 \\ 652.05 & 6622.82 & 803.64 \\ 2517.35 & 803.64 & 2947.63 \end{bmatrix}$$

---

[4] When there are q predictors, the df_t, df_c, df_{int}, df_g, and df_{res} are $(N - 1)$, q, $(q - 1)$, $(k - 1)$, and $N - qk - 2$, where q is the number of covariates.

[5] I have a confession to make. I fiddled around with the numbers to make the results plausible. When higher loadings were used, virtually all experimental error disappeared, which is unreasonable. When lower loadings were used, the error washed out nearly all effects with the particular set of random numbers I used.

Consequently, $\mathbf{SP}_w$, which is $\mathbf{SP}_t - (\mathbf{SP}_c + \mathbf{SP}_{int} + \mathbf{SP}_g)$, is

$$\begin{bmatrix} 1947.76 & 4.76 & 1160.06 \\ 4.76 & 6266.63 & 583.37 \\ 1160.06 & 583.37 & 1950.43 \end{bmatrix}$$

The first eigenanalysis involves $\mathbf{SP}_{res}^{-1}\mathbf{SP}_c$. Because the covariate has only 1 df, there is only one eigenvalue, which was .652. The F ratio obtained from the Pillai–Bartlett trace was 8.05, $p < .001$ with df of 3 and 37. Both the eigenvector (.019, .001, .005) and the univariate F ratios (24.33, .45, and 13.59) indicated that the covariate related most strongly to X_1 and not at all to X_2, which is essentially how it was constructed. The fact that the multivariate test proved significant indicates that the covariate did remove systematic variance from what would have been considered error in a MANOVA, a point to be expanded upon below. The mechanism is fundamentally the same as in the ANCOVA relative to the ANOVA (Chapter 5).

The eigenanalysis of $\mathbf{SP}_{res}^{-1}\mathbf{SP}_{int}$ deals with whether the slopes for individual groups could be assumed to be parallel. The first eigenvalue accounted for 99.2% of the total variance. This group x covariate effect was not significant by the Pillai–Bartlett criterion, $F(6, 76) = 2.09$. However, the interaction was significant by the Hotelling–Lawley and Wilks criterion. This discrepancy actually was minor, since the significance levels associated with the three measures are .064, .039, and .049. Accepting the null hypothesis means a willingness to assume the slopes are the same for the three groups, which in fact was true in the population.

Finally, the eigenanalysis of $\mathbf{SP}_{res}^{-1}\mathbf{SP}_g$ describes the overall groups effect. The two eigenvalues were .318 and .082, accounting for 79.4% and 20.6% of the variance. The effect was significant by the Pillai–Bartlett criterion, $F(6, 76) = 2.39$, $p < .05$. Hence, the three groups can be assumed to differ. The first eigenvector (.026, .006, −.020) and univariate F ratios (3.25, .79, and 1.61) indicate that the manipulation most strongly affected X_3 following the covariance adjustment. Only the first F ratio was significant.

I also ran the data as a MANOVA by eliminating the covariate from the model. The MANOVA design combines $\mathbf{SP}_c$, $\mathbf{SP}_{int}$, and $\mathbf{SP}_{res}$ into a single error matrix, $\mathbf{SP}_w$ (strictly speaking, the adjustment also removes some variance from $\mathbf{SP}_g$). I will not present the data, since the form is identical to that presented in the two-group MANOVA. The results were that the groups did *not* differ for the particular sample that I chose (in the world of simulated data, experiments sometimes *do not* replicate!). Recall that my first simulation did yield significance at the .04 level. However, the Pillai–Bartlett trace only had a p value .47!

This concludes the general topic of classification methods. The specific topic of null hypothesis testing has been considered in detail. I began with the relatively simple problem of determining whether two group profiles differ. The question may be answered in relatively unambiguous manner. I then considered the problem posed of examining possible differences when there are several groups. One important issue is whether the group mean differences are *concentrated* along a single dimension of variation or *diffused* along more than one dimension. One test (Roy's largest root) that is most powerful when the means are concentrated will not be most powerful when they are diffused (other problems with Roy's test were also noted). Three other tests—(1) the Hotelling–Lawley trace, (2) Wilks' lambda, and (3) the Pillai–Bartlett trace— were presented. These are more powerful for use with diffuse structures and generally provide acceptable results with a concentrated structure. The multivariate analysis of variance (MANOVA) and multivariate analysis of covariance (MANCOVA) were then presented.

I will now turn to a group of models that are broadly concerned with how *similar* two vectors (profiles) are. After discussing the general issue of how to define profile similarity, I will discuss a set of techniques known as *clustering*, which place observations into groups on the basis of their profile similarity. The remainder of Chapter 11 will deal with the problem of *canonical analysis*, which is concerned with forming linear combinations from two different sets of variables in order to maximize the correlation between the two.

11
Profile and Canonical Analysis

Chapter Overview

This chapter is largely concerned with questions related to how similar two vectors (profiles) are. The issue of vector similarity appears directly in many classification problems, as was seen in Chapter 9, in particular. Vector similarity leads into the process of forming groups based on the similarity of their vectors, *clustering*. However, it also appears indirectly whenever one wishes to make a linear combination obtained from one set of variables as similar as possible to a linear combination obtained from a second set of variables, which is the topic of *canonical analysis*.

I. PROFILE SIMILARITY—There are three common situations in which profile similarity is at issue: (1) comparing profiles obtained from two individuals, (2) comparing the similarity of an individual's profile to a group (composite) profile, and (3) comparing two group profiles. There are several ways to define profile similarity. In some cases, all that is needed is a definition of the *elevation* (level or height) of the profile, which may be indexed by the sum or average of the elements. In other cases, the *shape* is at issue, either in conjunction with, or independently of the level. Three measures which are sensitive to *shape* are (a) the *correlation* between profiles over elements, which is insensitive to elevation differences; (2) the *sum of cross products*, which is sensitive to elevation as well as shape; and (3) various forms of the d^2 measure, which may or may not be sensitive to elevation depending upon its definition. Examples of how the three types of measures may be used will be provided.

II. SIMPLE AND HIERARCHICAL CLUSTERING—Clustering is a generic term for procedures that group observations based on profile similarity. *Simple clustering* addresses the issue of assigning each of a set of profiles to a specific group in some optimal manner. Any given profile belongs to one, and only one, of the clusters. *Hierarchical clustering* takes an initial grouping (which may consist of individual profiles) and unites the two most similar groups into one subject to the constraint that an observation can belong to one and only one group (cluster). The process is repeated until eventually all observations belong to one large cluster. Simple and hierarchical clustering are the two most popular approaches to grouping although other forms are possible, such as *overlapping clustering*, in which an observation may belong to multiple clusters; of *fuzzy clustering*, in which observations may belong to a given cluster by degrees instead of all or none.

III. CANONICAL ANALYSIS—Canonical analysis is the process of forming optimal linear combinations from each of two sets of variables and evaluating the resulting correlation. This process bears many similarities to multiple regression, and the latter may be viewed as a special case in which one of the two sets consists of only a single variable. However, a form of eigenanalysis related to that used in discriminant analysis is required in canonical but not in regression analysis. *Redundancy analysis* is an important part of canonical analysis. It deals with the issue of how much variance in one data set is determined from the formation of a linear combination in the other data set. Finally, I note that canonical analysis is often an unproductive multivariate fishing expedition. Alternatives are discussed, which include relating sets of *principal components* from the two data sets.

This chapter will be concerned with two dominant themes. The first is *profile analysis*, which involves determining the similarity among two or more vectors. An important part of my discussion is a class of procedures called *clustering techniques*, which involves looking for latent groupings among the profiles based on their similarity. One popular type of clustering is called *hierarchical clustering* in which clusters are joined with other clusters in a sequential manner in an attempt to form "parent–offspring" relations among the clusters. There are other forms of clustering which have evoked less interest.

The second theme is *canonical analysis*, which was introduced briefly in the previous discussion on discriminant analysis. Canonical analysis can be viewed largely as an extension of multiple correlation and regression. Multiple correlation and regression deal with the "best" way to combine a set of variables to predict a single, scalar criterion. In canonical analysis, one forms pairs of linear combinations, one from each of the two sets of variables, in order to establish the strongest possible relations between the two sets.

The relation between the two themes is a bit subtle. In essence, this chapter as a whole is concerned with further issues in forming meaningful groupings of variables. Moreover, in both cases, dimensional analyses provided by the eigenstructure of symmetric matrices play an important role.

Profile Similarity

Similarity of Scalars

Much research has been guided by the principle that people who are similar in certain key respects (perhaps as inferred from some psychological tests) will also be similar in other respects. This principle does not always predict behavior well (cf. the converse statement that "opposites attract"), but it is a useful starting place for discussion. As it turns out, there are numerous methods of analysis, some of which had been considered as in the section of Chapter 9, which deals with classification.

There is one fundamental issue to be considered. Describing the similarity of two scalars is relatively simple. In most applications, it is sufficient to compute the *simple* or *absolute* difference. Thus, if Person *A* scores 115 on a test of cognitive ability (intelligence test) and Person *B* scores 120, this five-point difference may tell you all you need to know. The two people are more similar to one another in terms of their absolute difference than either is to Person *C* who scores only 95 on the same test.

One occasional complication is that certain applications demand one to determine *relative* differences. Relevant examples abound in the area of sensory psychophysics. In the 19th century, E.H. Weber noted the following. Suppose I have you lift a 2.0 gram weight (or *standard*) and then lift a series of weights (or *comparisons*) until you found one just noticeably heavier than the standard. For example, say you judged a weight of 2.04 grams as being noticeably heavier than the standard on half of the trials and reported no difference on the other half. The relevant measure of how similar the two weights are is the *relative difference* of .02 = [(2.04 − 2.00)/2.00], i.e., [(comparison − standard)/standard] and not the *absolute difference* of .04, because the relative difference predicts what would happen when a new standard of 10.0 grams is employed. To a good approximation, a weight of 10.2 grams, reflecting the same relative difference of .02, will be experienced as just noticeably different. An absolute difference of .04 grams would be far too small to be perceived in the latter case. Note that there is nothing mathematically wrong with computing the absolute difference; it just does not have the same meaning that the relative difference does. Also note that the computation requires the measures to possess a ratio scale (have a true zero point) for a relative difference to be meaningful. Many physical measures have a true zero point but few, if any, psychological measures do, so the absolute difference is used by default in most settings. All of my discussion of similarity in this chapter will involve absolute rather than relative differences, but keep in mind the possible utility of the latter concept.

Similarity of Vectors

Scalars, by definition, can vary in only one dimension. However, vectors can potentially vary along as many dimensions as there are elements in the vector, complicating the description of vector similarity immensely. Figure 11-1 illustrates pairs of vectors which (1) differ in *elevation*, but have the same *shape* (top), (2) have the same *elevation*, but differ in *shape* (center), and (3) differ in both *elevation* and *shape* (bottom).

The term "shape" does not necessarily denote how a profile looks, since its

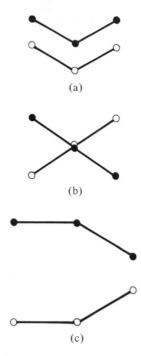

FIGURE 11-1. Some relations among pairs of profiles: (a) profiles differing in elevation; (b) profiles differing in shape; (c) profiles differing in shape and elevation.

appearance depends on the ordering of the elements, which can be arbitrary. The vector (10, 14, 21, 40) will appear to slope upward, whereas the vector (14, 10, 40, 21) will have an erratic appearance. However, these two vectors could actually represent alternative and acceptable ways of describing the same information.

In some situations, a particular ordering is imposed that allows one to make meaningful statements from shape differences. For example, psychologists who interpret MMPI profiles often distinguish between those that slope upward (which suggest "psychotic" symptoms) versus those that slope downward (which suggest "neurotic" symptoms). This slope difference is meaningful and interpretable because of the conventional ordering of the MMPI scales. Likewise, the successive trials of a learning experiment also imply a particular ordering of elements so that an upward slope reflecting the acquisition of knowledge can be visualized. In general, methods of profile analysis do *not* assume that the order in which the elements appear is meaningful.

No single measure thus fully describes how two profiles differ. Your application may suggest that you need only pay attention to profile elevation differences, to shape differences, or to both. To oversimplify things a bit, if you were involved in selecting individuals for a police force based on their MMPI profiles, you would wish to select on the basis of elevation (elevated profiles denoting maladjustment) and not be particularly concerned with the detailed reasons why, i.e., shape differences. Conversely, if you were diagnosing people to decide particular psychiatric treatments you might be primarily concerned with shape in order to determine which particular elements had elevated scores.

Profile similarity measures may be applied to compare (1) pairs of individual profiles, (2) an individual profile and a group profile (the topic of Chapters 8–10), or (3) a pair of group profiles. The first concerns questions like "how similar is Person A to Person B. The second concerns "how much is Person A like a member of Group X." Finally, the third question concerns "how similar are Groups X and Y." Logically, the same considerations hold in all three cases.

Measuring Profile Elevation

There are several ways to define profile elevation, depending on your needs. The simplest is the sum of the profile elements, which will often suffice. The matrix definition of the sum of the elements is given by Eq. (11-1a), where "e" is the generic symbol I will use for all profile elevation measures, "$\mathbf{1}$" is a unit vector of order K (1, 1, ..., where K is the number of profile elements), and "$\mathbf{x}$" is the profile in question. This formula is but a special case of the general definition of a linear combination as given by Eq. (1-1) in which the weights are all unity:

$$e = \mathbf{1}'\mathbf{x} \tag{11-1a}$$

$$e = (1/K)\mathbf{1}'\mathbf{x} \tag{11-1b}$$

$$e = (1/K)\mathbf{1}'\mathbf{R}^{-1}\mathbf{Z}_x \tag{11-1c}$$

$$e = (1/K)\mathbf{1}'\mathbf{C}^{-1}\mathbf{x} \tag{11-1d}$$

Sometimes, the average of the profile elements conveys information about elevation more directly than the sum even though the two measures are mathematically equivalent. For example, it would probably be more informative to learn that the average reaction time of a given subject in a typical learning experiment is 190 milliseconds per trial rather than the sum is 2080 milliseconds. Like any other type of arithmetic average, the average profile element is obtained simply by dividing the sum by K, as defined by Eq. (11-1b).

The sum and average of profile elements have two properties that may or may not be problematic. The first potential problem is that the variance of the elements affects e. Results can be useless when the units of the individual elements are arbitrary, unrelated, and vary widely in magnitude. For example, if one element of the profile were grade point average with a standard deviation of .2 and another were verbal SAT score with a standard deviation of 100, failure to adjust for the difference between the two scales would render the contribution of the grade point average almost totally negligible. Conversely, if the respective standard deviations are similar, the principle of "it don't make no nevermind" will make equal weighting satisfactory.

The second potential problem is that the covariance structure of the elements, specifically, the communalities (i.e., the covariance of an element with the other elements in the sense of Chapters 6 and 7), also affect e. For example, suppose a profile consists of responses to questions that fall in various categories. Also suppose that two questions from the same category correlate more highly than two questions from different categories. The more items within a given category, the more influence each question in that category will have. A difference in number of items per category might reflect intended differences or it might not. In the first case, the effects should remain; in the second case, the effects should not.

One way to correct for variability differences among elements while ignoring communality differences is to convert the profile elements to z scores over the set of profiles and to apply Eq. (11-1a) or (11-1b) to the z scores instead of raw scores. The symbol "z_x" denotes a profile whose elements were converted to z scores over the set of profiles. An alternative is to apply a weighting vector of reciprocal standard deviations to the raw scores rather than a unit vector. The two results will not be identical, but their properties will be equivalent.

It is unlikely that you would want to correct for communality differences but ignore variability differences. You can correct for both by means of Eq. (11-1c). This correction entails converting the profile elements to z scores and using the inverse of the correlation matrix among elements, $\mathbf{R}^{-1}$, to correct for the interrelations. An alternative, which is equivalent but not identical, is to apply the inverse of the variance–covariance matrix of raw scores, $\mathbf{C}^{-1}$, to $\mathbf{x}$ itself as described in Eq. (11-1d).

Always look for an ill-conditioned matrix when attempting to correct for the covariance structure. Profile elements are rarely even relatively independent of each other. *Always look at the determinants in question, $|R|$ and $|C|$, to see if they are negligibly small and do not attempt correction if the matrix is ill-conditioned.*[1] If $\mathbf{R}$ or $\mathbf{C}$ is ill-conditioned, combine highly correlated elements into a single element.

Finally, you may have some reason to use unequal weights in order to give more emphasis to certain elements over others. Unless the weights are substantially different from each other, differential weighting will have little overall effect. Also, your weights may counteract the effects of the variance and covariance adjustment. If that is the case, simply use one of the simpler procedures, Eq. (11-1a) or (11-1b), to begin with.

---

[1] The value of $|R|$ is affected only by the correlations. However, the value of $|C|$ reflects both the correlations and the scale units. In particular, $|C|$ can be small when the units have large variance even though the degree of intercorrelation is not objectionably large. When this is the case, solutions still will be unstable so that Eq. (11-1c) would be preferable to Eq. (11-1d). Using double precision computer calculations minimizes the problem.

The various definitions of e are not generally comparable with each other. Hence, you should not compare a simple sum obtained for a given profile with a variance-corrected sum directly.

Profile Similarity Based on Elevation Alone

The more similar two vectors are, the smaller the difference in their values of e. Hence, the difference in elevations of profiles $\mathbf{x}$ and $\mathbf{y}$, $e_x - e_y$, is a measure of *dissimilarity*. I will denote the elevation difference as d_e regardless of whether the profiles are in their original units or expressed as z scores. Note that the various Eqs. (11-1) can be expressed as $\mathbf{e}_x = \mathbf{t}'\mathbf{x}$, where $\mathbf{t}$ is a matrix of weights used to form linear combinations. Based on the properties of matrix addition and multiplication discussed in Chapter 3, d_e can be expressed either as $\mathbf{t}'\mathbf{x} - \mathbf{t}'\mathbf{y}$ or $\mathbf{t}'(\mathbf{x} - \mathbf{y})$. That is, you can subtract the elevation measure of $\mathbf{x}$ from the elevation measure of $\mathbf{y}$ or you can obtain the difference between the two vectors and then compute the elevation measure from the difference.

Numerical Example

Assume that a retail store chain sells phonograph records that are classified as (1) Popular/Rock, (2) Classical, and (3) Jazz, ignoring all other categories. All the stores have the same stock, but sales of the three categories of records vary. Assume that the owners of this hypothetical chain want you to use sales information to decide how to stock a given store to meet the demands of its clientele.[2]

Assume that the weekly sales of records in the three categories are $21,050, $8,210, and $9,270, averaged over stores during a suitable time period. Also, assume that the standard deviations over stores for the three categories are $2,205, $950, and $1,310. Sales of popular and classical records correlate .4 over stores, sales of popular and jazz records correlate .5, and sales of classical and jazz records correlate .8.

Consider two stores. Store X sold $21,321 worth of popular records, $8,835 worth of classical records, and $10,143 worth of jazz records. In contrast, Store Y sold $18,210 worth of popular records, $9,137 worth of classical records, and $7,974 worth of jazz records.

The total sales of Store X is $40,299 = (1,1,1)'(\$21,321, \$8,835, \$10,143) = \$21,321 + \$8,835 + \$10,143$. Similarly, the total sales of Store Y is $35,321.

[2] This particular example is different from most that you may encounter in psychology, because here "stores" rather than "people" form the unit of analysis. It will be most useful for you to bear with this particular problem, because you will encounter other situations in which "people" are not the unit of analysis. The one considered here, like several I have dealt with, is common in marketing. If you are a clinical psychology student, you may encounter problems in which hospitals form the unit of analysis. For example, you may wish to group hospitals on the basis of the socioeconomic characteristics of their patients.

The value of d_e is \$4,978, i.e., Store X sold roughly five thousand dollars more than Store Y over the target period. Adding a third store to the example (which I will do in the discussion of clustering below) will allow the difference to be described as relatively large or small and, consequently, the two stores as similar or dissimilar

The greater variability in sales of popular records over stores as compared to classical records is not an artifact of the measurement unit, since all three elements are measured in the same unit (dollars). To correct for differences in unit of measurement, convert the vector for store X ($\mathbf{x}$) to z-score form, $\mathbf{z}_x$, by using the preceding normative information furnished. The three elements of $\mathbf{z}_x$ are (\$21,321 − \$21,050)/\$2,205, (\$8,835 − \$8,210)/\$950, and (\$10,143 − \$9,270)/\$1,310. Hence, $\mathbf{z}_x = (.12, .66, .67)$. In a like manner, the z-score vector for Store $Y(\mathbf{z}_y)$ is $(−1.29, .97, −.99)$. Thus, Store X is roughly average in its sales of popular records and slightly above average in the sales of classical and jazz records, whereas Store Y is very poor in its sales of popular and jazz records and fairly good in its sales of classical records. Note, however, that this shape information is not relevant to those measures of profile similarity based on elevation alone. The two elevations are 1.45 and $−1.31$. Hence, d_e is 2.76.

Another procedure to correct for differences in variance is to use the reciprocal standard deviations. The weighting vector is $(1/2205, 1/950, 1/1310) = (.00045, .00105, .00076)$. If the weights are applied to $\mathbf{x}$, the result is 26.71, and if they are applied to $\mathbf{y}$, the result is 23.96. Hence, d_e is 2.75. Even though the individual elevations are not the same as in the previous case, the difference between the two (dissimilarity) is the same within rounding error.

The calculations used to correct for the covariance structure are as follows: First, I will apply Eq. (11-1c) to obtain e_x:

$$e_x = [1. \quad 1. \quad 1.] \begin{bmatrix} 1.00 & .40 & .50 \\ .40 & 1.00 & .80 \\ .50 & .80 & 1.00 \end{bmatrix}^{-1} \begin{bmatrix} .123 \\ .658 \\ .666 \end{bmatrix}$$

$$= [1. \quad 1. \quad 1.] \begin{bmatrix} 1.333 & .000 & -.667 \\ .000 & 2.778 & -.222 \\ -.667 & -2.222 & 3.111 \end{bmatrix} \begin{bmatrix} .123 \\ .658 \\ .666 \end{bmatrix}$$

$$= .595$$

Similarly, e_y is $−.536$ and d_e is 1.131.

The alternative is to use Eq. (10-1d), which produces

$$e_x = [1. \quad 1. \quad 1.] \begin{bmatrix} 4862025 & 837900 & 1444275 \\ 837900 & 902500 & 995600 \\ 1444275 & 995600 & 1716100 \end{bmatrix}^{-1} \begin{bmatrix} 21321 \\ 8835 \\ 7974 \end{bmatrix}$$

I will not proceed with the calculations. The value of $|R|$ of .27 is rather low but (debatably) high enough so that $\mathbf{R}^{-1}$ may be considered stable. Because the variances of the individual elements are quite large, $|C|$ is essentially 0. Consequently, $\mathbf{C}^{-1}$ is quite unstable so that computations should be based on z scores rather than raw scores. The reason is purely computational.

Finally, prior weights may be used. The above analyses made the implicit assumption that it was just as desirable to sell a given volume of popular records as it was that same volume of classical records or jazz records. In reality, though, the profit margins for the sales of the three different types of records may be quite different. For argument's sake, assume that the profits are .6, .4, and .3, e.g., that a dollar's worth of popular records at wholesale is sold at \$1.60 retail. The information would produce a weight vector of (1.6, 1.4, 1.3). Multiplying the vector by x yields $1.6 \times 21321 + 1.4 \times 8835 + 1.3 \times 10143 = 59668.5$ and multiplying weight vector by y yields 52294 for a difference of 7374.5.

Profile Similarity Based on Shape Information

There are a number of ways to incorporate shape information into a suitable index. For now, I will discuss indices that also incorporate level information. In a later section of the chapter, I will discuss how level differences among profile may be eliminated when it is not desired. I will emphasize the Mahalanobis d^2 measure and its variants because of their general theoretical importance.

Ignoring the issue of whether or not elevation is to affect the measure of similarity for a moment, three cases may be distinguished which parallel the preceding cases: (1) similarity measures based on the raw profiles, in which both the variances of the elements and their communalities affect the outcome; (2) similarity measures based on profiles that have been corrected for variability but not communality; and (3) similarity measures based on profiles that have been corrected for both variability and communality. Three suitable measures that incorporate elevation and shape information are given as Eqs. (11-2a), (11-2b), and (11-2c), respectively. These measures correspond to Eqs. (11-1a), (11-1b), and (11-1c). Equation (11-2d) is an alternative approach to correcting for both variance and communality, but it may run into the same problems as a result of the instability of $\mathbf{C}^{-1}$ that were previously discussed when the variances of individual elements are large. I have used the symbols "d^2" and "d_{se}^2" both to denote the similarity of the measures to previous discussion and to maintain consistency of notation for future discussion when shape and not elevation is allowed to affect the similarity measure. As before, the measures actually describe *dissimilarity*.

$$d^2 = d_{se}^2 = (\mathbf{x} - \mathbf{y})'(\mathbf{x} - \mathbf{y}) \tag{11-2a}$$

$$d^2 = d_{se}^2 = (\mathbf{z}_x - \mathbf{z}_y)'(\mathbf{z}_x - \mathbf{z}_y) \tag{11-2b}$$

$$d^2 = d_{se}^2 = (\mathbf{z}_x - \mathbf{z}_y)'\mathbf{R}^{-1}(\mathbf{z}_x - \mathbf{z}_y) \tag{11-2c}$$

$$d^2 = d_{se}^2 = (\mathbf{x} - \mathbf{y})'\mathbf{C}^{-1}(\mathbf{x} - \mathbf{y}) \tag{11-2d}$$

The similarity of all three measures described by Eqs. (11-2) to the original definition of Mahalanobis d^2 [Eq. (8-4)] should be noted. Both $(\mathbf{x} - \mathbf{y})$ and $(\mathbf{z}_x - \mathbf{z}_y)$ are difference vectors. In the original definition of d^2 given in Chapter 8, the inverse of a pooled within-group correlation matrix was used. Now, I will deal with the more general case of inverting a correlation matrix $(\mathbf{R}^{-1})$ or variance–covariance matrix $(\mathbf{C}^{-1})$, whichever is needed for the particular application. $\mathbf{C}$ and $\mathbf{R}$ are implicitly considered identity matrices whenever the covariance structure is ignored.

A Numerical Example

Applying Eq. (11-2a) to the present data yields the following:

$$(\mathbf{x} - \mathbf{y}) = \begin{bmatrix} 21321 \\ 8835 \\ 10143 \end{bmatrix} - \begin{bmatrix} 18210 \\ 9137 \\ 7974 \end{bmatrix} = \begin{bmatrix} 3111 \\ -302 \\ 2169 \end{bmatrix}$$

$$d^2 = d_{se}^2 = \begin{bmatrix} 3111 & -302 & 2169 \end{bmatrix} \times \begin{bmatrix} 3111 \\ -302 \\ 2169 \end{bmatrix}$$

$$= 14{,}474{,}086$$

The large value of d^2 reflects the squaring inherent in its definition and the units of measurement. The result may be more descriptive if the square root of d^2 (d) is obtained, which equals 3804.48. The d measure has the useful property of being in the original unit of measurement (dollars).

Applying Eq. (11-2b) leads to the following:

$$(\mathbf{z}_x - \mathbf{z}_y) = \begin{bmatrix} .122 \\ .658 \\ .666 \end{bmatrix} - \begin{bmatrix} -1.288 \\ .976 \\ -.989 \end{bmatrix} = \begin{bmatrix} 1.411 \\ -.317 \\ 1.656 \end{bmatrix}$$

$$d^2 = d_{se}^2 = \begin{bmatrix} 1.411 & -.317 & 1.656 \end{bmatrix} \times \begin{bmatrix} 1.411 \\ -.317 \\ 1.656 \end{bmatrix}$$

$$= 4.83$$

Transforming d^2 to d yields 2.20. Because the elements of $(\mathbf{z}_x - \mathbf{z}_y)$ are in z-score form, d will generally be more tractable than its counterpart defined in raw-score units. However, d will not itself be in z-score form.

Finally, using Eq. (11-2c) to correct for the intercorrelations among the profile elements yields

$$d^2 = d_{se}^2 = \begin{bmatrix} 1.411 & -.317 & 1.656 \end{bmatrix} \begin{bmatrix} 1.333 & .000 & -.667 & 1.411 \\ .000 & 2.777 & -2.222 & -.317 \\ -.667 & -2.222 & 3.111 & 1.656 \end{bmatrix}$$

$$= 10.68$$

The three measures are clearly different. The context of a particular problem will determine which procedure is preferable.

Correcting for Elevation

Elevation differences may be eliminated so that one may look at pure shape differences. One simple correction is to make the elevation of each profile equal zero by expressing the individual profile elements as deviations from the mean of the profile elements. The mean of Store X's popular, classical, and jazz elements is $(21321 + 8835 + 10143)/3 = 13433$, and the comparable mean of Store Y's elements is 11773.67. Subtracting the former from each element of $\mathbf{x}$ leads to an *elevation-corrected* x profile $= (7888, -4598, 3290)$. The elevation-corrected $\mathbf{y}$ profile is $(6436.33, -2636.67, -3799.67)$. Note that the sum of the three elements of both elevation-corrected profiles adds to zero.

The elevation-corrected difference between the profiles, obtained by subtraction, is $(1451.67, -1961.33, 509.667)$. Using Eq. (11-2a) to obtain the d^2 separating the two profiles leads to $(1451.67)^2 + (-1961.33)^2 + (508.68)^2$ or 6,213,925. The distance between the two stores is considerably less than it was prior to elevation-correction (14,474,086), because part of the original difference between the two was in their elevation; eliminating this difference makes the two stores more similar.

Dividing the elements of the elevation-corrected difference vector by the associated standard deviations yields an elevation-corrected difference vector in z-score form. Thus $(1451.67/2205, -1961.33/950, 508.68/1310) = (.658, -2.065, .389)$. Applying Eq. (11-2b) leads to a d^2 value of 4.84, which describes the effects of correcting the two stores' profiles for elevation and variance, but not communality. Applying Eq. (11-2c) leads to a value of 16.12, which describes the effects of correcting for elevation, variance, and communality.

Correlations, Covariances, and Cross Products as Alternative Indices of Similarity

An alternative measure of profile similarity is the correlation between the two profiles over elements. I will use the symbol "r_s" to denote the correlation between two profiles. Two profiles with identical shapes will have a r_s of 1.0, whereas two profiles whose elements are unrelated will have an r_s of .0. Note that a small value of r_s denotes *dissimilarity*, whereas a small value of Mahalanobis d^2 denotes *similarity*.

The r_s, like any other correlation, is sensitive to shape, but not elevation, differences. It also corrects for scale differences among the profile elements. There are other related statistics with different properties. The *covariance* between the two profiles (COV) is also sensitive to shape differences and insensitive to elevation differences, but it allows difference in variability among the units to affect the outcome. In contrast, the *sum of cross products* (CP) is sensitive to shape, elevation, and variability of the elements. One final and infrequently used alternative is to compute a CP measure using elements which have been divided by their standard deviations. This measure is sensitive to shape and elevation, but not variability, differences.[3]

The r_s and d^2 measure obtained from an elevation-corrected profile using Eq. (11-2a) are closely related. The relation is given by Eq. (11-3), where K denotes the number of profile elements.

$$r_s = 1 - d^2/2K \qquad (11\text{-}3)$$

The CP statistic relates to d_{se}^2 as indicated by Eq. (11-4). The quantities x^2 and y^2 are the sums of squares ($\mathbf{x'x}$ and $\mathbf{y'y}$, respectively) of the elements of $\mathbf{x}$ and $\mathbf{y}$.

$$CP = .5(x^2 + y^2 - d_{se}^2) \qquad (11\text{-}4)$$

Unlike matrices that contain d^2 measures, matrices containing values of CP, COV, or r_s measures of profile similarity are Gramian and hence factorable. Nunnally (1962) introduced raw-score factor analysis of matrices containing cross products rather than correlations into the psychology literature. The normal mode of factoring such matrices uses a component rather than a common factor model. The solution provides Euclidian distances among profiles as an index of dissimilarity. Raw-score factor analysis is analogous to the use of $\mathbf{R}^{-1}$ and $\mathbf{C}^{-1}$ in Eqs. (11-1c) and (11-1d), respectively. It is exploited in certain clustering routines, specifically the version employed by SAS.

Raw-score factor analysis, as used in the present context, differs from previous applications of factor analysis in three respects. First, the role of subjects and measures are reversed so that correlations (or covariances or cross products) describe the similarity among subjects over measures instead of the converse ("stores," in the above example, play the role of "subjects"). Second, the statistics obtained from the analysis will be different when covariances or cross products are obtained. The sum of the eigenvalues will equal the sum of the covariances or cross products, not the number of variables. Finally, structure loadings will describe covariances or cross products and not correlations. However, a crucial property of the result will be the same. The ratio of the first eigenvalue to the sum of all the eigenvalues describes the proportion of variance that can be accounted for by one dimension of variance; the ratio of the sum of the first two eigenvalues to the sum of all the eigenvalues describes the proportion of variance that can be accounted for by two dimensions, etc. You should examine the ratio when interpreting an SAS or other clustering routine based upon crossproduct analysis.

---

[3] The CP measure can, and frequently is, based on variables that have been standardized so as to eliminate differences in elevation and variability. Remember that r_s and COV involve profile elements expressed as deviations about the mean of the profile elements (and, in the case of r_s, the standard deviation) and not the mean over people. The CP measure is quite simply expressed as $\mathbf{x'y}$ or $\mathbf{y'x}$ for the two profiles, $\mathbf{x}$ and $\mathbf{y}$, respectively.

There are a number of other statistical procedures that can be used to compare profiles. One useful discussion is given in Cattell, Eber, and Tatsuoka (1970). Despite the advantages of alternatives in some cases, I will be emphasizing d^2 type statistics in my discussion because of their general utility.

Simple and Hierarchical Clustering

What I will call *simple* clustering is a set of methods to form a given number of groups based on their similarity. In principle, any of the measures thus far considered may be used as a basis for clustering, but, in practice, measures incorporated by the particular package you are using may be the most accessable to your analysis unless you are highly skilled with its use.

To introduce the topic, assume that there are now four stores whose total sales during the target time period are \$40,299 (Store X above), \$35,321 (Store Y above), \$33,329 (which I will call Store V), and \$27,191 (which I will call Store W). Now assume that one wishes to classify the stores into three groups, i.e., big stores, medium stores, and small stores, based on their *total* sales. Consider the problem as an example of a more complex task in which the number of stores (N) and the number of categories (p) are greater than 4 and 3, respectively. More importantly, consider the possibility that one might wish to form clusters based on the shape of the profiles, and not just elevation (total sales) in other applications.

The rank ordering of the stores in terms of total sales is X, Y, V, and W. There are several possible ways to group them. For example, one could call both X and Y "Large," V "Medium," and W "Small." However, one could also call X "Large," Y and V "Medium," and W "Small." There are many other possible ways to group the four stores, some of which are reasonable (X is "Large," Y is "Medium," and V and W are "Small"). Other groupings do not make sense because the rank ordering is disturbed. (Y is "Large," X and W are "Medium," and V is "Small"). You might prefer the second of the four groupings, in which Y and V are placed in the same cluster, because the two stores are closer to each other in their sales ($d_e = 1892$) than are X and Y ($d_e = 5078$), which is actually a quite reasonable thing to do. I will show you why this choice is, in fact, the most reasonable one to make.

One popular clustering criterion minimizes the *pooled within-group (within-clusters) variance* as a measure of classification error. The pooled within-group variance is a useful definition of error because it represents the extent to which observations within a cluster, which are treated as being equivalent, actually differ among themselves.

The pooled within-group variance associated with grouping stores V and Y into one cluster and leaving Stores X and W alone in separate clusters is computed as follows. The *sum of squares* within the cluster formed by V and Y is obtained by adding up the squared differences between each of the two profiles and their mean—(35221 + 33329)/2 or 34275. The differences between each profile and their mean are $(35221 - 34275) = 946$ for Store V and $(33329 - 34275) = -946$ for Store Y. Hence, the sum of squares is $(946)^2 + (-946)^2 = 894916 + 894916 = 1789832$. My computation is for demonstration purposes. In actuality, one would take advantage of the computational relation $\sum(X - X)^2 = \sum X^2 - (\sum X)^2/N$ just as one would in computing an ordinary variance.

There is but one profile in each of the two remaining clusters, which will always be true when forming clusters from individual observations. Consequently, the *pooled* within-group sum of squares is also 1,789,832. One df is needed to estimate the sum of squares for the two stores that were clustered (V and Y); none were needed to estimate the sums of squares for the remaining two stores. Consequently, the *pooled df* = 1.0, and the pooled within-group variance is the pooled sum of squares divided by the pooled df or 1,789,832.

In other forms of clustering, e.g., hierarchical clustering, clusters may be formed from pairs of other clusters, each of which will contain error. The df associated with each cluster is the number of profiles in the cluster minus one. The pooled df is the sum of the df associated with each cluster. However, the pooled df may be expressed more simply as the number of observations minus the number of clusters ($4 - 3 = 1$ in the present example).

The cluster formed from Stores V and Y has a pooled-within-group variance that is smaller than any other pooling of the four stores into three clusters. You may verify this as an exercise by obtaining the within-group variance for all other possible three-cluster groupings that can be formed. Consequently, the grouping of X alone, Y and V, and W alone is the "best" way to form three clusters based upon total sales, where "best" means "smallest pooled within-group variance."

The pooled within-group variance may be used to provide an alternative and equivalent definition of "best" based on the *squared multiple correlation* (R^2) between dummy codes for group membership and the appropriate profile measure (total sales). Note that this definition is one of "goodness," whereas a definition based on pooled within-group variance is one of "badness." In order to compute R^2, first one needs the total sum of squares of deviations associated with placing all the stores within a single cluster, i.e., the sum of squared deviations about the mean of all stores. The grand mean is $(40299 + 35321 + 33329 + 27181)/4$ or 34032.5. You may verify that the total sum of squares of the four observations about their mean is 88,367,219. The R^2 is 1.0 minus the ratio of the pooled within-class sum of squares (1,789,832) to the overall sum of squares (88,377,219) or .980. The arrangement producing the smallest pooled within-group variance for a given number of clusters will also produce the largest R^2 because of the equivalence of the two measures.

Hierarchical clustering usually involves starting with the individual stores. The first step is, as illustrated previously, to form the best three-cluster grouping based on a criterion such as minimizing the pooled within-group variance. In essence, Y and V are replaced as individual stores by their *average*, which is $(35221 + 33329)/2$. or 34275. At the next step, the two most similar clusters from this set of three are joined, leaving two clusters. *Choice of a merger is limited to existing clusters. You cannot take Store Y, once it has been merged with Store V, dissociate it from the cluster and pair it with a different store.* Once you have two clusters, all you can do is merge them into one large class, at which point the process ends. Thus, at any given stage of hierarchical clustering, a given cluster is the offspring of the merger of two "parent" clusters. *Clustering is the search for the "best" way, in a mathematical sense, to form k clusters out of a set of N profiles. In hierarchical clustering, one is also interested in finding the best* $(N - 1)$, $(N - 2)$, $(N - 3)$, ... *clusters and minimizing the error associated with each.*

As the clustering process continues, one also goes from minimum within-group variance (0), i.e., error, to maximum error. At the same time as within-group variance increases, explanation of the data becomes more parsimonious because their are fewer discrete entities to deal with. *A second goal of hierarchical clustering may be thought of as the search for the optimal tradeoff of error and parsimony, again in the mathematical sense. The problem is not unlike that of determining the number of important factors to keep in an exploratory factor analysis. However, there is even less general consensus as to how many clusters should be chosen.* The results of hierarchical clustering possess a "tree" structure, a terminology rather similar to that used in botany. Individual observations may be thought of as "leaves," which join to form small "branches"; small branches join to form larger "branches," until the "root" is reached.

I have perhaps lulled you into a bit of simplification by means of this example. Since stores were grouped on the basis of sales volume in dollars (elevation), there was no question as to what formed the clusters. In most cases, shape information also contributes to clustering so that an interpretive problem is present. *From the psychological, as opposed to mathematical standpoint, the major problem in clustering (simple or hierarchical) is in determining what the profiles within a given cluster have in common.*

The problem of defining clusters is like the problem of defining factors. You not only have to consider what profiles within clusters have in common, you also have to consider the role that chance may have played in forming the clusters. It is vital that you consider some means of replicating your cluster structure on a new group of observations. Prokop, Bradley, Margolis, and Gentry (1980) provide an illustration of how one may determine if clusters are replicable. Keep in mind that almost anybody with sufficient imagination can identify properties shared by a group of observations (profiles) no matter how spurious that basis.

There are other ways to group profiles than hierarchical clustering. *Overlapping* clusters allow a profile to be assigned to more than one cluster, although algorithms typically put constraints on the number of different clusters to which an observation may be assigned. *Fuzzy* clustering allow degrees of inclusiveness instead of all-or-none belongingness. I will not discuss overlapping or fuzzy clustering.

Numerical Example

To pursue the previous example, I have generated hypothetical data from 10 stores, using their sales profiles. The data include X and Y whose complete profiles were presented earlier, V and W whose total sales (but not profile) were given, and six new "Stores" A, B, C, D, E and F. The complete set of profiles is given in Table 11-1. The particular clustering criterion I used is the SAS default known as "Ward's method." It is based on the squared differences *uncorrected* for covariance structure, i.e., the results of using Eq. (11-2a). It is intended to merge clusters with small number of observations each and, hence, provide clusters with approximately the same numbers of observations as much as possible. The "centroid" and "average linkage" methods are optional alternatives that also correct for the covariance structure; the former simply being the Mahalanobis distance.

A component analysis of the 10 store by three element data matrix, which I will term $\mathbf{X}$, indicated that these profiles differed in two dimensions (the dimensionality of the 10 by 10 matrix $\mathbf{XX'}$ is the same as the dimensionality of the 3 by 3 matrix $\mathbf{X'X}$ so that the maximum number of dimensions of variation is 3). The first eigenvalue (26,653,358—remember, the analysis uses *raw scores*) accounted for 53% of the total variance and the second eigenvalue (19,796,487) accounted for 43%. Hence, the stores differ in more than simple elevation, which I intended since the problem would otherwise be rather dull if I constructed the numbers simply to have large and small stores.

The means of the three categories for the 10 stores (which are different from the hypothetical populations means given above because of sampling error) are 19758, 7950, and 8341. Their associated standard deviations are 4999, 3322, and 3735. The *root-mean-square total-sample standard deviation* is the square root of the average of the squared standard deviations: $[(1/3) \times (4999^2 + 3322^2 + 3735^2)]^{1/2} = 4088$. The result is an upper limit on error, reflecting what happens when the 10 stores are treated as a single cluster. It has $(N - 1)(K - 1) = 9 \times 2 = 18\ df$.

TABLE 11-1. Hypothetical sales figures for 10 stores

Store	Rock	Classical	Jazz
X	21321	8835	10143
Y	18210	9137	7974
V	13671	8137	11521
W	12121	9111	5959
A	14190	7450	7340
B	25075	12135	11234
C	21092	4356	6935
D	25112	3004	2135
E	25467	13121	15175
F	21324	4221	4998

The sum of the entire matrix of d^2 values is 9,025,030,252. There are 90 values (excluding the diagonals) and each has 2 df. The square root of $9,025,030,252/(90 \times 2)$ is 7080.89. It represents the *root-mean-square distance between observations*.

You may verify that the d^2 for Stores C and F is $(21092 - 21324)^2 + (4356 - 4221)^2 + (6935 - 4998)^2$ or 3,824,018. It is the smallest such value of d^2 in the set of 45 distinct values. Hence, Stores C and F are the first two to be linked.

Averaging Stores C and F into a single cluster produces the vector (21208, 4288.5, 5966.5). If one sums the squared deviations of this cluster from the remaining three profiles and divides by 3 (K is used instead of $K - 1$ as all three elements can vary), the result is the *root-mean-square standard deviation of the cluster*.

I have previously shown how a value of R^2 can be obtained as 1.0 minus the ratio of the pooled within-group sum of squares to the overall sum of squares. That value is .996. The *semipartial* R^2 is the difference between 1.0 and R^2 or .004. It reflects the decrement in R^2 produced by clustering. Depending upon the program, other statistics may be computed as guides.

In essence, the algorithm now replaces the individual d^2 values for Stores C and F with those based upon their average. The smallest value in the resulting 9×9 matrix involves Stores W and A. The RMS standard deviation of the new cluster is 1221.12, which, by definition, must be larger than that obtained with the first cluster though smallest among the remaining possibilities. The R^2 value based upon the two clusters drops to .986; hence, the semipartial R^2 for the new cluster is $.996 - .986$ or .01. The decrement in R^2 is also the smallest possible.

The next two clustering operations merge Stores X and Y and B and E, respectively. Up to now, only individual profiles have been linked. At the fifth step (five-cluster level) the first merger takes place between a cluster that has been formed (W and A) and another profile (V) to form a cluster based on three profiles. Step 6 merges Store D and C and F. All individual stores are now in a multi-store cluster. Next, step 7 merges the cluster consisting of Stores X and Y with the cluster representing Stores V, W, and A and step 8 merges the new cluster with the one representing Stores C, F, and D, and, finally, step 9 merges all profiles into one cluster. The sequence may be visualized in Fig. 11-2, which is the tree diagram obtained from SAS output.

I have edited the diagram slightly. Each row represents a step. The top or "root" row is the case in which all 10 stores are in one cluster, and the bottom or "leaf" row is the point prior to any clustering. Note that the first row is actually the last step in clustering and the bottom row is the starting point. The figure or *clustering history* is conventionally read from the bottom up. The symbols "XXXX" tie together stores within a cluster at each step and "." denotes stores which are not yet clustered.

As I noted before, the question of "how many clusters?" is like the question of "how many factors?," only the former question is even less well defined.

Name of observation or cluster

Store

X	Y	V	W	A	C	F	D	B	E

```
XXXXXXXXXXXXXXXXXXXXXXXXXXXXXXXXXXXXXXXXXXXXXXXXXXXXXXXXXXXXXXXXX
XXXXXXXXXXXXXXXXXXXXXXXXXXXXXXXXXXXXXXXXXXXXXXXXXXX         XXXXXXX
XXXXXXXXXXXXXXXXXXXXXXXXXXXX         XXXXXXXXXXXX         XXXXXXX
XXXXXX         XXXXXXXXXXXX         XXXXXXXXXXXX         XXXXXXX
XXXXXX         XXXXXXXXXXXX         XXXXXX         ·         XXXXXXX
XXXXXX         ·         XXXXXXX         XXXXXX         ·         XXXXXXX
XXXXXX         ·         XXXXXXX         XXXXXX         ·         ·     ·
·     ·     ·         XXXXXXX         XXXXXX         ·     ·     ·
·     ·     ·     ·     ·         XXXXXXX         ·     ·     ·
```

FIGURE 11-2. Tree diagram for hierarchical clustering data.

TABLE 11-2. Results of clustering obtained from
the data of Table 11-1

Number of clusters	Frequency of new cluster	RMS Std of new cluster	Semipartial R^2
9	2	798.3	0.004237
8	2	1221.1	0.009913
7	2	1553.2	0.016038
6	2	1666.2	0.018457
5	3	1847.8	0.035483
4	3	1956.2	0.046643
3	5	2563.9	0.113375
2	8	3471.9	0.335263
1	10	4088.2	0.420590

There are several statistics among those I have mentioned that may serve as a guide. To avoid cluttering things too much, I have edited the SAS output although what is called the "Cubic clustering criterion" is favored by many. The data are presented in Table 11-2. Unlike Fig. 11-1, the table is read "downward" so that successive rows represent *increases* in groupings.

In principle, one seeks the point (or "elbow") before which there is a relatively large increase in error, just as in a scree test (cf. Chapter 6). One strategy is to look at successive ratios of semipartial R^2 values. For example, going from 9 to 8 clusters involves R^2 values of .0043 and .0099. The ratio of the latter to the former is 2.30. The next ratio is .0160/.99 or 1.62. Continuing, the ratios are 1.15, 1.92, 1.31, 2.43, 2.95, and 1.25. The figure of 2.43 represents what happens when one goes from 4 clusters to 3. It appears to be an "elbow" in the error function. With only 10 stores to begin with, there is no solution with a good number of exemplars, but a four-cluster solution does have the additional advantage of being the first step in which each store was grouped with at least one other store. As you may see from Fig. 11-2, the four-cluster solution consists of stores (1) X and Y, (2) V, W, and A, (3) C, F, and D, and (4) D and E. The clusters are approximately balanced as to number of stores in each group so I will stop here and accept this solution.

The average profile for Group (1) stores is the vector (19760, 8906, 9058). This indicates that the sales of popular records are about average, but the sales of classical and jazz records are above average in this cluster. By contrast, the average profile for Group (2) stores is the vector (13327, 8232, 4472), which represents poor sales in all three categories. The average profile for Group (3) stores is (22509, 3860, 4689), which indicates very good sales of popular records but very poor sales of classical and jazz records. Finally, the profile for Group (4) stores is (252,271, 12628, 13204), which represents strong sales in all three categories. You might visualize the different clienteles of the four clusters. Perhaps the Group (3) stores heavily cater to teenagers. That takes us beyond the hypothetical data.

Looking at the history (the "hierarchical side") tells us when groups were added. For example, the Group (3) cluster started with C and F and only later picked up D. The point may be of interest. Nonetheless, in most applications, interest is in the "clusters" and not the "hierarchy" or how one got there.

Canonical Analysis

Goals of Canonical Analysis

As noted in the previous discussion of the linear discriminant function and elsewhere, canonical analysis functions as an extension of multiple regression. Whereas the latter is concerned with optimizing the relation between a set of predictors and a single criterion and hence between a vector and a scalar, canonical analysis is concerned with the optimal relations between two sets of variables and hence between pairs of vectors.

Before proceeding further, an editorial comment is in order. Canonical analysis, like any other multivariate model, is based on truly elegant mathematics. However, elegant mathematics is not the same thing as elegant application. All too often, canonical analysis is used as the basis for a fishing expedition where someone says "lets see what happens when we take variable set X (an ill-defined group of predictors) and relate them to variable set Y (an equally ill-defined set of criterion variables)." Considerable thought needs to go into a successful canonical analysis. Rather than continue on with my sermon on GIGO, I will now return to the discussion about how canonical analysis is performed (see Marascuilo & Levin, 1983, for similar remarks).

Basic Logic

By way of introduction, assume that you have two sets of variables that I will term the X set and the Y set. There are P variables in the X set and Q variables in the Y set. The temporal relation between the two is not important. That is, do not necessarily think of the X variables as predictors and the Y variables as criteria or vice versa. Rather, define the two sets in such a way that $P \leq Q$, i.e., you assign the set containing the lesser number of variables to X. As before, the matrix is based on N observations, each of which are measured on all of the X and Y variables.

The basic analysis proceeds through the following sequence. A set of beta weights is computed for the X set, designated $\boldsymbol{\beta}_{x1}$, and a set of weights are computed for the Y set, designated $\boldsymbol{\beta}_{y1}$ (since the computation of β weights are at issue, it is assumed that X and Y are standardized). The weights produce the largest possible correlation between a linear combination of X and a linear combination of Y, the *first canonical correlation*, symbolized as R_{c1}. The linear combinations of the X and the Y variables are called the *first canonical variates*.

The X and Y variables are then adjusted for their respective canonical variates, which leaves a set of X and a set of Y residuals. This adjustment process is analogous to correcting a single correlation matrix for the first PC before extracting the second PC (Chapter 6). The process is repeated using successive residuals. Linear combinations of X and Y residuals (*first-order residuals*) are formed to obtain the largest possible correlation between the two sets of residuals—the *second canonical correlation*, R_{c2}, which must be less than or equal to R_{c1}, by definition. The vectors of weights leading to the largest possible correlation among the residuals will be symbolized as $\boldsymbol{\beta}_{x2}$ and $\boldsymbol{\beta}_{y2}$.

Second-order residuals are then formed, and a third canonical correlation R_{c3} ($\leq R_{c2} \leq R_{c1}$) and associated canonical variates, $\boldsymbol{\beta}_{x3}$ and $\boldsymbol{\beta}_{y3}$, are formed, etc.

A total of P such canonical variates and associated canonical correlations can be formed, given the assumptions that $P \leq Q$ and that the number of observations upon which the correlations are based (N) is very large compared to both P and Q. I will denote the entire matrix of weights obtained from each of the $\boldsymbol{\beta}_{xi}$ vectors as $\mathbf{B}_x$ and the entire matrix of weights obtained from each of the $\boldsymbol{\beta}_{yi}$ vectors as $\mathbf{B}_y$. Assume that the weights for the relations are given as *column* vectors. Hence, $\mathbf{B}_x$ is of order $P \times P$ (though it will be asymmetric), and $\mathbf{B}_y$ is of order $Q \times P$. Some texts and computer packages transpose the relations. Hence, the equations I present may look slightly different from those presented in other texts. Note that $\mathbf{B}_x$ and $\mathbf{B}_y$ are *factor score coefficient* matrices in the sense of Chapters 6 and 7 since they convert observed scores to linear combinations.

Each step of the analysis will provide canonical variates for X and Y, $\boldsymbol{\beta}_{xi}$ and $\boldsymbol{\beta}_{yi}$, and associated canonical correlation, R_{ci}. as primary output. Just like any other correlational measure, R_{ci} may be squared to estimate the total variance that is explained by the canonical variates chosen at that step. Other results may also be derived. First, one may obtained the X structure, which, as in previous applications, consists of the correlations between the original

X variates and the canonical variate at that step. The Y structure may be obtained in an analogous fashion.

Next, one may determine how much of the variance within X has been explained by the canonical variate, β_{x1}, and how much of the variance within Y has been explained by the canonical variate, $\mathbf{b}_{y1}$. These two quantities will differ from one another, often substantially, and both will differ from the percentage of *total* variance explained by the first *pair* of canonical variates, which equals R_{ci}^2. Two questions that are even more significant to many investigators are how much variance in X is accounted for by knowledge of β_{y1} and vice versa. This pair of questions deals with how *redundant X and Y* are with respect to one another. The redundancy of the two sets is often the major question because the bottom line of many inquiries is how well one set of variables can account for variance in the other.

Redundancy Analysis

Even though you may obtain one or more large canonical correlations, it does not necessarily mean that the associated canonical variates will be very informative. For example, assume that X_1, X_2, and X_3 are a set of intelligence measures obtained from a group of grammar school children and that X_4 is the chronological age of the children. Now assume that Y_1 and Y_2 are some performance measures, and that Y_3 is also chronological age.

A moments reflection will demonstrate that R_{c1} must be 1.0 since it is possible to take a linear combination of the X variables, namely, X_4 alone, and a linear combination of the Y variables, namely, Y_3 alone, which correlate perfectly (as they are identical in actuality). However, this relation might or might not be very informative about the remaining measures in the sense of explaining a large proportion of X's or Y's total variance. Most intelligence measures are normed by age so that X_1, X_2, and X_3 will not correlate very highly with age. The process of norming, in effect, corrects for age. On the other hand, knowing the students' ages may tell you a great deal about Y_1 and Y_2 if these two measures tend to reflect maturation. Thus, knowing Y_3 may tell you little about X_1, X_2, or X_3, but knowing X_4 may tell you a great deal about Y_1 or Y_2.

In sum, when R_{c1} is large, it does not mean that you have extracted much variance *within* either the X or the Y set. Moreover, the proportion of total X variance that is explained by knowing an optimal linear combination of Y may be large or small, independently of the proportion of total Y variance that is explained by knowing an optimal linear combination of X. Incidentally, the reason that it actually makes sense to include age in both the X and the Y sets in this example is that all later canonical relations will be independent of age. My example also illustrates a type of multivariate covariance adjustment.

Redundancy analysis is concerned with how knowledge of X reduces your uncertainty about Y and vice versa. In general, knowing Y will explain a large amount of variance in X only when R_{ci} is high *and* the canonical variate is highly similar to one of the first few principal components of X. Even when the two conditions are met, the canonical variate for X may not correspond to an early principal component of Y, i.e., a redundancy relationship is not necessarily *symmetric*. Current approaches to canonical correlation analysis (Cooley & Lohnes, 1971; Stewart & Love, 1968) stress the importance of redundancy analysis statistics over canonical correlations.

The *redundancy* of X with respect to the ith canonical variate in Y, R_{dxi}, is the product of (a) the proportion of X variance accounted for by that canonical variate, which I will denote as v_{xi}, and (b) the proportion of total variance shared by the ith pair of canonical variates, which is R_{ci}^2. The redundancy describes the overlap in X and Y based on using Y to predict X. In a like manner, the redundancy of Y with respect to X, R_{dyi}, is the product of the proportion of Y variance accounted for by that canonical variate, v_{yi} and R_{ci}^2. I will express the collection of v_{xi} terms over the set of all canonical relations as $\mathbf{V}_x$, the collection of v_{yi} terms as $\mathbf{V}_y$, and the collection of squared canonical correlations as $\mathbf{R}^2$. Assume that all three are expressed as diagonal matrices. The relations among these matrices are expressed in Eqs. (11-5). Their computation will be discussed shortly.

$$\mathbf{R}_{dxi} = \mathbf{V}_x \mathbf{R}^2 \qquad (11\text{-}5a)$$

$$\mathbf{R}_{dyi} = \mathbf{V}_y \mathbf{R}^2 \qquad (11\text{-}5b)$$

Because successive canonical variates are orthogonal, values of $\mathbf{V}_x$, $\mathbf{V}_y$, $\mathbf{R}_{dx}$, $\mathbf{R}_{dy}$, and $\mathbf{R}^2$ can be summed. For example, $v_{x1} + v_{x2}$ of $\mathbf{V}_x$ is the proportion of variance in the X variables accounted for by the first two X canonical variates.

Basic Matrix Operations

The entire set of correlations, $\mathbf{R}$, can be viewed as a partitioned matrix of the following form:

$$\mathbf{R} = \begin{bmatrix} \mathbf{R}_{xx} & \mathbf{R}_{xy} \\ \mathbf{R}_{yx} & \mathbf{R}_{yy} \end{bmatrix}$$

Thus, the entire set of correlations among the $P + Q$ variables can be expressed in terms of (1) correlations within the set of X variables, $\mathbf{R}_{xx}$, (2) correlations within the set of Y variables, $\mathbf{R}_{yy}$, and (3) correlations between X and Y variables, $\mathbf{R}_{xy}$ and $\mathbf{R}_{yx}$—the two being transposes of one another. The submatrices $\mathbf{R}_{xx}$ and $\mathbf{R}_{yy}$ play the same role that the *predictor intercorrelation* matrix does in multiple correlation and regression; likewise, the submatrices $\mathbf{R}_{xy}$ and $\mathbf{R}_{yx}$ play the same role that *validities* do.

Before proceeding any further in the analysis, you should inspect $\mathbf{R}_{xy}$ (or $\mathbf{R}_{yx} = \mathbf{R}'_{xy}$). To repeat an old saw, you cannot use multivariate analysis to make silk purses out of univariate sows' ears. *If all of the elements of $\mathbf{R}_{xy}$ are smaller than, say $< .40$, forget the idea of performing a canonical analysis.* At the same time, it is quite possible for a relation between a set of X variables and a set of Y variables to be considerably stronger than any *individual* relation between a given X variable and the set of Y variables (multiple correlations) or vice versa, especially when the variables within each of the sets are relatively independent of one another. Be careful that you are not capitalizing upon chance.

The fundamental data of a canonical analysis are derived from an eigen-analysis of a $P \times P$ product matrix, which I will define as $\mathbf{A}$. The matrix $\mathbf{A}$ is defined by Eq. (11-6a). Had I reversed the roles of X and Y, the resulting order would be larger (g). It can be shown that the sum of the eigenvalues of the latter matrix equals the sum of the eigenvalues of $\mathbf{A}$ but the relation is not of practical use, as, in actuality, neither product matrix is computed. Both would be asymmetric and therefore difficult to analyze directly, as in discriminant analysis (cf. Chapter 8, pp. 256–257). The actual product matrix is defined as $\mathbf{A}^*$ in Eq. (11-6b). Conceptually, however, $\mathbf{A}$ is important to discuss.

$$\mathbf{A} = \mathbf{R}_{xx}^{-1}\mathbf{R}_{xy}\mathbf{R}_{yy}^{-1}\mathbf{R}_{yx} \qquad (11\text{-}6a)$$

$$\mathbf{A}^* = \mathbf{R}_{xx}^{-1/2}\mathbf{R}_{xy}\mathbf{R}_{yy}^{-1}\mathbf{R}_{yx}\mathbf{R}_{xx}^{-1/2} \qquad (11\text{-}6b)$$

This rather involved expression for $\mathbf{A}$ consists of two pairs of matrix products, $\mathbf{R}_{xx}^{-1}\mathbf{R}_{xy}$ and $\mathbf{R}_{yy}^{-1}\mathbf{R}_{yx}$. Each pair consists of (1) the inverse of a matrix containing predictor intercorrelations and (2) a matrix of validities. Hence, each pair is of the form of Eq. (4-10), which was used to obtain beta weights in multiple correlation. The only difference is that relevant terms here form a matrix, whereas in multiple correlation, the terms comprised a vector.

The data from $\mathbf{R}_{xx}^{-1}\mathbf{R}_{xy}$ can be used to perform a series of multiple regressions by treating each Y variable in turn as a criterion to be predicted from the set of X variables, and the data from $\mathbf{R}_{yy}^{-1}\mathbf{R}_{yx}$ can also be used to perform a series of multiple regressions by treating each X variable in turn as a criterion to be predicted from the set of Y variables. Specifically, the diagonals of $\mathbf{R}_{yx}\mathbf{R}_{xx}^{-1}\mathbf{R}_{xy}$ will contain values of R^2 predicting the individual Y variables and the diagonals of $\mathbf{R}_{xy}\mathbf{R}_{yy}^{-1}\mathbf{R}_{yx}$ will contain values of R^2 predicting the individual X variables.

The successive canonical correlations are simply the square roots of the eigenvectors of $\mathbf{A}$, and the canonical variates for X are the associated eigenvectors. The rather straightforward equations for the two relations are given as Eqs. (11-7a) and (11-7b). Since one obtains the eigenvectors of $\mathbf{A}^*$ rather than A, the computational formulas for $\mathbf{B}_x$ are given in Eq. (11-7c). The symbol "E" denotes a matrix containing the normalized eigenvectors of $\mathbf{A}^*$ expressed in columns. The symbol Λ denotes a diagonal matrix containing the reciprocal square roots of the eigenvalues of $\mathbf{A}$ (or $\mathbf{A}^*$, as the two sets of eigenvalues are identical), which are also the reciprocals of the canonical correlations.

The canonical variates for the larger Y set are a shade more involved to calculate and are given by Eq. (11-7c). The computation involves adding cross products of the beta weights predicting X from Y (given in $\mathbf{R}_{yy}^{-1}\mathbf{R}_{yx}$) and the canonical weights for X ($\boldsymbol{\beta}_{xi}$).

$$\mathbf{R}_{ci} = \Lambda_i^{1/2} \tag{11-7a}$$

$$\mathbf{B}_x = \mathbf{E} \tag{11-7b}$$

$$\mathbf{B}_x = \mathbf{R}_{xx}^{-1/2}\mathbf{V} \tag{11-7c}$$

$$\mathbf{B}_y = \mathbf{R}_{yy}^{-1}\mathbf{R}_{yx}\mathbf{B}_x\Lambda^{-1/2} \tag{11-7d}$$

Normally, canonical variates are scaled to unit variance. That is, the *side conditions* that $\boldsymbol{\beta}'_{xi}\mathbf{R}_{xx}\boldsymbol{\beta}_{xi} = \boldsymbol{\beta}'_{yi}\mathbf{R}_{yy}\boldsymbol{\beta}_{yi} = 1$ are introduced. Consequently, the diagonals of $\mathbf{B}'_x\mathbf{R}_{xx}\mathbf{B}_x$ and $\mathbf{B}'_y\mathbf{R}_{yy}\mathbf{B}_y$ are 1. This convention differs from that of multiple regression that yields predicted scores with a variance of R^2 to meet the least squares criterion.

The canonical structures of X and Y, $\mathbf{S}_x$ and $\mathbf{S}_y$, are respectively given by Eqs. (11-8a) and (11-8b). Both equations are of the same general form as Eq. (6-8), since the two involve the product of a matrix of beta weights and intercorrelations. In addition, it is possible to determine the correlations between variables in the X set and canonical variates derived from the Y sets. I will symbolize these correlations as "$\mathbf{S}_x(\mathbf{R}_y)$," defined by Eq. (11-8c). Conversely, one may also obtain correlations between variables in the Y set and canonical variates derived from the X set, denoted "$\mathbf{S}_y(\mathbf{R}_x)$," as defined in Eq. (11-8d).

$$\mathbf{S}_x = \mathbf{R}_{xx}\mathbf{B}_x \tag{11-8a}$$

$$\mathbf{S}_y = \mathbf{R}_{yy}\mathbf{B}_y \tag{11-8b}$$

$$\mathbf{S}_x(\mathbf{R}_y) = \mathbf{R}_{yx}\mathbf{B}_x \tag{11-8c}$$

$$\mathbf{S}_y(\mathbf{R}_x) = \mathbf{R}_{xy}\mathbf{B}_y \tag{11-8d}$$

Element s_{ij} of $\mathbf{S}_x$ is the correlation between canonical variate i and variable j. As in orthogonal factor analysis, the orthogonality of successive canonical variates allows two further useful sets of statistics. If the elements of $\mathbf{S}_x$ are squared and added over rows (canonical variates), the sum describes the proportion of variance in the jth variable that is explained by the canonical relations. The resultant is analogous to individual values of h^2 in factor analysis. Given our definition of $\mathbf{S}_x$ with the variables as columns, the relationship $\mathbf{S}'_x\mathbf{S}_x$ gives h^2-like variables along its diagonal. Hence, the jth diagonal of the matrix, which I will call $\mathbf{H}_x^2$, is the proportion of variance in variable j that has been explained through the set of canonical variates. $\mathbf{H}_y^2$ may be defined in an analogous manner.

In contrast, a second type of relationship, $(1/P)\mathbf{S}_x\mathbf{S}'_x$, provides factor variances along its diagonal. These factor variances comprise the $\mathbf{V}_x$ matrix used in redundancy analysis. The "$(1/P)$" term is present to define the *average* variances explained by individual variables over the number of X variables. These two important relations are given in Eqs. (11-9a) and (11-9b), respectively. Equations (11-9c) and (11-9d) give parallel formulas for variables in the Y set:

$$\mathbf{H}_x^2 = \mathrm{Diag}[\mathbf{S}_x'\mathbf{S}_x] \tag{11-9a}$$

$$\mathbf{V}_x = \mathrm{Diag}[(1/P)\mathbf{S}_x\mathbf{S}_x'] \tag{11-9b}$$

$$\mathbf{H}_y^2 = \mathrm{Diag}[\mathbf{S}_y'\mathbf{S}_y] \tag{11-9c}$$

$$\mathbf{V}_y = \mathrm{Diag}[(1/Q)\mathbf{S}_y\mathbf{S}_y'] \tag{11-9d}$$

The canonical variates may be correlated with principal components within each set of variables, which allows a more explicit description of the relation between the canonical variates (defined in terms of *external* criteria) and principal components (defined in terms of *internal* criteria). One uses Eq. (3-8) to correlate linear combinations and Eq. (6-10) to compute factor score weights for the principal components.

Statistical Inference

The most commonly performed statistical tests in canonical analysis are basically variants upon those discussed in the previous chapter. The tests are not carbon copies because the eigenvalues they use have slightly different properties as R^2 values here.

Wilks' lambda is commonly used as a basis for testing the omnibus null hypothesis that there is no linear relation between the X set of variables and the Y set of variables. The null hypothesis may be stated in several ways: (1) $\mathbf{R}_{xy}$ is a null matrix, (2) $\mathbf{R}_{ci} = 0$ for all P values of i, and that (3) $\mathbf{B}_x = \mathbf{B}_y = \boldsymbol{\beta}_{xi}$ (for all values of i) $= \boldsymbol{\beta}_{yi}$ (for all values of i) $= 0$. In the present case, Wilks' lambda is defined as

$$\lambda = \prod(1 - \lambda_i)$$
$$= \prod(1 - R_{ci}^2) \tag{11-10}$$

Wilks' lambda may be tested according to a chi-square approximation devised by Bartlett or an F approximation devised by Rao (1951), and the latter is generally preferred. It is defined in Eq. (11-11a), but two intermediate quantities, defined in Eqs. (11-11b) and (11-11c), are needed. The associated *df* are given in Eq. (11-11d). The Pillai–Bartlett, Hotelling–Lawley, and Roy tests may also be performed.

$$F = \frac{(ab - .5PQ + 1)}{PQ} \frac{(1 - \lambda^{1/b})}{\lambda^{1/b}} \tag{11-11a}$$

$$a = (N - 1) - .5(p + q \pm 1) \tag{11-11b}$$

$$b = \frac{|(PQ)^2 - 4|^{1/2}}{|P^2 + Q^2 - 5|} \quad \text{(unless } PQ = 2, \text{ in which case } b = 1) \tag{11-11c}$$

$$df_n = PQ$$

$$df_d = PQ - .5PQ + 1 \tag{11-11d}$$

Omnibus tests basically are designed to tell you whether you can assume some relations exist between the two sets. However, the tests tell you nothing about the degree of concentration. Bartlett's chi-square procedure can be adapted to sequential tests. That is, it can be applied to see if (1) at least one relation is present, (2) given that one relation is present, whether there is at least one more relation present in the residual matrix, etc.

First use Bartlett's χ^2 in the manner just described. Significance implies that the first canonical relation can be assumed not due to chance. If the test statistic is not significant, stop—there is no evidence that any relation exists between the two sets of variables.

Assuming that the first relation is significant, compute a new value of λ, which I will call λ_2 by deleting λ_1 when λ is computed. In other words, use limits of 2 to P instead of 1 to P in forming the product of the eigenvalues. The general form of the relation for steps 2, 3, ... is given by Eq. (11-12a), where K is the step number (two for the moment). You may still use Eq. (11-10) to obtain χ^2. However, the df are $(P-1)(Q-1)$ instead of PQ. The general form required for the df are given in Eq. (11-12b). Thus, if λ_1 and λ_2 are significant and λ_3 is not significant, retain two canonical variates for considerations. You may find that either or both relations are too weak to be of interest or is not interpretable in further analysis. The idea is the same as its counterpart in discriminant analysis (Chapter 10).

$$\lambda = \prod(1 - \lambda_i) \tag{11-12a}$$

$$df = (P - K + 1)(Q - K + 1) \tag{11-12b}$$

The calculations reflect the properties of standardized variables. Relevant operations may be performed upon the corresponding variance–covariance matrices to describe the results obtained with raw (unstandardized) variables. Alternatively, once the beta weights from the X and Y canonical variables weights have been derived, Eq. (4-5) may be employed to obtain b weights. (The intercept is not needed to calculate scores on canonical variates.)

Numerical Example

To maintain the spirit of the chapter, assume that you wish to learn more about sales in the various stores. Instead of trying to group them by similar patterns of sales, the problem is to relate sales in the three categories, which constitute the X variables, to demographics of the neighborhoods in which the stores are located, the Y variables which consists of (1) per capita income, (2) average number of teen age children per family, (3) educational level for the head of the household, and (4) mean age of family head. Assume that the data are derived from 1000 "stores" in a large chain.

Table 11-3 contains the resulting correlations among the entire set of seven measures, three X variables and four Y variables. The correlations are con-

TABLE 11-3. Correlations among variables in canonical analysis[a]

	POP	CLAS	JAZZ	INC	CHI	EDUC	AGE
Popular (POP)	1.000	.388	.491	.162	.545	.083	−.254
Classical (CLAS)	.388	1.000	.822	.464	.010	.608	.052
Jazz	.491	.822	1.000	.361	.213	.440	−.022
Income (INC)	.162	.464	.361	1.000	−.259	.633	.369
Children (CHI)	.545	.010	.213	−.259	1.000	.253	−.379
Education (EDUC)	.083	.608	.440	.633	−.253	1.000	.291
Age	−.254	.052	−.022	.369	−.379	.291	1.000
Can. Var. 1 for X	.756	.897	.813	.408	.332	.472	−.085
Can. Var. 2 for X	−.651	.439	.132	.224	−.452	.421	.289
Can. Var. 1 for Y	.534	.633	.575	.577	.470	.668	−.120
Can. Var. 2 for Y	−.370	.249	.075	.395	−.796	.741	.509

[a] Popular, Classical, and Jazz denote hypothetical sales of popular, classical, and jazz records, respectively. Income (INC) denotes family income; Children (CHI) denotes average number of teen age children per family; Education (EDUC) represents the educational level of the family head, and Age represents the age of the family head. "Can. Var." denotes canonical variate.

tained in the first seven rows. The table also contains other derived statistics, which I will refer to later. View the 7×7 matrix as consisting of four sub-matrices: (1) $\mathbf{R}_{xx}$ in the first three rows and first three columns, (2) $\mathbf{R}_{xy}$ in the first three rows and last four columns, (3) $\mathbf{R}_{yx} = \mathbf{R}'_{xy}$ in the last four rows and first three columns, and (4) $\mathbf{R}_{yy}$ in the last four rows and last four columns.

Applying Eq. (11-6b) to the submatrices leads to $\mathbf{A}^*$ (you may derive $\mathbf{R}_{xx}^{-1/2}$ yourself from $\mathbf{R}_{xx}$ as an exercise):

$$\mathbf{A}^* = \begin{bmatrix} 1.149 & .057 & -.611 \\ 0.000 & 1.753 & -1.445 \\ 0.000 & 0.000 & 1.000 \end{bmatrix} \times \begin{bmatrix} .162 & .545 & .083 & -.254 \\ .463 & .010 & .608 & .052 \\ .361 & .213 & .440 & -.022 \end{bmatrix}$$

$$\times \begin{bmatrix} 1.783 & .080 & -1.011 & -.333 \\ .080 & 1.202 & -.140 & .386 \\ -1.011 & .140 & 1.695 & -.067 \\ -.333 & .386 & -.067 & 1.289 \end{bmatrix} \times \begin{bmatrix} .162 & .464 & .361 \\ .545 & .010 & .213 \\ .083 & .608 & .440 \\ -.254 & .052 & -.021 \end{bmatrix}$$

$$\times \begin{bmatrix} 1.149 & 0.000 & 0.000 \\ .057 & 1.757 & 0.000 \\ -.611 & -1.445 & 1.000 \end{bmatrix} = \begin{bmatrix} .297 & -.066 & .137 \\ -.066 & .188 & .187 \\ .137 & .187 & .336 \end{bmatrix}$$

The three eigenvectors of the matrix are .4991, .3227, and .0004 (which you may also derive as an exercise). The three canonical correlations are therefore .706 ($.4991^{1/2}$), .568, and .021. Sequential χ^2 tests applied to the eigenvalues, based on Eq. (10-13), indicated that $\mathbf{R}_{c1}$ and $\mathbf{R}_{c2}$ were both significant ($p < .001$) but $\mathbf{R}_{c3}$ was not. The matrix of beta weights for X coefficients is given by application of Eq. (11-7c), using $\mathbf{R}_{xx}^{-1/2}$ and V.

$$\mathbf{B}_x = \begin{bmatrix} 1.149 & .057 & -.702 \\ .000 & 1.757 & -1.445 \\ .000 & .000 & 1.000 \end{bmatrix} \times \begin{bmatrix} .422 & -.804 & .417 \\ .400 & .579 & .710 \\ .813 & .133 & -.566 \end{bmatrix}$$

$$= \begin{bmatrix} .485 & -.924 & .480 \\ .727 & .972 & 1.272 \\ -.023 & -.212 & -1.848 \end{bmatrix}$$

Only the first two columns of $\mathbf{B}_x$ are of interest in view of the nonsignificance of $\mathbf{R}_{c3}$. Note that canonical variate I is primarily defined by sales of classical records and secondarily by sales of popular records. Conversely, canonical variate II is a bipolar factor that contrasts sales of classical records with sales of popular records. Jazz plays little direct role in either of the two canonical functions.

The determination of $\mathbf{B}_y$ involves the application of Eq. (11-7d) and the product of $\mathbf{R}_{yy}^{-1/2}$ (which I have not shown you), $\mathbf{R}_{xy}$, $\mathbf{B}_x$, and $\lambda^{-1/2}$:

$$\mathbf{B}_y = \begin{bmatrix} 1.783 & .080 & -1.011 & -.333 \\ .080 & 1.203 & .141 & .386 \\ -1.011 & .141 & 1.694 & -.066 \\ -.333 & .386 & -.067 & 1.289 \end{bmatrix} \times \begin{bmatrix} .162 & .545 & .083 & -.254 \\ .464 & .096 & .608 & .052 \\ .361 & .213 & .440 & -.021 \end{bmatrix}$$

$$\times \begin{bmatrix} .485 & -.924 & .480 \\ .727 & .972 & 1.272 \\ -.003 & -.212 & -1.848 \end{bmatrix} \times \begin{bmatrix} 1.415 & .000 & .000 \\ .000 & 1.761 & .000 \\ .000 & .000 & 47.543 \end{bmatrix}$$

$$= \begin{bmatrix} .431 & -.279 & .296 \\ .659 & -.625 & -.590 \\ .623 & .710 & -.038 \\ -.211 & .168 & -1.097 \end{bmatrix}$$

The first column of $\mathbf{B}_y$ is primarily defined by number of children and education with income also contributing. The second is defined by high education and the relative absence of children. Putting the information together with that obtained from $\mathbf{B}_x$, the data reveal two relations: (1) large families size, better equation, and, to a slightly lesser extent, income, are associated with sales of popular and classical records, but (2) well-educated small families tend to spend their money on classical records, whereas more poorly educated larger families spend their money on popular records, independently of the first relation. The results may make some sense (I tried, since I am the one that made up the data); my experience is that real problems generally do not provide as clearly interpretable results as my example did.

One should look at the canonical structures. The correlation between the individual X variables and the optimal linear combination of X variables, $\mathbf{S}_x$, is the product of the intercorrelations among the X variables ($\mathbf{R}_{xx}$) and the canonical variable weight matrix for X ($\mathbf{B}_x$):

$$\mathbf{S}_x = \begin{bmatrix} 1.000 & .388 & .491 \\ .388 & 1.000 & .822 \\ .491 & .822 & 1.000 \end{bmatrix} \times \begin{bmatrix} .485 & -.924 & .480 \\ .727 & .972 & 1.272 \\ -.023 & -.212 & -1.848 \end{bmatrix}$$

$$= \begin{bmatrix} .756 & -.651 & .065 \\ .897 & .439 & -.061 \\ .813 & .133 & -.567 \end{bmatrix}$$

The first column of $\mathbf{S}_x$ tells us that canonical variate I can be thought of as a general sales factor as jazz correlates quite highly with it, which is unlike the inference one would draw from the canonical variable weights. There is a difference between the structure and pattern matrices because sales of jazz records correlate highly with sales of classical records. The second column of $\mathbf{S}_x$ tells pretty much the same story for canonical variate II as was told by the canonical variable weights. By analogous computations involving an appropriately chosen combination of a correlation matrix and the canonical weights for Y, which I will not present, the remaining structures are:

$$\mathbf{S}_y = \begin{bmatrix} .577 & .395 & .020 \\ .470 & -.796 & -.024 \\ .668 & .741 & -.241 \\ -.120 & .509 & -.775 \end{bmatrix}$$

$$\mathbf{S}_x(\mathbf{R}_y) = \begin{bmatrix} .534 & -.370 & .001 \\ .633 & .249 & -.001 \\ .575 & .075 & -.012 \end{bmatrix}$$

$$\mathbf{S}_y(\mathbf{R}_x) = \begin{bmatrix} .408 & .224 & .000 \\ .332 & -.452 & -.005 \\ .472 & .421 & .000 \\ -.085 & .289 & .016 \end{bmatrix}$$

The Y structure, $\mathbf{S}_y$, is fairly similar to the canonical variable weight matrix for Y, $\mathbf{B}_y$, so it adds little new information. The structure relating X variables to Y canonical variates, $\mathbf{S}_x(\mathbf{R}_y)$, tells us that the composite formed from the demographic variables predicts the three sales categories to an approximately equal extent. The complementary structure relating Y variables to X canonical variates, $\mathbf{S}_y(\mathbf{R}_x)$, tells us (1) that the variable representing the sum of popular and classical record sales (which implicitly incorporates jazz sales in the structure) relates to an approximately equal extent to income, number of children, and education and is unrelated to age, and (2) that the variable representing classical versus popular record sales is positively correlated with education and negatively correlated with number of children to an approximately equal degree. Finally, all correlations with canonical variate III are negligible which is not surprising given the trivial magnitude of $\mathbf{R}_{c3}$ (.021).

Equation (11-9a) produces $\mathbf{H}_x^2$, a diagonal matrix of h^2 values (communalities) of the X variables as determined by the canonical variates. Determination of H_x^2 is equivalent to squaring and summing rows of S_x. Rather than use all three columns, I only used two, since I retained only the first two canonical variates. The resulting values are $.995 = (.756^2 + .651^2)$, $.998 = (.897^2 + .439^2)$, and $.679 = (.813^2 + .133^2)$ for popular, classical, and jazz records. Consequently, nearly all the variance in sales of popular and classical records can be explained by the two canonical variates. In other words, the factors derived from the X variables do in fact represent major dimensions of variation in X.

The variances of the X factors are obtained from Eq. (11-9b), which is equivalent to averaging the squared sum of column entries of S_x. The X factor variances are $.679 = (.756^2 + .896^2 + .813^2)/3.$, $.211 = (-.651^2 + .439^2 + .133^2)/3.$, and $.110 = (.065^2 + .241^2 + .567^2)/3$. Collectively, canonical variates I and II therefore explain $.920 = (.679 + .211)$ of the X variance.

Results obtained from applying the corresponding Eqs. (11-9c) and (11-9d) show that the h^2 values for the Y variables, based upon the first two canonical variates, are $.484$, $.857$, $.995$, and $.273$ and that the three canonical variates explain $.253$, $.400$, and $.165$ of the total variance. Thus, income and age are less well described by the factors than are number of children and education and the Y factors are less descriptive of the Y variable set than the X factors are descriptive of the X variable set.

Further evidence that the X canonical variates are the major dimensions of variation in the X set lies in the correlation between the X factors and the principal components of X. Canonical variate I correlated $.970$ with the first principal component because both measured general sales; canonical variate II correlated $.956$ with the second principal component because both measured popular vs. classical record sales, and canonical variate III correlated $.930$ with the third principal component because both measured jazz record sales.[4]

Equation (11-5a) may be used to perform a redundancy analysis, which describes how much of the variance in record sales (X) is determinable from knowledge of demographics (Y). Thus, the first canonical variate explains $.679$ of the X variance and R_{c1}^2 is $.4991$. Hence, knowledge of the optimal linear combination of Y explains $.339$ $(.679 \times .4991)$ of the X variance. In a like manner, the second canonical variate adds an additional $.068$ to the variance in X that can be explained by Y $(.211$, the variance explained by the second canonical variate, x $.3227$, $R_{c2}^2)$. The first canonical variate on the Y side therefore accounts for the bulk of the prediction possible within X.

Conversely, results obtained from applying Eq. (11-5b) indicate that the two canonical variates on the X side $(.127)$ accounted for roughly the same proportion of the variance on the Y $(.129)$. Seeing how knowledge of demographics

---

[4] The total set of canonical variates will always explain all of the variance in data set with the smaller number of variables because they comprise a full set of components, even though they are not principal components. That is, P (3, in the example) linearly independent components will account for all the X variance. Three components will not necessarily explain all the variance in the larger Y set as there are four variables in the Y set.

predicts record sales is probably of more interest than the converse, but both sets of results here are of interest. The canonical variates reflect important dimensions of variation within each of the set, but more importantly they also reflect important dimensions of *covariation*. The importance of the canonical variates is reflected in the fact that $\mathbf{R}_{xy}$ contains several large correlations between the two sets.

The data given above in conjunction with the material of Chapter 4 allow you to use multiple regression to predict sales within the three individual categories. As is consistent with previous discussion, the prediction of popular and classical record sales from the data is slightly better than the prediction of jazz record sales ($R^2 = .422, .463,$ and $.336,$ respectively).

Alternatives to Canonical Analysis

I have previously pointed out how real world applications of canonical analysis are likely to prove disappointing, especially when X and Y are simply grab bag collections of variables. One strategy I have used is to factor the X and Y variables individually in order to make sure I understand what properties the variables I measure have in common. I prefer a hypothesis-based (confirmatory) approach to an exploratory method, but the latter is often quite satisfactory when I do not have a well-formulated model. What I then do is to replace the raw variables with factors and look at the correlations between sets of factors. This outcome is mathematically far less elegant than canonical analysis and requires several additional steps. However, it is far more likely to produce interpretable correlations as it ensures that the "new" variables (the principal components) represent the "old" (original) variables well.

This concludes the discussion of profile and canonical analysis. This chapter first considered the general question of how to describe the similarity of two profiles. It was noted that "similarity" could be defined in several ways depending on such considerations as whether differences in elevation were relevant or not. The concept of similarity was applied to a class of procedures known as *clustering*, which groups observations on the basis of their similarity. A particular form of clustering, *hierarchical clustering*, was then considered. Hierarchical clustering consists of forming successive clusters from the merger of other clusters and/or individual profiles. The final major topic of the chapter was *canonical analysis*, which consists of forming linear combinations from each of two sets of variables that correlate maximally with one another. It was noted that considerable care should be taken to prevent the model from degenerating into a multivariate "fishing expedition."

I am now ready for the final chapter which deals with the analysis of scales. That chapter will consider topics relevant to the construction of tests, inventories, and the like. There will be some new concepts, but much of the next chapter will deal with problems in applying multivariate techniques, which were derived from models based upon continuous and often normally distributed variables, to analyze individual items, which are inherently discrete and nonnormal.

12
Analysis of Scales

Chapter Overview

Chapter 12 is concerned with the statistical properties of multiitem *scales*. A distinguishing characteristic of relevant analyses is that items are typically quite *unreliable* or "noisy" in the sense of containing considerable measurement error. The situation is therefore quite different from what was considered in the discussion of multiple regression—an important but contrasting model which assumed that the predictors were reliable. As was noted in the earlier discussion, small amounts of measurement error would not seriously impair the use of the regression model, but could produce spurious results when the predictors were highly unreliable.

I will now distinguish between *multivariate analysis*, which deals with linear combinations of elements that individually are reliable, and *psychometrics*, which deals with combining individual items or elements that are themselves quite unreliable into a totality (scale) that is itself reliable.

In previous discussion of the model for factor analysis, I pointed out that it is proper to factor analyze items despite the unreliability of the items. However, I also pointed out that certain problems were present in analyses conducted at the item level that were very unlikely to occur in analyses conducted at the scale level. I will now consider some of the problems of item-level factoring.

A formal course in psychometric theory deals with the many possible ways to combine items into scales. The simplest way is through the *linear* model in which each item is assigned a weight, and the resulting scale score is a weighted linear combination of the individual item responses. Moreover, the simplest form of linear model is the special case of the *centroid* model in which the weights are all equal. The score you obtain on most essay examinations illustrates a linear model in that each item is allotted a certain number of points. Your total score is the sum of the points awarded on each item. Most objective tests illustrate the centroid model in that you get one point for each correct answer. One important consideration is that more elaborate scoring rules typically provide scale scores that are correlated almost perfectly with a score obtained from the centroid model when there is a large number of items—one more case of "it don't make no nevermind." This chapter is largely devoted to the centroid model.

I. PROPERTIES OF INDIVIDUAL ITEMS—The most important thing to keep in mind about constructing items is to *keep the wording simple*. Alternative item formats are discussed. Issues relevant to correcting for guessing are considered. It is also noted that most, but not all, situations demand that the test discriminate at all levels of the trait continuum. Consequently, it is usually desirable to have items of high, medium, and low difficulty level (on an abilities test) or endorsement probability (on a personality or attitudinal test).

Additional basic properties of individual items are presented. Many analyses are based upon the *interitem correlations*. One very important property of an item is its *trace (item operating characteristic)*. An item trace describes the score on that item as a function of the strength of the trait measured by the item. One way to obtain an item trace is to split up a group of test takers on the basis of their total scale (test) score. For example, one might divide a class into the top 10%, the second 10%, etc., based on students' scores on the test as a whole. The percentage of students passing the item within each subgroup then defines the trace.

Item traces can be described in several ways, and several different types of traces are illustrated. However, the most important property of a trace as far as the centroid model is concerned is *monotonicity*. Monotonicity is concerned with whether the trace of a given item increases as the strength of the trait increases, at least probabilistically, i.e., whether more able subjects are more likely to answer the item in question correctly than less able subjects. Given that an item has a monotone trace, two parameters of its trace are important. *Item difficulty* is the average level of performance on the item, e.g., how probable is it that an average student will get a given item on a classroom test correct. *Item discrimination* deals with the difference in performance on the item between people who are high versus low on the trait, e.g., what is the difference in probability of passing a given item on a classroom test between students in the top versus bottom quarter of the class. Item discrimination can also be indexed by the *item-total correlation*, i.e., the correlation between performance on an individual item and the scale score.

II. TEST RELIABILITY—The topic of test *reliability* is concerned with "internal" properties of a scale, in contrast with test *validity*, which deals with "external" properties, i.e., how well the scale score relates to other related measures. Two types of reliability need be distinguished: (1) *temporal stability* is concerned with how repeatable a scale is when given at two different points in time, and (2) *homogeneity* or *internal consistency* is concerned with how strongly the systematic components of individual items are related to each other, i.e., do all items "measure the same thing."

The temporal stability of a scale is usually assessed by the *test−retest method* in which the scale is administered twice to the same group of subjects at different times and the correlation between the two test results is obtained. Determining the homogeneity of a scale is more complex. Several models have been proposed to define the homogeneity, of which the *domain sampling* model is a useful example. The domain sampling model assumes that individual items are sampled randomly from an infinite domain (pool or population) of items. The *reliability index* is the correlation between the score obtained from a sample of the items and the score obtained from all items in the population. By contrast, the *reliability coefficient* is the correlation between two random samples of test items. It can be shown that the *reliability index is the square root of the reliability coefficient.* The relation is important because the reliability index describes the upper limit of correlation between a scale score and any other measure. The reliability index may be thought of as the hypothetical correlation between a "fallible" and an "infallible" measure of a trait, whereas the reliability coefficient may be thought of as the potentially obtainable correlation between two independent "fallible" measures of the same trait.

The most popular measure of the reliability coefficient is known as *Cronbach's alpha*, which may be defined as *the proportion of variance in total test scores that is due to item covariances.* Several other terms are related to the reliability coefficient. The *standard error of measurement* describes the standard deviation of obtained scores for a given trait level that arise due to the unreliability of the scale. One may use it to estimate what the true scores would be if a scale were made perfectly reliable. The *Spearman–Brown prophecy formula* allows one to estimate what the reliability of a test would be if it were lengthened or shortened by a given factor. A distinction is made between the reliability of a *scale* (collection of items that are individually of limited reliability) and the reliability of a *linear combination* of scales that possess at least some degree of reliability.

One often asks the question of how many dimensions are represented by a set of items. Factor analysis is widely used to infer such dimensionalities. I will note that many item-level factoring falsely conclude that scales are multidimensional because the analyses do not take differences in item response level and other item statistics such as item variances into account. *Difficulty* factors are largely spurious factors defined on the basis of similarity of response level (or, by extension, other statistics such as item variance) rather than content. Such factors arise because items with different response levels will correlate more poorly, in general, with each other than like items with similar response levels. Some procedures to examine the potential confounding of *statistical* and *substantive* differences among items are discussed.

III. NUMERICAL EXAMPLE I: A UNIFACTOR SCALE—An example of a set of 20 items presumably measuring a single factor is presented.

IV. NUMERICAL EXAMPLE II: A TWO-FACTOR SCALE—An example of a scale intended to measure two factors is presented.

V. TEST VALIDITY—Three traditional forms of validity are discussed: (1) *criterion validity* deals with how well a scale predicts a specified external variable (criterion), (2) *content validity* deals with how well items were sampled from a given domain, and (3) *construct validity* deals with how well a scale fulfills properties ascribed to it by a relevant theory. Two aspects of construct validity are *convergent validity* which reflects how well a measure correlates with related measures and *divergent validity* which indicates how well the measure can discriminate among groups known to differ with respect to the underlying trait.

Many people think of the three types of validity as constituting three separate meanings. A more recent trend is to view the three terms as relating to a single concept; specifically, criterion validity and content validity are now commonly viewed as simply being part of the concept of construct validity. Test validation is not only an important academic topic; it has legal ramifications as well. If members of protected minorities, i.e., females, blacks, hispanics, orientals, or native Americans, perform less well as a group than white males on an employment test, the test must be shown to meet one of the definitions of validity. If a test cannot be shown to be valid and the test discriminates against a protected minority, costly legal repercussions may ensue.

The reliability of a test sets a limit upon its validity, although the failure of the underlying trait to predict the criterion usually imposes a much stronger limit. It is possible to estimate what the validity of a test would be if its reliability were altered—the *correction for attenuation*.

The last chapter will contain considerable information that is conceptually new. Much of it will be devoted to special problems that arise when analyses of the type discussed previously are conducted on items designed to measure attitudes, traits, and the like. The problems reflect, in large part, the issue of range restriction discussed back in the early chapters of this book. For a simple example, suppose you have two binary items, one of which is answered "yes" 50% of the time and the other is answered "yes" only 10% of the time. The difference in probability of endorsement will have a dramatic effect upon the correlation between the two items even when the underlying traits being tapped may be highly similar. Examples of two such items are "I eat chocolate ice cream at least once a week," and "I eat chocolate ice cream at least four times a week."

The difference between the material covered by a text in psychometric theory and a text in multivariate analysis is not sharp and there actually is much overlap. One important distinction may be made, however. A basic assumption to regression analysis is that the predictors are individually *reliable*—that which a variable measures is measured consistently, though not necessarily *validly*. (See the assumptions underlying multiple regression in Chapter 4, particularly those made concerning *predictors*.) Psychometric theory, on the other hand, can be viewed as dealing with problems of constructing a reliable *scale* from unreliable *items*.

I will use the term "item" to denote measurement of a specific bit of behavior and the term "scale" to denote a score derived from a set of items. The terms "scale" and "test" will be used interchangeably in this chapter. I will use the term "battery" to denote a set of scales, such as those on the MMPI.

In most real-world application, a scale score is derived from scores on individual items by means of a weighted sum, and the scale is therefore a linear combination of items. The resulting scale score may be thought of as the outcome of a particular psychometric model, the *linear* model. Moreover, in most cases, items are weighted equally, an important special case called the *centroid* model. I will devote nearly all discussion to the linear model and the special case of the centroid model because these models are the two most commonly used ones, but I will also breifly discuss some nonlinear scoring methods.

Properties of Individual Items

The distinction between individual items and scales parallels that commonly made between *molecular* and *molar* analyses. A single item involves a relatively discrete observation such as the response to "I plan to buy an automobile in the next year," "What is the square root of 25?," or "I am prone to migraine headaches." A scale, in contrast, involves aggregating scores from two or more items.

The reason for making a distinction between items and scales was elegantly stated by Lucy Van Pelt, nemesis of Charlie Brown in the comic strip *Peanuts*. Lucy asserted that "Individually, these five fingers mean nothing; put them together and you get a fighting force fearsome to behold." Applying her idea to psychometrics: responses to individual items on surveys, aptitude tests, or personality inventories often tell you very little about an individual, whereas the scale score that results may tell you a great deal.

As an example,[1] Item 45 of the MMPI is "I sleep fitfully." If a person endorses Item 45, he or she has one point added to his or her raw score on Scale 1, Hypochondriasis. This item belongs to the scale because it has previously been empirically determined that hypochondriacs, individuals that are inclined to exaggerate their ill health, are more likely to answer this question affirmatively than normals. This trend is fairly demonstrable. Nonetheless, many people who would be considered normal by any criteria including a normal score on the scale as a whole, may endorse this particular item, perhaps because they need a new mattress or roomate or they just misread the item in question. Similarly, many hypochondriacs reject the item, perhaps feeling that their fatal disease of the moment allows them to fall asleep easily. You can construct many such items for a target population of interest to endorse that will make the scale as a whole quite informative relative to individual items.

---

[1] I have slightly altered the wording of MMPI items because of copyright considerations.

The fact that responses to individual items are determined by a multiplicity of factors does not mean that you should never pay attention to them; it only means that you should consider the possibility of spurious factors. If I were using the MMPI to evaluate a person's suitability for work as a police officer and that person endorsed Item 205 which, again paraphrased, is "Sometimes I cannot help but steal things that belong to others," rest assured that I would want to follow up on that response.

There are two basic statistical properties of items to discuss: (1) item distributions, and (2) the relation of items to the scale as a whole, including, but not limited to their *traces* (also called *item operating characteristics*), a concept I will define shortly. Later, I will consider concepts such as *interitem correlations* and *reliability* which may be derived from more basic concepts, most specifically, the formula for the variance of a sum, Eq. (3-6).

Item Formats and Scoring

I would be remiss if I failed to mention a basic pragmatic point of item construction: *Keep its wording simple.* I have seen otherwise elegant psychometric analyses yield nothing because the items on the scale were so poorly phrased. One particular tendency I see among people who make up surveys is to construct long, convoluted items because they think that more useful results can be obtained with more precise wording. What usually happens is that nobody save the survey constructor can understand the real meaning of these items. Nunnally (1978), Hopkins and Stanley (1981), and Guilford (1954) are good sources for further information on item construction.

When making up multiple choice tests, such as classroom examinations, avoid giving out information about which alternative is correct by making its length consistently shorter or longer than the fillers (distractors). I also suggest that you do not include alternative like "All of the above," "None of the above," and, most of all, "(a) and (b) but not (c)." The ideal behind a multiple choice item is to have the test-taker identify which alternative is most nearly true. In some cases, truth is unequivocal—Abraham Lincoln was President during the Civil War and not Millard Fillmore. However, in a great many other cases, you are attempting to summarize generalities succinctly. A question with a "None of the above" or the like is really a double question—which alternative is most true *and* are any of the alternatives true. If you cannot think of enough simple alternatives (four as a rule), ask another question.

Correction for Guessing

For a long time, multiple choice tests often employed a correction for guessing by subtracting a fraction of the number of answers wrong from the number of correct answers, commonly $1/K$, where K is the number of alternatives. The idea was to eliminate the effect of "lucky guesses."

I find two problems with corrections for guessing and much prefer the simpler approach of telling people to answer all the items without penalty for wrong answers. One problem is that a person's willingness to risk a response becomes a variable apart from the skill being tested. The second is that the assumption assumes that subjects either know the item or guess at random. Everyone's own life experience speaks to the contrary. It is very rare that a person knows so little that he or she cannot correctly eliminate at least one alternative—guessing may occur but it is not completely blind. Consequently, the standard correction for guessing formula is predicated upon a rather naive model of guessing. Thus, simply make the test sufficiently long to separate those who are simply relying upon test taking strategies from those who know the material.

Item Distributions

An item distribution is simply a distribution of scores for a particular item. One point in favor of a binary scoring system is that a single measure can summarize all relevant properties of item distributions. That is, the proportion of people who answer the item in the keyed direction (a generic term that covers answering the question correctly in an abilities type of test) or *response level* also specifies the variability in response over subjects, the skewness, etc. This useful property of binary items is not the only consideration in deciding how to score items, though. Allowing partial credit on short ability types of tests (such as a typical essay examination with a relatively small number of items) or allowing the subject to express *degrees* of acceptance or rejection on attitudinal questions, can often provide even more useful data in many situations.

The point to note here is that a given item taps only a limited region of the underlying trait being measured, even when there are more than two responses available. Questions answered in the keyed direction a high percentage of the time (items with high response levels) discriminate people who are very low in the trait from the remainder of the population; questions with response levels of roughly .5 (assuming the items are dichotomous) discriminate the top from the bottom halves; and questions with low response levels discriminate people high in the trait from the remainder of the population.

You should let the objective of the test dictate the kinds of item distributions that are most desirable. Perhaps in the majority of cases, you will be interested in making discriminations throughout the trait continuum. In a typical class-room test, for example, you normally want at least some easy items to help separate D and F students and at least some difficult items to help separate A and B students. A scale consisting of items with varied response levels is called an *equidiscriminating test*. On the other hand, some circumstances dictate limiting response levels to a narrow range. The written test for the driver's license really needs identify only those people who are very ignorant of the law. It is doubtful that inclusion of, say items which tap literal memory of the state traffic law would produce better drivers. Hence, it is reasonable that a typical item on a written driver's license test be answered correctly by most, if not nearly all, test takers. Conversely, to the extent that tests like the MMPI are aimed at the identification of people who are at least moderately deviant, it is reasonable that most MMPI items consist of symptoms that are infrequently endorsed, which is essentially the case in reality.

Item distributions will influence scale score distributions. Scales comprised of items with low response levels will be positively skewed, whereas scales consisting of items with response levels near the midpoint of the range of response levels, i.e., .5 for binary items or equidiscriminating tests, will tend to have more symmetric distributions. However, the fact that items are imperfectly correlated means that the distribution of scale scores will tend to be more normally distributed than will individual item distributions. *Distribution of scale scores are not necessarily normally distributed and they often should not be. The presence of independent and random error in individual items is an influence (via the central limit theorem) toward normality. However, as I discussed in Chapter 2, there are other factors such as item intercorrelations and item distributions which lead the distribution away from normality.*[2]

Relation of Items to the Scale as a Whole

The item trace or item operating characteristic is the relation between that item and the underlying trait being measured. Figure 12-1 contains some different types of traces, which I will use to illustrate the importance of this concept.

Item traces can be obtained in several different ways depending on how one measures a given trait. Most commonly, it is defined as the score on the test as a whole. Assume that you had 1000 people take a test of cognitive ability (intelligence), consisting of a series of multiple choice items. You first compute the percentage of people passing the item, $P(c)$, among the lowest scoring 100. Then, repeat the process for the next lowest scoring group of 100, etc., until you have obtained $P(c)$ for each of the 10 subgroups. An alternative scoring method is to form blocks based on equal scale score units. For example you might form the bottom group of those scoring 2.0 z-score units or more below the mean, the next group of those scoring between -1.5 and -2.0 units, etc. Using this method will result in unequal numbers of people in each of the

---

[2] For example, MMPI scale scores are positively skewed, reflecting in large part the fact that answering its constituent items is largely admission of a symptom and is atypical, by definition. There is absolutely nothing wrong with scales just because they are skewed. However, scales that count the number of symptom admissions inherently are poor at discriminating among normals unless most of the symptoms are very common. Similarly, the written part of driver's license examinations does not discriminate the skills necessary for competitive driving or those needed by people like police officers from the average driver. The inherently *psychometric* limitation imposed by the rarity of many of the symptoms is one reason why many attempts at finding out characteristics of low scorers on MMPI scales have come to naught.

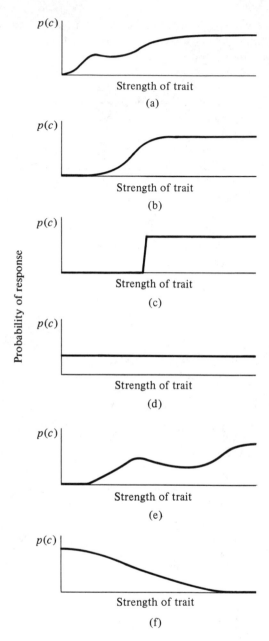

FIGURE 12-1. Theoretical item traces: (a) monotone ascending trace; (b) ogival trace; (c) deterministic trace; (d) nondiscriminating trace; (e) nonmonotone trace; (f) monotone descending trace.

groups. Still a third possibility is to define the trait externally to the particular scale. For example, you might define intelligence on the basis of an individually administered intelligence test. In all cases, the item trace will be defined by the percentage of people within each successive group passing that given item. Regardless of how the trait level is defined, fairly large samples are needed to obtain stable estimates of item traces.

Panel (a) of Fig. 12-1 tells you that the more ability one possesses, the more likely he or she is to pass the item, i.e., the item is *monotone ascending*. The linear model of test scoring, and, consequently, the special case of the centroid model, assume that items on the scale are monotone ascending, but that is all the models assume.

Panel (b) illustrates an *ogive* trace. Several statistical functions may give rise to ogives. Two of the most important are the *cumulative normal function* and the *logistic function*. (One could not tell the difference between the two forms of ogives visually.) Certain scaling models, generically known as *item response theory (IRT)* or *item trace models* (cf. Hulin, Drasgow, & Parsons, 1983; Thissen, 1982; Thissen, Steinberg, & Gerrard, 1986) capitalize upon properties of ogives. Specifically, the Rasch (1966a, 1966b; Lord & Novick, 1968) model assumes that items have logistic traces. Scales derived from ogival models have the property that one can compare scores of two individuals who answered totally different sets of items. Such models can be quite useful when you wish to test someone repeatedly and do not want their memory for specific items to influence the results. The basic idea underlying the model is that a value can be attached to each item based upon its trace—items with higher response level are given higher values. The values associated with the items evoking positive response are then used to estimate the scale score. It is not simply the *number* of items endorsed, but rather the *pattern* of endorsement that is critical for these models.[3]

Panel (c) illustrates a *deterministic trace*. A certain amount of ability, or threshold, is needed to pass the item. If your ability is below that threshold you are certain to fail that item, and if your ability is above that threshold,

---

[3] It is not uncommon for a scale that is acceptable by the standards of a linear model to be unacceptable when evaluated by IRT criteria. Thissen et al. (1986) provide an illustrative critique. However, Thissen et al.'s critique implies that a test which meets linear model standards but does not meet the standards of his particular IRT model is unacceptable. I do not agree with that position. Tests that meet the assumptions of various IRT models (some of which are more restrictive than his, others are less restrictive) have certain desirable properties. One such property is that it is possible to obtain a meaningful comparison between two people who answer totally different sets of items from the test. However, as long as that property is not necessary, e.g., as long as the two people answer the same set of items, a test that simply meets the linear model is quite satisfactory. In other words, I do not agree that it is proper to criticize a test that is constructed according to a fairly general model by applying the standards of a more restrictive model whose assumptions are not necessary to the use of the test. (This point is not intended as an endorsement of the particular test they criticized which may not meet linear model assumptions.)

you are certain to pass that item. A once-popular model called the *Guttman scale* employs items with deterministic traces. Because items with truly deterministic traces are practically never encountered, it is no longer favored by most psychometricians and has been replaced by ogival item response models.

Panel (d) illustrates an item that does not discriminate—people have the same probability of passing the item regardless of their ability level. Although it might technically be called "monotone," since it does not concave down, I will not consider a flat trace to be "monotone" because it has no useful psychometric property in scale construction. The general procedure of examining the relation between items and total score or *item analysis* typically reveals many such items in preliminary drafts of the tests.

Panel (e) illustrates a *nonmonotone* item. Such items imply that you can know too much to answer the item correctly. When a nonmonotone item occurs in a multiple choice test of cognitive ability, it indicates that one or more distractors is chosen with disproportionate frequency among the most able students. Such an item should be replaced or at least reworded. The reason is not the same as the arguments one gives to a teacher that alternative (c) is just as correct as alternative (d)—the criterion is empirical.[4]

Nonmonotonicity occurs regularly in attitudinal items, however. For example, consider an item like "We can handle the college expenses by having the government make low interest loans more available." Conservative students will probably reject the item because they oppose federal aid to education. On the other hand, liberal students would tend to believe in having the government subsidize college educations directly instead of in the form of loans. Thus, people at both poles are likely to reject the item but for completely different reasons.

Finally, panel (f) illustrates a *descending monotone item*. In most applications, such items simply reflect miskeying and may be made ascending monotone by reversing the direction of scoring.

Given that an item is monotone, there are two additional properties to consider: (1) its *response level* and (2) its *discriminatory capacity*. I have previously defined the response level, which is also known as the *difficulty level* in the context of ability tests. It may be summarized by the mean [or $P(c)$ if it is in binary format]. Thus, if an item on an anxiety scale were to be endorsed by 20% of the normative sample, it would have a response level of .2.

The discriminatory capacity of an item measures the extent to which it differentiates people high versus low on the trait. One way to define the discriminatory capacity is through the correlation of the item with the scale score or *item-total correlation*. Sometimes the item-total correlation is computed by deleting the score of the particular item from the total scale score in order to correct for the fact that the item itself also contributes to the total;

---

[4] In a great many cases, the nonmonotonicity may simply be due to sampling error so little "jiggles" in the trace can usually be ignored.

in other cases the correction is not made. If the scale consists of a large number of items, the correction will have little effect. I will denote the uncorrected item-total correlation as $r(u)$ and the corrected item-total correlation as $r(c)$. A third measure of the discriminatory capacity of an item is its loading on the first PC (b) of an item-level factor analysis, assuming the items measure only one factor.

Typically, item-total correlations are in the .3 to .4 range, at best, if the scale is at least of moderate length. The low correlations are just another instance of the fallibility of individual items.

Numerical Example

I took four items from Scale 2 (Depression or D) of the MMPI and obtained item traces from a sample of 1035 prison inmates placed into five groups on the basis of their total score. Hence, the group sizes are roughly 200 each (the sizes are not exactly equal because of some ties in total score). Group 1 had the lowest total score on Scale 2, i.e., was least depressed, and group 5 had the highest total score. The traces, as well as other statistics I am going to present are derived from real data.

I chose four items for demonstration purposes: #189 ("I feel weak quite often"), #248 ("Even thought there may be no reason, I sometimes feel excitedly happy"), #271 ("I do not blame people for taking advantage of a person who asks to be taken advantage of"), and #285 ("I occasionally like to hear dirty jokes"). Item 189 is keyed so that a "Yes" response reflects presence of the trait, i.e., is "correct," and items 248, 271, and 285 are keyed so that a "No" response reflects presence of the trait. Figure 12-2 contains the four traces.

Note that all four traces are essentially monotone—the slight dip in item 271 between groups 2 and 3 is within the limits of sampling error. The monotonicity indicates that the items fulfill the basic requirement of the centroid model used to score the scale. Note further that (1) items 271 and 248 (open square and circle) are at a higher level than items 285 and 189 (filled square and circle) and (2) items 248 and 189 (open and filled circle, respectively) have item traces that slope more steeply upward than do items 271 and 285 (open and filled square, respectively). The first finding indicates that the symptoms tapped by items 271 and 248 are more common than the symptoms tapped by items 285 and 189. The mean levels of the four items (.785, .568, .204, and .068, respectively) summarize their differences in response level. On the other hand, items 248 and 189 are more discriminating (at least for this particular population) with respect to depression. Their respective item-total correlations are .336 and .412, whereas the item-total correlations for items 271 and 285 are .224 and .242. In fact, the item-total correlation for item 189 was the highest of any of the 60 items which comprise the MMPI Depression scale.

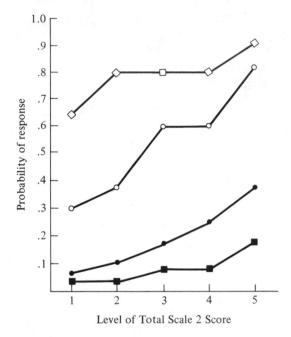

FIGURE 12-2. Traces for four actual MMPI items. Filled circle (●) = item 189; open circle (○) = item 248; filled square (■) = item 285; and open square (□) = item 271.

Test Reliability

The concept of test reliability deals generically with the alternative scale scores that are possible. Specifically, when one obtains a given scale score, one should consider that the score might have been different had (1) the test been taken at a different time, and (2) the test consisted of similar but slightly different items. The first concept is that of *temporal stability*, and the second is that of *internal consistency* as it relates to the degree to which items measure the same underlying trait. A synonym for internal consistency is *item homogeneity*.[5]

Certain measures are highly stable over time, such as those based upon knowledge of factual information obtained from adults. Still others vary widely over time. Measures of mood are a good example. One simple way to determine the temporal stability of a test or scale is to administer the same test twice to a suitably defined sample at two different times and correlate the results. This procedure is known as the *test–retest method*. Sometimes, you wish to extend the method to include several time periods since the correlation

---

[5] Some authors define the homogeneity of a scale in terms of its internal consistency *and* its dimensionality, in the factor analytic sense. I will not do so here. I will show you later that much of the evidence for the factorial complexity of scales is spurious.

between the two test results usually diminishes with the length of time separating the two test administrations.

The test–retest method is not suitable when memory of the content of the test is likely to influence the outcome of the second test. In some cases, it is possible to construct *parallel forms* of the test. Parallel forms imply that items on the two forms have equivalent internal consistencies. It is often fairly simple to construct parallel forms for tests of cognitive ability that consist of items like "How much is 34 times 14" and "How much is 27 times 19." These two items are probably tapping the same arithmatical ability so they can be randomly assigned to alternate forms. An experimental design nicety is to administer the alternate forms at random on the first testing so that half the subjects receive form "*A*" and half receive form "*B*." On retesting, those subjects given form "*A*" at the first time would receive form "*B*" at the second time and vice versa. Using this method, differences among the tests upon simultaneous administration can also be examined as a consequence.

The Logic of Internal Consistency Measures

Deriving the formulas necessary for specification of internal consistency is a bit more complicated to describe. It requires discussion of an appropriate model that is more specific than the linear or centroid models. Fortunately, the model provides a variety of useful deductions which go beyond the specification of internal consistency.

The Domain Sampling Model

One popular approach to the study of internal consistency is known as the *domain sampling model*. It assumes that items are sampled at random from a certain domain or universe. In some situations this ideal state can be achieved or at least closely approximated. For example, consider a test that contains of a series of addition problems involving pairs of five-digit numbers. The number of distinct problems is finite rather than infinite, as the model demands, but is sufficiently large—99999^2 to fit the assumption in a satisfactory manner.

Assume that a series of tests is to be constructed. Each test is made up of one or more items, but all tests have the same number of items (k). Hence, a subject can receive a score ranging from 0 to k each time he or she takes the test. Assume that there is no direct relation between test results, i.e., there are no practice effects so that each observation can be viewed as being drawn from a population of measures defined by the domain.

Subjects are unlikely to get identical scores each time they take the test. However, if the tests measure something in common, a subject who does well on one testing will probably do well on others. Likewise, a subject who does poorly on one testing will probably do poorly on others. One subject's successive scores may be 9, 8, 9, 9, 10, 7, ..., and another's may be 3, 4, 2, 2, 3, 4, ...

Consider the correlation between a given pair of tests, say the third test everyone takes and the ninth. There is nothing "special" about this particular pair of trials. Although the correlation across subjects on the two trials will differ from a like correlation obtained between the fourth trial and the sixth, it will only differ by chance. That correlation, or that between any other pair of tests can serve as an estimate of internal consistency, called the *reliability coefficient*. I will symbolize the reliability coefficient as "r_{xx}" to denote that it is the correlation between two individual tests, each of which is denoted x, and which differ only randomly.

One can obtain a second measure of reliability from the data by correlating the score on a given trial with the *total* (or the average, it does not matter) on all tests taken. This correlation is called the *reliability index*. I will symbolize the reliability index as r_{xt} to denote that it is the correlation between an individual test (x) and a total score (t). The reliability index will generally be larger in magnitude than the reliability coefficient for one very crucial reason—t is mathematically a more stable measure than x is for the same reason that the sum of any set of items (scale score) is more stable than an individual item score. The quantity t "averages out" the peculiarities of individual tests.

One very dramatic finding is that there is a simple relation between r_{xx} and r_{xt}, as given in Eqs. (12-1):

$$r_{xt} = r_{xx}^{1/2} \tag{12-1a}$$

$$r_{xx} = r_{xt}^2 \tag{12-1b}$$

The relation between the reliability coefficient and the reliability index is important because r_{xt} is an upper limit imposed by heterogeneity of content (unreliability) on validity (the correlation between test x and *any* other external variable). Hence, if r_{xx} is estimated to be .64, test x cannot correlate any higher than .8 with another test.[6]

Computing r_{xx} and Cronbach's Alpha

Obviously, one cannot sit around and administer an infinite number of tests nor expect that there is no practice effect. Hence, what is needed is a pragmatic formula, of which there are several, most of which were rendered obsolete by the availability of computers.[7] Nowadays, the most widely used way to estimate r_{xx} is through Cronbach's (1951) *alpha* measure.

The formula for Cronbach's alpha is given by Eq. (12-2). The symbol r_{xx} in Eq. (12-2) denotes the Cronbach alpha estimate of the reliability coefficient.

---

[6] It may seem surprising that test x can theoretically correlate .8 with another variable when the meaning of r_{xx} is the correlation of a test with a parallel form. The reason is that the other test can measure the same ability but more reliably. One way the test can correlate more highly with another test than with "itself" is for the other test to contain more items of the same nature.

[7] The method I am describing is implemented in SPSSX's RELIABILITY routine. Unfortunately, SAS does not have a comparable procedure even though relevant quantities can be readily programmed by PROC MATRIX.

There are other ways to define r_{xx} but I will not present them because nearly all are simply special cases or approximations that were popular before the advent of computers. Coefficient alpha is a function of the number of items on the test (K), the variance in total test scores over subjects, S^2, and the sum of the variances of individual items, $\sum s^2$.

$$r_{xx} = \frac{K(S^2 - \sum s^2)}{(K - 1)S^2}$$

$$= \frac{K[S(C) - S(D)]}{(K - 1)S(C)}$$

$$= \frac{K[S(D) - K]}{(K - 1)S(D)} \tag{12-2}$$

An alternative way to state the formula is a bit more edifying. Let $S(C)$ denote the sum of the elements of the variance–covariance matrix among items, **C**. It can be obtained from the relation $\mathbf{1'C1}$ where **1** is a unit matrix of order $K \times 1$. Similarly, let $S(D)$ be the sum of the diagonal elements of **C**. Equation (12-2) defines r_{xx} in terms of $S(C)$, $S(D)$, and K. Note that $S(C)$ equals the sum of variance in total test scores. Hence, it equals the sum of the item variances and twice the sum of the item covariances by Eq. (3-6b). Subtracting $S(D)$ from $S(C)$ simply leaves the item covariances. Ignoring the fraction $K/(K - 1)$, which is derived from the degrees of freedom and will be close to 1.0 in most cases, one can see that Cronbach's alpha equals *the fraction of variance in total test scores that is due to item covariances.* Coefficient alpha provides an additional instance in which an r^2-like variable (r_{xx} equals r_{xt}^2) is the ratio of true variance (variances shared by items) to total variance.

Numerical Example

In order to demonstrate the calculation of r_{xx} in the context of a problem with real data and maintain continuity throughout my discussion, I computed the reliability of scale L of the MMPI which consists of 15 items, all of which are keyed "false." The scale measures a person's naive defensiveness or lack of willingness to admit to even the most minor of flaws. Questions on the L scale are like "I occasionally use dirty words" or "Sometimes I get mad at people." Quite possibly there are a few individuals who never even said "Gosh," but the most plausible explanation for people who do not admit to any of the 15 Scale L items is that they are trying to put one over on the person administering the test rather than being candidate for sainthood.

Table 12-1 contains the basic data—the variance–covariance matrix among items. To keep the table compact, I have omitted the leading decimal point. The data are derived from 275 people who took the MMPI prior to seeking psychotherapy.

The sum of all 15^2 variances and covariances, $S(C)$, is 4.8937 and the sum

TABLE 12-1. Variance–covariance matrix of MMPI scale L items

248	020	035	−001	004	020	011
020	098	032	002	012	006	021
035	032	224	−001	−005	025	009
−001	002	−001	014	003	002	001
004	001	−005	003	025	−003	018
020	006	025	002	−003	098	021
011	021	009	001	018	021	135
010	030	020	000	011	033	030
045	−005	−006	000	−004	002	012
−008	012	000	−001	006	005	011
034	012	037	003	−003	026	015
191	022	021	002	000	008	013
020	038	044	005	010	031	045
033	004	021	008	−005	016	005
−007	−005	002	−001	−001	005	000

of the diagonal entries, $S(D)$, is 2.1291. Hence, r_{xx} is $15(4.8937 − 2.1291)/[(15 − 1)4.8937] = .605$. Taking the square root of r_{xx}, one can derive the r_{xt} (.778), which estimates the maximum correlation possible with an external criterion, i.e., the reliability index.

It is also possible to compute r_{xx} from the correlation matrix, $\mathbf{R}$, instead of the variance–covariance matrix, $\mathbf{C}$. The two estimates of r_{xx} will differ because the one obtained from $\mathbf{C}$ incorporates differences in item variance and the one obtained from $\mathbf{R}$ rescales each item to equal variance. A slight computational simplification is possible when r_{xx} is obtained from $\mathbf{R}$ since the equivalent of $S(D)$, the sum of the diagonal elements, is K—each of K values of r_{ii} being 1.0. Denoting the sum of the diagonal elements of $\mathbf{R}$ as $S(R)$, the resulting formula is given by Eq. (12-2c). The reliability obtained from $\mathbf{C}$ is .596. The similarity of the reliability coefficients obtained from $\mathbf{R}$ and from $\mathbf{C}$ reflects the tendency for items with larger variance (items about which subjects differ most) to also have the largest item to total correlations. Because item variances are typically quite similar to each other, I usually find little difference in r_{xx} obtained from $\mathbf{C}$ vs. r_{xx} obtained from $\mathbf{R}$.

Values of r_{xx} obtained from item analyses are standard output of the computer packages used in Educational Psychology to score classroom tests, among other applications (the programs stand alone and are unrelated to SAS, SPSSX, etc.). Often overlooked is the application of Cronbach's alpha to situations in which the data are not questionnaires. Specifically, suppose you had designed a study involving ratings of a series of subjects by three or more judges. Commonly people report the average intercorrelation among the judges, which underestimates the true reliability of scores derived from averaging the raters because the average only considers raters taken two at a time and not all at once. Coefficient alpha is one appropriate device to infer the interjudge reliability in such situations. In this case, however, I do recommend looking at values of r_{xx} obtained from $\mathbf{C}$ and $\mathbf{R}$ separately. It is not uncommon

010	045	−008	038	019	020	033	−008
029	−005	012	012	022	038	004	−005
020	006	−000	037	021	044	021	002
000	000	000	003	002	005	008	−001
011	−004	006	−002	000	010	−005	−001
033	002	005	026	008	032	016	005
030	012	011	015	013	045	005	000
246	027	020	023	028	034	018	−004
027	190	014	029	030	025	010	−008
020	014	052	008	004	008	010	001
023	029	008	250	011	035	020	−004
027	030	004	011	114	035	008	−002
034	025	008	035	035	143	021	000
018	010	010	020	008	021	245	002
−004	−008	001	−004	−002	000	002	039

to find mean ratings dominated by one rater who is inclined to use the extremes of the rating scale more often than the other judges. If that rater is responding to the same aspects of the stimuli as the others, it is appropriate to add the raw score ratings. However, if that judge is also ideosyncratic, the reliability of the sum will be attentuated. In the latter case, you often can increase the overall relability by converting each raters' raw data to z-scores and thereby weight them equally. Also, note that in any circumstance where K is small, the ratio of K to $(K - 1)$ can differ from 1.0 by more than a trivial amount.

The Standard Error of Measurement

The domain sampling model assumes that other observed scale scores are possible due to the sampling error inherent in item selection. The standard deviation of all possible outcomes is known as the *standard error of measurement* (s_{meas}). The logic in obtaining it involves attempting to predict the total score t from x and the concept is just a special case of the standard error of estimate defined in Eqs. (2-17c) and (2-17d) for z-score and raw-score forms, respectively. The true score, t, is the criterion estimated from x; hence, the correlation term used is r_{xt}. Equations (12-3a) and (12-3b) describe how one may obtain the standard error of measurement in the z-score and raw-score cases, respectively. Because of the square root relation between r_{xx}, which is normally the quantity one obtains, and r_{xt}, the more usual forms are given in Eqs. (12-3c) and (12-3d).

$$s_{meas} = (1 - r_{xt}^2)^{1/2} \qquad \text{(z-score form)} \qquad (12\text{-}3a)$$

$$s_{meas} = s_x(1 - r_{xt}^2)^{1/2} \qquad \text{(raw-score form)} \qquad (12\text{-}3b)$$

$$s_{meas} = (1 - r_{xx})^{1/2} \qquad \text{(z-score form)} \qquad (12\text{-}3c)$$

$$s_{meas} = s_x(1 - r_{xx})^{1/2} \qquad \text{(raw-score form)} \qquad (12\text{-}3d)$$

In the present case, s_x equals $C(S)^{1/2}$ or 4.8937. Hence, the standard error of measurement in z-score units is $(1 - .605)^{1/2}$ or .63 and 1.39 in raw score units. You can obtain a 95% two-tailed confidence interval by multiplying the standard error of measurement by 1.96, i.e., the interval is $r_{xx} \pm 1.96s_{meas}$. In a like manner, any other value of z may be chosen to obtain other degrees of confidence.

In many ways, the raw score form of the standard error of measurement is a more useful index of reliability than coefficient alpha is. Workers in the physical sciences are accustomed to describing the repeatability of measures in terms of their *tolerance*, or range of possible outcomes rather than as a correlation. In addition, the raw-score standard error of measurement tends to remain relatively stable across populations that differ in variability whereas r_{xx} will be heavily influenced by changes in variance. The effects of differences in variability are offset by the joint presence of s_x and r_{xx}. At the same time, r_{xx} is important in other mathematical respects to be described.

Estimating What True Scores Would Be in the Absence of Unreliability

Obtained scores contain sampling error which reflect the particular items chosen to assess a given trait. It is possible to estimate t, the score you would obtain if you could include every item from the domain in the test. However, your estimation of t is subject to the effects of regression toward the mean; a person whose obtained score x is above the mean probably has a value of t that is less than x but still above the mean, and vice versa for a person whose obtained score is below the mean. Equation 12-4 provides the estimated t score (t') in terms of r_{xx}, the mean of t ($\bar{t}$), the mean of x ($\bar{x}$), and x itself. One may let $\bar{t}$ be any convenient value, typically equal to $\bar{x}$, which I will do.

$$t' = r_{xx}(x - \bar{x}) + \bar{t} \qquad (12\text{-}4)$$

The value I obtained for $\bar{x}$ on scale L was 5.24 for the patient sample, in which r_{xx} was .605. Assume that a particular patient obtained a score of 8 on the scale. The estimate of the individual's score on a perfectly reliable scale, i.e., one based on all questions in the domain instead of the chosen 15, is $.605(8 - 5.24) + 5.24$ or 6.91 (assuming that true scores are normed to the same mean of 5.24 as the obtained scores). Note that confidence intervals obtained from the standard error of measurement should be placed symmetrically around the estimated true score ($t = 6.91$) instead of the observed score ($x = 8$).

Effects of Changes in Test Length

One of the fallouts of the domain sampling model is what is known as the *Spearman–Brown Prophecy formula*. This formula predicts how lengthening or shortening of a scale by inclusion or exclusion of items from the same domain will affect the scale's reliability. The formula is given as Eq. (12-5a), where r_{pp} is the reliability of a test that is increased by a factor of P relative to a test of given length whose r_{xx} is known.

$$r_{pp} = \frac{Pr_{xx}}{1 + (P - 1)r_{xx}} \tag{12-5a}$$

$$P = \frac{r_{pp}(1 - r_{xx})}{r_{xx}(1 - r_{pp})} \tag{12-5b}$$

Alternatively you may start with a given value of r_{xx} and wish to find out how much the test length must be changed to achieve a desired value of r_{pp}. The formula may be derived from (12-5a) by solving for P, and the result is given as Eq. (12-5b).

Thus, if one wished to triple scale L's length to 45 items, its new reliability would be $(3 \times .605)/[1. + (3 - 1).605] = .821$. Similarly, if one wished to ask by what factor the test would have to be lengthed to produce a r_{xx} of .90, the answer is $.90 \times (1 - .605)/[.605 \times (1 - .90)] = 5.87$, i.e., it would have to be increased by a factor of nearly 6. The formula assumes that the added or deleted items differ only randomly from the items already in the scale. The accuracy of the "prophecy" depends very much on the accuracy of the domain sampling. Stated another way, it depends upon your ability to generate additional items from the same content domain. In many tests of cognitive ability, you will literally be adding or deleting items at random as you attempt to alter the reliability of your test.

In most personality and educational testing situations, however, items within a scale will be fairly heterogeneous so that the model is probably far less applicable. When you shorten the test, you should delete the worst items so that the effects of shortening will be less drastic than predicted. Conversely, it is very likely that you have exhausted the best items in constructing the test so you may not be able find many additional items to increase the reliability of your test as well as the model predicts.

You may wish to play around with the formula. Note that it obeys the law of diminishing return: adding successive groups of P items has progressively less effect upon r_{xx}. Likewise, it is more difficult to make an already reliable scale more reliable than to make a test with an initially modest reliability more reliable.

Reliability of a Linear Combination of Tests (Scales)

Coefficient alpha's role is to compute the reliability of a composite measure from items which may be thought of as individually possessing little reliability. A rather different operation is to form linear combinations from scales (tests) where each scale has a determinable reliability. For example, it is natural to think of someone whose verbal SAT score exceeds his or her quantitative score as a "Liberal Arts type" and the converse as a "Science/Engineering type."

One's location along the bipolar dimension would be defined as the difference between the two parts of the SAT. Equation (12-6) can be used to compute the reliability of the composite (difference) score (r_{yy}). The symbol b_1 denotes the weight applied to the ith element, s_i^2 is the variance of the ith element, $r_{xx(i)}$ is the reliability of the ith elements, and s_t^2 is the variance of the composite. The quantity, s_t^2, may be obtained from the b_i and variance–covariance matrix among elements using Eq. (3-7) so that it need not be computed directly.

$$r_{yy} = 1 - \frac{(\sum b_i^2 s_i^2 - \sum b_i^2 s_i^2 r_{xx})}{S_t^2} \tag{12-6}$$

For example, suppose the verbal and quantitative scales each have a standard deviation of 10 and correlate .7. Further assume that the individual scale values of r_{xx} are .8. The variance–covariance matrix of the two scales is

$$\begin{bmatrix} 100 & 70 \\ 70 & 100 \end{bmatrix}$$

Hence, the variance of the difference, which constitutes s_y^2, is:

$$s_i^2 = [1 \quad -1] \times \begin{bmatrix} 100 & 70 \\ 70 & 100 \end{bmatrix} \times \begin{bmatrix} 1 \\ -1 \end{bmatrix}$$

$$= 60$$

The quantity $b_i^2 s_i^2$ is $[1^2 \times 100 + (-1)^2 \times 100]$ or 200. Likewise, the quantity $\sum b_i^2 s_i^2 r_{xx}$ is $[1^2 \times 100 \times .8 + (-1)^2 \times 100 \times .8]$ or 160. Consequently, the reliability of the composite is $1 - (200 - 160)/60 = 1 - 40/60 = 1 - .67 = .33$. Note how much lower the reliability of the composite (r_{yy}) is than the reliability of the components ($r_{xx(i)}$). *The reliability of a difference between two positively correlated quantities or the sum of two negatively correlated quantities will always be highly unreliable. The reason is that you are effectively subtracting out what is common to the components (general intelligence, in the SAT example), exaggerating the effects of measurement error. On the other hand, the reliability of the sum of two positively correlated quantities or the difference between two negatively correlated quantities will always be more reliable than the component reliabilities.*

You may verify that the reliability of the composite would be $1 - 40/200$ or .8 were the two tests to be unrelated. However, it is rather unlikely that two measures of cognitive ability would not be positively related unless they each measure two highly specialized skills like pitch perception and visual acuity.

When I write factor analytic programs, I commonly compute either coefficient alpha or use Eq. (12-6) to compute factor reliabilities, depending upon whether items or scales are the unit of analysis. The factor reliability in a scale-level analysis simply involves treating the factor as a linear combination. For any linear combination to have utility, it is necessary (but not sufficient) that it be reliable. A bipolar factor (cf. Chapter 6) derived from a set of positively intercorrelated variables will therefore be unreliable. Recall, however, that all but the first PC derived from a matrix of positive intercorrelations will be bipolar. Hence, one will be assigning negative weights to variables correlating positively with other variables, limiting the reliability. It is amazing how unreliable factors beyond the first few PCs are.[8]

Dimensionality and Item-Level Factoring

In most, but not all applications, the goal of forming a scale is to produce a unidimensional measure. Unidimensionality is most desirable when the scale is intended to measure a single trait. However, in many other applications, especially those of a highly applied nature, the criterion one attempts to predict is complex. One wishes to find a set of items that are also complex but which "hold together" and thereby tap the various attributes.

People commonly use item-level factoring to infer dimensionality of a given scale. Unfortunately, they typically employ the same procedures as they use in factoring correlations among scales. The results can be highly spurious or distorted, as I will demonstrate below.

The problem is that any correlation, whether based upon two scales or two items, is determined, in part, by how similar the two distributions are in shape. All things held equal, the more similar the distribution shapes are to one another, the higher the correlation. As I noted in Chapter 2, distributions of scale scores are typically not normal because of the effects of item intercorrelations. However, because you are adding over somewhat independent items, there will be a tendency *towards* normality that will make the distributions of two scales chosen at random be more alike than the distributions of two items (unless the item endorsement probabilities are similar).

Thus, no matter how similar two items are in content, they will differ substantially in distribution shape if their response levels are different. For example, suppose you ask a group of people the following two questions: (1) "I eat chocolate ice cream at least once a day" and (2) "I eat chocolate ice cream at least once a month." If you employ a binary response scale, the response level, standard deviation, and skewness of the two distributions will be determinable from one another. Assuming binary scoring makes discussion easier but is not intended as an argument away from using confidence rating (Likert) types of ratings. Because very few people will endorse the first question, it will have a low mean, small standard deviation and positive skew. Item (2) will have a high mean, more variability (probably, if not, one could ask the

---

[8] Mathematically, a reliability coefficient may be negative. Imagine a two-item test with a negative correlation between the two items, say $-.5$. Application of Eq. (12-6) yields an $S(C)$ value of 1 and an $S(D)$ value of 2 (assuming the items are standardized). Hence, r_{xx} is $[2 \times (1 - 2)]/(1 \times 1) = -2$. This negative value is anomalous given that the reliability can be expressed as the ratio of true score variance to total variance. The convention is to treat the reliability as .0, when a negative value emerges.

question about weekly consumption of ice cream), and negative skew. The difference in endorsement probabilities will severely *range-restrict* the correlation between the two items. Indeed, item (1) may even correlate more highly with an item like "I eat strawberry ice cream at least once a day" than with item (2). More broadly, the correlation between two items reflects both their *substantive (content-based) similarity* and their *statistical (distribution-based) similarity.*

When you factor a group of items dominated by a single factor, you are quite likely to obtain factors grouping items with similar distributions, regardless of their content. Factors that emerge because of similar distributional properties are known as *difficulty* factors, since they were first observed in the abilities domain where most factor analytic work was (and still probably is) done.

I generated two correlation matrices based upon 20 simulated variables to demonstrate difficulty factors. In the first, the individual variables were all normally distributed. The population correlations between pairs of variables were all .3. In the second, I dichotomized the first ten original variables at $z = +1.0$ and the remaining 10 at $z = -1.0$. The dichotomization reduced the correlation between pairs of variables which dichotomized at the same point, i.e., both at $z = +1.0$ or $z = -1.0$, to the .15 to .20 range. However, the effect of dichotomization was much more dramatic when two variables were split differently, i.e., one at $z = +1.0$ and the other at $z = -1.0$. The correlations were reduced to approximately .1.

When I performed a PC analysis upon the first data set, the results clearly supported a single factor solution: the first eigenvalue was 6.0, accounting for 30% of the total variance, and the second eigenvalue was .91. However, the first five eigenvalues of the second matrix were 3.19, 1.21, 1.07, 1.03, and .99 which would be interpreted as supporting a multidimensional structure, especially when one follows the defaults of computer packages. The difference between the two factor structures demonstrates how a purely statistical effect, differences in response level, can diffuse a factor structure in the sense of spreading factor variance spuriously across several factors.

Looking for Difficulty Factors

Investigators rarely look for difficulty factors in item-level factor analyses (or in other situations where the distributions of individual variables vary widely). I feel that this easily performed examination should be mandatory: *when you have identified the salient items (variables) defining factors, compute the means and standard deviations of the items on each factor. If you find large differences in means, e.g., if you find one factor includes mostly items with high response levels, another with intermediate response levels, and a third with low response levels, there is strong reason to attribute the factors to statistical rather than to substantive bases.*

One may look for difficulty factors more directly through confirmatory factor analysis. For example, suppose that you have a 10-item test which is supposed to measure a single trait. The results of factoring suggest more than one factor, perhaps because the first two eigenvalues both exceed 1.0. Form a factor composed of the items with the five highest means and a second factor composed of the remaining five items.[9] Using either an oblique multiple groups or LISREL solution, test the fit of the proposed factors. The resulting fit, relative to the fit of the first two PCs, is an index of the extent to which the evidence for multiple factors is statistical in nature.

If items are scored in binary format, one need only look at factors defined in terms of response level in order to evaluate the possible presence of difficulty factors as the response level fully describes the item distribution. If confidence ratings or some other form of multi response scoring is used, a definition based upon response level may not be sufficient. What I have done is to define one set of factors based upon similarity of response level, a second set of factors based upon similarity of item variances, and a third set of factors based upon similarity of item skewness. Bernstein, Teng, and Garbin (1986) illustrate the use of these statistical models to control for the effects of differences in item distributions.

Limitations on the Utility of Test Reliability

In the next section, I will consider the more important issue of test validity— the extent to which a scale measures what it purports to measure. There is an important linkage between the concepts of reliability and validity. Lack of reliability places a limit upon validity, though I will demonstrate that the limit is rather broad. Lack of validity in most tests is not due to lack of reliability—it is due to the fact that the scale measures only a portion of what one intends to measure. Moreover, the paradoxical situation can arise in which a test is too reliable to be optimally valid.

In order to understand how a test may be too reliable, note that a perfectly reliable scale is one in which all items intercorrelate perfectly. The implication is that the items have identical response levels—a situation that is like simply asking a person the same question repeatedly (cf. Cattell, Eber, & Tatsuoka, 1970). Suppose the particular response level were .5 (any other figure would do as well). Each item will dichotomize the population. Moreover, people get either perfect scores or zero scores. All items save one (and it does not matter which one) are redundant, since you could predict a person's score on all items when you know their score on any one particular item. Unfortunately, if that is the case, you will obtain no information beyond that. If a person passes one item, and therefore passes all items, you do not know whether he or she is

---

[9] The items may group more naturally into sets of unequal size, e.g., into one set of six items with a high response level and another set of four items with a low response level. When this is the case, these natural groupings should be used instead of an even split of five and five items.

slightly above average or extremely high in the trait being measured. Conversely, if a person fails one item, and therefore fails all items, you do not know whether he or she is slightly below average or extremely low in the trait being measured. To the extent there is more predictive information possible from knowing how far above or below average the individual is, information is lost. The practice of deliberately including items with various response levels is called *equidiscriminating test construction.*

The paradoxical state of affairs in which a test is too reliable to be valid is rare (I have never seen it happen in the real world). However, the underlying point is important. When you construct a test, make sure to measure at all points along the trait by choosing items that differ in their response levels.

Similar reasoning holds with regard to the direction of item scoring, most pertinent on personality tests. Items keyed "true" on the MMPI, for example, deal with *symptom admission,* whereas those keyed "false" deal with *symptom denial.* I have found in several situations that all things being held equal, items keyed in the same direction tend to correlate more highly with each other than items keyed in different directions (Bernstein & Eveland, 1982; Bernstein et al., 1986). This means that symptom admission is not the mirror image of symptom denial or, more generally, endorsing the presence of a trait is not the exact opposite of denying its absence. Even though having items keyed in different directions will therefore lower reliability (since it will lower the average interitem correlation), it is a good practice to have both positively and negatively keyed items.

In general, scales should be homogeneous in content so that you know you are measuring a single trait (or at least a small number of traits). On the other hand, they should be "statistically" heterogeneous in terms of their response level so that you can discriminate among people at all levels of the trait (unless your particular application requires you focus upon a particular level of the trait, as in MMPI scales where one is primarily interested in high scale scores (because high scores suggest the pathology that is of interest and low scores are generally difficult to interpret). Determining exactly what traits are being measured involves the issue of validity. If you desire to predict something that is factorially complex, it is probably better to develop multiple scales rather than increase the complexity of a given scale. However, the need for homogeneity should not be construed so narrowly that you are basically defining a trait on the basis of a very limited sampling of the possible content.

Numerical Example I: A Unifactor Scale

The following simulation is designed to illustrate some of the procedures involved in scale construction. The simulation involved a set of 20 "latent" (unobservable) variables. Seventeen were constructed with a loading of .65 on a single common factor (trait), i.e., each of the 17 items followed the general form: $X_j = .65F_1 + .79e_j$. The index j therefore denotes a particular item. One value of F_1 was generated for each of 200 "subjects" from a distribution that was Normal (0, 1). This value of F_1 represents a common factor score in the sense of Chapter 6. Separate values of e_j were generated for each of the 17 items. These unique factor scores were also obtained from distributions that were Normal (0, 1). In accord with the classical common factor model, the values of e_j were uncorrelated with each other as well as with F_1.

Basic statistical considerations imply that each latent variable, X_j, will have an expected mean of .0 because its mean will be the sum of the two component means, F_1 and e_j, each of which is 0. Similarly, Eq. (6-3) implies that each X_j will have a variance of 1.0, the sum of the variances of the orthogonal components, $.65^2$ and $.79^2$. Finally, because each of these 17 items has the same factor structure, they are *parallel* in the sense of Chapter 7. The population correlation between any given pair will be $.65^2$ or .4225 (cf. Chapter 6). These items constitute the *relevant set*. The variance of the systematic component, which is also .4225, is relatively high for an item-level analysis. Likewise, the error variance ($.79^2 = .6241$) is relatively low.

The factor pattern of the three remaining items (6, 11, and 18) followed the same general form. However, F_1 was set at .1. These items constituted the *irrelevant set*. One purpose of the analysis is to show that these three items will be eliminated from the scale, leaving the remaining 17 relevant items to form the unifactor scale. These items were also scaled to unit variance so all 20 latent variables may be thought of as *z*-scores.

These latent scores represent what a person's response *could* be *if* that person were able to respond along a continuum in a meaningful manner. However, subjects cannot do so because (1) the experimenter or test constructor forces them to answer in a limited number of categories and (2) even if they were allowed to respond with any number they wished, the inherent ability of humans to categorize is limited (Garner, 1960, 1962; Miller, 1956).

Consequently, all responses were dichotomized into categories I will label "0" and "1." The cutoffs were chosen at random from $z = -1.5$ to $z = +1.5$ for 15 of the 17 relevant items and for all three irrelevant items. The exceptional cutoffs were 2.1 for item 3 and -1.7 for item 15. In other words, if the cutoff happened to be $z = 1.0$ for a given latent variable, that latent variable would be transformed into a dichotomous variable with item "split," $P(0) = .84$ and $P(1) = .16$, within sampling error. As a result, the relevant item with cutoff of 2.1 was nearly always a "1." Even though its content was appropriate to the trait, it would not be discriminating, but for a different reason than the irrelevant items, i.e., in effect it was a constant. Similarly, the item with cutoff of -1.7 was also nondiscriminating since nearly all responses to it were a "0." Because no two items were dichotomized in the same way, the "observed" item responses were *not* parallel. Data from 200 "subjects" were generated.

Table 12-2 contains the relevant item statistics. The column denoted "Cutoff" denotes the randomly chosen (save for items 3 and 15) criterion value along the *z* axis. The next column, denoted "$P(1)$," contains the probability of a "1" response. It corresponds, within sampling error, to a normal curve of

TABLE 12-2. Statistics for 20 hypothetical
items on a proposed unifactor scale[a]

Item	Cutoff	P(1)	r(u)	r(c)	b
1	−1.21	.90	.40	.33	.39
2	1.23	.14	.53	.45	.56
3	2.10	.04	.31	.26	.34
4	1.33	.10	.47	.40	.49
5	−.15	.44	.54	.43	.55
6	−1.50	.93	.15	.08	.10
7	−.53	.68	.49	.38	.49
8	.13	.47	.60	.49	.60
9	.41	.43	.57	.44	.58
10	.31	.37	.61	.51	.63
11	.00	.42	.04	−.10	−.11
12	−1.43	.95	.33	.27	.32
13	.25	.40	.59	.48	.60
14	−1.50	.92	.31	.24	.30
15	−1.70	.98	.25	.21	.27
16	.85	.22	.50	.40	.51
17	.15	.43	.57	.47	.57
18	−.50	.68	.16	.02	.07
19	.04	.51	.56	.45	.57
20	.50	.29	.52	.41	.53

[a] "Cutoff" denotes the randomly chosen cutoff (in z-score units),
"P(1)" is the probability of a "1" response, "$r(u)$" is the correlation
between the item and the sum of all 20 items, *not* correcting for
item-total overlap, "$r(c)$" is the corrected item-total correlation,
and "b" is the loading of the item on the first PC.

the Cutoff, since the latent variables were defined as Normal $(0, 1)$. The next
column, denoted "$r(u)$," consists of the item-total correlation, *not* correcting
for overlap, i.e., not correcting for the fact that a given item enters into the
determination of the total score. The column denoted "$r(c)$" contains the
corresponding *corrected* item-total correlation, e.g., the corrected item-total
correlation for item 1 is the correlation between item 1 and the sum of items
2 to 20. Finally, the column marked "b" contains the loading of that item on
the first PC. All three measures, $r(u)$, $r(c)$, and b, can be viewed as indices of
the relevance of an item to the scale. Note that all three are actually *point–
biserial correlations*.

The following points may be noted from the table:

1. The three measures of whether an item belongs to the scale, $r(u)$, $r(c)$, and
   b, tell pretty much the same story, although $r(c)$ measures are generally
   smallest (since the spurious effects of item overlap are eliminated) and b
   measures are generally the largest (because the sum of the 20 b^2 values must
   be a maximum from the definition of a PC).
2. Irrelevant items 6, 11, and 18 have negligible $r(u)$, $r(c)$, and b values, as
   should be the case from their definition.
3. Items with a $P(1)$ values near .50 have the highest $r(u)$, $r(c)$, and b values,

e.g., 5, 8, and 9. They are least affected by the range restriction arising from dichotomization. *This does not necessarily mean they are the "best" items on a scale that is designed to measure at all levels of the trait. They are good at discriminating between high and low scorers, but other items are needed to discriminate within each of these two groups. Items at all response levels are needed unless one is simply interested in discriminating at some particular point, e.g., at one extreme, as in the MMPI.*

4. Items 3 and 15, on the other hand, have such extreme splits (.04 and .98) that their $r(u)$, $r(c)$, and b values are relatively small.

There were some other findings of interest not contained in the table:

1. Correlations between individual items were lower than item-total correlations because the totals contain less measurement error than the individual items do. Interitem correlations were generally in the .1 to .2 range, depending on the similarity of the $P(1)$ values. Were there no effects due to differences in item splits and were the scale sufficiently long, the average item-total correlation would be the square root of the average interitem correlation from Eq. (12-1) defining the relation between the reliability index (correlation between a "true" and a "fallible" scale) and the reliability coefficient (correlation between two "fallible" scales each containing independent error).

2. A total of seven eigenvalues in the item-level analysis exceeded 1.0, which makes them "important" by standards appropriate to scale-level exploratory analyses. The successive values were 4.31, 1.52, 1.24, 1.10, 1.07, 1.03, and 1.00. Since there were 20 variables, the first PC accounted 21.5% of the total variance. The presence of multiple components with eigenvalues greater than 1.0 reflects the heterogeneity of item response levels and not content. This is known to be true because the underlying data, prior to categorization, were constructed to contain only one factor.

3. The coefficient alpha reliability of the 20 items was .767, a value which is moderate, at best. As with any multiitem scale, the overall reliability is considerably higher than the interitem correlations (.1 to .2), reflecting the desired psychometric goal of making relatively reliable scale from unreliable items.

Given these initial results, one would definitely drop the three irrelevant items (6, 11, and 18). It is a matter of debate whether the two items with extreme splits (3 and 15) should also be dropped. I did so and reanalyzed the data, using a new random number seed which corresponds to a new, independent "sample." The major results were as follows:

1. Item-total correlations and the loading on the first PC increased in magnitude. For example, the first PC (based on 15 rather than 20 items) now accounted for 27.3% of the total variance; loadings on the component ranged from .31 to .61 with ten of the items loading at least .5. The composite was made more reliable through the exclusion of the three irrelevant items. Deleting the two items with extreme splits effectively eliminated a constant.

2. The reliability of the scale increased to .806.
3. *Despite the improvement from the original scale resulting from the deletion of the five items, scores based on the original 20 items correlated .969 with scores on the revised scale. Unless changes in the scale are substantial, the principle of "it don't make no nevermind" will generally hold.*

Numerical Example II: A Two-Factor Scale

The second example consists of evaluating a 12-item scale ostensibly designed so that items 1 to 6 measure one trait and items 7 to 12 measure a second trait. Assume that a preliminary form of the scale has been given to one "group." That group furnished the data necessary for item selection. The data at hand were derived from a second "group." The question is the adequacy of the final form. In actuality, my simulation defined the first six items in the form $X_j = .60F_{\mathrm{I}} + .10F_{\mathrm{II}} + .79e_j$ and the last six items in the form $X_j = .10F_{\mathrm{I}} + .60F_{\mathrm{II}} + .79e_j$. Items 1 to 6 are therefore parallel to each other, and items 7 to 12 are parallel to each other. Note that $.10^2 + .60^2 + .79^2 = 1.0$ so that each latent X_j is in z-score form, just as the latent data in the previous example. In contrast to the previous data, item responses were placed into one of five categories instead of simply being dichotomized. The cutoffs defining the response categories were chosen at random.

Table 12-3 contains various statistics of relevance to the scale. The columns denoted "Mean" and "sd" merely denote the mean rating along the five-point scale for each item and its associated standard deviation. The symbols "$r(u)$" and "$r(c)$" have their previous meaning of uncorrected and corrected item-total correlations, respectively. Note that in this example, Items 1 to 6 and 7

TABLE 12-3. Statistics for 12 hypothetical items on a proposed two-factor scale[a]

Item	Mean	sd	$r(u)$	$r(c)$	V_{I}	V_{II}	O_{I}	O_{II}	W_{I}	W_{II}
1	3.61	1.47	.64	.43	.66	.09	.64	.15	.64	.16
2	3.22	1.55	.67	.45	.64	.22	.66	.24	.67	.24
3	3.60	1.24	.59	.40	.61	.06	.62	.11	.59	.12
4	1.80	1.33	.51	.29	.54	−.08	.54	.03	.51	.04
5	2.49	1.72	.63	.36	.61	.06	.59	.15	.63	.15
6	1.80	1.35	.57	.35	.57	−.05	.58	.06	.57	.05
7	3.90	1.49	.54	.29	.06	.47	.10	.53	.10	.54
8	3.40	1.62	.63	.38	.23	.58	.23	.61	.24	.63
9	3.68	1.50	.63	.40	.08	.62	.13	.62	.14	.63
10	2.08	1.47	.64	.42	.13	.64	.18	.64	.19	.64
11	2.00	1.44	.59	.36	−.06	.64	.05	.59	.05	.59
12	1.62	1.17	.52	.23	−.08	.57	.03	.57	.03	.52

[a] "Mean" is the mean response along the five-point rating scale, "sd" is the standard deviation of each item, "$r(u)$" is the correlation between the item and the corresponding scale sum (items 1–6 or 7–12), *not* correcting for item-total overlap, "$r(c)$" is the corrected item-total correlation, "V_{I}" and "V_{II}" are loadings on the two varimax factors, "O_{I}" and "O_{II}" are structure elements for the two oblique multiple groups factors in which items were weighted equally (unweighted analysis), and "W_{I}" and "W_{II}" are structure elements for the two oblique multiple groups factors in which items were weighted in proportion to their standard deviation (weighted analysis).

to 12 are correlated with their respective and, hence, different, sums. Other entries in the table refer to a series of factor analyses to be discussed shortly. An additional statistic necessary when there are multiple scales is the correlation between each pair of subscales. The correlation between the present two scales is .22. Finally, the respective scale reliabilities are .64 and .63, which is in part a consequence of the small number of items per scale.

The item analysis provides the following points:

1. The $r(u)$ values are all relatively high.
2. The $r(c)$ values are considerably lower than the $r(u)$ values as compared to the previous example. This is because the scales are quite short.
3. Although the relation is not perfect due to sampling error, the magnitudes of $r(u)$ and $r(c)$ are related to the item standard deviations, another manifestation of range restriction.
4. The interscale correlation (.22) is sufficiently low for the two scales to be considered separable. However, the *observed* correlation needs be considered in the context of the *reliabilities* of the two scales (see *correction for attentuation*, below).

Another important set of results may be derived from factor analyses conducted upon the 12-item intercorrelation matrix. The columns labeled "V_I" and "V_{II}" denote the loadings on the two varimax factors derived from an exploratory factor analysis. By definition, the factors are orthogonal. The columns denoted "O_I" and "O_{II}" are derived from an oblique multiple groups confirmatory factor analysis in which items were weighted equally, i.e., an *unweighted* analysis of the item intercorrelation matrix. A second oblique multiple groups factor analysis used the item standard deviations as weights and corresponds to the results of factoring the item variance–covariance matrix. *No LISREL solution was obtained because I have found that the maximum likelihood estimation gives highly misleading results with categorical data like item responses* (Bernstein & Teng, 1986). Finally, a pseudofactor oblique multiple groups solution was obtained by assigning the odd-numbered items to one factor and the even-numbered items to a second factor. Note that in all cases I fixed the number of factors at two because that is what the model specifies. Some relevant results are:

1. Three eigenvalues exceeded 1.0. Their values were 2.66, 1.74, and 1.09. The fourth eigenvalue was .97. As noted at several points in this chapter, this reflects the heterogeneity of the response distributions rather than the presence of more than two dimensions of content. The first two PCs account for 36.71% of the total variance.
2. The varimax factors load as intended—items 1 to 6 load on Factor I, and items 7 to 12 load on factor II. Conversely, items 1 to 6 do *not* load on factor II and items 7 to 12 do not load on factor I. Even an exploratory solution was robust to detect the structure. As would be expected from Chapter 6, the first PC was a general factor and the second was a bipolar factor with items 1 to 6 having negative loadings and items 7 to 12 having positive loadings.

3. The structure elements of the unweighted oblique multiple groups solution are even more clearly supportive of the hypothesized pattern since the relevant weights are even larger. The two factors account for 36.41% of the total variance, which is extremely close to the 36.71%, the upper limit imposed by the first two PCs. The factor correlation of .203 is similar to the scale correlation; the slight difference reflects equal weighting versus the effects of differences in standard deviations.

4. The fit of the two weighted oblique multiple groups factors accounted for 36.43% of the total variance, which is nearly identical to the unweighted solution. This is another reflection of a main point of this book that different weightings applied to a correlation matrix that have the same signs will correlate highly with one another. Note that the $r(u)$ values and the structure elements are identical, by definition. (The correlation between the two factors is also identical to the correlation between the two scale scores of .22.)

5. The pseudofactor solution clearly accounted for less of the total variance (19.09%) and the factor correlation (.52) was much higher.

As an additional step, I took the PC factor weights from a different simulation, i.e., from a different random sample, and applied it to the present data. The fit of these *cross-validated PCs* was only 36.19% which is marginally less than the fit of the two models which use *a priori* weights (36.41% and 36.43%).

In sum, the two proposed scales fit nearly as well as the upper limit imposed by the PCs of the data set and actually better than the PCs obtained from a different random sample. They clearly fit better than an arbitrary grouping and were relatively independent. The scales could be lengthened to make them more reliable, depending upon the intended application.

Test Validity

Validity is concerned with the issue of whether a test measures what it is intended to measure. Several specific forms of validity have been proposed, but three particular concepts have appeared most frequently: (1) *criterion* validity,[10] which is concerned with the ability of a measure to correlate with

---

[10] The terms "predictive validity," "concurrent validity," and "postdictive" validity are sometimes treated as special cases to define the temporal relation between the measure and the criterion, denoting whether the measure was obtained before, at the same time, or after the criterion, respectively. The distinction is quite meaningful. A measure will typically have higher concurrent validity than predictive validity since various things may happen between the time you obtain the measure and the time you obtain the criterion. Since the effects occur independently of the predictor, they weaken the correlation. Because I am not making any assumptions about the temporal relations involved, I will use the term "measure" instead of the more common term "predictor" in my discussion.

a specific external measure or criterion; (2) *content* validity, which is concerned with the extent to which items comprising the measure sample the intended trait; and (3) *construct* validity, which is concerned with how well the measure relates to the underlying theory defining the properties of the trait. Two important aspects of construct validity are (1) *convergent validity*, which is defined by how well a measure relates to other measure of a similar nature, and (2) *divergent validity*, which is defined as how well a measure produces differences expected from the theory. For example, the convergent validity of a bathroom scale can be defined by correlating weights obtained from that scale with weights obtained from a previously calibrated scale (as one might use in a physician's office, for example) over a given sample. The divergent validity of the scale in question might be demonstrated by showing that males generally weigh more than females.

The three definitions of validity are often treated separately, as the following example typical of industrial applications indicates. You are interested in employing a test for personnel selection. According to Equal Employment Opportunity Commission (EEOC) *Guidelines*, if your test has any *adverse impact*, you must show that your test is valid according to one of the three definitions. Adverse impact occurs when the failure rate in one or more *protected minority groups* (females, hispanics, blacks, Asian-Americans, and native Americans) exceeds the failure rate among white males. The rule of thumb is that the disparity must be at least 20%, the "four-fifths" rule, before adverse impact is declared, and evidence for test validity required. As behavioral scientists, you should not use invalid selection devices in the first place, even if the devices do not have adverse impact.

In principle, a test may be quite valid even if its items do not correlate to the demands of the job or any behavioral theory as long as the resulting measure correlates with a suitable measure of performance on the job. If this is the case, the test in question would satisfy the definition of criterion validity. Similarly, if you can show that the items on the test involve the skills or knowledge the person needs to possess on the job (e.g., you have an applicant for a secretarial position type a letter), you can establish content validity and do not have to show that the score correlates with any performance rating or follows from any theory. Indeed, it might well be that all the secretaries pass the test. Were that to occur, there would not be any variance in the test so it could not correlate with any criterion.

Finally, you may show that a certain trait, perhaps emotional stability, is necessary for a given position, say police officer. You can show that MMPI scales meet the definition of measuring emotional instability, since normals get lower scores on the clinical scales than the target groups of emotionally unstable people. Consequently, the results provide evidence for the construct validity of the MMPI. According to EEOC guidelines, one need not hire psychotic police officers to see if they perform more poorly (predictive validity) or relate MMPI questions to the job demands (content validity).

My example makes it look like the three forms of validity are rather separate entities; in fact all are highly interdependent. Your initial choice of a test implied a theory, perhaps implicitly, of what the job entailed—you did not select items or tests at random. When you correlated scores on the test with the criterion, you probably first wanted to examine the performance ratings to insure that the raters were doing their own job validly and reliably. At a minimum, you probably should have at least two independent raters whose judgments should be highly correlated. The item content related to the demands of the task—you stand a better chance to develop a scale of emotional stability if you ask questions related to psychiatric symptoms than you do about preference for flavors of ice cream. The converse is not true, however. Just because an item looks like it is related to the trait, i.e., has what is traditionally called *face validity*, which is not a true form of validity, does not guarantee that it is valid in any of the three senses.

In other words, the three forms of validity are quite interdependent and the more recent trend is to view construct validity as a superordinate property that subsumes criterion validity and content validity. You must have some idea of what you are trying to measure before you develop the specific measure. Your idea will suggest possible correlates of the measure and the content of the measure.

Attenuation

Part of the validation process thus involves correlations between the measure and a criterion. The reliabilities of the measure and the criterion both affect the validity. What you obtain is a correlation between two observed scores. This observed correlation cannot exceed the correlation between "true" versions (termed "total" scores above) of the two scores. A *correction for attenuation* attempts to infer the correlations between the two true scores. The correction estimates the correlation between two measures with hypothesized reliabilities given their present correlation and reliabilities. There is an analogous relationship between an observed correlation and one corrected for attenuation, on the one hand, and a correlation between *components* and correlation between *common factors* (see Chapter 6), on the other. Equation (12-7) provides the formula for the correction for attenuation, where r_{xy} and r'_{xy} are the obtained and estimated correlation between measure and criterion, r_{xx} and r'_{xx} are the present and the projected reliabilities of the measure, and r_{yy} and r'_{yy} are the present and the projected reliabilities of the criterion.

$$r'_{xy} = r_{xy} \left[\frac{r'_{xx}}{r_{xx}} \frac{r'_{yy}}{r_{yy}} \right]^{1/2} \tag{12-7}$$

The correction for attenuation is derived from the idea that a reliability index is the upper limit of correlation between a fallible measure and any other measures. Suppose an observed measure predicts occupational success with a correlation of .3, has a reliability of .81, and the criterion has a reliability of .64. One could first estimate what would happen if the measure were made perfectly reliable but the criterion left as is. Thus, r'_{xx} is 1.0 and $r'_{yy} = r_{yy} = .64$, so the former drops out of the equation. The result therefore is $r'_{xy} = .3(1./.81)^{1/2} = .3(1./.9)$ or .33. The difference between r_{xy} and r'_{xy} is negligible. Unless a measure is *extremely* unreliable, not much is gained by correcting it for attenuation.

As an exercise, one may determine r'_{xy} if both the measure and the criterion were corrected for attenuation. The answer is $.3[(1 \times 1)/(.81 \times .64)]^{1/2} = .3[(1. \times 1.)/(.9 \times .8)] = .3/.72$ or .42. which is a larger gain, as you might expect since another source of unreliability is being eliminated. However, the correction is poor behavioral science even if it is acceptable mathematics. You probably have control over the predictor and might be able to add more items. (The Spearman–Brown prophecy formula can be employed to estimate how many additional items are needed to reach some level sufficiently close to 1.0—it may turn out to be impractically large.) You may or may not have control over the criterion. Perhaps the problem is that one rater is not adequate, but you can add more raters; in that case, the correction is appropriate. However, you may also be in the position of saying to your client "my predictive instrument is just fine but you have no idea of what constitutes a good employee." I doubt you will get far with that strategy.

This concludes the final chapter of the book. Psychometric theory was defined to reflect the process of making a reliable scale out of unreliable items. In contrast, multivariate analysis was defined as the process of forming linear combinations of elements that were individually unreliable. A particular, but rather general, psychometric approach to test construction, the linear model, was introduced. Properties of items were considered in order to discuss the process of item selection. Several meanings of reliability were noted and one important measure of reliability, Cronbach's alpha, were presented. The section concluded with a simulated test construction. Finally, the topic of validity, which is essentially the "bottom line" for any scale, was considered.

Appendix A
Tables of the Normal Curve

Areas and ordinates of the normal curve in terms of x/σ

(1)	(2)	(3)	(4)	(5)
z	A	B	C	y
Standard	Area from	Area in	Area in	Ordinate
score $\left(\dfrac{x}{\sigma}\right)$	mean to $\dfrac{x}{\sigma}$	larger portion	smaller portion	at $\dfrac{x}{\sigma}$
0.00	.0000	.5000	.5000	.3989
0.01	.0040	.5040	.4960	.3989
0.02	.0080	.5080	.4920	.3989
0.03	.0120	.5120	.4880	.3988
0.04	.0160	.5160	.4840	.3986
0.05	.0199	.5199	.4801	.3984
0.06	.0239	.5239	.4761	.3982
0.07	.0279	.5279	.4721	.3980
0.08	.0319	.5319	.4681	.3977
0.09	.0359	.5359	.4641	.3973
0.10	.0398	.5398	.4602	.3970
0.11	.0438	.5438	.4562	.3965
0.12	.0478	.5478	.4522	.3961
0.13	.0517	.5517	.4483	.3956
0.14	.0557	.5557	.4443	.3951
0.15	.0596	.5596	.4404	.3945
0.16	.0636	.5636	.4364	.3939
0.17	.0675	.5675	.4325	.3932
0.18	.0714	.5714	.4286	.3925
0.19	.0753	.5753	.4247	.3918
0.20	.0793	.5793	.4207	.3910
0.21	.0832	.5832	.4168	.3902
0.22	.0871	.5871	.4129	.3894
0.23	.0910	.5910	.4090	.3885
0.24	0.948	.5948	.4052	.3876
0.25	.0987	.5987	.4013	.3867
0.26	.1026	.6026	.3974	.3857
0.27	.1064	.6064	.3936	.3847

(1) z Standard score $\left(\dfrac{x}{\sigma}\right)$	(2) A Area from mean to $\dfrac{x}{\sigma}$	(3) B Area in larger portion	(4) C Area in smaller portion	(5) y Ordinate at $\dfrac{x}{\sigma}$
0.28	.1103	.6103	.3897	.3836
0.29	.1141	.6141	.3859	.3825
0.30	.1179	.6179	.3821	.3814
0.31	.1217	.6217	.3783	.3802
0.32	.1255	.6255	.3745	.3790
0.33	.1293	.6293	.3707	.3778
0.34	.1331	.6331	.3669	.3765
0.35	.1368	.6368	.3632	.3752
0.36	.1406	.6406	.3594	.3739
0.37	.1443	.6443	.3557	.3725
0.38	.1480	.6480	.3520	.3712
0.39	.1517	.6517	.3483	.3697
0.40	.1554	.6554	.3446	.3683
0.41	.1591	.6591	.3409	.3668
0.42	.1628	.6628	.3372	.3653
0.43	.1664	.6664	.3336	.3637
0.44	.1700	.6700	.3300	.3621
0.45	.1736	.6736	.3264	.3605
0.46	.1772	.6772	.3228	.3589
0.47	.1808	.6808	.3192	.3572
0.48	.1844	.6844	.3156	.3555
0.49	.1879	.6879	.3121	.3538
0.50	.1915	.6915	.3085	.3521
0.51	.1950	.6950	.3050	.3503
0.52	.1985	.6985	.3015	.3485
0.53	.2019	.7019	.2981	.3467
0.54	.2054	.7054	.2946	.3448
0.55	.2088	.7088	.2912	.3429
0.56	.2123	.7123	.2877	.3410
0.57	.2157	.7157	.2843	.3391
0.58	.2190	.7190	.2810	.3372
0.59	.2224	.7224	.2776	.3352
0.60	.2257	.7257	.2743	.3332
0.61	.2291	.7291	.2709	.3312
0.62	.2324	.7324	.2676	.3292
0.63	.2357	.7357	.2643	.3271
0.64	.2389	.7389	.2611	.3251
0.65	.2422	.7422	.2578	.3230
0.66	.2454	.7454	.2546	.3209
0.67	.2486	.7486	.2514	.3187
0.68	.2517	.7517	.2483	.3166
0.69	.2549	.7549	.2451	.3144

(1) z Standard score $\left(\dfrac{x}{\sigma}\right)$	(2) A Area from mean to $\dfrac{x}{\sigma}$	(3) B Area in larger portion	(4) C Area in smaller portion	(5) y Ordinate at $\dfrac{x}{\sigma}$
0.70	.2580	.7580	.2420	.3123
0.71	.2611	.7611	.2389	.3101
0.72	.2642	.7642	.2358	.3079
0.73	.2673	.7673	.2327	.3056
0.74	.2704	.7704	.2296	.3034
0.75	.2734	.7734	.2266	.3011
0.76	.2764	.7764	.2236	.2989
0.77	.2794	.7794	.2206	.2966
0.78	.2823	.7823	.2177	.2943
0.79	.2852	.7852	.2148	.2920
0.80	.2881	.7881	.2119	.2897
0.81	.2910	.7910	.2090	.2874
0.82	.2939	.7939	.2061	.2850
0.83	.2967	.7967	.2033	.2827
0.84	.2995	.7995	.2005	.2803
0.85	.3023	.8023	.1977	.2780
0.86	.3051	.8051	.1949	.2756
0.87	.3078	.8078	.1922	.2732
0.88	.3106	.8106	.1894	.2709
0.89	.3133	.8183	.1867	.2685
0.90	.3159	.8159	.1841	.2661
0.91	.3186	.8186	.1814	.2637
0.92	.3212	.8212	.1788	.2613
0.93	.3238	.8238	.1762	.2589
0.94	.3264	.8264	.1736	.2565
0.95	.3289	.8289	.1711	.2541
0.96	.3315	.8315	.1685	.2516
0.97	.3340	.8340	.1660	.2492
0.98	.3365	.8365	.1635	.2468
0.99	.3389	.8389	.1611	.2444
1.00	.3413	.8413	.1587	.2420
1.01	.3438	.8438	.1562	.2396
1.02	.3461	.8461	.1539	.2371
1.03	.3485	.8485	.1515	.2347
1.04	.3508	.8508	.1492	.2323
1.05	.3531	.8531	.1469	.2299
1.06	.3554	.8554	.1446	.2275
1.07	.3577	.8577	.1423	.2251
1.08	.3599	.8599	.1401	.2227
1.09	.3621	.8621	.1379	.2203
1.10	.3643	.8643	.1357	.2179
1.11	.3665	.8665	.1335	.2155
1.12	.3686	.8686	.1314	.2131

(1) z Standard score $\left(\dfrac{x}{\sigma}\right)$	(2) A Area from mean to $\dfrac{x}{\sigma}$	(3) B Area in larger portion	(4) C Area in smaller portion	(5) y Ordinate at $\dfrac{x}{\sigma}$
1.13	.3708	.8708	.1292	.2107
1.14	.3729	.8729	.1271	.2083
1.15	.3749	.8749	.1251	.2059
1.16	.3770	.8770	.1230	.2036
1.17	.3790	.8790	.1210	.2012
1.18	.3810	.8810	.1190	.1989
1.19	.3830	.8830	.1170	.1965
1.20	.3849	.8849	.1151	.1942
1.21	.3869	.8869	.1131	.1919
1.22	.3888	.8888	.1112	.1895
1.23	.3907	.8907	.1093	.1872
1.24	.3925	.8925	.1075	.1849
1.25	.3944	.8944	.1056	.1826
1.26	.3962	.8962	.1038	.1804
1.27	.3980	.8980	.1020	.1781
1.28	.3997	.8997	.1003	.1758
1.29	.4015	.9015	.0985	.1736
1.30	.4032	.9032	.0968	.1714
1.31	.4049	.9049	.0951	.1691
1.32	.4066	.9066	.0934	.1669
1.33	.4082	.9082	.0918	.1647
1.34	.4099	.9099	.0901	.1626
1.35	.4115	.9115	.0885	.1604
1.36	.4131	.9131	.0869	.1582
1.37	.4147	.9147	.0853	.1561
1.38	.4162	.9162	.0838	.1539
1.39	.4177	.9177	.0823	.1518
1.40	.4192	.9192	.0808	.1497
1.41	.4207	.9207	.0793	.1476
1.42	.4222	.9222	.0778	.1456
1.43	.4236	.9236	.0764	.1435
1.44	.4251	.9251	.0749	.1415
1.45	.4265	.9265	.0735	.1394
1.46	.4279	.9279	.0721	.1374
1.47	.4292	.9292	.0708	.1354
1.48	.4306	.9306	.0694	.1334
1.49	.4319	.9319	.0681	.1315
1.50	.4332	.9332	.0668	.1295
1.51	.4345	.9345	.0655	.1276
1.52	.4357	.9357	.0643	.1257
1.53	.4370	.9370	.0630	.1238
1.54	.4382	.9382	.0618	.1219

(1)	(2)	(3)	(4)	(5)
z	A	B	C	y
Standard score $\left(\dfrac{x}{\sigma}\right)$	Area from mean to $\dfrac{x}{\sigma}$	Area in larger portion	Area in smaller portion	Ordinate at $\dfrac{x}{\sigma}$
1.55	.4394	.9394	.0606	.1200
1.56	.4406	.9406	.0594	.1182
1.57	.4418	.9418	.0582	.1163
1.58	.4429	.9429	.0571	.1145
1.59	.4441	.9441	.0559	.1127
1.60	.4452	.9452	.0548	.1109
1.61	.4463	.9463	.0537	.1092
1.62	.4474	.9474	.0526	.1074
1.63	.4484	.9484	.0516	.1057
1.64	.4495	.9495	.0505	.1040
1.65	.4505	.9505	.0495	.1023
1.66	.4515	.9515	.0485	.1006
1.67	.4525	.9525	.0475	.0989
1.68	.4535	.9535	.0465	.0973
1.69	.4545	.9545	.0455	.0957
1.70	.4554	.9554	.0446	.0940
1.71	.4564	.9564	.0436	.0925
1.72	.4573	.9573	.0427	.0909
1.73	.4582	.9582	.0418	.0893
1.74	.4591	.9591	.0409	.0878
1.75	.4599	.9599	.0401	.0863
1.76	.4608	.9608	.0392	.0848
1.77	.4616	.9616	.0384	.0833
1.78	.4625	.9625	.0375	.0818
1.79	.4633	.9633	.0367	.0804
1.80	.4641	.9641	.0359	.0790
1.81	.4649	.9649	.0351	.0775
1.82	.4656	.9656	.0344	.0761
1.83	.4664	.9664	.0336	.0748
1.84	.4671	.9671	.0329	.0734
1.85	.4678	.9678	.0322	.0721
1.86	.4686	.9686	.0314	.0707
1.87	.4693	.9693	.0307	.0694
1.88	.4699	.9699	.0301	.0681
1.89	.4706	.9706	.0294	.0669
1.90	.4713	.9713	.0287	.0656
1.91	.4719	.9719	.0281	.0644
1.92	.4726	.9726	.0274	.0632
1.93	.4732	.9732	.0268	.0620
1.94	.4738	.9738	.0262	.0608
1.95	.4744	.9744	.0256	.0596
1.96	.4750	.9750	.0250	.0584
1.97	.4756	.9756	.0244	.0573

(1) z Standard score $\left(\dfrac{x}{\sigma}\right)$	(2) A Area from mean to $\dfrac{x}{\sigma}$	(3) B Area in larger portion	(4) C Area in smaller portion	(5) y Ordinate at $\dfrac{x}{\sigma}$
1.98	.4761	.9761	.0239	.0562
1.99	.4767	.9767	.0233	.0551
2.00	.4772	.9772	.0228	.0540
2.01	.4778	.9778	.0222	.0529
2.02	.4783	.9783	.0217	..0519
2.03	.4788	.9788	.0212	.0508
2.04	.4793	.9793	.0207	.0498
2.05	.4798	.9798	.0202	.0488
2.06	.4803	.9803	.0197	.0478
2.07	.4808	.9808	.0192	.0468
2.08	.4812	.9812	.0188	.0459
2.09	.4817	.9817	.0183	.0449
2.10	.4821	.9821	.0179	.0440
2.11	.4826	.9826	.0174	.0431
2.12	.4830	.9830	.0170	.0422
2.13	.4834	.9834	.0166	.0413
2.14	.4848	.9838	.0162	.0404
2.15	.4842	.9842	.0158	.0396
2.16	.4846	.9846	.0154	.0387
2.17	.4850	.9850	.0150	.0379
2.18	.4854	.9854	.0146	.0371
2.19	.4857	.9857	.0143	.0363
2.20	.4861	.9861	.0139	.0355
2.21	.4864	.9864	.0136	.0347
2.22	.4868	.9868	.0132	.0339
2.23	.4871	.9871	.0129	.0332
2.24	.4875	.9875	.0125	.0325
2.25	.4878	.9878	.0122	.0317
2.26	.4881	.9881	.0119	.0310
2.27	.4884	.9884	.0116	.0303
2.28	.4887	.9887	.0113	.0297
2.29	.4890	.9890	.0110	.0290
2.30	.4893	.9893	.0107	.0283
2.31	.4896	.9896	.0104	.0277
2.32	.4898	.9898	.0102	.0270
2.33	.4901	.9901	.0099	.0264
2.34	.4904	9904	.0096	.0258
2.35	.4906	.9906	.0094	.0252
2.36	.4909	.9909	.0091	.0246
2.37	.4911	.9911	.0089	.0241
2.38	.4913	.9913	.0087	.0235
2.39	.4916	.9916	.0084	.0229

(1)	(2)	(3)	(4)	(5)
z	A	B	C	y
Standard score $\left(\dfrac{x}{\sigma}\right)$	Area from mean to $\dfrac{x}{\sigma}$	Area in larger portion	Area in smaller portion	Ordinate at $\dfrac{x}{\sigma}$
2.40	.4918	.9918	.0082	.0224
2.41	.4920	.9920	.0080	.0219
2.42	.4922	.9922	.0078	.0213
2.43	.4925	.9925	.0075	.0208
2.44	.4927	.9927	.0073	.0203
2.45	.4929	.9929	.0071	.0198
2.46	.4931	.9931	.0069	.0194
2.47	.4932	.9932	.0068	.0189
2.48	.4934	.9934	.0066	.0184
2.49	.4936	.9936	.0064	.0180
2.50	.4938	.9938	.0062	.0175
2.51	.4940	.9940	.0060	.0171
2.52	.4941	.9941	.0059	.0167
2.53	.4943	.9943	.0057	.0163
2.54	.4945	.9945	.0055	.0158
2.55	.4946	.9946	.0054	.0154
2.56	.4948	.9948	.0052	.0154
2.57	.4949	.9949	.0051	.0147
2.58	.4951	.9951	.0049	.0143
2.59	.4952	.9952	.0048	.0139
2.60	.4953	.9953	.0047	.0136
2.61	.4955	.9955	.0045	.0132
2.62	.4956	.9956	.0044	.0129
2.63	.4957	.9957	.0043	.0126
2.64	.4959	.9959	.0041	.0122
2.65	.4960	.9960	.0040	.0119
2.66	.4961	.9961	.0039	.0116
2.67	.4962	.9962	.0038	.0113
2.68	.4963	.9963	.0037	.0110
2.69	.4964	.9964	.0036	.0107
2.70	.4965	.9965	.0035	.0104
2.71	.4966	.9966	.0034	.0101
2.72	.4967	.9967	.0033	.0099
2.73	.4968	.9968	.0032	.0096
2.74	.4969	.9969	.0031	.0093
2.75	.4970	.9970	.0030	.0091
2.76	.4971	.9971	.0029	.0088
2.77	.4972	.9972	.0028	.0086
2.78	.4973	.9973	.0027	.0084
2.79	.4974	.9974	.0026	.0081
2.80	.4974	.9974	.0026	.0079
2.81	.4975	.9975	.0025	.0077
2.82	.4976	.9976	.0024	.0075

(1) z Standard score $\left(\dfrac{x}{\sigma}\right)$	(2) A Area from mean to $\dfrac{x}{\sigma}$	(3) B Area in larger portion	(4) C Area in smaller portion	(5) y Ordinate at $\dfrac{x}{\sigma}$
2.83	.4977	.9977	.0023	.0073
2.84	.4977	.9977	.0023	.0071
2.85	.4978	.9978	.0022	.0069
2.86	.4979	.9979	.0021	.0067
2.87	.4979	.9979	.0021	.0065
2.88	.4980	.9980	.0020	.0063
2.89	.4981	.9981	.0019	.0061
2.90	.4981	.9981	.0019	.0060
2.91	.4982	.9982	.0018	.0058
2.92	.4982	.9982	.0018	.0056
2.93	.4983	.9983	.0017	.0055
2.94	.4984	.9984	.0016	.0053
2.95	.4984	.9984	.0016	.0051
2.96	.4985	.9985	.0015	.0050
2.97	.4985	.9985	.0015	.0048
2.98	.4986	.9986	.0014	.0047
2.99	.4986	.9986	.0014	.0046
3.00	.4987	.9987	.0013	.0044
3.01	.4987	.9987	.0013	.0043
3.02	.4987	.9987	.0013	.0042
3.03	.4988	.9988	.0012	.0040
3.04	.4988	.9988	.0012	.0039
3.05	.4989	.9989	.0011	.0038
3.06	.4989	.9989	.0011	.0037
3.07	.4989	.9989	.0011	.0036
3.08	.4990	.9990	.0010	.0035
3.09	.4990	.9990	.0010	.0034
3.10	.4990	.9990	.0010	.0033
3.11	.4991	.9991	.0009	.0032
3.12	.4991	.9991	.0009	.0031
3.13	.4991	.9991	.0009	.0030
3.14	.4992	.9992	.0008	.0029
3.15	.4992	.9992	.0008	.0028
3.16	.4992	.9992	.0008	.0027
3.17	.4992	.9992	.0008	.0026
3.18	.4993	.9993	.0007	.0025
3.19	.4993	.9993	.0007	.0025
3.20	.4993	.9993	.0007	.0024
3.21	.4993	.9993	.0007	.0023
3.22	.4994	.9994	.0006	.0022
3.23	.4994	.9994	.0006	.0022
3.24	.4994	.9994	.0006	.0021

(1) z Standard score $\left(\frac{x}{\sigma}\right)$	(2) A Area from mean to $\frac{x}{\sigma}$	(3) B Area in larger portion	(4) C Area in smaller portion	(5) y Ordinate at $\frac{x}{\sigma}$
3.30	.4995	.9995	.0005	.0017
3.40	.4997	.9997	.0003	.0012
3.50	.4998	.9998	.0002	.0009
3.60	.4998	.9998	.0002	.0006
3.70	.4999	.9999	.0001	.0004

Source: Overall, J.E., and Klett, C.J. (1972). *Applied multivariate analysis.* New York: McGraw-Hill.

Appendix B
Tables of F

The 5 (roman type) and 1 (boldface type) percent points for the distribution of F

	n_1 degrees of freedom (for greater mean square)																							
n_2	1	2	3	4	5	6	7	8	9	10	11	12	14	16	20	24	30	40	50	75	100	200	500	∞
1	161 **4,052**	200 **4,999**	216 **5,403**	225 **5,625**	230 **5,764**	234 **5,859**	237 **5,928**	239 **5,981**	241 **6,022**	242 **6,056**	243 **6,082**	244 **6,106**	245 **6,142**	246 **6,169**	248 **6,208**	249 **6,234**	250 **6,258**	251 **6,286**	252 **6,302**	253 **6,323**	253 **6,334**	254 **6,352**	254 **6,361**	254 **6,366**
2	18.51 **98.49**	19.00 **99.00**	19.16 **99.17**	19.25 **99.25**	19.30 **99.30**	19.33 **99.33**	19.36 **99.34**	19.37 **99.36**	19.38 **99.38**	19.39 **99.40**	19.40 **99.41**	19.41 **99.42**	19.42 **99.43**	19.43 **99.44**	19.44 **99.45**	19.45 **99.46**	19.46 **99.47**	19.47 **99.48**	19.47 **99.48**	19.48 **99.49**	19.49 **99.49**	19.49 **99.49**	19.50 **99.50**	19.50 **99.50**
3	10.13 **34.12**	9.55 **30.82**	9.28 **29.46**	9.12 **28.71**	9.01 **28.24**	8.94 **27.91**	8.88 **27.67**	8.84 **27.49**	8.81 **27.34**	8.78 **27.23**	8.76 **27.13**	8.74 **27.05**	8.71 **26.92**	8.69 **26.83**	8.66 **26.69**	8.64 **26.60**	8.62 **26.50**	8.60 **26.41**	8.58 **26.35**	8.57 **26.27**	8.56 **26.23**	8.54 **26.18**	8.54 **26.14**	8.53 **26.12**
4	7.71 **21.20**	6.94 **18.00**	6.59 **16.69**	6.39 **15.98**	6.26 **15.52**	6.16 **15.21**	6.09 **14.98**	6.04 **14.80**	6.00 **14.66**	5.96 **14.54**	5.93 **14.45**	5.91 **14.37**	5.87 **14.24**	5.84 **14.15**	5.80 **14.02**	5.77 **13.93**	5.74 **13.83**	5.71 **13.74**	5.70 **13.69**	5.68 **13.61**	5.66 **13.57**	5.65 **13.52**	5.64 **13.48**	5.63 **13.46**
5	6.61 **16.26**	5.79 **13.27**	5.41 **12.06**	5.19 **11.39**	5.05 **10.97**	4.95 **10.67**	4.88 **10.45**	4.82 **10.27**	4.78 **10.15**	4.74 **10.05**	4.70 **9.96**	4.68 **9.89**	4.64 **9.77**	4.60 **9.68**	4.56 **9.55**	4.53 **9.47**	4.50 **9.38**	4.46 **9.29**	4.44 **9.24**	4.42 **9.17**	4.40 **9.13**	4.38 **9.07**	4.37 **9.04**	4.36 **9.02**
6	5.99 **13.74**	5.14 **10.92**	4.76 **9.78**	4.53 **9.15**	4.39 **8.75**	4.28 **8.47**	4.21 **8.26**	4.15 **8.10**	4.10 **7.98**	4.06 **7.87**	4.03 **7.79**	4.00 **7.72**	3.96 **7.60**	3.92 **7.52**	3.87 **7.39**	3.84 **7.31**	3.81 **7.23**	3.77 **7.14**	3.75 **7.09**	3.72 **7.02**	3.71 **6.99**	3.69 **6.94**	3.68 **6.90**	3.67 **6.88**
7	5.59 **12.25**	4.74 **9.55**	4.35 **8.45**	4.12 **7.85**	3.97 **7.46**	3.87 **7.19**	3.79 **7.00**	3.73 **6.84**	3.68 **6.71**	3.63 **6.62**	3.60 **6.54**	3.57 **6.47**	3.52 **6.35**	3.49 **6.27**	3.44 **6.15**	3.41 **6.07**	3.38 **5.98**	3.34 **5.90**	3.32 **5.85**	3.29 **5.78**	3.28 **5.75**	3.25 **5.70**	3.24 **5.67**	3.23 **5.65**
8	5.32 **11.26**	4.46 **8.65**	4.07 **7.59**	3.84 **7.01**	3.69 **6.63**	3.58 **6.37**	3.50 **6.19**	3.44 **6.03**	3.39 **5.91**	3.34 **5.82**	3.31 **5.74**	3.28 **5.67**	3.23 **5.56**	3.20 **5.48**	3.15 **5.36**	3.12 **5.28**	3.08 **5.20**	3.05 **5.11**	3.03 **5.06**	3.00 **5.00**	2.98 **4.96**	2.96 **4.91**	2.94 **4.88**	2.93 **4.86**
9	5.12 **10.56**	4.26 **8.02**	3.86 **6.99**	3.63 **6.42**	3.48 **6.06**	3.37 **5.80**	3.29 **5.62**	3.23 **5.47**	3.18 **5.35**	3.13 **5.26**	3.10 **5.18**	3.07 **5.11**	3.02 **5.00**	2.98 **4.92**	2.93 **4.80**	2.90 **4.73**	2.86 **4.64**	2.82 **4.56**	2.80 **4.51**	2.77 **4.45**	2.76 **4.41**	2.73 **4.36**	2.72 **4.33**	2.71 **4.31**
10	4.96 **10.04**	4.10 **7.56**	3.71 **6.55**	3.48 **5.99**	3.33 **5.64**	3.22 **5.39**	3.14 **5.21**	3.07 **5.06**	3.02 **4.95**	2.97 **4.85**	2.94 **4.78**	2.91 **4.71**	2.86 **4.60**	2.82 **4.52**	2.77 **4.41**	2.74 **4.33**	2.70 **4.25**	2.67 **4.17**	2.64 **4.12**	2.61 **4.05**	2.59 **4.01**	2.56 **3.96**	2.55 **3.93**	2.54 **3.91**
11	4.84 **9.65**	3.98 **7.20**	3.59 **6.22**	3.36 **5.67**	3.20 **5.32**	3.09 **5.07**	3.01 **4.88**	2.95 **4.74**	2.90 **4.63**	2.86 **4.54**	2.82 **4.46**	2.79 **4.40**	2.74 **4.29**	2.70 **4.21**	2.65 **4.10**	2.61 **4.02**	2.57 **3.94**	2.53 **3.86**	2.50 **3.80**	2.47 **3.74**	2.45 **3.70**	2.42 **3.66**	2.41 **3.62**	2.40 **3.60**
12	4.75 **9.33**	3.88 **6.93**	3.49 **5.95**	3.26 **5.41**	3.11 **5.06**	3.00 **4.82**	2.92 **4.65**	2.85 **4.50**	2.80 **4.39**	2.76 **4.30**	2.72 **4.22**	2.69 **4.16**	2.64 **4.05**	2.60 **3.98**	2.54 **3.86**	2.50 **3.78**	2.46 **3.70**	2.42 **3.61**	2.40 **3.56**	2.36 **3.49**	2.35 **3.46**	2.32 **3.41**	2.31 **3.38**	2.30 **3.36**
13	4.67 **9.07**	3.80 **6.70**	3.41 **5.74**	3.18 **5.20**	3.02 **4.86**	2.92 **4.62**	2.84 **4.44**	2.77 **4.30**	2.72 **4.19**	2.67 **4.10**	2.63 **4.02**	2.60 **3.96**	2.55 **3.85**	2.51 **3.78**	2.46 **3.67**	2.42 **3.59**	2.38 **3.51**	2.34 **3.42**	2.32 **3.37**	2.28 **3.30**	2.26 **3.27**	2.24 **3.21**	2.22 **3.18**	2.21 **3.16**

14	2.13 / 3.00	2.14 / 3.02	2.16 / 3.06	2.19 / 3.11	2.21 / 3.14	2.24 / 3.21	2.27 / 3.26	2.31 / 3.34	2.35 / 3.43	2.39 / 3.51	2.44 / 3.62	2.48 / 3.70	2.53 / 3.80	2.56 / 3.86	2.60 / 3.94	2.65 / 4.03	2.70 / 4.14	2.77 / 4.28	2.85 / 4.46	2.96 / 4.69	3.11 / 5.03	3.34 / 5.56	3.74 / 6.51	4.60 / 8.86
15	2.07 / 2.87	2.08 / 2.89	2.10 / 2.92	2.12 / 2.97	2.15 / 3.00	2.18 / 3.07	2.21 / 3.12	2.25 / 3.20	2.29 / 3.29	2.33 / 3.36	2.39 / 3.48	2.43 / 3.56	2.48 / 3.67	2.51 / 3.73	2.55 / 3.80	2.59 / 3.89	2.64 / 4.00	2.70 / 4.14	2.79 / 4.32	2.90 / 4.56	3.06 / 4.89	3.29 / 5.42	3.68 / 6.36	4.54 / 8.68
16	2.01 / 2.75	2.02 / 2.77	2.04 / 2.80	2.07 / 2.86	2.09 / 2.89	2.13 / 2.96	2.16 / 3.01	2.20 / 3.10	2.24 / 3.18	2.28 / 3.25	2.33 / 3.37	2.37 / 3.45	2.42 / 3.55	2.45 / 3.61	2.49 / 3.69	2.54 / 3.78	2.59 / 3.89	2.66 / 4.03	2.74 / 4.20	2.85 / 4.44	3.01 / 4.77	3.24 / 5.29	3.63 / 6.23	4.49 / 8.53
17	1.96 / 2.65	1.97 / 2.67	1.99 / 2.70	2.02 / 2.76	2.04 / 2.79	2.08 / 2.86	2.11 / 2.92	2.15 / 3.00	2.19 / 3.08	2.23 / 3.16	2.29 / 3.27	2.33 / 3.35	2.38 / 3.45	2.41 / 3.52	2.45 / 3.59	2.50 / 3.68	2.55 / 3.79	2.62 / 3.93	2.70 / 4.10	2.81 / 4.34	2.96 / 4.67	3.20 / 5.18	3.59 / 6.11	4.45 / 8.40
18	1.92 / 2.57	1.93 / 2.59	1.95 / 2.62	1.98 / 2.68	2.00 / 2.71	2.04 / 2.78	2.07 / 2.83	2.11 / 2.91	2.15 / 3.00	2.19 / 3.07	2.25 / 3.19	2.29 / 3.27	2.34 / 3.37	2.37 / 3.44	2.41 / 3.51	2.46 / 3.60	2.51 / 3.71	2.58 / 3.85	2.66 / 4.01	2.77 / 4.25	2.93 / 4.58	3.16 / 5.09	3.55 / 6.01	4.41 / 8.28
19	1.88 / 2.49	1.90 / 2.51	1.91 / 2.54	1.94 / 2.60	1.96 / 2.63	2.00 / 2.70	2.02 / 2.76	2.07 / 2.84	2.11 / 2.92	2.15 / 3.00	2.21 / 3.12	2.26 / 3.19	2.31 / 3.30	2.34 / 3.36	2.38 / 3.43	2.43 / 3.52	2.48 / 3.63	2.55 / 3.77	2.63 / 3.94	2.74 / 4.17	2.90 / 4.50	3.13 / 5.01	3.52 / 5.93	4.38 / 8.18
20	1.84 / 2.42	1.85 / 2.44	1.87 / 2.47	1.90 / 2.53	1.92 / 2.56	1.96 / 2.63	1.99 / 2.69	2.04 / 2.77	2.08 / 2.86	2.12 / 2.94	2.18 / 3.05	2.23 / 3.13	2.28 / 3.23	2.31 / 3.30	2.35 / 3.37	2.40 / 3.45	2.45 / 3.56	2.52 / 3.71	2.60 / 3.87	2.71 / 4.10	2.87 / 4.43	3.10 / 4.94	3.49 / 5.85	4.35 / 8.10
21	1.81 / 2.36	1.82 / 2.38	1.84 / 2.42	1.87 / 2.47	1.89 / 2.51	1.93 / 2.58	1.96 / 2.63	2.00 / 2.72	2.05 / 2.80	2.09 / 2.88	2.15 / 2.99	2.20 / 3.07	2.25 / 3.17	2.28 / 3.24	2.32 / 3.31	2.37 / 3.40	2.42 / 3.51	2.49 / 3.65	2.57 / 3.81	2.68 / 4.04	2.84 / 4.37	3.07 / 4.87	3.47 / 5.78	4.32 / 8.02
22	1.78 / 2.31	1.80 / 2.33	1.81 / 2.37	1.84 / 2.42	1.87 / 2.46	1.91 / 2.53	1.93 / 2.58	1.98 / 2.67	2.03 / 2.75	2.07 / 2.83	2.13 / 2.94	2.18 / 3.02	2.23 / 3.12	2.26 / 3.18	2.30 / 3.26	2.35 / 3.35	2.40 / 3.45	2.47 / 3.59	2.55 / 3.76	2.66 / 3.99	2.82 / 4.31	3.05 / 4.82	3.44 / 5.72	4.30 / 7.94
23	1.76 / 2.26	1.77 / 2.28	1.79 / 2.32	1.82 / 2.37	1.84 / 2.41	1.88 / 2.48	1.91 / 2.53	1.96 / 2.62	2.00 / 2.70	2.04 / 2.78	2.10 / 2.89	2.14 / 2.97	2.20 / 3.07	2.24 / 3.14	2.28 / 3.21	2.32 / 3.30	2.38 / 3.41	2.45 / 3.54	2.53 / 3.71	2.64 / 3.94	2.80 / 4.26	3.03 / 4.76	3.42 / 5.66	4.28 / 7.88
24	1.73 / 2.21	1.74 / 2.23	1.76 / 2.27	1.80 / 2.33	1.82 / 2.36	1.86 / 2.44	1.89 / 2.49	1.94 / 2.58	1.98 / 2.66	2.02 / 2.74	2.09 / 2.85	2.13 / 2.93	2.18 / 3.03	2.22 / 3.09	2.26 / 3.17	2.30 / 3.25	2.36 / 3.36	2.43 / 3.50	2.51 / 3.67	2.62 / 3.90	2.78 / 4.22	3.01 / 4.72	3.40 / 5.61	4.26 / 7.82
25	1.71 / 2.17	1.72 / 2.19	1.74 / 2.23	1.77 / 2.29	1.80 / 2.32	1.84 / 2.40	1.87 / 2.45	1.92 / 2.54	1.96 / 2.62	2.00 / 2.70	2.06 / 2.81	2.11 / 2.89	2.16 / 2.99	2.20 / 3.05	2.24 / 3.13	2.28 / 3.21	2.34 / 3.32	2.41 / 3.46	2.49 / 3.63	2.60 / 3.86	2.76 / 4.18	2.99 / 4.68	3.38 / 5.57	4.24 / 7.77
26	1.69 / 2.13	1.70 / 2.15	1.72 / 2.19	1.76 / 2.25	1.78 / 2.28	1.82 / 2.36	1.85 / 2.41	1.90 / 2.50	1.95 / 2.58	1.99 / 2.66	2.05 / 2.77	2.10 / 2.86	2.15 / 2.96	2.18 / 3.02	2.22 / 3.09	2.27 / 3.17	2.32 / 3.29	2.39 / 3.42	2.47 / 3.59	2.59 / 3.82	2.74 / 4.14	2.98 / 4.64	3.37 / 5.53	4.22 / 7.72

n_1 degrees of freedom (for greater mean square)

n_2	1	2	3	4	5	6	7	8	9	10	11	12	14	16	20	24	30	40	50	75	100	200	500	∞
27	4.21 **7.68**	3.35 **5.49**	2.96 **4.60**	2.73 **4.11**	2.57 **3.79**	2.46 **3.56**	2.37 **3.39**	2.30 **3.26**	2.25 **3.14**	2.20 **3.06**	2.16 **2.98**	2.13 **2.93**	2.08 **2.83**	2.03 **2.74**	1.97 **2.63**	1.93 **2.55**	1.88 **2.47**	1.84 **2.38**	1.80 **2.33**	1.76 **2.25**	1.74 **2.21**	1.71 **2.16**	1.68 **2.12**	1.67 **2.10**
28	4.20 **7.64**	3.34 **5.45**	2.95 **4.57**	2.71 **4.07**	2.56 **3.76**	2.44 **3.53**	2.36 **3.36**	2.29 **3.23**	2.24 **3.11**	2.19 **3.03**	2.15 **2.95**	2.12 **2.90**	2.06 **2.80**	2.02 **2.71**	1.96 **2.60**	1.91 **2.52**	1.87 **2.44**	1.81 **2.35**	1.78 **2.30**	1.75 **2.22**	1.72 **2.18**	1.69 **2.13**	1.67 **2.09**	1.65 **2.06**
29	4.18 **7.60**	3.33 **5.42**	2.93 **4.54**	2.70 **4.04**	2.54 **3.73**	2.43 **3.50**	2.35 **3.33**	2.28 **3.20**	2.22 **3.08**	2.18 **3.00**	2.14 **2.92**	2.10 **2.87**	2.05 **2.77**	2.00 **2.68**	1.94 **2.57**	1.90 **2.49**	1.85 **2.41**	1.80 **2.32**	1.77 **2.27**	1.73 **2.19**	1.71 **2.15**	1.68 **2.10**	1.65 **2.06**	1.64 **2.03**
30	4.17 **7.56**	3.32 **5.39**	2.92 **4.51**	2.69 **4.02**	2.53 **3.70**	2.42 **3.47**	2.34 **3.30**	2.27 **3.17**	2.21 **3.06**	2.16 **2.98**	2.12 **2.90**	2.09 **2.84**	2.04 **2.74**	1.99 **2.66**	1.93 **2.55**	1.89 **2.47**	1.84 **2.38**	1.79 **2.29**	1.76 **2.24**	1.72 **2.16**	1.69 **2.13**	1.66 **2.07**	1.64 **2.03**	1.62 **2.01**
32	4.15 **7.50**	3.30 **5.34**	2.90 **4.46**	2.67 **3.97**	2.51 **3.66**	2.40 **3.42**	2.32 **3.25**	2.25 **3.12**	2.19 **3.01**	2.14 **2.94**	2.10 **2.86**	2.07 **2.80**	2.02 **2.70**	1.97 **2.62**	1.91 **2.51**	1.86 **2.42**	1.82 **2.34**	1.76 **2.25**	1.74 **2.20**	1.69 **2.12**	1.67 **2.08**	1.64 **2.02**	1.61 **1.98**	1.59 **1.96**
34	4.13 **7.44**	3.28 **5.29**	2.88 **4.42**	2.65 **3.93**	2.49 **3.61**	2.38 **3.38**	2.30 **3.21**	2.23 **3.08**	2.17 **2.97**	2.12 **2.89**	2.08 **2.82**	2.05 **2.76**	2.00 **2.66**	1.95 **2.58**	1.89 **2.47**	1.84 **2.38**	1.80 **2.30**	1.74 **2.21**	1.71 **2.15**	1.67 **2.08**	1.64 **2.04**	1.61 **1.98**	1.59 **1.94**	1.57 **1.91**
36	4.11 **7.39**	3.26 **5.25**	2.86 **4.38**	2.63 **3.89**	2.48 **3.58**	2.36 **3.35**	2.28 **3.18**	2.21 **3.04**	2.15 **2.94**	2.10 **2.86**	2.06 **2.78**	2.03 **2.72**	1.98 **2.62**	1.93 **2.54**	1.87 **2.43**	1.82 **2.35**	1.78 **2.26**	1.72 **2.17**	1.69 **2.12**	1.65 **2.04**	1.62 **2.00**	1.59 **1.94**	1.56 **1.90**	1.55 **1.87**
38	4.10 **7.35**	3.25 **5.21**	2.85 **4.34**	2.62 **3.86**	2.46 **3.54**	2.35 **3.32**	2.26 **3.15**	2.19 **3.02**	2.14 **2.91**	2.09 **2.82**	2.05 **2.75**	2.02 **2.69**	1.96 **2.59**	1.92 **2.51**	1.85 **2.40**	1.80 **2.32**	1.76 **2.22**	1.71 **2.14**	1.67 **2.08**	1.63 **2.00**	1.60 **1.97**	1.57 **1.90**	1.54 **1.86**	1.53 **1.84**
40	4.08 **7.31**	3.23 **5.18**	2.84 **4.31**	2.61 **3.83**	2.45 **3.51**	2.34 **3.29**	2.25 **3.12**	2.18 **2.99**	2.12 **2.88**	2.07 **2.80**	2.04 **2.73**	2.00 **2.66**	1.95 **2.56**	1.90 **2.49**	1.84 **2.37**	1.79 **2.29**	1.74 **2.20**	1.69 **2.11**	1.66 **2.05**	1.61 **1.97**	1.59 **1.94**	1.55 **1.88**	1.53 **1.84**	1.51 **1.81**
42	4.07 **7.27**	3.22 **5.15**	2.83 **4.29**	2.59 **3.80**	2.44 **3.49**	2.32 **3.26**	2.24 **3.10**	2.17 **2.96**	2.11 **2.86**	2.06 **2.77**	2.02 **2.70**	1.99 **2.64**	1.94 **2.54**	1.89 **2.46**	1.82 **2.35**	1.78 **2.26**	1.73 **2.17**	1.68 **2.08**	1.64 **2.02**	1.60 **1.94**	1.57 **1.91**	1.54 **1.85**	1.51 **1.80**	1.49 **1.78**
44	4.06 **7.24**	3.21 **5.12**	2.82 **4.26**	2.58 **3.78**	2.43 **3.46**	2.31 **3.24**	2.23 **3.07**	2.16 **2.94**	2.10 **2.84**	2.05 **2.75**	2.01 **2.68**	1.98 **2.62**	1.92 **2.52**	1.88 **2.44**	1.81 **2.32**	1.76 **2.24**	1.72 **2.15**	1.66 **2.06**	1.63 **2.00**	1.58 **1.92**	1.56 **1.88**	1.52 **1.82**	1.50 **1.78**	1.48 **1.75**
46	4.05 **7.21**	3.20 **5.10**	2.81 **4.24**	2.57 **3.76**	2.42 **3.44**	2.30 **3.22**	2.22 **3.05**	2.14 **2.92**	2.09 **2.82**	2.04 **2.73**	2.00 **2.66**	1.97 **2.60**	1.91 **2.50**	1.87 **2.42**	1.80 **2.30**	1.75 **2.22**	1.71 **2.13**	1.65 **2.04**	1.62 **1.98**	1.57 **1.90**	1.54 **1.86**	1.51 **1.80**	1.48 **1.76**	1.46 **1.72**
48	4.04 **7.19**	3.19 **5.08**	2.80 **4.22**	2.56 **3.74**	2.41 **3.42**	2.30 **3.20**	2.21 **3.04**	2.14 **2.90**	2.08 **2.80**	2.03 **2.71**	1.99 **2.64**	1.96 **2.58**	1.90 **2.48**	1.86 **2.40**	1.79 **2.28**	1.74 **2.20**	1.70 **2.11**	1.64 **2.02**	1.61 **1.96**	1.56 **1.88**	1.53 **1.84**	1.50 **1.78**	1.47 **1.73**	1.45 **1.70**

df																								
50	4.03	3.18	2.79	2.56	2.40	2.29	2.20	2.13	2.07	2.02	1.98	1.95	1.90	1.85	1.78	1.74	1.69	1.63	1.60	1.55	1.52	1.48	1.46	1.44
	7.17	**5.06**	**4.20**	**3.72**	**3.41**	**3.18**	**3.02**	**2.88**	**2.78**	**2.70**	**2.62**	**2.56**	**2.46**	**2.39**	**2.26**	**2.18**	**2.10**	**2.00**	**1.94**	**1.86**	**1.82**	**1.76**	**1.71**	**1.68**
55	4.02	3.17	2.78	2.54	2.38	2.27	2.18	2.11	2.05	2.00	1.97	1.93	1.88	1.83	1.76	1.72	1.67	1.61	1.58	1.52	1.50	1.46	1.43	1.41
	7.12	**5.01**	**4.16**	**3.68**	**3.37**	**3.15**	**2.98**	**2.85**	**2.75**	**2.66**	**2.59**	**2.53**	**2.43**	**2.35**	**2.23**	**2.15**	**2.06**	**1.96**	**1.90**	**1.82**	**1.78**	**1.71**	**1.66**	**1.64**
60	4.00	3.15	2.76	2.52	2.37	2.25	2.17	2.10	2.04	1.99	1.95	1.92	1.86	1.81	1.75	1.70	1.65	1.59	1.56	1.50	1.48	1.44	1.41	1.39
	7.08	**4.98**	**4.13**	**3.65**	**3.34**	**3.12**	**2.95**	**2.82**	**2.72**	**2.63**	**2.56**	**2.50**	**2.40**	**2.32**	**2.20**	**2.12**	**2.03**	**1.93**	**1.87**	**1.79**	**1.74**	**1.68**	**1.63**	**1.60**
65	3.99	3.14	2.75	2.51	2.36	2.24	2.15	2.08	2.02	1.98	1.94	1.90	1.85	1.80	1.73	1.68	1.63	1.57	1.54	1.49	1.46	1.42	1.39	1.37
	7.04	**4.95**	**4.10**	**3.62**	**3.31**	**3.09**	**2.93**	**2.79**	**2.70**	**2.61**	**2.54**	**2.47**	**2.37**	**2.30**	**2.18**	**2.09**	**2.00**	**1.90**	**1.84**	**1.76**	**1.71**	**1.64**	**1.60**	**1.56**
70	3.98	3.13	2.74	2.50	2.35	2.23	2.14	2.07	2.01	1.97	1.93	1.89	1.84	1.79	1.72	1.67	1.62	1.56	1.53	1.47	1.45	1.40	1.37	1.35
	7.01	**4.92**	**4.08**	**3.60**	**3.29**	**3.07**	**2.91**	**2.77**	**2.67**	**2.59**	**2.51**	**2.45**	**2.35**	**2.28**	**2.15**	**2.07**	**1.98**	**1.88**	**1.82**	**1.74**	**1.69**	**1.62**	**1.56**	**1.53**
80	3.96	3.11	2.72	2.48	2.33	2.21	2.12	2.05	1.99	1.95	1.91	1.88	1.82	1.77	1.70	1.65	1.60	1.54	1.51	1.45	1.42	1.38	1.35	1.32
	6.96	**4.88**	**4.04**	**3.56**	**3.25**	**3.04**	**2.87**	**2.74**	**2.64**	**2.55**	**2.48**	**2.41**	**2.32**	**2.24**	**2.11**	**2.03**	**1.94**	**1.84**	**1.78**	**1.70**	**1.65**	**1.57**	**1.52**	**1.49**
100	3.94	3.09	2.70	2.46	2.30	2.19	2.10	2.03	1.97	1.92	1.88	1.85	1.79	1.75	1.68	1.63	1.57	1.51	1.48	1.42	1.39	1.34	1.30	1.28
	6.90	**4.82**	**3.98**	**3.51**	**3.20**	**2.99**	**2.82**	**2.69**	**2.59**	**2.51**	**2.43**	**2.36**	**2.26**	**2.19**	**2.06**	**1.98**	**1.89**	**1.79**	**1.73**	**1.64**	**1.59**	**1.51**	**1.46**	**1.43**
125	3.92	3.07	2.68	2.44	2.29	2.17	2.08	2.01	1.95	1.90	1.86	1.83	1.77	1.72	1.65	1.60	1.55	1.49	1.45	1.39	1.36	1.31	1.27	1.25
	6.84	**4.78**	**3.94**	**3.47**	**3.17**	**2.95**	**2.79**	**2.65**	**2.56**	**2.47**	**2.40**	**2.33**	**2.23**	**2.15**	**2.03**	**1.94**	**1.85**	**1.75**	**1.68**	**1.59**	**1.54**	**1.46**	**1.40**	**1.37**
150	3.91	3.06	2.67	2.43	2.27	2.16	2.07	2.00	1.94	1.89	1.85	1.82	1.76	1.71	1.64	1.59	1.54	1.47	1.44	1.37	1.34	1.29	1.25	1.22
	6.81	**4.75**	**3.91**	**3.44**	**3.14**	**2.92**	**2.76**	**2.62**	**2.53**	**2.44**	**2.37**	**2.30**	**2.20**	**2.12**	**2.00**	**1.91**	**1.83**	**1.72**	**1.66**	**1.56**	**1.51**	**1.43**	**1.37**	**1.33**
200	3.89	3.04	2.65	2.41	2.26	2.14	2.05	1.98	1.92	1.87	1.83	1.80	1.74	1.69	1.62	1.57	1.52	1.45	1.42	1.35	1.32	1.26	1.22	1.19
	6.76	**4.71**	**3.88**	**3.41**	**3.11**	**2.90**	**2.73**	**2.60**	**2.50**	**2.41**	**2.34**	**2.28**	**2.17**	**2.09**	**1.97**	**1.88**	**1.79**	**1.69**	**1.62**	**1.53**	**1.48**	**1.39**	**1.33**	**1.28**
400	3.86	3.02	2.62	2.39	2.23	2.12	2.03	1.96	1.90	1.85	1.81	1.78	1.72	1.67	1.60	1.54	1.49	1.42	1.38	1.32	1.28	1.22	1.16	1.13
	6.70	**4.66**	**3.83**	**3.36**	**3.06**	**2.85**	**2.69**	**2.55**	**2.46**	**2.37**	**2.29**	**2.23**	**2.12**	**2.04**	**1.92**	**1.84**	**1.74**	**1.64**	**1.57**	**1.47**	**1.42**	**1.32**	**1.24**	**1.19**
1000	3.85	3.00	2.61	2.38	2.22	2.10	2.02	1.95	1.89	1.84	1.80	1.76	1.70	1.65	1.58	1.53	1.47	1.41	1.36	1.30	1.26	1.19	1.13	1.08
	6.66	**4.62**	**3.80**	**3.34**	**3.04**	**2.82**	**2.66**	**2.53**	**2.43**	**2.34**	**2.26**	**2.20**	**2.09**	**2.01**	**1.89**	**1.81**	**1.71**	**1.61**	**1.54**	**1.44**	**1.38**	**1.28**	**1.19**	**1.11**
∞	3.84	2.99	2.60	2.37	2.21	2.09	2.01	1.94	1.88	1.83	1.79	1.75	1.69	1.64	1.57	1.52	1.46	1.40	1.35	1.28	1.24	1.17	1.11	1.00
	6.64	**4.60**	**3.78**	**3.32**	**3.02**	**2.80**	**2.64**	**2.51**	**2.41**	**2.32**	**2.24**	**2.18**	**2.07**	**1.99**	**1.87**	**1.79**	**1.69**	**1.59**	**1.52**	**1.41**	**1.36**	**1.25**	**1.15**	**1.00**

Source: Reprinted by permission from STATISTICAL METHODS, Seventh Edition by George W. Snedecor and William G. Cochran © 1980 by Iowa State University Press, 2121 South State Ave., Ames, Iowa 50010.

Appendix C
Tables of χ^2

Upper percentage points of the χ^2 distribution

v \ Q	0.995	0.990	.0975	0.950	0.900	0.750	0.500
1	392704.10^{-10}	157088.10^{-9}	982069.10^{-9}	393214.10^{-8}	0.0157908	0.1015308	0.454937
2	0.0100251	0.0201007	0.0506356	0.102587	0.210720	0.575364	1.38629
3	0.0717212	0.114832	0.215795	0.351846	0.584375	1.212534	2.36597
4	0.206990	0.297110	0.484419	0.710721	1.063623	1.92255	3.35670
5	0.411740	0.554300	0.831211	1.145476	1.61031	2.67460	4.35146
6	0.675727	0.872085	1.237347	1.63539	2.20413	3.45460	5.34812
7	0.989265	1.239043	1.68987	2.16735	2.83311	4.25485	6.34581
8	1.344419	1.646482	2.17973	2.73264	3.48954	5.07064	7.34412
9	1.734926	2.087912	2.70039	3.32511	4.16816	5.89883	8.34283
10	2.15585	2.55821	3.24697	3.94030	4.86518	6.73720	9.34182
11	2.60321	3.05347	3.81575	4.57481	5.57779	7.58412	10.3410
12	3.07382	3.57056	4.40379	5.22603	6.30380	8.43842	11.3403
13	3.56503	4.10691	5.00874	5.89186	7.04150	9.29906	12.3398
14	4.07468	4.66043	5.62872	6.57063	7.78953	10.1653	13.3393
15	4.60094	5.22935	6.26214	7.26094	8.54675	11.0365	14.3389
16	5.14224	5.81221	6.90766	7.96164	9.31223	11.9122	15.3385
17	5.69724	6.40776	7.56418	8.67176	10.0852	12.7919	16.3381
18	6.26481	7.01491	8.23075	9.39046	10.8649	13.6753	17.3379
19	6.84398	7.63273	8.90655	10.1170	11.6509	14.5620	18.3376

20	19.3374	15.4518	12.4426	10.8508	9.59083	8.26040	7.43386
21	20.3372	16.3444	13.2396	11.5913	10.28293	8.89720	8.03366
22	21.3370	17.2396	14.0415	12.3380	10.9823	9.54249	8.64272
23	22.3369	18.1373	14.8479	13.0905	11.6885	10.19567	9.26042
24	23.3367	19.0372	15.6587	13.8484	12.4011	10.8564	9.88623
25	24.3366	19.9393	16.4734	14.6114	13.1197	11.5240	10.5197
26	25.3364	20.8434	17.2919	15.3791	13.8439	12.1981	11.1603
27	26.3363	21.7494	18.1138	16.1513	14.5733	12.8786	11.8076
28	27.3363	22.6572	18.9392	16.9279	15.3079	13.5648	12.4613
29	28.3362	23.5666	19.7677	17.7083	16.0471	14.2565	13.1211
30	29.3360	24.4776	20.5992	18.4926	16.7908	14.9535	13.7867
40	39.3354	33.6603	29.0505	26.5093	24.4331	22.1643	20.7065
50	49.3349	42.9421	37.6886	34.7642	32.3574	29.7067	27.9907
60	59.3347	52.2938	46.4589	43.1879	40.4817	37.4848	35.5346
70	69.3344	61.6983	55.3290	51.7393	48.7576	45.4418	43.2752
80	79.3343	71.1445	64.2778	60.3915	57.1532	53.5400	51.1720
90	89.3342	80.6247	73.2912	69.1260	65.6466	61.7541	59.1963
100	99.3341	90.1332	82.3581	77.9295	74.2219	70.0648	67.3276
z_Q	0.0000	-0.6745	-1.2816	-1.6449	-1.9600	-2.3263	-2.5758

v \ Q	0.250	0.100	0.050	0.025	0.010	0.005	0.001
1	1.32330	2.70554	3.84146	5.02389	6.63490	7.87944	10.828
2	2.77259	4.60517	5.99147	7.37776	9.21034	10.5966	13.816
3	4.10835	6.25139	7.81473	9.34840	11.3449	12.8381	16.266
4	5.38527	7.77944	9.48773	11.1433	13.2767	14.8602	18.467
5	6.62568	9.23635	11.0705	12.8325	15.0863	16.7496	20.515
6	7.84080	10.6446	12.5916	14.4494	16.8119	18.5476	22.458
7	9.03715	12.0170	14.0671	16.0128	18.4753	20.2777	24.322
8	10.2188	13.3616	15.5073	17.5346	20.0902	21.9550	26.125
9	11.3887	14.6837	16.9190	19.0228	21.6660	23.5893	27.877
10	12.5489	15.9871	18.3070	20.4831	23.2093	25.1882	29.588
11	13.7007	17.2750	19.6751	21.9200	24.7250	26.7569	31.264
12	14.8454	18.5494	21.0261	23.3367	26.2170	28.2995	32.909
13	15.9839	19.8119	22.3621	24.7356	27.6883	29.8194	34.528
14	17.1170	21.0642	23.6848	26.1190	29.1413	31.3193	36.123
15	18.2451	22.3072	24.9958	27.4884	30.5779	32.8013	37.697
16	19.3688	23.5418	26.2962	28.8454	31.9999	34.2672	39.252
17	20.4887	24.7690	27.5871	30.1910	33.4087	35.7185	40.790
18	21.6049	25.9894	28.8693	31.5264	34.8053	37.1564	42.312
19	22.7178	27.2036	30.1435	32.8532	36.1908	38.5822	43.820

20	23.8277	28.4120	31.4104	34.1696	37.5662	39.9968	45.315
21	24.9348	29.6151	32.6705	35.4789	38.9321	41.4010	46.797
22	26.0393	30.8133	33.9244	36.7807	40.2894	42.7956	48.268
23	27.1413	32.0069	35.1725	38.0757	41.6384	44.1813	49.728
24	28.2412	33.1963	36.4151	39.3641	42.9798	45.5585	51.179
25	29.3389	34.3816	37.6525	40.6465	44.3141	46.9278	52.620
26	30.4345	35.5631	38.8852	41.9232	45.6417	48.2899	54.052
27	31.5284	36.7412	40.1133	43.1944	46.9630	49.6449	55.476
28	32.6205	37.9159	41.3372	44.4607	48.2782	50.9933	56.892
29	33.7109	39.0875	42.5569	45.7222	49.5879	52.3356	58.302
30	34.7998	40.2560	43.7729	46.9792	50.8922	52.6720	59.703
40	45.6160	51.8050	55.7585	59.3417	63.6907	66.7659	73.402
50	56.3336	63.1671	67.5048	71.4202	76.1539	79.4900	86.661
60	66.9814	74.3970	79.0819	83.2976	88.3794	91.9517	99.607
70	77.5766	85.5271	90.5312	95.0231	100.425	104.215	112.317
80	88.1303	96.5782	101.879	106.629	112.329	116.321	124.839
90	98.6499	107.565	113.145	118.136	124.116	128.299	137.208
100	109.141	118.498	124.342	129.561	135.807	140.169	149.449
z_Q	+0.6745	+1.2816	+1.6449	+1.9600	+2.3263	+2.5758	+3.0902

Source: Reprinted by permission from *Biometrika Tables for Statisticians*, Vol. 1, Third Edition, E.S. Pearson and H.O. Hartley (Eds.) © 1966 by the Biometrika Trust.

Appendix D
Tables of Orthogonal Polynomial Coefficients

Coefficients of orthogonal polynomials

	J = 3		J = 4			J = 5			
	1	2	1	2	3	1	2	3	4
X_1	−1	1	−3	1	−1	−2	2	−1	1
X_2	0	−2	−1	−1	3	1	−1	2	−4
X_3	1	1	1	−1	−3	0	−2	0	6
X_4			3	1	1	1	−1	−2	−4
X_5						2	2	1	1
Σc_j^2	2	6	20	4	20	10	14	10	70

	J = 6					J = 7					
	1	2	3	4	5	1	2	3	4	5	6
X_1	−5	5	−5	1	−1	−3	5	−1	3	−1	1
X_2	−3	−1	7	−3	5	−2	0	1	−7	4	−6
X_3	−1	−4	4	2	−10	−1	−3	1	1	−5	15
X_4	1	−4	−4	2	10	0	−4	0	6	0	−20
X_5	3	−1	−7	−3	−5	1	−3	−1	1	5	15
X_6	5	5	5	1	1	2	0	−1	−7	−4	−6
X_7						3	5	1	3	1	1
Σc_j^2	70	84	180	28	252	28	84	6	154	84	924

	J = 8						J = 9					
	1	2	3	4	5	6	1	2	3	4	5	6
X_1	−7	7	−7	7	−7	1	−4	28	−14	14	−4	4
X_2	−5	1	5	−13	23	−5	−3	7	7	−21	11	−17
X_3	−3	−3	7	−3	−17	9	−2	−8	13	−11	−4	22
X_4	−1	−5	3	9	−15	−5	−1	−17	9	9	−9	1
X_5	1	−5	−3	9	15	−5	0	−20	0	18	0	−20
X_6	3	−3	−7	−3	17	9	1	−17	−9	9	9	1
X_7	5	1	−5	−13	−23	−5	2	−8	−13	−11	4	22
X_8	7	7	7	7	7	1	3	7	−7	−21	−11	−17
X_9							4	28	14	14	4	4
Σc_j^2	168	168	264	616	2184	264	60	2772	990	2002	468	1980

	J = 10						J = 11					
	1	2	3	4	5	6	1	2	3	4	5	6
X_1	−9	6	−42	18	−6	3	−5	15	−30	6	−3	15
X_2	−7	2	14	−22	14	−11	−4	6	6	−6	6	−48
X_3	−5	−1	35	−17	−1	10	−3	−1	22	−6	1	29
X_4	−3	−3	31	3	−11	6	−2	−6	23	−1	−4	36
X_5	−1	−4	12	18	−6	−8	−1	−9	14	4	−4	−12
X_6	1	−4	−12	18	6	−8	0	−10	0	6	0	−40
X_7	3	−3	−31	3	11	6	1	−9	−14	4	4	−12
X_8	5	−1	−35	−17	1	10	2	−6	−23	−1	4	36
X_9	7	2	−14	−22	−14	−11	3	−1	−22	−6	−1	29
X_{10}	9	6	42	18	6	3	4	6	−6	−6	−6	−48
X_{11}							5	15	30	6	3	15
Σc_j^2	330	132	8580	2860	780	660	110	858	4290	286	156	11220

	J = 12						J = 13					
	1	2	3	4	5	6	1	2	3	4	5	6
X_1	−11	55	−33	33	−33	11	−6	22	−11	99	−22	22
X_2	−9	25	3	−27	57	−31	−5	11	0	−66	33	−55
X_3	−7	1	21	−33	21	11	−4	2	6	−96	18	8
X_4	−5	−17	25	−13	−29	25	−3	−5	8	−54	−11	43
X_5	−3	−29	19	12	−44	4	−2	−10	7	11	−26	22
X_6	−1	−35	7	28	−20	−20	−1	−13	4	64	−20	−20
X_7	1	−35	−7	28	20	−20	0	−14	0	84	0	−40
X_8	3	−29	−19	12	44	4	1	−13	−4	64	20	−20
X_9	5	−17	−25	−13	29	25	2	−10	−7	11	26	22
X_{10}	7	1	−21	−33	−21	11	3	−5	−8	−54	11	43
X_{11}	9	25	−3	−27	−57	−31	4	2	−6	−96	−18	8
X_{12}	11	55	33	33	33	11	5	11	0	−66	−33	−55
X_{13}							6	22	11	99	22	22
Σc_j^2	572	12012	5148	8008	15912	4488	182	2002	572	68068	6188	14212

	J = 14						J = 15					
	1	2	3	4	5	6	1	2	3	4	5	6
X_1	−13	13	−143	143	−143	143	−7	91	−91	1001	−1001	143
X_2	−11	7	−11	−77	187	−319	−6	52	−13	−429	1144	−286
X_3	−9	2	66	−132	132	−11	−5	19	35	−869	979	−55
X_4	−7	−2	98	−92	−28	227	−4	−8	58	−704	44	176
X_5	−5	−5	95	−13	−139	185	−3	−29	61	−249	−751	197
X_6	−3	−7	67	63	−145	−25	−2	−44	49	251	−1000	50
X_7	−1	−8	24	108	−60	−200	−1	−53	27	621	−675	−125
X_8	1	−8	−24	108	60	−200	0	−56	0	756	0	−200
X_9	3	−7	−67	63	145	−25	1	−53	−27	621	675	−125
X_{10}	5	−5	−95	−13	139	185	2	−44	−49	251	1000	50
X_{11}	7	−2	−98	−92	28	227	3	−29	−61	−249	751	197
X_{12}	9	2	−66	−132	−132	−11	4	−8	−58	−704	−44	176
X_{13}	11	7	11	−77	−187	−319	5	19	−35	−869	−979	−55
X_{14}	13	13	143	143	143	143	6	52	13	−429	−1144	−286
X_{15}							7	91	91	1001	1001	143
Σc_j^2	910	728	97240	136136	235144	497420	280	37128	39780	6446460	10581480	426360

Source: STATISTICS, 3/e, by William L. Hays. Copyright © 1981 by CBS College Publishing. Reprinted by permission of Holt, Rinehart & Winston, Inc.

Problems

1. Correlate the following pair of variables, X and Y. If possible, perform the analysis both by hand (or using a hand calculator) and with a computer package such as SAS or SPSSX. Also report the simple descriptive statistics (mean and standard deviation) of X and Y. Also, compute the covariance of X and Y.

X	Y
59	16
67	28
63	21
56	15
61	20
66	28
58	18
63	27
55	15
58	14
58	18
53	18
52	10
69	29
64	26
60	16
67	24
57	19
57	13
55	17

(*Answer*)
$r = .88$, $X = 59.5$, $s_x = 4.9$, $Y = 19.6$, $s_y = 5.6$. The covariance is 24.15.

2. Repeat the analysis using the following data.

X	Y	
27	6	162
36	6	216
32	3	96
29	5	145
32	5	160
31	3	93
32	3	96
31	5	155
32	4	155
31	5	155
34	5	128
27	4	170
29	5	108
30	4	145
28	6	120
35	5	168
30	5	175
37	6	150
27	5	222
37	4	135
		148

(*Answer*)
$r = .0$, $X = 31.35$, $s_x = 3.17$, $Y = 4.70$, $s_y = .98$. The covariance is .0.

3. Repeat the analysis using the following data.

X	Y	XY
48	−11	−528
61	−18	−1098
56	−17	−952
54	−15	−810
45	−8	−360
49	−12	−588
53	−14	−742
50	−11	−550
52	−15	−780
56	−15	−840
58	−16	−928
61	−19	−1159
56	−16	−896
55	−17	−935
63	−23	−1449
53	−16	−848
51	−13	−663
54	−14	−756
46	−10	−460
54	−15	−810
		−16152

(*Answer*)
$r = -.95$, $X = 53.8$, $s_x = 4.8$, $Y = -14.8$, $s_y = 3.4$. The covariance is 15.61. −14.79

4. Take the data from each of the above three problems and obtain the regression of X on Y in both raw and standard score form. What are the standard errors of estimate in raw and standardized form?
(*Answer*)
(a) $Y' = 1.00X - 40.61$, $z'_y = .88z_x$, and $s_{y \cdot x} = 2.63$ (raw score) and .47 (standardized).
(b) $Y' = 4.68$, $z'_y = .0$, and $s_{y \cdot x} = 3.47$ (raw score) and 1.0 (standardized).
(c) $Y' = -.66X + 21.07$, $z'_y = -.95z_x$, and $s_{y \cdot x} = 1.05$ (raw score) and .31 (standardized).

5. Now, take the data from each of the above three problems and obtain the regression of Y on X in both raw and standard score form. What are the standard errors of estimate in raw and standardized form?
(*Answer*)
(a) $X' = .77Y + 44.72$, $z'_x = .88z_y$, and $s_{x \cdot y} = 2.30$ (raw score) and .47 (standardized).
(b) $X' = 31.32$, $z'_x = .0$, and $s_{x \cdot y} = .98$ (raw score) and 1.0 (standardized).
(c) $X' = -1.34Y + 33.90$, $z'_x = -.95z_y$, and $s_{x \cdot y} = 1.49$ (raw score) and .31 (standardized).

6. Generate scatterplots for the three data sets.

7. Let $r_{xw} = .7$, $r_{yw} = .7$, and $r_{xy} = .90$. Obtain (a) $r_{xw \cdot y}$, (b) $r_{(x-y)w}$, (c) $r_{yw \cdot x}$, and $r_{(y-x)w}$.
(*Answer*)
(a) $= .22$, (b) $= .16$, (c) $= .22$, (d) $= .16$.

8. Repeat problem 7, but let $r_{xy} = .0$.
(*Answer*)
(a) .98, (b) .70, (c) .98, (d) .70.

9. Now, let $r_{xw} = .7$, $r_{yw} = .0$, and $r_{xy} = .6$. Perform the same computations.
(*Answer*)
(a) .87, (b) .70, (c) $-.74$, (d) $-.52$.

PROBLEMS FOR CHAPTER 3

1. Construct an example of (a) a symmetric matrix, (b) a skew-symmetric matrix, (c) a diagonal matrix, (d) an identify matrix, (e) a triangular matrix, (f) a transformation matrix with an angle of 25 degrees, and (g) a 4 × 2 matrix. Now, transpose the matrix you constructed for part (g).

2. Let $\mathbf{A}$, $\mathbf{B}$, $\mathbf{c}$, and $\mathbf{d}$ be defined as follows:

$$\mathbf{A} = \begin{bmatrix} 3 & 5 & 1 \\ 2 & 4 & 3 \\ 5 & 7 & 10 \end{bmatrix}$$

$$\mathbf{B} = \begin{bmatrix} 2 & 1 & 9 \\ 0 & 1 & 4 \\ 11 & 2 & 4 \end{bmatrix}$$

$$\mathbf{c} = \begin{bmatrix} 1 \\ 4 \\ 3 \end{bmatrix}$$

$$\mathbf{d} = \begin{bmatrix} 2 \\ 1 \\ 8 \end{bmatrix}$$

Obtain: (a) $\mathbf{A} + \mathbf{B}$, (b) $\mathbf{A} - \mathbf{B}$, (c) $\mathbf{A} \times \mathbf{B}$, (d) $\mathbf{A} \times \mathbf{c}$, (e) $\mathbf{B} \times \mathbf{c}$, (f) $\mathbf{d}' \times \mathbf{A}$, (g) $\mathbf{d}' \times \mathbf{B}$, (h) $\mathbf{c} \times \mathbf{d}'$, (i) $\mathbf{d} \times \mathbf{c}'$, (j) $\mathbf{c}' \times \mathbf{d}$, and (k) $\mathbf{d}' \times \mathbf{c}$.
(*Answer*)

(a) $\mathbf{A} + \mathbf{B}$
$$\begin{bmatrix} 5 & 6 & 10 \\ 2 & 5 & 7 \\ 16 & 9 & 14 \end{bmatrix}$$

(b) $\mathbf{A} - \mathbf{B}$
$$\begin{bmatrix} 1 & 4 & -8 \\ 2 & 3 & -1 \\ -6 & 5 & 6 \end{bmatrix}$$

(c) $\mathbf{A} \times \mathbf{B}$
$$\begin{bmatrix} 17 & 10 & 51 \\ 37 & 12 & 46 \\ 120 & 32 & 13 \end{bmatrix}$$

(d) $\mathbf{A} \times \mathbf{c}$
$$\begin{bmatrix} 26 \\ 27 \\ 63 \end{bmatrix}$$

(e) $\mathbf{B} \times \mathbf{c}$
$$\begin{bmatrix} 33 \\ 16 \\ 31 \end{bmatrix}$$

(f) $\mathbf{d}' \times \mathbf{A}$ $\begin{bmatrix} 48 & 70 & 85 \end{bmatrix}$

(g) $\mathbf{d}' \times \mathbf{B}$ $\begin{bmatrix} 92 & 19 & 54 \end{bmatrix}$

(h) $\mathbf{c} \times \mathbf{d}'$
$$\begin{bmatrix} 2 & 1 & 8 \\ 8 & 4 & 32 \\ 6 & 3 & 24 \end{bmatrix}$$

(i) $\mathbf{d} \times \mathbf{c}'$
$$\begin{bmatrix} 2 & 8 & 6 \\ 1 & 4 & 3 \\ 8 & 32 & 24 \end{bmatrix}$$

(j) and (k) $\mathbf{c}' \times \mathbf{d} = \mathbf{d}' \times \mathbf{c} =$ 30

3. Take the following 4×3 matrix and (a) determine the length of each column vector, (b) determine the length of each row vector, (c) present a matrix with the columns normalized, and (d) present a matrix with the rows normalized.

$$\begin{bmatrix} 7 & 4 \\ 8 & 3 \\ 2 & 5 \\ 4 & 6 \end{bmatrix}$$

(*Answer*)
(a) 11.53 and 9.27

$$\begin{bmatrix} .61 & .43 \\ .69 & .32 \\ .17 & .54 \\ .35 & .65 \end{bmatrix}$$

(b) 8.06, 8.59, 5.39, and 7.21

(d) $\begin{bmatrix} .87 & .50 \\ .94 & .35 \\ .37 & .93 \\ .55 & .83 \end{bmatrix}$

4. Construct a 3×3 matrix which is of rank: (a) 0, (b) 1, (c) 2, and (d) 3.

5. Compute the determinants and inverses associated with the following matrices. Prove your result by multiplying the original matrix by its inverse. Also prove that the determinant of the inverse of each matrix equals the reciprocal of the determinant of the original matrix. What kind of matrix is each of these examples?

$$A = \begin{bmatrix} 2.00 & .75 \\ 1.03 & -.90 \end{bmatrix}$$

$$B = \begin{bmatrix} 16 & 0 & 0 & 0 \\ 0 & 25 & 0 & 0 \\ 0 & 0 & 24 & 0 \\ 0 & 0 & 0 & 8 \end{bmatrix}$$

(*Answer*)
(a) **A** is a square matrix, $[A] = 2.57$, and

$$A^{-1} = \begin{bmatrix} .35 & .29 \\ .40 & .77 \end{bmatrix}$$

(b) **B** is a diagonal matrix, $[B] = 38400$, and

$$B^{-1} = \begin{bmatrix} .062 & .000 & .000 & .000 \\ .000 & .004 & .000 & .000 \\ .000 & .000 & .041 & .000 \\ .000 & .000 & .000 & .125 \end{bmatrix}$$

(c) **C** is an orthonormal (transformation) matrix, $[C] = 1.0$, and

$$C^{-1} = \begin{bmatrix} .80 & .60 \\ -.60 & .80 \end{bmatrix}$$

6. The following is a 3×3 correlation matrix (**A**) and its inverse (A^{-1}). Assume the variable in the third column and row of **A** is to be deleted. Recompute A^{-1} by two

different methods. Prove your result by showing that the product of the reduced **A** and $\mathbf{A}^{-1}$ is an identity matrix.

$$\mathbf{A} = \begin{bmatrix} 1.0 & 0.6 & 0.3 & -0.1 \\ 0.6 & 1.0 & 0.2 & 0.7 \\ 0.3 & 0.2 & 1.0 & -0.3 \\ -0.1 & 0.7 & -0.3 & 1.0 \end{bmatrix}$$

$$\mathbf{A}^{-1} = \begin{bmatrix} -68.84 & 116.05 & -31.86 & -97.67 \\ 116.05 & -192.56 & 52.33 & 162.09 \\ -31.86 & 52.33 & -13.02 & -43.72 \\ -97.67 & 162.09 & -43.72 & -135.35 \end{bmatrix}$$

(*Answer*)

$$\mathbf{A}^{-1} = \begin{bmatrix} 1.65 & -.93 & -.31 \\ -.93 & 1.56 & -.03 \\ -.31 & -.03 & 1.10 \end{bmatrix}$$

7. Compute a correlation matrix from the following matrix of z-scores:

$$\begin{bmatrix} 0.8088 & -0.8967 & 0.9871 \\ 0.8879 & -0.3408 & -0.7828 \\ -0.5941 & -0.0665 & 1.2375 \\ 0.4133 & -0.4817 & 0.6468 \\ 1.0606 & 0.8712 & -0.6670 \\ 1.4429 & 1.5968 & -1.9072 \\ 0.2165 & 1.1355 & 0.1263 \\ -1.0482 & -1.4922 & 0.4522 \\ 0.8358 & 0.9617 & -1.0148 \\ -1.7119 & -1.1803 & -0.2440 \\ 0.0748 & -0.6570 & -0.2731 \\ -0.7794 & -0.5892 & 0.3897 \\ 1.0548 & -0.4482 & 2.1740 \\ 0.1176 & -0.3414 & 1.5964 \\ -1.1264 & -0.0334 & 0.6755 \\ 1.5174 & 0.9932 & -1.8991 \\ -0.3155 & 0.1063 & -0.4444 \\ -1.7599 & -0.4675 & 0.5675 \\ -1.1370 & 0.3830 & -0.9212 \\ 1.0077 & 0.1676 & -0.1122 \\ 0.3224 & -0.4186 & -0.2139 \\ -0.1206 & 1.0681 & -0.5853 \\ 0.9490 & 2.6040 & -1.0364 \\ -0.9333 & -1.4509 & 0.6549 \\ -1.1709 & -1.0085 & 0.5270 \end{bmatrix}$$

(*Answer*)

$$\begin{bmatrix} 1.000 & .557 & -0.346 \\ 0.557 & 1.000 & -0.614 \\ -0.346 & -0.614 & 1.000 \end{bmatrix}$$

8. Verify Eq. (3-6) by using the following data. Apply the equation to both the sum and the difference. Also verify that the mean of the sum is the sum of the means and the mean of the difference is the difference of the means (see the section entitled *the mean of a linear combination*):

X	Y
26	1
53	8
43	11
38	7
20	-7
29	1
36	6
30	-2
35	8
42	3

(*Answer*)
$X = 35.2$, $s_x = 9.51$, $Y = 3.6$, $s_y = 5.46$, and $r_{xy} = .797$. Therefore, the mean of the sum is 38.8, the standard deviation of the sum is 14.25, the mean of the difference is 31.6, and the standard deviation of the difference is 6.11.

9. Compute the eigenvalues and normalized eigenvectors of symmetric matrix **A** and asymmetric matrix **B**. Note that the sum of the cross products of the eigenvector elements of **A** is zero, but the sum of the cross products of the eigenvector elements of **B** is not zero.

$$\mathbf{A} = \begin{bmatrix} 15 & 4 \\ 4 & 10 \end{bmatrix}$$

$$\mathbf{B} = \begin{bmatrix} 15 & 16 \\ 1 & 10 \end{bmatrix}$$

(*Answer*)
The eigenvalues of both matrices and 17.217 and 7.783. However, the eigenvectors of **A** are (.87, .48) and (−.87, .48), whereas the eigenvectors of **B** are (.41, .91) and (−.13, .99).

PROBLEMS FOR CHAPTER 4

1. Using the following data in which X and Y are the predictors and C is the criterion, compute R, R^2, the standardized and raw score regression equations, and the F ratio associated with a test of the null hypothesis that $R = 0$. Perform the analysis both by hand, using Eqs. (4-4) to (4-6) and through an SPSSX, SAS, BMDP, or similar package. Also, use the data to verify Eqs. (4-7) to (4-9).

C	X	Y
12	98	23
9	92	26
14	111	36
11	118	25
8	98	28
15	87	39
11	101	20
8	108	27
9	100	24
7	86	19
10	81	32
15	101	34
14	111	34
10	112	24
16	109	39
9	89	34
17	112	39
13	91	31
6	88	21
9	100	25
11	117	26
14	98	35
14	110	34
11	88	31
14	111	37
12	110	21
10	94	31
9	87	30
11	114	27
16	103	38
14	109	37
14	106	32
9	90	25
10	98	24
12	100	27
15	113	34
16	101	39
9	124	23
10	92	34
8	96	28
10	94	23
10	97	29
16	110	42
14	111	32
12	108	24
10	94	34
9	87	28
11	98	25
12	98	33
10	94	21

(*Answer*)
$R = .82$, $R^2 = .6724$, $z_c' = .355z_x + .700z_y$, $C' = .096X + .318Y - 7.630$, $F(2, 47) = 48.04$, $p < .0001$.

2. Let $\mathbf{R} = $ a 2×2 correlation matrix with r_{xy} as its off-diagonal element and $\mathbf{v}$ be the vector containing the respective correlations of X and Y with C, using results obtained from problem 1. Obtain $\mathbf{R}^{-1}$ and compute R^2 and the standardized regression equation from these data.

3. Perform the same analyses upon the following data. What role does Y play in the analysis?

C	X	Y
19	98	71
12	86	64
15	93	62
16	96	61
10	101	73
16	88	68
19	82	58
9	84	57
14	91	65
14	62	49
12	69	56
19	76	53
15	90	60
15	100	67
17	102	69
8	108	82
19	104	70
18	94	71
10	74	57
12	90	64

(*Answer*)
$R = .38$, $R^2 = .1408$, $z'_c = .859z_x - .754z_y$, $C' = .298X - .218Y + 13.852$, $F(2,47) = 3.85$, $p < .03$. Y is a suppressor variable, as its correlation with C is effectively zero (.01) yet its beta weight is substantial $(-.753)$ due to its correlation with X.

4. In the following problem, let X, Y, and Z be predictors of C. Input the data to a compute package and analyze the results, providing the same results you obtained from the data of problem 1.

C	X	Y	Z
17	5	15	8
17	2	16	5
19	3	15	7
18	5	15	10
25	5	23	11
14	3	21	8
14	3	20	8
12	6	17	5
13	4	14	9
13	3	17	8
8	5	19	3
20	7	17	7

C	X	Y	Z
15	2	22	8
16	4	16	7
11	3	12	8
14	4	22	12
12	4	15	9
12	4	19	9
19	7	19	7
12	3	14	4
8	2	12	8
13	6	8	8
18	5	13	9
13	3	17	9
20	6	17	8
18	4	19	8
19	4	17	8
14	6	13	7
16	5	20	6
12	3	19	8
22	4	21	8
19	3	20	5
14	5	14	10
17	4	21	8
17	3	13	4
11	3	14	7
11	4	13	4
13	4	12	3
20	3	18	10
19	7	21	7
12	7	13	3
18	6	19	7
13	3	19	3
17	6	20	6
20	4	20	8
21	4	16	5
18	4	18	6
11	4	19	5
21	1	8	8
10	5	9	6
10	6	6	9
17	5	16	7
13	2	21	8
8	3	16	5
15	4	16	8
11	6	18	9
14	4	22	4
17	6	11	11
17	3	18	7
21	3	13	6

(*Answer*)
$R = .34$, $R^2 = .1197$, $z'_c = .104z_x + .256z_y + .199z_z$, $C' = .285X + .261Y + 371Z$, $F(3, 56) = 2.54$, ns.

5. Perform the same analysis upon the following data that was performed in answer to question 4.

C	X	Y	Z
11	6	20	8
17	4	14	9
14	5	23	6
17	4	13	4
15	5	18	8
16	6	12	6
9	3	17	7
16	5	12	4
7	0	16	6
9	4	21	4
22	5	16	7
18	4	12	9
11	4	13	9
23	8	23	10
14	4	20	9
11	2	12	3
11	4	9	10
15	5	16	9
17	6	19	7
5	4	15	7
21	4	22	8
15	0	12	6
12	5	12	7
15	7	12	6
19	5	19	9
20	4	3	9
14	6	20	6
14	5	14	5
13	3	15	8
18	4	19	11
26	5	25	6
14	3	14	5
7	3	15	6
10	3	12	8
10	2	13	8
23	5	21	10
12	5	16	9
12	5	14	9
9	3	15	7
24	4	19	8
13	4	19	10
11	2	17	8
9	3	10	8
11	7	14	9
17	6	14	8
14	6	17	7
19	4	23	7
13	4	18	6
17	7	13	8

C	X	Y	Z
16	5	16	8
18	4	15	6
16	6	5	8
14	6	17	8
14	5	18	7
16	3	26	7
16	6	18	6
7	4	25	9
13	3	10	8
18	3	29	7
8	5	11	10

(*Answer*)
$R = .41$, $R^2 = .1717$, $z'_c = .323z_x + .227z_y + .036z_z$, $C' = .945X + .209Y + .095Z$,
$F(3, 56) = 3.87$, $p < .02$.

6. Evaluate the proposition that the results obtained in the previous two problems simply reflect sampling error by performing a cross-validation. The following matrices provide the necessary information:

$$\mathbf{b}_a = \begin{bmatrix} 0.10402568 \\ 0.25631013 \\ 0.19865516 \end{bmatrix}$$

$$\mathbf{v}_a = \begin{bmatrix} 0.09816 \\ 0.26021 \\ 0.15290 \end{bmatrix}$$

$$\mathbf{R}_a = \begin{bmatrix} 1.00000 & -0.05466 & 0.04102 \\ -.05466 & 1.00000 & 0.04824 \\ 0.04102 & 0.04824 & 1.00000 \end{bmatrix}$$

$$\mathbf{b}_b = \begin{bmatrix} 0.32337802 \\ 0.22694046 \\ 0.03583207 \end{bmatrix}$$

$$\mathbf{v}_b = \begin{bmatrix} 0.34570 \\ 0.24874 \\ 0.09756 \end{bmatrix}$$

$$\mathbf{R}_b = \begin{bmatrix} 1.00000 & 0.06781 & 0.19339 \\ 0.06781 & 1.00000 & -0.00356 \\ 0.19339 & -0.00356 & 1.00000 \end{bmatrix}$$

Note: $\mathbf{b}_a$ is the vector of least squares beta weights obtained from the first sample, i.e., question 4, $\mathbf{R}_a$ is matrix of correlations among predictors of the first sample, and $\mathbf{v}_a$ is the validity vector. The $\mathbf{b}_b$, $\mathbf{R}_b$, and $\mathbf{v}_b$ are the corresponding data from the second sample, problem 5.
(*Answer*)
The data were, in fact, obtained from the same population (they actually were

generated with different random number seeds). The value of r^2 obtain by applying b_b to R_a is .0642, and the respective F-ratios are 1.76 and 2.04 ($df = 2$ and 56). Neither is significant.

7. How highly correlated are the predicted scores using b_a and b_b (a) within R_a and (b) within R_b?

(*Answer*)

(a) .73 and (b) .80 (note that the "It don't make no nevermind" principle is less applicable here than in many other situations because the correlations among the variables are relatively small).

8. Apply unit weights to the two correlation matrices. Determine r^2 and test the significance of the difference from the least squares R^2 values in the two samples.

(*Answer*)

The two values of r^2 are .1072 and .1362. The associated F ratios are <1.0 and 1.13 ($df = 2$ and 56). Note that unit weighting actually provided more stable results across samples than the least squares weights (although the difference was not significant).

9. The following matrices are the inverse of R_a and the inverse of the corresponding R^* matrix (the 4×4 matrix with the validities added). Use these data, as well as the preceding data from R_a to perform an "all subsets regression," i.e., compute values of R^2 associated with all combinations of the three predictors. Perform the computations using the matrix equations in the book. Then compare your results to the output of computer package performing the same analysis, e.g., SAS PROC RSQUARE.

(*Answer*)

Predictors	R^2
X	0.0096
Y	0.0463
Z	0.0677
X, Y	0.0543
X, Z	0.0803
Y, Z	0.1089
X, Y, Z	0.1197

PROBLEMS FOR CHAPTER 5

1. Assume that subjects are assigned to one of four groups in a learning task. Group A is a control Group, and Groups B, C, and D represent three different types of instructions. The data (percentage of words correctly recalled) are as follows. Perform an ANOVA: (a) by hand using the conventional (partitioning of sums of squares) method, (b) using a relevant computer package, (c) using dummy codes, (d) using effect codes, and (e) using orthogonal codes. Use Group A as the target Group and let the contrasts be: (1) Groups A and C versus Groups B and D, (2) Groups A and B versus Groups C and D, and (3) Groups A and D versus Groups B and C. Present the regression equations derived from the dummy, effect, and orthogonal coding. Indicate which comparisons are significant.

	Group		
A	B	C	D
13	9	37	33
4	11	37	7
26	11	23	13
26	19	25	13
21	13	31	−3

(*Answer*)

$F(3, 16) = 4.51$, $p < .02$. The raw score dummy code equation is $Y' = -5.4D_b + 12.6D_c - 5.4D_d + 18.0$, with only D_c significant. The effect code equation is $Y' = -5.85E_2 + 12.15E_c - 5.85E_d + 18.45$, with only E_c significant. Finally, the orthogonal code equation is $Y' = 3.15O_1 - 5.85O_2 - 3.15O_3$, with only O_2 (Groups A and B versus Groups C and D) significant.

2. Assume that each of 60 subjects had been exposed to one of three different advertisement and that half within each group were male and half were female. The following are recall scores for information presented in the advertisement. Analyze these data.

	Males			Females		
	Ad			Ad		
	Type			Type		
1	2	3	1	2	3	
19	31	23	29	24	23	
12	32	22	16	16	41	
30	20	16	38	22	38	
30	22	37	24	27	32	
25	27	15	25	27	29	
15	37	15	35	13	40	
16	16	37	25	10	44	
16	21	30	15	26	47	
22	21	31	22	8	28	
18	8	32	34	14	29	

(*Answer*)

$F(1, 54) = 3.03$, ns. for the sex effect, $F(2, 54) = 7.88$, $p < .001$ for Type of Ad, and $F(4, 48)$, $p < .02$ for the interaction.

3. Compute the simple effects of Type of Ad within sex for the above data.

(*Answer*)

$F(1, 54) = 1.26$ for males, ns, and $F(1, 54) = 11.09$, $p < .001$ for females. In other words, males responded equivalently to all three types of advertisements, but females recalled them differentially.

4. Assume the data from the study were as below because some subjects failed to show up for the study. Obtain each effect with all possible forms of correction, e.g., obtain the Type of Ad effect (1) ignoring Sex and the Interaction, (2) adjusting for Sex and ignoring the Interaction, (3) ignoring Sex and adjusting for the interaction, and (4) adjusting for both Sex and the Interaction.

	Males Ad Type			Females Ad Type		
	1	2	3	1	2	3
	19	31	23	29	24	23
	12	32	22	16	16	41
	30	20	16	38	22	38
	30	22	37	24	27	32
	25	27	15	25	27	29
	15	37	15	35	13	40
	16	16	37	25	10	44
	16	21	30	15	26	47
	22	21	31	22	8	28
	18	8	32	34	14	29

(*Answer*)

Effect	Adjusting for	F	p
Sex	—	.31	ns
Sex	Type	.41	ns
Sex	Interaction	*	
Sex	Type, Interaction	*	
Type	—	1.98	ns
Type	Sex	2.19	ns
Type	Interaction	*	
Type	Sex, Interaction	*	
Interaction	—	2.22	ns
Interaction	Sex	2.77	.04
Interaction	Type	2.19	ns
Interaction	Sex, Type	3.36	.04

Note: Effects designated by an asterisk (*) were not computable due to the correlation between the interaction and the main effects.

5. Assume that you ran a study like that in problem number 1, and obtained a covariate measure (X) for each subject, as well as the dependent variable (Y). Analyze the results, and be sure to test for homogeneity of regression.

	Group						
A		B		C		D	
Y	X	Y	X	Y	X	Y	X
13	7	28	32	24	12	16	7
26	32	14	12	15	13	26	23
21	17	22	31	13	−5	10	14
9	6	9	6	41	34	10	1
17	15	15	2	34	28	6	10

(*Answer*)
$F(1, 12) = 44.76$, $p < .0001$ for the Covariate, $F(3, 12) = 3.14$, ns, for the Groups × Covariate interaction, and $F(3, 12) < 1$, ns, for the Groups effect. Thus, the only determinant of Y is the covariate, X.

6. Now suppose a study of similar design yielded the following results. Analyze the data.

				Group				
	A		B		C		D	
Y	X	Y	X	Y	X	Y	X
21	16	24	17	25	16	28	16
22	17	23	16	24	17	29	15
21	16	23	17	24	15	28	16
21	16	23	16	26	16	28	16
21	16	23	15	25	16	28	17

(*Answer*)
$F(1, 12) = 5.74$, ns, for the Covariate, $F(3, 12) = 140.06$, $p < .0001$ for the Group $\times$ Covariate interaction, and $F(3, 12) = 2.80$, ns, for the Group effect. The significant interaction illustrates differences in slope among groups (X and Y are positively related in Groups A and B, unrelated in Group C, and negatively related in Group D).

7. Analyze the following data in two different ways: (1) as a repeated measure design with each of seven subjects tested under five conditions, and (2) as an independent groups design with subjects randomly assigned to each group.

		Treatment		
A	B	C	D	E
102	102	109	108	115
110	117	126	117	127
91	87	87	100	96
99	101	98	97	97
96	100	97	96	107
110	113	109	126	119
97	101	103	109	107

(*Answer*)
Viewed as a repeated design experiment, $F(4, 24) = 4.57$, $p < .01$. This is because the error term is Treatment $\times$ Subjects, whose mean square is 18.90 with 24 *df*. Viewed as an independent groups experiment, $F(4, 28) < 1$, ns. This is because the error term is subjects within groups whose mean square is 109.91 with 30 *df*. Though simulated, the outcome is typical of most situations.

PROBLEMS FOR CHAPTER 6

1. The following hypothetical data are derived from 50 subjects who took 10 tests of cognitive abilities, each scaled to a mean of 100 and a standard deviation of 15. The tests are designated X_1 to X_{10}. Explore their factor structure by means of a component analysis. (Note that in actual practice, the number of cases would be far too small; this problem, as well as the two that follow are included to demonstrate certain important raw data structures.)

Test

X_1	X_2	X_3	X_4	X_5	X_6	X_7	X_8	X_9	X_{10}
86	90	78	84	88	84	93	64	81	74
104	111	100	103	103	118	107	101	112	103
122	118	122	117	126	131	141	109	133	106
109	104	98	111	108	116	112	113	113	114
116	110	109	110	124	113	104	122	109	123
92	103	103	96	91	114	119	106	82	83
109	113	102	100	108	83	96	90	118	108
106	119	114	108	111	110	112	110	94	96
97	105	96	102	117	129	107	109	113	97
97	83	99	89	87	104	103	83	93	85
129	122	134	114	118	115	113	103	120	110
98	98	108	94	112	111	113	79	107	92
98	107	106	114	117	99	102	101	110	120
102	98	107	102	104	116	101	119	98	101
104	89	91	108	108	116	103	111	98	111
87	87	96	91	90	100	84	90	83	87
99	97	93	96	87	95	112	99	122	92
113	124	112	127	132	115	110	109	129	106
88	89	97	92	94	82	75	88	86	79
115	120	119	117	120	108	111	105	114	112
76	71	81	84	72	66	84	82	84	77
116	117	106	114	123	114	100	114	122	99
114	104	110	118	113	129	123	111	126	113
93	103	85	96	103	95	106	109	92	103
113	109	117	114	119	115	108	107	108	99
127	129	118	122	116	118	106	103	119	128
92	94	92	75	78	98	111	87	84	104
75	72	70	76	90	56	95	73	87	88
104	106	109	99	111	96	115	109	101	111
71	83	76	70	80	89	86	83	91	87
96	111	110	111	99	89	92	106	122	89
120	110	115	101	121	108	92	125	110	106
103	101	106	90	90	89	110	104	111	96
78	70	80	87	82	91	79	70	85	87
95	97	95	93	91	84	88	80	113	96
90	84	91	87	88	95	94	67	90	95
85	87	83	85	91	79	86	91	92	119
92	90	90	106	111	115	111	81	79	86
93	91	116	102	103	100	104	98	112	94
98	104	99	103	98	102	113	109	93	94
110	97	112	114	111	120	99	109	113	99
88	81	85	98	84	91	96	82	97	92
104	93	99	94	98	121	102	110	105	104
83	78	77	81	84	90	92	69	78	98
108	112	125	116	121	110	113	108	116	115
118	109	98	108	111	118	100	104	102	117
88	79	88	95	82	77	87	92	90	99
92	106	84	103	98	104	92	96	93	93
110	113	110	106	108	94	107	118	118	99
96	95	90	96	87	92	89	113	74	92

(*Answer*)

The first four eigenvalues are 6.87, .74, .56, and .50. By virtually any definition (number of eigenvalues > 1, scree, etc.), the data can be well represented by a single factor. The pattern for the first principal component, which accounts for .687 of the total variance, and the associated h^2 values is as follows. Note that tests X_1 to X_5 load more heavily upon the factor than do tests X_6 to X_{10}.

Variable	Component	h^2
X_1	.939	.882
X_2	.899	.808
X_3	.872	.761
X_4	.898	.806
X_5	.905	.819
X_6	.772	.596
X_7	.694	.482
X_8	.777	.603
X_9	.801	.642
X_{10}	.689	.474

Variables X_1 to X_5 were actually generated by equations of the form $Y = .90F + .43e$, and variables X_6 to X_{10} were generated by equations of the form $Y = .70F + .71e$. F and e are random normal deviates $(0, 1)$. F is common to all 10 equations and e is unique to each. Since $.90^2 + .43^2 = .70^2 + .71^2 = 1$ and e and F are independent, the variance of Y is 1.0.

2. Now, perform the same analysis upon the following data.

Test

X_1	X_2	X_3	X_4	X_5	X_6	X_7	X_8	X_9	X_{10}	X_{11}	X_{12}
123	101	111	119	107	116	64	80	74	85	79	87
90	109	97	91	100	92	101	98	91	94	89	98
121	147	117	137	130	123	102	122	117	128	125	125
120	105	92	95	97	117	106	98	114	105	114	109
102	89	80	112	116	104	64	65	84	87	91	79
89	103	96	125	116	119	88	107	100	91	94	96
84	87	105	89	101	88	98	121	126	105	107	110
103	78	107	89	86	103	100	82	91	85	104	98
97	105	111	113	104	119	90	102	86	88	100	84
114	77	108	95	112	91	108	106	119	121	106	109
118	104	105	100	114	106	99	109	95	106	92	94
76	79	111	109	114	102	110	98	111	97	100	101
103	112	94	101	95	98	108	119	116	113	116	106
119	143	111	133	106	122	85	107	115	98	94	94
81	90	92	101	94	97	105	99	110	111	106	126
95	92	98	91	94	88	89	86	76	86	80	91
69	89	87	86	80	92	120	122	105	116	126	114
126	101	123	104	88	98	95	87	108	99	91	101
90	107	74	95	106	95	106	108	94	102	106	100
111	119	114	108	107	107	85	111	103	102	89	94
88	85	102	110	95	100	93	89	64	73	91	100

						Test					
X_1	X_2	X_3	X_4	X_5	X_6	X_7	X_8	X_9	X_{10}	X_{11}	X_{12}
102	73	87	81	78	87	111	69	104	85	95	96
95	101	84	102	88	105	109	102	111	96	95	109
81	87	85	79	85	82	93	77	100	95	96	83
94	111	76	96	103	88	92	71	100	82	71	94
97	106	102	109	85	85	93	112	107	111	100	91
88	101	91	91	79	71	99	101	92	102	104	101
88	93	84	116	101	89	107	98	109	103	105	107
79	85	68	74	77	72	103	112	95	103	107	107
86	83	84	110	117	114	143	115	113	127	139	123
113	115	114	122	116	128	68	76	75	79	73	78
118	113	97	99	109	107	84	106	110	103	109	95
99	98	103	94	100	119	95	102	106	97	107	104
94	104	96	105	126	109	109	104	103	91	98	93
93	96	99	76	84	103	97	75	82	95	85	91
97	106	105	108	116	102	83	97	102	106	94	96
93	122	105	121	132	112	87	97	101	98	104	92
94	128	119	125	114	118	89	89	98	94	97	95
87	100	113	111	93	95	102	101	92	101	90	95
93	112	100	115	114	118	84	91	108	93	99	90
103	121	106	117	126	105	97	125	103	115	126	113
119	106	114	126	129	130	101	98	86	72	100	88
107	116	117	123	122	99	121	117	119	125	114	120
96	92	114	100	104	106	122	120	131	110	121	134
90	92	95	78	74	89	122	137	126	122	133	124
103	80	97	109	85	94	123	126	117	133	117	132
111	102	109	123	120	132	82	90	78	91	86	76
91	87	84	80	97	97	112	116	113	92	113	97
82	87	115	100	94	98	106	88	94	85	104	100
101	98	90	93	107	88	90	104	113	86	83	87

(*Answer*)

The first four eigenvalues are 4.76, 3.37, .82, and .74. The results thus strongly suggest a two-factor structure. The first two components account for .398 and .281. Together, they account for 67.9% of the total variance. The pattern and associated h^2 values for the principal components are as follows.

	Component		
Variable	I	II	h^2
X_1	−.428	.514	.447
X_2	−.371	.666	.581
X_3	−.347	.587	.464
X_4	−.464	.744	.768
X_5	−.425	.674	.635
X_6	−.530	.641	.691
X_7	.857	.508	.740
X_8	.700	.508	.748
X_9	.711	.392	.659
X_{10}	.753	.468	.786
X_{11}	.800	.395	.796
X_{12}	.840	.330	.815

Note that the results consist of a unipolar and a bipolar factor. More commonly, the unipolar factor will be the first principal component than the second, in contrast to what was observed here. Variables X_1 to X_3 tend to have lower communalities than variables X_4 to X_6 and variables X_7 to X_9 tend to have lower communalities than variables X_9 to X_{12}. Most importantly, variables X_1 to X_6 tend to have higher loadings on Component II than Component I, but the reverse is true of variables X_7 to X_{12}. The raw data suggest two relatively *independent* factors, which is actually how the data were generated. The outcome is not completely clear in the factor analysis because of the small sample size, but see problem 5, where the results will be clearer. Variables X_1 to X_3 were defined by equations of the form $Y = .63F_I + .77e$; variables X_4 to X_6 were defined by equations of the form $Y = .76F_I + .65e$; variables X_7 to X_9 were defined by equations of the form $Y = .76F_{II} + .65e$, and; variables X_{10} to X_{12} were defined by equations of the form $Y = .87F_{II} + .49e$.

3. Perform the same analysis upon the following raw data.

Test

X_1	X_2	X_3	X_4	X_5	X_6	X_7	X_8	X_9	X_{10}	X_{11}	X_{12}
118	96	107	112	100	109	69	85	79	88	82	90
87	106	95	87	96	88	100	96	90	93	87	97
125	151	121	142	135	128	113	132	128	135	132	133
122	106	94	97	99	119	109	101	116	106	116	110
97	84	76	105	109	97	66	66	86	88	92	80
87	101	94	123	114	116	92	112	104	94	97	99
85	87	106	90	102	89	98	121	126	106	107	110
102	77	105	87	83	100	98	80	89	84	103	96
96	104	110	111	102	117	97	109	93	93	104	89
117	79	110	98	116	95	110	108	121	123	108	110
116	102	104	98	112	104	101	111	97	107	93	95
77	80	111	110	115	103	111	99	111	98	101	101
106	115	98	106	99	103	108	119	117	113	116	106
118	142	110	131	104	120	92	114	122	103	99	99
85	94	96	107	100	104	100	93	105	108	103	123
93	90	96	88	91	85	89	87	76	86	80	91
72	91	89	90	84	96	114	116	100	113	122	110
124	99	121	101	85	95	99	91	112	102	94	104
90	107	74	95	106	95	106	108	93	102	106	100
109	117	112	105	104	105	89	115	107	104	92	96
85	83	100	107	91	96	94	91	65	74	92	101
101	71	85	80	76	85	107	65	100	83	92	93
97	103	85	105	90	108	107	100	109	95	93	107
79	86	83	76	83	79	86	71	93	90	91	78
90	108	72	91	98	83	89	68	97	80	69	91
97	107	103	110	86	86	92	112	106	110	100	90
88	101	91	91	80	72	93	95	86	97	100	97
89	94	84	117	102	90	106	98	108	103	104	106
82	88	70	77	81	76	93	103	85	97	100	100
95	92	92	122	129	126	140	112	110	126	138	122
106	108	107	111	106	117	78	86	85	85	79	84
118	113	96	98	108	106	85	108	111	104	110	96
100	99	103	95	101	120	98	105	109	99	109	106
93	104	96	104	125	108	112	107	106	93	100	95

Test

X_1	X_2	X_3	X_4	X_5	X_6	X_7	X_8	X_9	X_{10}	X_{11}	X_{12}
89	93	96	71	80	98	95	74	81	94	83	89
97	105	105	107	116	101	84	98	103	106	94	97
91	121	103	118	129	110	92	102	106	101	107	95
91	126	116	121	109	114	97	97	106	99	103	100
87	100	112	110	92	94	102	101	92	101	90	95
91	110	98	111	110	114	92	99	116	99	104	95
107	125	110	123	132	111	103	131	109	119	131	117
116	103	111	121	124	124	112	108	97	79	107	94
113	123	123	133	131	108	123	119	121	127	116	122
101	96	119	107	111	113	124	122	132	111	122	135
97	99	101	89	84	100	113	128	117	116	128	118
109	85	102	118	94	103	122	126	116	133	117	132
108	98	105	117	114	126	90	98	85	96	91	81
93	90	87	84	101	101	111	115	112	92	112	97
81	86	114	98	92	96	105	86	93	84	103	99
100	97	88	90	104	85	90	104	113	85	82	86

(*Answer*)
The first four eigenvalues are 5.78, 2.17, .84, and 77. The results thus also strongly imply a two-factor structure. The first two components account for .482 and .181, for a total of .603. Note the greater disparity between the variance accounted for by the two components compared to the previous example. The pattern and associated h^2 values for the principal components are as follows:

	Component		
Variable	I	II	h^2
X_1	.482	.453	.437
X_2	.565	.510	.580
X_3	.578	.348	.455
X_4	.714	.490	.750
X_5	.669	.415	.619
X_6	.662	.476	.664
X_7	.615	−.591	.728
X_8	.825	−.193	.718
X_9	.757	−.229	.626
X_{10}	.811	−.314	.755
X_{11}	.791	−.421	.803
X_{12}	.767	−.477	.817

As in the previous example, variables X_1, X_2, and X_3 are less well explained by the two factors (have lower h^2 values) than X_4, X_5, and X_6. Likewise, variables X_7, X_8, and X_9 are less well explained by the two factors than are X_{10}, X_{11}, and X_{12}. Once more, the results consist of a general factor and a bipolar factor, but, as occurs infrequently, the first factor is bipolar instead of the second. The key point is that the raw data suggest two *correlated* factors (see problem 6). Variables X_1 to X_3 were defined by equations of the form $Y = .2F_I + .6F_{II} + .77e$; variables X_4 to X_6 were defined by equations of the form $Y = .3F_I + .7F_{II} + .65e$; variables X_7 to X_9 were defined by equations of the form $Y = .7F_I + .3F_{II} + .65e$, and variables X_{10} to X_{12} were defined by equations of the form $Y = .85F_I + .2F_{II} + .49e$.

4. The following correlation matrix was obtained from 500 cases sampled from the same population as the raw data of problem 1. Analyze it: (1) by means of the method of principal components, (2) rotating the principal components to a varimax criterion, (3) by means of one or more common factor models, (4) rotating the common factors to a varimax criterion, (5) rotating the common factors to a quartimax criterion, and (6) rotating the common factors to a suitable oblique criterion.

	X_1	X_2	X_3	X_4	X_5	X_6	X_7	X_8	X_9	X_{10}
X_1	1.000	.827	.837	.824	.832	.661	.654	.652	.610	.667
X_2	.827	1.000	.801	.805	.802	.611	.629	.615	.614	.628
X_3	.837	.801	1.000	.816	.808	.634	.660	.640	.620	.661
X_4	.824	.805	.816	1.000	.812	.642	.642	.638	.615	.660
X_5	.832	.802	.808	.812	1.000	.620	.611	.648	.628	.646
X_6	.661	.611	.634	.642	.620	1.000	.494	.517	.449	.526
X_7	.654	.629	.660	.642	.611	.494	1.000	.490	.476	.524
X_8	.652	.615	.640	.638	.648	.517	.490	1.000	.474	.529
X_9	.610	.614	.620	.615	.628	.449	.476	.474	1.000	.489
X_{10}	.667	.628	.661	.660	.646	.526	.524	.529	.489	1.000

(*Answer*)

The first principal component accounts for .687 of the total variance, whereas the first principal axis (common factor) accounts for 1.000 of the common factor variance (the sum of the communalities within R). Since the data are well explained by a single factor, no rotation is possible.

Variable	Comp.	h^2	Common Factor	h^2
X_1	.921	.849	.922	.850
X_2	.893	.798	.886	.784
X_3	.910	.828	.907	.823
X_4	.908	.823	.904	.817
X_5	.902	.814	.897	.805
X_6	.741	.549	.703	.494
X_7	.744	.554	.707	.499
X_8	.748	.558	.710	.503
X_9	.718	.515	.677	.458
X_{10}	.763	.583	.728	.530

Because the original communalities were high, the common factor results are fairly similar to the component results.

5. Do the same thing with the following correlation matrix, which was derived from the same population as the data of problem 2. Conduct the following rotations: (1) varimax, using the component solution, (2) varimax, using the common factor solution, (3) quartimax, using the common factor solution, and (4) a suitable oblique transformation, using the common factor solution. Pay particular attention to the characteristics of the various transformations, e.g., the angles of rotation and the factor correlation within the oblique transformation.

	X_1	X_2	X_3	X_4	X_5	X_6	X_7	X_8	X_9	X_{10}	X_{11}	X_{12}
X_1	1.00	.42	.36	.44	.44	.46	.01	.00	.02	.56	.04	.05
X_2	.42	1.00	.41	.47	.48	.47	−.06	.03	−.05	−.02	−.02	−.02
X_3	.36	.41	1.00	.48	.44	.45	−.06	−.01	−.06	−.04	−.04	−.02
X_4	.44	.47	.48	1.00	.56	.54	−.10	−.00	−.06	−.02	−.04	−.03
X_5	.44	.48	.44	.56	1.00	.55	−0.8	.00	−.02	−.06	−.01	−.04
X_6	.46	.47	.45	.54	.55	1.00	−.05	−.04	−.05	−.03	−.03	−.03
X_7	.01	−.06	−.06	−.10	−.08	−.05	1.00	.62	.58	.69	.69	.70
X_8	.00	.01	−.01	−.00	.00	−.04	.62	1.00	.58	.68	.71	.70
X_9	.02	−.05	−.06	−.06	−.02	−.05	.58	.58	1.00	.64	.67	.66
X_{10}	.06	−.02	−.04	−.02	−.06	−.03	.69	.68	.64	1.00	.76	.78
X_{11}	.04	−.02	−.04	−.04	−.01	−.03	.69	.71	.67	.76	1.00	.78
X_{12}	.05	−.02	−.02	−.03	−.04	−.03	.70	.70	.66	.78	.78	1.00

(*Answer*)
The first two principal components account for .371 and .277 of the variance, for a total of .648. Their associated eigenvalues were 4.452 and 3.315. The first two principal axes account for .597 and .402 of the common factor (reduced) variance or 1.000 collectively. The eigenvalues of the reduced matrix were 4.147 and 2.800. The patterns associated with each of the component solutions are as follows (F_I and F_{II} are the principal components and V_I and V_{II} are the varimax rotations).

Variable	F_I	F_{II}	V_I	V_{II}	h^2
X_1	−.039	.692	.058	.691	.481
X_2	−.119	.712	−.018	.722	.521
X_3	−.134	.683	−.037	.695	.485
X_4	−.145	.776	−.036	.789	.623
X_5	−.137	.772	−.029	.784	.615
X_6	−.141	.771	−.032	.783	.614
X_7	.830	.051	.829	−.065	.691
X_8	.821	.131	.831	.016	.680
X_9	.794	.075	.796	−.036	.635
X_{10}	.881	.115	.888	−.008	.789
X_{11}	.892	.121	.900	−.004	.810
X_{12}	.892	.125	.901	−.001	.812

The common factor solutions are as follows: F_I and F_{II} are the unrotated principal axes, V_I and V_{II} are the varimax rotations, and O_I and O_{II} are oblique rotations, using the Harris/Kaiser orthoblique method as described in the SAS, 1985 manual; the quartimax solution is not presented as it was virtually indistinguishable from the varimax rotation).

Variable	F_I	F_{II}	V_I	V_{II}	O_I	O_{II}	h^2
X_1	−.023	.612	.049	.611	.612	.067	.375
X_2	−.095	.642	−.019	.649	.649	.000	.422
X_3	−.108	.609	−.036	.618	.617	−.017	.382
X_4	−.122	.735	−.035	.744	.744	−.012	.555
X_5	−.115	.728	−.028	.736	.737	−.006	.543
X_6	−.117	.727	−.031	.736	.736	−.009	.542

Variable	F_I	F_{II}	V_I	V_{II}	O_I	O_{II}	h^2
X_7	.788	.027	.785	−.066	−.052	.784	.621
X_8	.780	.105	.787	.013	.027	.788	.620
X_9	.741	.050	.742	−.037	−.024	.741	.551
X_{10}	.865	.092	.870	−.010	−.006	.870	.756
X_{11}	.883	.099	.887	−.005	.011	.888	.788
X_{12}	.884	.103	.890	−.002	.014	.890	.791

The first column of the transformation matrix for the component solutions is (.990, .139). The two elements respectively represent the cosine and sine of the angle of rotation jointly applied to F_I and F_{II} which transforms them into V_I and V_{II} (the matrix as a whole is skew-symmetric, as described in Chapter 3 because of the orthogonal nature of the transformation). Taking the inverse of either gives the angle of rotation at eight degrees (the same data indicate that F_I and V_I correlate .990). In other words, the transformation is minor and the rotations are nearly identical to the original factors, as may be seen by comparing the two matrices. The sine of the angle of transformation for the two orthogonal common factor rotations (varimax and quartimax) are both .118, which corresponds to an angle of rotation of only seven degrees. Similarly, the variances accounted for by the two varimax rotated principal components (.369 and .278) are nearly identical to the variances accounted for by the unrotated components. Similar trends held for the other rotations, which will not be repeated. One role of analytic rotations is to "even out" factor variances, but, because of the way the data were generated, they were nearly even to begin with. The oblique transformation involves two different angles of rotation for F_I and F_{II}. In the present case, the rotation was such that O_I was actually more similar to F_{II} than F_I and vice versa for O_{II} (it is perfectly proper to reverse the names of the two factors, but I did not do so). The correlation between the two factors was only .047. Consequently, the following factor structure is nearly identical to the factor pattern.

Variable	O_I	O_{II}
X_1	.609	.038
X_2	.649	−.030
X_3	.618	.047
X_4	.745	−.047
X_5	.737	−.041
X_6	.736	−.044
X_7	−.089	.786
X_8	−.010	.787
X_9	−.059	.742
X_{10}	−.036	.870
X_{11}	−.031	.887
X_{12}	−.028	.889

The "bottom line" is therefore that the data can be represented quite well by two orthogonal factors which account for nearly equal amounts of variance and that the common factor solutions are relatively similar to the component solutions. Test X_1 to X_3 have the lowest communality (are least well explained by the two factors, regardless of which set), and test X_{10} to X_{12} have the highest, reflecting, of course, the intent of the simulation.

6. Finally, perform the same analyses upon the following data.

	X_1	X_2	X_3	X_4	X_5	X_6	X_7	X_8	X_9	X_{10}	X_{11}	X_{12}
X_1	1.00	.42	.36	.44	.45	.47	.34	.32	.33	.35	.33	.35
X_2	.42	1.00	.40	.46	.47	.47	.26	.33	.27	.27	.27	.27
X_3	.36	.40	1.00	.48	.44	.44	.29	.32	.27	.27	.26	.29
X_4	.44	.46	.48	1.00	.44	.43	.34	.43	.36	.39	.37	.38
X_5	.44	.47	.44	.55	1.00	.54	.36	.43	.40	.34	.38	.36
X_6	.47	.47	.44	.54	.54	1.00	.39	.40	.38	.38	.38	.39
X_7	.34	.27	.28	.34	.36	.39	1.00	.61	.56	.68	.68	.68
X_8	.32	.33	.33	.43	.43	.40	.61	1.00	.57	.66	.70	.68
X_9	.33	.27	.27	.36	.40	.38	.56	.57	1.00	.63	.66	.65
X_{10}	.35	.27	.27	.39	.34	.38	.68	.67	.63	1.00	.76	.78
X_{11}	.32	.26	.26	.37	.38	.38	.68	.70	.66	.76	1.00	.78
X_{12}	.34	.27	.29	.38	.36	.39	.69	.68	.65	.78	.78	1.00

(*Answer*)
The first two principal components account for .497 and .146 of the variance, for a total of .643. Their associated eigenvalues were 5.967 and 1.098. The first two principal axes account for .810 and .190 of the reduced variance or 1.000 collectively. The eigenvalues of the reduced matrix were 5.580 and 1.309. The patterns associated with each of the component solutions are as follows (F_I and F_{II} are the principal components and V_I and V_{II} are the varimax rotations):

Variable	F_I	F_{II}	V_I	V_{II}	h^2
X_1	.586	.365	.231	.651	.477
X_2	.544	.494	.118	.725	.539
X_3	.535	.454	.136	.689	.493
X_4	.661	.418	.257	.738	.612
X_5	.656	.418	.253	.736	.606
X_6	.667	.400	.273	.728	.605
X_7	.761	−.311	.789	.230	.676
X_8	.789	−.232	.762	.309	.677
X_9	.742	−.267	.747	.253	.622
X_{10}	.806	−.373	.863	.210	.789
X_{11}	.812	−.391	.879	1.99	.813
X_{12}	.816	−.376	.873	.214	.807

The common factor solutions are as follows (because the quartimax rotation produced nearly identical results to the varimax rotation, it will not be presented).

Variable	F_I	F_{II}	V_I	V_{II}	O_I	O_{II}	h^2
X_1	.540	.302	.240	.570	.590	.045	.383
X_2	.502	.408	.145	.630	.698	−.092	.419
X_3	.491	.364	.163	.589	.643	−.054	.374
X_4	.627	.391	.254	.694	.734	.009	.546
X_5	.622	.392	.249	.692	.732	.004	.540
X_6	.632	.376	.267	.685	.717	.029	.540
X_7	.738	−.240	.729	.265	.037	.753	.602
X_8	.766	−.170	.708	.338	.132	.697	.616
X_9	.712	−.190	.678	.288	.084	.683	.543
X_{10}	.803	−.329	.836	.235	−.040	.891	.754
X_{11}	.815	−.355	.861	.222	−.065	.926	.790
X_{12}	.818	−.339	.853	.236	−.045	.912	.784

Unlike the previous problem, the angle of rotation was relatively large. The orthogonal transformations did make the contributions of the two varimax factors more nearly equal (.361 and .281). Note, however that the loadings on the two factors are more nearly equal than on the corresponding two factors from the previous problem. Because all factors are at least modestly correlated, it is not possible to achieve orthogonal "simple structure" so that each variable loads highly on only one of the two factors and nearly zero on the other.

The oblique rotation *looks* like simple structure has been achieved, but the two factors are highly correlated ($r = .605$). The factor variances are nearly equal (.362 and .422). However, the *indirect* contribution of the other factor produced by the factor correlation means that a given variable *correlates* highly with the "wrong" factor, e.g., even though the *pattern* element for factor O_{II} in predicting X_1 is small (.045), the *structure* weight is not small, as can be seen in the following matrix.

Variable	O_I	O_{II}
X_1	.617	.402
X_2	.642	.330
X_3	.609	.334
X_4	.739	.453
X_5	.735	.447
X_6	.734	.463
X_7	.493	.775
X_8	.554	.777
X_9	.497	.733
X_{10}	.500	.867
X_{11}	.496	.887
X_{12}	.507	.884

7. Plot the factors obtained in problems 5 and 6 graphically.

8. Use the appropriate option to generate factor scores for the data of problems 2 and 3 for both component and common factor models, with and without rotation. Then, obtain the means and standard deviations of the factor scores and the correlations between corresponding pairs, e.g., factors I and II for the principal components. Which ones have standard deviations of 1.0, and which pairs are actually uncorrelated?

PROBLEMS FOR CHAPTER 7

1. Take the 10×10 correlation matrix from problem 4 in Chapter 6. Generate the factor score coefficient vector associated with the first principal component. You may either do this by specifying the appropriate option in your computer package, e.g. "SCORE" in SAS, or by dividing each factor loading (b_i) by λ. Correlate this set of weights with the first centroid, i.e., equally weighted sum of all 10 variables. (*Answer*)
$r = .999$.

2. Correlate the factor score weights derived from the first principal component of the above matrix with the first principal component. Then, do the same thing with the first principal axis (common factor).

(*Answer*)
The correlation between the first principal component and scores on the first principal component is 1.0, which is inherent in a component solution. The correlation between the first principal axis and scores on the first principal axis depends on the method used to estimate the factor scores. The regression method (which is used by SAS and is probably the most commonly used method) led to a correlation of .989. Lack of perfect correlation is inherent in the common factor model although in many situations, such as the present, the deviation from 1.0 is trivial.

3. Take the data from problem 6 in Chapter 6. Factor variables 1 to 6 separately from variables 7 to 12. Compute the correlations between: (a) the first principal component of each data set and (b) the first principal axis of each data set.
(*Answer*)
(a) $r = .538$ and (b) $r = .481$.

4. The following pair of correlation matrices, **A** and **B**, were each derived from 50 subjects. Obtain the first principal component in each. Then, correlate the two within each correlation matrix, i.e., compute the correlation between the first principal component of **A** and the first principal component of **B** within correlation matrix **A** and within correlation matrix **B**. Finally, correlate the first principal component of **A** and the centroid (equally weighted linear combination) within **A** and do the same thing with the first principal component of **B** and the centroid within **B**.

$$
\mathbf{A} = \begin{bmatrix}
1.000 & .853 & .836 & .816 & .818 & .699 & .595 & .703 & .767 & .617 \\
.853 & 1.000 & .786 & .789 & .897 & .596 & .589 & .686 & .707 & .572 \\
.836 & .786 & 1.000 & .763 & .754 & .603 & .584 & .634 & .711 & .477 \\
.816 & .789 & .763 & 1.000 & .852 & .679 & .522 & .670 & .708 & .560 \\
.818 & .807 & .754 & .858 & 1.000 & .691 & .559 & .644 & .694 & .610 \\
.698 & .596 & .606 & .678 & .691 & 1.000 & .646 & .581 & .476 & .435 \\
.590 & .589 & .584 & .522 & .559 & .646 & 1.000 & .454 & .512 & .374 \\
.702 & .683 & .634 & .670 & .644 & .581 & .454 & 1.000 & .527 & .530 \\
.736 & .707 & .711 & .708 & .694 & .476 & .512 & .527 & 1.000 & .527 \\
.671 & .572 & .477 & .560 & .610 & .435 & .374 & .530 & .527 & 1.000
\end{bmatrix}
$$

$$
\mathbf{B} = \begin{bmatrix}
1.000 & .801 & .764 & .868 & .787 & .651 & .767 & .581 & .600 & .546 \\
.801 & 1.000 & .791 & .838 & .820 & .644 & .701 & .626 & .571 & .625 \\
.764 & .791 & 1.000 & .756 & .757 & .628 & .685 & .557 & .559 & .694 \\
.868 & .838 & .756 & 1.000 & .811 & .631 & .764 & .696 & .691 & .646 \\
.787 & .820 & .756 & .811 & 1.000 & .560 & .771 & .632 & .573 & .558 \\
.651 & .644 & .628 & .631 & .560 & 1.000 & .585 & .546 & .412 & .395 \\
.767 & .701 & .685 & .764 & .771 & .585 & 1.000 & .584 & .629 & .519 \\
.581 & .626 & .557 & .695 & .632 & .546 & .584 & 1.000 & .492 & .275 \\
.600 & .571 & .559 & .691 & .573 & .412 & .629 & .492 & 1.000 & .401 \\
.546 & .625 & .694 & .646 & .558 & .395 & .519 & .275 & .401 & 1.000
\end{bmatrix}
$$

(*Answer*)
The first principal component of **A** correlates .9998 with the first principal component of **B** within correlation matrix **A** and .9997 with the centroid. The first principal

component of **A** correlates .9999 with the first principal component of **B** within correlation matrix **B** and .9998 with the first centroid. The example is one more instance of "it don't make no nevermind" involving a matrix whose correlations are all modestly (matrix **A** is also the correlation matrix derived from problem 1 in Chapter 7, and matrix **B** was derived from the same structural equations but a different random number seed so that it differs from **A** only through sampling error).

5. Use the same correlation matrix but present the solutions defined from using: (a) variables X_1 to X_6 as one factor and X_7 to X_{12} as the other (which is the "correct" weak substantive model) and (b) the odd-numbered variables as one "pseudo-factor" and the even-numbered variables as the other "pseudo-factor."
(*Answer*)
The results for the "correct" substantive model, in the form of computer printouts from the OMG program, are as follows:

FACTOR STRUCTURE AND H**2

STRTHSQ	COL1	COL2	COL3
ROW1	0.699269	0.0340001	0.492863
ROW2	0.725466	−0.0322516	0.526309
ROW3	0.704195	−0.0470173	0.496234
ROW4	0.781891	−0.0487659	0.611648
ROW5	0.777189	−0.041383	0.604122
ROW6	0.778085	−0.0452688	0.605606
ROW7	−0.0770248	0.831352	0.693032
ROW8	−0.00649337	0.832712	0.69415
ROW9	−0.0512752	0.802209	0.643894
ROW10	−0.0277648	0.885364	0.783934
ROW11	−0.0248539	0.897409	0.805475
ROW12	−0.0208236	0.897992	0.806631

FACTOR VARIANCES (OMG AND PC)

FCTVAR	COL1	COL2	COL3
OMG FVAR	0.278532	0.36952	0.646991
PC FVAR	0.371012	0.276268	0.64728
PC CUM	0.371012	0.64728	0.64728

FACTOR INTERCORRELATIONS

RFACT	COL1	COL2
ROW1	1	−0.0404574
ROW2	−0.0404574	1

FACTOR PATTERN

PATTERN	COL1	COL2
ROW1	0.701793	0.0623928
ROW2	0.725349	−0.00290587
ROW3	0.703444	−0.0185578
ROW4	0.781197	−0.0171607
ROW5	0.776786	−0.00995629
ROW6	0.777526	−0.0138121

ROW7	−0.0434616	0.829594
ROW8	0.0272406	0.833814
ROW9	−0.0188508	0.801446
ROW10	0.00806794	0.88569
ROW11	0.0114717	0.897873
ROW12	0.0155323	0.898621

The results for the "pseudofactor model" are as follows:

FACTOR STRUCTURE AND H**2

STRTHSQ	COL1	COL2	COL3
ROW1	0.541637	0.396262	0.2962
ROW2	0.335162	0.53252	0.303565
ROW3	0.47368	0.351769	0.225814
ROW4	0.371598	0.543921	0.305165
ROW5	0.514165	0.411556	0.264421
ROW6	0.382298	0.53391	0.289421
ROW7	0.620005	0.498038	0.384547
ROW8	0.551469	0.653484	0.430168
ROW9	0.630127	0.478573	0.398157
ROW10	0.591376	0.664051	0.452528
ROW11	0.67842	0.601205	0.471281
ROW12	0.6148	0.668222	0.466253

FACTOR VARIANCES (OMG AND PC)

FCTVAR	COL1	COL2	COL3
OMG FVAR	0.287685	0.288973	0.357293
PC FVAR	0.371012	0.276268	0.64728
PC CUM	0.371012	0.64728	0.64728

FACTOR INTERCORRELATIONS

RFACT	COL1	COL2
ROW1	1	0.791607
ROW2	0.791607	1

FACTOR PATTERN

PATTERN	COL1	COL2
ROW1	0.610549	−0.0870531
ROW2	−0.231372	0.715676
ROW3	0.522866	−0.0621355
ROW4	−0.157953	0.668958
ROW5	0.50454	0.0121585
ROW6	−0.10807	0.619459
ROW7	0.60466	0.0193857
ROW8	0.0915125	0.581042
ROW9	0.67304	−0.0542101
ROW10	0.175995	0.524732
ROW11	0.542379	0.171855
ROW12	0.229889	0.486241

6. Now repeat the exercise with the data of problem 6, Chapter 6.
(*Answer*)
The result for the "correct" weak substantive model is:

STRTHSQ	COL1	COL2	COL3
ROW1	0.705175	0.394369	0.497595
ROW2	0.720891	0.327143	0.524838
ROW3	0.698665	0.331247	0.490915
ROW4	0.778589	0.445571	0.607217
ROW5	0.774099	0.442249	0.600177
ROW6	0.776793	0.454756	0.605335
ROW7	0.446319	0.824111	0.679172
ROW8	0.501099	0.826065	0.686933
ROW9	0.45036	0.795383	0.633355
ROW10	0.451483	0.882543	0.779634
ROW11	0.444972	0.895637	0.804057
ROW12	0.457545	0.893292	0.798704

FACTOR VARIANCES (OMG AND PC)

FCTVAR	COL1	COL2	COL3
OMG FVAR	0.38152	0.445532	0.642328
PC FVAR	0.497209	0.14574	0.642949
PC CUM	0.497209	0.642949	0.642949

FACTOR INTERCORRELATIONS

RFACT	COL1	COL2
ROW1	1	0.537768
ROW2	0.537768	1

FACTOR PATTERN

PATTERN	COL1	COL2
ROW1	0.693715	0.0213115
ROW2	0.76685	−0.0851562
ROW3	0.732311	−0.0625671
ROW4	0.75826	0.0378026
ROW5	0.754456	0.0365258
ROW6	0.748784	0.0520835
ROW7	0.00441521	0.821736
ROW8	0.0800037	0.783042
ROW9	0.0318347	0.778263
ROW10	−0.032528	0.900036
ROW11	−0.0515937	0.923382
ROW12	−0.0321319	0.910571

and the pseudofactor result is

FACTOR STRUCTURE AND H**2

STRTHSQ	COL1	COL2	COL3
ROW1	0.658404	0.529543	0.439121
ROW2	0.487767	0.631846	0.411831

ROW3	0.612463	0.49439	0.379497
ROW4	0.597228	0.721079	0.522265
ROW5	0.708329	0.605932	0.501814
ROW6	0.610353	0.717249	0.51469
ROW7	0.756379	0.671054	0.57352
ROW8	0.692156	0.790032	0.624633
ROW9	0.754269	0.644014	0.569071
ROW10	0.710673	0.787554	0.624172
ROW11	0.776537	0.732797	0.618656
ROW12	0.727314	0.790032	0.63249

FACTOR VARIANCES (OMG AND PC)

FCTVAR	COL1	COL2	COL3
OMG FVAR	0.461219	0.466352	0.534314
PC FVAR	0.497209	0.14574	0.642949
PC CUM	0.497209	0.642949	0.642949

FACTOR INTERCORRELATIONS

RFACT	COL1	COL2
ROW1	1	0.862026
ROW2	0.862026	1

FACTOR PATTERN

PATTERN	COL1	COL2
ROW1	0.785968	−0.147982
ROW2	−0.221478	0.822765
ROW3	0.725098	−0.130663
ROW4	−0.0948237	0.80282
ROW5	0.723984	−0.0181609
ROW6	−0.0308792	0.743867
ROW7	0.692506	0.0740967
ROW8	0.0433126	0.752696
ROW9	0.775025	−0.0240772
ROW10	0.123704	0.680917
ROW11	0.5638	0.246787
ROW12	0.180164	0.634727

PROBLEMS FOR CHAPTER 8

1. Assume that subjects are either normal (Group N) or impaired (Group I). Two measures, X_1 and X_2, are obtained from each. Describe the discriminant structure, including the univariate results, the total, between-group, and within-group correlations, the canonical correlation, the total, between-group and within-group canonical structure, the discriminant weights (both standardized and unstandardized, and the locations of the groups upon the discriminant function). Use a computer package to analyze the results. In addition, compute the discriminant weights using the methods described by Eq. (8-1). Then, draw scatterplots of the two groups on a single graph. Without performing any formal test (to be described in Chapter 10),

are the shapes of the two scatterplots reasonably similar except for location, i.e., are the two group homoscedastic.

Group	X_1	X_2
N	10	31
N	7	−14
N	15	−2
N	13	−11
N	13	2
N	10	8
N	2	2
N	12	24
N	24	25
N	12	2
N	−4	4
N	14	39
N	10	−5
N	−12	1
N	20	6
N	6	14
N	32	2
N	12	12
N	4	16
N	24	10
N	9	0
N	15	9
N	22	35
N	35	−18
N	6	−7
I	8	8
I	38	25
I	−4	−3
I	5	−13
I	24	27
I	−14	8
I	−5	6
I	3	0
I	6	9
I	22	12
I	21	31
I	23	9
I	−18	25
I	−7	12
I	13	38
I	17	27
I	12	47
I	−4	1
I	−2	7
I	−13	10
I	2	61
I	−6	34
I	−21	−16
I	0	13
I	17	4

(*Answer*)
The means for Group N on X_1 and X_2 are 12.44 and 7.40; the corresponding means for Group I are 4.68 and 18.28. The pooled within-group standard deviations for X_1 and X_2 are 12.70 and 16.40. The total, between-group, and within-group correlations are .13, -1.00 (of necessity, as there are but two groups), and .22. The canonical (multiple) correlation is .41. The total canonical structure is (.73, $-.58$); the between canonical structure is (1.0, -1.0) (again of necessity), and the within structure is (.70, $-.55$). The standardized weights are (.89, $-.75$), and the unstandardized (raw) weights are (.067, $-.045$). The locations of the two groups on the discriminant axis are .44 and $-.44$. The groups are in fact homoscedastic. In essence, the discriminant axis is simply the difference between the two measures, which, in turn, have a slight positive correlation within groups.

2. Do the same thing with the following data, in which Y_1 and Y_2 are the predictors.

Group	Y_1	Y_2
N	51	72
N	0	−21
N	28	11
N	15	−9
N	28	17
N	28	26
N	6	6
N	48	60
N	73	74
N	26	16
N	−4	4
N	67	92
N	15	0
N	−23	−10
N	46	32
N	26	34
N	66	36
N	36	36
N	24	36
N	58	44
N	18	9
N	39	33
N	79	92
N	52	−1
N	5	−8
I	24	24
I	101	88
I	−11	−10
I	−3	−21
I	75	78
I	−20	2
I	−4	7
I	6	3
I	21	24
I	56	46

Group	Y_1	Y_2
I	73	83
I	55	41
I	−11	32
I	−2	17
I	64	89
I	61	71
I	71	106
I	−7	−2
I	3	12
I	−16	7
I	65	124
I	22	62
I	−58	−53
N	13	26
I	38	25

(*Answer*)

The means for Group N on Y_1 and Y_2 are 32.28 and 27.24; the corresponding means for Group I are 24.64 and 35.24. The pooled within-group standard deviations for Y_1 and Y_2 are 33.11 and 37.68. The total, between-group, and within-group correlations are .85, −1.00, and .87. The canonical (multiple) correlation is .41. The total canonical structure is (−.29, .26); the between canonical structure is (1.0, −1.0), and the within structure is (−.26, .24). The standardized weights are (−1.98, 1.97), and the unstandardized (raw) weights are (−.060, .052). The locations of the two groups on the discriminant axis are .44 and −.44. The groups are in fact homoscedastic. In essence, the discriminant axis is simply the difference between the two measures, which, in turn, have a strong within-group correlation. In fact, the structure of the data in problems 1 and 2 are totally equivalent, as reflected in the identical canonical correlations and locations of the groups along the discriminant axis. The data were constructed so that $Y_1 = 2X_1 + X_2$ and $Y_2 = X_1 + 2X_2$.

3. Do the same thing with the following data set, where Y_1 and Y_2 are the predictors.

Group	Y_1	Y_2
N	51	−52
N	0	35
N	28	19
N	15	35
N	28	9
N	28	−6
N	6	−2
N	48	−36
N	73	−26
N	26	8
N	−4	−12
N	67	−64
N	15	20
N	−23	−14
N	46	8

Group	Y_1	Y_2
N	26	−22
N	66	28
N	36	−12
N	24	−28
N	58	4
N	18	9
N	39	−3
N	79	−48
N	52	71
N	5	20
I	24	−8
I	101	−12
I	−11	2
I	−3	31
I	75	−30
I	−20	−30
I	−4	−17
I	6	3
I	21	−12
I	56	−2
I	73	−41
I	55	5
I	−11	−68
I	−2	−31
I	64	−63
I	61	−37
I	71	−82
I	−7	−6
I	3	−16
I	−16	−33
I	65	−120
I	22	−74
I	−58	11
I	13	−26
I	38	9

(*Answer*)
The means for Group N on Y_1 and Y_2 are 32.28 and −2.36; the corresponding means for Group I are 24.64 and 25.88. The pooled within-group standard deviations for Y_1 and Y_2 are 33.11 and 32.48. The total, between-group, and within-group correlations are −.26, −1.00, and −.33, respectively. The canonical (multiple) correlation is .41. The total canonical structure is (.29, .85); the between canonical structure is (1.0, −1.0), and the within canonical structure is (.26, .83). The standardized weights are .60, 1.08, and the unstandardized (raw) weights are .02, .03. The locations of the two groups on the discriminant axis are .44 and −.44. The groups are in fact homoscedastic. In essence, the discriminant axis is simply the sum the two measures, which, in turn, have a strong within-group correlation. In fact, the structure of the data in problems 1 and 3 are totally equivalent, as reflected in the identical canonical correlations and locations of the groups along the discriminant axis. The data were constructed so that $Y_1 = 2X_1 + X_2$ and $Y_2 = X_1 − 2X_2$.

4. Do the same thing with the following data set, where Y_1 and Y_2 are the predictors.

Group	Y_1	Y_2
N	10	31
N	7	−14
N	15	−2
N	13	−11
N	13	2
N	10	8
N	2	2
N	12	24
N	24	25
N	12	2
N	−4	4
N	14	39
N	10	−5
N	−12	1
N	20	6
N	6	14
N	32	2
N	12	12
N	4	16
N	24	10
N	9	0
N	15	9
N	22	35
N	35	−18
N	6	−7
I	8	9
I	38	43
I	−4	−13
I	5	−33
I	24	47
I	−14	9
I	−5	5
I	3	−7
I	6	11
I	22	17
I	21	55
I	23	11
I	−18	43
I	−7	17
I	13	69
I	17	47
I	12	87
I	−4	−5
I	−2	7
I	−13	13
I	2	115
I	−6	61
I	−21	−39
I	0	19
I	17	1

(*Answer*)

The means for Group N on X_1 and X_2 are 12.44 and 7.40; the corresponding means for Group I are 4.68 and 23.56. The pooled within-group standard deviations for X_1 and X_2 are 12.70 and 27.44. The total, between-group, and within-group correlations are .13, -1.00, and .25, respectively. The canonical (multiple) correlation is .45. The total canonical structure is $(-.66, .64)$; the between canonical structure is $(1.0, -1.0)$, and the within structure is $(-.62, .60)$. The standardized weights are $(-.86, .84)$, and the unstandardized (raw) weights are $(-.067, .029)$. The locations of the two groups on the discriminant axis are .49 and $-.49$. The groups are in fact heteroscedastic. For example, Y_1 and Y_2 have a very high correlation within Group N ($r = .82$), but are essentially uncorrelated within Group I ($r = .12$).

5. Now, consider the following three groups (A, B, and C), which may be thought of as three divisions within a company. Let X_1, X_2, X_3, and X_4 be predictors used in making personnel decisions. Can you simplify the prediction equation?

Group	X_1	X_2	X_3	X_4
A	112	109	45	92
A	77	91	35	95
A	73	98	23	89
A	109	93	44	98
A	114	85	41	77
A	97	91	33	111
A	119	98	49	120
A	95	105	63	79
A	93	80	39	89
A	130	103	49	78
A	98	90	52	60
A	81	94	38	77
A	110	89	42	105
A	125	86	46	97
A	100	100	36	61
A	115	102	59	99
A	99	93	34	99
A	101	91	42	142
A	96	126	38	84
A	82	80	32	88
B	120	109	41	151
B	99	127	37	76
B	108	110	46	80
B	114	105	51	103
B	82	95	55	60
B	134	94	41	78
B	114	120	59	64
B	119	96	52	97
B	158	112	49	107
B	130	96	42	111
B	101	102	45	57
B	126	127	47	83
B	132	118	55	108
B	120	130	53	66
B	125	98	46	82

Group	X_1	X_2	X_3	X_4
B	110	108	33	71
B	173	94	64	90
B	104	111	60	48
B	91	82	33	99
B	144	100	46	79
C	100	117	48	65
C	111	109	53	51
C	101	112	52	96
C	143	102	71	78
C	140	108	49	113
C	125	114	47	81
C	130	106	52	92
C	104	113	62	70
C	149	92	49	91
C	130	110	61	81
C	117	113	63	121
C	126	96	54	87
C	128	100	51	88
C	122	130	54	85
C	112	126	45	73
C	137	91	75	79
C	125	101	39	77
C	136	116	69	97
C	129	93	57	84
C	139	92	59	78

(*Answer*)

The means for Group *A* are 101.30, 95.20, 42.00, and 92.00; the means for Group *B* are 120.20, 106.70, 47.75, and 85.50, and the means for Group *C* are 125.20, 107.05, 55.50, and 84.35. The pooled within-group standard deviations are 17.46, 11.63, 9.06, and 19.73. The total, between-group, and within-group correlation matrices are as follows:

$$
\mathbf{T} = \begin{bmatrix}
1.00 & .13 & .53 & .15 \\
.13 & 1.00 & .24 & -.17 \\
.53 & .24 & 1.00 & -.15 \\
.15 & -.17 & -.15 & 1.00
\end{bmatrix}
$$

$$
\mathbf{B} = \begin{bmatrix}
1.00 & .98 & .92 & -.99 \\
.98 & 1.00 & .83 & -.99 \\
.92 & .83 & 1.00 & -.89 \\
-.99 & -.99 & -.89 & 1.00
\end{bmatrix}
$$

$$
\mathbf{W} = \begin{bmatrix}
1.00 & -.12 & .38 & .29 \\
-.12 & 1.00 & .07 & -.11 \\
.38 & .06 & 1.00 & -.08 \\
.29 & -.11 & -.08 & 1.00
\end{bmatrix}
$$

The two canonical correlations are .67 and .28. Since the first one accounts for 90% of the total variance, the structure is concentrated so only the first one needs be considered (significance tests, considered in Chapter 10, will confirm this point). The total structure is (.76, .63, .73, −.25); the between structure is (.99, .98, .93, −.99), and the within structure is (.66, .52, .64, −.19). The standardized canonical coefficients are (.80, .60, .36, −.30), and the raw canonical coefficients are (.04, .05, .03, and −.02). Group A is located at −1.23 on the axis, Group B is located at .36, and Group C is located at .86. Various simplifications are possible. For example, the canonical correlation obtain using the sum of X_1, X_2, and X_3 with equal weights is .65, implying little would be lost with this equation.

6. Now, perform the same analysis upon the following data.

Group	X_1	X_2	X_3	X_4
A	104	93	49	34
A	98	93	40	29
A	103	104	28	24
A	112	99	35	41
A	88	86	35	49
A	113	109	56	59
A	107	80	38	40
A	83	105	44	39
A	102	88	30	44
A	76	84	32	21
A	91	98	50	46
A	124	110	29	36
A	85	113	40	39
A	117	108	42	38
A	104	96	44	67
A	151	102	32	24
A	92	91	32	37
A	156	99	28	52
A	90	78	37	29
A	102	96	35	34
B	100	109	20	32
B	125	118	41	31
B	120	115	49	41
B	151	136	46	37
B	148	117	34	50
B	111	102	25	35
B	133	117	56	60
B	156	137	40	57
B	112	112	28	30
B	115	112	26	30
B	117	127	60	70
B	109	83	18	41
B	119	106	50	37
B	117	97	42	29
B	100	103	36	18
B	136	114	32	49
B	132	108	35	39
B	143	117	33	38
B	112	103	35	33
B	115	120	43	26

Group	X_1	X_2	X_3	X_4
C	69	84	68	63
C	121	97	57	55
C	133	99	62	55
C	118	95	46	47
C	93	108	55	58
C	138	96	38	43
C	153	101	49	48
C	81	102	39	46
C	114	104	47	59
C	107	84	58	51
C	145	93	39	28
C	83	95	57	65
C	70	98	41	57
C	113	100	56	47
C	101	95	53	54
C	113	115	42	52
C	67	80	52	41
C	86	75	65	57
C	105	91	70	52
C	82	73	58	59

(*Answer*)
The means for Group A are 104.90, 96.60, 37.80, and 39.10; the means for Group B are 123.55, 112.65, 37.45, and 39.15, and the means for Group C are 104.60, 94.25, 52.60, and 51.85. The pooled within-group standard deviations are 21.19, 11.13, 9.13, and 11.03. The total, between-group, and within-group correlation matrices are as follows:

$$T = \begin{bmatrix} 1.00 & .56 & -.19 & -.06 \\ .56 & 1.00 & -.14 & -.01 \\ -.19 & -.14 & 1.00 & .62 \\ -.06 & -.01 & .62 & 1.00 \end{bmatrix}$$

$$B = \begin{bmatrix} 1.00 & .99 & -.53 & .51 \\ .99 & 1.00 & -.61 & -.60 \\ -.53 & -.61 & 1.00 & 1.00 \\ -.51 & -.60 & 1.00 & 1.00 \end{bmatrix}$$

$$W = \begin{bmatrix} 1.00 & .44 & -.09 & .04 \\ .44 & 1.00 & .12 & .22 \\ -.09 & .12 & 1.00 & .46 \\ .04 & .22 & .46 & 1.00 \end{bmatrix}$$

The two canonical correlations are .73 and .42. Since the magnitude of the second canonical correlation is also fairly large in this example, there is more evidence for diffusion, and it is reasonable to look at both functions (as would later be confirmed by significance tests). The total structure is (.45, .73, −.74, −.60) for the first function and (.52, .66, .59, .51) for the second; the between structure is (.83, .89, −.90, −.90) for the first function and (.55, .46, .42, .44) for the second, and the within structure is

(.33, .62, −.63, −.47) for the first function and (.51, .75, .67, .53) for the second. The standardized canonical coefficients are (−.05, .98, −.67, −.44) for the first function and (.36, .62, .71, .14) for the second, and the raw canonical coefficients are (.00, .07, −.06, −.04) for the first function and (.02, .04, .06, .02) for the second. Group A is located at (.11, −.64), Group B is located at (1.23, .36), and Group C is located at (−1.33, .27). The first function is thus essentially $X_2 − X_3 + X_4$. Group B obtains high scores (X_2 is large compared to X_3 and X_4) Group C obtains low scores, and Group A obtains average scores. The second function is essentially the sum with variables X_2 and X_3 weighted more heavily (which does not make much of a difference). Group A obtains very low scores and Groups B and C obtain scores of about the same magnitude which are modestly high.

PROBLEMS FOR CHAPTER 9

1. Assume that a signal detection study gave rise to the following six pairs of hit rates and false alarm rates. Draw the ROC curves in both probability and normal curve form. In addition, compute the likelihood ratios associated with each criterion. Do the data fit a particular model?

Criterion	1	2	3	4	5	6
$p(Y/s)$	.977	.933	.726	.500	.159	.040
$p(Y/n)$	.960	.894	.637	.401	.106	.023

(*Answer*)

Criterion	$p(Y/s)$	$p(Y/n)$	$z(Y/s)$	$z(Y/n)$	$l(z_i)$
1	.977	.960	2.00	1.75	.628
2	.933	.894	1.50	1.25	.710
3	.726	.637	.60	.35	.888
4	.500	.401	.00	−.25	1.031
5	.159	.106	−1.00	−1.25	1.322
6	.040	.023	−1.75	−2.00	1.592

The data fit an equal variance Gaussian model.

2. Perform the same analysis upon the following data.

Criterion	1	2	3	4	5	6
$p(Y/s)$	.841	.742	.681	.618	.520	.347
$p(Y/n)$	.841	.692	.579	.500	.308	.159

(*Answer*)

Criterion	$p(Y/s)$	$p(Y/n)$	$z(Y/s)$	$z(Y/n)$	$l(z_i)$
1	.841	.841	1.00	1.00	1.000
2	.742	.692	.65	.50	.818
3	.681	.579	.47	.20	.913
4	.618	.500	.30	.00	.954
5	.520	.308	.05	−.50	1.131
6	.347	.159	−.40	−1.00	1.521

The data fit an unequal variance Gaussian model.

3. Take the data from problem 5, Chapter 8. Verify that the vector of means for Group A is (104.9, 96.6, 37.8, 39.1). Assume that this represents an unknown score to be classified. Further assume that the prior odds are .7, .2, and .1, and that the values are .2, .3, and .5 for Groups A, B, and C, respectively. Perform an analysis paralleling that portrayed in Table 9-3.
(*Answer*)
Several salient decision variables are possible. The following table uses $2X_2 - (X_3 + X_4)$, although an argument can be made in favor of X_2 by itself or $X_2 - X_3 - X_4$.

		Variance					
		Pooled			Individual		
Method	Bayesian Variable	$p(A/X)$	$p(B/X)$	$p(C/X)$	$p(A/X)$	$p(B/X)$	$p(B/X)$
Salient	—	.527	.236	.237	.524	.176	.300
Salient	p	.839	.107	.054	.849	.081	.070
Salient	v	.358	.240	.403	.341	.171	.488
Salient	pv	.739	.142	.119	.742	.106	.152
Function I	—	.530	.284	.187	.522	.217	.261
Function I	p	.831	.127	.042	.840	.100	.060
Function I	v	.373	.299	.328	.348	.218	.435
Function I	pv	.738	.169	.093	.737	.132	.131
Both function	—	.914	.073	.013	.928	.063	.009
Both functions	p	.976	.022	.002	.980	.019	.001
Both functions	v	.867	.104	.030	.887	.090	.023
Both functions	pv	.962	.033	.005	.968	.028	.004
Mahalanobis distance	—	.914	.073	.013	.972	.027	.001
Mahalanobis distance	p	.976	.022	.002	.992	.008	.000
Mahalanobis distance	v	.866	.104	.030	.957	.040	.003
Mahalanobis distance	pv	.962	.033	.005	.988	.012	.000

4. Compute the percentage of correct classifications for each of the data sets described in Chapter 8. Assume that the base rates for the various groups within a given data set. Then, explore the consequences of altering the base rates.
(*Answer*)
Based upon Mahalanobis distance measures (SAS' procedure), 33 of 50 (66%) of the cases in data sets 1–3 would be correctly classified. They are the same because the three sets are linear transformations of one another. The corresponding figures are 36/50 (72%), 38/60 (63.3%), and 46/60 (76.7%) for the remaining data sets. If the package you employ uses a different basis of classification, your results may differ. Likewise, different percentages will obtain as the base rates are changed.

PROBLEMS FOR CHAPTER 10

1. Report (if available) or compute the various inferential statistics associated with the problems of Chapter 8, including Hotelling's T^2 values for the first four problems.
(*Answer*)
For problems 1–3, R^2 (reported under "Squared canonical correlations") = .166903, $F(2, 47) = 4.7080$, $T^2 = 9.616$, $p < .02$. Wilks' lambda (the likelihood of the particular mean difference vector) is .8331, Pillai's trace is .1669, the Hotelling–Lawley trace is .2003, and Roy's largest root is .2003. The results are identical because all three data sets are transformations of one another.

For problem 4, $R^2 = .200193$, $F(2, 47) = 5.8821$, $T^2 = 12.014$, $p < .01$. Wilks' lambda is .7998, Pillai's trace is .2002, the Hotelling–Lawley trace is .2503, and Roy's largest root is .2503.

For problem 5, the two squared canonical correlations are .4556 and .0824 (neither are R^2 values since there are three groups and therefore only two sets of dummy or other codes are needed), $F = 5.6019$ and 1.6467, $p < .001$ and ns. The two tests are respectively based upon 8 and 108 and 3 and 55 df. Wilks' lambda is .4995, Pillai's trace is .5381, the Hotelling–Lawley trace is .9269, and Roy's largest root is .8371. Thus, the first dimension of discrimination is significant, but the second is not.

For problem 6, the two squared canonical correlations are .5366 and .1778, $F(8, 108) = 8.37$ and $F(3, 55) = 3.96$, $ps < .001$ and .01. Wilks' lambda is .3810, Pillai's trace is .7144, the Hotelling–Lawley trace is 1.3743, and Roy's largest root is 1.1580. Thus, both dimensions of discrimination are significant.

2. Students were taught a computer language by one of three different methods. Method 1 consisted of using the large university mainframe computer, method 2 consisted of using the "Banana" personal computer, and method 3 consisted of using both. Two different instructors (A and B) taught 10 students by each of the three methods. The data obtained from the students consisted of SAT scores as an index of general academic ability, two hour examinations and a final examination. There were a possible 75 points on each of the hour examinations and 150 on the final. Use a MANOVA to test the effects of method, differences between the two instructors, and the the effects of their interaction upon the vector of examination scores, ignoring, for the moment, SAT scores. The data are as follows:

Method	Instructor	SAT	Exam 1	Exam 2	Final
1	A	396	30	34	86
1	A	371	15	20	67
1	A	498	19	31	43
1	A	598	37	30	85
1	A	542	38	24	79
1	A	556	29	26	63
1	A	673	42	34	94
1	A	649	35	42	123
1	A	459	25	16	75
1	A	730	53	44	95
1	B	487	47	45	123
1	B	270	29	38	96
1	B	539	49	42	104
1	B	557	56	41	112
1	B	384	43	48	91
1	B	672	57	57	138
1	B	520	44	45	88
1	B	690	48	46	103
1	B	617	49	73	95
1	B	375	32	31	83
2	A	634	51	53	82
2	A	435	42	65	74
2	A	530	49	57	92
2	A	361	42	44	102

Method	Instructor	SAT	Exam 1	Exam 2	Final
2	A	293	31	39	110
2	A	469	57	43	83
2	A	527	53	65	119
2	A	407	46	40	104
2	A	632	70	60	98
2	A	572	56	45	84
2	B	307	39	45	91
2	B	454	52	66	95
2	B	556	56	60	111
2	B	595	58	74	107
2	B	457	52	45	93
2	B	437	46	53	67
2	B	537	73	45	129
2	B	545	51	61	120
2	B	231	27	23	66
2	B	492	62	48	92
3	A	451	57	68	119
3	A	333	57	59	129
3	A	564	59	66	127
3	A	677	82	66	164
3	A	587	73	63	121
3	A	524	68	67	117
3	A	533	69	61	126
3	A	382	55	62	146
3	A	384	70	46	120
3	A	437	66	62	144
3	B	579	48	48	126
3	B	462	50	34	107
3	B	601	57	42	102
3	B	558	53	62	107
3	B	589	52	62	90
3	B	417	53	30	150
3	B	513	53	41	78
3	B	669	62	55	138
3	B	511	54	34	114
3	B	482	57	33	118

(*Answer*)
The effect of method is highly significant, which implies that the vectors for method 1 (38.85, 38.35, 92.15), method 2 (50.65, 51.55, 95.95), and method 3 (59.75, 53.05, 122.15) can be assumed different. Wilks' lambda is .4085, which corresponds to an F ratio of 9.78 with 6 and 104 df. Pillai's trace is .6809 which corresponds to an F ratio of 9.12 with 6 and 106 df. The Hotelling–Lawley trace is 1.2285 which corresponds to an F ratio of 10.44 with 6 and 102 df, and Roy's largest root is 1.012, which corresponds (approximately) to an F ratio of 17.88 with 3 and 53 df. All effects are significant well beyond the .001 level.

The structure is fairly well concentrated with the first eigenvalue accounting for 82.4% of the variance and the second accounting for 17.6%. The discriminant axis is (.0094, .0033, .0024) which means that groups are most different on the first test once all test scores are adjusted for each other. Univariate tests indicated that all three dependent variables different from each other well beyond the .001 level (these data will not be presented).

The overall difference between the vectors of mean test scores for the two instructors, (49.20, 47.73, 102.36) and (50.30, 47.57, 104.47) is not significant. Wilks' lambda is .9939; Pillai's trace is .0060; the Hotelling–Lawley trace is .0061, and Roy's largest root is .0061. All correspond to F ratios <1.0 with $df = 3$ and 52.

The interaction is significant. This means that the three vectors individually associated with instructor A, which are (32.3, 30.1, 81.0), (49.7, 51.1, 94.8), and (65.6, 62.0, 131.3), and the corresponding vectors associated with instructor B, which are (45.4, 46.6, 103.3), (51.6, 52.0, 97.1), and (53.9, 44.1, 113.0), differed following correction for the two main effect vectors. Wilks' lambda is .6170, $F(6, 104) = 4.73$; Pillai's trace is .3823, $F(6, 106) = 4.19$, the Hotelling–Lawley trace is .6204, $F(6, 102) = 5.27$, and Roy's largest root is .6199, $F(3, 53) = 10.95$, (all $ps < .001$). The first eigenvector accounted for 99.91% of the total variance so the interaction may be regarded as concentrated. The eigenvector is (.0040, .0087, .0024), which means that the joint effects of instructor and method are seen most strongly on the second examination, although univariate analyses indicated that the interaction is significant for all three dependent variables. The interaction reveals that instructor A does relatively poorly with method 1 and relatively well on method 3, compared to instructor B.

3. Now, use the SAT score as a covariate upon the preceding data.

(*Answer*)

The covariance adjustment strongly reduced experimental error so that its primary effect is to increase the significance levels of the main effect and the interaction. For example, Wilks' lambda decreased to .1544, which led to a corresponding increase in the associated F ratio for the main effect of Type of Method to 26.26, $p < .001$, with 6 and 102 df. Similarly, Wilks' lambda decreased to .2625 and the associated F ratio for the interaction increased to 16.18, $p < .001$. However, the main effect of Instructor remained nonsignificant with a Wilks' lambda of .9858, $F(3, 51) < 1$. Other criteria led to similar results. These increases in significance levels arise because the pretest measure (SAT) is correlated with each of the dependent variables. Consequently, removing its effect prior to assessing the main effects and interaction reduces experimental error, the goal of any covariance analysis.

However, the data were constructed so that SAT did not correlate to an equal extent with all three measures. Instead, SAT correlated most highly with test 1 ($r = .78$), next most highly with test 2 ($r = .62$), and least highly with the final examination ($r = .32$, a plausible outcome since the longer one is in the course, the more information specific to the course would determine performance). As a result, the error is reduced more for test 1 than for the final, which, in turn, meant that the discriminant axis is "tilted" toward the first test more. Specifically, the eigenvector associated with the Type of Method effect is (.0205, .0031, .0020), and the eigenvector associated with the Interaction is (.0181, .0123, .0005).

PROBLEMS FOR CHAPTER 11

1. Three individuals, A, B, and C, obtain vectors of (44, 17, 12), (34, 12, 8), and (50, 15, 8), respectively, on three measures whose means are 40, 15, and 12. The variance–covariance matrix of the three measures is:

$$\begin{bmatrix} 100 & 20 & 12 \\ 20 & 25 & 12 \\ 12 & 12 & 16 \end{bmatrix}$$

Describe the level of each profile as: (a) a raw-score sum, (b) a raw-score average, (c) a z-score sum, (c) a z-score average, and (d) a z-score sum, correcting for the intercorrelations among the variables.
(*Answer*)

	Profile		
	A	B	C
(b) z-score sum	24.33	18.00	24.33
(c) Raw score average	.80	−2.20	.00
(d) z-score average	.26	−.73	.00
(e) Correcting for R	.14	−.40	.04

Note that because the three profile elements have different variances, the results obtained from converting each element to a z-score are not equivalent to the raw score results.

2. Take the data of the previous problem and obtained d^2 measures of profile similarity for: (a) the raw measures, (b) the z-score measures, and (c) the z-score measures correcting for the correlations among the measures. Then, obtain cross-product (CP) and correlation measures of similarity for the raw score and z-score measures.
(*Answer*)

	1 vs. 2	1 vs. 3	2 vs. 3
(a) Raw score d^2	141.00	56.00	265.00
(b) z-score d^2	3.00	1.52	2.92
(c) d^2 correcting for R	1.69	1.89	2.89
(d) Raw score CP	1796.00	2551.00	1944.00
(e) z-score CP	−.48	.40	.40
(f) r based upon raw scores	1.00	1.00	1.00
(g) r based upon z-scores	1.00	.87	.87

The raw score correlations are largely artifacts of the scales used for the three measures, as they largely reflect the overall mean differences among the measures.

3. Correct the three profiles in question 1 for level and recompute the various indices obtained in that question.
(*Answer*)
The three new profiles are (19.67, −7.33, −12.33), (16, −6, 10), and (25.67, −9.33, −16.33) for A, B, and C, respectively. The z-score versions are (.13, .13, −.27), (.13, .13, −.27), and (1, 0, 1). Note that A and B therefore differ only as to level once differences in standard deviations of the profile elements are taken into account.
    The relevant indices are:

	Profile		
	A	B	C
(a) Raw score sum	0.00	0.00	0.00
(b) z-score sum	0.00	0.00	0.00
(c) Raw score average	0.00	0.00	0.00
(d) z-score average	0.00	0.00	0.00
(e) Correcting for R	.00	−.00	.04

Note that uncorrected "elevation" measures are .0 once a correction for level is introduced.

4. Now, compute d^2, CP, and correlation-based similarity measures for the level-corrected measures.
   (*Answer*)

	1 vs. 2	1 vs. 3	2 vs. 3
(a) Raw score d^2	20.67	56.00	144.67
(b) z-score d^2	0.00	1.31	1.31
(c) d^2 correcting for R	.00	1.84	1.84
(d) Raw score CP	482.00	774.67	630.00
(e) z-score CP	.11	.40	.40
(f) r based upon raw scores	1.00	1.00	1.00
(g) r based upon z-scores	1.00	.87	.87

The correlation measures do not change from the original (nonlevel-corrected case) because they were insensitive to level to begin with.

5. The following 45 profiles were constructed so that the first 15 belonged to one class, the next 15 to a second class, and the last 15 to a third class. Profiles in the second class were higher than profiles in the first class on the first three measures (X_1 to X_3) but equivalent on the last three measures (X_4 to X_6). The converse is true for profiles in the third class. Use a suitable clustering program to determine groupings. Do the various measures of fit change abruptly at three clusters? How well does a three-cluster solution reconstruct the actual classes?

X_1	X_2	X_3	X_4	X_5	X_6
49	51	40	50	53	57
53	45	55	45	53	56
50	52	54	47	40	45
43	42	40	54	53	50
57	61	44	54	60	51
40	47	45	60	49	46
48	42	41	48	35	35
56	47	50	57	51	55
63	52	60	57	53	57
46	63	55	50	56	52
48	46	51	52	48	47
60	51	61	70	71	71
44	44	44	42	43	37
74	88	74	52	60	54

X_1	X_2	X_3	X_4	X_5	X_6
49	40	56	47	50	46
55	63	50	42	48	40
67	57	68	51	43	45
82	76	83	64	61	55
83	73	77	65	57	61
65	70	79	69	60	59
79	75	78	71	62	71
63	65	64	42	43	43
61	62	72	73	57	66
67	74	75	60	56	72
66	63	71	52	52	52
74	61	66	41	45	47
73	57	74	36	43	46
73	63	73	50	49	45
82	83	79	61	67	66
70	62	67	55	59	49
41	52	43	85	87	90
62	61	63	76	80	72
56	56	59	67	63	66
52	69	50	79	85	77
57	58	66	56	74	60
55	48	54	81	73	76
62	65	54	80	77	81
61	56	63	56	75	60
47	56	48	60	54	59
43	58	46	73	74	72
61	55	57	77	73	74
52	40	45	72	64	69
35	44	37	59	57	68
60	55	55	72	66	63
51	63	60	58	62	63

(*Answer*)

Your results may differ because of differences in the algorithm. Using Ward's method, 12 members of Group 3 were placed in one cluster along with 1 member of Group 1; 13 members of Group 1, 1 member of Group 2, and 3 members of Group 3 were placed into a second cluster, and 14 members of Group 2 and 1 member of Group 1 were placed in the third cluster. The RMS standard deviations associated with 1 through 6 clusters are: 12.18, 10.89, 8.72, 7.37, 7.74, and 6.45 so the increase in homogeneity in going from two to three categories is relatively large. Likewise, the associated semipartial r^2 values were .31, .29. .10, .04, .04, and −.02. Finally, the R^2 values were .00, .31, .59, .69, .73, and .77. The latter two measures thus tell the same story.

6. Assume you had analyzed blood samples of 90 subjects to determine the levels of three hormones, H_1, H_2, and H_3. Also assume that you had obtained systolic blood pressure (S), diastolic blood pressure (D), and pulse rate measures (P) on these same subjects. What relations exist between these hypothetical hormones, on the one hand, and the blood pressure and pulse rate measures, on the other? The data are as follows:

H_1	H_2	H_3	D	S	P
4	6	9	83	82	81
5	5	8	96	82	80
5	6	6	102	72	62
4	4	5	98	82	70
5	8	6	99	88	71
4	5	6	108	79	65
4	4	4	99	68	48
5	5	8	102	81	78
6	6	9	109	83	80
4	8	7	105	85	73
4	5	7	102	78	66
6	6	15	97	97	02
4	4	4	96	75	51
7	13	6	126	88	77
4	4	6	106	80	64
3	4	1	85	72	44
4	3	6	93	68	51
6	7	8	114	82	67
6	6	6	114	79	76
4	6	8	112	82	73
5	7	10	109	83	90
4	5	3	92	68	48
4	4	8	110	79	83
4	7	10	92	78	92
4	4	8	91	75	62
5	4	2	96	70	54
5	3	3	98	68	53
5	4	5	102	73	51
6	8	7	110	87	83
4	4	5	101	81	57
3	5	10	88	91	92
5	6	7	112	86	66
5	5	6	100	72	56
4	8	8	99	90	74
5	6	4	105	81	47
5	4	6	111	80	72
5	7	6	107	83	79
5	5	6	97	81	48
4	5	2	100	65	45
3	6	4	101	80	65
5	5	7	106	80	69
4	2	5	98	73	61
3	3	5	77	67	59
5	5	4	108	74	52
4	7	4	101	71	52
5	5	9	110	88	86
4	5	6	99	83	67
4	2	2	97	66	43
4	3	10	91	81	81
5	5	3	105	68	64
5	3	3	95	69	47
4	6	7	98	78	79
2	1	8	81	83	90

H_1	H_2	H_3	D	S	P
4	4	9	96	84	78
4	3	8	91	82	82
5	5	10	104	93	98
3	2	3	84	69	41
4	3	8	94	83	78
6	7	6	109	79	61
3	3	8	93	79	80
4	3	8	82	91	72
5	5	5	88	81	59
5	5	7	95	74	74
5	9	8	109	87	92
7	7	6	116	85	76
5	5	8	104	75	63
5	6	5	111	75	60
5	6	6	109	76	62
5	7	8	97	92	91
6	8	8	106	95	93
4	4	7	100	77	66
4	3	8	81	74	76
5	7	7	97	85	74
5	4	4	100	72	53
6	8	10	114	88	84
6	7	5	115	78	62
5	5	5	111	72	54
5	5	8	96	78	83
5	7	5	99	70	52
3	3	6	82	77	63
6	7	9	117	80	76
5	6	6	95	77	73
5	4	5	105	76	55
4	5	6	98	79	60
5	9	10	108	88	94
5	9	9	111	85	81
4	4	4	91	72	60
4	4	2	83	58	34
5	6	6	103	75	66
5	6	5	98	78	60

(*Answer*)
The first two canonical correlations are highly significant ($R_c = .890$ and $.741$, $ps < .001$), but the third is not ($R_c = .125$).

The raw score formulas for the first canonical variate are $.016H_1 + .149H_2 + .373H_3$ and $.014S + .034D + .050P$. The corresponding standardized formulas are $.015z_{H_1} + .285z_{H_2} + .878z_{H_3}$ and $.132z_s + .252z_D + .750z_p$. The linear combination of hormones correlates $.343$, $.539$, and $.959$ with the individual hormone levels and $.300$, $.793$, and $.868$ with S, D, and P, respectively. Conversely, the linear combination of S, D, and P correlates $.337$, $.891$, and $.975$ with H_1, H_2, and H_3 and $.306$, $.480$, and $.854$ with S, D, and P, individually. The first canonical variate is thus a weighted sum of the three hormone measures, emphasizing H_3 vs. a weighted sum of S, D, and P, emphasizing P. It is primarily reflective of the substantial correlation between H_3 and P ($r = .866$).

The raw score formulas for the second canonical variate are $.801H_1 + .192H_2 - .199H_3$ and $.103S + .017D - .031P$. The corresponding standardized formulas are $.728z_{H_1} + .368z_{H_2} - .467z_{H_3}$ and $.978z_s + .127z_D - .453z_p$. The linear combination of hormones correlates .874, .687, and $-.238$ with the individual hormone levels and .692, .032, and $-.132$ with S, D, and P, respectively. Conversely, the linear combination of S, D, and P correlates .934, .043, and $-.179$ with H_1, H_2, and H_3 and .648 .509, and $-.176$ with S, D, and P, individually. The first canonical variate is thus a weighted sum of H_1 and H_2, minus H_3, emphasizing H_1 vs. basically the weighted differences of $S - P$, emphasizing S.

The two linear combinations of hormones individually account for 62.4% and 26.7% of their own variance, for a total of 89.1%. They also account for 49.4% and 14.6% of the variance in S, D, and P, for a total of 64.0%. Conversely, the two linear combinations of S, D, and P account for 71.8% and 23.7% of their own variance, for a total of 95.5%. Likewise, they account for 56.9% and 13.0% of the variance among the hormone measures, for a total of 69.9%.

PROBLEMS FOR CHAPTER 12

1. Suppose that tests A, B, and C have reliability coefficients of .8, .5, and .3. What is the maximum correlation each can have with some external criterion.
   (*Answer*)
   The maximum correlations (equal to the reliability indices) are .89, .71, and .55, which are the respective square roots of the reliability coefficients.

2. Now, suppose that tests D, E, and F correlate .4, .5, and .6 with some external criterion. What is the *minimum* value of their associated reliability coefficients can assume.
   (*Answer*)
   Assume that the above values are lower bounds on the reliability index. The reliability coefficients would be .16, .25, and .36, i.e., the squares of the obtained correlations.

3. A five-item test gave rise to the following variance–covariance matrix. Compute the reliability of the test.

$$\begin{bmatrix} 1.0000 & .4301 & .4230 & .2786 & .1615 \\ .4301 & .7775 & .4902 & .2288 & .1374 \\ .4230 & .4902 & 1.2370 & .2860 & .2010 \\ .2786 & .2288 & .2860 & .4681 & .0817 \\ .1615 & .1374 & .2010 & .0817 & .2681 \end{bmatrix}$$

   (*Answer*)
   $r_{xx} = .740$.

4. Assume each of the five items is rescaled to equal variance. Recompute the reliability, i.e., compute the reliability of the correlation matrix based upon the previous data.
   (*Answer*)
   $r_{xx} = .748$.

5. Assume that three raters, A, B, and C, evaluate the degree of maladjustment they perceive in 50 job applicants, using a 9-point rating scale (1 = most maladjusted). Compute: (a) the individual interjudge correlations, (b) their average, (c) coeffi-

cient alpha based upon the raw scores, and (d) coefficient alpha based upon equal weighting of each rater.

A	B	C
5	3	3
8	5	6
1	1	3
6	3	4
7	4	4
3	6	7
7	5	6
9	7	9
5	3	3
2	2	3
6	6	6
5	6	6
6	3	3
3	6	6
2	2	2
6	3	3
1	2	3
5	7	8
1	1	4
7	5	7
2	5	6
4	4	4
1	5	4
9	5	5
7	5	5
1	6	6
6	4	3
1	6	6
9	3	4
1	3	5
4	2	3
1	6	6
1	6	5
1	5	5
9	5	6
4	5	4
2	6	5
9	5	7
4	4	5
1	2	3
5	7	6
1	5	6
6	6	7
2	3	4
6	4	4
1	5	7
9	5	7
4	1	4
5	7	7
1	6	6

(*Answer*)

(a) .172, .242, and .813, (b) .409, (c) .574, (d) .675.

6. A test of cognitive ability is scaled to a mean of 100 and a standard deviation of 15. Its reliability coefficient is .64. What is the standard error of measurement in both raw and z-score terms? What would these standard errors become if the test's reliability is increased to .80?

(*Answer*)

(a) 9.0 and .60, and (b) 6.71 and .447.

7. Suppose person A obtains a score of 115 on the test considered in problem 6. What is the best estimate of the true score for the test in its present form? What would the best estimate be if the test were made more reliable?

(*Answer*)

(a) 109.6, and (b) 112.

8. A 70 item personality scale has a reliability coefficient of .80. (a) What would the reliability be if the test were doubled in length? (b) How many items would the test have to contain in order to have a reliability of .95? (c) What is the average interitem correlation, i.e., what would the reliability of the test be if it only consisted of one item?

(*Answer*)

(a) .89, (b) 332, (c) .05 (note how a test that is collectively of acceptable reliability consists of items with essentially no reliability of their own).

9. Assume that two tests each have a reliability of .7, the correlation between them is also .7, and their individual variances are 1.0 units each. What is the reliability of: (a) their sum and (b) their difference?

(*Answer*)

(a) .82 and (b) .00.

10. A psychologist develops a test to predict skill at widgetry. The test correlates .3 with actual widgetry and has a reliability coefficient of .70. The criterion (widgetry) has a reliability coefficient of .50. (a) What would the test's validity coefficient (correlation with actual widgetry) be if its reliability were increased to .9? (b) What would the test's reliability be if it were doubled in length? (c) How would the doubling in length affect the validity? (d) What would happen if the test were doubled in length *and* the reliability of the criterion were increased to .9? (e) What would happen to the validity if both predictor and criterion were made perfectly reliable?

(*Answer*)

(a) .34, (b) .82, (c) .32, (d) .43, (e) .51. Note, however, that although it may be possible to make the predictor more reliable, the unreliability in the criterion may be inherent in the measure so that neither of the last two outcomes may be obtainable. If so, very little you do will improve the validity of the predictor. The validity can equal .39 at most when the predictor is made perfectly reliable and the criterion is left as is.

11. One hundred students each take a six item test. Their results are as follows (0 = incorrect and 1 = correct). Do the data suggest the six items measure a single factor?

| | Item | | | | | |
Student	1	2	3	4	5	6
1	0	0	0	1	1	0
2	0	0	0	1	1	1
3	0	0	0	1	1	1
4	0	0	0	1	1	1
5	1	1	1	1	1	1
6	0	0	0	1	1	1
7	0	1	0	1	1	1
8	0	0	1	1	1	1
9	0	0	0	0	1	1
10	0	0	0	1	1	1
11	0	0	0	1	1	1
12	0	1	0	1	1	1
13	0	0	0	1	1	1
14	0	0	0	1	1	1
15	0	0	0	1	1	1
16	1	0	0	1	1	1
17	0	0	0	1	1	1
18	0	0	0	1	1	1
19	1	1	0	1	1	1
20	0	0	0	1	0	0
21	0	0	0	1	1	1
22	0	0	0	1	1	1
23	0	0	0	1	1	1
24	0	0	0	1	1	1
25	1	0	1	1	1	1
26	0	0	0	1	1	1
27	0	0	1	1	1	1
28	0	0	1	1	1	1
29	0	0	0	1	1	1
30	0	0	0	1	1	1
31	0	0	0	1	0	1
32	0	0	0	0	0	1
33	0	0	0	1	1	1
34	1	1	0	1	1	1
35	0	0	0	1	1	0
36	0	0	0	1	0	1
37	0	0	0	0	1	1
38	0	0	0	1	1	1
39	0	0	0	1	1	1
40	0	0	0	1	1	1
41	0	0	0	1	1	0
42	0	0	0	0	1	1
43	0	0	0	1	1	0
44	0	0	0	1	1	1
45	0	0	0	1	1	1
46	1	0	1	1	1	1
47	0	0	0	1	1	1
48	0	0	0	1	1	1
49	0	0	0	0	1	1
50	0	0	0	1	1	1

Student	Item					
	1	2	3	4	5	6
51	0	0	0	1	1	1
52	0	0	0	1	0	0
53	0	0	0	1	1	1
54	0	0	0	1	1	1
55	0	0	0	1	1	1
56	0	0	0	1	1	1
57	0	0	0	1	1	1
58	0	0	0	1	1	1
59	1	1	1	1	1	1
60	1	0	0	1	1	1
61	0	0	0	0	0	0
62	0	0	0	1	1	1
63	0	0	0	1	1	1
64	0	0	0	1	1	1
65	0	0	0	1	1	1
66	0	0	1	1	1	1
67	0	0	0	1	1	1
68	0	0	0	1	1	1
69	0	0	0	1	0	0
70	1	0	0	1	1	1
71	0	0	0	1	1	1
72	0	0	0	1	1	1
73	0	0	0	1	1	1
74	0	0	0	1	1	1
75	0	0	0	1	1	1
76	0	0	0	1	1	1
77	0	0	0	1	1	1
78	0	0	0	1	1	1
79	0	0	0	0	1	1
80	0	0	0	1	1	1
81	1	0	1	1	1	1
82	0	0	0	0	1	0
83	0	0	0	1	1	1
84	0	0	0	1	1	1
85	1	1	1	1	1	1
86	0	0	0	0	0	0
87	1	1	0	1	1	1
88	0	0	0	1	1	1
89	0	1	1	1	1	1
90	0	1	0	1	1	1
91	1	1	0	1	1	1
92	0	0	0	1	0	1
93	0	0	0	1	1	1
94	1	1	0	1	1	1
95	0	0	0	1	1	1
96	0	0	0	0	1	1
97	0	0	0	1	1	1
98	0	0	0	1	1	1
99	0	0	0	1	1	1
100	0	0	0	0	0	0

(*Answer*)

The eigenvalues of the correlation matrix are 2.18, 1.41, .77, .75, .47 and .41. The factor pattern, following a varimax rotation, is:

Item	Factor		h^2
	I	II	
1	.861	.088	.749
2	.792	.077	.632
3	.665	.098	.452
4	.125	.624	.405
5	.057	.828	.688
6	.071	.813	.666

Consequently, the six items *appear* to form two factors. One factor is defined by items 1, 2, and 3, and the other factor is defined by items 4, 5, and 6. Note, however, that the item p values are .14, .12, .11, .89, .90, and .89, respectively. Therefore, the two factors simply reflect the fact that items 1, 2, and 3 are difficult and 4, 5, and 6 are easy. They are classical *difficulty* factors.

References

Applebaum, M.I., & Cramer, E.M. (1974). Some problems in the nonorthogonal analysis of variance. *Psychological Bulletin, 81,* 335–343.

Atkinson, R.C. (1963). A variable sensitivity theory of signal detection. *Psychological Review, 70,* 91–106.

Bartlett, M.S. (1937). The statistical conception of mental factors. *British Journal of Psychology, 28,* 97–104.

Bartlett, M.S. (1950). Tests of significance in factor analysis. *British Journal of Psychology, 3,* 77–85.

Bentler, P.M. (1980). Multivariate analysis with latent variables: Causal modeling. *Annual Review of Psychology, 31,* 419–456.

Bentler, P.M. (1983). Some contributions to efficient statistics in structural models: Specification and estimation of moment structures. *Psychometrika, 48,* 493–517.

Bentler, P.M., & Bonnett, D.G. (1980). Significance tests and goodness of fit tests in the analysis of covariance structures. *Psychological Bulletin, 88,* 508–606.

Bernstein, I.H., & Eveland, D. (1982). State vs. trait anxiety: A case study in confirmatory factor analysis. *Personality and Individual Differences, 3,* 361–372.

Bernstein, I.H., Lin. T.-D., & McClellan, P. (1982). Cross- vs. within-racial judgments of attractiveness. *Perception and Psychophysics, 32,* 495–503.

Bernstein, I.H., & Garbin, C.P. (1985a). A comparison of alternative proposed subscale structures for MMPI scale 2. *Multivariate Behavior Research, 20,* 223–235.

Bernstein, I.H., & Garbin, C.P. (1985b). A simple set of salient weights for the major dimensions of MMPI scale variation. *Educational and Psychological Measurement, 45,* 771–787.

Bernstein, I.H., Garbin, C.P., & McClellan, P.G. (1983). A confirmatory factoring of the California Psychological Inventory. *Educational and Psychological Measurement, 43,* 687–691.

Bernstein, I.H., Schoenfeld, L.S., & Costello, R.L. (1982). Truncated component regression, multicollinearity and the MMPI's use in a police officer setting. *Multivariate Behavior Research, 17,* 99–116.

Bernstein, I.H., & Teng, G. (1986). Effects of item categorization and scale reliability upon factor structures. Unpublished manuscript.

Bernstein, I.H., Teng, G., & Garbin, C. P. (1986). A confirmatory factoring of the self-consciousness scale. *Multivariate Behaviorial Research, 21,* 459–475.

Blalock, H.M. (Ed.) (1971). *Causal models in the social sciences.* Chicago: Aldine.

Boneau, C.A. (1960). The effects of violations of assumptions underlying the *t* test.

Psychological Bulletin, 57, 291–309.

Box, G.E.P. (1950). Problems in the analysis of growth and linear curves. *Biometrika, 6,* 362–389.

Box, G.E.P. (1953). Nonnormality and tests on variance. *Biometrika, 40,* 318–335.

Browne, M.W. (1967). On oblique Procrustes rotation. *Psychometrika, 33,* 267–334.

Browne, M.W. (1972a). Orthogonal rotation to a partially specified target. *British Journal of Mathematical Statistics, 25,* 115–120.

Browne, M.W. (1972b). Oblique rotation to a partially specified target. *British Journal of Mathematical Statistics, 25,* 207–212.

Browne, M.W. (1974). Generalized least squares estimators in the analysis of covariance structures. *South African Statistical Journal, 8,* 1–24.

Brunswik, E. (1956). *Perception and the representative design of experiments* (2nd. ed.). Berkeley; University of California Press.

Buckles, M. (1982). Utilization of a semantic differential to measure attitudes of nurse-practitioners and consumers towards power, authority, and health care. Masters thesis, University of Texas–Arlington.

Burt, C.W. (1948). The factorial study of temperamental traits. *British Journal of Psychology (Statistical Section), 1,* 178–203.

BMDP (1982). *Biomedical computer programs: P-series.* Berkeley, Cal: University of California Press.

Carroll, J.B. (1953). An analytic solution for approximating simple structure in factor analysis. *Psychometrika, 18,* 23–38.

Cattell, R.C. (1957). *Personality and motivation structure and measurement.* New York: World Book Co.

Cattell, R.B. (1966). The scree test for the number of factors. *Multivariate Behavioral Research, 1,* 245–276.

Cattell, R.B. (1978). *The scientific use of factor analysis in behavioral and life sciences.* New York: Plenum.

Cattell, R.B., Eber, H.W., & Tatsuoka, M.M. (1970). *Handbook for the sixteen personality factor questionnaire (16PF).* Champaign, Il: Institute for Personality and Ability Testing.

Cliff, N.R. (1966). Orthogonal rotation to congruence. *Psychometrika, 31,* 33–42.

Cohen, J., & Cohen, P. (1975). *Applied multiple regression/correlation analysis for the behavioral sciences.* Hillsdale, NJ: Lawrence Erlbaum.

Cooley, W.W., & Lohnes, P.R. (1971). *Multivariate data analysis.* New York: Wiley.

Cronbach, L.J. (1951). Coefficient alpha and the internal structure of tests. *Psychometrika, 16,* 297–334.

Cronbach, L.J. (1957). The two disciplines of scientific psychology. *American Psychologist, 12,* 671–684.

Darlington, R.B. (1979). Multiple regression in psychological research and practice. *Psychological Bulletin, 69,* 161–182.

Draper, N.R., & Smith, H. (1981). *Applied regression analysis* (2nd. ed.). New York: Wiley.

Dulany, D.E., Jr. (1962). The place of hypotheses and intentions: An analysis of verbal control in verbal conditioning. In C.D. Spielberger (Ed.), *Behavior and awareness: A symposium of research and interpretation.* Durham, NC: Duke University Press.

Duncan, O.D. (1975). *Introduction to structural equation models.* New York: Academic Press.

Dunnett, C.W. (1955). A multiple comparison procedure for comparing several treatments with a control. *Journal of the American Statistical Association, 50,* 1096–1121.

Dunnett, C.W. (1964). New tables for multiple comparisons with a control. *Biometrics, 20,* 482–491.

Egan, J.P. (1975). *Signal detection theory and ROC analysis.* New York: Academic Press.

Eriksen, C.M. (1960). Discrimination and learning without awareness: A methodological survey and evaluation. *Psychological Review, 67,* 279–300.

Feller, W.H. (1957). *An introduction to probability theory and its applications* (Vol I., 2nd ed.). New York: Wiley.

Ferguson, G.A. (1954). The concept of parsimony in factor analysis. *Psychometrika, 19,* 281–290.

Fisher, R.A. (1921). On the "probable error" of a coefficient of correlation. *Metron, 1,* 1–32.

Fao, U.G. (1965). New developments in facet design and analysis. *Psychological Review, 72,* 262–274.

Ford, L.S. (1981). Interspecific relationships among cloud forest frogs in the genus *Eleutherodactylus.* Unpublished masters thesis, University of Texas–Arlington.

Gaito, J, (1965). Unequal intervals and unequal *n* in trend analyses. *Psychological Bulletin, 63,* 125–127.

Garbin, C.P., & Bernstein, I.H. (1984). Visual and haptic perception of three-dimensional solid forms. *Perception and Psychophysics, 36,* 104–110.

Garner, W.R. (1960). Rating scales, discriminability, and information transmission. *Psychological Review, 67,* 343–352.

Garner, W.R. (1962). *Uncertainty and structure as psychological concepts.* New York: Wiley.

Garner, W.R., Hake, H.W., & Eriksen, C.W. (1957). Operationalism and the concept of perception. *Psychological Review, 63,* 317–329.

Gerbring, D.W. & Hunter, J. E. (1980). The return to multiple groups: Analysis and critique of confirmatory factor analysis with LISREL. Unpublished manuscript.

Gorsuch, R.L. (1966). The general factor in the Test Anxiety Questionnaire. *Psychological Reports, 19,* 308.

Gorsuch, R.L. (1983). *Factor analysis* (2nd, ed.). Hillsdale, NJ: Lawrence Erlbaum.

Green, D.M., & Swets, J.A. (1967). *Signal detection theory and psychophysics.* New York: Wiley.

Guilford, J.P. (1954). *Psychometric methods* (2nd. ed.). New York: McGraw-Hill.

Guttman, L. (1952). Multiple group methods for common-factor analysis: Their basis, computation, and interpretation. *Psychometrika, 17,* 209–222.

Guttman, L. (1953). Image theory for the structure of quantitative variates. *Psychometrika, 18,* 277–296.

Guttman, L. (1954). Some necessary conditions for common factor analysis. *Psychometrika, 19,* 149–161.

Hake, H.W., & Rodwan, A.S. (1966). Perception and recognition. In J.B. Sidowski (Ed.), *Experimental methods and instrumentation in psychology.* New York: McGraw-Hill.

Harman, H.H., & Jones, W.H. (1966). Factor analysis by minimizing residuals. *Psychometrika, 31,* 351–368.

Harman, H.H. (1976). *Modern factor analysis* (3rd. ed., rev.). Chicago: University of Chicago Press.

Hays, W.L. (1981). *Statistics* (3rd ed.). New York: Holt, Rinehart, and Winston.

Heck, D.L. (1960). Charts of some upper percentage points of the distribution of the largest characteristic root. *Annals of Mathematical Statistics, 31,* 625–642.

Heise, D.R. (1975). *Causal Analysis.* New York: Wiley.

Hoaglin, D.C., Mosteller, F., & Tukey, J.W. (1983). *Understanding robust and exploratory data analysis.* New York: Wiley.

Holzinger, K.J., & Swineford, F. (1937). The bi-factor method. *Psychometrika, 2,* 41–54.

Holzinger, K.J. (1944). A simple method of factor analysis. *Psychometrika, 9,* 257–262.

Hopkins, K.D., & Stanley, J.C. (1981). *Educational and psychological measurement and evaluation* (6th ed.). Englewood Cliff, NJ: Prentice-Hall.

Horn, J.L. (1965). An empirical comparison of various methods for estimating common factor scores. *Educational and Psychological Measurements, 25,* 313–322.

Horst, P.W. (1963). *Matrix algebra for social scientists.* New York: Holt, Rinehart, and Winston.

Huberty, C.J. (1984). Issues in the use and interpretation of discriminant analysis. *Psychological Bulletin, 95,* 156–171.

Hulin, C.L., Drasgow, F., & Parsons, C.K. (1983). *Item response theory.* Homewood, IL: Dow Jones-Irwin.

Hunter, J.E., & Schmidt, F.L. (1976). Critical analysis of the statistical and ethical implications of various definitions of *Test Bias. Psychological Bulletin, 83,* 1053–1071.

Hurley, J., & Cattell, R.B. (1962). The Procrustes program: Producing direct rotation to test a hypothesized factor structure. *Behavioral Science, 7,* 258–262.

Jöreskog, K.G. (1967). Some contributions to maximum likelihood factor analysis. *Psychometrika, 32,* 443–482.

Jöreskog, K.G. (1969). A general approach to confirmatory maximum likelihood factor analysis. *Psychometrika, 34,* 183–202.

Jöreskog, K.G. (1974). Analyzing psychological data by structural analysis of covariance matrices, in R.C. Atkinson, D.H. Krantz, R.D. Luce, and P. Suppes (Eds.), *Contemporary developments in mathematical psychology* (Vol. II, pp. 1–64). San Francisco: Freeman.

Jöreskog, K.G., & Sörbom, D. (1986). *LISREL: Analysis of linear structural relationships by the method of maximum likelihood (Version VI).* Mooresville, IN: Scientific Software, Inc.

Kaiser, H.F. (1958). The varimax criterion for analytic rotation in factor analysis. *Psychometrika, 23,* 187–200.

Kaiser, H.F. (1960). The application of electronic computers to factor analysis. *Educational and Psychological Measurements, 20,* 141–151.

Kaiser, H.F. (1970). A second generation Little Jiffy. *Psychometrika, 35,* 401–417.

Kaiser, H.F., & Caffey, J. (1965) Alpha factor analysis. *Psychometrika, 30,* 1–14.

Kaiser, H.F., Hunka, S., & Bianchini, J. (1971). Relating factors between studies based upon different individuals. *Multivariate Behavioral Research, 6,* 409–422.

Kemeny, J.G., Mirkil, H., Snell, J.N., & Thompson, G.L. (1959). *Finite mathematical structures.* Englewood Cliffs, NJ: Prentice-Hall.

Kenny, D.A. (1979). *Correlation and causality.* New York: Wiley.

Keppel, G. (1982). *Design and analysis: A researcher's handbook* (2nd ed.). Englewood Cliffs, NJ: Prentice-Hall.

Kirk, R.E. (1968). *Experimental design: Procedures for the behavioral sciences.* Belmont, CA: Brooks-Cole.

Kmenta, J. (1971). *Elements of econometrics.* New York: Macmillan.

Kruskal, J.B., & Wish, M. (1978). *Multidimensional scaling.* Beverly Hills, CA: Sage Publications.

Laughlin, J.E. (1978). Comment on "Estimating coefficients in linear models: It don't make no nevermind." *Psychological Bulletin, 85,* 237–238.

Lawley, D.N. (1938). A generalization of Fisher's z test. *Biometrika, 30,* 180–187.

Lawley, D.N. (1939). Corrections to "A generalization of Fisher's z test." *Biometrika, 30,* 467–469.

Lindquist, E.F. (1953). *Design and analysis of experiments in psychology and education.* Boston: Houghton-Mifflin.

Long, J.S. (1983a). *Confirmatory factor analysis.* Beverly Hills, CA: Sage Publications.

Long, J.S. (1983b). *Covariance structure models.* Beverly Hills, CA: Sage Publications.

Lord, F.M., & Novick, M.R. (1968). *Statistical theories of mental test scores.* Reading, MA: Addison-Wesley.

Luce, R.D. (1959). *Individual choice behavior: A theoretical analysis.* New York: Wiley.

Luce, R.D. (1964). Detection and recognition. In R.D. Luce, R.R. Bush, and E. Galanter (Eds.), *Handbook of mathematical psychology* (Vol. 1, pp. 103–190). New York: Wiley.

Lykken, D.T. (1979). The detection of deception. *Psychological Bulletin, 86,* 47–53.

MacCallum, R. (1986). Specification searches in covariance structure modeling. *Psychological Bulletin, 100,* 107–120.

Marascuilo, L.A., & Levin, J.R. (1983). *Multivariate statistics in the social sciences: A researcher's guide.* Belmont, CA: Brooks-Cole.

Miller, G.A. (1956). The magical number seven, plus or minus two. *Psychological Review, 63,* 81–97.

Morris, J.D. (1982). Ridge regression and some alternative weighting techniques: A comment on Darlington. *Psychological Bulletin, 91,* 203–209.

Morrison, D.F. (1976). *Multivariate statistical methods* (2nd ed.). New York: McGraw-Hill.

Mosteller, F., & Tukey, J.W. (1977). *Data analysis and regression: A second course in statistics.* Reading, MA: Addison-Wesley.

Mulaik, S.A. (1972). *The foundations of factor analysis.* New York: McGraw-Hill.

Neder, J., & Wasserman, W. (1974). *Applied linear statistical models.* Homewood, Il: Irwin.

Nelson, T.O. (1986). ROC curves and measures of discrimination accuracy: A reply to Swets. *Psychological Bulletin, 100,* 128–132.

Neuhaus, J.O., & Wrigley, C. (1954). The quartimax method: An analytical approach to orthogonal simple structure. *British Journal of Statistical Psychology, 7,* 81–91.

Nunnally, J.C. (1962). The analysis of profile data. *Psychological Bulletin, 59,* 311–319.

Nunnally, J.C. (1978). *Psychometric theory* (2nd ed.). New York: McGraw-Hill.

O'Brien, R.G., & Kaiser, M.K. (1985). MANOVA method for analyzing repeated measures designs: An extensive primer. *Psychological Bulletin, 97,* 316–333.

Olson, C.L. (1974). Comparative robustness of six tests in multivariate analysis of variance. *Journal of the American Statistical Association, 69,* 894–908.

Olson, C.L. (1976). On choosing a test statistic in multivariate analysis of variance. *Psychological Bulletin, 83,* 579–586.

Overall, J.E., & Klett, C.J. (1972). *Applied multivariate analysis.* New York: McGraw-Hill.

Ozer, D.J. (1985). Correlation and the concept of determination. *Psychological Bulletin, 97,* 307–317.

Pagel, M.D., & Lunneborg, C.E. (1985). Empirical evaluation of ridge regresion. *Psychological Bulletin, 97,* 342–355.

Pedhazur, E.J. (1982). *Multiple regression in behavioral research* (2nd ed.). New York: Holt, Rinehart, and Winston.

Pillai, K.C.S. (1955). Some new test criteria in multivariate analysis. *Annals of Mathematical Statistics, 26*, 117–121.

Pillai, K.C.S. (1960). *Statistical tables for tests of multivariate hypotheses*. Manilla: Statistical Center, University of the Phillippines.

Pillai, K.C.S. (1965). On the distribution of the largest characteristic root of a matrix in multivariate analysis. *Biometrika, 52*, 405–414.

Price, B. (1977). Ridge regression: Application to nonexperimental data. *Psychological Bulletin, 84*, 759–766.

Prokop, C.K., Bradley, L.A., Margolis, R., & Gentry, W.D. (1980). Multivariate analyses of the MMPI profiles of patients with multiple pain complaints. *Journal of Personality Assessment, 44*, 246–252.

Pruzek, R.M., & Frederick, B.C. (1978). Weighting predictors in linear models: Alternatives to least squares and limitations of equal weights. *Psychological Bulletin, 85*, 254–266.

Rao, C.R. (1951). An asymptotic expansion of the distribution of Wilk's criterion. *Bulletin of the International Statistics Institute, 33*, 177–180.

Rao, C.R. (1955). Estimation and tests of significance in factor analysis. *Psychometrika, 20*, 92–111.

Rasch, G. (1966a). An individualistic approach to item analysis. In P.F. Lazarsfeld and N.W. Henry (Eds.), *Readings in mathematical social science*. Chicago: Science Research Associates.

Rasch, G. (1966b). An item analysis which takes individual differences into account. *British Journal of Mathematical and Statistical Psychology, 19*, 49–57.

Roy, S.N. (1953). On a heuristic method of test construction and its use in multivariate analysis. *Annals of Mathematical Statistics, 24*, 220–238.

Rozeboom, W.W. (1979). Ridge regression: Bonanza or beguilement. *Psychological Bulletin, 86*, 242–249.

Schoenberg, R. (1982). *MILS: A computer program to estimate the parameters of multiple indicator structure models*. Bethesda, MD: National Institutes of Health.

Schonemann, P.H., & Wang, M.M. (1972). Some new results in factor indeterminacy. *Psychometrika, 37*, 61–91.

Searle, S.R. (1966). *Matrix algebra for the biological sciences*. New York: Wiley.

Searle, S.R. (1971). *Linear models*. New York: Wiley.

Scheffe, H. (1959). *The analysis of variance*. New York: Wiley.

Shepard, R.N. (1958). Stimulus and response generalization: Tests of a model relating generalization to distance in psychological space. *Journal of Experimental Psychology, 55*, 509–523.

Spearman, C. (1904). "General intelligence" objectively determined and measured. *American Journal of Psychology, 15*, 201–293.

Steiger, J.H., & Ward, L.M. (1987). Factor analysis and the coefficient of determination. *Psychological Bulletin, 87*, 471–474.

Stevens, S.S. (1950). Mathematics, measurement, and psychophysics. In S.S. Stevens (Ed.), *Handbook of experimental psychology*. New York: Wiley.

Stewart, D.K., & Love, W.A. (1968). A general correlation index. *Psychological Bulletin, 70*, 160–163.

Stewart, D.W. (1981). The application and misapplication of factor analysis in marketing research. *Journal of Marketing Research, 18*, 51–62.

Swets, J.A., & Pickett, R. (1982). *Evaluation of diagnostic systems: Method from signal detection theory*. New York: Academic Press.

Swets, J.A. (1986a). Indices of discrimination or diagnostic accuracy: Their ROCs and implied models. *Psychological Bulletin, 99,* 100–117.

Swets, J.A. (1986b). Form of empirical ROCs in discrimination and diagnostic tasks: Implications for theory and measurement of performance. *Psychological Bulletin, 99,* 181–198.

SAS (1985). *SAS user's guide: Statistics* (Version 5 Edition). Cary, NC: SAS Institute, Inc.

SPSSX (1986). *SPSSX user's guide.* Chicago, IL: SPSSX.

Tanner, W.P., Jr., & Swets, J.A. (1954). A decision-making theory of visual detection. *Psychological Review, 61,* 401–409.

Tatsuoka, M.M. (1970). *Discriminant analysis.* Champaign, IL: Institute for Personality and Ability Testing.

Theodor, L.H., & Mandelcord, M.S. (1973). Hysterical blindness: A case report and study using a modern psychophysical technique. *Journal of Abnormal Psychology, 82,* 552–553.

Thissen, D. (1982). Marginal maximum likelihood estimation for the one-parameter logistic model. *Psychometrika, 47,* 175–186.

Thissen, D., Steinberg, L., & Gerrard, M. (1986). Beyond group-mean differences: The concept of item bias. *Psychological Bulletin, 99,* 118–128.

Thurstone, L.L. (1945). A multiple group method of factoring the correlation matrix. *Psychometrika, 10,* 73–78.

Thurstone, L.L. (1947). *Multiple factor analysis.* Chicago: University of Chicago Press.

Timm, N.H. (1975). *Multivariate analysis with applications in education and psychology.* Belmont, CA: Brooks-Cole.

Tucker, L.R. (1951). *A method for synthesis of factor analytic studies.* Personnel Research Section Report No. 984. Washington, DC: Department of the Army.

Wainer, H. (1976). Estimating coefficients in linear models: It don't make no never-mind. *Psychological Bulletin, 83,* 213–217.

Wainer, H. (1978). On the sensitivity of regression and regressors. *Psychological Bulletin, 85,* 267–273.

Wiggins, J.S. (1973). *Personality and prediction: Principles of personality assessment.* Reading, MA: Addison-Wesley.

Wilkinson, L. (1975). Response variable hypotheses in the multivariate analysis of variance. *Psychological Bulletin, 82,* 408–412.

Wilks, S.S. (1932). Certain generalizations in the analysis of variance. *Biometrika, 24,* 471–494.

Wilks, S.S. (1938). The large sample distribution of the likelihood ratio for testing composite hypotheses. *The Annals of Mathematical Statistics, 9,* 60–62.

Winer, B.J. (1971). *Statistical principles in experimental design* (2nd ed.). New York: McGraw-Hill.

Wright, S. (1934). The method of path coefficients. *Annals of Mathematical Statistics, 5,* 161–215.

Wrigley, C., & Neuhaus, J.O. (1955). The use of an electronic computer in principal axes factor analysis. *Journal of Educational Psychology, 46,* 31–41.

Author Index

Subject Index